W9-BEO-077

DECISION SYSTEMS FOR INVENTORY MANAGEMENT AND PRODUCTION PLANNING

WILEY SERIES IN
PRODUCTION/OPERATIONS MANAGEMENT

DECISION SYSTEMS FOR INVENTORY MANAGEMENT AND PRODUCTION PLANNING

Second Edition

Edward A. Silver
Professor of Management
The University of Calgary

Rein Peterson
Magna International Professor of Management Policy
York University

JOHN WILEY & SONS
New York Chichester Brisbane Toronto Singapore

Library of Congress Cataloging in Publication Data:

Silver, Edward A. (Edward Allen), 1937–
Decision systems for inventory management and production planning.

(Wiley series in production/operations management)
Rev. ed. of: Decision systems for inventory management and production planning/Rein Peterson, Edward A. Silver. ©1979.
Includes index.
1. Inventory control—Decision making. 2. Production planning—Decision making. I. Peterson, Rein, 1937–
II. Peterson, Rein, 1937– . Decision systems for inventory management and production planning. III. Title. IV. Series.

HD40.S54 1985 658.7′87 84-15179
ISBN 0-471-86782-9

Printed in the United States of America

10 9 8 7 6 5 4

To Maxine, Michelle, Norman, and Heidi
To Mari Ann, Michael Daniel,
and Jennifer Mai Charlotte

ABOUT THE AUTHORS

Edward A. Silver is a Professor of Management at the University of Calgary. Prior to his appointment at Calgary, he was a Professor of Management Sciences on the Faculty of Engineering at the University of Waterloo. He has also previously taught at Boston University and, as a visiting professor, at the Swiss Federal Polytechnique Institute in Lausanne, Switzerland.

A native of Montreal, Professor Silver completed a Bachelor of Civil Engineering at McGill University and a Science Doctorate in Operations Research at the Massachusetts Institute of Technology. He is a licensed professional engineer and is a member of a number of professional societies, including the American Production and Inventory Control Society, the Canadian Operational Research Society (of which he was the President in 1980–81), the Institute of Industrial Engineers, the Institute of Management Sciences, the International Society for Inventory Research, and the Operational Research Society (UK). Professor Silver has served in an editorial capacity for several journals and also has been the Chairman of the Grant Selection Committee for Industrial Engineering of the Natural Sciences and Engineering Research Council of Canada.

Professor Silver has presented seminars and talks at national and international meetings of a number of professional societies as well as at educational institutions throughout North America and Europe. He has published over 60 articles in a broad range of professional journals.

Professor Silver spent four years as a member of the Operations Research Group of the international consulting firm, Arthur D. Little, Inc. Subsequently, as President of MAXED & Associates, Inc., he has consulted for a wide variety of industrial and government organizations throughout North America. These consulting activities have addressed both tactical and strategic problems arising in the management of operations. Specific areas of application have included inventory management, production planning, logistics management, facilities layout, maintenance management, and distribution planning. An additional important activity has been his involvement in several executive development programs related to the production/inventory field.

Rein Peterson is the Magna International Professor of Management Policy on the Faculty of Administrative Studies, York University, Toronto, Canada. Formerly, he served the Faculty of Administrative Studies as Associate Dean, Director of Research, Coordinator of the Management Science Area, and as Chairman of the Faculty Council.

Born in Europe, he considers himself part Quebecois, having spent thirteen formative years in Montreal. Prior to his academic career, he worked as a prospector and as a professional engineer/project manager helping to locate and build iron mines, new towns, and railways in northern Quebec and Ontario.

He was awarded his Ph.D. at Cornell University, having received his M.B.A. from the University of Western Ontario and Bachelor of Engineering from McGill University. Before coming to York, Professor Peterson served on the faculties of Columbia University, Harpur College, and the University of Western Ontario.

Professor Peterson has served as an elected member of the Council of the Institute of Management Sciences (T.I.M.S.), and the editor in charge of a special issue of *Management Science*, and as Programme Director of the XXII International T.I.M.S. Conference in Kyoto, Japan.

He is an active consultant to business and government, and from 1980 to 1982 served as an officer and vice-president of the Cape Breton Development Corporation, where he was responsible for four departments: Corporate Planning, Management Information Systems, Research and Development, and Marketing.

PREFACE

Inventories are produced, used (for example, as raw materials, supplies, spare parts, and so forth), or distributed by *every* organization. Moreover, inventories represent a major investment from the perspectives of both individual firms and entire national economies. In addition, enormous costs are incurred in the planning, scheduling, control, and actual carrying out of replenishment (procurement or production) related activities.

Inventory management and production planning have been studied in considerable depth from a theoretical perspective. Yet, those of us who, through consulting work, come into close contact with managerial decision procedures in this area are repeatedly surprised to find how limited, and ad hoc, many of the existing decision systems actually are. The rate at which theory has been developed has far outstripped the rate at which decision practices of firms have been successfully upgraded. A major gap has existed between the theoretical solutions, on the one hand, and the real world problems, on the other.

Our primary objective in the first edition of the book was to bridge this gap through the development of *operational* inventory management and production planning decision systems that would allow management to capitalize on readily implementable improvements to current practices. Extensive feedback from both academicians and practitioners has been very gratifying in this regard. Our primary objective is unchanged in this revised edition. We hope to further bridge the gap with this *substantial* revision that incorporates ideas from our additional consulting and teaching experience and that uses certain aspects of feedback that we have received, as well as recent *practical* research findings.

Major changes made in this edition include:

1. An expanded treatment of the strategic issues of production planning and inventory management.
2. More emphasis on production-related material, that is, a more balanced coverage of inventory management and production planning.
3. Introduction of a unifying framework for planning, scheduling, and control in production situations.
4. A more balanced treatment of capacity-oriented process industry situations versus materials/labor-oriented fabrication/assembly industries.
5. Expanded coverage of Material Requirements Planning and its extensions, including Distribution Requirements Planning.
6. Substantial treatment of scheduling at a bottleneck production operation.

7. Discussion of the Japanese "Just-in-Time" Manufacturing philosophy and the associated details of a Kanban control system.
8. A major revamping and more comprehensive coverage of the strategy and tactics of forecasting.
9. Incorporation of the impacts of inflation.
10. Treatment of control procedures for repairable items.
11. Discussion of some of the latest developments in coordinated inventory control of families of items, multistage lot-sizing, and multiechelon inventory control.

In introducing new technical material and trimming some of the old material, the viewpoint adopted has been to stay away, as much as possible, from complicated mathematics and, instead, to give a primarily qualitative description of the complexity of a particular problem, the general approach taken, and the nature of the results (with appropriate literature references for readers wishing to pursue the specific topic in more depth). In the same vein, most mathematical proofs have been placed in Appendixes at the end of individual chapters. In addition, a few sections, requiring a level of mathematical understanding higher than the rest of the book, *have been marked with asterisks*. In all cases, these sections can be omitted without a loss of continuity. This style of presentation has been deliberately chosen so that sufficient material of interest is made available to the analytically inclined reader, while at the same time providing a meaningful text for a less analytically oriented audience.

Part One of the book presents a discussion of inventory management and production planning decisions as important components of total business strategy. Topics covered include the diverse nature of inventories, the complexity of production/inventory decision making, cost measurement, and an introduction to the important concept of exchange curves. A separate chapter is devoted to the determination of forecasting strategy and the selection of forecasting methods.

Part Two is concerned with traditional decision systems for the inventory control of individual items. The use of approximate decision rules, *based on sound logic*, permits realistic treatment of time-varying (for example, seasonal) demand, probabilistic demand, and the many different attitudes of management toward costing the risk of insufficient capacity in the short run.

Part Three deals with special classes of items, including the most important (Class A) and the large group of low-activity items (Class C). Also discussed are procedures for dealing with items that can be maintained in inventory for only relatively short periods of time—for example, style goods and perishable items.

Part Four addresses two types of coordination of groups of items in nonproduction contexts. First, there is the situation of a family of items, at a single stocking location, that share a common supplier or a common mode of transport. The second type of coordination is in a multiechelon framework where replenishment requests from one stocking point become part of the demand at another location.

Part Five is concerned with decision making in a production environment. A general framework for such decision making is presented. Two separate chapters deal with the details of short-range scheduling and control: one primarily for capacity-oriented flow production and the other for materials/labor-oriented fabrication/assembly situations.

Part Six discusses the important practical problems of planning, implementation, and control of large decision systems. We pool, in this section, our consulting experience with psychological-sociological research findings on bringing about change. The concluding chapter includes a discussion of *computerized* decision systems.

Extensive problem sections (substantially modified from the first edition) have been provided at the end of each chapter. *In addition, a large selection of supplementary problems are available in the Solutions Manual.* Finally, six case studies, entitled MIDAS Canada, are interwoven with the material in the text to provide a context for technical topics and a means of reference to existing managerial practice. *The cases can be utilized individually*, but it is recommended that Case A be read prior to dealing with any other case.

As was the situation with the first edition, the book should be of interest to faculty and students in programs of business administration, industrial/systems engineering, and management sciences/operations research. Although *the presentation is geared to a basic course in production planning, scheduling, and inventory management*, the inclusion of extensive references permits its use in advanced elective courses and as a starting point for research activities. At the same time, the book should continue to have broad appeal to practicing analysts and managers.

Possible paths through the book for different types of users include:

1. Industrial/systems engineering, management sciences/operations research programs:
   - **a.** One-term course on inventory management: Chapters 1–12 and 17–18.
   - **b.** One-term course primarily on production planning and control: Chapters 1–3, 4 (medium-range forecasting), 13–18, and Cases E–F.
2. Graduate business (MBA) programs (as a part of the production/operations management offerings or as an illustration of a functional area application of the management sciences approach to problem solving):
   - **a.** One-term course on inventory managment: Chapters 1–7, 11–12, 17–18, and Cases A–D.
   - **b.** One-term course primarily on production planning and control: Chapters 1–3, 4 (medium-range forecasting), 13–18, and Cases A–F.
3. Undergraduate business and community college programs: Chapters 1–7 and 9–10.

4. Managers exclusively interested in policy issues (perhaps on an executive development program basis): Chapters 1–4, 13, 17–18, and Cases A–F.
5. Practicing inventory/production managers and consultants (the latter both internal and external):
   a. As related to purchasing managers, industrial distributors, and retailers: Chapters 1–7, 9–12, 17–18, and Cases A–D.
   b. As related to manufacturing managers and production planners: All of the above as well as Chapters 13–16 and Cases E–F.

Most organizations face an increasingly competitive environment, both nationally and internationally, in the production and distribution of their goods. It is hoped that this revised edition of our text will help prepare readers to better cope with this complex decision environment.

E.A. Silver
R. Peterson

ACKNOWLEDGMENTS

Special mention must be made of two authorities in the field who, early in our careers, encouraged us to work in the general area of inventory management/production planning—namely, Robert G. Brown, as a colleague at Arthur D. Little, Inc., and Martin K. Starr, as a colleague at Columbia University.

The manuscript, as is often the case, had its origin in the teaching notes used by the authors for several years in courses they taught at Boston University, The University of Calgary, Columbia University, the Swiss Federal Polytechnique Institute, the University of Waterloo, the University of Western Ontario, and York University. A large number of students (including many part-time students holding employment in industry) have provided excellent critiques. We would like to particularly thank Maged Abo El-Ela, Blyth Archibald, Louis Brosseau, Ron Craig, Alan Daley, Paul Dixon, Robert Lamarre, John Miltenburg, and Robert Thompstone. A special note of appreciation is in order to Patricia Lundman, Russ McGillivray, and Ken Miller for their excellent work on the Solutions Manual.

A significant portion of the book has developed out of research supported by Grant Numbers A7417 and A1485 from the Natural Sciences and Engineering Research Council of Canada, Grant Number 9740-16 from the Defence Research Board of Canada, Grant Number 16-585 from the Canada Council, and Grant Number 69-151 from the Ford Foundation. The authors gratefully acknowledge this support. A special work of thanks is in order to The University of Calgary and to the Killam Foundation for providing a resident fellowship, thus permitting the completion of this revised edition.

A number of our professional colleagues have provided helpful comments concerning our earlier research papers, the first edition of the book, and the drafts of the revised edition. In addition, other colleagues have made available drafts of papers in the more advanced topic areas. We appreciate these important contributions from individuals such as Sven Axsäter (Linköping Institute of Technology, Sweden), Ken Baker (Dartmouth College), Éva Barancsi (Karl Marx University, Hungary), Peter Bell (University of Western Ontario), Bill Berry (University of Iowa), Gabriel Bitran (MIT), Joseph Blackburn (Vanderbilt University), Jim Bookbinder (University of Waterloo), Robert G. Brown (Materials Management Systems Inc.), Elwood Buffa (UCLA), F. Eric Burke (University of Waterloo), John Buzacott (University of Waterloo), Robert Carbone (Laval University), Attila Chikán (Karl Marx University, Hungary), Andrew Clark (CACI, Inc.), Morris Cohen (University of Pennsylvania), Donald Daly (York University), Chandrasekhar Das (University of Saskatchewan), W.

Steven Demmy (Wright State University), Adolf Diegel (University of Natal, South Africa), Richard Ehrhardt (University of North Carolina), Hamilton Emmons (Case Western Reserve University), Michael Florian (University of Montreal), Leonard Fortuin (N. V. Philips, Netherlands), James Freeland (University of Virginia), S. K. Goyal (Concordia University), Stephen Graves (MIT), Donald Gross (The George Washington University), Robert Hall (Indiana University), Warren Hausman (Stanford University), Jack Hayya (Pennsylvania State University), Arnoldo Hax (MIT), David Herron (SRI International), Charles Holt (University of Texas), Donald Iglehart (Stanford University), Edward Ignall (Columbia University), Colin Lewis (University of Aston, England), Alan Kaplan (U.S. Army Inventory Research Office), W. J. Kennedy (University of Utah), Jack Kleijnen (Katholieke Hogeschool Tilburg, Netherlands), Morton Klein (Columbia University), Ernest Koenigsberg (University of California), Peter Kubat (University of Rochester), Howard Kunreuther (University of Pennsylvania), Marc Lambrecht (Katholieke Universiteit Leuven, Belgium), Alastair MacCormick (University of Auckland, New Zealand), Michael Magazine (University of Waterloo), Harlan Meal (MIT), Robert Millen (Northeastern University), Jeffrey Miller (Boston University), John Muckstadt (Cornell University), Eliezer Naddor (Johns Hopkins University), Colin New (Cranfield School of Management, England), Steven Nahmias (University of Santa Clara), E. F. Peter Newson (University of Western Ontario), Kenji Okano (Matsuyama University, Japan), Muhittin Oral (Laval University), John Papageorgiou (University of Massachusetts), Michael Peters (Louisiana State University), Graham Rand (University of Lancaster, England), Philip Rhodes (Price Waterhouse & Co.), Eric Ritchie (University of Lancaster, England), L. S. Rosen (York University), Bernard Rosenman (U.S. Army Inventory Research Office), Alan Saipe (Thorne, Stevenson & Kellogg), Christoph Schneeweiss (Universitat Mannheim, West Germany), Helmut Schneider (Freie Universitate Berlin, West Germany), David Schrady (Naval Postgraduate School), Lee Schwarz (Purdue University), Paul Schweitzer (University of Rochester), Suresh Sethi (University of Toronto), D. James Smith (D. J. Smith Consultants), Stephen Smith (Xerox Corporation), Tibor Szandtner (Woods, Gordon & Co.), Andrew Szendrovits (McMaster University), Sam Taylor (University of Wyoming), L. Joseph Thomas (Cornell University), Henk Tijms (Vrije Universiteit Amsterdam, Netherlands), Paul van Beek (Agricultural University and Philips' Industries, Netherlands), Luk Van Wassenhove (Katholieke Universiteit Leuven, Belgium), Paul Vincent (Department of National Defence), Urban Wemmerlov (Indiana University), D. Clay Whybark (Indiana University), Jack Williams (University of Notre Dame), and Gene Woolsey (Colorado School of Mines). We apologize to any contributing colleagues inadvertently omitted from this list.

Our thanks are extended to the following individuals who provided extremely helpful reviews of the first edition or this book: John Buzacott (University of Waterloo), D. Ross Cowan (University of Michigan), James Freeland (University of Virginia), Warren Hausman (Stanford University), Henrik

Jönsson (University of Calgary), Solon Morgan (Drexel University), Gary Scudder (University of Minnesota), and George Wilson (Lehigh University).

A number of senior managers also have had an influence on the development of this book—for example, J. Alexander, formerly President, A. L. & W. Sports; E. Brewer, Controller, CIBA-GEIGY; D. B. McCaskill, former President of Connaught Labs Ltd.; and R. Walker, formerly Vice-President, Manufacturing, Fuller Brush Co.

Finally, on such a major task a special word of thanks is necessary for those individuals who have edited, typed, and proofread the many drafts of the manuscript. These appreciated people include Joan Davidson, Diane Hammar, and Mari Peterson on the first edition, and Nora Corbett and Karen Lehman on this manuscript.

E. A. S.
R. P.

CONTENTS

PART ONE

THE CONTEXT AND IMPORTANCE OF INVENTORY MANAGEMENT AND PRODUCTION PLANNING DECISIONS

A lack of agreement with regard to the relative importance and role of production and inventories in overall business strategy has impeded the introduction of modern methods of decision making. Too many in top management have tended to view inventory as a result of a year-end accounting of "all the dumb things we undertook last year." Furthermore, production has often been viewed as a necessary evil, simply contributing to the cost of operations. Analysts, for their part, have too readily adapted formulations of inventory management and production planning decisions that are largely mathematical in content and that too often have not adequately captured the realities of the managerial context.

In Chapter 1 we discuss the importance of inventories from the perspective of both individual firms and entire national economies. We then describe various statistical properties of inventories. The role of aggregate inventories in the business cycle is also discussed.

Chapter 2 presents an overview of corporate decision making and the rationale for why production should be a key component of corporate strategy. Strategic choices in production planning and inventory management are identified.

Chapter 3 is concerned with the complexity of the decisions made in production planning and inventory management. Several aids, both conceptual and physical, for dealing with this complexity are presented. These include the identification of a number of key variables affecting decision making.

Since managerial expectations about the future have such a tremendous impact on inventory management and production planning decisions, forecasting the demand variable is given special treatment in a separate chapter. In Chapter 4 we present a number of strategies and techniques that could be adopted to cope with the unknown future.

CHAPTER 1

The Nature and Importance of Inventories

Every organization produces, uses (for example, as supplies, spare parts, etc.), or distributes inventories. According to Statistics Canada the total inventories owned by Canadian manufacturers are in the neighborhood of $30 billion. Furthermore, on average, 34 percent of the current assets and 90 percent of the working capital of a typical company in the United States are invested in inventories. In addition, considerable labor costs (clerical and managerial) are incurred in the control of inventories. Herron (1979) reports that for many firms, inventory costs are approximately as large as *before-tax* operating profits. Thus, we see that even a small percentage reduction in costs will be transformed into a huge absolute savings, when viewed from a national or international perspective.

As implied above, inventories have an important impact on the usual aggregate scorecards of management's performance—namely, on the balance sheet and the income statement.[1] First, inventories are classified as one of the current assets of an organization; thus, *all other things being equal*, a reduction in inventories lowers assets relative to liabilities. However, the funds freed by a reduction in inventories normally would be used to acquire other types of assets or to reduce liabilities. Such actions directly influence the so-called *current ratio*, the ratio of current assets to current liabilities, which is the most commonly used measure of liquidity.

Income statements represent the flow of revenues and expenses for a given period (for example, one year). Specifically,

$$\text{Operating profit} = \text{Revenue} - \text{Operating expenses} \tag{1.1}$$

[1]Droms (1979) provides a nontechnical description of financial reports.

Changes in inventory levels can affect both of the terms on the right side of Eq. 1.1. First, sales revenue can be influenced by a different allocation of inventories among specific items. Second, operating expenses can be altered through changes in aggregate inventory levels in that inventory carrying charges represent a significant component of such expenses. The labor component of operating expenses can also be reduced by more effective scheduling and control of inventories of individual items.

Finally, one of the most common measures of managerial performance is the *return on investment (ROI)*, which represents the profit (after taxes) divided by the average investment (or level of assets). From the above discussion it is clear that inventories have an important impact on the ROI (also see Problem 1.1).

1.1 A BRIEF HISTORY

Some three hundred years ago the management of inventories was a relatively simple matter. Inventories were considered by merchants, producers, and policy makers primarily as a measure of wealth. The wealth and power of a business or a country were assessed in terms of how many bushels of wheat, heads of cattle, pounds of gold, and so forth, were stored in warehouses. Pappilon (1697) in writing about inventories argued that:

> *The stock or riches of the kingdom doth not only consist of our money, but also in our commodities and ships for trade and magazines furnished with all necessary materials.*

In this century, starting in the 1920s, decision makers began to put an increased emphasis on the liquidity of assets, such as inventories, until fast turnover became a goal to be pursued for its own sake in many organizations. Whitin (1957) reported that:

> *Inventories are often referred to as the "graveyard" of American business, as surplus stocks have been a principal cause of business failures. Inventories are also considered a destabilizing influence in business cycles. . . . Businessmen have developed an almost pathological fear of increasing inventories.*

Most of the pathological fears to which Whitin refers date from the period 1920–21 when the first "Inventory Depression" was recognized; it caused, in turn, a phenomenon commonly known as "hand-to-mouth buying" throughout the American economy (McGill, 1927). As the name suggests, during this depression, much emphasis was placed on the necessity of achieving rapid rates of inventory turnover. In this book we define inventory turnover as

$$\text{Inventory turnover} = \frac{\text{Annual sales or usage (at cost)}}{\text{Average inventory (in \$)}} \tag{1.2}$$

Some managers overreacted by trying to achieve near zero inventories—with disastrous results. Top management in many companies had completely reversed their attitude *from 250 years earlier* regarding the desirability of holding inventory.

High inflation rates, which became common in the 1970s in all world economies, altered permanently the spending patterns of individuals, companies, and governments. By the late 1970s the prime interest rate (the fee charged to the most preferred borrowers) had, in some developed countries, such as Canada, surpassed 20 percent per annum. Astronomical rates became commonplace in less developed countries.

Inventories are today viewed by most senior management as a large potential risk and seldom as a measure of wealth. A constant nagging fear persists in the minds of most policy makers that merchandise stocked in excess of actual demand may require drastic price cuts, so that it can be sold before it becomes worthless as a result of obsolescence through style or technological changes. Obsolescence is, in fact, of relatively recent origin, but promises to be of increasing importance in the future as product life cycles become shorter and shorter.[2]

Most managers today recognize the importance of balancing the advantages and disadvantages of carrying inventories. Nevertheless, some of the old fears still linger on. As one company president expressed it to us:

> *I agree that inventories play a crucial role in my operations. But I cannot lose sight of the other side of the coin. While inventories are something I need to survive, they also represent stuff I can get stuck with.*

But *balancing* the advantages and disadvantages of inventory investment in the future may not be as simple as in the past. In 1980 the Japanese automobile industry overtook that of the United States. Toyota became the world's second largest producer. It sold more automobiles than the entire car industry of the United Kingdom, and Japanese sales surpassed those of France in Francophone Africa. Japan's systems of production planning, inventory management, and organizational design were credited as being the main strategic vehicles of bringing about this amazing feat. The Japanese had demonstrated a weakness in the Western approach to strategic management, recognized earlier by Skinner (1969):

> *Manufacturing has too long been dominated by experts and specialists. . . . As a result, top executives tend to avoid involvement in manufacturing policy making . . . a function that* could *be a valuable asset and be tied to corporate strategy. . . .*

[2]Product life cycles will be discussed in Chapter 2. All products go through a period of low sales during introduction, followed by a period of growth. Eventually sales decline and production is discontinued.

It may seem odd to think of manufacturing as anything other than a competitive weapon, yet the history of the U.S. auto industry shows that by the late 1950s manufacturing had become a neutral factor in competition. Except perhaps for their reliance on economies of scale, they tended to compete by means of styling, marketing, and dealership networks. Research by Abernathy et al. (1981) has shown that a valid explanation of the Japanese success must start with the factor of "process yield," an amalgam of management practices and systems connected with inventory management and production planning and control. While we were thinking in terms of optimal buffer stocks and order quantities, the Japanese were examining trade-offs between different types of production systems. They developed a production system that effectively eliminated the need for any significant amount of inventory. Such a system (to be discussed in Chapters 2 and 16) required extensive organizational readjustments and investments that only the most senior levels of executives could authorize.

What has happened is now logically obvious. Inventory management decision systems in the new international industrial competition of the future can no longer be designed separately from their production process contexts. Inventory management, production planning, and corporate strategy are all closely linked together, a point to which we return in Chapter 2.

1.2 WHY AGGREGATE INVENTORY INVESTMENT FLUCTUATES: THE BUSINESS CYCLE

That total dollar inventory investment in any economy fluctuates in response to a complex set of factors is an empirical fact. Inventory investment is one of the most volatile components of an economy. During business cycles, changes in the rate of inventory investment have been larger in magnitude than those in any one of the other volatile components of the economy, such as expenditures on plant and equipment, housing, or durable consumption.

Much has been written as a result of empirical studies of aggregate inventory behavior in the economy (Lovell, 1964; Mack, 1967). It is generally agreed that expectations about the future held collectively by decision makers in the economy are the major determinants of whether and to what degree inventory investment will fluctuate. The severity of inventory fluctuations depends on the degree to which expectations are in error and on the speed with which decision makers are capable of reacting to errors in their expectations in a rational manner. Expectations about the future have been shown to depend on the following variables: the trend of recent sales and new orders, the volume of unfilled orders, price pressures, the level of inventories in the recent past, the ratio of sales to inventories (turnover ratio), interest rates on business loans, the current level of employment, and the types of decision-making systems used by management.

Many economists have tried to compile comprehensive models of the business cycle to explain all patterns of fluctuations that have occurred historically. (See, for example, Evans, 1969.) No one has succeeded, to date, in building an all-purpose model. The major point which seems to emerge from all this research is that each cycle has in the past been somewhat different, especially with regard to its exact timing and relative magnitude. However, some underlying common variables, which can be gleaned from past cycles, about the recurrent timing of the cyclical process are illustrated in Figure 1.1.

We start describing the cycle in Figure 1.1 at point A where, because of over-optimistic expectations, too many products are manufactured by the economy and cannot be sold. These surplus goods increase aggregate inventories to the extent that producers start to reduce the scale of their operations until the rate of sale exceeds the rate of production of goods. The resulting disinvestment in inventories creates a recession during which prices, production, and profits fall and unemployment is prevalent. For example, *Time* magazine on May 10, 1982 reported that in the U.S. economy

> *Inventory liquidation has been driving the economy steadily lower since last December. . . . Companies have been emptying warehouses, trimming stock piles and cutting back orders from suppliers. This was the major cause of the 3.9% drop in the gross national product during the first quarter . . . with interest rates high and sales projections dismal. . . . few businesses seem eager to start hastily rebuilding their stocks to former levels.*

Eventually, an economic recovery is generated by a slowing in the rate of inventory liquidation. Some top managers, expecting that prices will recover, start to slowly expand their operations while costs are low. More and more firms slowly start to hire additional labor, purchase more raw materials, and

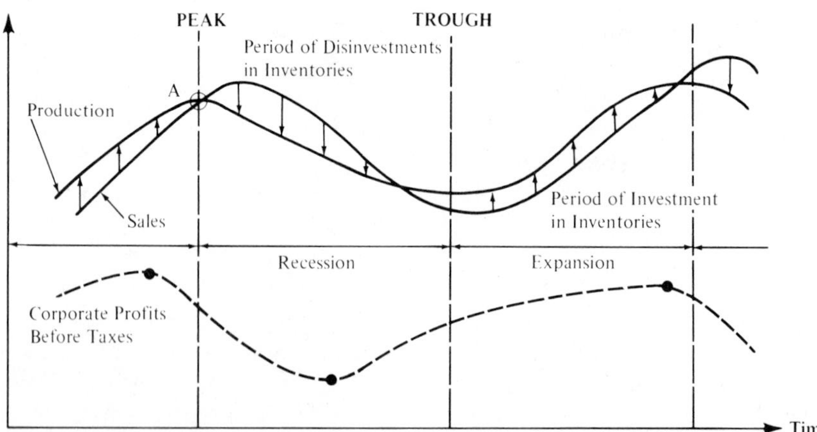

FIGURE 1.1 The Business Cycle

thereby infuse more money into circulation in the economy. To illustrate, *Business Week* on May 2, 1983 stated

> *For the past year and a half, most businesses have chopped inventories by record amounts to barebone levels, and companies are standing by, ready to gear up their production lines as they have in past recoveries.*

Consumers, with money to spend once again, start to bid up prices of available goods. Once prices of goods start to rise, more and more executives get on the bandwagon by expanding their operations and thereby accentuate the expansionary phase of the cycle. The boom that results eventually is brought to an end when costs of materials are bid up once again by competing firms, when labor unions begin demanding higher wages, and when the scarcity of money for further expansion causes the banks to raise their interest rates. The crisis phase which follows is a period of uncertainty and hesitation on the part of consumers and business. Executives find that their warehouses are restocked with excess inventory that, once again, cannot be sold. The business cycle then is ready to repeat itself as explained above.

This explanation is, of course, highly simplified, but it does illustrate the main forces, especially the role of inventories, at work during each cycle. Note that the expectations of business and consumers as well as the ability of decision makers to react quickly and correctly to change are important determinants of the length and severity of a cycle.

In Figure 1.1 the following key relationships are illustrated by the data. The peaks and troughs in corporate profits before taxes precede the peaks and troughs in production. Inventory investment lags slightly and thereby contributes to higher cyclical amplitudes in production than are really necessary.

1.3 PRODUCTIVITY AND PERFORMANCE OF EXISTING PRODUCTION PLANNING AND INVENTORY MANAGEMENT DECISION SYSTEMS

In this section we first look at comparisons among different countries. Then we examine differences in performance within specific industries.

1.3.1 Comparisons by Industries Across Countries

Historically, in the United States and other Western countries, productivity improvement has been pursued through reducing the amount of direct manufacturing labor expended per unit of output. Herron (1979) has shown that a considerably greater potential for productivity improvement lies in "working smarter" in the areas of production planning and inventory management. Table 1.1, based partly on the work of Ray (1981), shows that in materials management, Japanese firms are able to work with considerably less working capital invested in inventories than firms in several other countries. Furthermore, while stockturn[3] figures in other countries are either declining or relatively stable, Japan's stockturn numbers are increasing in most industries. (The Japanese performance, in large part, is the result of the successful implementation of a stockless production philosophy, a topic to be discussed in Chapter 2.) The data indicate that substantial savings in inventory investment are possible in most of the industries listed in Canada, the United States, and the United Kingdom.

1.3.2 Comparisons within Industries

Companies are relatively successful in managing the productivity of their investment in inventories, but a surprising number of organizations leave decisions in this crucial area to rules of thumb, guesswork, or chance. A majority of organizations consider inventory control a middle or lower management responsibility—a technical subject consisting of mathematical formulas, cost accounting, measurement, and the drudgery of keeping track of thousands of individual items of stock.

Hupp (1969), using data that were originally compiled by Dun's *Review* on the inventory management policies of merchants (retailers and wholesalers) from 17 industries, concluded that:

> *If the typical unsuccessful company did as well as a successful one, it could double its sales with no increase in quantity of goods on hand. Or, with no change in sales, it could reduce stock by 50 percent.*

That is, a typical "successful company" (on basis of profitability) seemed to turn over its inventories twice as often as an "unsuccessful" one in the same industry. According to Hupp, the companies studied sold the same goods, hired the same type of operating personnel, and had access to the same tools and techniques of successful inventory management. The one major factor that was not the same in all companies studied was the attitude of top management. In the more successful companies top management tended to become more directly involved with aggregate inventory and production planning policy determination by considering it as an integral part of corporate strategy.

In similar research carried out by Hill (1974) companies in the retail and wholesale trades were found typically to have greater top management involvement in the management of inventories. In most other industries top management tended to become concerned only from time to time if inventory got "out-of-line," which often meant higher than at the same time last year. More concern was also likely to be expressed when money supply from conven-

[3] Ray's "stockturn" terminology is synonomous with our "turnover ratio."

TABLE 1.1 Median Stockturns, 1974–1978 by Country[a]

Industry	Canada	United States	United Kingdom	Japan
1. Wood products	2.7 (2.7–3.3)	3.2 (3.1–3.4)	1.5 (1.5–1.4)	5.2 (3.9–7.0)
2. Paper products	3.2 (3.9–3.8)	4.0 (4.0–4.1)	2.5 (2.5–2.7)	3.6 (3.6–4.5)
3. Industrial chemicals	2.2 (3.0–2.1)	3.6 (3.9–3.7)	2.0 (2.3–1.9)	2.6 (2.8–3.3)
4. Petroleum refineries	0.9 (1.2–0.8)	2.4 (2.2–2.8)	0.8 (0.8–0.7)	0.7 (0.8–0.8)
5. Iron and steel	1.7 (2.3–1.9)	2.2 (3.2–2.5)	1.4 (2.0–1.4)	1.5 (2.3–2.0)
6. Metal products	2.4 (2.4–2.4)	2.7 (2.6–2.8)	2.0 (1.5–1.9)	4.2 (4.0–4.6)
7. Motor vehicles	2.7 (3.5–2.7)	4.1 (3.4–4.2)	1.7 (2.0–1.7)	5.9 (4.9–7.3)
8. Manufacturing	2.4 (2.6–2.4)	3.0 (2.9–3.1)	1.8 (1.8–1.7)	2.8 (2.7–3.4)

[a]The 1974 and 1978 figures are in parentheses.

tional sources became so tight that a reduction in the investment in inventory was perceived as being the most ready source of cash in the short-run perspective.

About half of the organizations studied by Hall had neither predetermined budgets nor limits on inventory. Most of the representatives of the organizations interviewed said they had had some *aggregate* inventory budgets or limits that were usually arbitrarily set in terms of number of days supply, flat dollar limits, or as a percentage of total sales. Many organizations interviewed were attempting to shift the burden of inventory investment to a greater degree on their suppliers.

The above discussion shows that differences exist within industries. To properly design a production/inventory decision system for a specific firm we need to know far more than just the industry of which it is a part. Specifically, as we will discuss in Chapters 2 and 3, we need to know the specific organizational setting, the general objectives of management, the number of distinct items involved, the technical capabilities of support staff, among other things.

1.4 THE TURNOVER RATIO AND INVENTORY MANAGEMENT

Although inventory turnover is an adequate indicator for comparing current to past performance within the same company or division, it can be misleading when making comparisons among companies and industries. It is not true that a higher turnover is always preferable. Nevertheless, inventory turnover is a simple, easy to use yardstick that is comparable in use to the payback period in investment analysis. Its use as a quick reporting tool, in a context which is understood by all, explains its warranted popularity in practice.

The following anecdote is distilled from Garwood (1980). A U.S. company manufactured its own castings and machined them in large lot sizes. Other parts were fabricated from bar stock and assembled with other purchased parts. The bar stock parts were more profitable, because the company had developed a distinctive competence in manufacturing these parts at a lower cost than its competitors in the same general industry group. However, they did require a higher inventory investment. Because they manufactured most of the parts, raw material had to be in-process for a longer period of time than if purchased complete. To increase inventory turnover all they would have to do is to buy more and make less. In short, the nature of a business and existing strategic competitive advantages have significant effects on the determination of an appropriate inventory investment and the resulting turnover. Improving profitability rather than reducing inventory investment, per se, is the real name of the game. Right? Wrong! The president of this firm issued an edict to cut inventory to achieve 4.5 turns or else! This target was set arbitrarily to meet the industry average. The controller recalculated the decision rules for inventory ordering so as to establish a limit on material receipts that would yield the necessary material inventory reduction to achieve the turnover target. Lot sizes were chopped to stretch out deliveries of purchased and manufactured material. Manpower in manufacturing was also cut to limit labor input. Shipments continued for a few months as warehouse inventories were depleted. Customer service degenerated when finished goods and component inventories bottomed out. Rampant stockouts created massive, expensive expediting. The smaller lot sizes drove up the product cost, and the profits plummeted.

Garwood also reports that Richard S. Sloma, an experienced Chief Executive for several companies, including Division President of ITT and CEO of Bastian-Blessing, Inc., wrote in his book, *No Nonsense Management*:

> *A typical directive from a General Manager who is running scared is a bold "Cut the inventory." Such a directive (if his subordinates pursue it seriously) will certainly lead to a reduction, but it will inevitably be the wrong items that are cut—by the wrong amounts—and at the wrong time. . . . You'll reduce quantities on purchase orders and postpone deliveries and you'll get your reduction this month. However, shipments next month will be jeopardized, which will lead to further profit erosion, which will lead to further inventory and production cuts, which will eventually lead to (bankruptcy). . . .*

1.5 SOME STATISTICAL PROPERTIES OF AGGREGATE INVENTORIES

First, the importance and magnitude of inventory investment vary from one industry to another, as well as with the type and location of the firm within a distribution system of an industry. Second, in most companies a small percent of the products account for a large percent of the total annual dollar usage.

1.5.1 The Distribution of Inventories within Industries

In some industries, from the point of view of top management, the problem is primarily one of controlling raw materials; in others it is one of controlling finished goods; whereas, for example, in the capital goods industry, most organizational effort must be concentrated on the control of work-in-process inventories. Tables 1.2 and 1.3 provide illustrations.

In the case of manufacturers of railroad rolling stock and the garment industry, production is carried out primarily to specific customer order. One simply does not stock many diesel engines because of the tremendous cost of carrying inventory. One stocks a minimum of finished goods in the garment industry because of the vagaries of taste and style. However, note that in the latter case considerable inventory investment is tied up in work-in-process, presumably in readiness for a quick response to cues from the marketplace.

1.5.2 The Distribution by Annual Dollar Usage Value (DBV) within a Firm

Managerial decisions regarding inventories must ultimately be made at the level of an individual item or product. The specific unit of stock to be controlled will be called a *stock keeping unit (or s.k.u.), where an s.k.u. will be defined as an item of stock that is completely specified as to function, style, size, color, and,*

TABLE 1.2 The Relative Concentration of Inventory Investment across Three Canadian Industries[a] (in percent of total inventory investment)

	Raw Materials	Work-in-Process	Finished Goods
Iron and steel mills	50	29	21
Railroad rolling stock manufacturers	40	52	8
Rubber tires manufacturers	15	10	75

[a]Based on figures reported in "Inventories, Shipments and Orders in Manufacturing Industries." *Statistics Canada*, 1969.

TABLE 1.3 Inventory Distribution in Three U.S. Industries (percent of total inventory investment)[a]

	Raw Material	Work-in-Process	Manufacturer's Finished Goods	In the Distribution System
Capital goods	60	16	24	0
Garment industry	28	60	4	8
Consumer goods	4	12	28	56

[a]Adopted from D. D. Hall (1966), "Hard Nosed Inventory Management." In *The Manufacturing Man and His Job* (R. E. Finley and H. R. Pioboro, Editors). The American Management Association, Inc.

usually, location. For example, the same style shoes in two different sizes would constitute two different s.k.u. Each combination of size and grade of steel rod in raw stock constitutes a separate s.k.u. An oil company must regard each segregation of crude as a separate s.k.u. A tire manufacturer would normally treat the exact tire at two geographically remote locations as two distinct s.k.u. Note that the above type of classification system can result in the demand for two s.k.u. being highly correlated in practice, because a certain portion of customers will always be willing to substitute, for example, a blue widget for one that is red.[4] As we will see, particularly in Chapters 11, 12, and 16, decision rules often must coordinate the control of a number of distinct s.k.u.

Close examination of a large number of actual multi-s.k.u. inventory systems has revealed a useful statistical regularity in the usage rates of different items. Typically, somewhere on the order of 20 percent of the s.k.u. account for 80 percent of the total annual dollar usage. This suggests that all s.k.u. in a firm's inventory should not be controlled to the same extent, a discussion to which we return later. Figure 1.2 illustrates graphically the typical Distribution by Value (DBV) observed empirically in practice. Incidentally, the same DBV concept is applicable to a wide variety of other phenomena such as the distribution of (1) incomes within a population of individuals, (2) donation sizes among a group of donors, and so forth.

A DBV curve can be developed as follows: The value v, in dollars per unit, and the annual usage (or demand) D, in specific units, of each s.k.u. in inventory are identified. Then, the product Dv is calculated for each s.k.u., and the Dv values for all s.k.u. are ranked in descending order starting with the largest value as in Table 1.4. Subsequently the corresponding values of the cumulative percentages of total dollar usage and the cumulative percent of the total number of s.k.u. in inventory are plotted on a graph such as Figure 1.2. Experience has revealed that inventories of consumer goods will typically show a lesser concentration in the higher value s.k.u. than will an inventory of industrial s.k.u. Furthermore, as we find in Chapter 17, often a particular mathematical distribution provides an adequate fit to the DBV and thus permits relatively simple estimation of the *aggregate* effects of different inventory control policies.

A table, such as Table 1.4, is one of the most valuable tools for handling the diversity of disaggregate inventories because it helps to identify the s.k.u. that are the most important. These s.k.u. will be assigned a higher priority in the allocation of management time and financial resources in any decision system we design. Note that the ranking is on the basis of Dv. (As will be discussed in Chapter 3, other factors can be used for ranking items for managerial purposes, for example, by space requirements, by perishability, etc.) Both the usage (D) and the cost (v) of an item are continually subject to change. As a result, the relative priority assigned to any product is also always changing. That is, the DBV is a dynamic, not a static, concept.

[4]In practice, of course, one can define an s.k.u. in other (for example, less detailed) ways depending on the decision being made and the level of detail at which one wants to control inventories.

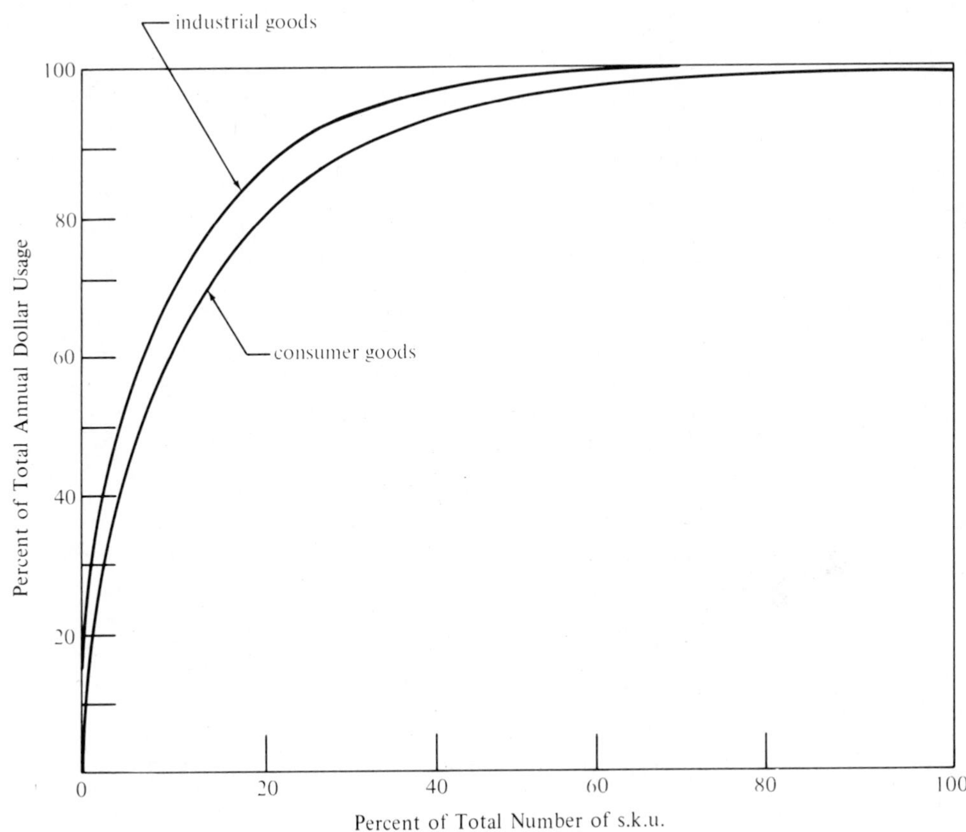

FIGURE 1.2 Distribution by Value of s.k.u.'s

TABLE 1.4 Example Listing of s.k.u. by Descending Dollar Usage

Sequential Number	s.k.u. I.D.	Cumulative Percent of s.k.u.	Annual Usage Value (Dv)	Cumulative Usage	Cumulative Percent of Total Usage
1	—	0.5	$3,000	$3,000	13.3
2	—	1.0	2,600	5,600	24.9
3	—	1.5	2,300	7,900	35.1
—	—	—	—	—	—
—	—	—	—	—	—
—	—	—	—	—	—
—	—	—	—	22,498	—
199	—	99.5	2	22,500	100.0
200	—	100.0	0	22,500	100.0

1.6 SUMMARY

In this chapter we first examined the importance of inventories. Further evidence of this importance is provided by the emergence and growth of two major professional societies. The first, the American Production and Inventory Control Society (founded in 1957 and with affiliated organizations in a number of other countries) now has a membership exceeding 50,000. In 1983 the International Society of Inventory Research was founded. Its interests encompass macro (industry and government level) as well as micro (level of the individual s.k.u. or firm) aspects of inventory management.

In this chapter we also looked at the nature of inventories in detail and found them to be diverse physically, statistically, and from the point of view of the values held by policy makers who manage inventory at the level of the economy and the firm. While we have made much of managing inventory, decision makers should not expect to be able to eliminate all inventory investments. Certain systematic inventory fluctuations are an unavoidable part of doing business:

1. Most industries face a seasonal demand for their products and services. As a result, desired inventory levels must also be seasonal, to some degree.
2. All corporate planning is based on forecasts which, after the fact, will always turn out to be in error to some degree. As a result, inventory levels must always be adjusted, post hoc, to match reality.
3. The amount of managerial effort and expense needed to eliminate or even control *all* inventories may prove to be uneconomical.

PROBLEMS

1.1 As stated in the introduction to the chapter, on the average, 34 percent of the current assets of a typical company are invested in inventories. An important financial performance measure is the return on investment:

$$\text{ROI} = \frac{\text{Profit}}{\text{Total assets}}$$

a. Consider the typical company and assume that it has a ratio

$$\frac{\text{Current assets}}{\text{Total assets}} = 0.40$$

What impact will a 25 percent decrease in inventory have on the ROI? What percent decrease in inventories is needed to double the ROI?

b. Develop an algebraic expression for the impact on ROI of an x percent decrease in inventories when

$$\frac{\text{Current assets}}{\text{Total assets}} = f$$

1.2 Select two appropriate, recent articles from a newspaper and identify how their contents could impinge on decision making in production planning and inventory management.

1.3 Read the article "Trimming Stocks," *The Wall Street Journal*, May 6, 1975, on the front page. Summarize the three main issues regarding inventories discussed, and comment.

1.4 Why do inflation and supply shortages tend to increase real inventories? What is the effect of a reduction in the rate of inflation on inventory investment?

1.5 Analyze the financial statements for the last five years of two companies from different industries. (For example, a grocery chain and an electronic goods manufacturer.) Calculate their turnover ratios. Try to explain why their turnover ratios are different. Are there any trends apparent that can be explained?

1.6 Investigate the inventory control procedures at a *small* (owner-managed) company. When does a company become too small to have its inventories managed scientifically?

1.7 Have a class representative (or representatives) select a *random* sample of 30 items stocked in your university bookstore. For each item obtain an estimate of Dv (from records or from the manager of the store). Prepare a Distribution by Value table and graph. (See Table 1.4 and Figure 1.2.)

REFERENCES

Abernathy, W. J., K. B. Clark, and A. M. Kantrow (1981). "The New Industrial Competition." *Harvard Business Review*, Vol. 59, No. 5, pp. 68–81.

Droms, W. G. (1979). *Finance and Accounting for Nonfinancial Managers.* Addison-Wesley, Reading, Massachusetts.

Evans, M. K. (1969). *Macroeconomic Activity: Theory, Forecasting and Control.* Harper and Row, New York, pp. 321–345.

Garwood, R. D. (1980). "Inventory Turns—A Dangerous Comparative Indicator." *1979–80 Hot Lists*, R. D. Garwood, Inc., Atlanta, Georgia.

Herron, D. P. (1979). "Managing Physical Distribution for Profit." *Harvard Business Review*, Vol. 57, No. 3, pp. 121–132.

Hill, R. E. (1974). "Does Top Management Manage Inventory?" *Production and Inventory Management*, Vol. 15, No. 1, pp. 32–36.

Hupp, B. W. (1969). "Inventory Policy Is a Top Management Responsibility." In *Readings in Physical Distribution Management* (D. J. Bowersox, B. J. Lalonde, and E. W. Smykay, Editors), Macmillan, New York, pp. 179–184.

Lovell, M. C. (1964). "Determinants of Inventory Investment." In *Models of Income Distribution* (I. Friend, Editor), Princeton University Press, Princeton, N.J.

Mack, R. P. (1967). *Information Expectations and Inventory Fluctuations.* Columbia University Press, New York.

McGill, H. N. (1927). "Hand to Mouth Buying and Its Effect on Business." *Industrial Management*, Vol. 73, No. 6.

Pappilon, A. (1697). "A Treatise Concerning the East India Trade (1677)." A 1697 reprint quoted in J. Viner (1937), *Studies in the Theory of International Trade*, Harper, New York, p. 20.

Ray, D. L. (1981). "Assessing U.K. Manufacturing Industry's Inventory Management Performance." *Focus on PDM (Journal of the Institute of Physical Distribution Management, U.K.)*, No. 27, pp. 5–11.

Skinner, W. (1969). "Manufacturing—Missing Link in Corporate Strategy." *Harvard Business Review*, Vol. 47, No. 3, pp. 136–145.

Whitin, T. M.(1957). *The Theory of Inventory Management.* Princeton University Press, Princeton, New Jersey, p. 219.

CHAPTER 2

Strategic Issues in Production Planning and Inventory Management

Reuter (1983) has succinctly summarized the history of production management in the United States during the twentieth century:

> *This country prospered and grew mightily in the first 60 years of the twentieth century amid firms largely dominated and run by production men. During World War II and for a number of years afterward, engineers, manufacturing managers, and production controllers were the glamour boys of industry as they met war-time needs and the subsequent pent-up, post-war civilian demands. Once the post-war backlog of orders for consumer goods was satisfied and the supply pipelines became full, the problem was over-production, and the challenge was to find markets for industry's excess capacity. Later came a need for tax shelters, diversification, and acquisition, which demanded new management skills in marketing, accounting, finance, and law. The educational establishment responded by training increasing numbers of people in these areas.*
>
> *During the late 1950s and through the mid-1970s, production and operations management went through a period of decline. The period was one of affluence and surplus. Production managers were taken for granted and lost status in corporate councils. For years top management ignored the production function while concentrating on marketing and finance. As time passed and management ranks were filled with other than production/operations management (POM) types, top management made strategic planning and operating decisions without taking into sufficient account the capabilities and limitations of the POM function.*

It is becoming evident that new manufacturing technologies are revolutionizing manufacturing worldwide. Related to the above quote, the increasingly automatic factories of the future will result in a new systems orientation to strategic management and will, at last, make production a part of the top management team. Technological changes currently underway will change not only how industry makes goods, but also the way in which management thinks about the role of manufacturing. Manufacturing will become increasingly total-systems based, which "promises a revolution the likes of which business has not seen since the introduction of mechanized power in the eighteenth century" (Thompson and Paris, 1982).

By the early 1980s, it became evident that many Japanese companies had mastered this new basis for industrial competition. The Japanese cost and quality advantages were shown to originate from the painstaking, strategic management of people, materials, and equipment—that is, in superior manufacturing performance. Despite the publicity given to Japan's experimentation with industrial robots and advanced plants, the evidence suggested that U.S. producers had maintained roughly comparable levels of process equipment. An explanation of Japanese success had more to do

> *with the factor of "process yield," and an amalgam of management practices and systems connected with production planning and control. . . . The Japanese advantage has far more to do with the interaction of materials control systems, maintenance practices, and employee involvement [Abernathy et al. 1981].*

Many of the management techniques used by the Japanese were not new. They had been generally available for years. What was different was the intensity and degree of commitment with which standard production planning and inventory management concepts were being applied. As a resource-poor and technologically dependent country, Japan had the most to gain from improving production concepts borrowed from the West.

In Section 2.1 we briefly discuss the nature of corporate strategy and how it relates to decision making in production planning and inventory management. Section 2.2 deals with an important ingredient of decision making—namely, the specification of appropriate measures of effectiveness. Key strategic issues in the production management area include the choice of the specific types of production/inventory planning, scheduling, and control systems as well as the particular decision rules for selecting values of the various control parameters. These, in turn, are very much dependent on the nature of the products and production processes involved. Thus, Sections 2.3 to 2.5 relate to the product life cycle, a dichotomy between two types of processing environments and, finally, a simultaneous representation of the product-process situation of any specific firm. With this as a backdrop we turn, in Section 2.6, to the choice of strategies in production planning and inventory management. Section 2.7 elaborates on one of these strategic choices, namely Just-in-Time Manufacturing.

2.1 CORPORATE STRATEGY AND THE ROLE OF TOP MANAGEMENT

It is not our intention to cover the topic of strategic planning in any depth. There are a number of texts on this topic (see, for example, Bower,1966; Hofer and Schendel, 1978; Steiner and Miner, 1982; and Thompson and Strickland, 1983). Instead, our objective is to show that decision making in the production and inventory areas must not be done in a vacuum, as is too often the case in practice, but rather must be coordinated with decisions in other functional areas by means of corporate strategic planning.

The key organizational role of top managers is strategic business planning. Senior management has the responsibility for defining in broad outline what needs to be done, and how and when it should be done. Top management also must act as the final arbiter of conflicts among operating divisions and has the ultimate responsibility for seeing that the general competitive environment is monitored and adapted to effectively.

Hofer and Schendel (1978) define an organization's strategy as the

> *fundamental pattern of present and planned resource developments and environmental interactions that indicates how the organization will achieve its objectives.*

In most business organizations 4 levels of strategy can be delineated (listed from the highest to the lowest level):

1. **Enterprise Strategy:** What role does the organization play in the economy and in society? What should be its legal form and how should it maintain its moral legitimacy?
2. **Corporate Strategy:** What set of businesses or markets should the corporation serve? How should resources be deployed among the businesses?
3. **Business Strategy:** How should the organization compete in each particular industry or product/market segment? On the basis of price, service, or what other factor?
4. **Functional Area Strategy:** At this level the principal focus of strategy is on the maximization of resource productivity and the development of distinctive competences.

While each level of strategy can be seen as being distinct, they must fit together to form a coherent and consistent whole. Typically, each level is constrained by the next higher one.

Most formal corporate planning systems encompass the following 14 processes according to Bower (1966) who, as managing director of the management consulting firm McKinsey and Company, implemented many such systems:[1]

[1]For another viewpoint on several of these issues see Peters and Waterman (1982).

1. **Setting Objectives:** Deciding on the business or businesses in which the company or division should engage and on other fundamentals that will guide and characterize the business. (Such as gaining a competitive advantage over other companies in an industry by developing more effective production planning and inventory management systems.)
2. **Planning Strategy:** Developing concepts, ideas, and plans for achieving objectives successfully, and for meeting and beating competition.
3. **Establishing Goals:** Deciding on achievement targets shorter in time range or narrower in scope than the objectives, but designed as specific subobjectives in making operational plans for carrying out strategy. (The Japanese automobile industry has increased inventory turnover every year for the last 10 years without reducing quality or service.)
4. **Developing a Company Philosophy:** Establishing the beliefs, values, attitudes, and unwritten guidelines that add up to "the way we do things around here."
5. **Establishing Policies:** Deciding on plans of action to guide the performance of all major activities in carrying out strategy in accordance with company philosophy.
6. **Planning the Organization Structure:** Developing the plan of organization—the "harness" that helps people pull together in performing activities in accordance with strategy, philosophy, and policies. (Some corporations adopt a functional form: marketing, production, etc.; others are divisionalized by product/market groupings; most are a mixture of the two.)
7. **Providing Personnel:** Recruiting, selecting, and developing people to fill the positions required by the organization plan selected.
8. **Establishing Procedures:** Determining and prescribing how all important and recurrent activities will be carried out. (Including, for example, production quantities and order-triggering mechanisms.)
9. **Providing Facilities:** Providing the plant, equipment, warehouse space, and other facilities required to carry on the business.
10. **Providing Capital:** Making sure the business has the money and credit needed for physical facilities and working capital (including inventory investment).
11. **Setting Standards:** Establishing measures of performance that will best enable the business to achieve its long-term objectives successfully. (Including acceptable stockout levels, finished goods availability off the shelf, etc.)
12. **Establishing Management Programs and Operational Plans:** Developing programs and plans governing activities and the use of resources that, when carried out in accordance with the established strategy, policies, procedures, and standards, will enable people to achieve particular goals.
13. **Providing Control Information:** Supplying facts and figures to help people follow the strategy, policies, procedures, and programs, and measure their own performance against established plans and standards.

14. **Activating People:** Commanding and motivating people up and down the line to act in accordance with philosophy, policies, procedures, and standards in carrying out the plans of the company.

We will have more to say on strategic planning in Chapter 13 where a specific framework for decision making in a production environment will be developed.

2.2 MEASURES OF EFFECTIVENESS FOR PRODUCTION PLANNING AND INVENTORY MANAGEMENT DECISIONS

Analysts in the production/inventory area have tended to concentrate on a single quantifiable measure of effectiveness such as cost or contribution to profit and overhead, sometimes recognizing certain constraints such as limited space, desired customer service, and so forth. In actual fact, of course, the impact of decisions is not restricted to a single measure of effectiveness. The appropriate measures of effectiveness should relate back to the underlying objectives of management. Unfortunately, some of the following objectives are very difficult to quantify:

1. Minimizing political conflicts (in terms of the competing interests) within the organization. (Figure 2.1 illustrates the behavioral/political conflicts in the management of inventories.)
2. Maintaining a high level of flexibility to cope with an uncertain future.
3. Maximizing the chance of survival of the firm or the individual manager's position within the organization.
4. Keeping at an acceptable level the amount of human effort expended in the planning and operation of a decision system.

Moreover, as will be discussed in Chapter 3, even some of the more tangible cost factors are very difficult to estimate in practice.

From the perspective of top management, the measures of effectiveness used must be aggregate in nature. Management is concerned with *overall* inventory levels and customer service levels (by broad classes of items) as opposed to, for example, minimization of costs on an individual s.k.u. basis. Furthermore, rather than optimization in the absolute sense, a more appealing justification for a new or modified decision system is that it simply provides significant improvements (in terms of one or more measures of effectiveness) over an existing system. The implications, in terms of the nature of mathematical modeling to be used, will be discussed in Section 2.6 as well as in Chapter 3.

One other complexity is that certain decisions in the production planning and inventory management area should not necessarily be made in isolation from decisions in other areas. As an illustration, both Schwarz (1981) and Wagner

A. Organizational forces pushing for *higher* inventory:

1. Middle to senior management, in general, prefer higher buffer stocks to cover mistakes and inefficiencies in their operations that they have not been able to remove. Their promotion and reward depend on smooth operations.

2. Production management prefers higher inventories because they allow:
   - Lower operating costs
   - Longer production runs
   - More in-process stock
   - Higher raw materials levels

3. Marketing/sales management prefer higher inventories because they make it possible to provide:
   - Better customer service
   - Shorter lead times
   - Higher order fill rates
   - Full product lines
   - More new products
   - More flexibility

B. Organizational forces pushing for *lower* inventory:

1. When a corporation faces difficult times one of the first actions examined is lower inventory investment—that is, reducing the organizational slack present in the form of buffer stocks. "We must tighten our belts!"

2. Finance/accounting management are rewarded for:
   - Reducing working capital requirements
   - Demonstrating higher return on investment on the money tied up in inventories
   - Increasing profits by reducing carrying costs
   - Keeping better records on managers who may be overly using inventory buffers
   - Diverting money tied up in inventory into other, more profitable investments

FIGURE 2.1 Managing Inventory Means Managing Conflict

(1974) point out that there are important interactions between the design of a physical distribution system (for example, the number, nature, and location of warehouses) and the selection of an appropriate inventory management system (Chapter 12 will deal further with this particular issue.) Constable and Whybark (1978) and Herron (1979) address another type of interaction, namely, between transportation (shipping) decisions and those of inventory management. Another interaction, vividly portrayed by the success of Japanese management systems, is between inventory management and quality assurance. In this text we do not develop mathematical models that directly deal with these large-scale interactive problems. However, in several places further descriptive advice will be presented.

In the next three sections we digress somewhat to lay a further part of the foundation needed for our subsequent discussion of the choice of strategies in the production/inventory functional area.

2.3 A KEY MARKETING CONCEPT—THE PRODUCT LIFE CYCLE

The lifetime sales of many branded products reveal a typical pattern of development, as shown in Figure 2.2. The length of this so-called life cycle appears to be governed by the rate of technological change, the rate of market acceptance, and the ease of competitive entry (Dean, 1950).

Each year, some new dress styles are introduced in the knowledge that their whole life cycle may last only a season (a few months). Other products, such as commercial aircraft, are expected to be competitive for decades. Some products have been known to begin a new cycle or to revert to an earlier stage as a result of the discovery of new uses, the appearance of new users, or the invention of new features. Kotler (1967) cites the example of television sales, which have exhibited a history of spurts as new sizes of screens were introduced, and the advent of color television, which put sales back to an earlier, rapid growth stage in that industry. Although the life cycle is an idealized concept, three basic generalizations seem to hold (Kotler, 1967):

1. Products have a limited life. They are introduced to the market, may (or may not) pass through a strong growth phase, and eventually degenerate or disappear.
2. Product profits tend to follow a predictable course through the life cycle. Profits are absent in the introductory stage, tend to increase substantially in the growth stage, slow down and then stabilize in the maturity and saturation stages, and can disappear in the decline stage.
3. Products require a different marketing, production planning, inventory management, and financial strategy in each stage. The emphasis given to the different functional areas must also change.

When product life cycles are reasonably short, associated production processes must be designed to be reusable or multipurpose in nature. Alternatively, the amount of investment in single-purpose equipment must be recoverable before the product becomes obsolete. Moreover, the appropriate planning, scheduling, and control systems to use for an individual product are likely to change as the relative importance of the item changes during its life cycle. In particular, special control aspects for the development and saturation stages of Figure 2.2 will be discussed in Chapters 4, 6, 8, and 9.

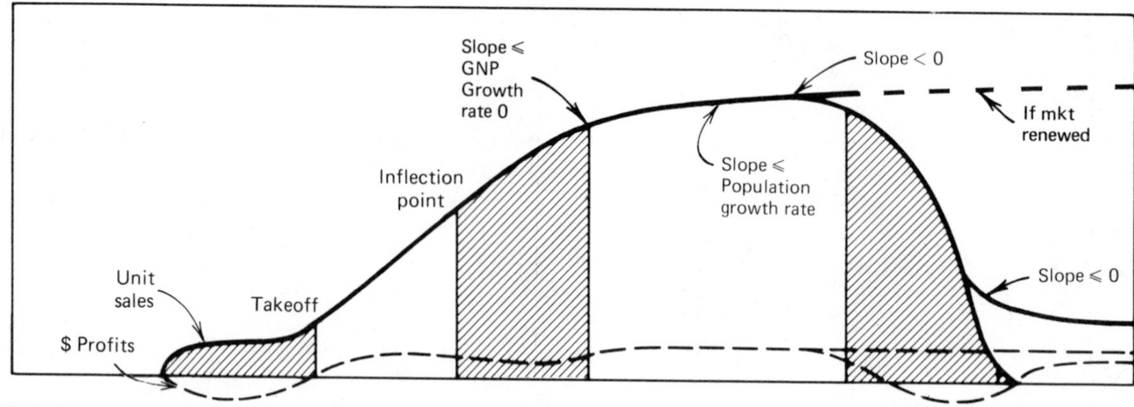

Stage	Development	Growth	Shakeout	Maturity	Saturation		
					Saturation	Decline	Petrification
Market growth rate	Slight	Very large	Large	GNP growth	Population growth	Negative	Stable
Change in growth rate	Little	Increases rapidly	Decreases rapidly	Decreases slowly	Little	Decreases rapidly, then slow; may increase then slow[a]	Little
Number of segments	Very few	Some	Some	Some to many		Few	Few
Technological change in product design	Very great	Great	Moderate	Slight	Slight[b]	Slight	Slight
Technological change in process design	Slight	Slight/ moderate	Very great	Great/ moderate	Slight	Slight	Slight
Major functional concern	R & D	Engineering	Production	Marketing distribution, finance		Finance	Marketing and finance

[a]The rate of change of the market growth rate usually only increases during the decline stage of those products that do not die, that is, that enter the petrification stage of evolution.

[b]Although the rate of technological change in the basic design of the product is usually low during these stages of market evolution, the probability of a major breakthrough to a different kind of product that performs the same function increases substantially during these stages of evolution.

Source: Charles W. Hofer (1977). "Conceptual Constructs for Formulating Corporate and Business Strategy." (Dover, Mass.: Case Teachers Association, #BP-0041, p. 7.) Copyright © 1977 by Charles W. Hofer. Reprinted by permission.

FIGURE 2.2 The Fundamental Stages of Product/Market Evolution

2.4 PROCESS VERSUS FABRICATION/ ASSEMBLY INDUSTRIES

We distinguish initially between two broad classes of industries—process versus fabrication/assembly—because the differences between them have important implications in terms of the choice of strategy for production planning and inventory management. Typical illustrations of process industry products include chemicals (plastics, drugs, soaps, fertilizers, etc.), refined petroleum and metal products, foods and beverages, and paper goods. Fabrication/assembly products encompass, for example, automobiles, home furnishings, machine tools, electrical equipment, computers, industrial machinery, and apparel. As we will see, the differences between these two categories include product/market characteristics, the nature of the production equipment, inputs to the production process, and other manufacturing characteristics. In what follows we draw, in particular, on the work of Taylor et al. (1981).

2.4.1 Product and Market Characteristics

The contrast in product and market characteristics can be seen in Table 2.1. Clearly, there are significant differences between the two types of industries. In particular, because of the more standardized nature of products in the process industries, there tends to be more production to stock (as opposed to order) than there is in fabrication/assembly.

2.4.2 The Nature of the Equipment and Inputs to the Production Process

By inputs we mean raw materials, manpower, and energy. Again, there are important differences between the two industry groups as evidenced by Table 2.2. Specifically, we note that process industries tend to be more capital intensive. For example, in the United States in 1979 the average gross plant per

TABLE 2.1 Differences in Product and Market Characteristics

	Type of Industry	
Characteristics	Process	Fabrication/Assembly
Number of customers	Less	More
Number of products	Less	More
Product differentiation	More standardized (commodities)	More customized
Marketing characteristics	Availability/price	Features of products
Demand for intermediate products	Higher	Lower

TABLE 2.2 Differences in Equipment and Production Inputs

	Type of Industry	
Characteristics	Process	Fabrication/Assembly
Capital versus labor/material intensive	Capital	Labor/material
Level of automation	Higher	Lower
Nature of production layout	Flow	Job shop or flow
Flexibility of output	Less	More
Capacity	Well defined	Vague
Lead times for expansion	Higher	Lower
Reliability of equipment	Higher needs	Lower needs
Nature of maintenance	Shutdown	More on a component basis
Number of raw materials	Lower	Higher
Variability of raw materials	Higher	Lower
Energy usage	Higher	Lower

employee for process industries was $60,000, whereas that for fabrication/assembly was only $17,000.[2] This is partly a consequence of higher average automation in the process environment.

Process industries tend to have a flow-type layout; that is, materials flow through various processing operations in a fixed routing. However, particularly in fabrication, the flow is by numerous, different, and largely unconstrained paths.[3] The production lines in the process context tend to be dedicated to a relatively small number of products with comparatively little flexibility to change either the rate or the nature of the output. In this environment capacity is quite well defined by the limiting (or bottleneck) operation, whereas with fabrication/assembly both the bottleneck and the associated capacity tend to shift with the nature of the work load (which products are being produced and in what quantities).

Because of the relatively expensive equipment and plant involved and the relatively low flexibility in output rate, process industries tend to run at full capacity (that is, 3 shifts per day, 7 days per week) when they are operating. This and the flow nature of the process necessitate highly reliable equipment, which, in turn, normally requires substantial preventive maintenance. Such maintenance is usually carried out when the entire operation is shut down for an extended period of time. Moreover, much longer lead times are typically involved in changing the capacity in a process industry (partly because of environmental concerns, but also because of the nature of the plant and equipment involved).

[2]From *Financial Dynamics*, Standard and Poor's Compustat Service, Inc., 1979.

[3]However, use of the concept of group technology (see, for example, Wild, 1972) tends to lead to a significant amount of flow layout even in fabrication.

The number of raw materials used tends to be lower in process situations as compared with fabrication/assembly; in fact, *coordination of raw materials, components, and so on, as well as required labor input, is a major concern in fabrication/assembly*. However, there can be more natural variability in the characteristics of these raw materials in the process context (for example, ingredients from agricultural or mineral sources). Furthermore, energy usage is quite high in certain process industries (for example, smelter and refining operations).

2.4.3 Other Manufacturing Characteristics

Differences in other manufacturing characteristics are illustrated in Table 2.3. Several of these are a direct consequence of factors identified in the preceding two subsections.

Although there may be relatively few products run on a particular flow line in the process industries, the products do tend to group into families according to a natural sequence. An example would be paints, where the natural sequence of changes would be to darker and darker colors with a major changeover (once a cycle) from the darkest to the lightest color. As a consequence, in contrast with fabrication/assembly, a major concern is ascertaining the appropriate sequence and the time interval between consecutive cycles among the products. The relative similarity of items run on the same line in the process context also makes it easier to aggregate demand data, running hours, and so forth, than is the case in fabrication/assembly.

The flow nature of production in the process industries leads to less work-in-process inventories than is the case, for example, in the job shop context of fabrication. This relative lack of buffering stock, in turn, implies a crucial need for adequate supplies of the relatively few raw materials, as well as reliable equipment. However, in this case the same line of reasoning applies to high-volume assembly lines.

There can be considerable yield variability in certain operations in process industries. Thus, variable mixes of ingredients (recipes) and running times are more common in process than in fabrication/assembly industries. An interest-

TABLE 2.3 Differences in Other Manufacturing Characteristics

	Type of Industry	
Characteristics	Process	Fabrication/Assembly
Families of items	Primary concern	Less concern
Aggregation of data	Easier	More difficult
Work-in-process inventory	Lower	Higher
Yield variability	Higher	Lower
By-products	More	Less
Need for traceability	Higher	Lower

ing discussion of this point with respect to McCormick and Company, a major processor and distributor of food flavorings, is provided by Bolander et al. (1981).

There tends to be more by-products in process situations. Some of these are desirable and can be sold at a higher return than the primary products (such is the case, for example, in the meat-packing industry). Others may be highly undesirable and subject to government restrictions, such as the toxic wastes resulting from chemical reactions.

Finally, the nature of certain process industry products, such as drugs and foods, necessitates *lot tracing*—the ability to ascertain which ingredients were used and under what conditions as each output unit was produced.

2.5 THE PRODUCT-PROCESS MATRIX

Recall that we are striving to divide production and inventory situations into classes that require somewhat different strategies and procedures for planning and control. The product life cycle and the process versus fabrication/assembly dichotomy have been major steps in that direction. However, Hayes and Wheelwright (1979a, 1979b) present a concept that provides us with considerable further insight. They point out that while

> *the product life cycle pattern . . . does provide a provocative framework for thinking about the growth and development of a new product . . . one of the major shortcomings of this approach, however, is that it concentrates on marketing implications (only) . . . It implies that other aspects of the business and industry environment (somehow) move in concert. . . .*

In fact, most manufacturing processes in practice also go through a cycle of evolution (the process cycle). Typically, they start from a relatively flexible, "fluid" state, making few of a kind products, that are labor intensive and generally not very cost efficient and move to a state that is less flexible, increasingly standardized, mechanized, automated, and capital intensive. Hayes and Wheelright suggested that the product life and process life cycle stages cannot be considered separately. One cannot proceed from one level of mechanization to another, for example, without making some adjustments to the products and management decision systems involved. Nor can new products be added or others discontinued without considering the effect on production process utilization.

Hayes and Wheelwright encapsulated the above remarks into a graphical representation known as a product-process matrix. Rather than showing their original form of the matrix we have portrayed in Figure 2.3 an adapted version (based partly on suggestions in Schmenner, 1981, and Taylor et al., 1981) that is more suitable for our purposes. The columns of the matrix represent (in a more condensed version than Figure 2.2) the product life cycle phases, going from the great variety associated with startup products on the left-hand side, to stand-

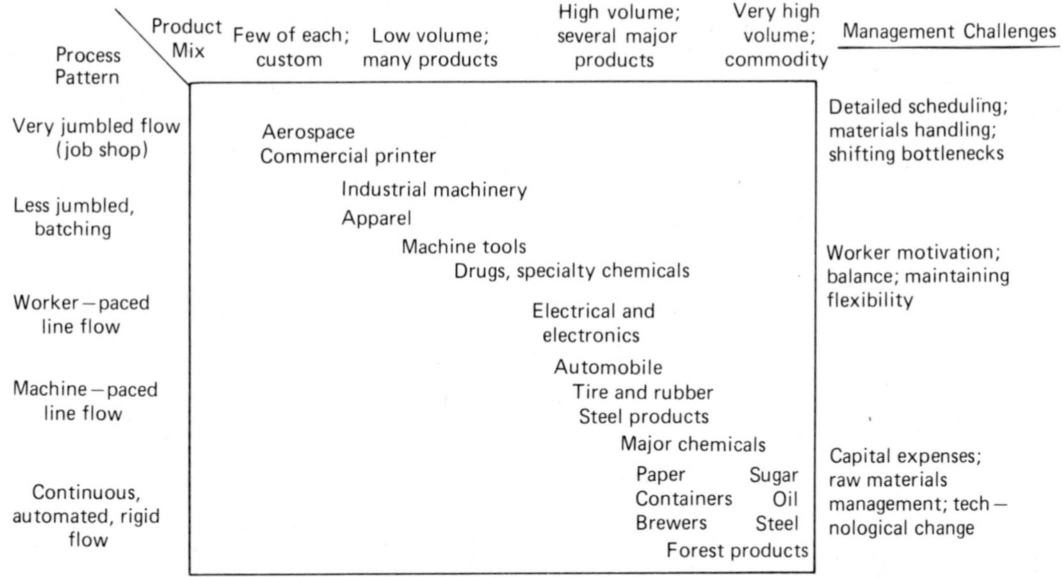

FIGURE 2.3 Product-Process Matrix

ardized commodity products on the right-hand side. The rows represent the major stages through which a production process tends to pass in going from a relatively fluid to a highly standardized form. Most production organizations find themselves more or less along the diagonal. A number of illustrations are shown in the figure. We see that, by and large, fabrication is in the top left corner, process industries toward the bottom right corner, and assembly in the middle. However, there are some exceptions. For example, drugs and specialty chemicals, which are process industry products, are centrally located whereas containers and steel products, which involve some fabrication, are toward the bottom right. Hayes and Wheelwright discuss the strategic implications of nondiagonal positions.

To provide additional insight we draw on the work of Schonberger (1983) who points out that the strategy for production planning, scheduling, and inventory management should depend on how easily one can associate raw material and part requirements with the schedule of end products. As we will now show, there is a direct connection between the position on the product-process matrix and the ease of the aforementioned association. In the lower right-hand corner of Figure 2.3 the association tends to be quite easy (continuous flow systems). This position is, by and large, occupied by capacity-oriented process industries.[4] As

[4]In Chapters 13 to 16, where we address in detail decision making in production contexts, we will primarily use the dichotomy of capacity-oriented process industries versus materials and labor-oriented fabrication/assembly industries.

one moves up to the left and passes through high-volume assembly into lower volume assembly and batching, the association becomes increasingly difficult. In this region one is dealing primarily with materials and labor-oriented fabrication/assembly industries.[5] Finally, in the top left-hand corner, where fabrication is dominant, the association may again become easier but, where production here is primarily to order, detailed, advanced planning and scheduling are likely not feasible.

2.6 THE CHOICE OF STRATEGIES IN THE PRODUCTION PLANNING AND INVENTORY MANAGEMENT FUNCTIONAL AREA

The previous several sections have laid the foundation for a discussion of strategy in production planning and inventory management. In this section we first discuss the various possible systems available for production planning, scheduling, and inventory management. Subsequently, the impact of some of the new, computer-related technology is mentioned. Finally, we address the implications, in terms of the type and amount of mathematical modeling, of the choice among the possible decision systems.

2.6.1 Possible Types of Planning and Control Systems

Possible types of systems for production planning, scheduling, and inventory management are summarized in Table 2.4. Also shown in Figure 2.4 are the corresponding positions in the product-process matrix. Note that the matrix does not really include the important segment (shown in Table 2.4) of nonmanufacturing organizations, the latter encompassing distributors, retailers, and wholesalers, as well as all service industries (including government agencies) that use various types of supplies, spare parts, and so forth. This nonmanufacturing segment represents a major focus of our book.

2.6.2 The Impact of Computer-Related Technologies

The above discussion, as well as that in Section 2.5, is likely to be tempered somewhat by the continued development of computer-related technology such as computer-aided design (CAD), robotics, and computer-aided manufacturing (CAM). Specifically, this new technology will continue to reduce the contrast

[5]See footnote 4.

TABLE 2.4 Types of Systems for Production Planning, Scheduling, and Inventory Management

System	Relevant Chapters of Text	Nature of Relevant Industries	Primary Focus of System
Job shop	a	Low-volume fabrication	Flexibility to cope with a myriad of different orders
Economic order quantities,[b] reorder points, etc.	5–11	Nonmanufacturing	Reduction of inventory-related costs while maintaining high customer service
Multistage economic order quantities,[b] reorder points, etc.	12–16	Distribution	"
		Capacity-oriented	High utilization of capacity at reasonable cost
Material Requirements Planning	13, 16	Batching, low-volume assembly	Effective coordination of material and labor needs
Just-in-Time Manufacturing	2 (Section 2.7), 16	High-volume, repetitive assembly/ fabrication	Minimization of setup times and inventories, with associated high quality levels

[a]Discussed briefly in Chapter 13.

[b]This includes variations on economic order quantities (for example, quantity discounts, coordination of items procured from the same supplier,etc.).

between production processes at either end of the diagonal in Figure 2.3. Some of the advantages of job shop flexibility will become available to continuous flow production processes, and vice versa.

The range of robots available is depicted in Table 2.5. "Programming" in the table refers to the software instruction that can be given to the robot, ranging from relatively simple to complex and reprogrammable. The "tasks performed" refers to the nature of the jobs carried out by the robot in terms of the number of separate steps and discrete operations. The effect on production planning and inventory management will clearly be dramatic. Unlike traditional automation (the first row of Table 2.5) where operations are performed in unison, in a machining center each separate unit can now operate independently, but can be linked to an overall computerized production plan. These machine center robots will provide greater flexibility in production scheduling by reducing setup and changeover costs through the use of microprocessors and by making it possible

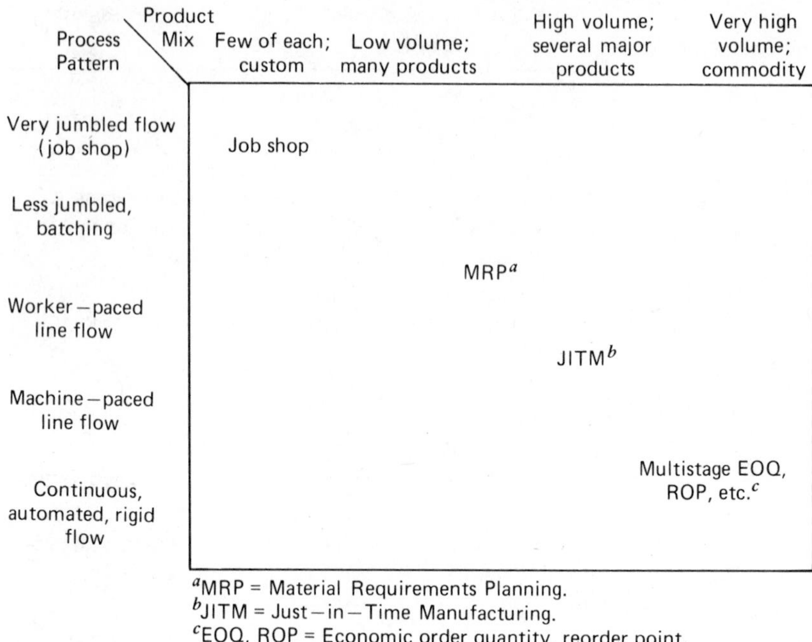

FIGURE 2.4 Positions of Possible Systems on the Product-Process Matrix

TABLE 2.5 Classification of Robots

	Tasks Performed	
Programming	Single	Multiple
Simple	Fixed-sequence robots	Numeric control robots
Complex	Machine center robots	Sensor-aided robots

Source: C. J. McMillan(1982), "Robotics: Will the Corporation Be Managed by Machines?" *Cost and Management*, Vol. 56, No. 4, pp. 1–7.

to automate very simple tasks at fairly low costs—for example, conveyor and materials handling systems. According to McMillan (1982),

> *For large firms, robotics may bring the opportunity to introduce enormous flexibility in production scheduling for diverse products on the same assembly line, even for small batches. Existing assembly-line forms must deal in large volume to operate economically, because the alternative to small lots is higher inventory. . . . The small firm will have the opportunity of entering many market segments normally reserved for large firms because, within certain volume ranges, robotics will equalize costs for big firms and small firms alike.*

Buzacott and Shanthikumar (1980) define a flexible manufacturing system (FMS) as "a set of machines . . . linked by a material handling system all under central computer control." An FMS makes the automated production of complex workpieces in small and medium lot sizes technically feasible and economically possible. The goal is to establish a smooth flow through the plant so that at any moment one piece is waiting at each work station, another has just been finished, while a third piece is being worked on. The production quantity is effectively one. Actual in-process stocks are determined by machine balance, capacity, breakdowns, and so on.

2.6.3 Three Types of Modeling Strategies

The choice of a decision system within the framework of either Table 2.4 or Figure 2.4 has broad implications in terms of the nature and amount of mathematical modeling that is utilized. Prior to discussing the different types of modeling strategies, we wish to emphasize that the results of *any* mathematical analysis *must* be made consistent with overall corporate strategy (Section 2.1) and *must* be tempered by the behavioral and political realities (see Stainton, 1983) of the organization under study (as discussed in Section 2.2). In particular, a proper problem diagnosis is often more important than the subsequent analysis (see Lockett, 1981) and, in some cases, corporate strategy and the behavioral or political circumstances may rule out the meaningful use of any mathematical model.

There are three types of strategies that involve some modeling:

1. Detailed modeling and analytic selection of the values of a *limited* number of decision variables.
2. Broader scope modeling, with less attempt at optimization.
3. Minimization of inventories with very little in the way of associated mathematical models.

We now discuss the first two of these. Because the third encompasses a radically different philosophy requiring more explanation, we leave its treatment to Section 2.7.

Detailed Modeling and Analytic Selection of the Values of a Limited Number of Decision Variables

The strategy here is to develop a mathematical model that permits the selection of the values of a limited set of variables so that some reasonable measure of effectiveness can be optimized. A classical example (to be treated in Chapter 5) is the economic order quantity which, under certain assumptions, minimizes the total of ordering and inventory carrying costs per unit time. The mathematical model may permit a deductive (closed-form) solution, an iterative solution (such as in the Simplex Method of linear programming), or a solution by some form of trial-and-error procedure (such as in the use of a simulation model).

Broader Scope Modeling with Less Optimization

Here the strategy is to attempt to develop a more realistic model of the particular situation. However, the added realism often prevents any clearly defined optimization; in fact, there may not even be a mathematically stated objective function. One strives for a feasible solution that one hopes will provide reasonable performance. This is the philosophy underlying Material Requirements Planning (to be discussed in Chapters 13 and 16).

2.7 THE STRATEGIC ASPECTS OF STOCKLESS PRODUCTION

Much of the Japanese success in international markets has been the result of the adoption of stockless production, a concept first introduced by the Toyota Motor Corporation. Stockless production is a total manufacturing system encompassing product design, equipment selection, materials management, quality assurance, job design, and productivity improvement (see, for example, Hall, 1983, and O'Connor, 1982). Inventories are reduced as much as possible to increase productivity (possibly by automation), to improve quality, and to reduce production lead times (hence, customer response times). The production/material control system is called Just-in-Time Manufacturing (JITM).[6]

2.7.1 The General Nature of the System

Stockless production is appropriate in a high-volume, repetitive manufacturing environment. The different stages of production are tightly linked with very little in-process inventories. Final assembly needs dictate the inflow of subassemblies, triggering the production of new subassemblies, and so on. Each feeding work center produces only what its following (or consuming) work center uses to satisfy the assembly schedule. The associated manual information system is known as Kanban (the Japanese word for a card). The details of Kanban will be presented in Chapter 16. For now, all that is important is that the amount of in-process inventory between any two work centers is strictly (and easily) controllable by the number of cards assigned to that particular pair of centers.

In working toward stockless production, an organization follows a set of systematic steps:

1. The need for high levels of quality (both in-house and with suppliers) is given extreme emphasis.
2. Setup or changeover times are reduced as much as possible (very low setup times permit the economic production of small lot sizes as well as increasing the utilization of equipment).

[6]The usual abbreviation is JIT; for convenience we have incorporated the noun "manufacturing" into the abbreviation.

3. Lot sizes are reduced as much as possible and standardized.
4. Once the plant is in reasonable balance (in terms of stable, roughly equal workloads at the different work centers) inventory is systematically reduced (by removing Kanban cards). Each reduction usually leads to the identification of a problem (bottleneck) area.
5. The problem is resolved in a cost-effective fashion (for example, by procedural changes, equipment adjustments, etc.).

Steps 4 and 5 are repeated over and over until no further improvements can be realized or until zero inventory is achieved between pairs of work centers. In the latter case, one then investigates the possibility of automated piece-by-piece transfer between the two centers.

A useful analogy (see, for example, O'Connor, 1982) to the above philosophy and approach is to liken inventories to water in a river. When the water is at a high level, dangerous rocks (obstacles to higher productivity) below the surface are concealed. As the water (inventory) level is lowered, the rocks (underlying problems) are identified and removed, thus keeping the waterway open (improving productivity) at a lower water (inventory) level.

2.7.2 Prerequisities and Benefits

There are impressive benefits to be gained through the adoption of the stockless production philosophy. Qualitatively, these include (1) lower space requirements, (2) reduced inventory handling and control costs, (3) less money needed for financing inventories, (4) increased productivity, (5) higher quality levels, and (6) reduced lead times. An illustration of specific results achieved in Japan is shown in Table 2.6.

Stockless production is not the end-all for every organization. For it to be truly effective, there are several conditions that must first exist or be developed, specifically, (1) employee motivation and mutual trust between workers and

TABLE 2.6 Results of Stockless Production Programs in Japan

Company	Time Since Program Started[a] (years)	Manufacturing Inventory (% of original value)	Lead Time (% of original value)	Percent Increase in Labor Productivity
Auto parts	3	45%	40%	50%
Electrical components	3	16	20	80
Electronic products	4	30	25	60
Motorcycles	2	20	50	50

[a]These are results after the first round of the programs at each company, but stockless production programs never stop. Each program continues to yield improvements year after year.

Source: J. Nakane and R. W. Hall (1983). "Management Specs for Stockless Production." *Harvard Business Review*, Vol. 61, No. 3, p. 89.

management (culturally much more likely in Japan than in other countries)—a tremendous responsibility is thrown onto the individual workers (see Kamata, 1982, for a scathing attack on the system); (2) multiskilled work force (to provide flexibility in scheduling); (3) special relationship with suppliers; (4) extremely high levels of quality; and (5) high-volume, repetitive manufacturing. A report on management opinions related to the U.S. automobile industry, prepared by the consulting firm of Arthur Andersen and Company (1983), sheds further light on these issues.

2.8 SUMMARY

In this chapter we have examined a number of strategic issues related to production planning and inventory management. In these times of rapid technological change and increased international competition, these issues are of extreme importance from a national perspective. In much of the remainder of the book our attention will be addressed to less global concerns, specifically how best to design and operate a production planning and inventory management decision system *within a specific organization and given the process technology and the market environment.* Nevertheless, we would hope that the reader will not lose sight of the broader perspective of this chapter.

PROBLEMS

2.1 In Section 2.2 mention was made of an interaction between the design of a physical distribution system and the choice of an inventory management system. Briefly comment on this interaction.

2.2 Examine the interaction specified in Section 2.2 again, but now between the choice of a transportation mode and the selection of inventory decision rules.

2.3 *Briefly* comment on how inventory management might interact with each of the following functional areas of the firm:

a. Maintenance

b. Quality control

c. Distribution (shipping)

2.4 With respect to the product-process matrix of Figure 2.3, in what area do you feel there is the greatest threat, posed by developing countries, to North American industry? What is the implication in terms of future needs in production planning, scheduling, and control in North American organizations?

2.5 Which decision categories among the following are considered traditionally operational in North American companies and strategic in Japanese companies?

a. Capacity planning

b. Production planning and inventory management

c. Facilities planning

d. Process technology

Explain your choice of categories briefly.

2.6 The type of operation characterized by a large volume of identical or similar products flowing through identical stages of production is typical in which of the following industries?

a. Aerospace

b. Automobiles

c. Machine tools

For such a situation, which type of production planning and inventory management system is appropriate? Explain your reasoning.

2.7 A management decision system designed for providing information on how well a business is doing, relative to other businesses in the same industry segment, is appropriate for:

a. Top management

b. Middle management

c. Marketing management

d. Factory Management

e. Office staff

Explain the reasoning behind your choice.

2.8 Using Figure 2.2, describe the appropriate production planning and inventory management strategy that you would recommend at each stage of product/market evolution. Would your recommendation change from one industry to another? Illustrate your answer by selecting two different products.

2.9 In a report, concerning the U.S. automobile industry by Arthur Andersen and Company (1983), the following statements are made:

In (our) survey questionnaire, we defined just-in-time as a management approach on the elimination of waste, including unnecessary inventory, scrap, rework, indirect labor, and non-productive machines, etc. However, responses indicate a misunderstanding of and disagreement over just-in-time approaches. . . .

Quick setups and production of smaller lot sizes are likely to be an important consideration for suppliers at all *tiers in the supply pipeline.*

Quantum leaps in quality improvement are required to implement just-in-time and the required investment will not be a major constraint to implementation.

Electronically created, stored, and transmitted data will become the norm by 1988 . . . communication of data between vehicle manufacturers and suppliers is now being established. Perhaps a "high tech" version of Kanban will evolve in the U.S.

Comment on this quote, using the discussion in this book, your experience, and other publications that are available in the library.

REFERENCES

Abernathy, W. J., K. B. Clark, and A. M. Kantrow (1981). "The New Industrial Competition." *Harvard Business Review*, Vol. 59, No. 5, pp. 68–81.

Arthur Andersen and Company (1983). *The Changing U.S. Automobile Industry*. Chicago, pp. 33–46.

Bolander, S. F., R. C. Heard, S. M. Seward, and S. G. Taylor (1981). *Manufacturing Planning and Control in Process Industries*. American Production and Inventory Control Society, Falls Church, Virginia.

Bower, M. (1966). *The Will to Manage: Corporate Success Through Programmed Management*. McGraw-Hill, New York, pp. 17–18.

Buzacott, J. A., and J. G. Shanthikumar (1980). "Models for Understanding Flexible Manufacturing Systems." *AIIE Transactions*, Vol. 12, No. 4, pp. 339–350.

Constable, G., and D. C. Whybark (1978). "The Interaction of Transportation and Inventory Decisions." *Decision Sciences*, Vol. 9, No. 4, pp. 688–699.

Dean, J. (1950). "Pricing Polices for New Products." *Harvard Business Review*, Vol. 28, No. 6, p. 28.

Hall, R. W. (1983). *Zero Inventories*. Dow-Jones, Irwin, Homewood, Illinois.

Hayes, R. H., and S. C. Wheelwright (1979a). "Link Manufacturing Process and Product Life Cycles." *Harvard Business Review*, Vol. 57, No. 1, pp. 133–140.

Hayes, R. H., and S. C. Wheelwright (1979b). "The Dynamics of Process-Product Life Cycles." *Harvard Business Review*, Vol. 57, No. 2, pp. 127–136.

Herron, D. P. (1979). "Managing Physical Distribution for Profit." *Harvard Business Review*, Vol. 57, No. 3, pp. 121–132.

Hofer, C., and D. Schendel (1978). *Strategy Formulation: Analytical Concepts*. West, St. Paul, Minnesota.

Kamata, S. (1982). *Japan in the Passing Lane: An Insider's Account of Life in a Japanese Auto Factory*. Pantheon Books, New York.

Kotler, P. (1967). *Marketing Management: Analysis, Planning, and Control*. Prentice-Hall, Englewood Cliffs, N.J.

Lockett, A. G. (1981). "The Management of Stocks—Some Case Histories." *OMEGA*, Vol. 9, No. 6, pp. 595–604.

McMillan, C. J. (1982). "Robotics: Will the Corporation Be Managed by Machines?" *Cost and Management*, Vol. 56, No. 4, pp. 2–7.

Nakane, J., and R. W. Hall (1983). "Management Specs for Stockless Production." *Harvard Business Review*, Vol. 61, No. 3, pp. 84–91.

O'Connor, B. J. (1982). "How Do the Japanese Get Higher Productivity Than We Do?" *Proceedings of the 25th Annual International Conference of the American Production and Inventory Control Society*, pp. 477–481.

Peters, T. J., and R. H. Waterman (1982). *In Search of Excellence*. Harper & Row, New York.

Reuter, V. G. (1983). "Trends in Production Management Education and Training." *Industrial Management*, Vol. 25, No. 3, pp. 1–3.

Schmenner, R. W. (1981). *Production/Operations Management: Concepts and Situations*. Science Research Associates Inc., Chicago, Illinois, p. 124.

Schonberger, R. J. (1983). "Applications of Single-Card and Dual-Card Kanban." *INTERFACES*, Vol. 13, No. 4, pp. 56–67.

Schwarz, L. B. (1981). "Physical Distribution: The Analysis of Inventory and Location." *AIIE Transactions*, Vol. 13, No. 2, pp. 138–150.

Stainton, R. S. (1983). "Behavioural Aspects of Stock Control." Paper presented at the National Conference of the Operational Research Society, Bristol, United Kingdom.

Steiner, G. A., and J. B. Miner (1982). *Management Policy and Strategy*. MacMillan, New York.

Taylor, S. G., S. M. Seward, and S. F. Bolander (1981). "Why the Process Industries Are Different." *Production and Inventory Management*, Vol. 22, No. 4, pp. 9–24.

Thompson, A. A., Jr., and A. J. Strickland III (1983). *Strategy Formulation and Implementation, Task of the General Manager*. Business Publications, Plano, Texas.

Thompson, H., and M. Paris (1982). "The Changing Face of Manufacturing Technology." *The Journal of Business Strategy*, Vol. 3, No.1, pp. 45–52.

Wagner, H. M. (1974). "The Design of Production and Inventory Systems for Multifacility and Multiwarehouse Companies." *Operations Research*, Vol. 22, No. 2, pp. 278–291.

Wild, R. (1972). *Mass-Production Management*. John Wiley & Sons, London, Chapter 8.

Zanakis, S. H., L. M. Austin, D. C. Nowading, and E. A. Silver (1980). "From Teaching to Implementing Inventory Management: Problems of Translation." *INTERFACES*, Vol. 10, No. 6, pp. 103–110.

Case A

MIDAS CANADA CORPORATION*

NOTE: Throughout the book we refer to examples that are related to the decision systems explained in the MIDAS case series. We have written the chapters so that they can be read without a detailed knowledge of the cases. Nevertheless, the reader is encouraged to read the cases for a fuller appreciation of the points of view we are trying to express.

The MIDAS Canada Corporation is a wholly owned Canadian subsidiary of a large international conglomerate with head offices located in England (see Figure 1). The company's Canadian facilities, namely, an assembly plant and warehouse, were located in Toronto, Ontario. It distributed, in Canada and the United States, "Superchrome" branded high-technical, quality-sensitized films, papers, and processing chemicals from a modern, highly efficient plant in Germany where an active ongoing product research and development program was maintained. From Japan, MIDAS imported "Takashi" branded X-ray Systems which it installed and maintained through service contracts in hospitals and private clinics. The Canadian company also assembled, under license from MIDAS International, two lines of film processing equipment: the manually operated MIDAS Stabilization Processor, used for rapid development of black and white paper, and the Midamatic, a much more expensive automatic rapid processor of X-Ray film.

A total of $1.1 million was invested in inventories in Toronto on May 31, 1984 and distributed among 2103 stock keeping units (s.k.u.) as shown in Table 1. On May 31, 1984, a total of 14 s.k.u. were out of stock, a situation which the Inventory Control Manager labeled as being "normal and typical for this time of year."

The industry in Canada was dominated by one large company and was served by seven other companies, one of which was MIDAS. Keen competition was prevalent both as to price and technical quality. Most customers displayed fierce brand loyalty and were quite proficient in their ability to judge the technical quality of a film, a processing chemical, or a paper offered for sale.

The Canadian company usually employed more than 60 persons and had an annual sales of over $8 million. It was organized into four sales divisions: the X-ray Film Division, the Professional Products Division, the Industrial Products Division, and the Equipment Division. The organization chart is given in Figure 2.

*The MIDAS cases describe actual decisions systems which are based on consulting experiences of the authors. They do not describe the situation at any single company, but are in fact a compendium of actual situations which have been compressed into the environment of a single firm and industry for discussion and illustrative purposes. The cases are not intended as presentations of either effective or ineffective ways of handling administrative problems.

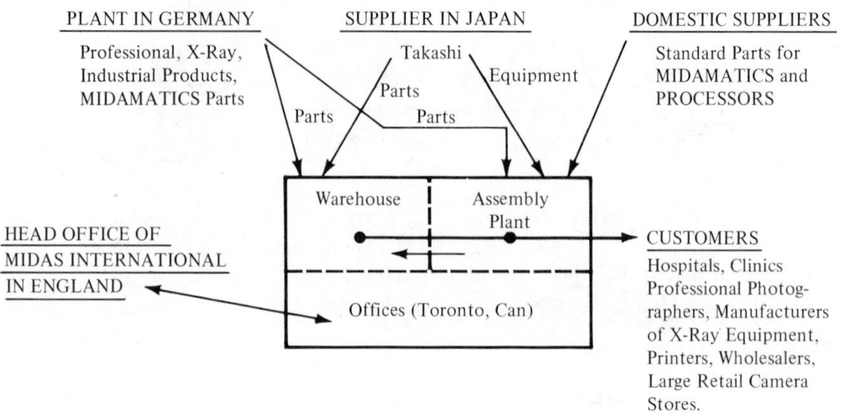

FIGURE 1 Product Flowchart

TABLE 1 Composition of Inventory Investment for Midas Canada Corporation

Division	No. of s.k.u. (1)	Turnover Ratio[a] (2)	Annual Sales—1984 Forecast (3)	Total Inventory (31/5/84) (4)	Finished Goods: Cycle Stock (5)	Finished Goods: Safety Stock (6)	Work in Process (7)	Raw Materials (8)	Seasonal Inventory (9)
Equipment	644	6.84	$5,168,000[b]	$ 453,100	$ 50,800[c]	$123,300[c]	$153,000[d]	$123,000[e]	$3,000[f]
X-ray	207	3.93	690,000	105,300	32,700	71,400	—	—	1,200
Industrial	403	3.89	1,070,000	165,100	46,900	116,350	—	—	1,850[g]
Professional	849	4.20	1,740,000	248,700	72,400	173,200	—	—	3,100[g]
(Obsolete)	—	0.00	0	128,000[h]	—	—	—	—	—
Overall	2,103	4.73	$8,668,000	$1,100,200	$202,800	$484,250	$153,000	$123,000	$9,150

[a]Cost of goods sold assumed to be 60 percent of sales.

[b]Sales of spare parts amounted to $968,000.

[c]Spare parts of Midamatics, Processors, and Takashi system only.

[d]Mostly semifinished Midamatics being assembled.

[e]$91,000 of Midamatic parts and $32,000 of Processor parts awaiting assembly.

[f]Processors only.

[g]Repackaged bulk chemicals only.

[h]Estimated value of dead stock, currently not listed in sales catalogue.

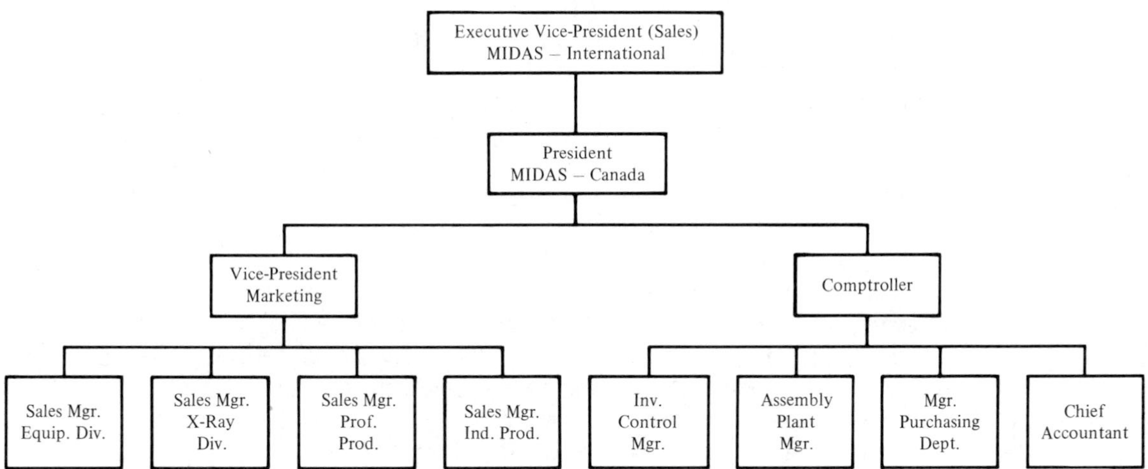

FIGURE 2 Organization Chart

THE EQUIPMENT DIVISION

The Equipment Division was by far the largest division in the company, accounting for about 60 percent of total sales. Whereas the other three divisions acted merely as sales agents for products manufactured in Germany, the Equipment Division sold products that it either assembled, or installed itself. The division was divided into two functions: the sales office and the Assembly Plant. The Assembly Plant consisted of 17 employees reporting to a manager. Four salespersons and a manager operated the sales office.

Stabilization Processors were assembled from standard parts available in Canada. In the case of Midamatics, 60 percent of the components were imported from Germany, with the remainder being available from suppliers in Canada. Spare parts for the repair and maintenance of existing Processors and Midamatics were kept in inventory and were listed as "finished goods"; see Table 1, columns 5 and 6. During May 1984, 14 Midamatics and 311 Processors were assembled. Parts for these machines were stored separately, even though they were identical to the spare parts that were used for repairs and maintenance of existing machines. Parts for assembly were listed as "Raw Materials"; see Table 1, column 8. Company policy did not allow any assembled Midamatics or Processors to be kept in finished goods inventory. However, because of production smoothing considerations (to be discussed in detail in Case E) during May 1984, some assembled Processors were in inventory in anticipation of future sales and were listed as "Seasonal Inventory"; see Table 1, column 9.

All chemicals arrived from Germany in 800-liter drums or in 100-kilogram barrels and were repackaged and labeled by the Equipment Division in 4-liter plastic bottles (sold four to a carton) or into envelopes and boxes weighing up to 2 kilograms,and sold either singly or up to 6 to a carton. The use of large bulk containers significantly reduced the cost of shipment from Germany. During May 1984, some bulk chemicals had been repackaged ahead of immediate needs to help with work load smoothing in the Assembly Plant. These inventories became the responsibility of the X-Ray Division, the Industrial Products Division, or the Professional Products Division, respectively, and were listed under "Seasonal Inventory" in Table 1, column 9.

The Assembly Plant also installed Takashi X-Ray Systems. No original Takashi equipment was kept in inventory. The company ordered the X-Ray equipment directly from the Japanese manufacturer only after successfully bidding on a contract. Such contracts stipulated an installed price plus a fee for maintaining the equipment in continuous repair. A selection of replacement parts was kept in inventory; see columns 5 and 6 in Table 1.

The vice-president in charge of marketing felt that

In the future we will have to keep some of the more popular original units in stock. These installations are not as customized as some people around here like to think. The long lead time between getting the bid and delivery from Japan is hurting us. We cannot compete with some of the larger companies on delivery, and therefore must try to beat them on price or on post-installation service. We are in danger of not even being invited to bid on jobs which require quick turnaround. For example, a lot of hospitals are currently in the process of upgrading their X-ray systems and demand fast delivery once they have made up their mind to allocate some funds from the budget for this purpose.

The Inventory Control Manager commented:

We offer the best repair and installation service in the industry. Our products and prices are competitive and profitable. However, success has generated its own problems; it is getting increasingly more difficult to promise fast delivery on our Midamatics because of the steadily increasing work load on our assembly facilities in Toronto. The Assembly Plant is always complaining that our orders arrive in bunches instead of being spaced out over the year and that we are always rushing them to get faster delivery.

I believe that a good design engineer could look at our Takashi, Midamatic and Stabilizer lines and reduce, through product standardization, the number of different screws, nuts, bolts, and brackets that we now keep in inventory. I think that in this way the work load in the Assembly Plant could probably be made more manageable.

THE X-RAY FILM DIVISION

Two types of X-ray film (rapid process and manual process), in many sizes, were sold through nine dealers who also manufactured X-ray equipment and usually carried a complete line of various technical supplies for hospitals, clinics, and veterinary hospitals. Some film was sold directly to the federal and provincial governments and to larger hospital group purchasing departments through competitive bids that quoted prices that were close to those charged to MIDAS dealers. All X-ray film was manufactured in Germany, where it was dated upon manufacture. Each quantity of film sold subsequently received a further code number which recorded the date of sale to a MIDAS dealer. According to the Inventory Control Manager,

Like fresh food, photographic sensitized materials deteriorate with age. As with some foods it is possible to halt the process of deterioration by, for example, freezing. But with most photographic papers and films, it is commercially uneconomical to do so.

The division also sold chemicals that were used to develop X-ray film. These included liquid developers, fixers and starters, and various powdered substances. Chemicals were packed by the Equipment Division from bulk shipments made from Germany.

In addition to the above fast moving items,the X-ray Division also sold a variety of supplementary products. These consisted of Tungsten screens, used by technicians to get better contrast, and cassettes which made it easier to handle film.

THE INDUSTRIAL PRODUCTS DIVISION

In addition to X-ray film, MIDAS Canada distributed specialized films and stabilization papers, along with dry and liquid developing chemicals, to industrial printers, craft jobbers, and large in-house captive printing shops. Four company salespersons called on the larger offset printing, letterpress, and rotogravure plants in Canada and in the northern portion of the United States. In addition, about one-third of the division's sales were handled through wholesalers who sold a variety of other kinds of printers' supplies.

PROFESSIONAL PRODUCTS DIVISION

This division sold 90 percent of its products to wholesalers who, in turn, supplied retail camera stores. Products included general-purpose photographic films and papers, stabilization papers, general-purpose flat films, black and while roll films, and a variety of dry and wet developing chemicals. A total of 849 s.k.u. were kept in inventory, including 10 s.k.u. of "Superchrome" film, which were kept in a specially designed, climate-controlled room kept at 2 degrees centigrade, under lock and key. These items were display transparency color films available in flat or in roll form and used by professional photographers. Only a select, small number of professional photographers bought these films directly from MIDAS. These very expensive films had a life of less than 12 months and were considered by professional photographers to be at the forefront of current technological development. The Inventory Control Manager commented that

I don't let anyone else handle these films but myself. I worry at night about that darn air-conditioning unit failing on me. With good reason, we jokingly refer to the climate-controlled room as Fort Knox.

PRODUCT IDENTIFICATION

All stock keeping units were identified by a 3-letter, 3-number code. The first letter identified the selling division: X for X-ray, I for Industrial Products, P for Professional Products, and E for the Equipment Division. The second letter recorded whether the product was produced for stock by the plant in Germany (Code: S) or was manufactured to order (Code: M). If the item was available domestically in Canada, the second letter was coded D.

The third letter was either F, C, P, or M, identifying the s.k.u. as being either film, chemical, paper, or some other miscellaneous item, respectively. This was true for all divisions except for products in the Equipment Division where the third letter (either M, S, T, or C) identified the s.k.u. as being a part of either the Midamatic, Stabilizer, Takashi, or common to more than one product line, respectively. For example, s.k.u. XMF-014 identified a film (product number 14) manufactured to order in Germany and sold by the X-ray Division.

COMPANY POLICY REGARDING INVENTORIES

No written, formal set of guidelines existed regarding the control of inventories. The final responsibility for inventory management rested with the company's Comptroller. The Comptroller believed that

Because there is no certainty of how customers will store our films . . . our own stocks must be kept as low as possible, consistent of course with maintaining reasonable customer delivery. Therefore at any time, we try to maintain several orders outstanding on the plant in Germany for the same stock keeping unit. The basic idea is to keep a steady flow of material moving from Germany to our warehouse. In this way the stock sits for only a short time on our shelves before being sold—about 3 months on average. Besides, by doing this, we keep our book inventories low. The head office in England does not invoice us until 30 days after the date of shipment from Germany. As a result, the more stock we keep in the pipeline the better we look on the balance sheet.

Case B

MIDAS CANADA CORPORATION*

In this case we describe how inventory transactions were recorded and how the level of inventory for each of the 2103 s.k.u. was monitored. Also described is the warehouse receiving, preparation, and control system.

THE INVENTORY RECORDING AND CONTROL SYSTEM

The inventory recording and control system at MIDAS was manual and was based on a commercially available "Vertical Visi-Record" card system. For each s.k.u. three cards were kept in sequence in a bin on wheels (also called a tub file) which was located in the Stock Keeping Clerk's office. These three cards were called the Record Card (Figure 1), the Travel Card (Figure 2), and the Backorder Card (Figure 3).

The Record Card (Figure 1) recorded the dates of all transactions in column 1, the Sales Order or Purchase Order numbers in column 2, the quantities received in column 3, and the balances on order in column 4. In column 5 was recorded the number issued on a particular sales order. In column 6 the cumulative number of units issued during the current month to date was calculated.

Balance on hand was recorded in column 7. Column 8 was reserved for recording any quantities that were held in abeyance for an important expected order or demand but for which a sales order had not as yet been issued. The last column recorded the balance available, which was calculated from:

$$\text{Balance available} = \text{balance on order} + \text{balance on hand} - \text{quantity allocated}$$

For example, on Figure 1, on May 28 three units of IMM-177 were issued via sales order number 73149, resulting in a total issued to date of 129, a balance on hand of 273, and a balance available of 673. A total of 400 units remained on order from the plant in Germany. Similarly, on June 4 an order for 120 units was placed on purchase order number 35373. On June 5 a shipment of 200 units arrived as a result of purchase order number 34999, placed several weeks earlier.

On the top right-hand corner of the Record Card was recorded the allowed minimum balance available. If the balance available dropped to or below the

---

*The MIDAS cases describe actual decision systems that are based on the consulting experiences of the authors. They do not describe the situation at any single company, but are in fact a compendium of actual situations that have been compressed into the environment of a single firm and industry for illustrative purposes. The cases are not intended as presentations of either effective or ineffective ways of handling administrative problems.

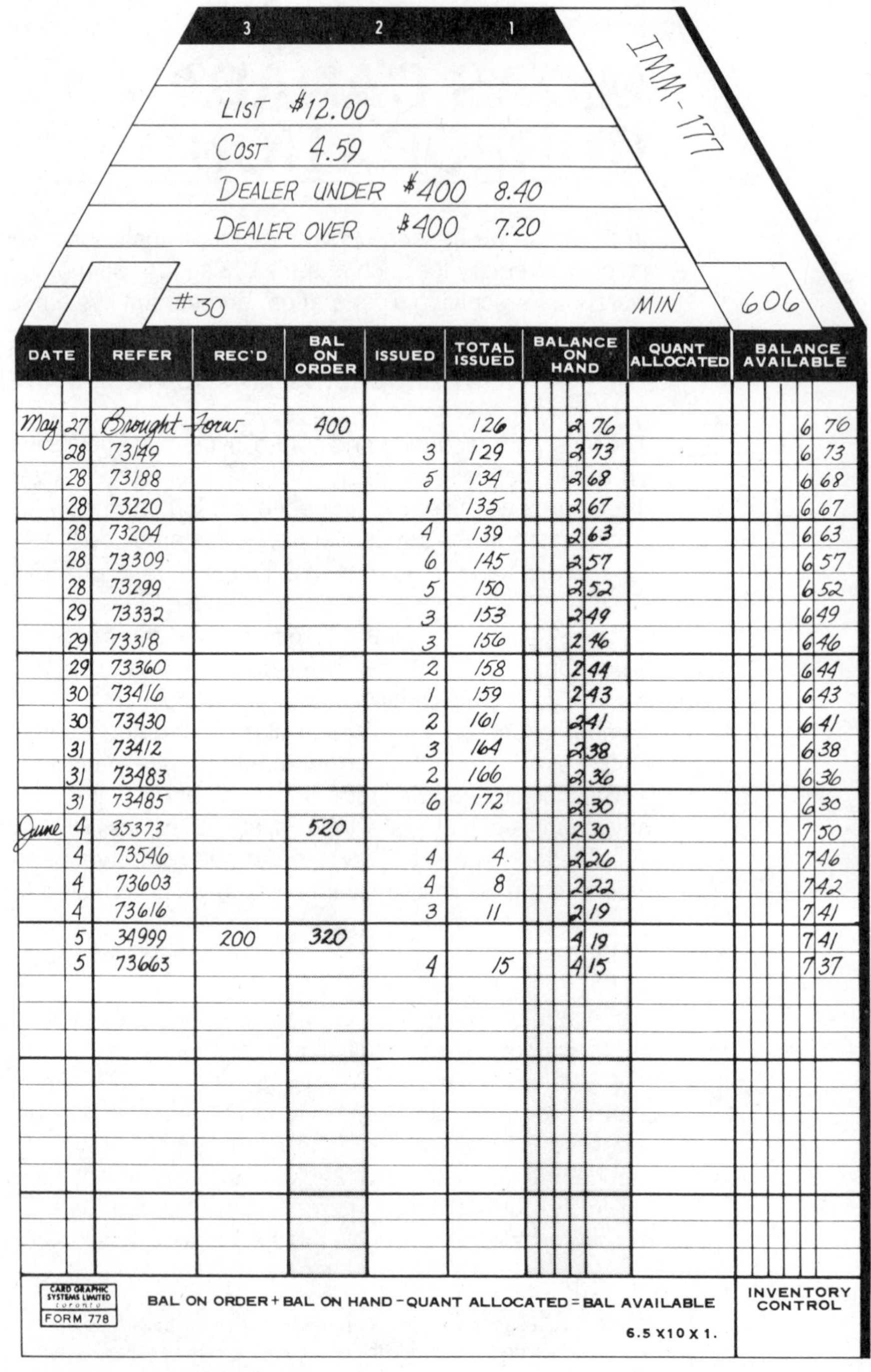

3 2 1

IMM-177

LIST $12.00
COST 4.59
DEALER UNDER $400 8.40
DEALER OVER $400 7.20

#30 MIN 606

DATE		REFER	REC'D	BAL ON ORDER	ISSUED	TOTAL ISSUED	BALANCE ON HAND	QUANT ALLOCATED	BALANCE AVAILABLE
May	27	Brought Forw.		400		126	276		676
	28	73149			3	129	273		673
	28	73188			5	134	268		668
	28	73220			1	135	267		667
	28	73204			4	139	263		663
	28	73309			6	145	257		657
	28	73299			5	150	252		652
	29	73332			3	153	249		649
	29	73318			3	156	246		646
	29	73360			2	158	244		644
	30	73416			1	159	243		643
	30	73430			2	161	241		641
	31	73412			3	164	238		638
	31	73483			2	166	236		636
	31	73485			6	172	230		630
June	4	35373		520			230		750
	4	73546			4	4	226		746
	4	73603			4	8	222		742
	4	73616			3	11	219		741
	5	34999	200	320			419		741
	5	73663			4	15	415		737

CARD GRAPHIC SYSTEMS LIMITED toronto FORM 778

BAL ON ORDER + BAL ON HAND − QUANT ALLOCATED = BAL AVAILABLE

6.5 X10 X 1.

INVENTORY CONTROL

FIGURE 1 MIDAS Canada Corporation—The Record Card

specified figure, then this was a signal for placing an order for more units. The minimum available balance for IMM-177 for June was given as 606. The order placed on June 4 was placed at an available balance level of 630 units. Apparently, the Inventory Control Manager decided to place the order at that point rather than wait a few more days until the balance available dropped closer to 606.

Also on top of the Record Card were listed the retail list price, the cost of IMM-177 to MIDAS Canada, and the prices charged to dealers as a function of their annual dollar purchase volume from MIDAS. On the top left-hand corner of the card was recorded the number of Record Cards that had been filled for a particular s.k.u. The Record Card illustrated in Figure 1 was the 30th card to date that had been used to record transactions regarding IMM-177.

When the balance available (column 9, Figure 1) dropped below the minimum balance available allowed, listed on top of the Record Card (i.e., 606 for IMM-177), the Inventory Clerk pulled the Travel Card (Figure 2) from the vertical tub file. The clerk recorded in column 1 the current balance available (from column 9 of the Record Card), the date in column 2, and suggested an order quantity in column 3. Then he sent the Travel Card to the Inventory Control Manager who determined the actual quantity to be ordered. The Inventory Control Manager in turn recorded the date on which he processed the order in column 4 and placed his initials in column 5. His decision as to the quantity to be ordered appeared in column 8. In the past the Inventory Control Manager had usually ordered the difference between the maximum balance available which was listed on the top right-hand corner of the Travel Card (for example, for IMM-177, the maximum was 757) and the current balance available as given in column 1.* However, he was free to round off the actual quantity ordered or to ignore the rule if, in his opinion, impending future events made an alternative quantity more attractive. This was especially true for special items such as Superchrome and the more expensive, slow-moving Professional and Industrial Products. For such items the Inventory Control Manager admitted that he went completely "by the seat of his pants." He relied heavily on his intimate knowledge of the industry, his customers and suppliers, some of whom he had dealt with over 23 years.

Note that column 1 of Figure 2 is actually labeled "Balance on Hand." In the past the Inventory Control Manager had based his ordering decisions on the balance-on-hand figures, as suggested by the Vertical Visi-Record card system. After a while he found it very difficult to keep track of outstanding orders and started to base his decisions on the balance available figures. As a result, column 1 of Figure 2 was in fact mislabelled on all the Travel Cards. The Inventory Control Manager was somewhat unsure whether he had done the right thing:

I've always wondered how other people who use Visi-cards manage to make decisions using The Travel Card as it was originally intended?

---

*The determination of maximum and minimum levels of balance available will be discussed in Case D of MIDAS Canada Corporation.

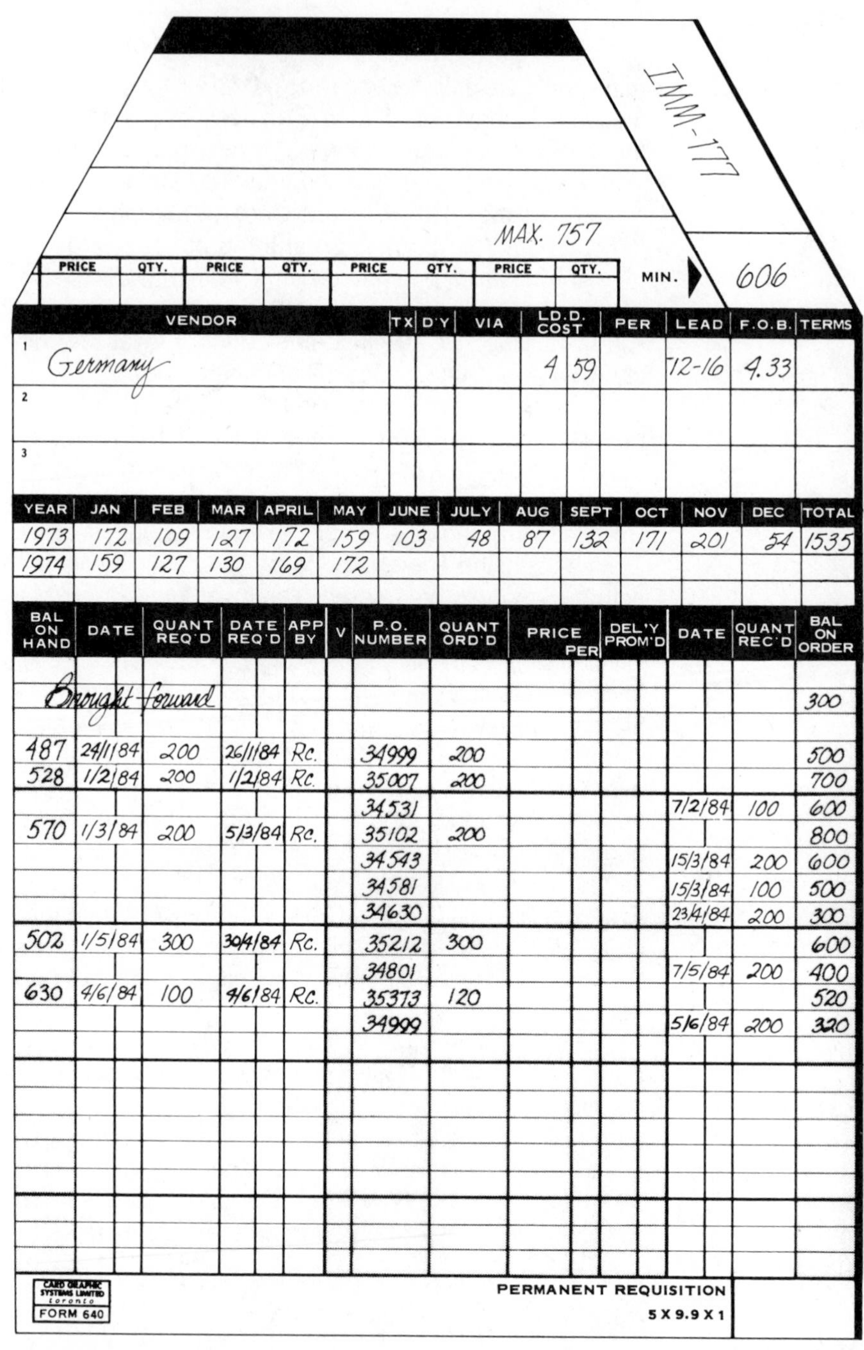

IMM-177

MAX. 757

PRICE	QTY.	PRICE	QTY.	PRICE	QTY.	PRICE	QTY.	MIN. 606

	VENDOR	TX	D'Y	VIA	LD.D. COST		PER	LEAD	F.O.B.	TERMS
1	Germany				4	59		12-16	4.33	
2										
3										

YEAR	JAN	FEB	MAR	APRIL	MAY	JUNE	JULY	AUG	SEPT	OCT	NOV	DEC	TOTAL
1973	172	109	127	172	159	103	48	87	132	171	201	54	1535
1974	159	127	130	169	172								

BAL ON HAND	DATE	QUANT REQ'D	DATE REQ'D	APP BY	V	P.O. NUMBER	QUANT ORD'D	PRICE PER	DEL'Y PROM'D	DATE	QUANT REC'D	BAL ON ORDER
Brought forward												300
487	24/1/84	200	26/1/84	Rc.		34999	200					500
528	1/2/84	200	1/2/84	Rc.		35007	200					700
						34531				7/2/84	100	600
570	1/3/84	200	5/3/84	Rc.		35102	200					800
						34543				15/3/84	200	600
						34581				15/3/84	100	500
						34630				23/4/84	200	300
502	1/5/84	300	30/4/84	Rc.		35212	300					600
						34801				7/5/84	200	400
630	4/6/84	100	4/6/84	Rc.		35373	120					520
						34999				5/6/84	200	320

CARD GRAPHIC SYSTEMS LIMITED Toronto
FORM 640

PERMANENT REQUISITION
5 X 9.9 X 1

FIGURE 2 MIDAS Canada Corporation—The Travel Card

After determining the order quantity the Inventory Control Manager sent the Travel Card to the purchasing department. There a clerk typed up a purchase order, entered the purchase order number in column 7 of Figure 2, and returned the Travel Card to the Inventory Control Clerk, who then updated the balance on order columns on both the Record and Travel Cards.

For example, on January 24, 1984, the Inventory Control Clerk noticed that the balance available had fallen to 487, which was below the minimum allowed for January.* She pulled the Travel Card and sent it to the Inventory Control Manager who processed the order on January 26, agreeing to place an order for 200 units. The Travel Card was then sent to purchasing where a purchase order number of 34999 was assigned and a purchase order was typed up. Then the Travel card was returned to the Inventory Control Clerk who updated the balance on order from 300 to 500.

Also recorded on the Travel card was the arrival of orders. When an order had been received and checked by the warehouse, a copy of the accompanying packing slip was forwarded to the Inventory Control Clerk. Note that on the bottom line of Figure 2 a quantity of 200 units on purchase order 34999 arrived on June 5, reducing the balance on order to 320.

On the top of the Travel Card were recorded the maximum and minimum allowable available balances, as well as the vendor's name, his prices, and the estimated lead time needed to get delivery. IMM-177 was supplied exclusively by the MIDAS International plant in Germany. When more than one vendor was available, such as for some domestically available parts for the assembly of Midamatics and Processors, the Inventory Control Manager was responsible for deciding which vendor would get an order. In such cases he would record the vendor number under the column headed "V," along with the price per unit and promised delivery dates in the appropriate columns.

During the second week of March 1984 IMM-177 was out of stock. In such cases the Inventory Control Clerk filled out the Backorder Card (Figure 3) and notified the Inventory Control Manager. Customer sales orders that were on backorder were listed in the order they were received. Note that once the delayed order arrived on March 15 (see Figure 2) the backorders were filled in the same order that they had been received. In this particular case the Inventory Control Manager dispatched a panel truck to pick up the order from the railway station rather than wait for regular delivery. The extra cost of expediting the order in this manner was charged to the Industrial Products Division, whose product was involved.

THE WAREHOUSE RECEIVING, PREPARATION, AND CONTROL SYSTEM

Orders normally arrived at the warehouse by railroad car or by truck in cardboard cases along with a packing slip. An invoice had usually preceded the shipment by

*Each month has a different set of maxima and minima, which will be discussed in Case D.

DESCRIPTION: IMM-177

DATE	CUSTOMER	REF NO	QUANTITY ORDERED	QUANTITY SHIPPED	QUANTITY BACK ORDERED	TOTAL BACK ORDERED
7/3/84	Goldare	2387	12	5	7	7
7/3/84	Black	2372	4		4	11
7/3/84	Jones	2378	5		5	16
8/3/84	B&W	2427	2		2	18
8/3/84	Kenny's	2404	3		3	21
12/3/84	Weinberg	2409	3		3	24
13/3/84	United	2381	6		6	30
15/3/84		2387			7	23
15/3/84		2372			4	19
15/3/84		2378			5	14
15/3/84		2427			2	12
15/3/84		2404			3	9
15/3/84		2409			3	6
15/3/84		2381			6	0

CARD GRAPHIC SYSTEMS LIMITED Toronto FORM 805 — CARD GRAPHIC BACK ORDER CONTROL — 5.5X7.7X1

FIGURE 3 MIDAS Canada Corporation—The Backorder Card

mail. The packing slip, the invoice, and the original purchase order were compared. Only if discrepancies were noted, was the box opened to determine its exact contents. Otherwise the boxes were stored without being opened. A copy of the packing slip was sent to the Inventory Control Clerk to notify her of the arrival of orders.

For each arriving box a Case Card (see Figure 4) was prepared by cutting the description of its contents from the packing slip and pasting it on a 4 × 6 inch file card. (Cut and paste was used to minimize clerical errors.) Each carton also received an identification number. Under such a system, inventory of the same s.k.u

		Case No. 7664
17	XMF-014	
100	IMM-177	
75	XMF-038	
4	PMP-747	
30	PMF-198	
50	PMF-231	

FIGURE 4 MIDAS Canada Corporation—The Case Card

IMM-177

DATE	CASE	IN	RMDR.	RMDR.	RMDR.	DATE	CASE	IN	RMDR.	RMDR.	RMDR.
11/1/84	7664	100		100/0	7/2						
7/2/84	8355	100		100/0	14/2						
15/3/84	8498	200		200/0	15/3						
15/3/84	8499	100		100/0	26/3						
23/4/84	8548	200		200/0	2/5						
7/5/84	8586	200		200/0	20/5						
5/6/84	9090	200									

FIGURE 5 MIDAS Canada Corporation—The Case Control Card

could be located in several different cartons. For this reason a Case Control Card (see Figure 5) was also prepared listing the date of arrival, the quantity, and the carton numbers where stock pertaining to a particular s.k.u. was located. Inventory was stored in cartons, because in this form it took up less space and provided a simple first-in, first-out system of stock use.

About one month's sales of inventory was kept loose on metal shelves from which stock pickers daily compiled orders to be sent to customers. No record was kept of how much of a particular s.k.u. was left on the shelf at any moment. It was the responsibility of the warehouseman to visually keep the shelves stocked from the packing cartons described above. To guide the warehouseman, on the edge of each shelf, directly under the product's location, was recorded the amount that represented approximately one month's sales. When a shelf location became depleted, the warehouseman consulted the Case Control Card for that particular s.k.u. He recorded the date on the card and the quantity of stock he was removing from the carton in question. For example, according to Figure 5, on February 7, he removed 100 units of IMM-177, leaving a zero balance in case 7664 which had arrived in the warehouse on January 11, 1984. Upon removing the 100 units from case 7664, he also recorded this fact on the Case Card (Figure 4).

The President, on several occasions, commented on the existing control systems as follows:

The present system seems to involve a tremendous amount of paper handling, recording, and checking. Even with all this activity we seem to lose considerable amounts of stock, through pilferage I presume. After all, everyone is interested in photography to some extent. Although I must admit that some stock just gets lost in the boxes and is found much later either damaged, too old to be sold, or is no longer in our sales catalogues. Surely the present system could be improved on!

CHAPTER 3

Coping with the Complex Decisions of Production Planning and Inventory Management

In this chapter we first discuss, in Sections 3.1 and 3.2, the complexity of production planning and inventory management decisions (even without considering interactions with other functional areas, as was outlined in Section 2.2 of Chapter 2). Then, in Sections 3.3 to 3.6, we present various aids for coping with the complexity. Section 3.7 provides some suggestions concerning the use of mathematical models. Finally, Sections 3.8 and 3.9 are concerned with two very different approaches for estimating relevant cost factors identified earlier in the chapter.

3.1 THE DIVERSITY OF STOCK KEEPING UNITS

Some military organizations stock over 600,000 items in inventory. Large retailers, such as department stores, carry about 100,000 goods for sale. A typical medium-sized manufacturing concern keeps in inventory approximately 10,000 types of raw materials, parts, and finished goods.

Items produced and held in inventory can differ in many ways. They may differ in cost, weight, volume, color, or physical shape. Units may be stored in crates, in barrels, on pallets, in cardboard boxes, or loose on shelves. They may be packaged by the thousands or singly. They may be perishable because of deterioration over time, perishable through theft and pilferage, or subject to obsolescence because of style or technology. Some items are stored in dust-proof, temperature-controlled rooms, while others can lie in mud, exposed to the elements.

Demand for items also can occur in many ways. Items may be withdrawn from inventory by the thousands, by the dozen, or unit by unit. They may be substitutes for each other, so that, if one item is out of stock, the user is usually willing to accept another. Items can also be complements; that is, customers will not accept one item unless another is also available. Units could be picked up by a customer, or they may have to be delivered by company-owned vehicles or shipped by rail, boat, airplane, or transport truck. Some customers are willing to wait for certain types of products; others expect immediate service on demand. Many customers will order more than one type of product on each purchase order submitted.

Goods also arrive for inventory by a variety of modes and in quantities that can differ from how they will eventually be demanded. Some goods arrive damaged; others differ in number or kind from that which was requisitioned (from a supplier or from an in-house production operation). Some items are unavailable because of strikes or other difficulties in-house or at a supplier's plant. Delivery of an order may take hours, weeks, or even several months.

Decision making in production planning and inventory management is therefore basically a *problem of coping with large numbers and with a diversity of factors external and internal to the organization*. Some decision systems for inventory management and production planning fail in practice simply because of this basic diverse nature of inventories. For example, Whitin (1957), who examined the collapse of inventory decision systems at several U.S. military establishments, concluded that:

> *The failure of the National Military Establishment to establish effective inventory control has been to a large extent due to the sheer magnitude of the task.*

We have seen tremendous progress in the technology of inventory control since 1957, including the successful installation of a very modern inventory control system by the aforementoned National Military Establishment. But one basic fact remains: production planning and inventory management is still a problem of managing large numbers of units of a diverse nature. On an individual item basis, answers must be provided to three basic questions:

1. How often should the inventory status be determined?
2. When should the item be ordered?
3. How much of the item should be requested on any particular order?

Moreover, the detailed daily individual s.k.u. decisions must, *in the aggregate*, be consistent with the overall objectives of management.

3.2 THE BOUNDED RATIONALITY OF A HUMAN BEING

An inescapable fact alluded to in the first two chapters was the need to view the inventory management and production planning problem from a systems standpoint. Before we plunge into a detailed discussion of the possible solutions to the problem as we have posed it, let us consider explicitly and realistically our expectations regarding the nature of the results we seek.

Simon (1957) has pointed out that all decision makers approach complex problems with a framework or model that simplifies the real situation encountered. A human being's brain is simply incapable of absorbing and rationalizing *all* of the many relevant factors in a complex decision situation. A decision maker cannot effectively conceive of the totality of a large system without assistance from extracerebral systems. All decision makers are forced to ignore some relevant aspects of a complex problem and base their decisions on a smaller number of carefully selected factors. These selected factors always reflect decision makers' personal biases, abilities, and perceptions of the realities they think they face, as well as the decision technology that is available to them at any point in time.

The decisions of production planning and inventory management are complex. They extend beyond the intuitive powers of most decision makers because of the many interconnected systems, both physical and conceptual, that have to be coordinated, rationalized, adapted to, or controlled. The decisions must be viewed *simultaneously* from the point of view of: the individual s.k.u. in its relation to other similar s.k.u., the total aggregate inventory investment, the master plan of the organization, the production-distribution systems of suppliers and customers, and the economy as a whole.

The challenge is therefore twofold. Since a decision maker's ability to cope with diversity is limited, decision systems and rules must be designed to help expand the bounds put upon that individual's ability to rationalize. However, since most decision makers probably have already developed personalized approaches to the inventory decision, decision systems have to be designed and their use advocated in the context of existing resources and managerial capabilities.

Inventory management and production planning as practiced today, like the practice of accounting, because of the predominance of numerical data and a relatively long history, are mixtures of economically sound theory, accepted industrial practices, tested personalized approaches, and outright fallacies. Our goal in this book is to influence the amount of sound theory that actually gets used, while trying to clarify existing fallacies. However, one must accept the fact that existing theory is, and will be, for some time to come, insufficient to do the whole job. There will always be room for personalized, tested-in-practice, approaches to fill the gaps in theory. Therefore, within this book, we in effect weave our own brand of personalized approaches with theory. This is why, from an intellectual point of view, we find inventory management and production decisions both challenging and exciting.

3.3 DECISION AIDS FOR MANAGING THE PRODUCTION AND INVENTORIES OF DIVERSE INDIVIDUAL ITEMS

The managerial aids are basically of two kinds, conceptual and physical.

3.3.1 Conceptual Aids

We can think of the following list as conceptual aids to our decision making.

1. Decisions in an organization can be considered as a hierarchy—extending from long-range strategic planning, through medium-range tactical planning, to short-range operational control. Typically, different levels of management deal with the three classes of decisions. We have more to say about such a hierarchy, specifically related to production situations, in Chapter 13.

2. Another related type of hierarchy can be conceptualized with respect to decision making in production planning and inventory management. At the highest level one chooses a particular type (or types) of control system(s). At the next level one selects the values of specific parameters within a chosen system (for example, the desired level of customer service). Finally, one operationalizes the system, including data collection, calculations, reporting of results, and so forth (Brown, 1982).

3. The large number of physical units of inventory can be classified into a smaller number of relatively homogeneous organizational categories. Managers then manage inventories in the context of this smaller number of decision classifications (to be discussed in Section 3.4).

4. The complexity of production planning and inventory management decisions can be reduced by identifying, through analysis and empirical research, only the most important variables for explicit consideration (for example, ordering costs and demand rates). This is an especially important essence of the operational theory that we expound in this book.

3.3.2 Physical Aids

The following encompass possible decision aids.

1. Decision makers often resort to mechanized procedures that collect and summarize environmental data and that, based on the use of mathematical modeling, suggest solutions to specific problems. On the basis of such, more compact information, the decision maker can deal more quickly and effectively with a larger number of decisions. This book places a major emphasis on this type of decision aid. Within this category we include the use of graphs, tables, programmable calculators (see, for example, Brout, 1981, and Krupp, 1977), and *interactive* computer routines.

2. A decision maker's physical span of control can also be expanded by harnessing the *principle of management by exception* through the use of computer-based or manual clerical systems that free the manager from the mass of unimportant routine situations. Agreed on decision rules are used within computer systems or by clerks on a routine basis. When the system or clerk encounters factors that cannot be handled routinely, only then is the situation brought to the attention of higher level decision makers. If computerized reporting is used, care must be taken to ensure that exceptional situations are properly highlighted.

3.4 FUNCTIONAL CLASSIFICATIONS OF INVENTORIES

In answering the question "How much inventory is enough?" the most common mistake made in practice is that the turnover ratio is used uniformly across many s.k.u. to control inventories with little regard to their differing functions or the degree of compatibility between individual items. As Plossl (1971) reports, the inventory planning decision often gets delegated to a controller who in sheer frustration imposes controls on categories of inventories that had previously been defined *for accounting purposes only*. Examples include the *same* specified turnover ratio for *all* raw material categories or the *same* inventory limits (expressed as a percent of sales) on *all* regional divisions. While turnover ratio and percent of sales measures are useful tools for reporting results after the fact, we will discover that they should not be applied uniformly for control purposes.

We recommend five broad decision categories for controlling aggregate inventories: cycle stock, safety (or buffer) stock, anticipation inventories, pipeline inventories, and decoupling stock. In our opinion, senior management can and must express an opinion on how much aggregate inventory is required in each of these broad categories. While we cannot expect that such opinions will always be in the form of clear-cut, simple answers, the categorization focuses our attention on viewing inventories as being controllable and not as the "residue of the sum total of all the mistakes we made over the past year."

Cycle inventories result from an attempt to order or produce in batches instead of one unit at a time. The amount of inventory on hand, at any point, that results from such batches is called *cycle stock*. The reasons for batch replenishments include (1) to achieve economies of scale (because of large setup costs), (2) to achieve quantity discounts in purchase price or freight cost, and (3) to satisfy technological restrictions such as the fixed size of a processing tank in a chemical process. The amount of cycle stock on hand at any time depends directly on how frequently orders are placed. As we will see, this can be determined in part by senior management who can specify the desired tradeoff between the cost of ordering and the cost of having cycle stock on hand. A major consideration in Chapters 5, 6, 8, 11, and 15 will be the determination of appropriate cycle stocks.

Safety stock is the amount of inventory kept on hand, on the average, to allow for the uncertainty of demand and the uncertainty of supply in the short run. Safety stocks are not needed when the future rate of demand and the length of time it takes to get complete delivery of an order are known with certainty. The level of safety stock is controllable in the sense that this investment is directly related to the level of desired customer service (that is, how often customer demand is met from stock). The determination of safety stock levels in response to prespecified managerial measures of customer service will be discussed in Chapters 7 to 12.

Anticipation inventory consists of stock accumulated in advance of an expected peak in sales. When demand is regularly lower than average during some parts of the year, excess inventory (above cycle and safety stock) can be built up so that, during the period of high anticipated requirements, extra demand can be serviced from stock rather than from, for example, working overtime in the plant (that is, the aggregate production rate is stabilized through the use of anticipatory stock). Anticipation stock can also occur because of seasonality on the supply side. For example, tomatoes, which ripen during a rather short period, are processed into ketchup which is sold throughout the year. Climatic conditions, such as in the Arctic, can cause shipments to be restricted to certain times of the year, thus introducing anticipatory inventory. Anticipation stocks can also consist of inventories built up to deal with labor strikes, war crises, or any other events that are expected to result in a period of time during which the possible rate of acquisition of s.k.u. into inventory is likely to be lower than the rate of demand. Chapter 14 will deal with the rational determination of anticipation inventories as a part of production planning.

Pipeline (work-in-process) inventories include goods in transit (for example, in physical pipelines, on trucks, or in railway cars) between levels of a multiechelon distribution system or between adjacent work stations in an assembly line. The pipeline inventory of an item between two adjacent locations is proportional to the usage rate of the item and to the transit time between the locations. Pipeline inventories will be considered in Chapters 12 and 16.

Decoupling stock is used in a multiechelon situation to permit the separation of decision making at the different echelons. For example, decoupling inventory allows decentralized decision making at branch warehouses without every decision at a branch having an immediate impact on the central operations (production and storage) of the organization. Chapter 12, in particular, will include a discussion related to decoupling stocks.

Note that our five functional categories were defined in order to concentrate attention on the organizational purposes of the inventories, especially with regard to control and manageability, rather than accounting scorekeeping (for example, raw materials, supplies, finished components, etc.). Most managers are intuitively aware of the functions that inventories in each of the five conceptual categories must play. Some of the benefits (and costs) may even be measured by existing cost accounting systems. However, most accounting systems will not keep track of opportunity costs, such as customer disservice through lost sales or the costs of extra paperwork generated by an order that must be expedited to meet an unexpected emergency.

While it will not always be possible to precisely measure the costs and benefits of each subgroup of inventories, many experienced managers have garnered over the years a sense of perspective regarding the effect of reducing or increasing the amount of inventory investment allocated into each of these five different functional categories. One of our goals in this book is the development of procedures to harness this experiential perspective, along with measurable costs and benefits and analytical techniques, to yield better decisions from an overall systems viewpoint.

It is quite possible that an individual manager may not have had sufficient experience to have developed an intuitive feel for the five functional categories that we have defined above. This could be the case especially in respect to the many phases of a large organization's operations. In such cases, instead of classifying a company's total aggregate inventory investment, it may be more meaningful to a manager to deal with a smaller inventory investment, such as in a divisional grouping. In Case A of the MIDAS Corporation, the four sales managers of the X-ray, Industrial, Professional, and Equipment divisions felt qualified to provide an opinion as to how much inventory was enough for only their own divisions. The Inventory Control Manager, on the other hand, categorized total company inventory investment into imported, purchased domestically, or manufactured items for purposes of cost-benefit tradeoffs.

Meaningful functional groupings do vary from organization to organization. But, from a theoretical and practical viewpoint, at some point, the five organizational categories—cycle stock, safety stock, anticipation stock, pipeline inventories, and decoupling stock—need to be analyzed from a cost-benefit standpoint to provide an aggregate perspective for the control of individual s.k.u.

3.5 IMPORTANT FACTORS FOR DECISION MAKING

Through empirical studies and deductive mathematical modeling a number of factors have been identified that are important with respect to production planning and inventory decisions.

3.5.1 Cost Factors

Here we briefly describe a number of cost factors. Sections 3.8 and 3.9 will be concerned with estimating their values. The discussion of one other type of cost, the cost of changing the aggregate production rate or work force size, will be left until Chapter 14 where, for the first time, we deal with medium-range aggregate production planning problems in which such costs are relevant.

The Unit Value or Unit Variable Cost, v

The unit value (denoted by the symbol v) of an item is expressed in dollars per unit. For a merchant[1] it is simply the price (including freight) paid to the supplier. It can depend, via quantity discounts, on the size of the replenishment. For producers, the unit value of an item is usually more difficult to determine. However, one thing is certain; it is seldom the conventional accounting or "book value" assigned in most organizations. The value of an item ideally should measure the actual amount of money (variable cost) that has been spent on the s.k.u. to make it available for usage (either for fulfilling customer demand or for internal usage as a component of some other items). As we will see in Section 3.8, the determination of v is not an easy task.

The unit value is important for two reasons. First, the total acquisition (or production) costs per year clearly depend on its value. Second, the cost of carrying an item in inventory depends on v.

The Cost of Carrying Items in Inventory

The cost of carrying items in inventory includes the opportunity cost of the money invested, the expenses incurred in running a warehouse, the costs of special storage requirements, deterioration of stock, obsolescence, insurance, and taxes. The most common convention of costing is to use

$$\text{Carrying costs per year} = \bar{I}vr \tag{3.1}$$

where $\bar{I}$ is the average inventory in units (hence $\bar{I}v$ is the average inventory expressed in dollars),[2] and r is the carrying charge, the cost in dollars of carrying one dollar of inventory for one year.

By far the largest portion of the carrying charge is made up of the opportunity costs of the capital tied up that otherwise could be used elsewhere in an organization and the opportunity costs of warehouse space claimed by inventories. Neither of these costs are measured by traditional accounting systems.

The opportunity cost of capital can be defined easily enough. It is, theoretically speaking, the return on investment that could be earned on the next most attractive opportunity that cannot be taken advantage of because of a decision to invest the available funds in inventories. Such a marginal cost concept is difficult to implement in practice. For one thing, the next most attractive investment opportunity can change from day to day. Does this mean that the

---

[1]We use the term merchant to denote a nonproducer.

[2]Sirianni (1979) has proposed a graphical procedure for evaluating $\bar{I}v$, particularly useful for the case where raw materials are converted into work-in-process (for example, components and subassemblies) and then into finished goods (see Problem 3.9).

cost of the capital portion of carrying should also be changed from day to day? From a theoretical point of view, the answer is yes. In practice such fluctuation is difficult to administer; instead, the cost of capital is set at some level by decree and is changed only if major changes have taken place in a company's environment. For example, after due consideration by senior management, a policy is declared that "only investments which earn more than a specificed percent can be implemented." The cost of capital used, of course, has to depend on the degree of risk inherent in an investment. (For the same reason the banks charge a higher rate of interest on second mortgages than on the first.) As a result, in practice the opportunity cost of capital can range from the banks' prime lending rate to 50 percent and higher for small companies that are suffering from severe capital rationing (shortages) because they lack the collateral to attract additional sources of working capital. Inventory investment, at least in total, is usually considered to be of relatively low risk because in most cases it can be converted to cash relatively quickly. However, the degree of risk inherent in inventory investment varies from organization to organization. Some of the most important impediments to quick conversion to cash can be obsolescence, deterioration, pilferage, and the danger of a lack of immediate demand at normal price. Each of these factors increases the cost of capital over and above the prime rate because of a possible lack of opportunity of quick cash conversion.

The value of r is not only dependent on the relative riskiness of s.k.u., it also depends on the costs of storage that are a function of bulkiness, weight, special handling requirements, insurance, and possibly taxes. Such detailed attention is seldom given to all s.k.u. in inventory. To make the inventory decision more manageable both from a theoretical and practical point of view a single value of r is usually assumed to apply for most items. Note from Eq. 3.1 that this assumes that more expensive items are apt to be riskier to carry and more expensive to handle or store. Such a convenient relationship doesn't always hold true for all s.k.u.[3] Note that r itself could depend on the total size of the inventory; for example, r would increase if a company had to begin using outside warehousing.

The Ordering or Setup Cost, A

The symbol A denotes the fixed cost (independent of the size of the replenishment) associated with a replenishment. For a merchant it is called an ordering cost and it includes the cost of order forms, postage, telephone calls, authorization,[4] typing of orders, receiving, (possibly) inspection, following up on unexpected situations, and handling of vendor invoices. The production setup cost includes many of the aforementioned components but, in addition, there are also other costs related to interrupted production. For example, the wages of a skilled mechanic who has to adjust the production facilities to allow production of the ordered s.k.u. can be considerable. Then, once a setup is completed, there

[3]In principle, one could instead use $\bar{I}h$ where h is the cost to carry one *unit* in inventory for a year.

[4]The level of authorization may depend on the dollar size of the replenishment; for example, special authorization from a senior executive may be needed if the order exceeds $500.

usually follows a period of time during which the facility is unlikely to produce within rated effectiveness. During this period the production worker "learns" to get used to the new setup, procedures, and materials. Scrap costs are likely to be higher than normal while the worker adjusts to the new procedures, gradually reaching full efficiency. The latter two factors are normally called the "learning effect" and these costs are taken as a part of the setup cost because they are the result of a decision to place an order (see, for example, Conway and Schultz, 1969). Finally, notice that during the setup and learning period opportunity costs are, in effect, incurred because production time on the machines is being lost during which some other item could be manufactured. Hence, the latter opportunity cost is only incurred if the production facility in question is being operated at capacity.

The Costs of Insufficient Capacity in the Short Run

These costs could also be called the costs of avoiding stockouts and the costs incurred when stockouts take place. In the case of a producer they include the expenses that result from the tearing down of existing production setups to run emergency orders and the attendant costs of expediting and rescheduling, split lots, and so forth. For a merchant emergency shipments or substitution of a less profitable item can contribute to the costs. The costs mentioned so far can be estimated reasonably well. However, in addition there are costs that can result from not servicing customer demand. These are much more nebulous. Will the customer be willing to wait while the item is backordered or is the sale lost for good? How much goodwill is lost as a result of the inability to be of immediate service—will the customer ever return? Will the customer's colleagues be told of our disservice? Such questions can in principle be answered empirically through an actual study for only a limited number of s.k.u. For most items the risks and costs inherent in disservice have to remain a matter of educated, considered opinion, not unlike the determination of the risks inherent in carrying inventories. In Chapter 7 we examine a number of different methods of modeling the costs of disservice.

System Control Costs

There are costs associated with the operation of the particular decision system selected. These include the costs of data acquisition, data storage, and computation. In addition, there are less tangible costs of human interpretation of results, training, alienation of employees, and so on. Although difficult to quantify, this category of "costs" may be crucial in the choice of one decision system over another.

3.5.2 Other Key Variables

Figure 3.1 provides a rather extensive listing of potentially important variables. We elaborate on just three factors.

Service Requirements	*Ordering Characteristics*
• Customer expectations • Competitive practices • Lead time required • Order completeness required • Ability to influence and control customers • Special requirements with big customers	• Order timing • Order size • Advanced information for large orders • Extent of open or standing orders • Delay in order processing
Demand Patterns	*Supply Situation*
• Variability • Seasonality • Extent of deals and promotions • Ability to forecast • Any dependent demand? • Substitution?	• Lead times • Reliability • Flexibility • Ability to expedite • Minimum orders • Discounts (volume, freight) • Availability
Cost Factors	*Other Issues*
• Stockout (pipeline versus customer) • Carrying costs • Expediting • Write-offs • Space • Spoilage, etc.	• ABC pattern • Timing and quality of information • Number of stocking locations • Who bears the cost of inventory?

Source: Based on A. Saipe, Partner, Thorne Stevenson & Kellogg, "Managing Distribution Inventories," Executive Development Programme, York University, Toronto, Canada, September 12, 1982.

FIGURE 3.1 Inventory Planning Decision Variables

Replenishment Lead Time, L

A stockout can only occur during periods when the inventory on hand is "low." Our decision as to when an order should be placed will always be predicated on how low the inventory should be allowed to be depleted, so that the expected number of s.k.u. demanded during a replenishment lead time will not result in a stockout more often than a specified number of times. We define the *replenishment lead time,* as the time that elapses from the moment at which it is decided to place an order, until it is physically on the shelf for satisfying customer demands. The symbol L will be used to denote the replenishment lead time. It is convenient to think of the lead time as being made up of five distinct components:[5]

[5]The discussion deals specifically with the case of an external (purchased) replenishment but is also conceptually applicable for internal (production) replenishments.

1. Administrative time at the stocking point (order preparation time): the time that elapses from the moment at which it is decided to place the order until it is actually transmitted from the stocking point.
2. Transit time to the supplier: this may be negligible if the order is placed electronically or by telephone, but transit time can be several days if a mailing system is used.
3. Time at the supplier: this time constitutes the primary variable component. Its duration is materially influenced by the supplier's stock situation when the order arrives.
4. Transit time back to the stocking point.
5. Time from order receipt until it is available on the shelf: this time is often neglected when it should not be. Contributing factors include inspection and cataloging.

We will see that the variability of demand over L can be the result of several causes. If demand varies in a reasonably predictable manner *depending on time of the year*, we say it is *seasonal*. If it is essentially unpredictable, we label the variability *random*. Demand over lead time also varies because the time between ordering and receipt of goods is seldom constant. Strikes, inclement weather, or supplier production problems can delay delivery. During periods of low sales, lead times can turn out to be longer than expected because the supplier is accumulating orders to take advantage of the efficiency inherent in longer production runs. On the other hand, longer lead times can result because high demand is causing backlog in the supplier's plant. Finally, in periods of short supply, it may be impossible to acquire desired quantities of items, even after *any* lead time.

Production versus Nonproduction

Decisions in a production context are inherently more complicated than those in nonproduction situations. There are capacity constraints at work centers as well as an interdependency of demand among finished products and their components. Gregory et al. (1983) note that the production and inventory planning and control procedures for a firm should depend on (1) whether production is to stock or to order (which, in turn, depends on the relation between customer promise time and production lead time) and (2) whether purchasing is for known production or anticipated production (a function of the purchasing lead time). Chapters 13 to 16 will specifically address production situations.

Demand Pattern

Besides the factors listed in Figure 3.1, we mention the importance of the stage in the life cycle (Section 2.3 of Chapter 2) of a product. Different control procedures are appropriate for new, mature, and declining items. The nature of the item can also influence the demand pattern; for example, the demand for spare parts is likely to be less predictable than the requirements for components of an internally produced item.

3.6 THE A-B-C CLASSIFICATION AS A BASIS FOR DESIGNING INDIVIDUAL-ITEM DECISION MODELS

Many existing inventory management systems can be significantly improved on by simply adopting decision rules that do not treat all s.k.u. or all categories of aggregate inventory investment equivalently. Certainly, in the case of MIDAS (Canada) Corporation, an expensive line of film such as Superchrome deserves more managerial attention than the less expensive miscellaneous hardware items, such as sheet metal screws, used to assemble Stabilization Processors. Similarly, in designing a decision system MIDAS must take into account the fact that it can have more control over the finished goods inventory produced by the Assembly Department than over the amount of inventory in the pipeline between the plant in Germany and the warehouse in Toronto. On what basis, then, should the amount of operating funds and managerial effort available be allocated to controlling each of the many s.k.u. in inventory?

In Chapter 1, we saw, through a Distribution by Value analysis, that somewhere on the order of 20 percent of the s.k.u. account for approximately 80 percent of the total annual dollar usage (ΣDv). Assuming that s.k.u. with higher annual dollar volume deserve more managerial attention, because they can potentially yield higher profits, we recommend the assigning of a priority rating to each and every s.k.u. in inventory according to its Dv value. It is common to use three priority ratings: A (most important), B (intermediate in importance), and C (least important).

Other bases for an A-B-C type of classification are sometimes used. Some large-volume consumer distribution centers plan the allocation of warehousing space on the basis of usage rate and cubic feet per unit. The s.k.u.'s with high usage and large cubic feet are stored closer to the retail sales counter. Similarly a distribution by (profit $\times$ volume) per s.k.u. is sometimes used to identify the best-selling products. Items at the lower end of such an A-B-C curve become candidates for being discontinued. Finally, if top management wants to reclassify any items differently from the procedures described, because they believe (for example) that blue widgets are crucial to their operation, so be it.

The number of categories appropriate for a particular company depends on its circumstances and the degree to which it wishes to differentiate the amount of effort allocated to various groupings of s.k.u. For example, one can always subdivide the Distribution by Value into further categories such as "moderately important," etc., as long as the resulting categories receive differentiated treatment in terms of how much expense and managerial time is allocated to controlling the s.k.u. within them. A minimum of three categories is almost aways used, and we use this number to present the basic concepts involved.

Class A items should receive the most personalized attention from management. The first 5 to 10 percent of the s.k.u., as ranked by the Distribution by Value analysis, are usually designated for this, the class of most important items. Usually these items also account for somewhere in the neighborhood of 50 percent or more of the total annual dollar movement ($\Sigma\, Dv$) of the population of items under consideration.

At MIDAS careful attention was given to A items, especially regarding the level of customer service being achieved. Some of the most expensive Superchrome items were not even stocked; instead, salespersons placed orders in such a way as to ensure the arrival of the goods by air freight from Germany as soon as the relatively small number of individual customers actually needed a film of this type. For other A items, the Inventory Control Manager was directly responsible for monitoring and expediting any orders that seemed to be in danger of not being filled within the normal lead time period. In Chapters 6, 8, 10, 11, and 12 we discuss decision systems that are suitable for use with class A items.

Class B items are of secondary importance in relation to class A. These items, because of their Dv values or other considerations, rate a moderate but significant, amount of attention. The largest number of s.k.u. fall into this category. Usually more than 50 percent of total s.k.u., accounting for most of the remaining 50 percent of the annual dollar usage, are worthy of being labeled B items in any inventory. Some books on inventory control tend to recommend a somewhat lower portion of total s.k.u. for the B category. When a computer facility is available we suggest that as many s.k.u. as possible be monitored and controlled by a computer-based system, with management-by-exception intervention routines appended. Given the increasing costs of clerical labor and the attendant potential costs of human error, versus the constantly decreasing cost of data processing, we believe this propensity toward greater computerization will continue to look more attractive in the future. Having a larger proportion of s.k.u. on a computer system has also the advantage of making a larger data bank available for more effective and timely management reporting and sales analysis.

In Chapters 5, 6, 7, 10, and 11 of the book we present a large number of decision systems that are suitable for use with class B items. Some of the decision rules are also useful for controlling A items, although in the case of A items such rules are *more* apt to be overruled by managerial intervention. Furthermore, model parameters, such as costs and the estimates of demand, will be reviewed more often for A items.

Class C items are the relatively numerous remaining s.k.u. that make up only a minor part of total dollar investment. For these s.k.u. decision systems must be kept as simple as possible. One objective of A-B-C classification is to identify this third large group of s.k.u. that can potentially consume a large amount of data processing and record keeping time. Typically, for low-value items most companies try to keep a relatively large number of units on hand to minimize the amount of inconvenience that could be caused by a stockout of such insignificant parts.

For C items especially, and to a lesser degree for the others, as much grouping as possible of s.k.u. into control groups based on similar annual usage rates, common suppliers, similar seasonal patterns, same end users, common lead times, and so on, is desirable to reduce the total number of discrete decisions that must be processed.[6] Each control group can be designed to operate using a single order rule and monitoring system; for example, if one s.k.u. in the group requires an order because of low inventories, most of the other items will also be ordered at the same time to save on the cost of decision making. Two bin systems, because they require a minimum of paperwork, are especially popular for controlling class C items. They will be discussed in Chapters 7 and 9 of this book. Coordinated control systems will be presented in Chapter 11.

The classification into A-B-C categories at MIDAS had the objective of trying to put as many s.k.u. on a class B, computer-based decision system as possible.[7] Items that required special individualized attention were classified as "A." All remaining items were put into category C as shown in Table 3.1. Note the relatively small number of s.k.u. in class A and the low total dollar volume in class C. While Figure 3.2 is typical, the precise number of members in each of the above categories depends, of course, on how spread out the Distribution by Value curve actually is. For example, the greater the spread of the distribution, the more s.k.u. fall into class C.

An A-B-C classification need not be done on the basis of the Distribution by Value curve *alone*. Recall that management should feel free to move s.k.u. between categories on the basis of other criteria. For example, some inexpensive s.k.u. may be classified as "A" simply because they are crucial to the operation of

TABLE 3.1 A-B-C Classification for MIDAS Professional Products Division

Classification	Number of s.k.u.	Percent s.k.u.	ΣDv (dollars)	ΣDv Percent of Total Dv
A. s.k.u. with $Dv \geq \$6,000$	66	7.8	\$961,404.60	53.6
B. s.k.u. with $240 \leq Dv \leq \$6,000$	561	66.1	\$808,943.05	45.1
C. s.k.u. with $Dv \leq \$240$	222	26.1	\$23,317.65	1.3
Totals	849	100.0	\$1,793,665.30	100.0

[6]At MIDAS, because most of the films were supplied from Germany, common lead times for large classes of products were not unusual. Within these classes a large number of s.k.u. (especially the same films cut to different sizes) exhibited similar demand and seasonal patterns.

[7]For smaller inventory systems that are not computerized, the same logic makes sense. Instead of computers, one could try to routinize automatic decision making by use of manual-based clerical systems. Under such circumstances the fraction of s.k.u. classified as B items should probably be reduced somewhat and the fraction of C items should increase to take advantage of the lower costs of less paperwork and clerical handling.

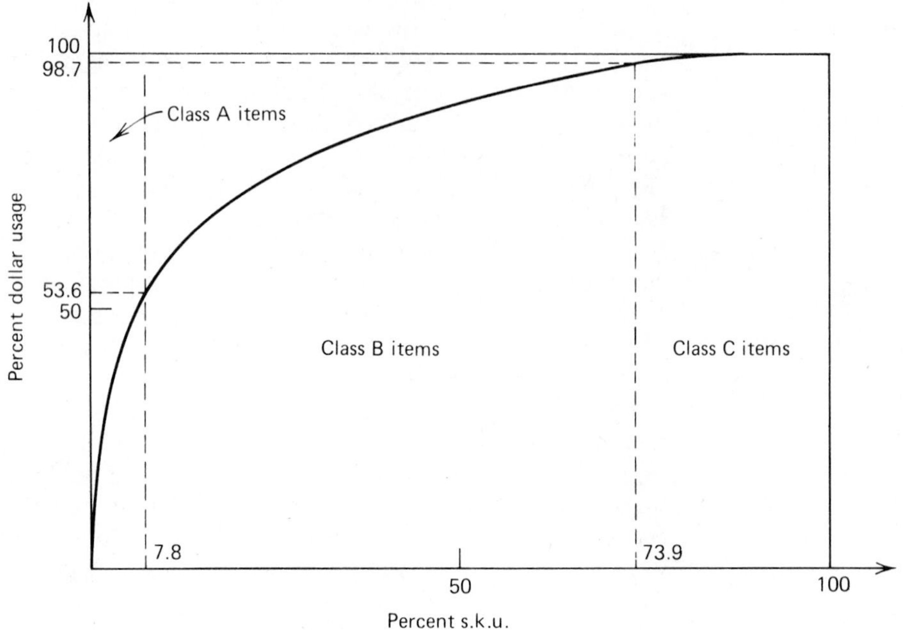

FIGURE 3.2 MIDAS Professional Products Division A-B-C Classification

the firm. The Distribution by (dollar) Value curve provides only a quick, but rough, first cut at the categorization eventually used.

3.7 THE ART OF MODELING

In developing a mathematical model *to aid* in decision making one is faced with the difficult task of incorporating the important factors, yet keeping the model as simple as possible. Incorrect modeling can lead to costly, erroneous decisions. As models become more elaborate they require more managerial time, take more time to design and maintain, are more subject to problems of personnel turnover, and require more advocation with top management and everyone else in an organization (that is, system control costs are increased). There is considerable art in developing an appropriate model; thus a completely prescriptive approach is not possible. There are some excellent references (see, for example, Ackoff and Sasieni, 1968; Little, 1970; Morris, 1967; and White, 1975) on the general topic of modeling. In particular, Little recommends that decision models should be understandable to the decision maker (particularly the underlying assumptions), complete, evolutionary, easy to control, easy to communicate with, robust (that is, insensitive to errors in input data, etc.), and adaptive. We now list a number of suggestions that analysts may find helpful in modeling complex production/inventory situations.(Another, more technical, point is also shown in the Appendix to this chapter.)

1. As discussed in Chapter 2 (see Section 2.2), the measures of effectiveness used in a model must be consistent with the objectives of the organization.

2. One is usually not looking for absolute optimization but instead for significant improvements over current operations. Thus, we advocate the development and use of so-called heuristic decision rules. These are procedures, based on sound logic, that are designed to yield reasonable, not necessarily mathematically optimal, answers to complex real problems (see Müller-Merbach, 1981; Silver et al., 1980).

3. A model should permit results to be presented in a form suitable (appropriately aggregated) for managerial review.

4. One should start with as simple a model as possible, only adding complexities as necessary. The initial, simpler versions of the model, if nothing else, provide useful insights into the form of the solution. We have found it helpful in multi-item problems to first consider the simplest cases of 2 items, then 3 items, and so on. In the same vein, it is worthwhile to analyze the special case of a zero lead time before generalizing to a nonzero lead time. We recall the incident of an overzealous mathematician who was employed by a consulting firm. Given a problem to solve involving just two items, he proceeded to wipe out the study budget by first solving the problem for the general case of n items and then substituting $n = 2$ in the very last step. In the same vein, one should introduce probabilistic elements with extreme caution in that many practicing managers have severe conceptual difficulties with probabilistic reasoning. Throughout the text we first deal with deterministic situations, with the resulting decision rules then being modified for probabilistic environments. Moreover, results are often insensitive to the particular probability distribution used for a specific random variable having a given mean and variance (see, for example, Naddor, 1978); thus a mathematically convenient distribution can be used (for example, the normal distribution described in Appendix B at the end of the book).

5. In most cases in the text we advocate modeling that leads to analytic decision rules (implementable through the use of formulas, tables, graphs, etc.). However, particularly when there are dynamic or sequential[8] effects with uncertainty present (for example, forecast errors), it may not be possible to analytically derive (through deductive mathematical reasoning) which of two or more alternative courses of action is best to use in a particular decision situation. In such a case, one can turn to the use of simulation, which still involves a model of the system. However, now, instead of using deductive mathematical reasoning, one instead, through the model, simulates through time the behavior of the real system under each alternative of interest. Conceptually, the approach is identical with that of using a physical simulation model of a prototype system—for example, the use of a small-scale hydraulic model of a series of reservoirs on a river system. More basically, prior to even considering possible courses of action, simulation can be used to simply obtain a better understand-

[8]An example of a sequential effect would be the following: if A occurs before B, then C results; but if B occurs before A, then D takes place.

ing of the system under study (perhaps via the development of a descriptive analytic model of the system). References on simulation include Fishman (1978), Law and Kelton (1982), Shannon (1975), and Silver (1980).

6. Where it is known a priori that the solution to a problem will possess a certain property, this information should be used, if possible, to simplify the modeling or the solution process. For example, White (1969) points out that in any reasonable solution to a problem a very costly event (such as a stockout) will only occur on an infrequent basis. By neglecting these infrequent occurrences, we can simplify the modeling and obtain a straightforward trial solution of the problem. Once this trial solution is found the above assumption is tested. If it turns out to be reasonable, as is often the case, the trial solution becomes the final solution.

7. When facing a new problem, one should at least attempt to show an equivalence with a different problem for which a solution method is already known (see Naddor, 1966; Nahmias, 1981).

3.8 EXPLICIT MEASUREMENT OF COSTS

It often comes as a surprise to technically trained individuals that cost accountants and managers cannot always determine exactly the costs of some of the variables they specify in their models. According to L. S. Rosen,[9]

> *Many aspects of accounting have developed over time on the basis of conventions that have been widely adopted simply because some people feel that they have proven to be useful in practice. What is not often appreciated by nonaccountants is the fact that we possess no magic formulas or methods for measuring relevant costs for a specific managerial decision. Different costs are relevant for different purposes; and unless the user's needs are known the wrong type of cost can be furnished by an accountant. . . . Many costs assembled for stockholder's financial reports, for example, are particularly useless or dangerous for other purposes because highly arbitrary methods are used to allocate costs to different functions of a business.*

That cost measurement is in practice a problem that has not been conclusively solved, is evident from the fact that a number of alternative cost accounting systems are in use. The basic problem arises because it is not possible and often is not economical to trace all costs (variable, semivariable, or fixed) to each and every individual s.k.u. in inventory. An allocation process that distributes, somewhat arbitrarily, fixed or overhead costs across all units is inevitable. Rosen (1974) categorizes some of the many possible cost systems, and we have summarized these in Table 3.2.

In Table 3.2, column 1, *process costing* is defined as an accounting method whereby all costs are collected by cost centers such as the paint shop, the

[9]Private correspondence (L. S. Rosen is Professor of Accounting at York University, Toronto).

TABLE 3.2 Costing and Control Alternatives

(1) Basic Characteristic of System	(2) Which Valuation? Actual? Predetermined? Standard?	(3) Include vs. Exclude Fixed Manufacturing Overhead in Inventory Cost?
A Process costing methods	A Actual direct material Actual direct labor Actual manufacturing overhead	A Full absorption costing (includes fixed portion of manufacturing overhead)
	B Actual direct material Actual direct labor Predetermined manufacturing overhead	
B Job order costing methods	C Actual direct material Predetermined direct labor, overhead	B Direct variable costing (does not include fixed portion of manufacturing overhead)
	D Standard direct material Standard direct labor Standard manufacturing overhead	

warehouse, etc. After a predetermined collection period, each s.k.u. that passed through the process will get allocated a share of the total costs incurred in the cost center. For example, all chairs painted in a particular month could be allocated exactly the same painting cost (which could be different the next month).

Alternatively, *job order costing* could be used. Under this accounting method a particular order for chairs would be kept track of as it progressed through the shop, and all costs incurred by this particular order would be recorded. Thereby the "cost" of producing the same chair under either of the two costing systems could be very different. The reason for having these two different systems in practice is simple. The job order costing system is more expensive in terms of the amount of bookkeeping required but provides information for more detailed cost control than process costing. (Note that the accountant has to select between decision systems for collecting and keeping track of costs just like we must design inventory/production decision systems that are appropriate in terms of the level of sophistication warranted.)

In addition to selecting between bookkeeping systems the accountant must decide on the basis of valuation. There are four choices according to column 2 of Table 3.2. Under *standard costing* the materials, labor, and factory overhead are charged against each production unit in accordance with a standard (hourly) rate regardless of how much actual effort (time) it takes. Any deficit (negative variance) between total standard costs charged and actual costs incurred over a costing period (say a year) is charged as a separate expense item on the income statement and does not end up as part of the cost of an item, v. Alternatively, surpluses (positive variances), that is, where production takes less time than the standard, can artificially inflate v unless all items produced are revalued at the end of an accounting year. The possibility of a difference between standard and actual costs results from the fact that standards may have been set for different purposes or they may have been set at ideal, long-run, or perceived "normal" rates that turn out, after the fact, to be unattainable. Existing standards can also be out of date and not indicative of prevailing conditions.

Under *actual costing*, the product cost v is determined on the basis of accumulated actual cost directly incurred during a given period. Materials, labor, and overhead costs are accumulated, which are then spread over all units produced during the period. Note that, as a result, the cost of a given item may vary from one period to another.

The term *predetermined* in Table 3.2 refers to the allocation of costs to an s.k.u. based on short-term budgets as opposed to engineered standards. Predetermined cost allocations are usually somewhat arbitrary and may not reflect the amount of expense (as could be determined from a careful engineering study) incurred by a s.k.u. Predetermined costing has the virtue of ensuring that, from an accounting point of view, all costs incurred over a costing period get allocated somewhere.

Cost accounting systems are further differentiated in column 3 of Table 3.2 by whether they utilize absorption costing or direct costing. Under *absorption costing* (also called full costing) little distinction is made between fixed and variable manufacturing costs. All overhead costs are charged according to some formula, such as percent of direct labor hours used, to the product being manufactured. The concept of *direct costing* involves the classification of costs into fixed and variable elements. Costs that are a function of time rather than volume are classified as fixed and are not charged to individual s.k.u. For example, all fixed manufacturing expenses, executive and supervisory salaries, and general office expenses are usually considered to be fixed since they are not directly a function of volume. However, note that some costs are in fact semivariable; they vary only with large fluctuations in volume. A doubling of the production rate, for example, could make it necessary to hire extra supervisory personnel.

Semivariable costs (Figure 3.3) in practice are often handled by assuming that volume can be predicted with sufficient accuracy so that over a relevant range, costs can be viewed as being only of two kinds: variable and fixed. This is not always a simple matter.

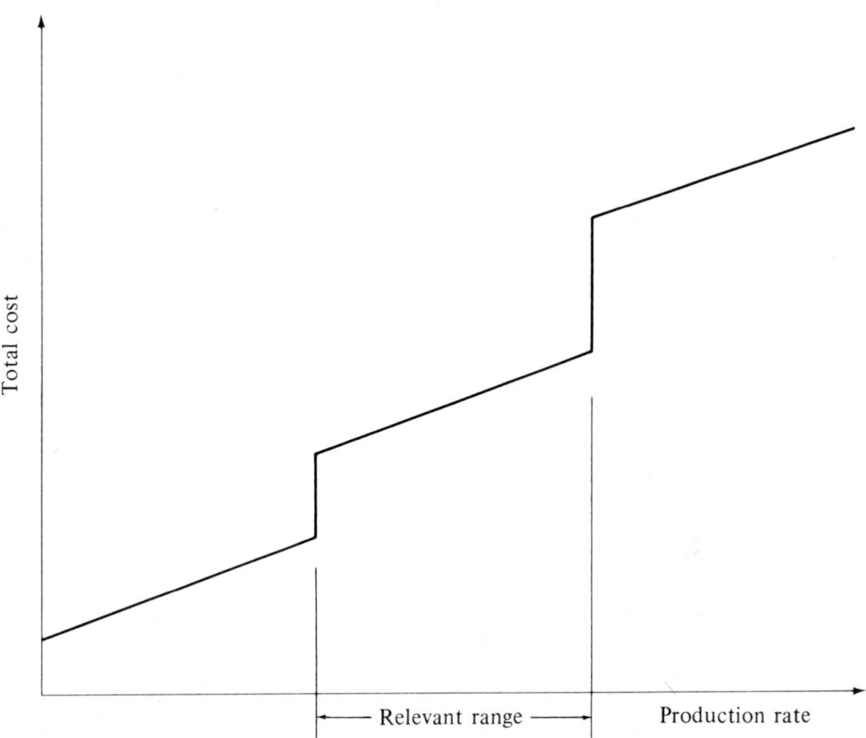

FIGURE 3.3 Semivariable Costs

It should be clear that the first step in any attempt at explicit cost measurement has to be a determination of what assumptions are made by the existing cost accounting system within a firm. As Rosen points out, a small business needing information for external reporting and bookkeeping purposes may choose from Table 3.2 a system (one selection from each of the 3 columns) that is A-A-A because it may be the least costly from a bookkeeping standpoint. A similar company wishing to postpone tax payments may choose A-A-B, and so forth.

Note that while the above description of costing systems provides many options, the most important costs of all, from an inventory planning standpoint, do not appear at all. Inventory and production planning decisions require the estimation of *opportunity costs*. These costs do not appear in conventional accounting records. Accountants are primarily concerned with the recording of *historical costs*, whereas decision makers must anticipate *future costs* so that they can be avoided if possible. Existing cost data in standard accounting records therefore may not be relevant to decision making or at best have to be recast to be useful.

To a decision maker a *relevant cost* is a cost that will be incurred in the *future* if a particular action is chosen. Alternatively, it could be a cost that can be avoided if a particular course of action is not chosen. Therefore, overall overhead costs are only relevant if they can be affected by an inventory planning decision. Allocated (predetermined) overhead, based on some ad hoc formula which is useful for financial reporting purposes, generally is not relevant for our purposes. One must therefore carefully examine the costing procedures of an organization from the point of view of their relevancy to the decision at hand.

3.9 IMPLICIT COST MEASUREMENT AND EXCHANGE CURVES

Suppose we examine carefully the existing accounting systems of a firm and determine the particular species with which we are dealing. Suppose further that we modify the historical cost data to the best of our ability to reflect the opportunity costs involved. Then, finally, suppose we use the most advanced techniques of inventory control to determine the appropriate inventory investment, *based on our adjusted costs*. What if this "appropriate" total investment in inventories that we propose turns out to be larger than top management is willing to accept?

Two possible conclusions could be drawn. First, one could argue that we did not correctly determine the relevant costs and that we did not allow properly for the opportunity costs involved. Second, one could argue that top management is wrong. But what to do? In this regard, the key lies in realizing that *the inventory planning decision deals with the design of an entire system: consisting of an ordering function, a warehousing system, and the servicing of customer demand—all to top management specification*. One can not focus on an individual s.k.u. and ask: What is the *marginal cost* of stocking this or that individual item without considering its impact on other s.k.u. or on the system as a whole! Brown (1967) argues that there is no "correct" value for r, the cost of carrying inventories, in the accounting-explicit measurement sense. Instead, the carrying charge r, he says, is a top management policy variable that can be changed from time to time to meet the changing environment. As Welsh (1979) has stated, "It is the boss' inalienable right and responsibility to decide what total inventory he wishes to authorize." The only "correct" value of r, according to Brown, is the one that results in a total system where aggregate investment, total number of orders per year, and the overall customer service level are in agreement with what top management wants. For example, the specification of a low r value would generate a system with relatively large inventory investment, good customer service, and low order replenishment expenses. Alternatively, higher values of r would encourage carrying of less inventories, poorer customer service, and higher ordering costs.

There is of course, no reason, from a theoretical point of view, why all costs (including A, v, and the cost of disservice) could not be considered as policy variables. In practice this is in effect what is often done, at least partially, by many inventory consultants. An attempt is first made to measure all costs explicitly to provide some baseline data ("ballpark" estimates). Thereupon the resulting inventory decision system is modified to conform to all aggregate specifications. Only cost estimates that serve the cause of attaining the aggregate specifications get ultimately used during implementation. Such an approach is feasible in practice partly because most of the decision models for production planning and inventory management are relatively insensitive to errors in cost measurement. In Chapters 5 and 7 we describe in detail a methodology called *exchange curves*, for designing inventory decision systems using cost information and policy variables specified by top management. For now we just give a brief overview illustration for the decision of choosing order quantities for a population of items.

For the economic order quantity decision rule (to be discussed in Chapter 5), it turns out that the order quantity of an individual item depends on the ratio A/r. As A/r increases, the order quantity increases; hence the average inventory level of the item increases and the number of replenishments per year decreases. These same general effects apply for all items in the population under consideration. Therefore, as A/r increases, the *total* average inventory (in dollars) increases and the *total* number of replenishments per year decreases. Thus, an aggregate curve is traced as A/r is varied (as shown in Figure 3.4). If management selects a desired aggregate operating point on the curve, this *implies* a

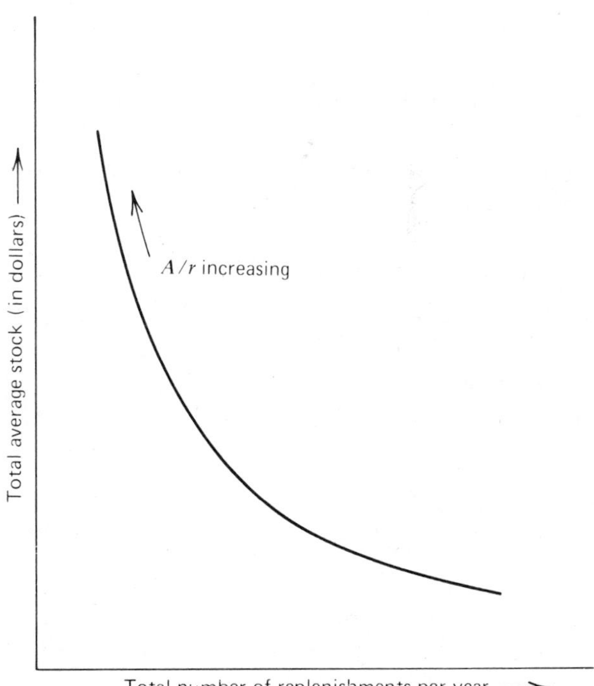

FIGURE 3.4 Example of Exchange Curve

value of A/r. Use of this A/r value in the economic order quantity formula for each item will give the desired aggregate operating characteristics.

3.10 SUMMARY

In this chapter we have discussed the complexity of decision making in production planning and inventory management. A wide variety of decision aids to cope with this complexity were identified. In the next and last chapter in this part of the book we turn to the topic of demand forecasting in that an estimate of future demand is clearly needed for all decisions in the production/inventory area.

APPENDIX TO CHAPTER 3
TWO APPROACHES TO DETERMINING EXPECTED COSTS PER UNIT TIME

Throughout the book the basic approach we use in establishing the expected total relevant costs per unit time will follow these steps:

1. Determine the average inventory level ($\bar{I}$), in units.
2. Carrying costs per year = $\bar{I}vr$.
3. Determine the average number of replenishments per year (N).
4. Replenishment costs per year[10] = NA.
5. Determine the expected shortage costs per replenishment cycle, say W.
6. Expected shortage costs per year = NW.
7. Total expected costs per year = sum of the results of steps 2, 4, and 6.

If the inventory process has a natural regenerative point where the same state repeats periodically, then a different approach, using a key result of renewal theory, is possible. Each time that the regenerative point is reached a cycle of the process is said to begin. The time between consecutive regenerative points is known as the length of the cycle, which we denote by T_c.

There is a set of costs (carrying, replenishment, and shortage) associated with each cycle. Let us denote the total of these costs by C_c. This quantity is almost certainly a random variable because its value depends on the demand process that is usually random in nature.

A fundamental result of renewal theory (see, for example, Ross, 1970), which holds under very general conditions, is:[11]

$$\text{Expected total relevant costs per unit time} = \frac{E(C_c)}{E(T_c)} \tag{3.2}$$

The key point is that in a complicated process it may be easier to evaluate each of $E(C_c)$ and $E(T_c)$ instead of the left-hand side of Eq. 3.2 directly. See Silver (1976) for an illustration of this approach.

---

[10]The discussion here neglects the possibility of quantity discounts.

[11]$E(x)$ is the expected or average value of the random variable x.

PROBLEMS

3.1 In Case A of the MIDAS Corporation a number of problems that require top management input are raised:

1. Should the Takashi subassemblies be stocked?

2. Should Midamatics be assembled only to order?

3. Should a major program be undertaken to reduce the number of s.k.u. through product standardization?

4. Should MIDAS continue to stock Superchrome given its high costs of storage and low volume?

5. Should MIDAS continue to keep its book inventories low and the pipeline from Germany full of many small orders?

a. How do you think top management would go about resolving the above issues?

b. Do you agree that top management can and should resolve the above issues?

c. Which of the above issues do you think operating management would be capable of handling *alone*?

3.2 Draw a flowchart that traces the flow of paperwork, information, and the decision points within the procedures described in Case B of the MIDAS Corporation. Are there any deficiencies that could lead to clerical or managerial error? Are they in a position to upgrade the decision-making rules within their system? Recommend changes by pointing out how your procedures would be superior. Illustrate your modifications in your flowchart.

3.3 *Briefly* describe the inventory management problem(s) faced by a typical small neighborhood restaurant. Point out differences in the inventory problem(s) faced by a particular store in a more specialized chain such as McDonald's or Kentucky Fried Chicken.

3.4 Comment on the following statement: "Optimization models, because they make unrealistic assumptions and are difficult for the user to comprehend, are useless in production planning and inventory management."

3.5 Discuss the fundamental differences in approach required to analyze the following two types of inventory control problems:

a. A one-opportunity type of purchase that promises large savings

b. A situation where the options remain the same from one buying opportunity to the next

3.6 It has been argued that the fixed cost of a setup A is not really fixed but can vary throughout the year when the production workload is seasonal. Discuss and include the implications in terms of the impact on replenishment lot sizes.

3.7 Assuming that you have no data on total annual dollar movement (ΣDv), which of the following s.k.u. (and under what circumstances) should be classified as A, B, or C items?

a. Spare parts for a discontinued piece of manufacturing equipment

b. Bolts and washers

c. Subassemblies

d. Imported s.k.u.'s for resale

e. Motor oil

f. Perishable food stuffs

g. A Right Handed PS-37R-01

h. Widget invented by the company owner's nephew

i. Platinum bushings

j. Describe and classify one example of A, B, and C from your experience

If, in addition, you were supplied with figures on the annual dollar movement (Dv) for each s.k.u., how could such figures affect your classification above? What other information would you like to have?

3.8 An inventory, mostly made up of machined parts, consisted of 6000 s.k.u. valued (at full cost) by the accounting department at $420,000. The company had recently built a new warehouse at a cost of $185,000 which was financed through a 12 percent mortgage. The building was to be depreciated on a 25-year basis. The company's credit rating was sound, and a bank loan of $50,000 was under negotiation with the bank. The main operating costs per year in the new warehouse were estimated to be as follows:

Municipal and other taxes	$5,732.67
Insurance on building and contents	3,200.00
Heating/air conditioning	12,500.00
Electricity and water	3,200.00
Labor (supervisor, 3 clerks, and a half-time janitor)[a]	69,000.00
Pilferage	5,000.00
Obsolescence	5,000.00
Total	$103,632.67

[a]Includes 60 percent manufacturing overhead.

It was estimated that on the average each s.k.u. involved one dollar of labor cost per dollar of material cost.

a. Recommend a value for the carrying cost r in \$/\$/year.

b. Suppose that your recommended value for r is accepted by management and the accounting department. You proceed to calculate the economic order quantities for all 6000 items and discover that the new warehouse is too small to physically accommodate all the inventory that is indicated by your calculations. What action would you take now?

c. Alternatively suppose that your recommended value for r is accepted by management and the accounting department, but that the total dollar investment (based on economic order quantities) that you estimate will be needed is approximately $800,000. Top management is unwilling to have a total investment greater than $500,000. What action would you take under such a circumstance?

3.9 Using Figure 3.5, in this problem assume that raw materials and purchased parts each represent 30 percent of the cost of goods sold and that value added (labor plus factory overhead) constitutes the remaining 40 percent. Also assume that each production cycle involves the production of 1000 units of finished goods, each valued (at cost) at $10/unit. In each case depicted in Figure 3.5, ascertain the appropriate *overall* value of $\bar{I}v$ (that is, the average inventory level, expressed in dollars). Also describe, in terms of the production and demand processes, how each of the patterns could result.

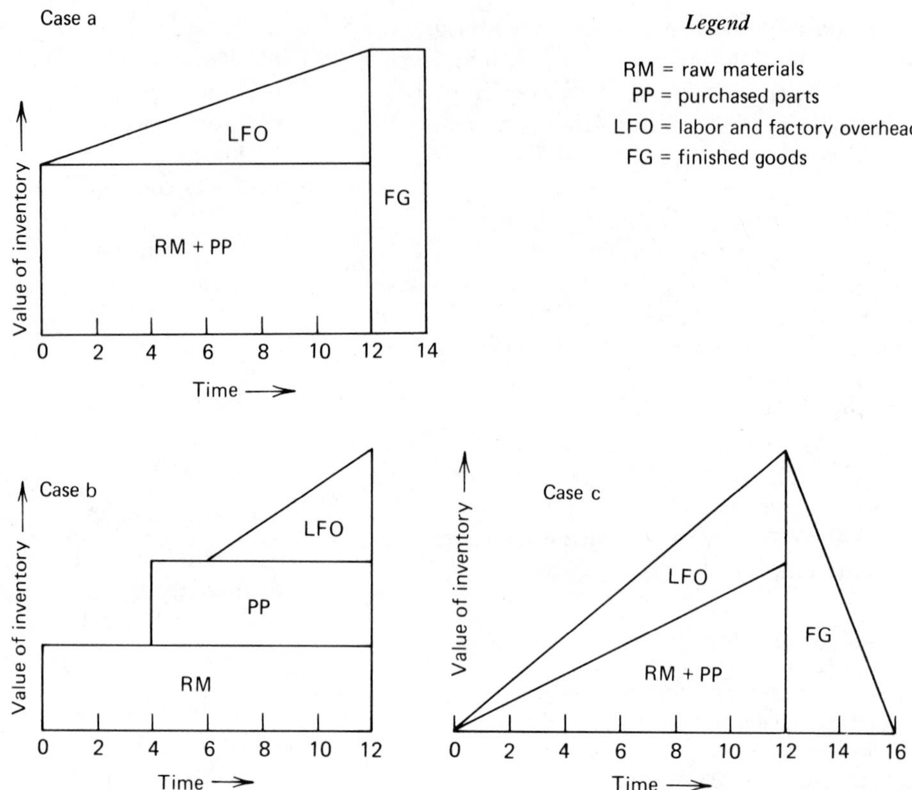

FIGURE 3.5 Inventory Valuation Problem 3.9

REFERENCES

Ackoff, R., and M. Sasieni (1968). *Fundamentals of Operations Research.* John Wiley & Sons, New York, Chapters 1–4.

Brout, D. (1981). "Scientific Management of Inventory on a Hand-Held Calculator." *INTERFACES*, Vol. 11, No. 6, pp. 57–69.

Brown, R. G. (1967). *Decision Rules for Inventory Management.* Holt, Rinehart and Winston, New York, pp. 29–31.

Brown, R. G. (1982). *Advanced Service Parts Inventory Control.* Materials Management Systems, Inc., Norwich, Vermont, Chapter 15.

Conway, R. W., and A. Schultz (1969). "The Manufacturing Progress Function." *Journal of Industrial Engineering*, Vol. X, No. 1, pp. 39–54.

Fishman, G. S. (1978). *Principles of Discrete Event Simulation.* Wiley-Interscience, New York.

Girling, A. J., and P. W. Morgan (1973). "Exchange Curves for Fixing Batch Quantities." *OMEGA*, Vol. 1, No. 2, pp. 241–245.

Gregory, G., S. A. Klesniks, and J. A. Piper (1983). "Batch Production Decisions and the Small Firm." *Journal of the Operational Research Society*, Vol. 34, No. 6, pp. 469–477.

Gross, D., C. M. Harris, and P. D. Robers (1972). "Bridging the Gap Between Mathematical Inventory Theory and the Construction of a Workable Model—A Case Study." *International Journal of Production Research*, Vol. 10, No. 3, pp. 201–214.

Hax, A. C., and D. Candea (1979). "Inventory Management." *Technical Report No. 168*, Operations Research Center, Massachusetts Institute of Technology, Cambridge, Massachusetts.

Krupp, J. (1977). "Programmable Calculators: The New Materials Management Tool." *Production and Inventory Management*, Vol. 18, No. 4, pp. 88–103.

Lalonde, B. J., and D. M. Lambert (1977). "A Methodology for Calculating Inventory Carrying Costs." *International Journal of Physical Distribution*, Vol. 7, No. 4, pp. 195–231.

Law, A. M., and W. D. Kelton (1982). *Simulation Modeling and Analysis.* McGraw-Hill, New York.

Little, J. D. C. (1970). "Models and Managers: The Concept of a Decision Calculus." *Management Science*, Vol. 16, No. 8, pp. 466–485.

Morgan, J. I. (1963). "Questions for Solving the Inventory Problem." *Harvard Business Review*, Vol. 41, No. 1, pp. 95–110.

Morris, W. T. (1967). "On the Art of Modelling." *Management Science*, Vol. 13, No. 12, pp. 707–717.

Müller-Merbach, H. (1981). "Heuristics and Their Design: A Survey." *European Journal of Operational Research*, Vol. 8, pp. 1–23.

Naddor, E. (1966). *Inventory Systems.* John Wiley & Sons, New York, Chapter 10.

Naddor, E. (1978). "Sensitivity to Distributions in Inventory Systems." *Management Science*, Vol. 24, No. 16, pp. 1769–1772.

Nahmias, S. (1981). "Approximation Techniques for Several Stochastic Inventory Models." *Computers and Operations Research*, Vol. 8, No. 3, pp. 141–158.

Plossl, G. W. (1971). "How Much Inventory Is Enough? *Production and Inventory Management*, Vol. 12, No. 2, pp. 1–22.

Rosen, L. S. (1974). *Topics in Managerial Accounting*, second edition. McGraw-Hill, Ryerson, Toronto.

Ross, S. (1970). *Applied Probability Models with Optimization Applications*. Holden-Day, San Francisco, California, pp. 52–53.

Shannon, R. E. (1975). *Systems Simulation: The Art and Science*. Prentice-Hall, Englewood Cliffs, New Jersey.

Silver, E. A. (1976). "Establishing the Order Quantity When the Amount Received Is Uncertain." *INFOR*, Vol. 14, No. 1, pp. 32–39.

Silver, E. A. (1980). "A Tutorial on Simulation (with Emphasis on Operations Management Applications)." *Tijdschrift voor Economie en Management*, Vol. 25, No. 1, pp. 77–103.

Silver, E. A., R. V. V. Vidal, and D. de Werra (1980). "A Tutorial on Heuristic Methods." *European Journal of Operational Research*, Vol. 5, pp. 153–162.

Simon, H. A. (1957). *Models of Man, Social and Rational*. John Wiley & Sons, New York, pp. 196–206.

Sirianni, N. C. (1979). "Inventory: How Much Do You Really Need?" *Production Magazine*, November, pp. 70–74.

Welsh, W. E. (1979). "Management's Role in Inventory Control." *Production and Inventory Management*, Vol. 20, No. 3, pp. 85–95.

White, D. J. (1969). "Problems Involving Infrequent but Significant Contingencies." *Operational Research Quarterly*, Vol. 20, No. 1, pp. 45–57.

White, D. J. (1975). *Decision Methodology*. John Wiley & Sons, London.

Whitin, T. M. (1957). *The Theory of Inventory Management*. Princeton University Press, Princeton, New Jersey, p. 219.

Case C

MIDAS CANADA CORPORATION*

Four times a year each of the managers of the four sales divisions prepared Sales Target Reports that estimated the dollar sales by quarter for each major product category for the 12-month period ahead. (See Table 1.) The Inventory Control Manager, in turn, prepared from the Sales Target Reports a number of reports that became the bases for planning. One set of summaries, called *Purchase Budgets*, he submitted to production planners in Germany. Purchase Budgets stated how many square meters in total of each type of photographic paper, for example, MIDAS Canada was going to buy in each of the next four quarters. The sales of individual s.k.u. were not forecasted on Purchase Budgets; only major product groupings such as major grades of paper and bulk chemicals were projected. The quantities stated in the Purchase Budget for the most imminent quarter were considered to be firm commitments; subsequent quarterly estimates could be modified later on if the need arose.

He also used the Sales Target Reports to prepare *Sales Forecasts* (in units) for the Assembly Plant, from which the Master Plan for the Equipment Division was compiled twice a year. The Master Plan stated the number of units of each product line that were to be assembled or repackaged each month, how many workers were required to carry out planned production, and how much inventory would be carried from one month to the next. In converting dollar sales estimates to units the Inventory Control Manager used a number of rules of thumb. He figured that on the average a Processor would sell for $500, a Midamatic for $25,000, and that bulk chemicals would yield approximately $4 per kilogram or $0.50 per liter.

According to the Inventory Control Manager:

A lot of discussion goes on between the Sales Managers and myself before the Purchase Budgets are prepared. I don't accept the Sales Targets at face value. As everyone knows, sales personnel are eternal optimists. I have been in this business 23 years and have a pretty good feel for what is reasonable and what is not. Unfortunately, because of the large number of products, I don't have the time nor the labor to actually go back and check in detail the sales history on each product every time.Now and then they slip one past me.

---

*The MIDAS cases describe actual decision systems that are based on the consulting experiences of the authors. They do not describe the situation at any single company, but are in fact a compendium of actual situations that have been compressed into the environment of a single firm and industry for illustrative purposes. The cases are not intended as presentations of either effective or ineffective ways of handling administrative problems.

TABLE 1 Timing of Sales Target Reports

Time of Preparation	Period Estimated
October	January to December
January	April to March
April	July to June
July	October to September

SALES FORECASTS OF INDIVIDUAL ITEMS

For most of the 2103 s.k.u. in inventory no forecast of future sales was made. Once a month the Inventory Control Manager and the Comptroller, along with 3 assistants, reviewed the sales of all items by summing the sales over the most recent 5-month period using the data recorded on Travel Cards (see Figure 2, Case B). These 5-month totals became the bases for determining order points and order quantities that will be discussed in Case D.

These monthly sessions usually lasted two 12-hour days and were referred to as "marathons." It was generally agreed that the manual updating system was becoming overly burdensome. During the year the head office Computer Center in England started to summarize past sales of individual s.k.u. and product groups in an effort to help out. Unfortunately, these computer printouts arrived in Toronto sometimes several months out of date and utilized methods that were not completely understood by the Toronto office. As a result, MIDAS Canada was considering, during the latter part of 1984, the installation of a small computer of their own to handle all the record keeping, sales forecasting, and order generation currently being done manually.

Stock keeping units needed for the assembly of Processors, Midamatics, and Takashi Systems were "forecasted" differently and were not a part of the marathon sessions. Four times a year the Inventory Control Manager calculated the number of assembled products (Processors, for example) that would be sold in a particular month from the Sales Target Reports. Then, in turn, he broke down each Processor into subcomponents and parts that had to be ordered. For example, each Processor consisted of 4 EDM-001 parts, 1 EDM-002 part, 6 EDM-003 parts, etc. By multiplying the number of each s.k.u. needed per Processor by the number of Processors forcasted for any month, he was able to determine the total number of each s.k.u. needed each month to meet the assembly schedule. Such a procedure, commonly referred to as explosion into components, was one of the key factors in the Assembly Plant planning system. The Inventory Control Manager kept no safety stocks in assembly parts, and ordered only enough parts to meet the demand per month forecasted through explosion of predicted demand for Processors, Midamatics, and Takashi Systems, because he felt that the explosion method of forecasting yielded quantities that were almost certain to accrue.

For some of the most expensive s.k.u. (A items) neither of the above two procedures were used. For specialty items, such as Superchrome, which were kept locked in a climate-controlled vault, the Inventory Control Manager prepared sales estimates every month by telephoning some of his key large customers and asking them to estimate their needs for a one-month period, two months ahead. (It took 2 to 4 weeks to receive delivery from Germany for specialty items such as Superchrome.) These estimates were considered as commitments by the Inventory Control Manager, who guaranteed delivery of orders up to the level estimated by the key customers telephoned by him. If a key customer habitually overestimated his actual sales of specialty items, then the Inventory Control Manager either dropped him from his list of customers whom he telephoned or asked the customer to sign a sales order that committed him to a fixed order quantity. The Inventory Control Manager usually ordered 10 to 20 percent more of each specialty item than was estimated by the customers whom he telephoned. Customers not on his telephone list had to take their chances of getting their orders serviced from the 10 to 20 percent increment which he added to the committed orders. Committed orders were recorded separately as "Quantities Allocated" on the Record Card (see column 8, Figure 1, in Case B).

For the remaining specialty items the Inventory Control Manager assumed that the demand this year would be approximately the same as last year. In such cases he defined last year's demand as being the sum of actual sales plus the number of backorders (see Figure 3, Case B) that were not filled. Only under unusual circumstances did he depart from this procedure, by multiplying last year's demand by an additional factor, in response to information that came to his attention.

In reviewing the existing forecasting procedures the Inventory Control Manager admitted that he found them very time-consuming. He also worried about what would happen when he retired from the Company:

The computer forecasts are of no use to me. All they do is report back to me the data that I mailed to them in the first place. We would be better off if they took my figures and carried out the sums and multiplications we have to go through during our marathon sessions. But the computer forecasts arrive too late from England to be of any use and appear to be less accurate than my own—especially for seasonal items. Apparently they use some sort of a mathematical model called triple exponential smoothing. I can't see how they can make up for all the intuitive judgments I have to make, on the spot, in coming up with my own estimates of future sales. I sometimes worry about what will happen when someone, with less experience than I, takes over my job when I retire. There are not too many of us old timers around any more.

CHAPTER 4

Forecasting Systems for Production Planning and Inventory Management

The demand pattern for a particular item (or group of related items) can be considered as a time series of separate values (for example, the total demands occurring day by day). Clearly, for effective decision making in production planning and inventory management one needs predictions (or forecasts) of the demands in *future* periods. In particular, if it takes longer to procure or make parts and to manufacture the associated product than the customers are willing to wait for delivery, then forecasts of demand are essential.

We need forecasts to set up performance standards for customer service, to plan the allocation of total inventory investment, to place replenishment orders, to identify needs for additional production capacity, and to choose between alternative operating strategies. Only one thing is certain after such decisions are made—*the forecasts will be in error*. Planning and control procedures should thus reflect the presence of such errors.

Forecasting is concerned with predicting the future. Forecasts can be based on a combination of an extrapolation of what has been observed in the past (what we call *statistical forecasting*) and informed judgments about future events. Informed judgments can include knowledge of firm orders (from external customers or preplanned shipments between locations within a single organization or preplanned usage of service parts, for example, in preventive maintenance) as well as marketing judgments (such as the impacts of promotions, competitor reactions, general economic conditions, etc.).

The overall framework of a suggested forecasting system is shown in Figure 4.1. The human judgment we have mentioned is a crucial ingredient. Note also that, as the actual demand in a period is observed, it is compared with the earlier forecast so that we can measure the associated error in the forecast. It is important to monitor these errors for at least three reasons. First, the quantity of safety (or buffer) stock needed to provide adequate customer service will depend (as we will see in Chapter 7) on the sizes of the forecast errors. Second, the statistical forecast is based on an assumed underlying mathematical model with specific values for its parameters. The sizes and directions (plus or minus) of the forecast errors should suggest possible changes in the values of the parameters of the model or even in the form of the model itself (for example, introducing a seasonal component, when such a component was not already present). Finally, the errors can provide a monitor and feedback on the performance of the subjective input component of the forecasts.

In Section 4.1 we present a strategic overview of forecasting, including the choice of which items to forecast and what management should expect from an effective forecasting system. The next several sections specifically address the statistical forecasting aspects of the system. Section 4.2 discusses the plausible components of mathematical models of a demand time series. Then, in Section 4.3 we present the three steps involved in the use of a mathematical model—namely (1) the selection of a general form of the model, (2) the choice of values for the parameters within the model, and, finally, (3) the use of the model for forecasting purposes. Although the emphasis in this chapter, with regard to statistical forecasting, is on individual-item, short-range forecasting (needed for inventory management and production scheduling) we do briefly present

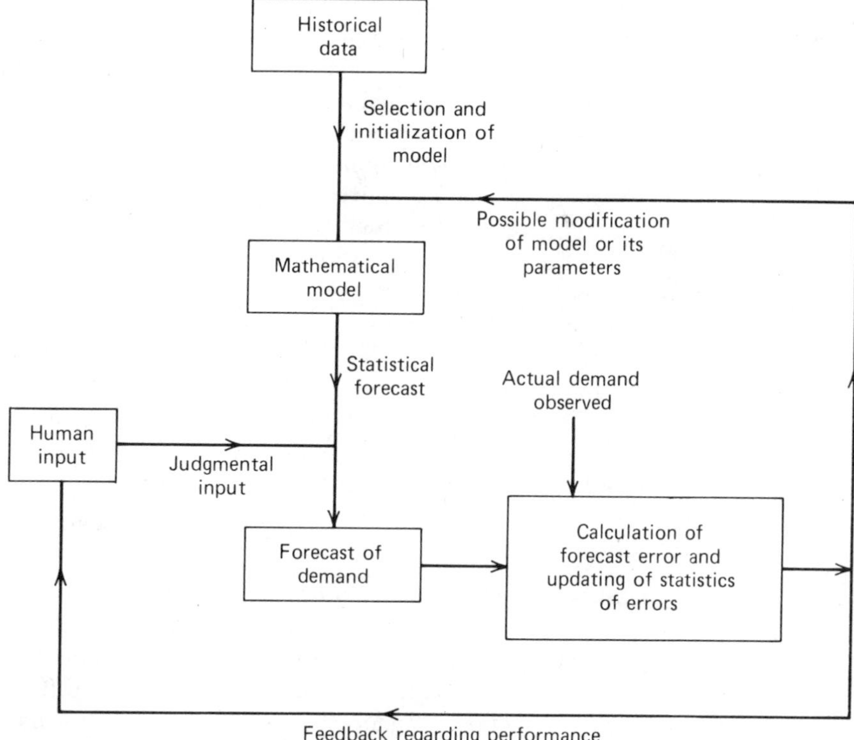

FIGURE 4.1 A Suggested Forecasting System

material appropriate to medium-range aggregate forecasting (useful for production planning) in Section 4.4. This is followed, in Section 4.5, by a detailed discussion of several different procedures for short-range forecasting, with particular emphasis on what is called *exponential smoothing*. Section 4.6 is concerned with various measures of forecast errors needed for establishing safety stocks and also for monitoring forecasting performance. Section 4.7 addresses how to deal with unusual kinds of demand. Then, in Section 4.8 we have considerable discussion concerning how to encourage and use the human judgment input to forecasting. Issues concerning special classes of items are raised in Section 4.9. Finally, in Section 4.10 we return to tactical and strategic issues, specifically to the choice among different forecasting procedures.

4.1 A STRATEGIC OVERVIEW OF FORECASTING

In this section we focus on the general nature of the forecasting system, addressing cost considerations, which items to forecast, and human involvement.

Throughout this chapter and, in fact, most of the book we implicitly assume that demand is an exogenous variable when, in actual fact, our ability to service customer requests on a timely basis will, of course, influence the demand for our products, at least in the long run. Thus, to at least some extent, our decisions, which are based on demand forecasts, will affect the actual demand that transpires. With the current state of the art it is not possible to develop an *operational*, global model that explicitly includes this type of two-way interaction, particularly on an individual item basis. Thus, to a large extent, we treat demand as an exogenous variable but, where possible, we attempt to incorporate the effects of actions such as promotions, price reductions, and so forth. In addition, in production/inventory decision making we emphasize investigations of the sensitivity of decisions and associated costs to inaccuracies in demand forecasting.

In principle, in choosing among forecasting procedures one is concerned with keeping the expected total relevant costs up to some future decision horizon as low as possible. The costs should include both the cost of obtaining a forecast and the *cost in use* of the forecasting errors made:

$$E(\text{Total cost of using a procedure}) =$$
$$E(\text{Cost of operating the procedure}) + E(\text{Cost of resulting forecast errors}) \tag{4.1}$$

In practice, however, the application of this apparently simple expected total cost criterion is quite limited because it is very difficult to measure the relative costs of the resulting forecast errors. But this does not mean that one should not even try to make the tradeoffs shown graphically in Figure 4.2. In an excellent article on choosing between forecasting techniques, Chambers, Mullick, and Smith (1971) provide some data on the relative cost of operating various fore-

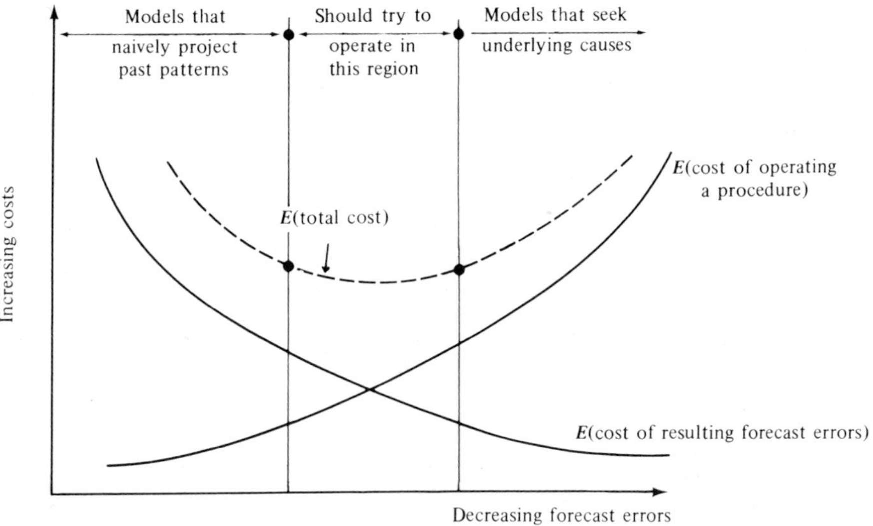

FIGURE 4.2 Cost of Forecasting versus Cost of Inaccuracy

casting procedures in the computing environment that existed at Corning Glass Works in 1970. More important, they spell out in considerable detail, with examples, the tradeoffs that need to be made in Figure 4.2.

There are two important points to be emphasized with regard to the two cost components shown in Eq. 4.1 and Figure 4.2. First, the expected costs of errors in short-range, individual-item forecasts are likely to be much smaller than those associated with longer term forecasts made for aggregate inventory management and production planning decisions. Second, a larger number of short-term, individual-item forecasts are needed in comparison with forecasts for longer term decision making. This is because of the higher frequency (in time) of short-run decisions. Moreover, production *planning* decisions are aggregate in nature, so that longer term forecasts are only typically needed on an aggregate basis for an entire group of items—for example, all the items produced at a particular work center. All of this suggests that different types of procedures are appropriate for short-term forecasts versus longer term forecasts. Specifically, a much higher expense (including managerial involvement) is justified for the relatively infrequent, but extremely important, longer range forecasts. In contrast, with respect to individual-item, short-term needs one is looking for relatively inexpensive procedures. Moreover, even within this last category consideration should be given to using different procedures for items of different importance. Specifically, A items should be individually subjected on a routine basis to managerial attention in conjunction with the use of some form of statistical forecasting model. B items, on the other hand, should involve statistical forecasting with manual intervention only for exceptions. Finally, in most cases the demand for individual C items should not be forecasted at all. (A simple method of estimating the demand rates of C items will be presented in Chapter 9 in conjunction with inventory control procedures for such items.)

Another important strategic issue is how much emphasis to place on statistical forecasting, that is, on an extrapolation of history. For items where the majority of the direct demand is from external customers statistical forecasting is a reasonable approach. On the other hand, if the bulk of the usage of an item is as a component of several other items and the assembly or fabrication schedules of the parent items are established well ahead of time, then explosion from firm usage requirements is clearly preferred to statistical extrapolation of historical usage of the component. This distinction will be emphasized particularly in Chapter 16 when we discuss the topic of Material Requirements Planning.

There is another important issue that relates to forecasting within the aforementioned context of fabricated or assembled items. As an illustration let us consider the case of a manufacturer of farm equipment—for example, tractors. One initially would think in terms of some form of forecasting for the different possible finished tractors. However, there may be a number of options (for example, choice of engine, starter, number of gears, color, umbrella canopy or not, etc.) so that the total number of distinct combinations becomes extremely large. Under such circumstances one should *not* attempt to forecast the demand for each of this myriad of possibilities but rather the forecasts (and associated production planning/inventory management) should begin at the option level. We return to this important topic in Chapter 13.

Production and inventory personnel have a very different perspective on forecasting than do marketing individuals. As McLaughlin (1979) has reported, production-oriented approaches are primarily pushing techniques in which history is extrapolated. In contrast, market-oriented approaches are primarily pulling techniques in which the forecasts are obtained by analysis of the customer needs and the environment. Our framework of Figure 4.1 provides for both types of input. Again, the relative amounts of marketing input (which tend to be of a more subjective nature) depend on the short- versus medium-term split and on the importance of the individual item in the short run. However, for important production/inventory decisions human involvement in, and the *ultimate responsibility* for, forecasts is essential. It would appear from our experience and that of others (see, for example, Garwood, 1980; Kallina, 1978) that a prerequisite for effective human involvement in forecasting is a transparency in the basic statistical forecasting procedure. Only if the individual understands the assumptions of the underlying model, can he or she apply subjective adjustments to incorporate the effects of factors not included in the model. Kallina (1978), reporting on experiences with a sophisticated model at the American Can Company, comments

> *A point made repeatedly by these individuals* (nontechnical line managers) *was that the model had become mistrusted not only because of the forecast errors themselves, but also because the model technicians were unable to explain these errors (or the model itself) except in arcane terms "unintelligible to laymen."*

In summary, from the viewpoint of inventory management and production planning an ideal forecasting system should:

1. Estimate expected demand (in physical units in the short run, but likely in a more aggregate unit, such as dollars or machine hours, in longer term forecasts).
2. Estimate probable range of actual demand around the expected value (that is, forecast errors).
3. Be timely—provide forecasts sufficiently in advance of any decision that must be made.
4. Have forecasts updated periodically so that revisions to decisions taken can be made promptly.
5. Balance the costs of forecast errors made versus the costs of generating forecasts.
6. Allow human judgment to override mechanical forecasts.
7. Be robust; that is, provide forecasts that are not overly sensitive to uncontrollable factors.

Finally an *appropriate forecasting strategy* for any organization depends on:

1. The number and the competence of existing forecasters. (In most companies no one person can do it all.)
2. The amount of budget made available for generating forecasts.
3. The availability of computer-based data processing facilities.
4. The purpose of the forecasts, including the timing and accuracy required.
5. The availability and extent of historical and current data.
6. The ability of decision makers (managers) to cope with sophisticated statistical or other rational approaches.

4.2 THE COMPONENTS OF TIME SERIES ANALYSIS

Any time series can be thought of as being composed of five components: level (a), trend (b), seasonal variations (F), cyclical movements (C), and irregular random fluctuations (ε). Level captures the scale of a time series (as shown in Figure 4.3; if only a level was present, the series would be constant with time). Trend identifies the rate of growth or decline of a series over time (see Figure 4.4, which illustrates a positive linear trend). Seasonal variations can be of two kinds: (1) those resulting from natural forces and (2) those arising from manmade conventions. For example, in the northern United States and in Canada, the intensity of many types of economic activity depends on prevailing weather conditions. On the other hand, department store sales increase before Easter and Christmas, a circumstance related to manmade events. Figure 4.5 shows an illustrative annual seasonal pattern. Cyclical variations or alternations be-

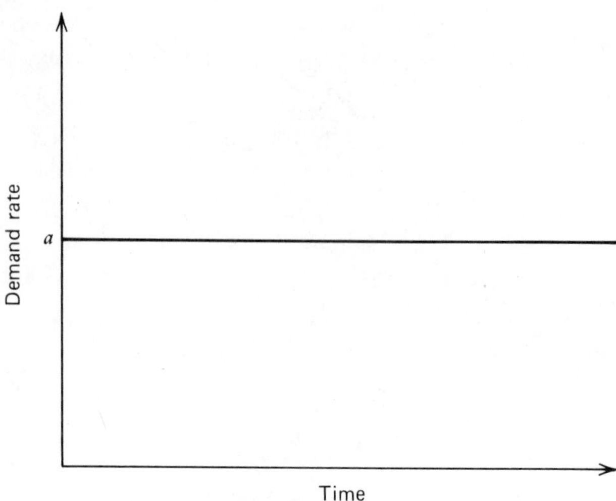

FIGURE 4.3 Level Demand

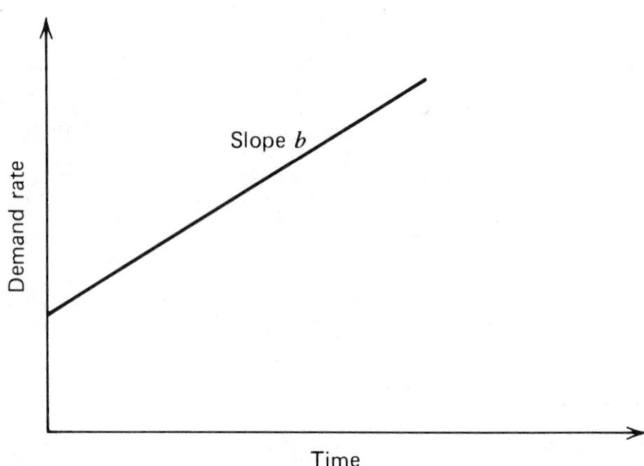

FIGURE 4.4 Linear Trend

tween expansion and contraction of economic activity are the result of business cycles. Irregular fluctuations in time series analysis are the residue that remain after the effects of the other four components are identified and removed from the time series. Such fluctuations may be the result of *unusual* weather conditions, *unexpected* labor strife and all other forms of *unpredictable* events. In any case, they represent our ignorance as to what else may be affecting the time series we are studying.

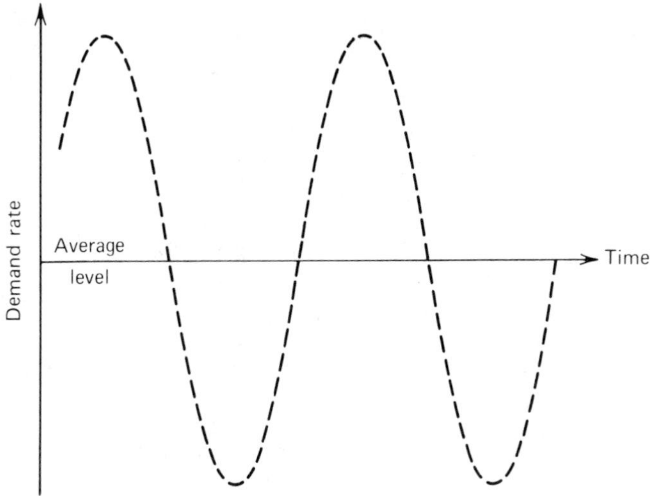

FIGURE 4.5 Illustrative Seasonal Pattern

Using these concepts one can formulate a *multiplicative model* of a time series:

$$\text{Demand} = (\text{Trend}) \cdot (\text{Seasonal}) \cdot (\text{Cyclic}) \cdot (\text{Irregular})$$
$$= b \cdot F \cdot C \cdot \varepsilon \tag{4.2}$$

or an *additive model*:

$$\text{Demand in period } t = (\text{Level}) + (\text{Trend}) + (\text{Seasonal}) + (\text{Cyclic}) + (\text{Irregular})$$
$$x_t = a + bt + F_t + C_t + \varepsilon_t \tag{4.3}$$

or a *mixed model* (partly additive, partly multiplicative). There are statistical procedures for isolating the components. We comment further on this topic later in the chapter, but our discussion will be restricted to models that, in general, do *not* incorporate cyclical effects (in that we concentrate on short- to medium-term forecasts).

4.3 THE THREE STEPS INVOLVED IN STATISTICALLY FORECASTING A TIME SERIES

It is conceptually useful to think in terms of three distinct steps involved in statistically forecasting a time series of demands for an individual stock keeping unit (or the aggregated demand for a group of related items). In this section we provide an overview of these steps. Considerable further detail will appear in later sections. The steps are

Step 1 Selection of an appropriate underlying model of the demand pattern through time.

Step 2 Selection of the values for the parameters inherent in the model.

Step 3 Use of the model (selected in Step 1) and the parameter values (chosen in Step 2) to forecast the future demands.

As discussed in Section 4.1, the choice of the general type of underlying model to use for a particular item (or aggregated group of items) depends very much on cost considerations. The more sophisticated models are really only appropriate for (1) medium- or long-term forecasting of aggregated time series and (2) perhaps for short-term forecasts of A items. Trend and particularly seasonal components should be introduced *with care* in the case of B items. An analysis of historical data (often woefully unavailable in companies embarking on the introduction of formalized forecasting procedures) should suggest the general types of models (for example, seasonal or not, additive or multiplicative, etc.) that would appear to be appropriate for given time series. In addition, managerial knowledge of a particular market is invaluable in suggesting the presence of trends or seasonal patterns.

Once a general form of model is tentatively selected, it is necessary to estimate the values of any parameters of that model. Estimation can be based on some form of statistical fit to historical data—for example, a least squares criterion will be discussed in Section 4.4.1. Alternatively, particularly when there is limited or no historical data available, the estimates of parameters are made on essentially a subjective basis—for example, saying that a new item in a family of comparable items will have a seasonal pattern similar to that of well-established members of the family.

In the event that historical data exist, the time series generated by the tentatively selected model (and its estimated parameter values) can be compared with the historical pattern. If the fit is judged inadequate, then it is necessary to iterate back through Steps 1 and 2.

Once we are satisfied with the assumed underlying model, then in Step 3 it is used, with the estimated values of its parameters, to forecast future demands. This procedure, of course, implicitly assumes that the model and its parameter values will not change appreciably over the period being forecasted. If such changes can be predicted, then appropriate *subjective* adjustments in parameter values and in the nature of the model itself are called for.

As we described earlier (see Figure 4.1), as forecasts are made and errors are observed, this provides us with additional information for adjusting estimates of the parameter values and for judging the suitability of the model in use.

4.4 SOME AGGREGATE MEDIUM-RANGE FORECASTING METHODS

In this section we provide a *brief* overview of *some* of the common models and procedures useful for medium and longer term forecasting of aggregate time series. Such forecasts are an important input to the aggregate production planning procedures to be discussed in Chapter 14. Our intention is simply to make the reader aware of the *general* nature of the available methodology and to provide references where further details can be found. Moreover, there are several longer range forecasting techniques that we will not even mention. An excellent starting point for someone desiring more information on either medium- or long-term forecasting is the article by Makridakis and Wheelwright (1979a).

In Section 4.2 we showed both a multiplicative and an additive model (Eqs. 4.2 and 4.3), each giving demand as a function of level, trend, seasonal, and cyclical components. In actual fact, it may be necessary to first apply a transformation to the demand data in order to achieve a reasonable fit with one of these models. The added complexity of such a transformation is warranted in medium-range forecasting where we are dealing with relatively few (aggregated) time series and forecasts. A class of transformations that has proved useful in practice (see Newbold, 1979) is

$$T(x_t) = \begin{cases} \dfrac{x_t - 1}{\lambda} & \lambda \neq 0 \\ \\ \ln x_t & \lambda = 0 \end{cases} \tag{4.4}$$

where λ is a constant.

To summarize, $T(x_t)$, as opposed to x_t, would be modeled and forecasted. Then, for any given forecast of $T(x_t)$ the corresponding x_t would be obtained by inverting the transformation, that is, solving Eq. 4.4 for x_t in terms of T; that is,

$$x_t = \begin{cases} \lambda T + 1 & \lambda \neq 0 \\ e^T & \lambda = 0 \end{cases} \tag{4.5}$$

4.4.1 Regression Procedures

For illustrative purposes we show only the simple, but common, case of an underlying model that assumes that demand is a linear function of time:

$$x_t = a + bt + \varepsilon_t \tag{4.6}$$

A least squares criterion is used to estimate values, denoted by $\hat{a}$ and $\hat{b}$, of the parameters a and b. The resulting modeled value of x_t, denoted by $\hat{x}_t$, is then given by

$$\hat{x}_t = \hat{a} + \hat{b}t \tag{4.7}$$

If there are n actual historical observations[1] x_t (for $t = 1, 2, \ldots, n$), then the least squares criterion involves the selection of $\hat{a}$ and $\hat{b}$ to minimize the sum of the squares of the n differences between x_t and $\hat{x}_t$; that is,

$$S = \sum_{t=1}^{n} (x_t - \hat{a} - \hat{b}t)^2 \tag{4.8}$$

Through the use of calculus one can show that

$$\hat{b} = \frac{\sum_{t=1}^{n} tx_t - \frac{n+1}{2} \sum_{t=1}^{n} x_t}{\sum_{t=1}^{n} t^2 - \left(\sum_{t=1}^{n} t\right)^2 / n} \tag{4.9}$$

and

$$\hat{a} = \sum_{t=1}^{n} x_t/n - \hat{b}(n+1)/2 \tag{4.10}$$

Fitting such a model to the aggregate demand data for PSF films shown in Table 4.1, we obtain

$$\hat{x}_t = 2961 + 48.68t \tag{4.11}$$

Once the parameters a and b are estimated, the model of Eq. 4.7 can be used to forecast (extrapolate) the demand in a future period. For example, use of Eq. 4.11 gives an estimate of demand for PSF films in October 1984 (period 22) as being 4032 packages. There are also statistical procedures for estimating the adequacy of the straight-line fit and for developing a confidence interval around the forecast (extrapolated) value for any future period. Details are available in several sources such as Bowker and Lieberman (1972) and Hamburg (1977).

[1]Strictly speaking one should not use the same symbol x_t for a random variable (in Eq. 4.6) and an actual observed value of that variable. Later in the text we distinguish between the two cases by adding a subscript "zero," as in $x_{t,0}$, to designate an actual realization of the variable. In this chapter, where there is already the one subscript t, we choose to not explicitly show the difference.

TABLE 4.1 Demand Data for MIDAS PSF Films

Year	Month	Period, t	x_t (packages)
1983	January	1	3025
	February	2	3047
	March	3	3079
	April	4	3136
	May	5	3268
	June	6	3242
	July	7	3285
	August	8	3334
	September	9	3407
	October	10	3410
	November	11	3499
	December	12	3598
1984	January	13	3596
	February	14	3721
	March	15	3745
	April	16	3650
	May	17	3746
	June	18	3775
	July	19	3906
	August	20	3973

Our discussion to here has assumed that the independent variable used in the regression is the time period t. More generally, multiple regression includes two or more exogeneous variables. Moreover, in autoregression the demand in period t is postulated as a function of the demand itself in earlier periods. As an illustration of the latter we might have

$$x_t = a_1 + a_2 x_{t-1} + \varepsilon_t$$

which postulates that the demand in period t is a linear function of the demand in period $t - 1$ plus an error term. A generalization to a system of autoregressive equations in several variables to be forecast, as well as some exogeneous variables, leads one into the field of econometric forecasting (see, for example, Maddala, 1977). This includes the use of so-called *leading indicators*. A variable y is said to be a leading indicator of another variable x if changes in x are *anticipated* by changes in y. Multiple regression is sometimes referred to as forecasting by association in that the variable of interest is forecasted indirectly by its association with other variables.

4.4.2 The Box-Jenkins Approach

Box and Jenkins (1976) have had a profound effect on the field of statistical forecasting. They have suggested a broad class of underlying statistical models of demand patterns, as well as a procedure for selecting an appropriate member of the class based on the historical data available. Conceptually the models are more complex than either the simple regression models (outlined in Section 4.4.1) or the exponential smoothing procedures (to be covered in Section 4.5). However, this complexity (and its associated additional costs) affords an opportunity for more accurate forecasting, which is certainly of interest at the medium-term, aggregate level.

For simplicity in exposition, most of our discussion will be restricted to the case of nonseasonal models. The so-called *autoregressive-moving average* (or ARMA) class of models of the demand pattern x_t can be represented as follows:

$$x_t = \phi_1 x_{t-1} + \phi_2 x_{t-2} + \cdots + \phi_p x_{t-p} + \varepsilon_t + \theta_1 \varepsilon_{t-1} + \theta_2 \varepsilon_{t-2} + \cdots + \theta_q \varepsilon_{t-q} \tag{4.12}$$

where the ε's are so-called *white noise*, namely, independent, normally distributed variables with mean 0 and a constant variance, and the ϕ's, θ's, p, and q are constants.

Equation 4.12 can be considered as a representation of x_t in terms of a linear combination of history (the ϕx autoregressive terms) and unpredictable random components (the $\theta\varepsilon$ moving average terms). Anderson (1976, p. 45) reports that many *stationary* time series are adequately represented by ARMA models with $p + q \leq 2$, that is, at most three terms on the right side of Eq. 4.12. As an illustration, the following shows the case of $p = 1$, $q = 1$:

$$x_t = \phi_1 x_{t-1} + \varepsilon_t + \theta_1 \varepsilon_{t-1}$$

The adjective *stationary* was used in the preceding paragraph. In fact, Eq. 4.12 implies that the x_t series is stationary with time (that is, its expected value and standard deviation do not change with time). At least two circumstances can invalid this assumption. First, there may be a trend (linear or higher order) in the underlying process. The Box-Jenkins approach can cope with this by using a new variable $z_t^{(d)}$ that represents a differencing of x values:

*Recall that a few sections, requiring a level of mathematical understanding higher than the rest of the book, have been marked with asterisks. In all cases, these sections can be omitted without a loss of continuity.

$$
\begin{aligned}
z_t^{(1)} &= x_t - x_{t-1} && \text{(first order difference)} \\
z_t^{(2)} &= z_t^{(1)} - z_{t-1}^{(1)} = x_t - 2x_{t-1} + x_{t-2} && \text{(second order difference)} \\
&\;\;\vdots && \;\;\vdots \\
z_t^{(d)} &= z_t^{(d-1)} - z_{t-1}^{(d-1)} && (d\text{th order difference})
\end{aligned}
\tag{4.13}
$$

To illustrate, if there is a linear trend in the x_t's, the first order difference will produce $z_t^{(1)}$'s that are independent of t. Quite often first order differencing (that is, $d = 1$) is sufficient to produce stationarity. Using $z_t^{(d)}$ instead of x_t in Eq. 4.12, we obtain what is called an ARIMA (p, d, q) model. Other types of transformations (see, for example, Eq. 4.4) can be used.

Another important situation that gives nonstationarity in the x's is seasonality. Again, the Box-Jenkins approach handles this by introducing into Eq. 4.12 additional terms of the form

$$\phi_{1s}\, x_{t-s} + \phi_{2s}\, x_{t-2s} + \cdots + \phi_{vs}\, x_{t-vs}$$

or

$$\theta_{1s}\, \varepsilon_{t-s} + \theta_{2s}\, \varepsilon_{t-2s} + \cdots + \theta_{ws}\, \varepsilon_{t-ws}$$

where v, w, the ϕ's and θ's are again constants, and s is the number of periods in the season. These representations say that the value of the time series in period t is related to the situation exactly 1, 2, etc., seasons previous; that is, there is a seasonally repeating effect.

In Section 4.3 we discussed three steps involved in statistically forecasting a time series: selection of a model, estimation of the parameters of the model, and use of the model for forecasting purposes. The Box-Jenkins approach involves considerable elaboration on the first two of these steps, in that there is such a rich class of models from which to choose. Specifically, the suggested approach involves stages of specification, identification, estimation, and verification (see Newbold, 1979, or Anderson, 1976, for further details). We define these terms in this way:

Specification A statement of exactly which class of models is under possible consideration (for example, ARMA models).

Identification Choice of a tentative model from the class (for example, selection of p and q values for the ARMA class) using the historical data and knowledge of the theoretical properties of the various eligible models.

Estimation Statistical estimation (using a least squares criterion) of the parameters of the selected model (for example, the ϕ's and θ's of the specific ARMA model selected).

Verification Checking the adequacy of the selected model in terms of explaining the given data. Statistical tests are available particularly with respect to whether or not the residuals exhibit a white noise behavior. In the event that they do not, their statistical properties suggest changes in the model; thus one, in effect, loops back to the identification stage.

In summary, Box and Jenkins have developed a powerful, but relatively complex, statistical forecasting methodology. The complexity prohibits its use on a routine basis for *short*-term forecasting of individual items. However, it can be of significant net benefit in some *medium*-term, aggregate forecasting situations.

4.5 INDIVIDUAL-ITEM, SHORT-TERM FORECASTING: MODELS AND PROCEDURES

In this major section of the chapter we concentrate on procedures for estimating model parameters; these procedures have been found to be effective (reasonably accurate) in terms of short-term forecasts for individual s.k.u. In addition, they are relatively simple, in contrast with the methods of the previous section, and thus are practical to use (relatively low system costs) for the high volume of individual-item, short-term forecasts.

We restrict attention to procedures that are appropriate for *at least* one of the following assumed underlying models of x_t, the demand in period t:[2]

$$x_t = a + \varepsilon_t \quad \text{(Level model)} \tag{4.14}$$

$$x_t = a + bt + \varepsilon_t \quad \text{(Trend model)} \tag{4.15}$$

$$x_t = (a + bt)\,F_t + \varepsilon_t \quad \text{(Multiplicative trend-seasonal model)} \tag{4.16}$$

where, as earlier,

a = a level

b = a (linear) trend

F_t = a seasonal coefficient (index) appropriate for period t

and the ε_t's = independent random variables with mean 0 and constant variance σ^2

(*Note*: We do *not* necessarily require that the ε's are normally distributed.)

[2]In a few cases we consider the more general case where x_t can also depend on x and ε values from earlier time periods.

Of course, we never know the exact values of the parameters in Eqs. 4.14 to 4.16. To make matters worse, the true values are likely to change with the passage of time (for example, the arrival of a new competitor in the market is likely to reduce the level or trend by removing part of the market share currently held by the product being forecasted). Consequently, the procedures to be discussed will be concerned with *estimating* current values of the parameters of the specific model under consideration. There are two distinct aspects to estimation. First, there is the question of obtaining initial estimates prior to using the model for forecasting purposes. Second, there is the updating of the most recent estimates as we observe the demand (and hence the forecast error) in the latest period. For each procedure we discuss these two different dimensions of estimation.

4.5.1 The Simple Moving Average

Underlying Demand Model

The simple moving average method is appropriate when demand is modeled as in Eq. 4.14:

$$x_t = a + \varepsilon_t \tag{4.17}$$

that is, a level with random noise. As mentioned above, the parameter a is not really known and is subject to random changes from time to time.

Updating Procedure

The simple N-period moving average, as of the end of period t, is given by

$$\bar{x}_{t,N} = (x_t + x_{t-1} + x_{t-2} + \cdots + x_{t-N+1})/N \tag{4.18}$$

where the x's are actual, observed demands in the corresponding periods. The estimate of a as of the end of period t is then

$$\hat{a}_t = \bar{x}_{t,N} \tag{4.19}$$

One can show that this estimate of a results from minimizing the sum of squares of errors over the preceding N periods (see Problem 4.3). A slightly simpler version (for updating purposes) of the N-period moving average is easily developed from Eq. 4.18 as

$$\bar{x}_{t,N} = \bar{x}_{t-1,N} + (x_t - x_{t-N})/N \tag{4.20}$$

Note from Eq. 4.18 that the moving average is simply the mean of the N most recent observations. Provided that the model of Eq. 4.17 holds, we know from basic probability that $\bar{x}_{t,N}$ or $\hat{a}_t$ is distributed with mean a and standard deviation $\sigma_\varepsilon/\sqrt{N}$. The larger N is, the more precise will be the estimate, provided Eq. 4.17 continues to apply over the whole period. However, if there is a change in the parameter a, a small value of N is preferable because it will give more weight to recent data, and thus will pick up the change more quickly. Typical N values that are used run from 3 to as high as 12. Recall that at MIDAS all inventory decision rules were based, in effect, on a five-month moving average forecast of demand.

Initialization

In terms of initialization, an N-period moving average should not really be used until there are N periods of history available. In actual fact, if early forecasts are essential, one can use a smaller number of periods in the initial stages.

Forecasting

Because of the (level) nature of the model of Eq. 4.17, it is appropriate to use our estimate $\hat{a}_t$ as a forecast at the end of period t for *any* future period:

$$\hat{x}_{t,t+\tau} = \hat{a}_t \tag{4.21}$$

where $\hat{x}_{t,t+\tau}$ is the forecast, made at the end of period t, of demand in period $t + \tau$ (for $\tau = 1, 2, 3, \ldots$).

Illustration

For MIDAS product PSF-008, a film ordered from Germany, columns 1 to 3 of Table 4.2 show the demand data during 1984. The five-month moving averages, beginning as of the end of May 1984, are shown in column 4 and the associated one-month ahead forecasts in column 6. We comment further on the results of Table 4.2 in the next section when we discuss the topic of simple exponential smoothing.

General Comments

There are two significant drawbacks to the simple moving average procedure. First, N periods of historical data must be stored for each s.k.u. Second, equal weight is given to the N most recent pieces of historical data with no weight to data prior to that. Intuitively, it seems inappropriate to completely discount the earlier data.

Finally we mention that there are moving average procedures available for more complicated underlying models. For example, Johnson and Montgomery (1974) present the procedure appropriate for the trend model of Eq. 4.15.

TABLE 4.2 Moving Average and Simple Exponential Smoothing Forecasts for PSF-008, using $N = 5$ and $\alpha = 1/3$ (all data in 100 square meters)

Year (1)	Month t (2)	Demand x_t (3)	5-Month Moving Average $\bar{x}_{t,5}$ (4)	Exponentially Smoothed Average (5)	Forecasts $\hat{x}_{t,t+1} = \bar{x}_{t,5}$ (6)	Forecasts $\hat{x}_{t,t+1} = \hat{a}_t$ (7)
1984	1	52				
	2	48				
	3	36		(50.0)		
	4	49		(49.7)		
	5	65	50.0	(54.8)	50.0	54.8[a]
	6	54	50.4	54.5	50.4	54.5[a]
	7	60	52.8	56.3	52.8[a]	56.3
	8	48	55.2	53.6	55.2	53.6[a]
	9	51	55.6	52.7	55.6	52.7[a]
	10	62	55.0	55.8	55.0	55.8[a]
	11	66	57.4	59.2	57.4	59.2[a]
	12	62	57.8	60.1	57.8	60.1
1985	13					

[a]Closer to actual sales in period $t + 1$.

4.5.2 Simple Exponential Smoothing

The procedure to be described in this subsection is probably the most widely used statistical method for short-term forecasting. As we will see, it is intuitively appealing and very simple to employ.

Underlying Demand Model

As in the case of moving averages, the basic underlying demand pattern assumed is that of Eq. 4.14, which, for convenience, we repeat here:

$$x_t = a + \varepsilon_t \tag{4.22}$$

However, later we will mention that the procedure is actually appropriate for a somewhat wider range of demand models.

Updating Procedure

We wish to estimate the parameter a in Eq. 4.22. Recall that in Sections 4.4.1 and 4.5.1 we used a least squares regression on historical data to estimate parameters of the underlying models. However, we pointed out that regular least squares gives equal weight to all historical data considered. Simple exponential smoothing, the procedure to be described, can be derived by selecting $\hat{a}_t$, the estimate of a at the end of period t, in order to minimize the following sum of *discounted* squares of residuals.

$$S' = \sum_{j=0}^{\infty} d^j \, (x_{t-j} - \hat{a}_t)^2 \tag{4.23}$$

where

d = a discount factor ($0 < d < 1$)

x_{t-j} = the *actual* demand in period $t - j$

Note that, because $d < 1$, the weighting given to historical data decreases *geometrically* as one goes back in time. Exponential smoothing would really be more appropriately named geometric smoothing (an exponential curve is a continuous approximation to geometrically decaying points). The minimization of Eq. 4.23 is carried out in the Appendix to this chapter. The resulting estimate of a satisfies the following updating formula

$$\hat{a}_t = \alpha x_t + (1 - \alpha)\hat{a}_{t-1} \tag{4.24}$$

where

$\alpha = 1 - d$ is known as the smoothing constant

In addition, it can be shown (see, for example, Johnson and Montgomery, 1974) that $\hat{a}_t$ is an unbiased estimate of a; that is, $E(\hat{a}_t) = a$.

Equation 4.24 can be manipulated as follows:

$$\hat{a}_t = \hat{a}_{t-1} + \alpha(x_t - \hat{a}_{t-1})$$

or

$$\hat{a}_t = \hat{a}_{t-1} + \alpha \, e_t \tag{4.25}$$

where

e_t = the error in period t between the actual demand x_t and the forecast $\hat{a}_{t-1}$ made at the end of the previous period ($t - 1$)

Equation 4.25 states that the new estimate of the level is the old estimate plus a fraction of the most recent error (see also Figure 4.6). Practically speaking, one doesn't ever really know whether any particular error results from a random fluctuation or whether a significant shift in a has occurred. As a result, the simple exponential smoothing model hedges by assuming that only a fraction of

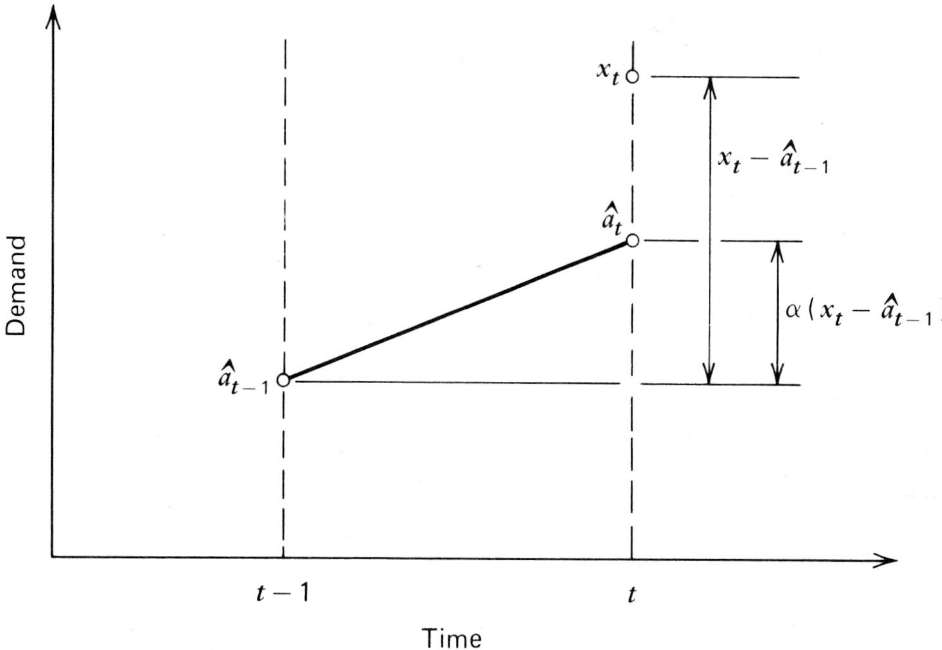

FIGURE 4.6 The Components of an Exponentially Smoothed Level

the forecast error should be used to revise the estimate of a. Note from Eq. 4.24 that as α tends toward 0 our estimate is unchanged by the latest piece of information, while as α moves toward 1 more and more weight is placed on the demand observed in the last period. In Section 4.5.5 we comment on the selection of an appropriate value of the smoothing constant.

The updating procedure of Eq. 4.24 can also be shown to minimize the mean squared error of the one-period-ahead forecast for the following models that are both somewhat more general than that of Eq. 4.22.

Case 1 (Details can be found in Harrison, 1967.)

$$x_t = a_t + \varepsilon_t$$

with

$$a_t = a_{t-1} + \delta_t$$

where the δ_t's are random changes with mean 0 and independent of the ε_t's; that is, the level is subject to random changes through time (which is what we have *implicitly* assumed earlier).

Case 2 (See Goodman, 1974, for details.) The x_t's are generated by an ARIMA (0, 1, 1) process. In other words, from Eqs. 4.12 and 4.13, we have

$$x_t = x_{t-1} + \varepsilon_t + \theta_1 \varepsilon_{t-1}$$

The geometric weighting of historical data in exponential smoothing can also be seen by substituting a corresponding relation for $\hat{a}_{t-1}$ in Eq. 4.24, and then repeating for $\hat{a}_{t-2}$, etc. This gives

$$\begin{aligned}\hat{a}_t &= \alpha x_t + (1 - \alpha)[\alpha x_{t-1} + (1 - \alpha)\hat{a}_{t-2}]\\ &= \alpha x_t + \alpha(1 - \alpha)x_{t-1} + (1 - \alpha)^2[\alpha x_{t-2} + (1 - \alpha)\hat{a}_{t-3}]\\ &= \alpha x_t + \alpha(1 - \alpha)x_{t-1} + \alpha(1 - \alpha)^2 x_{t-2} + \cdots \end{aligned} \tag{4.26}$$

We see the contrast with moving averages where the last N observations were given equal weight. In addition, the recursion relationship of Eq. 4.24 shows that only one value of a and the most recent x_t need be retained, a significant data storage savings compared with the situation of moving averages.

From the weighting of the terms in Eq. 4.26, one can ascertain (see Problem 4.4) that the average age of the data encompassed in $\hat{a}_t$ is $1/\alpha$ periods. In an N-month moving average the average age of the data used is $(N + 1)/2$. Equalizing the average ages gives the following relationship between α and N:

$$\alpha = 2/(N + 1) \tag{4.27}$$

Initialization

Where significant historical data exist, one simply uses the average demand in the first several periods as the initial estimate of a. The numerical illustration will demonstrate this point. The case where inadequate history exists will be addressed in Section 4.9.1.

Forecasting

As mentioned earlier $\hat{a}_t$ is an unbiased estimate, as of the end of period t, of the parameter a, where the latter, according to Eq. 4.22, is the expected demand in *any* future period. Thus our forecast, made at the end of period t, for any future period $t + \tau$ is

$$\hat{x}_{t,t+\tau} = \hat{a}_t \tag{4.28}$$

For deciding when to place a replenishment order and how much to order we will be interested in the *total* forecast over several unit time periods (for example, the replenishment lead time may be 4 months, while the forecast update period is

1 month). If we let $\hat{x}_{t,t,u}$ be the forecast, made at the end of period t, of total demand from time t (end of period t) to time u, then from Eq. 4.28 we have

$$\hat{x}_{t,t,u} = (u - t)\hat{a}_t \tag{4.29}$$

Illustration

We use the same example of MIDAS product PSF-008 as was employed earlier to illustrate a 5-period moving average. In addition, for comparison we select the smoothing constant to give the equivalence condition of Eq. 4.27; that is,

$$\alpha = 2/(5 + 1) = 1/3$$

(In actual fact, as will be discussed later, one would normally not use such a high value of α.)

In Table 4.2, the average of the first 5 months' sales (50.0) is taken as the initial value for the exponentially smoothed average and plotted opposite $t = 3$, the midpoint of the 5-month range of the average. Then the exponentially smooth average in column 5 for month 4 is calculated by using Eq. 4.24:

$$\begin{aligned}\hat{a}_4 &= \frac{1}{3}x_4 + \frac{2}{3}\hat{a}_3 \\ &= \frac{1}{3}(49) + \frac{2}{3}(50) \\ &= 49.7\end{aligned}$$

The same procedure was repeated for all subsequent months. For months 4 and 5 no exponentially smooth forecasts were issued to allow the effect of setting initial conditions at $\hat{a}_3 = 50.0$ to be smoothed out. This is commonly referred to as the "run-in period." Rather than using $\hat{a}_3 = 50.0$, one could instead set $\hat{a}_0 = 50.0$, and thus make the run-in time equal to 5 periods.

Using Eq. 4.28 "exponential smoothing" forecasts were calculated for each period from period 6 onward. These are shown in column 7 of Table 4.2. Note from columns 6 and 7 that the exponential smoothing forecast outperforms the five-month moving average forecast for 6 of the 7 months of 1984. This appears to be a result of the fact that by using $\alpha = 1/3$, the simple exponential smoothing forecast is made more responsive to recent sales data variation than the five-month moving average. Since the time series x_t appears to be undergoing changes, this degree of responsiveness appears to be warranted for the particular example shown.

General Comments

In summary, simple exponential smoothing is an easy to understand, effective procedure to use when the underlying demand model is composed of level and random components. Even when the underlying demand process is more complicated, exponential smoothing can be used as part of an updating procedure. For example, Steece and Wood (1979) use a Box-Jenkins ARIMA model for the aggregate demand time series of an entire class of items, and then use simple exponential smoothing to update the estimate of a particular item's demand as a fraction of the aggregate.

4.5.3 Exponential Smoothing for a Trend Model

The simple smoothing procedure presented in the previous subsection is based on a model without a trend and therefore is inappropriate when the underlying demand pattern involves a significant trend. A somewhat more complicated smoothing procedure is needed when such a trend is present.

Underlying Demand Model

The basic underlying model of demand is the pattern of Eq. 4.15 which we repeat here.

$$x_t = a + bt + \varepsilon_t \tag{4.30}$$

Again, reference will be made later to somewhat more general models for which the suggested smoothing procedure is appropriate.

Updating Procedure

Holt (1957) suggested a procedure that is a natural extension of simple exponential smoothing:

$$\hat{a}_t = \alpha_{HW}\, x_t + (1 - \alpha_{HW})(\hat{a}_{t-1} + \hat{b}_{t-1}) \tag{4.31}$$

and

$$\hat{b}_t = \beta_{HW}(\hat{a}_t - \hat{a}_{t-1}) + (1 - \beta_{HW})\hat{b}_{t-1} \tag{4.32}$$

where α_{HW} and β_{HW} are smoothing constants (we use the subscripts HW to represent Holt-Winters since these smoothing constants will be part of a procedure of Winters', to be discussed in Section 4.5.4) and, for the demand model of Eq. 4.30, the difference $\hat{a}_t - \hat{a}_{t-1}$ is an estimate of the actual trend in period t.

Harrison (1967), among others, has shown that the Holt procedure minimizes the expected one-period-ahead, mean-square forecast error for the trend model of Eq. 4.30—in fact, for a more general model where independent random changes in both a and b are possible each period, in addition to the random noise (the ε's).

We use Holt's updating as part of a popular procedure, to be described in Section 4.5.4, for dealing with an underlying model involving both trend and seasonal components. However, in the current subsection, where there is no seasonality, we recommend instead a single parameter procedure suggested by Brown (1963), which turns out to be a special case of Holt's method. Besides involving only a single smoothing parameter, Brown's procedure again has the intuitively appealing property of being derived from minimizing the sum of geometrically weighted forecast errors (similar to the basis for the simple exponential smoothing procedure of Eq. 4.24). Brown's updating equations are (see Problem 4.6)

$$\hat{a}_t = [1 - (1 - \alpha)^2]x_t + (1 - \alpha)^2(\hat{a}_{t-1} + \hat{b}_{t-1}) \tag{4.33}$$

and

$$\hat{b}_t = \left[\frac{\alpha^2}{1 - (1 - \alpha)^2}\right](\hat{a}_t - \hat{a}_{t-1}) + \left[1 - \frac{\alpha^2}{1 - (1 - \alpha)^2}\right]\hat{b}_{t-1} \tag{4.34}$$

where α is the single smoothing constant involved ($\alpha = 1 - d$ again, where d is the discount factor used in the geometrically weighted sum of squares).

Note that Eqs. 4.33 and 4.34 are the special case of Holt's updating Eqs. 4.31 and 4.32, where

$$\alpha_{HW} = [1 - (1 - \alpha)^2] \tag{4.35}$$

$$\beta_{HW} = \frac{\alpha^2}{1 - (1 - \alpha)^2} \tag{4.36}$$

In Section 4.5.5 we address the issue of the selection of the α value.

At the end of this subsection we will comment on two other updating procedures, suggested in the literature, that have turned out to be equivalent with Brown's procedure in Eqs. 4.33 and 4.34.

Initialization

Typically, the initial values of the level (a) and the trend (b) are ascertained by doing a regular (unweighted) least squares regression on the historical data available. Suppose that there are n periods of data available. Smoothing will begin with the next period after this preliminary data. Thus we would like to have the level a computed relative to an origin at the end of the last period of the fitted data; that is, we should number the historical periods $0, -1, -2, -3, \ldots,$

$-(n-1)$ going back in time.[3] In other words, we wish to select a_0 and b_0 to minimize

$$S = \sum_{t=-n+1}^{0} [x_t - (\hat{a}_0 + t\hat{b}_0)]^2$$

Through the use of calculus one obtains

$$\hat{a}_0 = \frac{6}{n(n+1)} \sum_t tx_t + \frac{2(2n-1)}{n(n+1)} \sum_t x_t \tag{4.37}$$

and

$$\hat{b}_0 = \frac{12}{n(n^2-1)} \sum_t tx_t + \frac{6}{n(n+1)} \sum_t x_t \tag{4.38}$$

where all the summations range over the integers $-(n-1), -(n-2), \ldots, -2, -1, 0$.

Where this initial regression is a relatively straightforward matter, the reader might ask why we don't simply redo a regression after each additional period of information instead of resorting to the smoothing procedure of Eqs. 4.33 and 4.34. There are two important reasons. First, the regression gives *equal* weight to all historical information, whereas the smoothing reduces the weight geometrically as we go back in time. Second, regression is computationally prohibitive on a repetitive basis for short-term forecasting.

The case where there is insufficient history for regression initialization will be treated in Section 4.9.1.

Forecasting

Because of the underlying model of Eq. 4.30, we know that

$$\hat{x}_{t,t+\tau} = \hat{a}_t + \hat{b}_t\tau \tag{4.39}$$

where

$\hat{x}_{t,t+\tau}$ = the forecast, made at the end of period t, of the demand in period $t+\tau$

---

[3]Alternatively, we might wish to see a run-in period as earlier, in which case the origin would be shifted to the start of the run-in period. If there are m periods to run in, then the $\hat{a}_0$ parameter to use is that found from Eq. 4.37 minus $m\hat{b}_0$.

Also the forecast, made at the end of period t, of *cumulative* demand from time t (end of period t) to time u (end of period u) is

$$\hat{x}_{t,t,u} = \sum_{\tau=1}^{u-t} (\hat{a}_t + \hat{b}_t \tau) \tag{4.40}$$

When u is not exactly an integer, the last term in the summation should cover an appropriate fraction of the last period.

Illustration

Consider another MIDAS product PSF-016 where it is reasonable to assume that demand is growing, approximately linearly, with time. Table 4.3 shows demand data for 15 consecutive months. Suppose that the first 6 months of data (January 1984 through June 1984) are used to estimate $\hat{a}_0$ and $\hat{b}_0$. Use of Eqs. 4.37 and 4.38 gives

$$\hat{a}_0 = 27.19 \qquad \text{and} \qquad \hat{b}_0 = 1.34$$

Suppose we do not use a run-in period and directly use these to forecast demand in July 1984 ($t = 1$), employing Eq. 4.39. This gives us $\hat{x}_{0,1} = 28.53$. The resulting error in July 1984 is $27 - 28.53$ or -1.53. The parameters a and b are updated through the use of Eqs. 4.33 and 4.34[4] and a forecast $\hat{x}_{1,2}$ is made at the end of July 1984, and so on. Continuing in this fashion, we obtain the results in the last four columns of Table 4.3.

Updating Procedures Equivalent to That Suggested in Eqs. 4.33 and 4.34

There are other updating procedures that have been suggested in the literature for the underlying trend model of Eq. 4.30. We specifically mention two that turn out to be equivalent to the procedure suggested in Eqs. 4.33 and 4.34.

The first, known as double exponential smoothing, was also suggested by Brown(1963). In double smoothing, rather than updating the coefficients a and b directly as in Eqs. 4.33 and 4.34, two smoothing statistics are updated:

$$S_t = \alpha x_t + (1 - \alpha) S_{t-1} \tag{4.41}$$

and

$$S_t^{(2)} = \alpha S_t + (1 - \alpha) S_{t-1}^{(2)} \tag{4.42}$$

[4]An α value of 1/3 is used to be consistent with the earlier smoothing examples. As mentioned earlier, one would normally use a somewhat smaller α value.

TABLE 4.3 Illustration of Forecasting with a Trend Model for PSF-016 (all data in 100 square meters)

Year	Month	t	x_t	$e_t = x_t - \hat{x}_{t-1,t}$	$\hat{a}_t$	$\hat{b}_t$	$\hat{x}_{t,t+1} = \hat{a}_t + \hat{b}_t$
1984	January	−5	20				
	February	−4	25				
	March	−3	21				
	April	−2	22				
	May	−1	27				
	June	0	28		27.19	1.34	28.53
	July	1	27	−1.53	27.68	1.17	28.85
	August	2	30	1.15	29.49	1.30	30.79
	September	3	34	3.21	32.57	1.66	34.23
	October	4	25	−9.23	29.10	0.63	29.73
	November	5	25	−4.73	27.10	0.10	27.20
	December	6	26	−1.20	25.98	−0.14	25.84
1985	January	7	36	10.16	31.48	0.99	32.47
	February	8	41	8.53	37.21	1.94	39.15
	March	9	39	−0.15	39.06	1.92	40.98

where

S_t = single smoothed statistic

$S_t^{(2)}$ = double smoothed statistic

Note that Eq. 4.41 is equivalent to the single updating of Eq. 4.24 used in Section 4.5.2 for the case of just a level (that is, no trend). Brown shows that the coefficients $\hat{a}_t$ and $\hat{b}_t$ can be expressed in terms of S_t and $S_t^{(2)}$ as follows:

$$\hat{a}_t = 2S_t - S_t^{(2)} \tag{4.43}$$

and

$$\hat{b}_t = \frac{\alpha}{1-\alpha}(S_t - S_t^{(2)}) \tag{4.44}$$

In addition, he demonstrates that the procedure of Eqs. 4.41 to 4.44 is completely equivalent to what, we believe, is the intuitively more appealing procedure of Eqs. 4.33 and 4.34.

The second procedure, suggested by Goodman (1974), also has considerable intuitive appeal. He uses a concept, call *twicing*, first suggested by Tukey (1971). The idea is to use *simple* exponential smoothing on the time series to develop forecasts $\hat{x}_{t-1,t}$ and from these compute residuals $r_t = x_t - \hat{x}_{t-1}$. Then simple exponential smoothing is *reapplied* to the new residual time series r_t

to develop "forecasts" $\hat{r}_{t-1,t}$. The actual forecasts to use in *twicing* are $\hat{x}_{t-1,t} + \hat{r}_{t-1,t}$. Goodman shows that this procedure minimizes the mean square error for one-period-ahead forecasts when the underlying demand pattern is of the form ARIMA (0, 2, 2).[5] He also shows that the *twicing* procedure is equivalent with the above discussed, double exponential smoothing method, which we have just seen is, in turn, equivalent with the procedure of Eqs. 4.33 and 4.34.

4.5.4 The Winters Exponential Smoothing Procedure for a Seasonal Model

In many organizations there are a number of individual s.k.u. that exhibit demand patterns with significant seasonality. Examples include lawnmowers, skiing equipment, fertilizer, ice cream, heating fuel, among other things. For individual items the most common forecasting update period is 1 month. However, in our illustration, to keep the amount of computations manageable, we use a quarterly (tri-monthly) update period. Incidentially, the procedure to be discussed, is certainly of potential use in aggregate, medium-range forecasting, in which case, quarterly periods are more meaningful.

Underlying Model

The underlying model assumed is that of Eq. 4.16:

$$x_t = (a + bt) F_t + \varepsilon_t \tag{4.45}$$

where

a = the level

b = the linear trend

F_t = a seasonal index (coefficient) appropriate for period t

ε_t's = independent random variables with mean 0 and constant variance σ^2

The season is assumed to be of length P periods and the seasonal indices are normalized so that, at any point, the sum of the indices over a full season is exactly equal to P. With an annual season $P = 12$ for a 1-month forecast interval and $P = 4$ for a quarterly interval. Seasonal models are also applicable for a weekly "season" (for example, demand for medical services at the emergency facilities of a hospital) or even a daily "season" (for example, customer demand for electrical energy as a function of the time of the day). The special case when all of the F's equal unity returns us to the situation of a nonseasonal trend model.

[5] See Eqs. 4.12 and 4.13.

Updating Procedure

To repetitively use the model of Eq. 4.45 for forecasting purposes, we must have estimates of a, b, and the F's. Winters (1960) first suggested the following procedure, which is *not* optimal in the sense, for example, of minimizing mean square forecast errors. However, it is intuitively appealing and is a natural extension of the Holt procedure[6] for a trend model (see Eqs. 4.31 and 4.32). Specifically, the parameters are updated according to the following three equations.

$$\hat{a}_t = \alpha_{HW}(x_t/\hat{F}_{t-P}) + (1 - \alpha_{HW})(\hat{a}_{t-1} + \hat{b}_{t-1}) \tag{4.46}$$

$$\hat{b}_t = \beta_{HW}(\hat{a}_t - \hat{a}_{t-1}) + (1 - \beta_{HW})\hat{b}_{t-1} \tag{4.47}$$

$$\hat{F}_t = \gamma_{HW}(x_t/\hat{a}_t) + (1 - \gamma_{HW})\hat{F}_{t-P} \tag{4.48}$$

where α_{HW}, β_{HW}, and γ_{HW} are the three smoothing constants that all lie between 0 and 1. The selection of their values will be covered in Section 4.5.5.

In Eq. 4.46 the term $x_t/\hat{F}_{t-p}$ reflects an estimate of the deseasonalized actual demand in period t in that $\hat{F}_{t-p}$ was the estimate of the seasonal index for the most recent (P periods earlier) equivalent period in the seasonal cycle. The rest of the terms in Eqs. 4.46 and 4.47 are equivalent to those shown earlier in the nonseasonal Holt procedure (see Eqs. 4.31 and 4.32). In Eq. 4.48 the term $x_t/\hat{a}_t$ provides an estimate of the seasonal factor based on the latest demand observation. Thus, Eq. 4.48, consistent with all of the earlier exponential smoothing equations, reflects a linear combination of the historical estimate and the estimate based on the latest piece of data. At all times we wish to have the sum of the indices through an entire season add to P. Thus, when a specific index is updated, we renormalize all indices to achieve this equality. A numerical illustration will be shown after a discussion of the initialization and forecasting procedures.

Initialization

With both trend and seasonal factors present, the initialization becomes considerably more complicated. One has to properly separate out the trend and seasonal effects in the historical data. Several different initialization procedures have been suggested, but we restrict our attention to the most commonly used method, the so-called *ratio to moving average procedure* (which differs from Winters' original suggestion). This approach can effectively handle changes in the underlying trend during the historical period. In addition, it tends to eliminate cyclical effects (which we are not explicitly considering). Further details are available in Hamburg (1977).

Ideally, from a statistical standpoint, one would like to have several seasons

[6]Actually, the single smoothing constant approach of Brown (see Eqs. 4.33 and 4.34) could equally well be used in lieu of the Holt method, as was advocated in Section 4.5.3.

worth of data because each specific seasonal period (for example, the month of June) occurs only once per season (year). However, using too much history, one runs the risk of the seasonal pattern having changed during the history, so that the early portion is no longer representative of current, let alone, future conditions. As a compromise we suggest a minimum of 4 complete seasons, using 5 or 6 (with care) if that much is available. The case where insufficient data exist will be treated in Section 4.9.1.

There are several steps in the procedure. We use the example, shown in Table 4.4 and Figure 4.7, of quarterly sales (in 1981 to 1984) for product EDM-617, a bracket used by the MIDAS assembly department.

Step 1 Initial Estimation of Level (Including Trend) at Each Historical Period
The demand in any historical period is assumed to be composed of trend (incorporating the level), seasonal, and random components. To estimate the seasonal indices we must first remove the trend effect. The trend point (that is, the level) for any particular period t is estimated by a moving average of a full season (that is, P periods) centered at period t. A full season is used in order to have the moving average free of seasonal effects. Because the most common seasons have an even number of periods ($P = 4$ or 12), the standard P-period moving average

TABLE 4.4 Initialization of Seasonal Model for Item EDM-617

Year	Quarter	Period t	Demand x_t	4-Period Total	Centered 4-Period Moving Average	Estimate of F_t
(1)	(2)	(3)	(4)	(5)	(6)	$(7) = \frac{(4)}{(6)}$
1981	1	−15	43			
	2	−14	57			
				217		
	3	−13	71		55.1	1.29
				224		
	4	−12	46		56.5	0.81
				228		
1982	1	−11	50		58.8	0.85
				242		
	2	−10	61		60.6	1.01
				243		
	3	− 9	85		62.3	1.36
				255		
	4	− 8	47		65.4	0.72
				268		
1983	1	− 7	62		67.1	0.92
				269		
	2	− 6	74		67.4	1.10
				270		
	3	− 5	86		66.9	1.29
				265		
	4	− 4	48		66.8	0.72
				269		
1984	1	− 3	57		69.3	0.82
				285		
	2	− 2	78		72.9	1.07
				298		
	3	− 1	102			
	4	0	61			

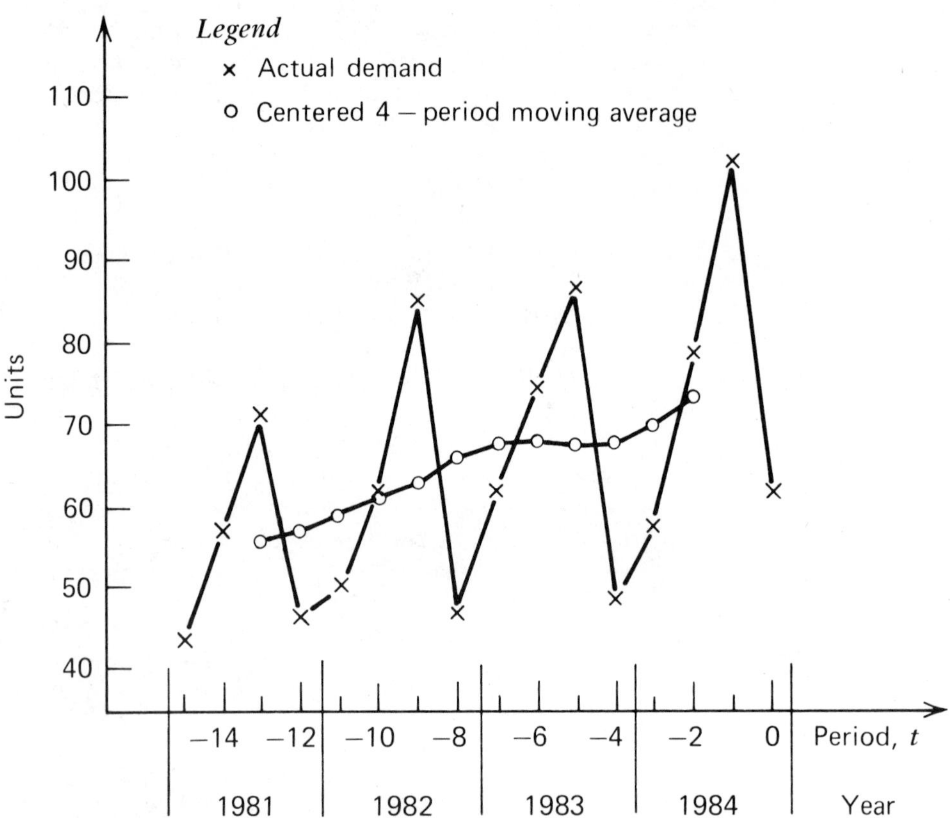

FIGURE 4.7 Historical Data for Item EDM-617

ends up being centered between two periods, not right at the middle of a period as desired. To overcome this problem we take the average of two consecutive moving averages. There is a slightly more efficient, equivalent computational procedure that is illustrated in Table 4.4. In column 5 we show 4-period moving *totals* (rather than averages) centered in the middle of the data from which they were computed. For example, the first entry of 217 is located between the 2nd and 3rd quarters of 1981 because it was computed from the data of the four quarters of 1981. Each entry in column 6 is the total of the surrounding two entries in column 5, divided by 8. These centered moving averages are also portrayed in Figure 4.7.

Step 2 Estimates of Seasonal Factors The estimate of the seasonal factor (column 7 of Table 4.4) for any particular historical period t is obtained by dividing the demand x_t (column 4) by the centered moving average (column 6). Note that, because of the moving average procedure, we cannot obtain estimates for the first half-season (first two quarters of 1981) nor for the last half-season (last two quarters of 1984). Estimates still include the random components. In an effort to dampen the random effect we average the seasonal factors for similar periods in different years. For example, in Table 4.4 the average of the 3rd quarter factors is (1.29 + 1.36 + 1.29)/3 or 1.31. The averages obtained in this fashion are shown in column 2 of Table 4.5. The total of the averages need not add up to exactly P (4 in our example). Thus, we normalize to obtain estimates of seasonal indices that total to P. The results are shown in column 3 of Table 4.5.

Step 3 Estimating $\hat{a}_0$ and $\hat{b}_0$ We still need estimates of the level and trend terms in Eq. 4.16. Using the seasonal indices found in Step 2 we deseasonalize the data as shown in Table 4.6. The results are also shown graphically in Figure 4.8. They are reasonably close to the centered moving averages found in Table 4.4, the reason being that, in this example, the seasonal coefficients found in Table 4.4 do not fluctuate very much from year to year. In any event, a regression line is now fit to the data of column 6 in Table 4.6 using the procedure of Eqs. 4.37 and 4.38 of subsection 4.5.3. This gives us estimates $\hat{a}_0$ and $\hat{b}_0$ as of the end of 1984 (the end of period 0). The resulting line is shown in Figure 4.8; the parameter values are

$$\hat{a}_0 = 76.91 \qquad \hat{b}_0 = 1.68$$

Again, one could use an earlier origin (with $\hat{a}_0$ appropriately adjusted) and an associated run-in period through the rest of the historical data. Also, in the event that the plotted data indicate a shift in trend part way through the history, the regression line should only be fit to the latest data (beyond the shift).

Forecasting

The underlying model includes level, trend, and seasonal factors. As of the end of period t we have

$$\hat{x}_{t,t+\tau} = (\hat{a}_t + \hat{b}_t\tau)\,\hat{F}_{t+\tau-P} \tag{4.49}$$

TABLE 4.5 Initial Seasonal Indices for Item EDM-617

Quarter i (1)	Average Estimate (2)	Normalized Index F_i (3)
1	0.86	0.86
2	1.06	1.07
3	1.31	1.32
4	0.75	0.75
Total	3.98	4.00

TABLE 4.6 Calculations to Estimate $\hat{a}_0$ and $\hat{b}_0$ for Item EDM-617

Year (1)	Quarter (2)	Period t (3)	Demand x_t (4)	F_t (5)	Estimate of Level $(6) = \frac{(4)}{(5)}$
1981	1	−15	43	0.86	50.0
	2	−14	57	1.07	53.3
	3	−13	71	1.32	53.8
	4	−12	46	0.75	61.3
1982	1	−11	50	0.86	58.1
	2	−10	61	1.07	57.0
	3	− 9	85	1.32	64.4
	4	− 8	47	0.75	62.7
1983	1	− 7	62	0.86	72.1
	2	− 6	74	1.07	69.2
	3	− 5	86	1.32	65.2
	4	− 4	48	0.75	64.0
1984	1	− 3	57	0.86	66.3
	2	− 2	78	1.07	72.9
	3	− 1	102	1.32	77.3
	4	0	61	0.75	81.3

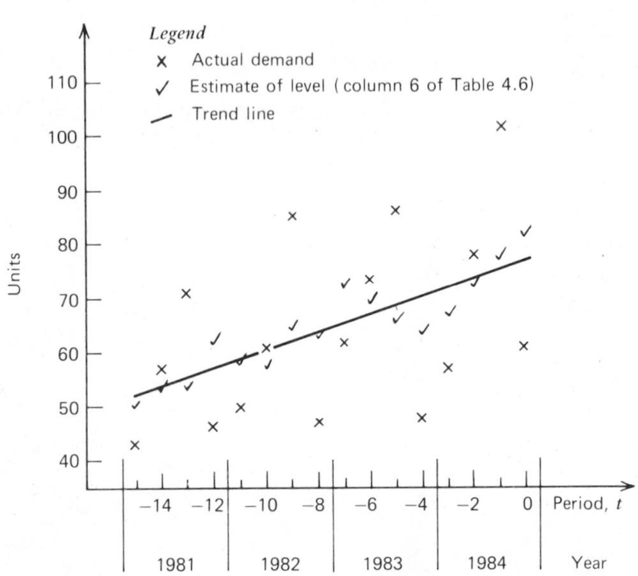

FIGURE 4.8 Determination of Trend Line for Item EDM-617

where $\hat{x}_{t,t+\tau}$ is the forecast, made at the end of period t, of demand in period $t + \tau$ and $\hat{F}_{t+\tau-P}$ is the most recent estimate of the seasonal index for period $L + \tau$. (This assumes $\tau \leq P$; the last *direct* update of $\hat{F}_{t+\tau-P}$ was made in period $t + \tau - P$. However, when any other seasonal index is updated, renormalization could cause $F_{t+\tau-P}$ to change somewhat.)

The forecast of cumulative demand from the beginning of period $t + 1$ through to the end of period u is given by

$$\hat{x}_{t,t,u} = \sum_{\tau=1}^{u-t} \hat{x}_{t,t+\tau} \tag{4.50}$$

where again, if u is not an integer, the last term in the summation reflects an appropriate proportion of the last period.

Illustration

We again use the item EDM-617. First, consider the forecast $\hat{x}_{0,1}$ of the demand in the 1st quarter of 1985 made at the end of 1984. The previous 1st quarter was $t = -3$. From Table 4.5 we thus have $\hat{F}_{-3} = 0.86$. Also $\hat{a}_0 = 76.91$ and $\hat{b}_0 = 1.68$. Thus, from Eq. 4.49 we have

$$\begin{aligned} \hat{x}_{0,1} &= (76.91 + 1.68)0.86 \\ &= 67.6 \text{ units} \end{aligned}$$

Similarly, the forecasts at the end of 1984 for the other three quarters of 1985 are

$$\begin{aligned} \hat{x}_{0,2} &= (76.91 + 3.36)1.07 = 85.9 \text{ units} \\ \hat{x}_{0,3} &= (76.91 + 5.04)1.32 = 108.2 \text{ units} \\ \hat{x}_{0,4} &= (76.91 + 6.72)0.75 = 62.7 \text{ units} \end{aligned}$$

Suppose that the actual demand in the 1st quarter of 1985 was 75 units. The level, trend, and seasonality factors can now be updated (revised). Assume that the smoothing constants α_{HW}, β_{HW}, and γ_{HW} have values 0.2, 0.1, and 0.3, respectively. From Eq. 4.46 the revised value of the level is given by

$$\begin{aligned} \hat{a}_1 &= \alpha_{HW}(x_1/\hat{F}_{-3}) + (1 - \alpha_{HW})(\hat{a}_0 + \hat{b}_0) \\ &= 0.2(75/0.86) + 0.8(76.91 + 1.68) \\ &= 80.31 \end{aligned}$$

Next, from Eq. 4.47 the revised estimate of the trend is given by

$$\begin{aligned}\hat{b}_1 &= \beta_{HW}(\hat{a}_1 - \hat{a}_0) + (1 - \beta_{HW})\hat{b}_0\\ &= 0.1(80.31 - 76.91) + 0.9(1.68)\\ &= 1.85\end{aligned}$$

Then, by using Eq. 4.48, we obtain the updated estimate of the seasonality factor for the 1st quarter as

$$\begin{aligned}\hat{F}_1 &= \gamma_{HW}(x_1/\hat{a}_1) + (1 - \gamma_{HW})\hat{F}_{-3}\\ &= 0.3(75/80.31) + 0.7(0.86)\\ &= 0.88\end{aligned}$$

Because of the change in this seasonality factor we renormalize the four seasonality factors so that they again add to 4:

$$1.07 + 1.32 + 0.75 + 0.88 = 4.02$$

Therefore,

$$\hat{F}_{-2} = 1.07 \times \frac{4.00}{4.02} = 1.06$$

$$\hat{F}_{-1} = 1.32 \times \frac{4.00}{4.02} = 1.31$$

$$\hat{F}_0 = 0.75 \times \frac{4.00}{4.02} = 0.75$$

$$\hat{F}_1 = 0.88 \times \frac{4.00}{4.02} = 0.88$$

$$\textit{Total} = 4.00$$

Note that demand for period 1 was forecast (at the end of period 0) as 67.6 units. Actual demand turned out to be 75 units; that is, demand was underforecast by 7.4 units. Because of this forecast error, the level was adjusted upward from 76.91 to 80.31—an increase of 3.40 units, considerably more than was predicted by the original trend value of 1.68 units. Moreover, the estimate of the trend was increased from 1.68 to 1.85, and the estimate of the seasonality factor was raised from 0.86 to 0.88.

The new estimates of the parameters can now be used in Eq. 4.49 to provide a revised set of forecasts as of the end of period 1 (the 1st quarter of 1985). To illustrate the forecast of demand in the 2nd quarter of 1985:

$$\begin{aligned}\hat{x}_{1,2} &= (\hat{a}_1 + \hat{b}_1)\hat{F}_{-2} \\ &= (80.31 + 1.85)(1.06) \\ &= 87.1 \text{ units}\end{aligned}$$

The forecasts for the remaining two quarters of 1985 are also shown in Table 4.7.

Once the figure for actual sales in quarter 2 of 1985 becomes available, the above procedures must be repeated—the parameters (level, trend, and seasonal factors) revised and a new set of revised forecasts issued.

General Comments

Clearly, updating, forecasting, and particularly initialization are considerably more complicated with a seasonal model than was the case with the earlier nonseasonal models. Thus, the decision to use a seasonal model should be taken with care (see also McLeavey et al., 1981). In the initialization stage, if the initial F's are all close to unity or fluctuate widely from season to season, then a seasonal model is probably inappropriate.

There are other, quite different approaches to dealing with seasonality. In particular Brown (1981, Chapter 9), among others, argues for the use of a transcendental model that is a mix of sine waves. This approach has the merit of being more parsimonious (less parameters than seasonal indices) and hence tends to be more stable, particularly when the demand level is quite low. However, we feel that this advantage is usually outweighed by the much more intuitively understandable nature of the seasonal indices model.

Finally, there are certain "seasonal" effects whose changing nature can be predicted. One of the best examples is the Easter holiday that some years occurs in March and some in April. Thus, monthly data can be distorted by this effect, yet such distortion can be anticipated. Another anomalous situation arises where it is crucial (perhaps for production scheduling purposes) to use monthly data to forecast the demand rate *per day*. Under these circumstances one should take account of varying numbers of days from month to month. In other circumstances it is simply adequate to consider the differing numbers of days as being part of the contribution to differing seasonal factors.

TABLE 4.7 Effect of Forecast Errors in Period 1 on Forecasts of Demand for Later Periods

Calendar Time	Period t	Forecast Calculated at End of Period 0	Forecast Calculated at End of Period 1
1st quarter 1985	1	67.6	75.0 (actual)
2nd quarter 1985	2	85.9	87.1
3rd quarter 1985	3	108.2	110.1
4th quarter 1985	4	62.7	64.4

4.5.5 Selection of Smoothing Constants

We now address the choice of the smoothing constants for the various smoothing procedures discussed earlier. For the moment attention is restricted to a *static* choice, that is, values that will essentially remain unchanged over time for any particular s.k.u. In Section 4.6.4 the case where the smoothing constants can vary with time, so-called *adaptive smoothing*, will be treated.

There is a basic tradeoff in the choice of the values of the smoothing constants. Small values, which give little weight to the most recent data, hence considerable weight to the history, are appropriate under stable conditions—they effectively smooth out most of the random noise. On the other hand, if the parameters of the underlying demand model are changing appreciably with time, then higher values of the smoothing constants are in order, in that they give more weight to recent data and thus more quickly bring the parameter estimates into line with the true changed values. Unfortuntely, we are never really sure whether forecast errors are a result of random (transient) noise or a real change in one or more of the parameter values in the underlying demand model. Therefore, a compromise must be made in choosing the values of the smoothing constants. Harrison (1967) has quantified this compromise under special assumptions about the inherent variability of the model parameters. Related to the same issue, all other factors being equal, the smoothing constants should increase with the length of the forecast update period, in that the likelihood of changes in the model parameters increases with the passage of time.

In general, we suggest the use of a search experiment to establish reasonable values of the smoothing constants within the context of the demand patterns of any specific organization. For each of a number of representative items, the following experiment should be conducted. The available demand history is divided into two sections. The first section is used to initialize the model parameters in the updating procedure selected. Then with these initial values, the smoothing is carried through the second portion of the data, using a specific combination of values for the smoothing constants. Some appropriate measure of effectiveness (for example, the sum of the squared forecast errors or the mean absolute error, the latter to be discussed in Section 4.6.1) is evaluated. This is repeated, on a grid search basis, to find the combination of values of smoothing constants that minimizes the measure of effectiveness across a class of similar items. In actual fact, exact minimization is not required because the measures of effectiveness always tend to be quite insensitive to deviations of the smoothing constants from their best values. Furthermore, we wish to use only a few sets of smoothing constants, each set being employed for a broad class of items. Moreover, any case where minimization occurs when unusually large values are used for the smoothing constants should be viewed with caution. As an illustration, a large value (greater than 0.3) of α in the simple smoothing procedure should raise the question of the validity of the assumed underlying level model. The high smoothing constant, in this case, suggests that perhaps a trend model is more appropriate. Further discussion on the above type of search can be found in Winters (1960) and Gardner and Dannenbring (1980).

Keeping the above suggestions in mind we now present, for each of the smoothing procedures discussed earlier, ranges of reasonable values of the parameters found through our experience and that of several other individuals, as reported in the literature.

Simple Exponential Smoothing

Recall from Eq. 4.24 that the updating procedure is

$$\hat{a}_t = \alpha x_t + (1 - \alpha)\hat{a}_{t-1}$$

The likely range of α is 0.01 to 0.30 with a compromise value of 0.10 often being quite reasonable.

Smoothing for a Trend Model

Earlier we suggested use of Brown's single parameter updating method. For reference purposes we repeat Eqs. 4.33 and 4.34.

$$\hat{a}_t = [1 - (1 - \alpha)^2]x_t + (1 - \alpha)^2(\hat{a}_{t-1} + \hat{b}_{t-1}) \tag{4.51}$$

$$\hat{b}_t = \left[\frac{\alpha^2}{1 - (1 - \alpha)^2}\right](\hat{a}_t - \hat{a}_{t-1}) + \left[1 - \frac{\alpha^2}{1 - (1 - \alpha)^2}\right]\hat{b}_{t-1} \tag{4.52}$$

The range of α values prescribed under simple smoothing are also applicable here.

The Winters Seasonal Smoothing

Repeating Eqs. 4.46 to 4.48 the updating procedure is

$$\hat{a}_t = \alpha_{HW}(x_t/\hat{F}_{t-P}) + (1 - \alpha_{HW})(\hat{a}_{t-1} + \hat{b}_{t-1}) \tag{4.53}$$

$$\hat{b}_t = \beta_{HW}(\hat{a}_t - \hat{a}_{t-1}) + (1 - \beta_{HW})\hat{b}_{t-1} \tag{4.54}$$

$$\hat{F}_t = \gamma_{HW}(x_t/\hat{a}_t) + (1 - \gamma_{HW})\hat{F}_{t-P} \tag{4.55}$$

As pointed out earlier (in Eqs. 4.35 and 4.36) Eqs. 4.51 and 4.52 are a special case of the Holt procedure where

$$\alpha_{HW} = [1 - (1 - \alpha)^2] \tag{4.56}$$

and

$$\beta_{HW} = \frac{\alpha^2}{1 - (1 - \alpha)^2} \tag{4.57}$$

This suggests that reasonable guidelines for choices of α_{HW} and β_{HW} in Eqs. 4.53 and 4.54 are provided by substituting the above suggested α values

TABLE 4.8 Reasonable Values of Smoothing Constants in the Winters Procedure

	Underlying α Value	α_{HW}	β_{HW}	γ_{HW}
Upper end of range	0.30	0.51	0.176	0.50
Reasonable single value	0.10	0.19	0.053	0.10
Lower end of range	0.01	0.02	0.005	0.05

Note: For stability purposes (see McClain and Thomas, 1973) the value of β_{HW} should be kept well below that of α_{HW}.

into Eqs. 4.56 and 4.57. The results are shown in Table 4.8 along with suggested values of γ_{HW}, the latter found through experimentation. Again, we emphasize that, where possible, a search experiment should be conducted with demand data for the particular population of items involved.

4.6 MEASURES OF FORECAST ERRORS

As mentioned earlier, all that we can say for certain about a forecast of demand is that it will be in error. Statistics of the errors are needed for at least two important reasons. First, as we will see in Chapter 7, the service provided to customers will depend on the distribution of forecast errors, including the standard deviation of the distribution. Second, as we will develop in Section 4.6.3, decisions concerning the adequacy of a particular forecast model will depend on a measure of the bias in recent forecasts.

Although in this section we concentrate on characterizing forecast errors, we hasten to emphasize that the production planner/ inventory manager should not just passively accept a particular distribution of forecast errors. Specifically, if there is a large bias or variability present, one should seek the underlying causes and, where practical, corrective actions should be taken to reduce the bias or variability.

4.6.1 Measures of Variability

As will be demonstrated in Chapter 7, for purposes of establishing the safety stock of an individual item (to provide an appropriate level of customer service), we will need an estimate of the standard deviation (σ_L) of the errors of forecasts of total demand over a period of duration[7] L (the replenishment lead time). In the current subsection we concentrate on estimating σ_1, the standard deviation of errors of forecasts of demand made for *unit* (forecast update interval) periods.

[7]Our discussion here is restricted to the case of continuous review systems where the key time interval in establishing safety stocks is the lead time L. In periodic review systems (review interval R) the key interval is $R + L$, as will be discussed in Chapter 7.

In Section 4.6.2 we discuss the conversion of the estimate of σ_1 to an estimate of σ_L. The procedures to be discussed are appropriate for A and B items. C items will be handled by simpler methods to be presented later.

Suppose that we had two types of information for each of n unit time periods (forecast update periods), specifically (1) the actual observed demands, $x_1, x_2, \ldots, x_n$ and (2) the one-period-ahead forecasts (by some particular forecasting procedure) $\hat{x}_{0,1}, \hat{x}_{1,2}, \ldots, \hat{x}_{n-1,n}$, where, as earlier, $\hat{x}_{t,t+1}$ is the forecast, made at the end of period t, of demand in period $t + 1$. A logical estimate of σ_1 would be the usual sample standard deviation (s_1) of the individual errors $x_1 - \hat{x}_{0,1}, x_2 - \hat{x}_{1,2}, \ldots, x_n - \hat{x}_{n-1,n}$. Computation of s_1 involves finding the average of the errors $\bar{x}$, calculating $x_1 - \hat{x}_{0,1} - \bar{x}, x_2 - \hat{x}_{1,2} - \bar{x}, \ldots$, squaring these differences, summing the squares, dividing by $n - 1$, and then taking the square root.[8] This creates no problem if a computer is routinely available for the particular company under consideration. However, a more serious drawback is that the meaning of s_1 *cannot* be easily interpreted to practitioners. Primarily for this latter reason we advocate the continued use of an alternative measure of variability, the mean absolute deviation (MAD), which was originally recommended for its computational simplicity. For the aforementioned data the estimate of the MAD would be[9]

$$\text{MAD} = \sum_{t=1}^{n} |x_t - \hat{x}_{t-1,t}|/n \tag{4.58}$$

The term $x_t - \hat{x}_{t-1,t}$ is the error (e_t) or the *deviation* in the forecast for period t. The vertical lines indicate that we take the *absolute* value of the difference.[10] Finally, the *mean* of the absolute deviations results by the summation and division by n.

Numerical Illustration

Consider an item with the demands and forecasts as shown for six periods in Table 4.9 and Figure 4.9. Using Eq. 4.58 the resulting estimate of MAD is

$$\text{MAD} = \sum_{t=1}^{6} |e_t|/6 = 32/6 = 5.33 \text{ units}$$

[8]If $\bar{x}$ can be assumed to be approximately 0, then the computations are somewhat simplified through the elimination of the need to subtract $\bar{x}$ in each case.

[9]In principle, MAD should have a subscript 1 to denote that one-period-ahead forecasts are involved. In this text we only evaluate MAD under such circumstances; thus we suppress the subscript.

[10]
$$|y| = \begin{cases} y & \text{if } y \geq 0 \\ -y & \text{if } y < 0 \end{cases}$$

TABLE 4.9 Illustration of Computation of MAD

Period t	1	2	3	4	5	6	
Actual demand x_t	100	87	89	87	95	85	
One-period-ahead forecast made at end of previous period $\hat{x}_{t-1,t}$	90	92	91	91	90	91	
Error or deviation $e_t = x_t - \hat{x}_{t-1,t}$	10	−5	−2	−4	5	−6	
Absolute deviation $\lvert e_t \rvert$	10	5	2	4	5	6	= 32 total

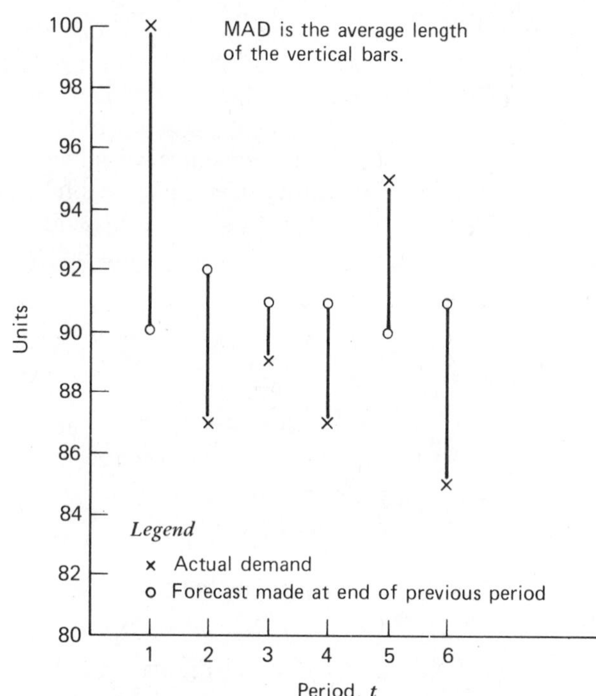

FIGURE 4.9 Illustration of the MAD

As seen in Figure 4.9 the MAD has the appealing graphical interpretation of being the average distance (ignoring direction) between the actual demand in a period and the forecast of that demand. This simple graphical explanation is in marked contrast with the case of the sample standard deviation.

Conversion of MAD to σ_1

Although it is a sample measure of variability of one-period-ahead forecast errors, the MAD is not the same as the sample standard deviation s_1. For the normal distribution one can show that the following relationship holds between the true MAD (the average absolute deviation from the mean) and the true standard deviation σ:

$$\sigma = \sqrt{\pi/2}\ \text{(true MAD)} \simeq 1.25\ \text{(true MAD)}$$

Thus, where we will be primarily advocating the use of the normal distribution, it makes sense to estimate σ_1 via

$$\hat{\sigma}_1 = 1.25\ \text{MAD} \tag{4.59}$$

Incidentally, for several common distributions, besides the normal, the theoretical conversion factor from the MAD to σ is not very different from 1.25.

To summarize, we are suggesting the indirect route of Eqs. 4.58 and 4.59 to estimate σ_1 rather than the usual sample standard deviation s_1. The latter is more efficient (somewhat more accurate in a statistical sense), but the former is somewhat simpler to compute and, *more important*, MAD has the simple graphical interpretation discussed in connection with Figure 4.9.

Updating of MAD

In theory one could use Eq. 4.58 to update the estimate of MAD_1 each time an additional period's information became available. Instead, we advocate a simple exponential smoothing form of updating:

$$\text{MAD}_t = \omega|x_t - \hat{x}_{t-1,t}| + (1 - \omega)\text{MAD}_{t-1} \tag{4.60}$$

where MAD_t is the estimate of MAD at the end of period t and ω is a smoothing constant. (A small value of ω, namely, between 0.01 and 0.10, should normally be used.)

There are two reasons for using Eq. 4.60 instead of Eq. 4.58. First, storage of an indefinitely long history is required for the use of Eq. 4.58, whereas only the most recent MAD_{t-1} need be stored for Eq. 4.60. Second, in using Eq. 4.58 each period of history is given equal weight. In contrast geometrically decaying weights occur through the use of Eq. 4.60. In fact, these arguments are identical to those presented earlier in the chapter when we advocated exponential smoothing, instead of repeated least squares regression, for updating the forecasts themselves.

Initialization of MAD

For each of the forecasting procedures discussed in Section 4.5 we suggested a method for estimating initial values of the parameters of the underlying model of demand, using sufficient available historical data. For such a situation the initial estimate of MAD is obtained through the use of the following equation that is closely related to Eq. 4.58.

$$\text{MAD}_0 = \sum_{t=-n+1}^{0} |x_t - \tilde{x}_t|/(n-p) \tag{4.61}$$

where the n historical periods are numbered from 0 (the most recent period) back through $-1, -2$, to $(-n+1)$, and $\tilde{x}_t$ is the estimate of x_t resulting from the underlying demand model when the estimates of its p parameters are obtained from the historical data. (For example, if the underlying model was a linear trend, $x_t = a + bt$, then p would be 2 and $\tilde{x}_t$ would be $\hat{a}_0 + \hat{b}_0 t$.)

The denominator in Eq. 4.61 is $n - p$, rather than n, to reflect that our estimate of MAD is based on an *ex-post* fit to the data where the data have already been used to estimate the p parameters of the model.

The case where insufficient historical information exists will be treated under the category of new items in Section 4.9.1.

Illustration

In Table 4.3 of Section 4.5.3 we showed the initialization of a trend model using six periods of historical information. The estimated values of the two parameters were $\hat{a}_0 = 27.19$ and $\hat{b}_0 = 1.34$. The original demand data and the $\tilde{x}_t$ values are shown in Table 4.10. By using Eq. 4.61, we obtain

$$\begin{aligned}\text{MAD}_0 &= \sum_{t=-5}^{0} |x_t - \tilde{x}_t|/(6-2) \\ &= (10.30)/4 \\ &= 2.58\end{aligned}$$

TABLE 4.10 Illustration of Computation of MAD_0 for the Example of Table 4.3

$\hat{a}_0 = 27.19 \quad \hat{b}_0 = 1.34$

t	x_t	$\tilde{x}_t = \hat{a}_0 + \hat{b}_0 t$	$\lvert x_t - \tilde{x}_t \rvert$
−5	20	20.49	0.49
−4	25	21.83	3.17
−3	21	23.17	2.17
−2	22	24.51	2.51
−1	27	25.85	1.15
0	28	27.19	0.81
		Total	10.30

4.6.2 Estimating the Standard Deviation of Forecast Errors over a Lead Time (or a Review Interval Plus a Lead Time)[11]

As mentioned earlier, the replenishment lead time is unlikely to be equal to the forecast update interval. Thus we need a method of converting $\hat{\sigma}_1$ (our estimate of σ_1) to $\hat{\sigma}_L$ (the corresponding estimate of σ_L). The *exact* relationship between σ_L and σ_1 depends in a complicated fashion on the specific underlying demand model, the forecast updating procedure, and the values of the smoothing constants used (see, for example, Brown, 1963 or Harrison, 1967). One of the reasons for the complexity is that the smoothing procedure introduces a degree of dependence between the forecast errors in separate periods. Fortunately, however, we have found that for most inventory systems the following model satisfactorily captures empirically the required relationship:

$$\hat{\sigma}_L = L^c \hat{\sigma}_1 \tag{4.62}$$

where

$\hat{\sigma}_L$ = estimate of the standard deviation of forecast errors over a lead time of duration L basic (forecast update) periods (L need *not* be an integer)

$\hat{\sigma}_1$ = estimate of the standard deviation of forecast errors over a basic (forecast update) period

c = coefficient that must be estimated empirically

To check the reasonableness of Eq. 4.62 for the MIDAS Professional Products inventory, we proceed as follows. We select 10 representative s.k.u.—6 from the A category and 4 from the B category, for which 7 years of historical monthly demand data are available. Using the first 4 years of data, we initialize the Winters exponential smoothing model by the procedures described in Section 4.5.4. That is, for each of the 10 representative s.k.u., we obtain the data needed to initialize the Winters forecast equation (Eq. 4.49):

$$\hat{x}_{t,t+\tau} = (\hat{a}_t + \hat{b}_t\tau)\hat{F}_{t+\tau-P} \tag{4.63}$$

Then for the fifth, sixth, and seventh years of the demand data, Eq. 4.63, along with the Winters updating procedures described in Eqs. 4.46, 4.47, and 4.48, is used to issue the forecasts listed in Table 4.11. In all cases the model parameters are updated monthly. For each forecast in Table 4.11, the forecast figure is

[11]Our discussion here is restricted to the case of continuous review systems, where the key time interval in establishing safety stocks is the lead time L. We discuss the case of periodic review in Chapter 7.

TABLE 4.11 Forecasts Simulated to Estimate *c*

Length of L	Forecasts		Number of Forecasts for Each s.k.u.
1	$\hat{x}_{t,t+1}$	$t = 0, 1, 2, \ldots, 35$	36
2	$\sum_{\tau=1}^{2} \hat{x}_{t,t+\tau}$	$t = 0, 2, 4, \ldots, 34$	18
3	$\sum_{\tau=1}^{3} \hat{x}_{t,t+\tau}$	$t = 0, 3, 6, \ldots, 33$	12
.	.	.	.
.	.	.	.
.	.	.	.
6	$\sum_{\tau=1}^{6} \hat{x}_{t,t+\tau}$	$t = 0, 6, 12, \ldots, 30$	6

compared to the actual demand that resulted over the immediate period of duration L and the associated forecast error is computed by using

$$\text{Forecast error} = e_t(L) = \sum_{\tau=1}^{L} \hat{x}_{t,t+\tau} - \sum_{\tau=1}^{L} x_{t+\tau} \tag{4.64}$$

For each value of L the sample standard deviation of forecast errors is computed and used as an estimate of σ_L,

$$\hat{\sigma}_L = s_L = \left\{ \frac{1}{n-1} \sum_t [e_t(L) - \bar{e}(L)]^2 \right\}^{1/2}$$

where

$\bar{e}(L) = \Sigma_t\, e_t(L)/n$ is the average error for the L under consideration

n = number of lead times of length L used (see the right-hand column of Table 4.11)

As a result of all of the above calculations, there are 10 values (one for each of the s.k.u.) of $\hat{\sigma}_L$ for each of $L = 1, 2, 3, \ldots, 6$. For each s.k.u. the 5 values of

$\hat{\sigma}_L/\hat{\sigma}_1$ are computed for $L = 2, 3, 4, 5, 6$. The 50 values of log $(\hat{\sigma}_L/\hat{\sigma}_1)$ are then plotted against log L, as shown in Figure 4.10. Eq. 4.62 can be written as:

$$\hat{\sigma}_L/\hat{\sigma}_1 = L^c \qquad \text{or} \qquad \log(\hat{\sigma}_L/\hat{\sigma}_1) = c \log L$$

Therefore, the slope of the line through the origin that gives a reasonable fit to the 50 data points is an estimate of c. The line with slope $c = 0.5$, plotted in Figure 4.10, gives a reasonable fit. For MIDAS we choose to use this approximation, which gives:

$$\begin{aligned} \log(\hat{\sigma}_L/\hat{\sigma}_1) &= 0.50 \log L \\ \hat{\sigma}_L &= L^{0.50}\hat{\sigma}_1 \\ &= \sqrt{L}\,\hat{\sigma}_1 \end{aligned} \tag{4.65}$$

The result of Eq. 4.65 could also be obtained by assuming that in an L period forecast the errors in consecutive periods are independent and each has standard deviation σ_1. In actual fact, both of these assumptions are violated to some extent; nevertheless the empirical behavior of Eq. 4.65 is often quite reasonable. However, we hasten to recommend that an analysis, such as that leading to Figure 4.10, be carried out for any system under consideration. If a straight line through the origin is a reasonable fit, then its slope, which need not be 0.5, gives the estimate of c in Eq. 4.62.

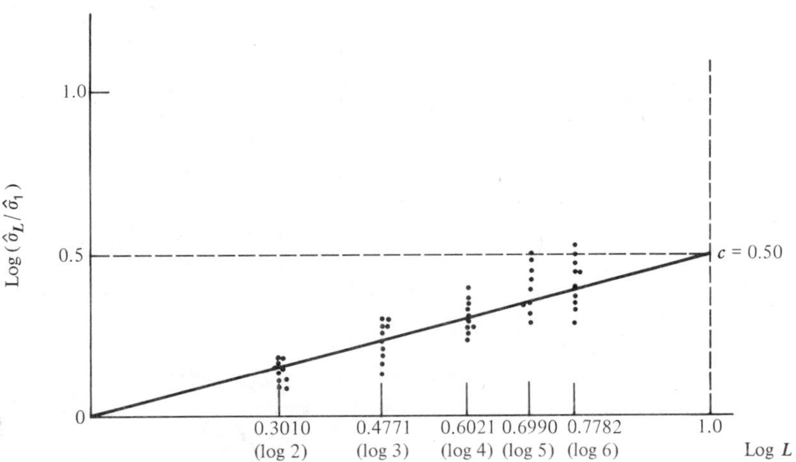

FIGURE 4.10 Relative Standard Deviations of Forecast Errors versus Lead Time[12]

[12]The linear graph paper used here requires the computation of logarithims before plotting. This can be avoided by the use of special log-log paper.

4.6.3 Measures of Bias in Forecasts

We use the word *bias* to indicate that, on the average, the forecasts are substantially above or below the actual demands. A bias signals that the parameters of the underlying demand model have been inaccurately estimated or that the model itself is incorrect. Where forecasts are used for production planning and inventory management decision making, clearly either of these situations is undesirable. Because of the random component in a demand pattern, it is not easy to detect an underlying bias; the noise tends to camouflage it. In this subsection we discuss three of the more common measures of bias; then in Section 4.6.4 subsequent corrective actions will be presented.

Smoothed Error Tracking Signal

Trigg (1964) suggested the use of a so-called *smoothed error tracking signal* defined by

$$T_t = z_t/\text{MAD}_t \tag{4.66}$$

where

T_t = value of the smoothed error tracking signal at the end of period t

MAD_t = mean absolute deviation of one-period-ahead forecast errors as of the end of period t (updated as in Eq. 4.60)

z_t = smoothed forecast error at the end of period t

z is updated in a fashion analogous to MAD, except the signs of the errors are retained:

$$z_t = \omega(x_t - \hat{x}_{t-1,t}) + (1 - \omega)z_{t-1} \tag{4.67}$$

where ω is the same smoothing constant as used to update MAD.

Illustration Consider an item where at the end of period $t - 1$ we have the following values:

$\hat{x}_{t-1,t} = 100$ units (forecast of demand in period t)

$\text{MAD}_{t-1} = 6.8$ units

$z_{t-1} = 2.1$ units

Suppose we use $\omega = 0.1$ and the demand in period t turns out to be 92 units. Then, from Eq. 4.60,

$$\begin{aligned}\text{MAD}_t &= 0.1|92 - 100| + 0.9(6.8)\\ &= 0.1(8) + 0.9(6.8)\\ &= 6.92 \text{ units}\end{aligned}$$

Also Eq. 4.67 gives

$$\begin{aligned}z_t &= 0.1(92 - 100) + 0.9(2.1)\\ &= 0.1(-8) + 0.9(2.1)\\ &= 1.09 \text{ units}\end{aligned}$$

Note that the relatively large *negative* forecast error in period t has increased MAD slightly but has caused z to become closer to 0 in that z_{t-1} was positive.

For an unbiased forecasting procedure the smoothed forecast error z_t should fluctuate about zero. Consider two consecutive forecast errors, one of which is positive, the other negative. It is seen from Eq. 4.67 that in the computation of z_t the effects of these two errors will tend to cancel one another. In contrast, in the computation of MAD_t, where the absolute value of e_t is taken, no canceling occurs. Continuing this line of reasoning, we can write that

$$-\text{MAD}_t \leq z_t \leq \text{MAD}_t$$

The limiting equalities are achieved if all errors are positive or if all errors are negative. From Eq. 4.66 the equivalent limits on the tracking signal T_t are

$$-1 \leq T_t \leq 1$$

Moreover, T_t will be close to one of the limits if most of the errors are of the same sign, an indication that the forecasting system is biased (most of the forecasts are too high or most of the forecasts are too low).

A potential drawback of the smoothed error signal is that, because of the smoothing, there can be a significant lag before an actual change in the model (or its parameter values) is identified. Moreover, it is not easy to identify ex-post exactly when the change took place. The next measure of bias to be discussed is more effective in this latter regard.

Cumulative Sum of Forecast Errors

Harrison and Davies (1964) suggested the use of cumulative sum techniques to monitor the bias in a forecasting procedure. Specifically, the cumulative sum of forecast errors is computed recursively using

$$C_t = C_{t-1} + e_t \tag{4.68}$$

where

C_t = cumulative sum of forecast errors as of the end of period t

$e_t = x_t - \hat{x}_{t-1,t}$ = one-period-ahead forecast error in period t

As with the smoothed error (z_t) it is advisable to normalize with respect to the MAD; that is, use

$$U_t = C_t/\text{MAD}_t \tag{4.69}$$

where U_t is the cumulative sum tracking signal.

U_t is not restricted to the range -1 to $+1$. Nevertheless, if the forecasting procedure is unbiased, U_t should fluctuate around 0.

An interesting property of the cumulative sum C_t is that on a graphical plot, if a straight line fit to it is reasonable over several periods, then the *slope* of the straight line gives us an estimate of the average bias of a single period forecast. In fact, more advanced versions of the cumulative sum technique are based on the graphical use of V-masks designed to detect a certain amount of bias within a specific number of periods. Further details are available in Brown (1971) or Lewis (1982).

Serial Correlation (or Autocorrelation) of Forecast Errors

The serial correlation of a time series measures the degree of dependence between successive observations in the series. With an appropriate forecasting model, there should be negligible correlation between separate forecast errors. If significant positive correlation exists, then this indicates that forecast errors of the same sign tend to follow one another. This, in turn, signals the likelihood of errors in the specification of the demand model or its parameter values. Further details on the computation and properties of serial correlation can be found in several books on probability and statistics (see, for example, Burington and May, 1958 or Cox and Miller, 1965).

4.6.4 Corrective Actions in Statistical Forecasting

As discussed above, there are at least three different measures of *potential* bias caused by incorrect specification of the underlying demand model or inaccurate estimates of the values of its parameters. We use the adjective "potential" because large absolute values of the tracking signals and substantial serial correlation can, from time to time, be simply generated from the random component in the demand pattern. In this regard McKenzie (1978) has developed statistical properties of the smoothed error tracking signal. The choice of threshold (or critical) values of the signals or serial correlation is completely analogous to the choice of the boundaries between acceptance and rejection in statistical hypothesis testing. There are two types of potential errors. First, we can take a corrective action when nothing has really changed. Second, we can do nothing when, in fact, a fundamental change has taken place. The choice of the threshold (or critical) values of the bias measures involves a, usually implicit, tradeoff between these two types of errors.

There are two general types of corrective actions that can be used. The first, which tends to be utilized in a more automated mode, is to increase the values of the smoothing constants in the hope that the form of the underlying model is still correct and all that is needed is to more quickly smooth the parameter estimates closer to their true, but unknown, values. The second type of corrective action is more substantive. It typically involves human intervention to make significant changes in the parameter estimates or in the form of the demand model itself. Within this general framework, for simplicity, our illustrative discussion will be restricted primarily to the case of a level demand model and to where the measure of bias is the smoothed error tracking signal. However, references for further details on several other cases will be given.

Changing the Smoothing Constants—Adaptive Forecasting

As discussed above, the implicit assumption is that the underlying model is still correct. Recall from Eq. 4.66 that the smoothed error tracking signal is given by

$$T_t = z_t/\text{MAD}_t \qquad (4.70)$$

and furthermore we deduced that $-1 \leq T_t \leq 1$. The general idea of adaptive smoothing is that the smoothing constants are increased (that is, smoothing becomes faster) when T_t gets too far away from 0, while smoothing is decreased as T_t returns closer to 0. We discuss four of the better known adaptive forecasting techniques where we have somewhat modified a categorization (see Table 4.12) first shown by Roberts and Whybark (1974).

TABLE 4.12 Classification of Adaptive Techniques

Method of Selecting α	Periodic evaluaton	Continuous evaluation
Unconstrained or Computed Value of Smoothing Constant	Eilon and Elmaleh	Trigg and Leach
Constrained or Pre-specified Choice of Smoothing Constant	Chow	Whybark

The Eilon and Elmaleh (1970) approach to adaptive smoothing consists of setting the smoothing constant α to a fixed value, whereupon forecasts are made for a specified number of periods (called the evaluation interval). At the end of the evaluation interval, forecast errors are computed (ex post) using the demand time series that actually occurred. Forecast errors are also computed for a range of permitted values ($\alpha = 0.1$ to 0.9) to see what size forecast errors *would have* resulted if one of these values of α has been used over the evaluation interval. The permitted value of the constant that would have minimized the forecast error variance over the historical evaluation interval is then used until the next evaluation interval. The procedure is repeated periodically over and over again.

Chow (1965) proposed a procedure whereby one computes three forecasts each period. The first forecast is developed using a base value of α, and the others using $\alpha_H = \alpha + 0.05$ and $\alpha_L = \alpha - 0.05$. If, over the evaluation period, the MAD using α is less than that using α_H or α_L, no change is made in α. However, if the MAD using α_H or α_L is lower, then α is changed to α_H or α_L for subsequent smoothing. Furthermore, all MADs are reset to 0 and the process is repeated for the next evaluation period, but with the new base α value. Extensions of Chow's approach to the case of Holt's trend model (having two smoothing constants) have been developed by Roberts and Reed (1969) and Montgomery (1970).

Trigg and Leach (1967) suggested a continuous evaluation approach that consists of setting the smoothing constant to be used in period $t + 1$ equal to the absolute value of the tracking signal at the end of period t:

$$\alpha_{t+1} = |T_t| \tag{4.71}$$

that is, the further T_t is from 0, the larger the smoothing constant becomes. Extensions to the cases of the Holt trend updating procedure and Winters seasonal updating have been suggested by Gilchrist (1976) and Flowers (1980), respectively. In particular, Flowers developed guidelines for how to choose upper limits to be placed on the smoothing constants α_{HW}, β_{HW}, and γ_{HW} when one attempts to set them equal to the tracking signal T_t.

An alternative approach to continuous adaptation was suggested by Whybark (1973). A base value of 0.2 is used for α. The value of α is changed only when errors exceed specified control limits. If the error in a single period is larger in absolute value than $4\sigma_1$ (that is, 5 MAD) or if two consecutive errors exceed $1.2\sigma_1$ (that is, 1.5 MAD), then α is increased to 0.8 for one period, reduced to 0.4 for the next period, and then reset to 0.2.

Unfortunately, although all four of the above mentioned procedures have intuitive appeal, recent research findings (see for example, Ekern, 1981; Flowers, 1980; Gardner and Dannenbring, 1980) would seem to imply that adaptive methods are not necessarily better than regular, nonadaptive smoothing. In particular, there are dangers of instabilities being introduced by the attempt at adaptation. Consequently, we suggest that careful testing be undertaken with actual time series from the organization under study before any automatic adaptive procedure is adopted.

Human Intervention

Where sufficient bias exists or where smoothing constants remain at high levels it may be appropriate to call for human intervention. Sufficient bias could be defined by

$$T_t > f \tag{4.72}$$

where f is a threshold fraction, or by

$$C_t > k \text{ MAD}$$

where k is some threshold multiple.

The choice of f or k implicitly involves the aforementioned tradeoff between two types of errors—namely (1) not intervening when such an action is necessary and (2) intervening when it is unnecessary. Lower thresholds would be used for A, as opposed to B items, the reason being that the first type of error is relatively more expensive for A items and for B items we would like to keep interventions on an exception basis. In actual practice a reasonable way to establish f or k is by trial and error in order to provide a reasonable intervention workload in an *aggregate* sense. Plausible initial values are $f = 0.4$ and $k = 5$.

Significant assistance can be provided to the intervener through a display of several periods of recent actual demands and forecasts made by the most current version of the model. This information can be made available in hard copy or video display format. The individual involved, on seeing the display, should attempt to ascertain the reason for the recent poor performance. There may be factors, external to the model, that have recently changed, such as

1. A temporary effect—for example, a sales promotion.
2. A more permanent effect—for example, a new competitive product or a new market penetration.

A temporary effect could lead to human override of forecasts for a few periods. On the other hand, a more permanent effect could be incorporated by manually adjusting parameter values or by even changing the nature of the demand model. If the visual display indicates that the change occurred several periods in the past, it may be appropriate to reinitialize the model using only data since the suspected time of the change.

4.6.5 Probability Distributions of Forecast Errors

As we will see in Chapter 7, the selection of safety stocks to provide adequate customer service will depend not just on the standard deviation of forecast errors over the replenishment lead time but, instead, on the whole probability distribution of such errors. Of particular concern will be the probabilities of large positive values of the errors (demand minus forecasts) in that such errors can lead to serious stockout situations.

Through most of this book we recommend the use of a normal distribution of forecast errors for three reasons. First, empirically the normal distribution usually provides a better fit to data than most other suggested distributions. Second, particularly if the lead time (or lead time plus review interval) is long, forecast errors in many periods are added together, so we would expect a normal distribution through the Central Limit Theorem. Finally, the normal leads to analytically tractable results. Nevertheless, particularly for expensive, slow-moving items it may be appropriate to use an alternative distribution such as the exponential, Gamma, Poisson, or negative binomial. In any event, before making a choice one should at least perform a relatively simple test of the fit of the normal distribution to the observed forecast errors for each of a number of representative items. Specifically, there is special normal probability paper such that the cumulative distribution of a normal distribution will appear as a straight line on it. Thus one can plot the empirical cumulative distribution and observe how closely it is fit by a straight line. (This is similar in nature to the test of a lognormal distribution as a fit to the distribution by value across a population of items, as will be described in the Appendix to Chapter 17.)

4.7 HANDLING ANOMALOUS DEMAND

In general, one should have a healthy suspicion of data that are purported to represent actual customer demand period by period. First, in many organizations sales or even just shipments to customers are recorded as opposed to demand. If not properly interpreted, a series of periods in which a stockout situation existed would imply no demand in each of those periods. Furthermore, if backordering is permitted, the periods immediately following the stockout may show sales or shipments well above the actual demands in those periods. Both Wecker (1978) and Bell (1981) have presented approaches for forecasting when stockouts distort the demand data.

Furthermore, recording and transmission errors can distort the demand picture. Certain types of demand also may not be normally handled on a routine basis by the production/stocking point under consideration and thus should not be incorporated in the forecast updating. For example, unusually large customer orders may be shunted back to the higher level of supply (to illustrate, orders larger than a certain size may be directly shipped from a central warehouse rather than via the usual mode of transshipment through a regional branch warehouse). Finally, there may be certain temporary changes in the demand pattern (for example, effects of promotions and price changes) that should be filtered out prior to updating.

A useful aid in monitoring anomalous demand is to have an exception signal trigger human investigation when the "demand" stated for a particular period differs from the forecast by more than k MAD where a k value of 4 to 5 is not unreasonable.

4.8 INCORPORATION OF HUMAN JUDGMENT

An overall framework for forecasting was shown in Figure 4.1. In it, the input of human judgment played a key role. In Sections 4.6.4 and 4.7 we have already seen evidence of manual intervention in an essentially *reactive* fashion, that is, responding to signals of forecast bias or unusual demand levels. Now we concentrate on the *anticipatory* use of human judgment. However, clearly there is considerable overlap in that a reactive response will often initiate an anticipatory input.

Obviously managerial judgment as input is essential in medium-range, aggregate forecasting. The ensuing decisions concerning work force levels, operating hours, seasonal inventory levels, and so forth, are of major importance to an organization and thus justify the devotion of a considerable amount of managerial time. Moreover, there are relatively few time series to be forecasted because of the aggregation procedure. One approach that has proved helpful is the Delphi method (see Basu and Schroeder, 1977, for the discussion of an illustrative use). Most of the remaining discussion will concentrate on shorter range forecasting, but many of the ideas are also applicable in the medium range.

4.8.1 Factors Where Judgment Input Is Needed

There are a number of factors, normally not included in a statistical forecasting model, where judgment input is clearly needed. These factors can be categorized along two different dimensions. First, there are factors external to the organization versus those internally influenced. Second, the duration of the effects of a factor can be temporary versus more or less permanent. Our discussion will concentrate on the first type of categorization.

Factors external to the organization include

1. The general economic situation (for example, the inflation rate, the cost of borrowing capital, the unemployment rate)
2. Government regulations such as subsidies, import duties and/or quotas, pollution restrictions, safety standards, etc.
3. Competitor actions
4. Potential labor stoppages at the customer level (users of our products)
5. Consumer preferences (particularly with regard to style goods)

Important factors internal to the organization encompass

1. Price changes
2. Promotions
3. Advertising

4. Engineering changes that, for example, will improve the reliability of a product, thus reducing the demand for spares
5. Introduction of substitute products—a classic example was the effect on the sales of slide rules that resulted from the introduction of hand calculators
6. Opening a new distribution outlet for an existing product
7. The pipeline filling effect associated with the introduction of a new product—a temporary surge of demand will occur simply to initially place appropriate levels of inventory at the various stocking points

Related to internal factors is the need to ensure that the total (in dollars) of statistical forecasts of individual items agrees reasonably well with the aggregate financial plan of the organization. Some adjustments may be needed (see, for example, Muir and Newberry, 1981).

Some success has been achieved in introducing some of the above judgmental factors into a form of the statistical forecasting model known as Bayesian forecasting. The general approach is discussed by Harrison and Stevens (1971, 1976) and an interesting application is presented by Johnston and Harrison (1980).

4.8.2 Guidelines for the Input and Monitoring of Judgment

It is advisable to think in terms of a small committee being responsible for the provision of judgmental input. Ideally, the membership should include a representive from marketing, production/inventory management, engineering/design, and an individual with a broad perspective (for example, from planning, systems, or management sciences). Meetings should be held on the order of once per month.

This committee is likely to be concerned with groups or families of items, perhaps by geographic region. The starting point in each case should be the objective (statistical) forecast, aggregated across the appropriate group of items. In addition, recent demand history and associated forecasts should be available on request, ideally in a real-time video display mode. Provision should be made for easy input of adjustments of forecasts. Typically, the computer would simply automatically prorate a family adjustment back to the individual-item forecasts according to the recent fractions of family demand represented by the individual items.

It is important to provide feedback on the performance of the judgmental input. This is accomplished by retaining both the original statistical forecast and the revised (through judgment) forecast. When the actual demand materializes, one can then show the statistical forecast error and the error of the judgmental forecast. In fact, a report can be developed listing the difference of the two errors (likely normalized by dividing by the MAD or σ) for each family of items forecasted. The listing can be ranked by relative performance of the two methods. The intention should not be to *externally* evaluate the human input; instead, the objective should be to provide a mechanism for the committee members themselves to learn from their earlier successes and failures. Further discussion on this topic can be found in Landau (1976).

4.9 DEALING WITH SPECIAL CLASSES OF INDIVIDUAL ITEMS

The procedures discussed to this stage in the chapter should be of use for a major portion of the items handled by a typical organization. However, there are special classes of items where caution must be exercised. The intention of this section is to provide some insights concerning each of several special classes. In addition, forecasting issues related to one other class, so-called style goods items, will be covered in Chapter 10.

4.9.1 Items with Limited History

Here we finally address the issue of initialization of the exponential smoothing procedures of Section 4.5 when there is insufficient historical data to use the methods suggested earlier for obtaining estimates of the parameters a, b, F's, and MAD. Incidentally, there are two reasons for an item having insufficient historical data. First the item may be a relatively new product (that is, early in its product life cycle, as discussed in Section 2.3 of Chapter 2). Second, when a new control system is introduced in an organization, there may simply not be sufficient historical records even though the item has had sales for a considerable period of time.

For an item with insufficient history a knowledgeable individual (likely a member of the judgmental input committee) should estimate

1. Total demand in the first year.
2. Total demand in the second year.

} Together these give an estimate of the level and trend.

3. Seasonal pattern (if appropriate)—most likely this would be provided by saying that the item's seasonal behavior should be the same as an existing individual item or group of items.

It is important to provide a graphical feedback of the implied 2-year demand pattern so that adjustments can be made, if necessary. Higher than normal smoothing should be used in the first several periods because of the relative inaccuracy of the initial estimates of the parameters.

The MAD of an item with insufficient history is estimated using an empirical relationship between MAD and the demand level a found to hold for more established items in the same inventory population. In particular, a relationship that has been observed to give a reasonable fit for many organizations is of the form[13]

$$\text{MAD} = c_1 a^{c_2} \tag{4.73}$$

or equivalently

$$\log \text{MAD} = \log c_1 + c_2 \log a \tag{4.74}$$

where c_1 and c_2 are regression coefficients typically with $0.5 < c_2 < 1$.

The relationship of Eq. 4.74 will plot as a straight line on log-log graph paper. For the 849 s.k.u. from the MIDAS Corporation's Professional Products Division we fitted the following equation by regression:

$$\text{MAD} = 1.04(D/12)^{0.65} \tag{4.75}$$

where MAD is the mean absolute deviation of forecast errors over a 1-month update period, and D is the annual demand rate.

Relationships other than Eq. 4.73 have been suggested in the literature (see, for example, Hausman and Kirby, 1970; Kaplan, 1974; Stevens, 1974). Also a relationship, such as Eq. 4.75, can be used on an on-going basis as needed to estimate the MAD of any C items in that C items are not statistically forecasted; hence errors are not recorded.

Illustration

Consider a new item with an estimated level of 300 units per year. Use of Eq. 4.75 gives an initial estimate of MAD as

$$\begin{aligned} \text{MAD} &= 1.04(300/12)^{0.65} \\ &= 8.43 \text{ units} \end{aligned}$$

4.9.2 Intermittent and Erratic Demand

The exponential smoothing forecast methods described earlier have been found to be rather ineffective where transactions (not necessarily unit-sized) occur on a somewhat infrequent basis. To illustrate this point, let us consider a particularly simple situation where only transactions of a single size j occur exactly every n periods of time. Suppose that simple exponential smoothing (level only)

---

[13] Sometimes a somewhat different form of Eq. 4.73 is used, namely,

$$\sigma_1 v = c_1 (av)^{c_2}$$

where v is the unit variable cost of an item.

with a smoothing constant α is used and the updating is done every unit period, that is,

$$\hat{a}_t = \alpha x_t + (1 - \alpha)\hat{a}_{t-1} \tag{4.76}$$

and

$$\hat{x}_{t,t+1} = a_t \tag{4.77}$$

where, as earlier,

x_t = demand in period t

$\hat{a}_t$ = estimate of the level at the end of period t

$\hat{x}_{t,t+1}$ = forecast, made at the end of period t, of demand in period $t + 1$

In the context of our special case we have

$$x_t = \begin{cases} j & t = 1, n + 1, 2n + 1, 3n + 1, \ldots \\ 0 & \text{otherwise} \end{cases}$$

where we have rather arbitrarily said that the first demand occurs in period 1. For low values of t the forecasts depend on the initial estimate $\hat{a}_0$. However, as t gets larger and larger, the effect of this initial term dies out. Therefore, we would expect that for large t the forecasts would settle into a pattern repeating every n units of time (where n is the cycle time of the simple demand pattern).[14] Suppose we have reached this stable situation and we let $\hat{a}_0$ represent the forecast just before a period in which a transaction occurs. The transaction is of size j, and no other transaction occurs for the next $n - 1$ periods. By updating, according to Eq. 4.76, we obtain the forecast just before the next transaction occurs as

$$(1 - \alpha)^n \hat{a}_0 + \alpha(1 - \alpha)^{n-1}j$$

But this must again equal $\hat{a}_0$. Therefore,

$$\hat{a}_0 = (1 - \alpha)^n \hat{a}_0 + \alpha(1 - \alpha)^{n-1}j$$

or

$$\hat{a}_0 = \frac{\alpha(1 - \alpha)^{n-1}j}{1 - (1 - \alpha)^n} \tag{4.78}$$

[14]There are more rigorous methods than the one we use for developing the pattern of forecasts. One involves the use of transform methods (see Croston, 1972).

Furthermore, the forecast u periods later (where $0 < u \leq n$) is

$$\hat{a}_u = \alpha(1 - \alpha)^{u-1}j + (1 - \alpha)^u \hat{a}_0$$

Using Eq. 4.78, this becomes

$$\hat{a}_u = \frac{\alpha(1 - \alpha)^{u-1}j}{1 - (1 - \alpha)^n} \qquad u = 1, 2, 3, \ldots, n - 1 \tag{4.79}$$

The forecasts in a typical n period cycle are shown in Figure 4.11 (illustrated for $n = 6$ and $\alpha = 0.2$). It is found that, immediately after the demand transaction, the forecast exceeds the average demand per period, and thereafter throughout the cycle the forecast decreases, dropping below the average demand by the end of the cycle. In other words, for a deterministic demand pattern exponential smoothing produces a saw-tooth type forecast.

This illustration is a symptom of an undesirable performance of exponential smoothing under the more general situation of infrequent[15] transactions, not necessarily all of the same size. For such a situation it is preferable to forecast two separate components of the demand process—namely, the time between consecutive transactions and the magnitude of individual transactions—that is, we let

$$x_t = y_t z_t \tag{4.80}$$

where

$$y_t = \begin{cases} 1 & \text{if a transaction occurs} \\ 0 & \text{otherwise} \end{cases}$$

and z_t is the size of the transaction.

If we define a quantity n as the number of periods between transactions and if demands in separate periods are considered independent, then the occurrence or nonoccurrence of a transaction in a period can be considered as a Bernoulli process with probability of occurrence being $1/n$; that is

$$\text{prob}\ (y_t = 1) = 1/n$$

and

$$\text{prob}\ (y_t = 0) = 1 - 1/n$$

[15]Infrequent in the sense that the average time between transactions is considerably larger than the unit period, the latter being the interval of forecast updating.

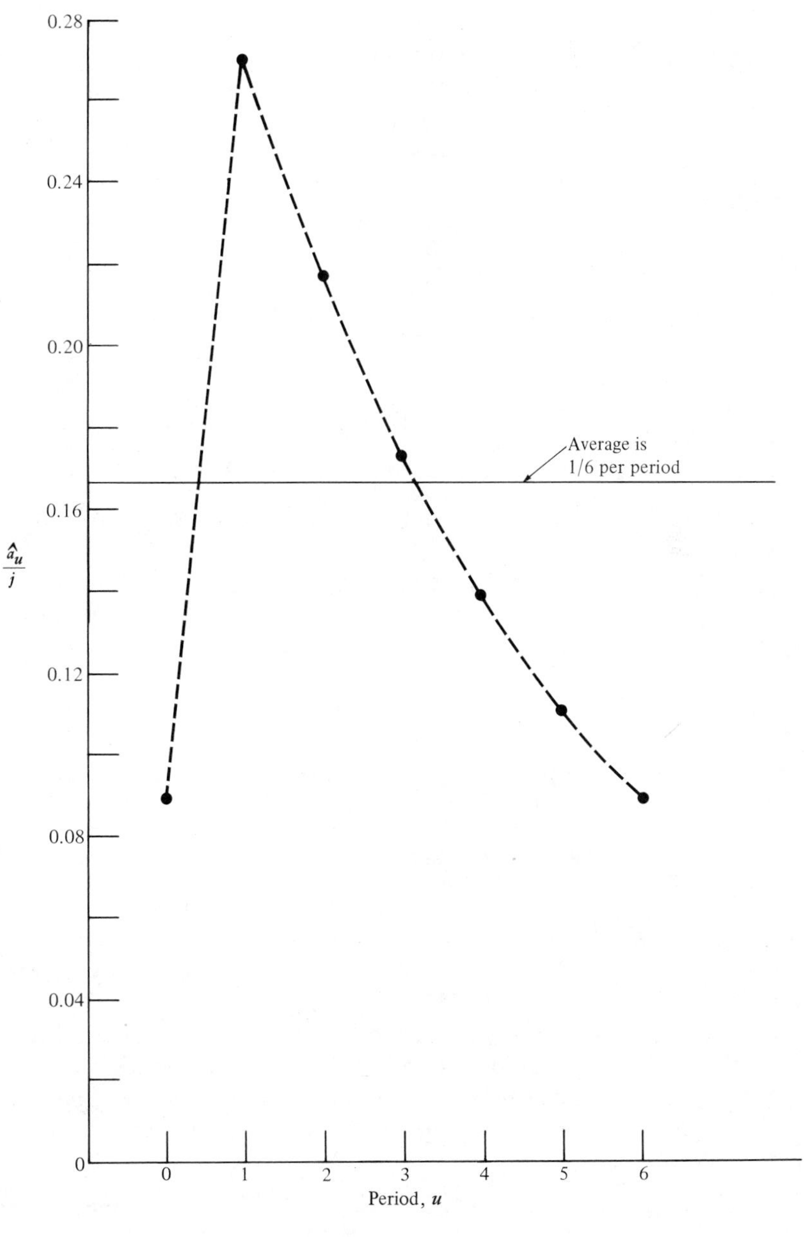

Note: Demand is $x_u = \begin{cases} j & u = 1, 7, 13 \ldots \\ 0 & \text{otherwise} \end{cases}$

FIGURE 4.11 Typical Behavior of Exponential Smoothing for Deterministic Intermittent Demand

Within this framework and assuming that transaction sizes are normally distributed, Croston (1972) recommends the following reasonable updating procedure: If $x_t = 0$ (that is, no demand occurs),

1. Transaction size estimates are not updated
2. $\hat{n}_t = \hat{n}_{t-1}$

If $x_t > 0$ (that is, a transaction occurs),

1. $\hat{z}_t = \alpha x_t + (1 - \alpha)\hat{z}_{t-1}$
2. $\hat{n}_t = \alpha n_t + (1 - \alpha)\hat{n}_{t-1}$

where

n_t = number of periods since the last transaction

$\hat{n}_t$ = estimated value of n at the end of period t

$\hat{z}_t$ = estimate, at the end of period t, of the average transaction size

Croston argues that forecasts for replenishment purposes will usually be needed immediately after a transaction. He shows that the forecast at that time, namely,

$$\hat{z}_t/\hat{n}_t$$

is preferable to that obtained by simple exponential smoothing for two reasons:

1. It is unbiased, whereas the simple smoothing forecast is not.
2. It has a lower variance than does the simple smoothing forecast.

However, Croston warns that the infrequent updating (only when a transaction occurs) introduces a marked lag in responding to actual changes in the underlying parameters. Therefore, he rightfully stresses the importance of control signals to identify deviations.

A key quantity to use in establishing the safety stock for an intermittently demanded item is MAD(z), the mean absolute deviation of the sizes of *nonzero* sized transactions. This quantity is only updated each time that a transaction occurs. The updating equation is of the form

$$\text{New MAD}(z) = \omega|x_t - \hat{z}_{t-1}| + (1 - \omega)\text{Old MAD}(z) \qquad x_t > 0 \tag{4.81}$$

In establishing the safety stock, account must also be taken of the fact that there is a nonzero chance of no transaction occurring in a period. Johnston (1980) suggests an alternate method for directly estimating σ_1 for an intermittent demand item.

An item is said to have an erratic demand pattern if the variability is large relative to the mean. Brown(1977) operationalizes this by saying that demand is erratic when $\hat{\sigma}_1 > \hat{a}$ where $\hat{\sigma}_1$ is obtained by a fit to history, as in Section 4.6.1. In such a case he suggests restricting the underlying model to the case of only a level and a random component. Another reference on this topic is Muir (1980).

4.9.3 Replacement or Service Parts

In the case of replacement or service parts we have more information than is usually available in a demand forecasting situation. In particular, the requirements for replacement parts depend on the failure rate of operating equipment which, in turn, depends on the time stream of the introduction of new (or repaired) pieces of equipment as well as the distribution of the service life of the equipment. Although it is relatively easy to state the above relationship, it is quite another thing to operationalize it. In particular, the mathematics become extremely involved and also it is neither easy to maintain the required records nor to estimate the service life distribution. Keilson and Kubat (1984) have developed tractable results for the special case where new equipment is introduced according to a time-varying Poisson distribution and failures also occur according to a Poisson process. Other references on the topic include Brown (1982), Kendrick (1961), and Ritchie and Wilcox (1977). Incidentally, a closely related problem is the forecasting of the returns of rented items or containers (for example, soft drink bottles, beer kegs, etc.).

4.9.4 Terminal Demand

Here we are dealing with exactly the opposite situation from that in Section 4.9.1. Now we are nearing the end of the demand pattern (life cycle) for a particular item. It has been empirically observed (see, for example, Brown,1981; Fortuin, 1980) that in the terminal phase of demand the pattern tends to decrease geometrically with time; that is, the demand in period $t + 1$ is a constant fraction (f) of the demand in period t. Mathematically, we then have

$$x_{t+1} = fx_t$$

or, more generally,

$$x_t = f^t x_0 \qquad t = 0, 1, 2, \ldots \tag{4.82}$$

In this last equation, the time origin has been placed at the beginning of, or somewhere during, the terminal phase of the pattern.

Taking logarithms of Eq. 4.82 reveals that

$$\log x_t = t \log f + \log x_0 \tag{4.83}$$

Thus a plot of x_t versus t on semilogarithmic graph paper should produce a straight line with slope $\log f$. Such a line can be fit by standard regression techniques, and Brown (1981) has developed an expression for the variance of an extrapolated forecast into the future as a function of the residual variance of the historical fit, the number of historical data points used in the fit, and how far into the future the projection is made.

If the origin is placed at the current period, and the current level is x_0, then an estimate of the all-time future requirements is given by

$$\begin{aligned} \text{ATR} &= \sum_{\tau=1}^{\infty} \hat{x}_{0,\tau} \\ &= \sum_{\tau=1}^{\infty} f^{\tau} x_0 \qquad \text{(from Eq. 4.82)} \\ &= \frac{f}{1-f} x_0 \qquad (4.84) \end{aligned}$$

Illustration

Consider a particular spare part used on a 1970s make of automobile. Suppose that the demand has begun dropping off geometrically with a factor $f = 0.81$ and the demand level in the current year is 115 units. From Eq. 4.84 the all-time future requirements are estimated to be

$$\text{ATR} = \frac{0.81}{0.19}(115) \simeq 490 \text{ units}$$

4.10 ASSESSING FORECASTING PROCEDURES: TACTICS AND STRATEGY

In this section we first address a tactical question—namely, measuring and comparing the statistical accuracies of different forecasting procedures. Then, we return to issues of a more strategic nature.

4.10.1 Statistical Accuracy of Forecasts

As mentioned above, here we restrict our attention to measuring and comparing the statistical accuracies of different forecast procedures. The first point to note is that there are several possible measures of forecast accuracy—for example, the MAD, the sample variance, the sample bias, any of these normalized by the mean demand level, and so forth. No single measure is universally best. In fact, forecast accuracy is only a surrogate for overall production/inventory system performance (encompassing the uses of the forecasts). The surrogate is usually justified in terms of keeping the evaluation procedure of a manageable size. We return to this point in Section 4.10.2 and also to a more general discussion of evaluation in Chapter 17.

Besides the choice of several possible statistical measures of forecast accuracy, there is the added problem of not even being able to make *valid* statistical claims about the relative sizes of the same measure achieved by two different forecasting procedures. The reason for this is that the two series of forecast errors are correlated to an unknown extent (Peterson, 1969).

To complicate matters, it can be shown that a linear combination of forecasts from two or more procedures can outperform *all* of those individual procedures. In theory, the best combination of procedures depends on the value of the measure of variability (for example, the MAD) for each individual procedure as well as the correlation between the results of the procedures (see Bates and Granger, 1969; Bunn, 1977; Dickinson, 1973, 1975; Peterson and Lamont, 1972). However, it is difficult to accurately estimate these quantities. Hence, if combinations of forecasts are to be considered, we recommend trying combinations, only two at a time, and starting with equal weights. Lewis (1978) also discusses simple combinations of objective and judgmental forecasts.

In developing relative measures of accuracy it is crucial to use an *ex-ante*, as opposed to an *ex-post*, testing procedure. In an ex-post approach the forecast model and updating procedure are tested on the *same* data from which the model form or smoothing constant values were selected. In contrast, the ex-ante method involves testing with an entirely different set of data—usually accomplished by using a first part of the historical information for fitting purposes and the remaining portion for testing. Performance on ex-post tests can be a very poor indicator of ex-ante performance, and it is the latter that is of practical interest. The reader is encouraged to consult the article by Fildes and Howell (1979) for further discussion and references.

Numerous tests that have measured the statistical accuracy of different forecasting procedures have been reported in the literature. However, of primary interest is the comprehensive study undertaken by Makridakis et al. (1982). It involved some 1001 time series including both micro- and macro-level data as well as monthly, quarterly, and annual forecast update intervals. All of the common statistical forecasting procedures (from very simple to quite complex) were tested, and a number of measures of statistical accuracy were obtained for each combination of procedure and time series. Some of the salient findings were the following:

1. Significant differences in forecast accuracy occurred as a function of the micro/macro classification. On micro data (the case in individual-item forecasting) the relatively simple methods did much better than the statistically sophisticated methodologies. In turn, the latter were better for macro data (the case in our medium or even longer term forecasting).
2. For horizons of 1 to 6 periods ahead, simple exponential smoothing, Holt and Brown trend procedures, and the Winters method performed well. For horizons of 7 or more periods, a more complicated procedure, developed by Lewandowski (1979), showed the best performance.

3. Deseasonalization of the data by the ratio to moving average method (what we have suggested earlier in this chapter) did as well as much more sophisticated deseasonalization procedures.
4. Adaptive methods did *not* outperform nonadaptive methods.
5. A simple average of six of the simpler statistical methods did somewhat better than any of the individual methods and also outperformed a combination of the methods that *in theory* was supposed to give the best results.
6. In general, sophisticated methods did not produce more accurate results than did the simpler methods.

In summary, the results of this major international study lend strong support to the forecasting procedures that we have advocated in this chapter.

4.10.2 Some Issues of a More Strategic Nature

As Fildes (1979) has pointed out, two questions dominate any assessment of a forecasting procedure. First, are the results statistically satisfactory (the topic covered in Section 4.10.1)? Second, will the procedure, once developed, be used and perform in a cost-effective fashion? In Fildes' words "it is the latter that is often of more concern to the practicing forecaster." This view is shared by the authors of the *Study Guide* for the Certification Program of the American Production and Inventory Control Society (see Blagg et al., 1980):

> *Forecasting is not done for its own sake; it is meaningful only as it relates to and supports decision making within the production system. Hence, managerial considerations regarding cost, effectiveness, and appropriateness of the forecasting function must be a part of the domain of forecasting.*

As discussed in Section 4.1, cost performance refers to the overall system costs associated with production/inventory decision making, which are affected by the choice of forecasting procedure. Earlier we mentioned that it has often been advocated that the statistical accuracy of a forecasting method should be used as a surrogate for the portion of system costs associated with forecast errors. Unfortunately, studies (see, for example, Gotwals, 1981; Muller et al., 1977) have shown that traditional error measures do *not* necessarily relate to overall system costs. Thus, where possible, a choice between forecasting procedures should be based partly on a comparative simulation test of system costs using historical data or a trial run on new data (see Kallina, 1978; Rosenman, 1984, for further discussion).

Closely related to the above is the desirable property of robustness (Fildes, 1979). The choice of a particular demand model and updating procedure should again be at least partially based on an insensitivity to the data quality, missing observations, outliers, and so forth. We hope the suggestions made in Section 4.7 would benefit any selected procedure from a standpoint of robustness.

Studies by Adam and Ebert (1976) and Mabert (1975) have compared objective (statistical model) forecasts with judgmental forecasts. Interestingly enough, the objective forecasts, on the average, outperformed the subjective forecasts. However, as argued earlier, we feel that there is a need for a combination of forecasts generated from the two sources. To have meaningful subjective input, the manager must be able to understand the underlying assumptions and general idea of the statistical model. This is an important reason for why we have placed so much emphasis on the relatively simple exponential smoothing procedures. A more extreme view of the need for simplicity is offered by Smith (1978). Moreover, in Chapters 12 and 16, where there will be a more explicit dependence of demand among different s.k.u. (multiechelon inventory systems and multistage production processes), we will emphasize a different type of forecasting that involves explosion of *known* future usage.

Related to the usefulness of a forecasting system, Makridakis and Wheelwright (1979b) have listed a number of potential organizational blocks to improved forecasting. Of specific interest here are (1) bias and (2) credibility and communication. By bias we mean that in many organizations there is incentive for a forecast to *not* represent the most likely outcome but, instead, to serve as a self-fulfilling goal. For example, sales personnel may deliberately provide low forecasts if they are rewarded for exceeding target levels based, at least in part, on the forecasted values. In terms of credibility, we mean that the forecasts may lack relevance or *appear* to lack relevance. The latter often results from a lack of proper communication between the forecast analyst and the decision maker.

In conclusion we recall the experience of one of the authors who was once asked to mediate between competing forecasting groups at a large international corporation. Each group was obviously very sophisticated in mathematical time series analysis and very clever in coaxing the most obscure of patterns out of historical data through spectral analysis. None of the nine highly trained mathematician-forecasters involved had every really closely examined a retail outlet or wholesaler through which the products that they forecasted were being sold. To most of them, products were characterized by amplitudes and phase angles.

Top management for their part were somewhat intimidated with all the apparent computerized sophistication (as was the author initially). Little collaboration existed between the users and the producers of forecasts. Management and analysts both ignored the fact that *you really cannot foretell the future with great accuracy*. Tactics without any overall strategy prevailed. On closer examination, it became clear that management was not taking the mathematicians' forecasts seriously, because they didn't understand how they were being generated. The problem that brought matters to a head involved the entrance of an aggressive competitor into the market who claimed through massive advertising that the company's basic product concept was technologically obsolete. It took top management several weeks to react because they were unable to determine the extent of the impact on their sales until wholesalers and retailers started to refuse previously planned shipments.

Eventually the situation was resolved as follows. Instead of trying to foretell the future, top management agreed to set up better procedures that would allow the company to *quickly react to forecast errors as soon as their magnitude was determined.* This involved a basic change in management philosophy. No longer were forecast errors a surprise event. They were fully anticipated, and everyone in the decision hierarchy prepared contingency plans in response. All agreed that it was at least equally as important to develop techniques for responding to errors, as it was to try to measure and predict them. In the process, six of the high-powered time series analysts were laid off, resulting in a substantial reduction of overall costs associated with forecasting as well as in a better *forecasting strategy.*

APPENDIX TO CHAPTER 4
DERIVATION OF SIMPLE EXPONENTIAL SMOOTHING

From Eq. 4.23, we know that we wish to select $\hat{a}_t$ in order to minimize

$$S' = \sum_{j=0}^{\infty} d^j (x_{t-j} - \hat{a}_t)^2$$

By setting $dS'/d\hat{a}_t = 0$, we obtain

$$-2 \sum_{j=0}^{\infty} d^j (x_{t-j} - \hat{a}_t) = 0$$

or

$$\hat{a}_t \sum_{j=0}^{\infty} d^j = \sum_{j=0}^{\infty} d^j x_{t-j} \tag{4.85}$$

Now

$$\sum_{j=0}^{\infty} d^j = \frac{1}{1-d}$$

Therefore, Eq. 4.85 becomes

$$\begin{aligned} \hat{a}_t &= (1-d) \sum_{j=0}^{\infty} d^j x_{t-j} \\ &= (1-d)(x_t + \sum_{j=1}^{\infty} d^j x_{t-j}) \end{aligned} \tag{4.86}$$

By substituting $r = j - 1$ in the summation, we obtain

$$\hat{a}_t = (1-d)x_t + (1-d)d \sum_{r=0}^{\infty} d^r x_{t-1-r} \tag{4.87}$$

From Eq. 4.86 we see that

$$(1 - d) \sum_{r=0}^{\infty} d^r x_{t-1-r} = \hat{a}_{t-1}$$

By substituting into Eq. 4.87, there follows

$$\begin{aligned} \hat{a}_t &= (1 - d)x_t + d\hat{a}_{t-1} \\ &= \alpha x_t + (1 - \alpha)\hat{a}_{t-1} \qquad \text{where } \alpha = 1 - d \end{aligned}$$

PROBLEMS

4.1 Suspose that the following were sales of beer in the Kitchener-Waterloo area by month for the 3 years shown:

	Jan.	Feb.	Mar.	Apr.	May	June
1968	73	69	68	64	65	98
1969	80	81	83	69	91	140
1970	95	66	81	100	93	116

	July	Aug.	Sept.	Oct.	Nov.	Dec.
1968	114	122	74	56	72	153
1969	152	170	97	122	78	177
1970	195	194	101	197	80	189

a. Plot the data roughly to scale.

b. Is there a trend present?

c. Is there any seasonality? Discuss.

d. Are there any anomalies? Discuss.

e. What is your forecast of demand for January 1971? For June 1971?

4.2 Southern Consolidated manufactures gas turbines. Some of the parts are bought from outside, while the important ones are made in the company's plant. CZ-43 is an important part that wears out in approximately two years and has to be replaced. This means CZ-43 has to be manufactured not only to meet demand at the assembly line but also to satisfy its demand as a spare part. The gas turbine was first sold in 1971 and the demand for CZ-43 for 1971–1984 is given below. Forecast the total demand for CZ-43 for 1985.

Year	Demand as Spare Part	Demand for Assembly	Total Demand
1971	3	87	90
1972	6	48	54
1973	14	43	57
1974	30	31	61
1975	41	49	90
1976	46	31	77
1977	42	37	79
1978	60	42	102
1979	58	47	105
1980	67	32	99
1981	70	25	95
1982	58	29	87
1983	57	30	87
1984	85	23	108

4.3 Under the assumption of a level model, that is,

$$x_t = a + \varepsilon_t$$

show that the choice of a to minimize

$$S = \sum_{j=t-N+1}^{t} (x_j - a_t)^2$$

where x_j is the actual demand in period j, is given by

$$\hat{a}_t = (x_t + x_{t-1} + x_{t-2} + \cdots + x_{t-N+1})/N$$

4.4 Prove that the *average* age of the data used in the estimate of Eq. 4.26 is given by $1/\alpha$.

4.5 The number of violent crimes in each of the last 6 weeks in the Hill Road Precinct has been:

Week j	1	2	3	4	5	6
Incidents x_j	83	106	95	91	110	108

a. Use a 2-week moving average to forecast the incidents in each of weeks 7 and 10. Also compute the MAD based on the incidents and forecasts for periods 1 to 6. To initialize, assume $x_{-1} = x_0 = 100$.

b. Detective Bick Melker suggests the use of simple (single) exponential smoothing with $\alpha = 0.1$. Use such a procedure to develop forecasts of incidents in weeks 7 and 10 for Hill Road. Initialize with $\hat{a}_0 = 100$. Also compute the MAD.

c. Without redoing all the computations, what would be the forecast of incidents in week 7 using exponential smoothing if $\hat{a}_0$ was 90 instead of 100?

4.6 Brown's updating equations, developed from discounted least squares, for the case of a trend model are actually given by

$$\hat{a}_t = x_t + (1 - \alpha)^2 (\hat{a}_{t-1} + \hat{b}_{t-1} - x_t)$$

and

$$\hat{b}_t = \hat{b}_{t-1} - \alpha^2 (\hat{a}_{t-1} + \hat{b}_{t-1} - x_t)$$

Show that these two equations are equivalent to Eqs. 4.33 and 4.34.

4.7 The demand for a particular model of microcomputer at a particular outlet of Radio Hut has had the following pattern during the past 15 weeks:

Week t	1	2	3	4	5	6	7	8
Demand x_t	34	40	34	36	40	42	46	50

Week t	9	10	11	12	13	14	15
Demand x_t	55	49	49	53	63	69	65

A systems analyst at Radio Hut believes that demand should be trending upward; thus she wishes to evaluate the use of exponential smoothing with a trend model.

a. Use the first 5 weeks of data in Eqs. 4.37 and 4.38 to obtain estimates of $\hat{a}$ and $\hat{b}$ as of the end of week 5.

b. Using an α value of 0.15, employ exponential smoothing to update $\hat{a}$ and $\hat{b}$ and show the forecasts for weeks 6, 7, . . . , 16 made at the start of each of these periods. Also, what is the forecast, made at the end of week 15, of the demand in week 20?

4.8 Union Gas reports the following (normalized) figures for gas consumption by households in a metropolitan area of Ontario:

	Jan.	Feb.	Mar.	Apr.	May	June
1972	196	196	173	105	75	39
1973	227	217	197	110	88	51
1974	216	218	193	120	99	59
1975	228					

	July	Aug.	Sept.	Oct.	Nov.	Dec.
1972	13	20	37	73	108	191
1973	27	23	41	90	107	172
1974	33	37	59	95	128	201

a. Using a simple (single) exponential smoothing model (with $\alpha = 0.10$), determine the forecast for consumption in (1) February 1975 and (2) June 1976.

b. Do the same using the Winters seasonal smoothing model with $\alpha_{HW} = 0.20$, $\beta_{HW} = 0.05$, and $\gamma_{HW} = 0.10$. Use the first 2 years of data for initialization purposes.

c. Plot the demand data and the two sets of forecasts roughly to scale. Does there appear to be a point of abrupt change in the demand pattern? Discuss your results briefly.

4.9 For purposes of calculating the safety stock of a particular item, we are interested in having an estimate of the MAD of forecast errors. No historical forecasts are available, but historical monthly demand data for three years are available. An analyst on your staff has proposed the following procedure for estimating the MAD:

Step 1 Plot the three years of data.

Step 2 Fit the best straight line to it (either by eye or through a statistical fit).

Step 3 For each month find the absolute deviation

$$|e_t| = |x_t - \tilde{x}_t|$$

where x_t is the actual demand in month t and $\tilde{x}_t$ is the value read off the straight line (found in Step 2) at month t.

Step 4 MAD = average value of $|e_t|$ over the 36 months.

a. Discuss why the MAD found by the above procedure might be *lower* than that actually achievable by statistical forecasting.

b. Discuss why the MAD found by the above procedure might be substantially *higher* than that actually achievable by a forecasting procedure.

Hint: The use of diagrams may be helpful.

4.10 Compare the ability of the Trigg-Leach and Whybark adaptive smoothing methods to track the following time series of demands.

Month t	1	2	3	4	5	6
Demand x_t	281	226	239	287	290	265

Month t	7	8	9	10	11	12
Demand x_t	281	290	287	296	280	275

Assume $MAD_0 = 10$, $z_0 = 0$, $\hat{x}_{0,1} = 200$, $\omega = 0.1$, $\sigma_1 = 1.25$ MAD. Also simple exponential smoothing forecasts are made with $\alpha = 0.5$. Plot the three sets of forecasts, as well as actual demands, and discuss your results briefly.

4.11 In current times give an illustration of an item fitting into each of the following special classes not using the specific examples in the text (use your everyday experiences at work or elsewhere).

a. Limited history

b. Intermittent demand

c. Erratic demand

d. Replacement parts

e. Terminal demand

4.12 Suppose that the demand rate for an item could be modeled as a *continuous* linearly decreasing function of time:

$$x_t = a - bt \qquad a > 0, b > 0$$

where $t = 0$ is the present time. Compute an estimate of the all-time future requirements.

4.13 Suppose you have been hired by a company to install a forecasting system for about 5000 B items. You suggest the use of exponential smoothing and the manager to whom you report is not happy about this. He says "Exponential smoothing is nothing but a massaging of historical data. It takes no account of our pricing strategy (for example, special sales at certain times of the year), our competitors' actions, etc."

a. How would you respond to this criticism?

b. If the manager insisted on having pricing effects built into the forecasting model, briefly outline how you would proceed to do this, including what data you would attempt to obtain.

4.14 For Case C of MIDAS Corporation, draw a flowchart that summarizes all the different methods used by the company to develop forecasts for s.k.u.

a. Which s.k.u. are explicitly forecasted and which are not? Do you agree with their approach? (You may also wish to read Case D.)

b. Would you allow the Inventory Control Manager to continue to override explicit decision rules at his own discretion?

c. How do you react to the Inventory Control Manager's quote at the end of Case C? What action do you recommend?

d. Comment on the attempted computerization of forecasting procedures at MIDAS. Is the company ready for sophisticated methods?

4.15 Evaluate the forecasting procedures described in Case C of the MIDAS Corporation in terms of the discussion in Section 4.1. Do they have a good forecasting system?

REFERENCES

Adam, E. E., and R. J. Ebert (1976). "A Comparison of Human and Statistical Forecasting." *AIIE Transactions*, Vol. 8, pp. 120–127.

Anderson, O. D. (1976). *Time Series Analysis and Forecasting: The Box-Jenkins Approach.* Butterworths, London.

Anderson, O. D. (1977). "A First Class Cast of Forecasters at King's."*Operational Research Quarterly*, Vol. 28, No. 3ii, pp. 749–752.

Basu, S., and R. C. Schroeder (1977). "Incorporating Judgements in Sales Forecasts: Application of the Delphi Method at American Hoist & Derrick." *INTERFACES*, Vol. 7, No. 3, pp. 18–27.

Bates, J. M., and C. W. Granger (1969). "The Combination of Forecasts." *Operational Research Quarterly*, Vol. 20, No. 4, pp. 451–468.

Bell, P. (1981). "Adaptive Forecasting with Many Stockouts." *Journal of the Operational Research Society*, Vol. 32, No. 10, pp. 865–873.

Blagg, B., G. Brandenburg, R. Conti, D. Fogarty, T. Hoffman, R. Martins, J. Muir, P. Rosa, and T. Vollman (1980). *APICS Certification Program Study Guide and Review Course Outline.* American Production and Inventory Control Society, Falls Church, Virginia.

Bowker, A. H., and G. J. Lieberman (1972). *Engineering Statistics*, second edition. Prentice-Hall, Englewood Cliffs, New Jersey, Chapter 9.

Box, G. E. P., and G. Jenkins (1976). *Time Series Analysis; Forecasting and Control*, second edition. Holden-Day, San Francisco, California.

Brown, R. G. (1963). *Smoothing, Forecasting and Prediction.* Prentice-Hall, Englewood Cliffs, New Jersey, Chapter 9.

Brown, R. G. (1971). "Detection of Turning Points in a Time Series." *Decision Sciences*, Vol. 2, No. 4, pp. 383–403.

Brown, R. G. (1977). *Materials Management Systems.* John Wiley & Sons, New York.

Brown, R. G. (1981). "Confidence in All-Time Supply Forecasts." *Working Memorandum 181*, Materials Management Systems, Inc., Norwich, Vermont.

Brown, R. G. (1982). *Advanced Service Parts Inventory Control.* Materials Management Systems, Inc., Norwich, Vermont.

Bunn, D. W. (1977). "A Comparative Evaluation of the Outperformance and Minimum Variance Procedures for the Linear Synthesis of Forecasts." *Operational Research Quarterly*, Vol. 28, No. 3ii, pp. 653–662.

Burington, R. S., and D. C. May (1958). *Handbook of Probability and Statistics with Tables.* Handbook Publishers, Inc., Sandusky, Ohio.

Chambers, J. C., S. K. Mullick, and D. D. Smith (1971). "How to Choose the Right Forecasting Technique." *Harvard Business Review*, Vol. 49, pp. 45–74.

Chow, W. M. (1965). "Adaptive Control of the Exponential Smoothing Constant." *Journal of Industrial Engineering*, Vol. 16, No. 5, pp. 314–317.

Cleveland, W. P., and G. C. Tiao (1976). "Decomposition of Seasonal Time Series: A Model for the Census X-11 Program. *Journal of the American Statistical Association*, Vol. 71, pp. 581–587.

Cox, D. R., and H. D. Miller (1965). *The Theory of Stochastic Processes.* John Wiley & Sons, New York.

Croston, J. D. (1972). "Forecasting and Stock Control for Intermittent Demands." *Operational Research Quarterly*, Vol. 23, No. 3, pp. 289–303.

Dancer, R., and C. Gray (1977). "An Empirical Investigation of Constant and Adaptive Computer Forecasting Models for Inventory Control." *Decision Sciences*, Vol. 8, pp. 228–238.

Dickinson, J. P. (1973). "Some Statistical Results in the Combination of Forecasts." *Operational Research Quarterly*, Vol. 24, No. 2, pp. 253–260.

Dickinson, J. P. (1975). "Some Comments on the Combination of Forecasts." *Operational Research Quarterly*, Vol. 26, No. 1, pp. 205–210.

Domnick, F. (1977). "When to Order? How Much to Order? Two Basic Questions Answered Using the Class Seasonal Approach." *Production and Inventory Management*, Vol. 18, No. 2, pp. 48–55.

Eilon, S., and J. Elmaleh (1970). "Adaptive Limits in Inventory Control." *Management Science*, Vol. 16, No. 8, pp. B533–B548.

Ekern, S. (1981). "Adaptive Exponential Smoothing Revisited." *Journal of the Operational Research Society*, Vol. 32, No. 9, pp. 775–782.

Fildes, R. (1979). "Quantitative Forecasting—The State of the Art: Extrapolative Models." *Journal of the Operational Research Society*, Vol. 30, No. 8, pp. 691–710.

Fildes, R., and S. Howell (1979). "On Selecting a Forecasting Model." In *Forecasting* (S. Makridakis and S. L. Wheelwright, Editors), Volume 12, Studies in the Management Sciences, North Holland, Amsterdam, pp. 297–312.

Flowers, A. D. (1980). "A Simulation Study of Smoothing Constant Limits for an Adaptive Forecasting System." *Journal of Operations Management*, Vol. 1, No. 2, pp. 85–94.

Fortuin, L. (1980). "The All-Time Requirements of Spare Parts for Service After Sales—Theoretical Analysis and Practical Results." *International Journal of Operations & Production Management*, Vol. 1, No. 1, pp. 59–70.

Gardner, E. S., and D. G. Dannenbring (1980). "Forecasting with Exponential Smoothing: Some Guidelines for Model Selection." *Decision Sciences*, Vol. 11, No. 2, pp. 370–383.

Garwood, R. D. (1980). "Why Can't Sales Forecast?" Third Issue of 1979–80 *Hot List*, R. D. Garwood, Inc., Atlanta, Georgia.

Gilchrist, W. (1976). *Statistical Forecasting*. John Wiley & Sons, London.

Goodman, M. L. (1974). "A Look at Higher-Order Exponential Smoothing for Forecasting." *Operations Research*, Vol. 22, No. 4, pp. 880–888.

Gotwals, E. P. (1981). "Evaluation of Forecast Methods in an Inventory Management System—An Empirical Study." *Technical Report TR 81-5*, U.S. Army Inventory Research Office, Philadelphia.

Hamburg, M. (1977). *Statistical Analysis for Decision Making*, second edition. Harcourt Brace Jovanovich, New York, pp. 365–384, 450–456, 468–477.

Harrison, P. J. (1965). "Short-Term Sales Forecasting." *Applied Statistics*, Vol. 14, pp. 102–139.

Harrison, P. J. (1967). "Exponential Smoothing and Short-Term Sales Forecasting." *Management Science*, Vol. 13, No. 11, pp. 821–842.

Harrison, P. J., and O. Davies (1964). "The Use of Cumulative Sum (CUSUM) Techniques for the Control of Product Demand." *Operations Research*, Vol. 12, No. 2, pp. 325–333.

Harrison, P. J., and C. F. Stevens (1971). "A Bayesian Approach to Short Term Forecasting." *Operational Research Quarterly*, Vol. 22, pp. 341–362.

Harrison, P. J. and C. F. Stevens (1976). "Bayesian Forecasting." *Journal of the Royal Statistical Society*, Vol. B38, pp. 205–228.

Hausman, W. H., and R. M. Kirby (1970). "Estimating Standard Deviations for Inventory Control." *AIIE Transactions*, Vol. 11, No. 1, pp. 78–81.

Holt, C. C. (1957). "Forecasting Seasonals and Trends by Exponentially Weighted Moving Averages." *O.N.R. Memorandum No. 52*, Carnegie Institute of Technology, Pittsburgh, Pennsylvania.

Johnson, L. A., and D. C. Montgomery (1974). *Operations Research in Production Planning, Scheduling and Inventory Control*. John Wiley & Sons, New York, Chapter 6.

Johnston, F. R. (1980). "An Interactive Stock Control System with a Strategic Management Role." *Journal of the Operational Research Society*, Vol. 31, No. 12, pp. 1069–1084.

Johnston, F. R., and P. J. Harrison (1980). "The Application of Forecasting in the Alcoholic Drinks Industry." *Journal of the Operational Research Society*, Vol. 31, No. 8, pp. 699–709.

Kallina, C. (1978). "Development and Implementation of a Simple Short Range Forecasting Model—A Case Study." *INTERFACES*, Vol. 8, No. 3, pp. 32–41.

Kaplan, A. J. (1974). "Estimation of Demand Variability Parameters." *IRO Report No. 183*, USAMC Inventory Research Office, Frankford Arsenal, Philadelphia.

Keilson, J., and P. Kubat (1984). "Parts and Service Demand Distribution Generated by Primary Production. To appear in *European Journal of Operational Research*.

Kendrick, C. (1961). "Estimation of Service Requirements for Production Purposes." *International Journal of Production Research*, Vol. 1, pp. 1–12.

Landau, E. (1976). "On the Non-Statistical Aspects of Statistical Forecasting. *Proceedings of the 19th Annual International Conference of the American Production and Inventory Control Society*, pp. 294–304.

Lewandowski, R. (1979). *La Prévision à Court Terme*. Dunod, Paris.

Lewis, C. D. (1978). "The Versatility of the Exponential Smoother's Portfolio of Skills." *Production and Inventory Management*, Vol. 19, No. 2, pp. 53–66.

Lewis, C. D. (1982). *Industrial and Business Forecasting Methods*. Butterworths, London.

Mabert, V. A. (1975). "Statistical versus Sales Force–Executive Opinion Short Range Forecasts: A Time Series Analysis Case Study." Working Paper, Krannert Graduate School, Purdue University, West Lafayette, Indiana.

Maddala, G. (1977). *Econometrics*. McGraw-Hill, New York, Chapter 11.

Makridakis, S., A. Andersen, R. Carbone, R. Fildes, M. Hibon, R. Lewandowski, J. Newton, E. Parzen, and R. Winkler (1982). "The Accuracy of Extrapolation (Time Series) Methods: Results of a Forecasting Competition." *Journal of Forecasting*, Vol. 1, pp. 111–153.

Makridakis, S., and S. C. Wheelwright (1979a). "Forecasting: Framework and Overview." In *Forecasting* (S. Makridakis and S. C. Wheelwright, Editors), Volume 12, Studies in the Management Sciences, North Holland, Amsterdam, pp. 1–15.

Makridakis, S., and S. C. Wheelwright (1979b). "Forecasting the Future and the Future of Forecasting." In *Forecasting* (S. Makridakis and S. C. Wheelwright, Editors), Volume 12, Studies in the Management Sciences, North Holland, Amsterdam, pp. 329–352.

McClain, J. O. (1974). "Dynamics of Exponential Smoothing with Trend Seasonal Terms." *Management Science*, Vol. 20, No. 9, pp. 1300–1304.

McClain, J. O., and L. J. Thomas (1973). "Response Variance Tradeoffs in Adaptive Forecasting." *Operations Research*, Vol. 21, No. 2, pp. 554–568.

McKenzie, E. (1978). "The Monitoring of Exponentially Weighted Forecasts." *Journal of the Operational Research Society*, Vol. 29, No. 5, pp. 449–458.

McLaughlin, R. L. (1979). "Organizational Forecasting: Its Achievements and Limitations." In *Forecasting* (S. Makridakis and S. C. Wheelwright, Editors), Volume 12, Studies in the Management Sciences, North Holland, Amsterdam, pp. 17–30.

McLeavey, D. W., T. S. Lee, and E. E. Adam (1981). "An Empirical Evaluation of Individual Item Forecasting Models." *Decision Sciences*, Vol. 12, No. 4, pp. 708–714.

Montgomery, D. C. (1970). "Adaptive Control of Exponential Smoothing Parameters by Evolutionary Operation." *AIIE Transactions*, Vol. 2, No. 3, pp. 268–269.

Muir, J. W. (1980). "Forecasting Items with Irregular Demand." *Proceedings of the 23rd Annual International Conference of the American Production and Inventory Control Society*, pp. 143–145.

Muir, J. W., and T. Newberry (1981). "Management's Role in a Forecasting System." *Proceedings of the 24th Annual International Conference of the American Production and Inventory Control Society*, pp. 16–19.

Muller, H., W. Bruggeman and S. de Samblanckx (1977). "Forecasting Accuracy, Cost Minimization and Investment Optimization in Inventory Management." MI 76/1-40, Rijksuniversiteit, Gent, Belgium.

Newbold, P. (1979). "Time-Series Model Building and Forecasting: A Survey." *In Forecasting* (S. Makridakis and S. C. Wheelwright, Editors), Volume 12, Studies in the Management Sciences, North Holland, Amsterdam, pp. 59–73.

Peterson, R. (1969). "A Note on the Determination of Optimal Forecasting Strategy." *Management Science*, Vol. 16, No. 4, pp. B165–B169.

Peterson, R., and J. G. D. Lamont (1972). "On the Consolidation of Competing Forecasts." *Proceedings of the 15th Annual International Conference of the American Production and Inventory Control Society*, pp. 1–11.

Ritchie, E., and P. Wilcox (1977). "Renewal Theory Forecasting for Stock Control." *European Journal of Operational Research*, Vol. 1, pp. 90–93.

Roberts, S. D., and R. Reed (1969). "The Development of a Self-Adaptive Forecasting Technique." *AIIE Transactions*, Vol. 1, No. 4, pp. 314–322.

Roberts, S. D., and C. D. Whybark (1974). "Adaptive Forecasting Techniques." *International Journal of Production Research*, Vol. 12, No. 6, pp. 635–645.

Rosenman, B. B. (1984). "Evaluating Forecasting Models." To appear in *INTERFACES*.

Smith, B. T. (1978). *Focus Forecasting: Computer Techniques for Inventory Control*. CBI Publishing Company, Inc., Boston, Massachusetts.

Steece, B., and S. Wood (1979). "An ARIMA-Based Methodology for Forecasting in a Multi-Item Environment." In *Forecasting* (S. Makridakis and S. C. Wheelwright, Editors), Volume 12, Studies in the Management Sciences, North Holland, Amsterdam, pp. 167–187.

Stevens, C. F. (1974). "On the Variability of Demand for Families of Items." *Operational Research Quarterly*, Vol. 25, No. 3, pp. 411–419.

Trigg, D. W. (1964). "Monitoring a Forecast System." *Operational Research Quarterly*, Vol. 15, pp. 271–274.

Trigg, D. W., and A. G. Leach (1967). "Exponential Smoothing with an Adaptive Response Rate." *Operational Research Quarterly*, Vol. 18, No. 1, pp. 53–59.

Tukey, J. (1971). *Exploratory Data Analysis, Volume III*. Addison-Wesley, Reading, Massachusetts.

Wecker, W. (1978). "Predicting Demand from Sales Data in the Presence of Stockouts." *Management Science*, Vol. 24, No. 10, pp. 1043–1054.

Whybark, D. C. (1973). "A Comparison of Adaptive Forecasting Techniques." *Logistic Transportation Review*, Vol. 9, No. 1, pp. 13–26.

Winters, P. R. (1960). "Forecasting Sales by Exponentially Weighted Moving Averages." *Management Science*, Vol. 6, pp. 324–342.

PART TWO

TRADITIONAL REPLENISHMENT SYSTEMS FOR MANAGING INDIVIDUAL-ITEM INVENTORIES

In the first part of this book we have laid the groundwork in terms of specifying the environment, goals, constraints, relevant costs, and forecast inputs of production/inventory decisions. Now we turn our attention to the detailed logic for short-range decision making in situations of a strictly inventory (that is, nonproduction) nature. We are concerned primarily with decision making on an individual item or stock keeping unit (s.k.u.) basis. However, as discussed in Chapter 3, aggregate considerations will often still play a crucial role in the following manner: in most of the decision rules there is a parameter whose value can be implicitly specified through selecting an operating point on an exchange curve that shows the aggregate consequences (across a population of inventoried items) of using different values of this policy parameter. Management can select the aggregate operating point, thus implying a value of the parameter that is to be used in the item by item decision rules.

Within this part of the book we deal with the so-called B items which, as we have seen earlier, comprise the majority of items in a typical inventory situation. Unlike for C items, which will be handled in Part Three, there are usually significant savings to be derived from the use of a reasonably sophisticated control system. On the other hand, the potential savings per inventoried item are not of the same order of magnitude as those realizable for individual A items. The combination of these two factors dictates that a hybrid system be used that combines the relative advantages of human and machine. The management by exception control system, often automated (possibly manual rather than computerized, depending on the total usage volume of the items involved), that we describe is reasonably sophisticated, requiring human intervention on a relatively infrequent basis. Such automated control systems, when applied in practice, have resulted in significant improvements in the control of B items.

In Chapter 5 we first answer the question of how much to replenish in the context of an *approximately level demand pattern*. Next, in Chapter 6, we consider the more general situation of a demand pattern, where the mean or forecast demand changes appreciably with time, an obvious example being that of a seasonal demand pattern. The relaxation to this more general case considerably complicates the analysis. Therefore, the suggested decision system is based on a reasonable heuristic decision rule.

Chapter 7 is concerned, for the most part, with the situation where the *average* demand rate stays approximately level with time, but there is a random component present; that is, the mean or forecast demand stays constant or changes slowly with time, but there definitely are appreciable forecast errors. When demand is known only in a probabilistic sense, two additional questions must be answered: "How often should we review the stock status?" "When should we place a replenishment order?"

All of the material in Chapters 5 through 7 ignores possible benefits of coordinating the replenishments of two or more items. We return to this important topic in Chapters 11 and 12 of Part Four.

We begin with Case D of the MIDAS Corporation. Its contents should be kept in mind while reading Chapters 5 to 7.

Case D

MIDAS CANADA CORPORATION*

The company's stated inventory control policy was "to have zero stockouts." Since customers could obtain almost equivalent products in most cases from a competitor, it was the opinion of the President of MIDAS Canada that every effort should be made to avoid back orders or stockouts. Air freight at a cost of approximately $2.50 per kilogram was sometimes used to meet the demand from an important large customer. However, if a large customer placed an unusually large order without prior warning that depleted the available stocks, then it was the company's policy to bill him for part of the costs of air freight involved. On occasion MIDAS filled an important customer's order by supplying a competitor's film at below retail price, thereby absorbing a loss on the sale.

On slow-moving items company sales personnel were instructed to make no delivery promises until they had checked with the Inventory Control Manager. Some customers were asked to sign a noncancellable purchase order and, if their credit rating was poor, a deposit was required before an order was accepted. The Inventory Control Manager tried to order all slow-moving items directly from Germany and thereby keep a minimum of inventory on hand of slow-moving s.k.u.

LEAD TIMES

The length of the lead time for receiving delivery depended on whether the plant in Germany produced the particular item for stock or to order. Because films tended to deteriorate over time, only the more popular items were manufactured for stock. Parts for Midamatics and items sold by the Industrial and Professional Products Divisions, which were stocked by the plant in Germany, arrived at the warehouse 8 to 12 weeks after an order was placed. Made-to-order items took longer, with the lead time varying from 12 to 16 weeks. The plant in Germany grouped orders whenever possible and shipped them via specially designed containers that could be unloaded directly from a cargo ship onto a railroad flatcar in Halifax, Nova Scotia, and then delivered directly to the MIDAS warehouse in Toronto, Ontario.

---

*The MIDAS cases describe actual decision systems that are based on consulting experiences of the authors. They do not describe the situation at any single company, but are in fact a compendium of actual situations that have been compressed into the environment of a single firm and industry for illustrative purposes. The cases are not intended as presentations of either effective or ineffective ways of handling administrative problems.

Superchrome was shipped from Germany by air cargo and arrived at the plant 2 to 4 weeks after an order was placed, depending on the work load at the manufacturing plant. Superchrome products were made to order.

All X-ray films were produced to order and received special handling throughout the production-shipping process. As a result, the lead time for these s.k.u. was shorter, varying from 8 to 10 weeks. The remaining products sold by the X-ray Division had lead times similar to the Professional and Industrial Products described above. For chemicals, an additional one to two weeks during some months of the year had to be allowed, in addition to the 8 to 12 weeks lead time for delivery from Germany, so that bulk shipments could be repackaged appropriately.

Takashi products arrived through the port of Vancouver on the west coast of Canada. Most items ordered by MIDAS were stocked by the Japanese manufacturer and arrived from 10 to 12 weeks after an order was placed. Because delicate optical instruments were involved, extra care was taken throughout shipment to minimize breakage. Nevertheless, some breakage inevitably occurred and one could never be sure of the exact quantity of goods that arrived safely.

The remaining miscellaneous items and parts, mostly used by the Assembly Plant and which were obtained domestically in Canada, had lead times that varied from zero to two weeks. Many items were available on the same day from suppliers located in the Toronto area, provided MIDAS sent a truck to pick up the goods.

Lead times for assembled Midamatics and Stabilization Processors had been always less than 2 weeks during 1984. Because of the increasing demand for both types of equipment, the company was starting to build some Processors for finished goods inventory during slack periods.

THE DETERMINATION OF ORDER QUANTITIES AND ORDER POINTS

Once a month, the Inventory Control Manager and the Comptroller, along with three assistants, calculated by hand, during "a two-day marathon session," for all but the most expensive s.k.u. and the parts used to assemble Processors and Midamatics, the total sales over the most recent 5-month period. The total sales figure over the last 5-month period became the order-up-to-quantity (called the "Maximum" by the Company). Whenever an order was placed the quantity ordered was taken as the difference between the "Maximum" and the current balance available (see Figures 1 and 2, Case B). Eighty percent of the "Maximum" quantity was then taken as the order point (called the "Minimum" by the Company). Such systems are commonly referred to by practitioners as Min/Max Inventory Control Systems. (See Table 1.)

The newly computed Min/Max quantities were compared to the ordering rules computed during the previous month and adjustments were made, when deemed appropriate, to Travel Cards of individual s.k.u. (see the top right-hand corner of Figure 2, Case B). The Inventory Control Manager did not blindly follow the 5-month rule described above. He sometimes modified the order-up-to-quantities and order points because of some future events that he knew would take place.

TABLE 1 Inventory Control Work Sheet

s.k.u.	Month 1	Month 2	Sales Month 3	Month 4	Month 5	Maximum = 5 Month Total	Order Point = 0.8 × Maximum
EDM-008	52	48	36	39	65	240	192
PMF-298	8	12	14	18	23	75	60
PSF-107	402	368	374	396	376	1916	1533
IMM-177	159	127	130	169	172	757	606
.	.	.	.	.	.	.	.
.	.	.	.	.	.	.	.
.	.	.	.	.	.	.	.

Parts for the assembly of Midamatics and Processors were not ordered in the above manner. The Inventory Control Manager tried to order the exact number of parts required each month to meet the planned assembly schedule. The parts for assembly and for repairs were kept physically separate. The Inventory Control Manager explained that:

Repair personnel used to be lax in keeping track of spare parts they needed. They felt that they could always dip into the stock of parts which had been ordered for assembly if they ran short. By doing this they upset our assembly schedules several times. By separating the two inventories, we put a stop to that practice. Although I must admit that now we sometimes borrow from the stock of spare parts to meet unexpected demand for our assembled end-products. On occasion, because of this practice, we have been a little short of spare parts. I've often wondered whether there was any way of combining the inventory for both types of parts so that there would be enough safety stock to meet emergencies from either of the two sources.

For very expensive items, such as all X-ray and Superchrome films, the Inventory Control Manager personally placed orders once a month. He tried to order only enough items to meet actual sales for the one-month period, one lead time period ahead. In most cases these orders were in response to noncancellable purchase orders placed by customers, or commitments made to him over the telephone by customers he deemed dependable. He usually ordered 10 to 20 percent more than the number of units he was able to identify through purchase orders or commitments to meet unexpected demand.

PROPOSED CHANGES TO EXISTING ORDERING PROCEDURES

By the Summer of 1984 MIDAS Canada had decided to explore the possibility of setting up computerized procedures for controlling inventories, for generating more timely sales reports, and for helping to reduce the amount of manual clerical accounting procedures currently in use. The Comptroller took this opportunity to review the current ordering rules that were based on the total sales during the 5 most recent months' sales, as explained above. The Comptroller had always felt that the total dollar investment in inventories was too high. He also agreed with the Vice-President of Sales that the Company had failed to meet its stated policy of "zero stockouts." Based on a number of investigations and calculations, he proposed the new system of calculating order quantities and order points described in Figure 1.

MIDAS CANADA CORPORATION

Inter-Office Memo

To: Inventory Control Manager

From: The Comptroller's Office

I have made a study of our present method of calculating Order Points and it seems to me that it has the following weaknesses:

1. We use 5 months of historical sales as a basis for our planning. That means that what happened 4 or 5 months ago weighs as heavily on what we order, as what happened last month.

2. The varying lead times of different products are not taken into account.

However it does appear to me that in the majority of cases these two points do offset each other, except that we seem to have too many overstocks of slow movers and understocks of fast movers. I propose that until further notice the following method be adopted for calculating Maximums. We have agreed that our products should at all times carry a 6 weeks' buffer stock. In addition we allow for 4 weeks of off-take inventory* that gets used up during the reorder cycle, for a total of 10 weeks inventory. Therefore, for an item that has, on the average, a lead time of 8 weeks the factor becomes (assuming 3 months = 13 weeks):

$$\frac{10 + 8}{13} \times \text{(3 months sales)} = 138\% \times \text{(3 months sales)}$$

Similarly for 10 week and 12 week lead times the factors become respectively 154% and 169%.

Order Points (Minimums) should continue to be calculated as being 80% of Maximum. The Maximum for most of our products under this proposed system will be 20 weeks sales, of which the 4 week reorder cycle is 20%, leaving 80% of Maximum as our Order Point just as before.

*By off-take inventory the Comptroller presumably meant cycle stock.

FIGURE 1

The Inventory Control Manager was asked to comment on the Comptroller's proposal:

As far as I am concerned, one set of rules is as good as another as long as I am allowed the freedom to modify the calculated order quantities when I need to. I think the proposed change will probably be an improvement over our previous methods because it takes account of lead times. But it does not solve a big problem I face each quarter—which is making sure that all the individual orders placed add up to the total I committed the Company to in the Purchase Budgets which I submitted to the production planners in Germany.*

---

*For a description of Purchase Budgets, see Case C.

CHAPTER 5

An Order Quantity Decision System for the Case of Approximately Level Demand

In this chapter we are concerned with the question of how large a replenishment quantity to use under rather stable conditions (any changes in parameters occur slowly over time). Furthermore, there is relatively little or no uncertainty concerning the level of demand. This simplified situation is a reasonable approximation of reality on certain occasions. However, more important, the results obtained turn out to be major components of the decision systems when parameters change with time or demand is probabilistic. In addition, the intention is to *not* have a completely automated replenishment system. Instead, a manual override capability is essential for several reasons, including (1) provision for the incorporation of factors not included in the underlying mathematical model and (2) the cultivation of a sense of accountability and responsibility on the part of the decision makers.

In Section 5.1 we discuss the rather severe assumptions needed in the derivation of the economic order quantity (EOQ). This is followed in Section 5.2 by the actual derivation. In Section 5.3 we show that the total relevant costs are not seriously affected by somewhat large deviations of the replenishment quantity away from the minimizing value. This robust property of the economic order quantity is important from an operational standpoint. Section 5.4 is concerned with aids, such as tables and graphs, in which items are grouped into broad categories to make implementation easier, particularly in a noncomputerized system. The important situation of quantity discounts is handled in Section 5.5. This is followed, in Section 5.6, by the incorporation of the effects of inflation. Section 5.7 deals with several types of limitations on replenishment quantities ignored in the earlier development of the EOQ. Other potentially important factors are incorporated in Section 5.8. The derivation of the basic EOQ includes two cost parameters: (1) the carrying charge r and (2) the fixed cost per replenishment A. As discussed in Chapter 3, one or both of the values of these parameters may be explicitly evaluated or may be implicitly specified through looking at the aggregate consequences of using different values of r (or A/r) and then selecting a suitable aggregate operating point, which implies an r (or A/r) value. Section 5.9 shows how to develop the exchange curves, a crucial step in this latter (implicit) approach.

5.1 ASSUMPTIONS LEADING TO THE BASIC ECONOMIC ORDER QUANTITY (EOQ)

Let us first stipulate the assumptions. Some of these may appear to be far removed from reality but, as we will see, the EOQ forms an important building block in the majority of decision systems that we advocate.The reader is asked to bear with us since considerable discussion will be directed to this point later in this and subsequent chapters.

1. The demand rate is constant and deterministic (that is, the item is in the mature stage of the product life cycle, as discussed in Section 2.3 of Chapter 2).
2. The order quantity need not be an integral number of units, and there are no minimum or maximum restrictions on its size.
3. The unit variable cost does not depend on the replenishment quantity; in particular, there are no discounts in either the unit purchase cost or the unit transportation cost.
4. The cost factors do not change appreciably with time; in particular, inflation is at a low level.
5. The item is treated entirely independently of other items; that is, benefits from joint review or replenishment do not exist or are simply ignored.
6. The replenishment lead time is of zero duration; as we will see later, extension to a *known* nonzero duration creates no problem.
7. No shortages are allowed.
8. The *entire* order quantity is delivered at the same time.

All of these assumptions will be relaxed later in this chapter or elsewhere in the book. For example, situations where the demand rate changes appreciably with time (that is, the first assumption is violated) will be treated in Chapters 6 and 9. However, in the derivation of the fundamental version of the economic order quantity, it is necessary that they be satisfied.

5.2 DERIVATION OF THE ECONOMIC ORDER QUANTITY

In determining the appropriate order quantity, we use the criterion of minimization of total relevant costs, relevant in the sense that they are truly affected by the choice of the order quantity. We emphasize that in some situations there may be certain, perhaps intangible, relevant costs that are *not* included in the model to be discussed. This is one of the reasons for our mention of the need for a manual override capability. We also remind the reader that cost minimization need not be the only appropriate criterion; for example, Buzacott (1979) discusses viewing the holding of an item in inventory as an investment and hence making the ordering decision to maximize an appropriate measure of the performance of the investment.

Returning to the consideration of costs, as discussed in Chapter 3, there are five fundamental categories of costs:

1. Basic production or purchase costs
2. Inventory carrying costs
3. Costs of insufficient capacity in the short run
4. Control system costs
5. Costs of changing work force sizes and production rates

The fifth category is not relevant for the item-by-item control which we are considering here. Also, given that we are restricting our attention to a particular type of control system (an order quantity system), the control system costs are not influenced by the exact value of the order quantity. Hence, they need not be taken into account when selecting the value of the order quantity.

Because of the deterministic nature of the demand, the only cost relevant to the third category would be that which is caused by the decision maker deliberately choosing to run short of inventory before making a replenishment. For now, we ignore the possibility of allowing planned shortages.

Therefore, we are left with only the first two types of costs being relevant to the economic selection of the replenishment quantity.

Before proceeding further, let us introduce some notation:

Q—the replenishment order quantity, in units.

A—the fixed cost component (independent of the magnitude of the replenishment quantity) incurred with each replenishment, in dollars. (This cost component has been discussed at length in Chapter 3.)

v—the unit variable cost of the item. This is not the selling price of the item, but rather its value (immediately *after* the replenishment operation now under consideration) in terms of raw materials and value added through processing and assembly operations. The dimensions are \$/unit.

r—the carrying charge, the cost of having one dollar of the item tied up in inventory for a unit time interval (normally one year); that is, the dimensions are \$/\$/unit time. (Again, this cost component was discussed at length in Chapter 3.)

D—the demand rate of the item, in units/unit time.

TRC(Q)—the total relevant costs per unit time, that is, the sum of those costs per unit time which can be influenced by the order quantity Q. The dimensions are \$/unit time.

Because the parameters involved are assumed to not change with time, it is reasonable (and, indeed, mathematically optimal) to think in terms of using the same order quantity, Q, each time that a replenishment is made. Furthermore, because (1) demand is deterministic, (2) the replenishment lead time is zero, and (3) we have chosen to not allow planned shortages, it is clear that each replenishment will be made when the inventory level is exactly at zero. A graphical portrayal of the inventory level with time is shown in Figure 5.1.

Note that the time between replenishments is given by Q/D, the time to deplete Q units at a rate of D units per unit time. (D is the usage over a period of time; normally 12 months is used.) Therefore, the number of replenishments per unit time is D/Q. Associated with each of these is a replenishment cost given by $A + Qv$, where one of our assumptions ensures that the unit variable cost v does not depend on Q. Therefore, the replenishment costs per unit time (C_r) are given by

$$C_r = (A + Qv)D/Q$$

or

$$C_r = AD/Q + Dv \tag{5.1}$$

The second component in Eq. 5.1 is seen to be independent of Q and, hence, can have no effect on the determination of the best Q value. (It represents the constant acquisition cost of the item per unit time which cannot be affected by the magnitude of the order quantity.) Therefore, it will be neglected in future discussions.[1]

As discussed in Chapter 3, the common method of determining the costs of carrying inventory over a unit time period is through the relation

$$C_c = \bar{I}vr$$

where $\bar{I}$ is the average inventory level, in units. The average height of the sawtooth diagram of Figure 5.1 is $Q/2$. Therefore,

$$C_c = Qvr/2 \tag{5.2}$$

[1]The Dv component will be of crucial interest in Section 5.5 where, in the case of quantity discounts, v depends on Q.

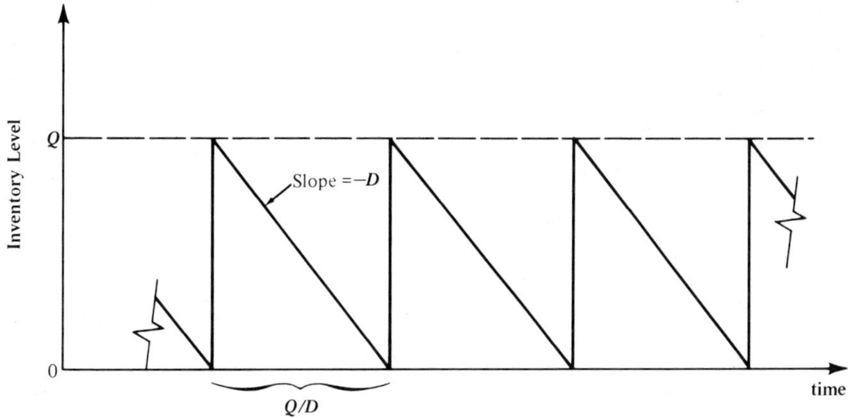

FIGURE 5.1 Behavior of Inventory Level with Time

Combining Eqs. 5.1 and 5.2 and neglecting the Dv term, as discussed above, we have that the total relevant costs per unit time are given by

$$\mathrm{TRC}(Q) = Qvr/2 + AD/Q \tag{5.3}$$

The two components of Eq. 5.3 and their total are plotted for an illustrative numerical example in Figure 5.2. It is seen that the replenishment costs per unit time decrease as Q increases (there are fewer replenishments), whereas the carrying costs increase with Q (a larger Q means a larger average inventory). The sum of the two costs is a u-shaped function with a minimum which can be found in a number of ways. (Adding the neglected Dv term would simply shift every point on the total cost curve up by Dv; hence, the location of the minimum would not change.) One convenient way to find the minimum is to use the necessary condition that the tangent or slope of the curve is zero at the minimum:[2]

$$\frac{d\,\mathrm{TRC}(Q)}{dQ} = 0$$

[2]A second condition for a minimum, namely, that the second derivative is positive, is also satisfied:

$$\frac{d^2\mathrm{TRC}(Q)}{dQ^2} = 2AD/Q^3 > 0 \qquad \text{for any } Q > 0$$

that is,

$$\frac{vr}{2} - \frac{AD}{Q^2} = 0$$

$$Q_{\text{opt}} \quad \text{or} \quad \text{EOQ} = \sqrt{\frac{2AD}{vr}} \tag{5.4}$$

This is the economic order quantity (also known as the Wilson lot size). This is one of the earliest and most well-known results of inventory theory (see, for example, Mennell, 1961). Substituting the equation for the EOQ back into Eq. 5.3, we find that the two cost components are equal at the EOQ and we obtain the simple and useful result

$$\text{TRC(EOQ)} = \sqrt{2ADvr} \tag{5.5}$$

It should be emphasized that the equality of the two cost components ($Qvr/2$ and AD/Q) at the point where their sum is minimized is a very special property of the particular cost functions considered here; it certainly does not hold in general.

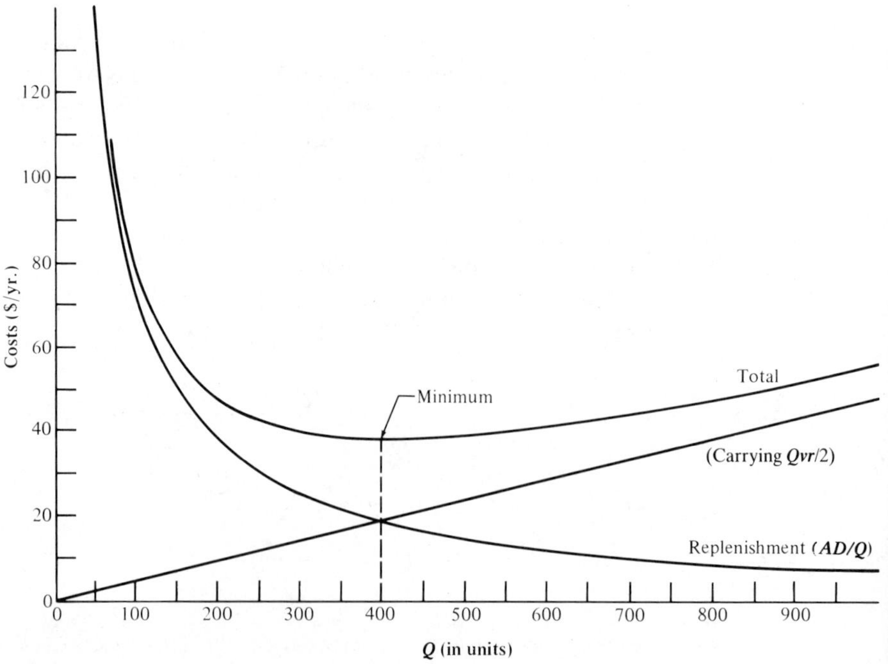

FIGURE 5.2 Costs as Functions of the Replenishment Quantity

The economic order quantity minimizes the total relevant costs under a given set of circumstances. It may in fact be more appropriate to *first* find ways of driving down the fixed cost A or the carrying charge r. This would lower the whole total cost curve in Figure 5.2. This is part of the Japanese "Just-in-Time" system (discussed in Chapter 2) in which A is reduced as much as possible. Also note from Eq. 5.4 that a lower A value will reduce the EOQ and thus the average inventory level.

The EOQ can also be expressed as a time supply, for example, as the number of months of demand that it will satisfy. This time supply, T_{EOQ}, is given by

$$T_{\text{EOQ}} = \frac{12\text{EOQ}}{D} = \sqrt{\frac{288A}{rDv}} \tag{5.6}$$

MIDAS' new decision rules suggested by the comptroller (see Case D) imply a replenishment quantity

$$Q = (2 + 0.2L)D/52$$

where L is the replenishment lead time, in weeks. Expressed in months of supply, this is

$$T_Q = \frac{12Q}{D} = \frac{3}{13}(2 + 0.2L)$$

Ignoring for now the dependence on the value of L, this says that MIDAS' decision rule would lead to items having the same time supply of replenishment even if they had different values of A, D, or v. The EOQ result of Eq. 5.6 shows that the time supply should depend on these factors (in fact, only items having the same value of the ratio A/Dv should have the same time supply); therefore, there is room for improvement over MIDAS' rule, the latter not having been developed from explicit cost considerations. Note that Eq. 5.4 illustrates, among other points, that the preferred order quantity goes up as the square root of demand rather than being directly proportional to the D value.

We can also convert the EOQ to an implied turnover ratio (annual demand rate divided by the average inventory level):

$$TR = \frac{D}{\bar{I}} = \frac{D}{\text{EOQ}/2} = \sqrt{\frac{2Dvr}{A}} \tag{5.7}$$

a result which is again seen to depend on the individual item factors D, v, and A. In particular, all other things remaining constant, we see that the turnover ratio increases in proportion to the square root of the demand rate, D.

Numerical Illustration (Illustrated in Figure 5.2)

Consider item EDM-073, a 3-ohm resistor used in the assembly of Midamatics. The demand for this item has been relatively level over time at a rate of 2400 units/yr. The unit variable cost of the resistor is \$0.40/unit and the fixed cost per replenishment is estimated to be \$3.20. Suppose further that an r value of 0.24 \$/\$/yr is appropriate to use. Then Eq. 5.4 gives

$$\text{EOQ} = \sqrt{\frac{2 \times \$3.20 \times 2400 \text{ units/yr}}{\$0.40/\text{unit} \times 0.24 \ \$/\$/\text{yr}}}$$

$$= 400 \text{ units, that is, a 2-month supply } (D/6).$$

Note that the dimensions appropriately cancel. This would not be the case, for example, if D and r were not defined on the same unit time basis.

Equation 5.5 reveals that the total relevant costs per year for the resistor are

$$\text{TRC(EOQ)} = \sqrt{2 \times \$3.20 \times 2400 \text{ units/yr} \times \$0.40/\text{unit} \times 0.24/\text{yr}}$$

$$= \$38.40/\text{yr}$$

A check on the computations is provided by noting that substitution of $Q = 400$ units in Eq. 5.3 gives a value of \$19.20/yr to each of the two terms.

For this item, which has a lead time of 8 weeks, the MIDAS decision rule gives

$$Q = (2 + 0.2 \times 8)2400/52$$

$$\simeq 166 \text{ units (or 0.83 months of supply)}$$

a value considerably below the EOQ. Substitution of $Q = 166$ into Eq. 5.3 reveals that the total relevant costs for item EDM-073 using the MIDAS rule are \$54.23/yr or some 41.2 percent higher than the costs incurred under use of the EOQ.

5.3 SENSITIVITY ANALYSIS

We now show that the costs are insensitive to errors in selecting the exact size of a replenishment quantity. Referring back to Figure 5.2, note that the total cost curve is quite shallow in the neighborhood of the EOQ. This indicates that reasonable sized deviations from the EOQ will have little impact on the total relevant costs incurred. Mathematically, suppose we use a quantity Q' which deviates from the EOQ according to the following relation:

$$Q' = (1 + p)\text{EOQ}$$

that is, $100p$ is the percentage deviation of Q' from the EOQ. The percentage cost penalty (PCP) for using Q' instead of the EOQ is given by

$$\text{PCP} = \frac{\text{TRC}(Q') - \text{TRC(EOQ)}}{\text{TRC(EOQ)}} \times 100$$

As shown in Section 1 of the Appendix to this chapter,

$$\text{PCP} = 50\left(\frac{p^2}{1+p}\right) \tag{5.8}$$

This expression is plotted in Figure 5.3. It is clear that even for values of p significantly different from zero the associated cost penalties are quite small.

To illustrate, consider the MIDAS item EDM-073 which was used as a numerical example in Section 5.2. The economic order quantity was found to be 400 units. Suppose that, instead, a value of 550 units was used; 550 is 1.375×400. Therefore, $p = 0.375$. Equation 5.8 or Figure 5.3 reveals that the percentage increase in total relevant costs is only 5.1 percent.

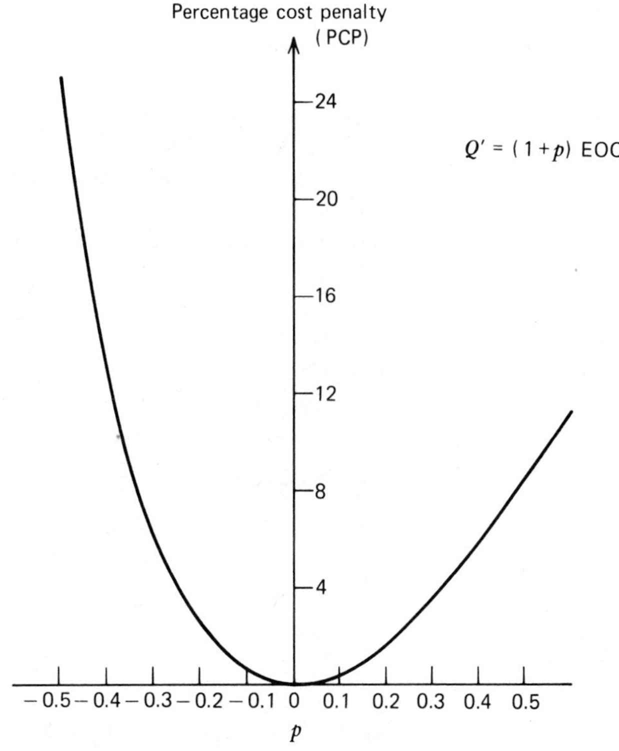

FIGURE 5.3 Cost Penalty for Using a Q' Value Different from the EOQ

The insensitivity of total costs to the exact value of Q used has two important implications. First, use of an incorrect value of Q can result from inaccurate estimates of one or more of the parameters D, A, v, and r which are used to calculate the EOQ.[3] The conclusion is that it is not worth making accurate estimates of these input parameters if considerable effort is involved; in most cases inexpensive, crude estimates should suffice. Second, certain order quantities may have additional appeal over the EOQ (for nonfinancial reasons or because of physical constraints which are not included in the basic EOQ model). The shallow nature of the total cost curve indicates that such values can be used provided that they are reasonably close to the EOQ. This seemingly trivial result is one of the important cornerstones of operational inventory control. Without this flexibility, implementable decision systems would be much more difficult to design. A detailed reference on sensitivity analysis is Juckler (1970).

5.4 IMPLEMENTATION AIDS

Despite the simplicity of the EOQ formula of Eq. 5.4, it may often be unreasonable to expect a stock clerk to compute the square root relationship manually and correctly on a consistent basis for many s.k.u. Consequently, several aids have been developed.

Special-purpose slide rules and nomographs (see Davis, 1963) are two types of aids. These are essentially mechanical devices. In addition, programmable calculators can be used to compute EOQ's as well as most of the more elaborate decision rules to be discussed in later sections of the book. References on the use of programmable calculators include Brout (1981), Krupp (1977), and Silver (1979).

It should be emphasized that, even if a computer is available, it may be advantageous, at least initially, to use either of two other types of aids—namely, graphical or tabular methods. Such aids are more intuitively appealing to a practitioner than is the output from a computer. Moreover, they involve the grouping of items into broad categories that also facilitates implementation. Thus, we now show illustrations of graphical and table lookup procedures.

5.4.1 Graphical Procedures

We illustrate only one of several possibilities. From Eq. 5.6 we have that the EOQ expressed as a time supply is given by

$$T_{\text{EOQ}} = \sqrt{\frac{2A}{r}}\sqrt{\frac{1}{Dv}}$$

[3]It is worth noting that the cost penalty can actually be zero even if D, A, v, and r are inaccurately estimated, as long as the resulting ratio AD/vr is correct. For example, if both D and v are overestimated by the same percentage, the resulting EOQ will be the same as that resulting from use of the correct D and v values.

in years (if D is measured in units/yr).

$$T_{\text{EOQ}} = \sqrt{\frac{288A}{r}}\sqrt{\frac{1}{Dv}} \tag{5.9}$$

in months (if D is measured in units/yr). For a given value of A, Eq. 5.9 can be plotted as a function of Dv (assuming r is known). Repeating for several values of A results in a number of curves, as indicated in Figure 5.4. (If more than one r value was possible, more than one set of curves would be necessary.) The steps in using such a graph are as follows:

1. Evaluate Dv for the item under consideration.
2. Look up this Dv value on the horizontal axis and move vertically to intersect the curve with the A value appropriate for the item.
3. Move across horizontally from the intersection point to read the T_{EOQ} (in months) on the vertical scale.
4. The EOQ is then given by

$$\text{EOQ} = \frac{D}{12}T_{\text{EOQ}}$$

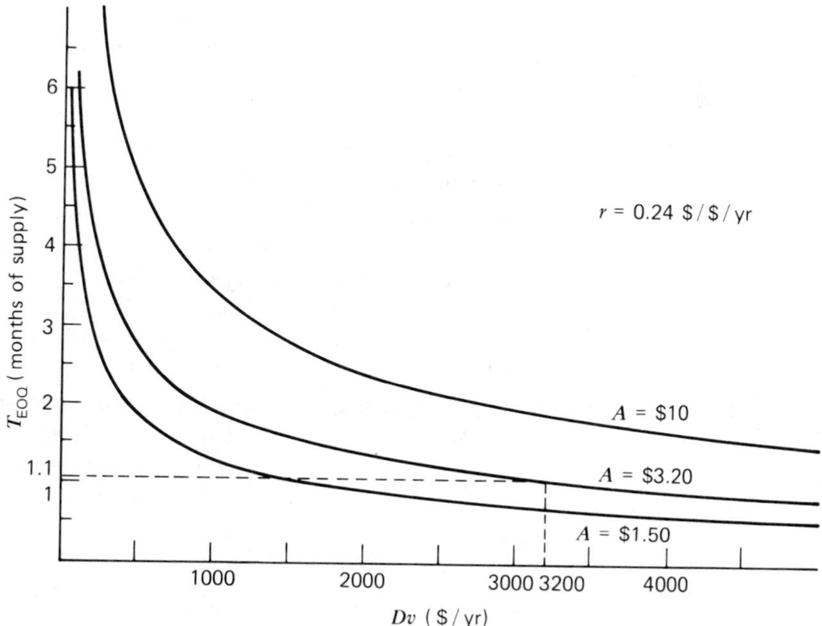

FIGURE 5.4 A Graphical Aid for Determining the EOQ

Numerical Illustration

Consider product ISF-017, a box of 100 sheets of $8\frac{1}{2}$ in. × 11 in. stabilization paper sold by the Industrial Products Division. This product has been observed to have a relatively constant demand rate (D) of 200 boxes/yr. The unit variable cost (v) is \$16/box. Also assume that it is reasonable to use A = \$3.20 and r = 0.24 \$/\$/yr.
We have

$$Dv = \$3200/\text{yr}$$

As shown in Figure 5.4, the intersection of a vertical line at \$3200/yr and the curve corresponding to an A value of \$3.20 results in a T_{EOQ} of approximately 1.1 months. The replenishment quantity is thus

$$\begin{aligned}\text{EOQ} &\simeq (200/12 \text{ boxes/mo}) \times 1.1 \text{ mo} \\ &= 18 \text{ boxes}\end{aligned}$$

This method gives the true EOQ value, at least to the accuracy of reading the graph; hence, the cost error, if any, is negligible.

5.4.2 Table Lookups

The basic idea here is that one value of the order quantity (perhaps expressed as a time supply) is used over a range of one or more of the parameters. There is an economic tradeoff involved. The larger the number of ranges, the smaller are the percentage cost penalties resulting from not using the exact EOQ. However, the difficulty of compiling and using the tables increases with the number of ranges involved. Further relevant discussion can be found in Chakravarty (1981), Crouch and Oglesby (1978), Donaldson (1981), and Maxwell and Singh (1983).

To illustrate let us consider a table usable for a set of MIDAS items having the same values of A and r. Suppose we deal with a group of items with A = \$3.20 and r = 0.24 \$/\$/yr. Furthermore, let us assume that management feels that the replenishment quantity of any item should be restricted to one of nine possible time supplies—namely, $\frac{1}{4}$, $\frac{1}{2}$, $\frac{3}{4}$, 1, 2, 3, 4, 5, 6, and 12 months. Table 5.1 shows the months of supply to use as a function of the annual dollar usage (Dv) of the item under consideration. A numerical illustration of the use of the table will be given shortly. First, let us discuss how such a table is constructed.

Use of T months of supply is equivalent to use of a quantity $Q = DT/12$ provided D is measured in units/year which are the most common units. Use of Eq. 5.3 gives

$$\text{TRC (using } T \text{ months)} = \frac{DTvr}{24} + \frac{12A}{T}$$

TABLE 5.1 Tabular Aid for Use of EOQ (For A = \$3.20 and r = 0.24 \$/\$/yr)

For Annual Dollar Usage (Dv) in This Range	Use This Number of Months of Supply
$30{,}720 \leq Dv$	$\frac{1}{4}$ ($\simeq$ 1 week)
$10{,}240 \leq Dv < 30{,}720$	$\frac{1}{2}$ ($\simeq$ 2 weeks)
$5{,}120 \leq Dv < 10{,}240$	$\frac{3}{4}$ ($\simeq$ 3 weeks)
$1{,}920 \leq Dv < 5{,}120$	1
$640 \leq Dv < 1{,}920$	2
$320 \leq Dv < 640$	3
$160 \leq Dv < 320$	4
$53 \leq Dv < 160$	6
$Dv < 53$	12

Now consider two *adjacent* allowable values of the months of supply, call them T_1 and T_2. Equating the total relevant costs using T_1 months with that using T_2 months, we obtain the value of Dv at which we are indifferent to using T_1 and T_2:

$$\frac{DT_1vr}{24} + \frac{12A}{T_1} = \frac{DT_2vr}{24} + \frac{12A}{T_2}$$

This reduces to

$$(Dv)_{\text{indifference}} = \frac{288A}{T_1T_2r}$$

To illustrate, for the given values of A and r in the MIDAS example, the indifference point for 1 month and 2 months is

$$(Dv)_{\text{indifference}} = \frac{288 \times 3.20}{1 \times 2 \times 0.24} = \$1{,}920/\text{yr}$$

In a similar fashion we can develop the rest of Table 5.1.

It should be emphasized that more than one value of A (and perhaps r) is likely to exist across a population of items. In such a case, a set of tables would be required, one for each of a number of possible A (and, perhaps, r) values.

Numerical Illustration

We use the same example as in the graphical case. Thus,

$$Dv = \$3200/\text{yr}$$

The table indicates that a 1-month supply should be used. Therefore.

$$Q = \frac{D}{12} = 16.7$$

say 17 boxes; that is, the film should be replenished in orders of 17 boxes. (The exact EOQ for this item is 18 boxes and the increase in costs for using 17 instead turns out to be only 0.3 percent.)

5.5 QUANTITY DISCOUNTS

A number of assumptions were made in Section 5.1 in order to derive the basic economic order quantity. One of the most severe of these was that the unit variable cost v did not depend on the replenishment quantity. In many practical situations quantity discounts (on basic purchase price or transportation costs) exist. We must be able to modify the EOQ to cope with these conditions.

We restrict our attention to the most common type of discount structure, namely, that of an "all-units" discount. (The less common situation of an *incremental* discount structure has been treated by Hadley and Whitin, 1963). For the case of a single breakpoint, the unit variable cost behaves as follows:

$$v = \begin{cases} v_0 & 0 \leq Q < Q_b \\ v_0(1 - d) & Q_b \leq Q \end{cases}$$

where v_0 is the basic unit cost without a discount and d is the discount expressed as a decimal fraction, given on *all* units when the replenishment quantity is equal to or greater than the breakpoint, Q_b. The *total* acquisition cost as a function of Q is shown in Figure 5.5. Note the discontinuity at the breakpoint.

Now, it is essential to include the Dv component in a cost expression which is to be used for determining the best replenishment quantity. Proceeding exactly as in Section 5.2, but retaining the Dv component, we end up with two expressions for the total relevant costs, that is, for $0 \leq Q < Q_b$,

$$\text{TRC}(Q) = Qv_0r/2 + AD/Q + Dv_0 \tag{5.10}$$

and for $Q_b \leq Q$

$$\text{TRC}(Q) = Qv_0(1 - d)r/2 + AD/Q + Dv_0(1 - d) \tag{5.11}$$

Although Eqs. 5.10 and 5.11 are valid for nonoverlapping regions of Q, it is useful, in deriving an algorithm for finding the best Q, to compare the two cost expressions at the same value of Q. A term-by-term comparison of the right-hand sides of the equations reveals that Eq. 5.11 gives a lower TRC (Q) than does Eq. 5.10 for the same Q. Therefore, if the lowest point on the Eq. 5.11 curve is a

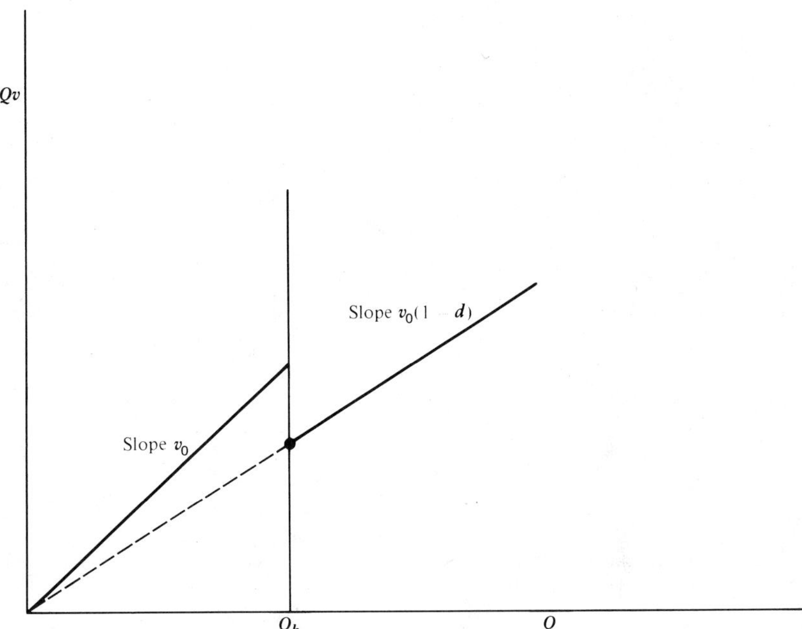

FIGURE 5.5 "All-Units" Quantity Discount

valid one (that is, at least as large as Q_b), it must be the optimum, since it is the lowest point on the lower curve.

In the usual situation where the economic order quantity (without a discount) is below the breakpoint, the decision of whether to go for the discount hinges on a tradeoff between extra carrying costs versus a reduction in the acquisition costs (primarily the reduction in the unit value, but also a benefit from fewer replenishments per unit time). Where the reduction in acquisition costs is larger than the extra carrying costs, the use of Q_b is preferable, as shown in part *a* of Figure 5.6. Where the extra carrying costs dominate, the best solution is still the EOQ (with no discount), as shown in part *b* of Figure 5.6. However, there is one other possibility—namely, that Q_b is relatively low, and it may be attractive to go to the local minimum (low point) on the curve of Eq. 5.11. This is the EOQ (with discount) and this case is shown in part *c* of Figure 5.6.

Taking advantage of the above property of Eq. 5.11 as being the lower curve, the steps of an efficient algorithm for finding the best value of Q are:

Step 1 Compute the economic order quantity when the discount is applicable, that is,

$$\text{EOQ (discount)} = \sqrt{\frac{2AD}{v_0(1-d)r}}$$

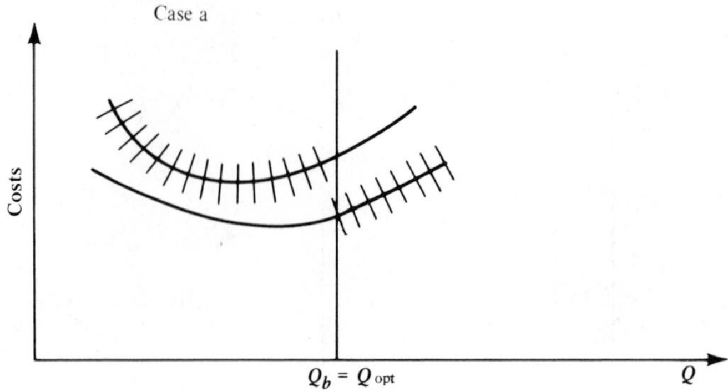

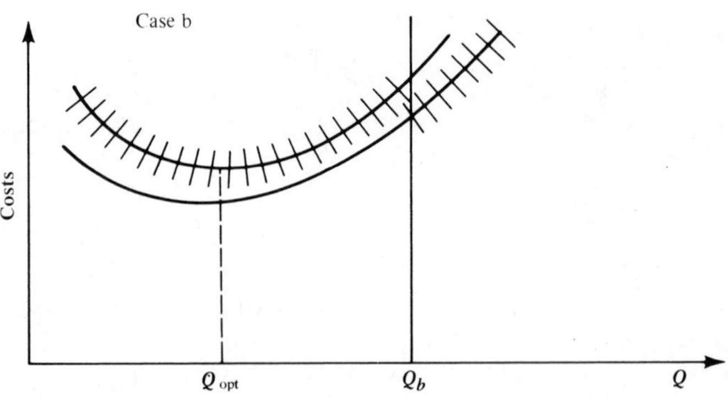

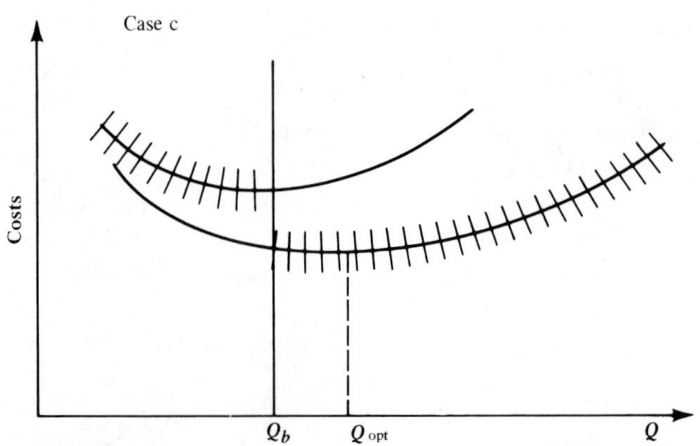

FIGURE 5.6 Total Relevant Costs under "All-Units" Discount

Step 2 Compare EOQ(d) with Q_b. If EOQ(d) $\geqslant Q_b$, then EOQ(d) is the best order quantity (case c of Figure 5.6).

If EOQ(d) $< Q_b$, go to Step 3.

Step 3 Evaluate

$$\text{TRC (EOQ)} = \sqrt{2ADv_0r} + Dv_0$$

and TRC(Q_b), using Eq. 5.11.

If TRC (EOQ) < TRC (Q_b), the best order quantity is the EOQ without a discount (case b of Figure 5.6), given by

$$\text{EOQ (no discount)} = \sqrt{\frac{2AD}{v_0r}}$$

If TRC (EOQ) > TRC (Q_b), the best order quantity is Q_b (case a of Figure 5.6).

This logic can easily be extended to the case of several breakpoints with increasing discounts. The best order quantity is always at a breakpoint or at a feasible EOQ. Kuzdrall and Britney (1982) have used a somewhat different approach that is useful when there is a large number of different discounts. Their method estimates the supplier's fixed and variable costs from a given schedule of discounts and breakpoints.

Numerical Illustrations

Consider items EDM-010, EDM-012, and EDM-027, three components used in the assembly of Midamatics. The supplier offers the same discount structure for each of the items and discounts are based on replenishment sizes of the *individual* items. The relevant characteristics of the items are given below.

Item	D (units/yr)	v_0 ($/unit)	A ($)	r ($/$/yr)
EDM-010	416	14.20	1.50	0.24
EDM-012	104	3.10	1.50	0.24
EDM-027	4160	2.40	1.50	0.24

Because of convenience in manufacturing and shipping, the supplier offers a 2 percent discount on any replenishment of 100 units or higher of a single item.

The computations are as follows:

EDM-010 (An Illustration of Case *a* of Figure 5.6)

Step 1 EOQ (discount) = 19 units < 100 units.

Step 2 EOQ (discount) < Q_b; therefore, go to step 3.

Step 3

$$\text{TRC (EOQ)} = \sqrt{2 \times 1.50 \times 416 \times 14.20 \times 0.24} + 416 \times 14.20$$
$$= \$5972.42/\text{yr}$$

$$\text{TRC } (Q_b) = \text{TRC } (100) = \frac{100 \times 14.20 \times 0.98 \times 0.24}{2} + \frac{1.50 \times 416}{100}$$
$$+ 416 \times 14.20 \times 0.98$$
$$= \$5962.29/\text{yr}$$

TRC (EOQ) > TRC (Q_b). Therefore, the best order quantity to use is Q_b, that is, 100 units.

EDM-012 (An Illustration of Case *b* of Figure 5.6)

Step 1 EOQ (discount) = 21 units < 100 units.

Step 2 EOQ (discount) < Q_b; therefore, go to step 3.

Step 3

$$\text{TRC (EOQ)} = \sqrt{2 \times 1.50 \times 104 \times 3.10 \times 0.24} + 104 \times 3.10$$
$$= \$337.64/\text{yr}$$

$$\text{TRC } (Q_b) = \text{TRC } (100) = \frac{100 \times 3.10 \times 0.98 \times 0.24}{2} + \frac{1.50 \times 104}{100}$$
$$+ 104 \times 3.10 \times 0.98$$
$$= \$353.97/\text{yr}$$

TRC (EOQ) < (TRC (Q_b). Therefore, use the EOQ without a discount; that is,

$$\text{EOQ} = \sqrt{\frac{2 \times 1.50 \times 104}{3.10 \times 0.24}} \simeq 20 \text{ units}$$

EDM-027 (An Illustration of Case *c* of Figure 5.6)

Step 1

$$\text{EOQ (discount)} = \sqrt{\frac{2 \times 1.50 \times 4160}{2.40 \times 0.98 \times 0.24}} = 149 \text{ units} > 100 \text{ units}$$

Step 2 EOQ (discount) is greater than Q_b. Therefore, the Q to use is 149 units (perhaps rounded to 150 for convenience).

In an all-units discount situation a possible strategy is to buy Q_b units to achieve the discount; then dispose of some of the units, at some unit cost (or revenue), to reduce inventory carrying costs. An application of this philosophy is the case where an entire car of a train is reserved, but not completely filled, by a shipment. Sethi (1984) has analyzed this more general situation.

Managers, buyers, purchasing agents, among others, rather than dealing with single items in isolation, often think in terms of a group of items purchased from a particular vendor. Thus, a potentially important discount can be achieved by having a total order, involving two or more items, exceeding some breakpoint level. This topic will be addressed in Chapter 11 where we will be concerned with coordinated replenishment strategies.

It should be mentioned that, in trying to achieve a quantity discount, one must be concerned about the implications of a large time supply, a topic to be discussed in Section 5.7.

5.6 ACCOUNTING FOR INFLATION

One of the assumptions in the derivation of the economic order quantity was that the inflation rate was at a negligible level. In recent times most countries have been confronted with fluctuating inflation rates that often have been far from negligible. In this section we investigate the impact of inflation on the choice of replenishment quantities.

There are several options available in terms of modeling the effects of inflation on costs and revenues. We restrict our attention to the case where the fixed replenishment cost A and the unit variable cost v are affected in the same fashion by inflation. A more elaborate model would be necessary if inflation had a different impact on the two types of costs. Moreover, the effects on revenue depend on the choice of pricing policy adopted by the organization (possibly subject to government regulation). In Section 5.6.1 we investigate the case where (selling) price changes are made independent of the replenishment strategy. A special case is where the unit selling price p is assumed to increase continuously at the inflation rate (in the same fashion as A and v). Then, in Section 5.6.2, the result will be shown for the situation where the price is adjusted only once for each replenishment lot. Thus, in this latter case, revenue, as well as costs, now depends on the sizes of the replenishments.

An *exact* analysis in the presence of inflation would be extremely complicated. The reason is that costs varying with time, in principle, should lead to the replenishment quantity changing with time. At any point in time our primary concern is with choosing the value of *only* the very next replenishment. To obtain a tractable analytic result, we assume that all future replenishments will be of the *same* size as the current replenishment, contrary to what the above discussion would suggest. This assumption is not as serious as it would first appear. In particular, at the time of the next replenishment we would recompute a *new* value for that replenishment, reflecting any changes in cost (and other) parameters that have taken place in the interim. Second, we employ discounting so that assumptions about future lot sizes should not have an appreciable effect on the *current* decision. This is an illustration of a heuristic solution procedure, a method, based on analytic and intuitive reasoning, that is not optimal but should result in a reasonable solution. Finally, we do *not* treat the case where quantity discounts are available. When discounts are available, the best order quantity may be quite insensitive to inflation in that the breakpoint value often is the best solution over a wide range of parameter values (see Gaither, 1981).

5.6.1 Price Established Independent of Ordering Policy

Because the price is established independent of the ordering policy (perhaps pricing is set by market forces external to the company under consideration), we can restrict our attention, as earlier, to the minimization of costs. However, because costs are changing with time, we cannot compare costs over a typical year as in Section 5.2. Instead, we resort to a common tool of investment analysis, namely, the use of the present value (PV) of the stream of future costs.

Suppose that the continuous discount rate is denoted by r, that is, a cost of c at time t has a present value of ce^{-rt}. (We deliberately use the symbol r because, as we will see, the discount rate is equivalent mathematically to what we have earlier called the carrying charge.[4]) Note that e is the constant 2.71829. . . . We denote the continuous inflation rate by i. Thus, if A and v are the cost factors at time zero, then their values at time t are Ae^{it} and ve^{it}, respectively. With a demand rate of D and an order of size Q received at time 0, the present value of the stream of costs is given by[5]

$$\begin{aligned} \text{PV}(Q) &= A + Qv + (A + Qv)e^{iQ/D}\,e^{-rQ/D} \\ &\quad + (A + Qv)e^{2iQ/D}\,e^{-2rQ/D} + \cdots \\ &= (A + Qv)(1 + e^{-(r-i)Q/D} + e^{-2(r-i)Q/D} + \cdots) \\ &= (A + Qv)\frac{1}{1 - e^{-(r-i)Q/D}} \end{aligned} \tag{5.12}$$

[4]Gurnani (1983) presents a more exact, present value analysis, where carrying costs (other than the cost of capital) are included as well as a discount factor.

[5]The derivation uses the fact that

$$1 + a + a^2 + \cdots = \frac{1}{1-a} \qquad 0 \leq a < 1$$

For a minimum, we set $d\text{PV}(Q)/dQ = 0$. As shown in Section 2 of the Appendix of this chapter, the result is

$$e^{(r-i)Q/D} = 1 + \left(\frac{A}{v} + Q\right)\left(\frac{r-i}{D}\right)$$

For $(r - i)Q/D << 1$, which is a reasonable assumption, this equation can be simplified further by approximating the exponential term ($e^x \simeq 1 + x + x^2/2$ for $x << 1$). Again, in the Appendix we obtain the following result:

$$Q_{\text{opt}} = \sqrt{\frac{2AD}{v(r-i)}} = \text{EOQ}\sqrt{\frac{1}{1 - i/r}} \qquad (5.13)$$

that is, the EOQ multiplied by a correction factor. Note that, when there is negligible inflation ($i = 0$), this is nothing more than the economic order quantity. Hence, our justification for using the symbol r for the discount rate. Buzacott (1975) has developed a somewhat more exact decision rule, for which the result of Eq. 5.13 is usually a good approximation.

In an inflationary environment when price is set independent of ordering policy, the profit per unit increases with time since the last replenishment; thus, intuitively, the replenishment quantity should be larger than under no inflation. Equation 5.13 indicates this type of behavior.

The cost penalty associated with using the EOQ (that ignores inflation) can be found from

$$\text{PCP} = \frac{\text{PV(EOQ)} - \text{PV}(Q_{\text{opt}})}{PV(Q_{\text{opt}})} \times 100 \qquad (5.14)$$

where PV(Q) is given by Eq. 5.12. The percentage cost penalty increases as i approaches r but, as shown in this chapter's Appendix, it reaches a limiting value of $100\sqrt{Ar/2Dv}$, which tends to be quite small (although it is a percentage of the *total* cost, the latter including the Dv term).

Numerical Illustration

Let us reconsider the MIDAS item EDM-073 that was used in Section 5.2. Its parameter values were

$D = 2400$ units/yr $\qquad v = \$0.40$/unit

$A = \$3.20 \qquad r = 0.24$ \$/\$/yr

The EOQ under no inflation was found to be 400 units. Use of Eq. 5.13 produces the behavior shown in Table 5.2 for different values of i. The percentage cost penalties computed from Eq. 5.14 are also presented in Table 5.2 and are seen to be extremely small.

TABLE 5.2 Effects of Inflation on Choice of Order Quantity for Item EDM-073

i	0	0.02	0.05	0.10	0.20	0.22	0.24
Q_{opt}	400	418	450	524	980	1386	∞
PCP of Using EOQ	0	0.0025	0.021	0.105	0.687	1.26	2.0

5.6.2 Price Set as a Fixed Fractional Markup on Unit Variable Cost

Let us denote the unit selling price established by the company as p. Suppose that a replenishment order is paid for at unit variable cost $v(t)$ at time t and the next order will be paid for at time $t + T$. Then a fixed fractional markup (f) implies

$$p(t + \tau) = v(t)(1 + f) \qquad 0 \leq \tau < T \tag{5.15}$$

$v(t)$ depends on the inflation rate as in the previous subsection; thus the unit selling price also depends on the inflation rate and on the order quantity Q, the latter in that $T = Q/D$ in Eq. 5.15. Consequently, here both costs *and revenues* are influenced by the choice of the order quantity Q. An appropriate criterion is to select Q in order to maximize the present value of revenues minus costs. Buzacott (1975) uses an analysis similar to that presented above[6] to obtain

$$Q_{opt} = \sqrt{\frac{2AD}{v(r + fi)}} = \text{EOQ}\,\frac{1}{\sqrt{1 + fi/r}} \tag{5.16}$$

When the markup for the sale of a *whole* replenishment lot is set as a fixed fraction of the unit variable cost at the *start* of a cycle and costs are increasing because of inflation, intuitively one should reduce the order quantity from the EOQ position in order to be able to keep the selling price more closely in line with a markup f on the *current* unit variable cost. Equation 5.16 reflects this intuitive behavior. It is seen that, as the product fi increases, Q_{opt} becomes smaller relative to the EOQ.

5.7 LIMITS ON ORDER SIZES

The basic economic order quantity that we derived earlier considers only the costs of replenishing and carrying inventory. All the variables used reflect only financial considerations. There are a number of possible physical constraints, not explicitly included in the model, that might prevent use of the so-called best solution derived from the model. We look at some of these constraints in sections 5.7.1, 5.7.2, and 5.7.3.

[6]An added complexity is that the revenue is a continuous function of time that must be discounted.

5.7.1 Maximum Time Supply or Capacity Restriction

1. The shelf life (SL) of the commodity may be an important factor. Previously we derived the economic order quantity expressed as a time supply as

$$T_{\text{EOQ}} = \frac{\text{EOQ}}{D} = \sqrt{\frac{2A}{Dvr}}$$

As illustrated graphically in Figure 5.7, if this quantity exceeds the allowable shelf life SL, then the best feasible order quantity to use (that is, it produces the lowest feasible point on the cost curve) is the shelf life quantity itself,

$$Q_{\text{SL}} = D(\text{SL})$$

2. Even without a shelf life limitation, an EOQ that represents a very long time supply may be unrealistic for other reasons. A long time supply takes us well out into the future where demand becomes uncertain and obsolescence can become of significant concern. This is an important constraint on class C items, as we will see in a later chapter. A good example of obsolescence would be an impending engineering change.

3. There may be a storage capacity limitation on the replenishment size for an item (for example, the entire replenishment must fit in a dedicated storage bin). Equivalently, in production situations (to be discussed in Chapters 15 and 16) there may be a finite production capacity available for the item or a group of related items. A capacity limitation is mathematically equivalent to a shelf life restriction.

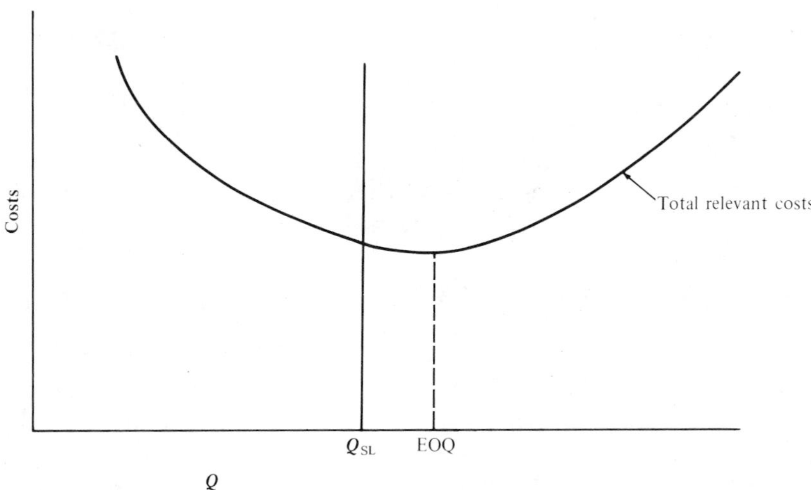

FIGURE 5.7 Case of a Shelf-Life Constraint

5.7.2 Minimum Order Quantity

The supplier may specify a minimum allowable order quantity. A similar situation exists in an in-house production operation where there is a lower limit on an order quantity that can be realistically considered. If the EOQ is less than this quantity, then the best allowable order quantity is the supplier or production minimum.

5.7.3 Discrete Units

The economic order quantity, as given by Eq. 5.4, will likely result in a nonintegral number of units. However, it can be shown mathematically (and is obvious from the form of the total cost curve of Figure 5.2) that the best integer value of Q has to be one of the two integers surrounding the best (noninteger) solution given by Eq. 5.4. For simplicity, we recommend simply rounding the result of Eq. 5.4, that is, the EOQ, to the nearest integer.[7]

Certain commodities are sold in pack sizes containing more than one unit; for example, MIDAS sells a certain type of film in a package of six units. Therefore, it makes sense to restrict a replenishment quantity to integer multiples of six units. In fact, if a new unit, corresponding to six of the old unit, is defined, then we're back to the basic situation of requiring an integer number of (the new) units in a replenishment quantity.

There is another possible restriction on the replenishment quantity very similar to that of discrete units, namely, the situation where the replenishment must cover an integral number of periods of demand. Again, we simply find the optimal continuous Q expressed as a time supply (see Eq. 5.6) and round to the nearest integer value of the time supply.

5.8 INCORPORATION OF OTHER FACTORS

In this section we briefly discuss four further modifications of the basic economic order quantity that result from the relaxation of one or more of the assumptions required in the earlier derivation. The treatment of one other important situation—namely, where the quantity supplied does not necessarily exactly match the quantity ordered—can be found in Silver (1976).

5.8.1 Nonzero Constant Lead Time That Is Known with Certainty

As long as demand remains deterministic, the introduction of a known nonzero replenishment lead time (L) presents no difficulty. The inventory diagram of

[7]Strictly speaking, one should evaluate the total costs, using Eq. 5.3, for each of the two surrounding integers and pick the integer having the lower costs. However, rounding produces trivial percentage cost penalties except possibly when the EOQ is in the range of only 1 or 2 units.

Figure 5.1 is unchanged. When the inventory level hits DL an order is placed and it arrives exactly L time units later just as the inventory hits zero. The costs are unaltered so that the best order quantity is still given by Eq. 5.4. As we will see in Chapter 7, a nonzero lead time considerably complicates matters when demand is probabilistic.

5.8.2 Finite Replenishment Rate

One of the assumptions inherent in the derivation of the EOQ was that the whole replenishment quantity arrives at the same time. If, instead, we assume that it becomes available at a rate of m per unit time (the production rate of the machinery used to produce the item), then the sawtoothed diagram of Figure 5.1 is modified to that of Figure 5.8. All that changes from the earlier derivation is the average inventory level which is now $Q(1 - D/m)/2$. The total relevant costs are given by

$$\text{TRC}\,(Q) = \frac{Q(1 - D/m)vr}{2} + \frac{AD}{Q}$$

and the best Q value is now the finite replenishment economic order quantity,

$$\begin{aligned} \text{FREOQ} &= \sqrt{\frac{2AD}{vr(1 - D/m)}} \\ &= \text{EOQ} \cdot \frac{1}{\sqrt{(1 - D/m)}} \end{aligned} \tag{5.17}$$

that is, the EOQ again multiplied by a correction factor. The magnitude of this correction factor for various values of D/m is shown in Figure 5.9. Also shown are the cost penalties caused by ignoring the correction and simply using the

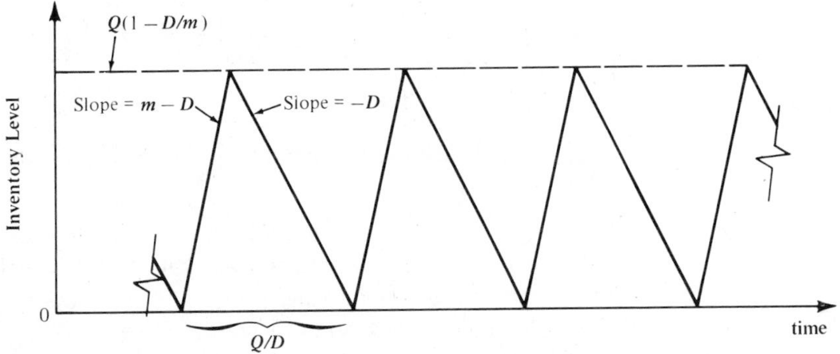

FIGURE 5.8 Case of a Finite Replenishment Rate

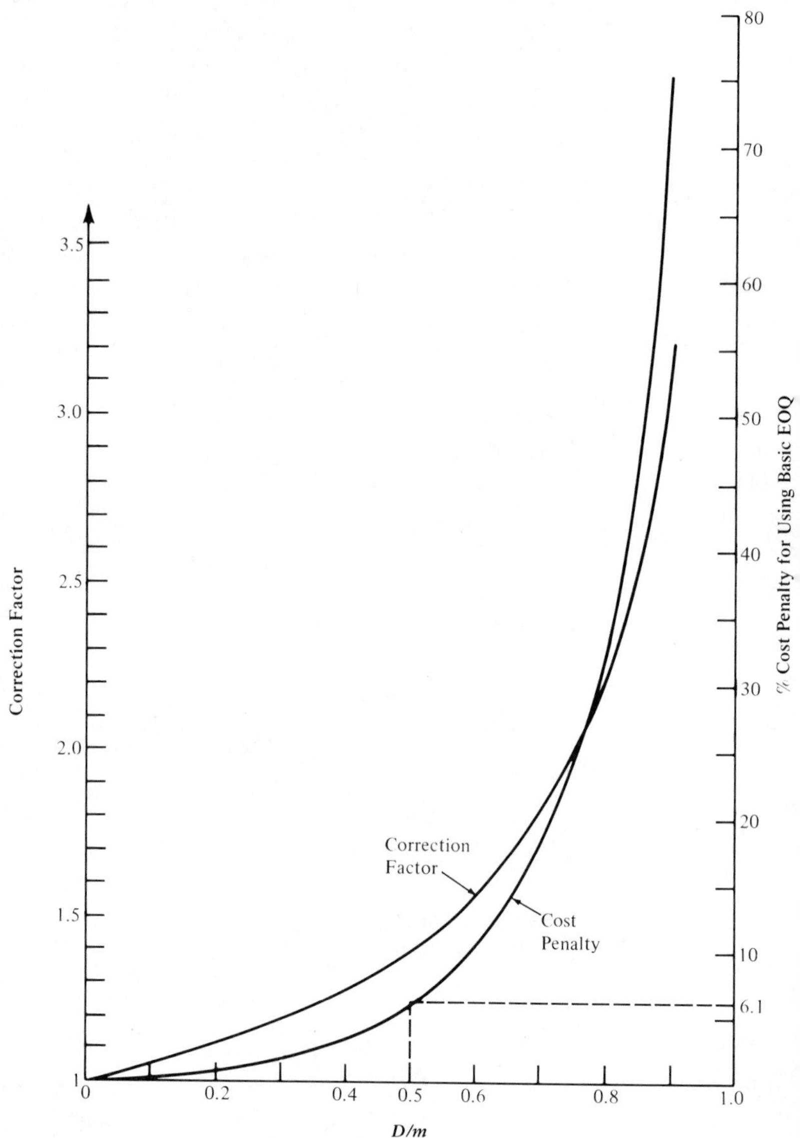

FIGURE 5.9 Use of EOQ When There Is a Finite Replenishment Rate

basic EOQ. It is clear that D/m has to be fairly large before the cost penalty becomes significant; for example, even when D/m is 0.5 (that is, the demand rate is one-half of the production rate), the cost penalty for neglecting the finite nature of the production rate is only 6.1 percent.

Note that as D/m gets very small (equivalent to instantaneous production of the entire lot), the FREOQ reduces to the EOQ as it should. Moreover, as D/m

tends to unity, Eq. 5.17 suggests we produce an indefinitely large lot, which makes sense in that demand exactly matches the production rate. For $D/m > 1$, the model breaks down because the capacity of the machine is insufficient to keep up with the demand. However, the model is still useful under these circumstances. To illustrate, suppose that $D = 1.6m$. Here, one would dedicate one machine to the product (with no changeover costs) and produce the remaining $0.6m$ in finite lot sizes on a second machine, where the latter machine's capacity would likely be shared with other items. An example, encountered by one of the authors in a consulting assignment, involved the bottling/canning operations of a large North American brewery where the fastest moving item had a bottling line dedicated to it. Further discussion on the sharing of production equipment among several items will be presented in Chapters 15 and 16.

5.8.3 Different Type of Carrying Charge

In Section 5.2 we assumed that the carrying charge was directly proportional to the average inventory level measured in dollars. Modifications are possible. Each can be handled with the resulting order quantity expression being somewhat more complex than Eq. 5.4.

To illustrate, consider the situation where costs depend on area or volume considerations as well as the value of the inventory. (It is intuitive that it should cost more per unit time to store a dollar of feathers than a dollar of coal.) Suppose that there is a charge of w dollars per unit time per cubic foot of space allocated to an item. Assume that this space must be sufficient to handle the maximum inventory level of the item. One situation where such a change would be appropriate is where items are maintained in separate bins and a specific bin size (which must house the maximum inventory) is allocated to an item. The best replenishment quantity under these circumstances is

$$\sqrt{\frac{2AD}{2hw + vr}}$$

where h is the volume (in cubic feet) occupied per unit of the item.

5.8.4 Multiple Setup Costs

Consider the situation of an item where the costs of a replenishment depend on the quantity in the following fashion:

Q Range	Cost
$0 < Q \leq Q_0$	$A + Qv$
$Q_0 < Q \leq 2Q_0$	$2A + Qv$
$2Q_0 < Q \leq 3Q_0$	$3A + Qv$

One interpretation is that the item is produced in some type of container (for example, a vat) of fixed capacity Q_0 and there is a fixed cost A associated with the use of each container. Another interpretation relates to transportation costs where Q_0 might be the capacity of a rail car.

Under the above cost structure Aucamp (1982) has shown that the best solution is either the standard EOQ or one of the two surrounding *integer* multiples of Q_0.

5.8.5 A Special Opportunity to Procure

An important situation, often faced by both producers and merchants, is a one-time opportunity to procure an item at a reduced unit cost (a particular case being where this is the last opportunity to replenish before a price rise).

Because of the change in one of the parameters (the unit cost), the current order quantity certainly can differ from future order quantities. (These future quantities will all be identical—namely, the EOQ with the new unit cost.) Thus the simple sawtooth pattern of Figure 5.1 no longer necessarily applies. Hence, we cannot base our analysis on the average inventory level and number of replenishments in a typical year (or other unit of time). Instead, in comparing two possible choices for the current value of the order quantity Q, strictly speaking, we should compare costs out to a point in time where the two alternatives leave us in an identical inventory state. To illustrate, suppose that the demand rate is 100 units/month and the new EOQ will be 200 units. Furthermore, suppose that two alternatives under consideration for the current order quantity are 200 and 400 units. As shown in Figure 5.10, an appropriate horizon for cost comparison would be 4 months because, for both alternatives, the inventory level would be zero at that point in time. A comparison of costs out to 1.95 months, for example, would be biased in favor of the 200 unit alternative because the imminent (0.05 months later) setup cost under this alternative would not be included. An exact (present value) comparison for all alternatives is rather complex mathematically, particularly when there is a continuum of choices for the order quantity.

We instead recommend an approximate approach, suggested by Naddor (1966). Let the decision variable, the current order quantity, be denoted by Q. Let the current unit cost be v_1 and the future unit cost be $v_2 (v_2 > v_1)$. The economic order quantity, after the price rise, is given by Eq. 5.4 as

$$\mathrm{EOQ}_2 = \sqrt{\frac{2AD}{v_2 r}} \tag{5.18}$$

Furthermore, from Eq. 5.5 the costs per unit time are then

$$\mathrm{TRC}\,(\mathrm{EOQ}_2) = \sqrt{2ADv_2 r} + Dv_2 \tag{5.19}$$

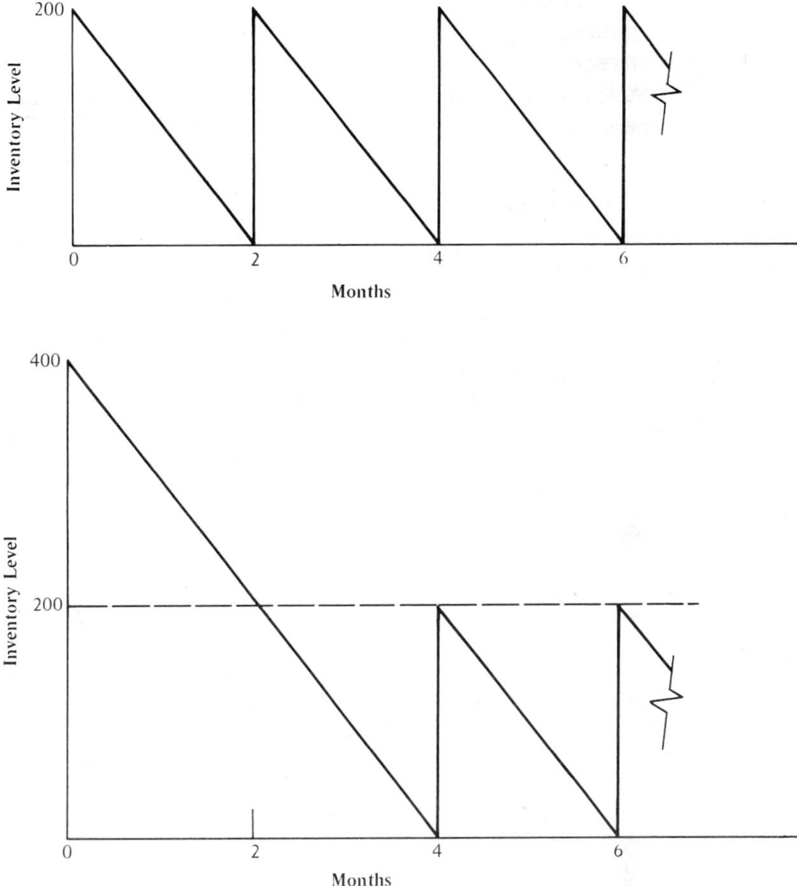

FIGURE 5.10 Comparison of Two Alternatives When the Order Quantity Changes with Time

If the current order quantity is of size Q, then it will last for Q/D units of time. The average inventory during this period is $Q/2$. Hence, the total costs out to time Q/D are

$$TC(Q) = A + Qv_1 + \frac{Q}{2}v_1\frac{Q}{D}r$$

$$= A + Qv_1 + \frac{Q^2 v_1 r}{2D} \tag{5.20}$$

Consider the extreme case where Q was set equal to 0 so that the price increase would occur and we would immediately start ordering the new EOQ_2. Under this strategy total costs out to some time T would be, from Eq. 5.19,

$$T \cdot \sqrt{2ADv_2r} + DTv_2$$

It is reasonable to select the value of Q to maximize

$$F(Q) = Q/D \sqrt{2ADv_2r} + Qv_2 - TC(Q) \tag{5.21}$$

the improvement in total cost out to time Q/D achieved by ordering Q at the old price instead of not ordering anything at the old price. It can be shown that use of this criterion need not lead to the exact cost minimizing solution. Again, we are opting for a heuristic procedure for selecting the value of the decision variable (in this case Q). A convenient approach to maximizing $F(Q)$ is to set $dF(Q)/dQ = 0$. From Eqs. 5.20 and 5.21

$$F(Q) = \frac{Q}{D}\sqrt{2ADv_2r} + Qv_2 - A - Qv_1 - \frac{Q^2v_1r}{2D}$$

$$\frac{dF(Q)}{dQ} = \frac{1}{D}\sqrt{2ADv_2r} + v_2 - v_1 - \frac{Qv_1r}{D} = 0 \tag{5.22}$$

or

$$Q_{\text{opt}} = \frac{\sqrt{2ADv_2r}}{v_1r} + \frac{v_2 - v_1}{v_1}\frac{D}{r}$$

that is,

$$Q_{\text{opt}} = \frac{v_2}{v_1}\text{EOQ}_2 + \frac{v_2 - v_1}{v_1}\frac{D}{r} \tag{5.23}$$

The above analysis implicitly assumed that the initial inventory (at the moment that the special opportunity replenishment was to be made) was 0. If instead the inventory was I_0, then one can show that Q_{opt} becomes the result of Eq. 5.23 minus I_0; that is, Eq. 5.23 gives the appropriate order-up-to-level.

Other analyses of this problem are presented by Brown(1982) and McClain and Thomas (1980). The latter authors, in particular, use a marginal approach that very quickly gives a decision rule. However, the rule, unlike Eq. 5.23, is not easily extendable to the case of multiple items, a case to be discussed in a moment. Miltenburg (1982) has shown that the Brown and Naddor decision rules give very similar results on a broad range of problems.

Numerical Illustration

Consider a particular Toronto-based X-ray film dealer supplied by MIDAS. Suppose that MIDAS announces a price increase for product XMF-082 from \$28.00/box to \$30.00/box. The dealer uses approximately 80 boxes per year and estimates the fixed cost per order to be \$1.50 and the carrying charge as 0.20 \$/\$/yr.

From Eq. 5.18

$$EOQ_2 = \sqrt{\frac{2 \times 1.50 \times 80}{30.00 \times 0.2}} \simeq 6 \text{ boxes}$$

Then, Eq. 5.23 gives

$$Q_{\text{opt}} = \frac{30.00}{28.00}(6) + \frac{2.00}{28.00}\,\frac{80}{0.2}$$
$$= 35.3, \text{ say } 35 \text{ boxes}$$

The increase in unit price from \$28.00/box to \$30.00/box (a 7 percent increase) causes a one-time procurement quantity of 35 boxes instead of 6 boxes (an increase of almost 500 percent!), a much higher sensitivity than in the basic EOQ itself (see Section 5.3).

Substitution of each of $Q = 6$ and $Q = 35$ into Eq. 5.22 gives

$$F(6) = \$12.09$$

and

$$F(35) = = \$42.23$$

so that the one-time cost savings of using the order quantity of 35 boxes is (42.23 − 12.09) or \$30.14.

Two additional points are worth making:

1. The one-time purchase is likely to represent a large time supply. Obsolescence and other forms of uncertainty may dictate an upper limit on this time supply.
2. The multi-item case, where a vendor offers a one-time price break on a range of products, is obviously of interest. In such a situation there is likely to be a constraint on the total amount that can be spent on the one-time purchase or on the total inventory (because of warehouse capacity). For illustrative

purposes, let us consider the case of a constraint on the total amount that can be spent. For notation let

D_i = usage rate of item i, in units/yr

A_i = fixed setup cost of item i, in dollars

v_{1i} = unit cost of item i in the special opportunity to buy, in \$/unit

v_{2i} = unit cost of item i in the future, in \$/unit

Q_i = amount, in units, of item i to be purchased in the special buy

EOQ_{2i} = economic order quantity of item i in units, under the future unit cost

n = number of items in the group under consideration (we assume in the sequel that the items are numbered 1, 2, 3, . . . , n)

W = maximum total amount, in dollars, that can be spent on the special buy

Then, the procedure for selecting the Q_i's is as follows:

Step 1 Determine the unconstrained best Q_i's by the analog of Eq. 5.23, namely,

$$Q_i^* = \frac{v_{2i}}{v_{1i}} \text{EOQ}_{2i} + \frac{v_{2i} - v_{1i}}{v_{1i}} \frac{D_i}{r} \qquad i = 1, 2, \ldots, n \tag{5.24}$$

Step 2 Calculate the total dollar value of the unconstrained Q_i's and compare with the constraining value; thus from Eq. 5.24

$$\sum_{i=1}^{n} Q_i^* v_{1i} = \sum_{i=1}^{n} [v_{2i} \text{EOQ}_{2i} + (v_{2i} - v_{1i}) D_i / r] \tag{5.25}$$

If $\Sigma_{i=1}^n Q_i^* v_{1i} \leq W$, we use the Q_i^*'s of Step 1. If not, we go to Step 3.

Step 3 Compute the constrained best Q_i values. (The derivation is shown in Section 3 of the Appendix of this chapter):

$$Q_i^* = \frac{v_{2i}}{v_{1i}}\left(\text{EOQ}_{2i} + \frac{D_i}{r}\right) - \frac{D_i}{\Sigma_{j=1}^n D_j v_{1j}} \times \left[\sum_{j=1}^{n} v_{2j}\left(\text{EOQ}_{2j} + \frac{D_j}{r}\right) - W\right] \qquad i = 1, 2, \ldots, n \tag{5.26}$$

5.9 SELECTION OF THE CARRYING CHARGE (r), THE FIXED COST PER REPLENISHMENT (A), OR THE RATIO A/r BASED ON AGGREGATE CONSIDERATIONS—THE EXCHANGE CURVE

Often it is difficult to explicitly determine an appropriate value of the carrying charge r or the fixed cost per replenishment A from basic cost considerations. An alternate method, which we discussed in Chapter 3, takes account of the aggregate viewpoint of management. In this and later sections we derive the relationships and graphs that we earlier asked you to accept on faith. For a population of inventoried items management may impose an aggregate constraint of one of the following forms:

1. The average total inventory cannot exceed a certain dollar value.
2. The total fixed cost (or total number) of replenishments per unit time (for example, one year) must be less than a certain value.
3. We should operate at a point where the tradeoff (exchange) between average inventory and cost (or number) of replenishments per unit time is at some reasonable prescribed value.

We restrict our attention to the case where the fixed cost per replenishment for item i, denoted by A_i, cannot be determined explicitly but it is reasonable to assume that a common value of A holds (at least approximately) for all items in the portion of the inventory population under consideration. We designate the demand rate, unit variable cost, and order quantity of item i by D_i, v_i, and Q_i, respectively. We also let n be the number of items in the population. (The case where the A_i's are *explicitly* predetermined can be treated in a similar fashion.)

As shown in Section 4 of the Appendix of this chapter, if we use an economic order quantity for each item, we obtain the total average (or cycle) stock in dollars,

$$\text{TCS} = \sqrt{\frac{A}{r}}\,\frac{1}{\sqrt{2}}\sum_{i=1}^{n}\sqrt{D_i v_i} \tag{5.27}$$

and the total number of replenishments per unit time,

$$N = \sqrt{\frac{r}{A}}\,\frac{1}{\sqrt{2}}\sum_{i=1}^{n}\sqrt{D_i v_i} \tag{5.28}$$

Both TCS and N are seen to depend on the value of the ratio A/r. Multiplication of Eqs. 5.27 and 5.28 gives

$$(\text{TCS})(N) = \tfrac{1}{2}\left(\sum_{i=1}^{n} \sqrt{D_i v_i}\right)^2 \tag{5.29}$$

which is an hyperbola. Moreover, the division of Eq. 5.27 by Eq. 5.28 gives

$$\frac{\text{TCS}}{N} = \frac{A}{r} \tag{5.30}$$

so that any point on the hyperbolic curve implies a value of A/r. Of course, if either A or r is known explicitly, the implicit value of A/r implies a value of the one remaining unknown parameter.

To summarize, when an EOQ strategy[8] is used for each item, management can select a desired point on the tradeoff curve (with associated aggregate conditions), thus implying an appropriate value of r, A, or A/r (the latter parameters can now be thought of as management control variables). It should be noted that the use of r as a policy variable is closely related to a technique known as LIMIT (Lot-size Inventory Management Interpolation Technique) discussed by Eaton (1964).

Exchange Curve for the MIDAS Professional Products Division

The Professional Products Division includes 849 items, the majority of which are purchased from the same supplier in Germany. Therefore, it is realistic to think in terms of a fixed setup cost A, which does not vary appreciably from item to item. Based on a detailed study of costs and policy factors, management decided to set the value of A at \$3.20. A computer routine was used to generate the exchange curve of Figure 5.11. The $D_i v_i$ values needed in Eq. 5.29 were already available from the distribution-by-value analysis of Chapter 1. Two other points are also shown on Figure 5.11.

1. Current operating procedure (estimated by using the most recent replenishment quantity actually used for each of the items in the division)

---

[8]When an aggregate constraint is to be satisfied, it is not obvious that the best strategy for an individual item is to use an EOQ-type order quantity. In fact, the more mathematically oriented reader may wish to verify that, for example, minimization of the total number of replenishments per unit time subject to a specified total average stock (or minimization of total average stock subject to a specified total number of replenishments per unit time) does indeed lead to an EOQ-type formula. If a Lagrange multiplier approach is used, the multiplier turns out to be identical with r/A (or A/r). An introduction to the use of Lagrange multipliers in constrained optimization is provided in Appendix A.

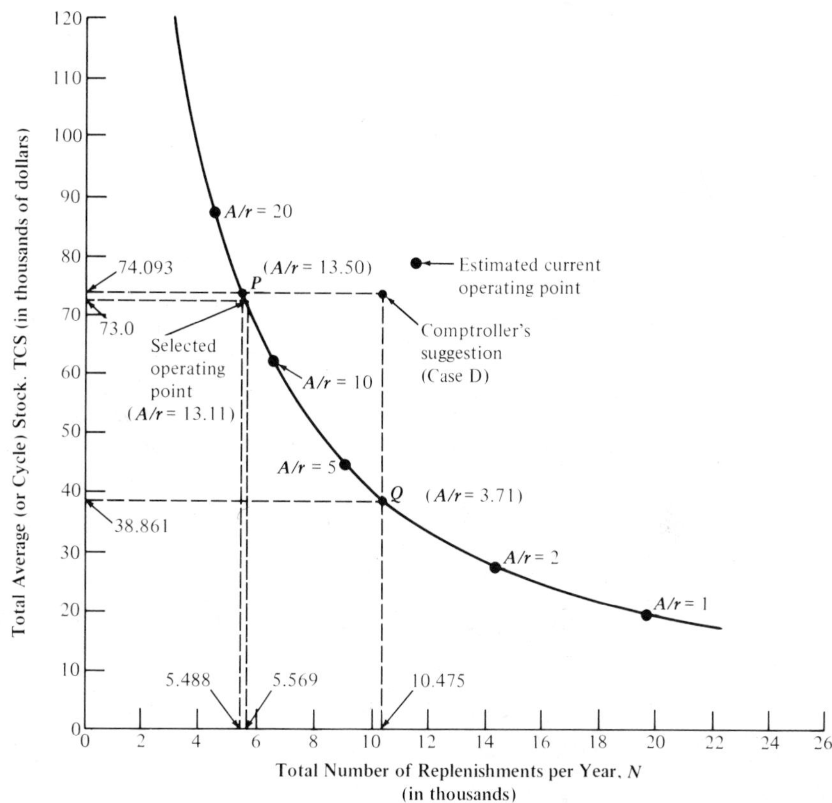

FIGURE 5.11 Aggregated Consequences of Different A/r Values—An Exchange Curve for the Professional Products Division of MIDAS

2. The Q_i's implied by the decision rules suggested by the comptroller (Figure 1 of Case D)

It is seen that the comptroller's suggestion is preferable to current operating rules because it reduces both the total cycle stock and the total number of replenishments per year. However, further improvements are possible through the use of economic order quantities with a suitable value of A/r. (This is because the comptroller's logic does not explicitly take economic factors into account—some inexpensive items are ordered too frequently while some fast-movers are not ordered often enough.) At one extreme, by operating at point P (with an implied A/r of 13.50), the same total cycle stock is achieved as by the comptroller's rule but the total number of replenishments per year is reduced from 10,475 to 5488 (a 47.6 percent reduction). Point Q (with an implied A/r of 3.71) represents the opposite extreme where the same total number of replenishments is achieved as by the comptroller's rule, but the total cycle stock is cut from \$74,093 to \$38,861 (a 47.6 percent reduction). Decreases, compared with the comptroller's rule, are possible in both aggregate measures at any point between P and Q. Suppose management has agreed that a total cycle stock of \$73,000 is a reasonable aggregate operating condition. The associated A/r value (using Eq. 5.27) is 13.11. Since A has been explicitly determined, we have that

$$r = A \div A/r = 3.20 \div 13.11 = 0.244 \text{ \$/\$/yr}$$

Rather than using a three decimal value for r, we choose to round to 0.24 \$/\$/yr for convenience in subsequent calculations.

To summarize, exchange curves permit us to show improvements (in terms of aggregate performance measures) over current operating practices. From a top management perspective this is far more appealing than the fact that the EOQ minimizes total costs on an individual item basis (particularly when the individual cost factors are so difficult to estimate). Other aggregate estimation procedures will be discussed in Chapter 17.

5.10 SUMMARY

In this chapter we have specified a procedure for selecting the appropriate size of a replenishment quantity under demand conditions that are essentially static in nature, the assumption being that the demand rate is at a constant level that does not change with time. Under a rigorous set of additional assumptions the resulting order quantity is the well-known square root, economic order quantity.

We argued that one or both of the parameters r and A may be very difficult to obtain from explicit cost considerations. In such a case it was shown that a value of r, A, or A/r can be implicitly specified by selecting a desired operating point on an aggregate exchange curve of total average stock versus total number or costs of replenishments per year.

Sizeable deviations of the order quantity away from the optimum value were seen to produce rather small cost errors. This robust feature of the EOQ helps justify its widespread use in practice. Often, the limited savings achievable do not justify the effort required to develop overly sophisticated variations of the EOQ. Nevertheless, as conditions change with time it becomes necessary to recompute the appropriate value of the order quantity. A general discussion of the updating of control parameters will be presented as part of implementation issues in Chapter 17.

Several simple modifications of the basic EOQ have been discussed; these modifications make the results more widely applicable. In the next chapter we develop a practical procedure for coping with situations where the average or forecast demand rate varies appreciably with time. Three other important extensions will be left to later chapters, namely,

1. Situations where demand is no longer deterministic (Chapter 7)

2. Situations where savings in replenishment costs are possible through the coordination of two or more items at the same stocking point (Chapter 11)
3. Situations (referred to as multiechelon) where the replenishment quantities of serially related production or storage facilities should not be treated independently (Chapter 12)

In each of these circumstances we will find that the basic EOQ plays an important role.

APPENDIX TO CHAPTER 5
DERIVATIONS

1. PENALTY FOR USING AN ERRONEOUS VALUE OF THE REPLENISHMENT QUANTITY

The percentage cost penalty is

$$\text{PCP} = \frac{\text{TRC}(Q') - \text{TRC}(\text{EOQ})}{\text{TRC}(\text{EOQ})} \times 100 \tag{5.31}$$

where

$$Q' = (1 + p)\text{EOQ} = (1 + p)\sqrt{\frac{2AD}{vr}}$$

Substituting this Q' expression into the Eq. 5.3 representation of TRC, we obtain

$$\begin{aligned} \text{TRC}(Q') &= (1 + p)\sqrt{\frac{ADvr}{2}} + \frac{1}{1+p}\sqrt{\frac{ADvr}{2}} \\ &= \sqrt{2ADvr}\ \tfrac{1}{2}\left(1 + p + \frac{1}{1+p}\right) \end{aligned} \tag{5.32}$$

Also from Eq. 5.5

$$\text{TRC}(\text{EOQ}) = \sqrt{2ADvr} \tag{5.33}$$

Substituting the results of Eqs. 5.32 and 5.33 into Eq. 5.31 gives

$$\text{PCP} = \left[\frac{1}{2}\left(1 + p + \frac{1}{1+p}\right) - 1\right] \times 100$$

or

$$\text{PCP} = 50\left(\frac{1}{1+p} - 1 + p\right) = 50\left(\frac{p^2}{1+p}\right)$$

2. ORDER QUANTITY UNDER INFLATION

Equation 5.12 is

$$\mathrm{PV}(Q) = (A + Qv)\frac{1}{1 - e^{-(r-i)Q/D}}$$

$$\frac{d\mathrm{PV}(Q)}{dQ} = \frac{(1 - e^{-(r-i)Q/D})v - (A + Qv)\left(\dfrac{r-i}{D}\right)e^{-(r-i)Q/D}}{[1 - e^{-(r-i)Q/D}]^2} = 0$$

The numerator must be zero, which (dividing through by v) implies

$$1 - e^{-(r-i)Q/D} - \left(\frac{A}{v} + Q\right)\left(\frac{r-i}{D}\right)e^{-(r-i)Q/D} = 0$$

This simplifies to

$$e^{(r-i)Q/D} = 1 + \left(\frac{A}{v} + Q\right)\left(\frac{r-i}{D}\right)$$

Approximating e^x by $1 + x + x^2/2$ gives

$$1 + \frac{(r-i)Q}{D} + \frac{(r-i)^2Q^2}{2D^2} \simeq 1 + \left(\frac{A}{v}\right)\left(\frac{r-i}{D}\right) + \frac{Q(r-i)}{D}$$

This solves for

$$Q_{\mathrm{opt}} \simeq \sqrt{\frac{2AD}{v(r-i)}}$$

From Eqs. 5.12 and 5.14 the percentage cost penalty for using the EOQ instead of the Q_{opt} is

$$\mathrm{PCP} = \left[\frac{A + \mathrm{EOQ}v}{A + Q_{\mathrm{opt}}v}\,\frac{1 - e^{-(r-i)Q_{\mathrm{opt}}/D}}{1 - e^{-(r-i)\mathrm{EOQ}/D}} - 1\right] \times 100$$

Substituting from Eq. 5.13 gives

$$\mathrm{PCP} = \left[\frac{A + \sqrt{\dfrac{2ADv}{r}}}{A + \sqrt{\dfrac{2ADv}{(r-i)}}}\,\frac{1 - e^{-(r-i)\sqrt{2A/(r-i)Dv}}}{1 - e^{-(r-i)\sqrt{2A/rDv}}} - 1\right] \times 100 \qquad (5.34)$$

As $x \to 0$ we know that $e^{-x} \simeq 1 - x$. Using this result in Eq. 5.34 leads, after some simplification, to

$$\text{PCP} = \left[\frac{\sqrt{\dfrac{Ar}{2Dv}} + 1}{\sqrt{\dfrac{Ar}{2Dv}} + \sqrt{\dfrac{r}{r-i}}} \frac{\sqrt{r}}{\sqrt{r-i}} - 1 \right] \times 100$$

$$= \left[\frac{\sqrt{\dfrac{Ar}{2Dv}} + 1}{\sqrt{\dfrac{A(r-i)}{2Dv}} + 1} - 1 \right] \times 100$$

As $i \to r$ we obtain

$$\text{PCP} = \sqrt{Ar/2Dv} \times 100$$

3. MULTI-ITEM SPECIAL OPPORTUNITY TO PROCURE

As in Section 5.8.5, we would like to pick each Q_i so as to maximize

$$\frac{Q_i}{D_i} \sqrt{2A_i D_i v_{2i} r} + Q_i v_{2i} - A_i - Q_i v_{1i} - \frac{Q_i^2 v_{1i} r}{2D_i}$$

However, there is the constraint (which we now know is binding because of the answer to Step 2 which caused us to go to Step 3)

$$\sum_{i=1}^{n} Q_i v_{1i} = W \tag{5.35}$$

We use a standard constrained optimization procedure, the Lagrange multiplier approach (see Appendix A at the end of the book). We maximize

$$L(Q_i\text{'s}, M) = \sum_{i=1}^{n} \left[\frac{Q_i}{D_i} \sqrt{2A_i D_i v_{2i} r} + Q_i v_{2i} - A_i - Q_i v_{1i} - \frac{Q_i^2 v_{1i} r}{2D_i} \right] - M \left(\sum_{i=1}^{n} Q_i v_{1i} - W \right)$$

where M is a Lagrange multiplier.

Taking partial derivatives and setting them to zero,

$$\frac{\partial L}{\partial M} = 0$$

gives Eq. 5.35, and

$$\frac{\partial L}{\partial Q_j} = 0 \qquad (j = 1, 2, \ldots, n)$$

leads to

$$Q_j^* = \frac{v_{2j}}{v_{1j}} \,\mathrm{EOQ}_{2j} + \frac{v_{2j} - (M+1)v_{1j}}{v_{1j}} \frac{D_j}{r} \qquad (j = 1, 2, \ldots, n) \tag{5.36}$$

where Q_i^* is the best constrained value of Q_j.

Therefore,

$$Q_j^* v_{1j} = v_{2j} \,\mathrm{EOQ}_{2j} + [v_{2j} - (M+1)v_{1j}] \frac{D_j}{r} \tag{5.37}$$

Summing Eq. 5.37 over j and using Eq. 5.35, there follows

$$\sum_{j=1}^{n} v_{2j} \,\mathrm{EOQ}_{2j} + \sum_{j=1}^{n} [v_{2j} - (M+1)v_{1j}] \frac{D_j}{r} = W$$

This is solved for $M + 1$ and the result is substituted into Eq. 5.37, producing Eq. 5.26 of the main text.

4. EXCHANGE CURVE EQUATIONS WHEN A/r IS CONSTANT ACROSS ALL ITEMS

Suppose that we have n items in the population and we designate item i's characteristics by v_i and D_i. The total average (or cycle) stock in dollars

$$\mathrm{TCS} = \sum_{i=1}^{n} \frac{Q_i v_i}{2}$$

and the total number of replenishment per unit time

$$N = \sum_{i=1}^{n} D_i/Q_i$$

If we use the EOQ for each item, we have, from Eq. 5.4,

$$Q_i = \sqrt{\frac{2AD_i}{v_i r}}$$

Therefore,

$$\text{TCS} = \sum_{i=1}^{n} \sqrt{\frac{AD_i v_i}{2r}} = \sqrt{\frac{A}{r}} \frac{1}{\sqrt{2}} \sum_{i=1}^{n} \sqrt{D_i v_i}$$

which is Eq. 5.27.

Also,

$$N = \sum_{i=1}^{n} \sqrt{\frac{D_i v_i r}{2A}} = \sqrt{\frac{r}{A}} \frac{1}{\sqrt{2}} \sum_{i=1}^{n} \sqrt{D_i v_i}$$

which is Eq. 5.28.

PROBLEMS

5.1

a. For MIDAS item EDM-073, used as an illustration in Section 5.2, suppose that A was changed to \$12.80. Now find

1. EOQ in units

2. EOQ in dollars

3. EOQ as a months of supply

Does the effect of the change in A make sense?

b. For the same item suppose that A was still \$3.20 but r was increased from 0.24/yr to 0.30/yr. Find the same quantities requested in part a. Does the effect of the change in r make sense?

5.2 Demand for a product at a depot is at a constant rate of 250 units per week. The product is supplied to the depot from the factory. The factory cost is \$10 per unit, while the total cost of a shipment from the factory to the depot when the shipment has size M is given by

$$\text{Shipment cost} = \$50 + \$2\,M$$

The inventory carrying cost in \$/\$/week is 0.004. Determine the appropriate shipment size.

5.3 MIDAS can load and package their own brand of 35-mm slide film, or buy prepacked rolls of "Discount" brand film. If they load their own film, there is a production setup cost of \$20. The finished product is valued at \$1.23 a roll, and the production rate is 500 rolls/day. "Discount" film costs MIDAS \$1.26 per roll and the fixed ordering charge is \$3/order. In either case, an inventory carrying charge of 0.24 \$/\$/yr would be used by the company. Demand for this item is 10,000 rolls per year. From the standpoint of replenishment and carrying costs, what should the company do? What other considerations might affect the decision?

5.4 A manufacturing firm located in Calgary produces an item in a 3-month time supply. An analyst, attempting to introduce a more logical approach to selecting run quantities, has obtained the following estimates of characteristics of the item:

$$D = 4000 \text{ units/yr}$$
$$A = \$5$$
$$v = \$4 \text{ per } 100 \text{ units}$$
$$r = 0.25 \text{ \$/\$/yr}$$

Note: Assume that the production rate is much larger than D.

a. What is the economic order quantity of the item?

b. What is the time between consecutive replenishments of the item when the EOQ is used?

c. The production manager insists that the A = \$5 figure has been pulled out of the air, that is, it is only a guess. Therefore, he insists on using his simple 3-month supply rule. Indicate how you would find the range of A values for which the EOQ (based on A = \$5) would be preferable (in terms of a lower total of replenishment and carrying costs) to the 3-month supply.

5.5 Suppose that all of the assumptions of the EOQ derivation hold except that we now allow backorders (that is, we deliberately let the stock level run negative before we order; backordered requests are completely filled out of the replenishment). Now there are two decision variables: Q and s (the level below zero at which we place an order).

a. Using a sketch and geometrical considerations, find the average on-hand inventory level and the average level of backorders.

b. Suppose that there is a cost $B_2 v$ per unit backordered (independent of how long the unit is backordered) where B_2 is a dimensionless factor. Find the best settings of Q and s as a function of A, D, v, r, and B_2.

c. Repeat part b but now with a cost $B_3 v$ per unit backordered *per unit time*. The dimensions of B_3 are equivalent to those for r.

5.6 The famous Ernie of "Sesame Street" continually faces replenishment decisions concerning his cookie supply. The Cookie Monster devours the cookies at an average rate of 200 per day. The biscuits cost \$0.03 each. Ernie is getting fed up with having to go to the store once a week. His friend, Bert, has offered to do a study to help Ernie with his problem.

a. If Ernie is implicitly following an EOQ policy, what can Bert say about the implicit values of the two missing parameters?

b. Suppose that the store offered a special of 10,000 cookies for \$200. Should Ernie take advantage of the offer? Discuss. (*Hint:* Consult your local TV listing for the timing of and channel selection for "Sesame Street.")

5.7 U. R. Sick Labs manufactures penicillin. Briefly discuss special considerations required in establishing the run quantity of such an item.

5.8 Table 5.1 was developed based on management specifying permitted values of the order quantity expressed as a time supply. Suppose instead that order quantities (in units) were specified.

a. Develop an indifference condition between two *adjacent* permitted values, namely Q_1 and Q_2.

b. For $A = \$10$ and $r = 0.25$ \$/\$/yr, develop a table, similar to Table 5.1 (although the variable involving D and v need not necessarily be Dv), for Q values of 1, 10, 50, 100, 200, 500, and 1000 units.

c. For an item with $D = 500$ units/yr and $v = 0.10$ \$/unit, what is the *exact* EOQ? What Q does the table suggest using? What is the cost penalty associated with the use of this approximate Q value?

5.9 A mining company routinely replaces a specific part on a certain type of equipment. The usage rate is 40 per week and there is no significant seasonality. The supplier of the part offers the following all-units discount structure.

Range of Q	Unit Cost
$0 < Q < 300$ units	\$10.00
$300 \leq Q$	9.70

The fixed cost of a replenishment is estimated to be \$25 and a carrying charge of 0.26 \$/\$/yr is used by the company.

a. What replenishment size should be used?

b. If the supplier was interested in having the mining company acquire at least 500 units at a time, what is the largest unit price they could charge for an order of 500 units?

5.10 The supplier of a product wants to discourage *large* quantity purchases. Suppose that all of the assumptions of the basic EOQ apply except that a *reverse* quantity discount is applicable; that is, the unit variable cost is given by

$$v = \begin{cases} v_0 & 0 < Q < Q_b \\ v_0(1+d) & Q_b \leq Q \end{cases} \quad \text{where } d > 0$$

a. Write an expression (or expressions) for the total relevant costs per year as a function of the order quantity Q. Introduce (and define) whatever other symbols you feel are necessary.

b. Using graphical sketches, indicate the possible positions of the best order quantity (as is done in Figure 5.6 for the *regular* discount case).

c. What is the best order quantity for an item with the following characteristics:

Demand rate = 50,000 units/yr

Fixed setup cost per replenishment = \$10

$v = \$1.00/\text{unit}$

$d = 0.005$

Selling price = \$1.44/unit

Carrying charge = 0.20 \$/\$/yr

$Q_b = 1500$ units

5.11 A particular product is produced on a fabrication line. Using the finite replenishment EOQ model, the suggested run quantity is 1000 units. On a particular day of production, this item is being run near the end of a shift and the supervisor, instead of stopping at 1000 units and having to set up for a new item (which would make her performance look bad in terms of total output), continues to produce the item to the end of the shift, resulting in a total production quantity of 2000 units. Discuss how you would analyze whether or not she made a decision that was attractive from a company standpoint. Include comments on possible intangible factors.

5.12 Consider an inventory with but four items with the following characteristics:

Item i	D_i (units/yr)	v_i (\$/unit)
1	7200	2.00
2	4000	0.90
3	500	5.00
4	100	0.81

The inventory manager vehemently argues that there is no way that he can evaluate A and r; however, he is prepared to admit that A/r is reasonably constant across the items. He has been following an ordering policy of using a 4-month time supply of each item. He has been under pressure from the comptroller to reduce the average inventory level by 25 percent. Therefore, he is about to adopt a 3-month time supply.

a. Develop an EOQ aggregate exchange curve.

b. What are the values of TCS and N for $A/r = 200$?

c. What A/r value gives the same TCS as the current rule?

d. What A/r value gives the same N as the proposed rule?

e. Use the curve to suggest an option(s) open to the manager that is (are) preferable to his proposed action.

5.13 In Figure 1 of MIDAS Case D it was pointed out that the comptroller was advocating a min-max system with specific rules for computing the minimum and maximum levels of each item. Suppose that for each item the values of A, v, D, L, and r could be reasonably accurately ascertained.

a. Indicate how you would estimate the approximate cost savings of selecting the order quantity of an item through EOQ considerations rather than by the comptroller's method. (*Hint:* Assume that the order quantity is approximately equal to the difference between the maximum and minimum levels.)

b. Illustrate for the following item: A = \$3.20; v = \$10; D = 900 units/yr; L = 10 weeks; r = 0.24 \$/\$/yr.

REFERENCES

Aucamp, D. (1982). "Nonlinear Freight Costs in the EOQ Problem." *European Journal of Operational Research*, Vol. 9, pp. 61−63.

Brout, D. (1981). "Scientific Management of Inventory on a Hand-Held Calculator." *INTERFACES*, Vol. 11, No. 6, pp. 57−69.

Brown, R. G. (1982). *Advanced Service Parts Inventory Control.* Materials Management Systems, Inc., Norwich, Vermont, Chapter 11.

Buzacott, J. A. (1975). "Economic Order Quantities with Inflation." *Operational Research Quarterly*, Vol. 26, No. 3, pp. 553−558.

Buzacott, J. A. (1979). "Inventory as an Investment: A Review of Models and Issues." *Working Paper 79−013*, Department of Industrial Engineering, University of Toronto, Toronto, Ontario, Canada.

Chakravarty, A. K. (1981). "Multi-Item Inventory Aggregation into Groups." *Journal of the Operational Research Society*, Vol. 32, No. 1, pp. 19−26.

Crouch, R., and S. Oglesby (1978). "Optimization of a Few Lot Sizes to Cover a Range of Requirements." *Journal of the Operational Research Society*, Vol. 29, No. 9, pp. 897−904.

Das, C. (1977). "Economic Lot Size Models." In *Encylopedia of Computer Science and Technology.* (J. Belzer, A. G. Holzman, and A. Kent, editors), Marcel Dekker, New York, Vol. 8, pp. 52−75.

Davis, G. B. (1963). "The Preparation and Use of Nomographs." Chapter 15 in *Scientific Inventory Management*, J. Buchan and E. Koenigsberg. Prentice-Hall, Englewood Cliffs, New Jersey.

Donaldson, W. A. (1981). "Grouping of Inventory Items by Review Period." *Journal of the Operational Research Society*, Vol. 32, No. 12, pp. 1075−1076.

Eaton, J. A. (1964). "New—The LIMIT Technique." *Modern Materials Handling*, Vol. 19, No. 2, pp. 38−43.

Gaither, N. (1981). "The Effects of Inflation and Fuel Scarcity upon Inventory Policies." *Production and Inventory Management*, Vol. 22, No. 2, pp. 37−48.

Girling, A., and R. Morgan (1973). "Exchange Curves for Fixing Batch Quantities." *OMEGA*, Vol. 1, No. 2, pp. 241−245.

Gurnani, C. (1983). "Economic Analysis of Inventory Systems." *International Journal of Production Research*, Vol. 21, No. 2, pp.261−277.

Hadley, G., and T. Whitin (1963). *Analysis of Inventory Systems.* Prentice-Hall, Englewood Cliffs, New Jersey, pp. 66−68.

Juckler, F. (1970). *Modèles de Gestion des Stocks et Coûts Marginaux.* Vandeur, Louvain, Belgium.

Krupp, J. (1977). "Programmable Calculators: The New Materials Management Tool." *Production and Inventory Management*, Vol. 18, No. 4, pp. 88−103.

Kuzdrall, P., and R. Britney (1982). "Total Setup Lot Sizing with Quantity Discounts." *Decision Sciences*, Vol. 13, No. 1, pp. 101−112.

Lev, B., H. Weiss, and A. Soyster (1981). "Optimal Ordering Policies When Anticipating Parameter Changes in EOQ Systems." *Naval Research Logistics Quarterly*, Vol. 28, No. 2, pp. 267−279.

Maxwell, W. L., and H. Singh (1983). "The Effect of Restricting Cycle Times in the Economic Lot Scheduling Problem." *IIE Transactions*, Vol. 15, No. 3, pp. 235−241.

McClain, J. O., and L. J. Thomas (1980). *Operations Management: Production of Goods and*

Services. Prentice-Hall, Englewood Cliffs, New Jersey, pp. 278–279.

Mennell, R. F. (1961). "Early History of the Economical Lot Size." *APICS Quarterly Bulletin*, Vol. 2, No. 2, pp. 14–22.

Miltenburg, G. J. (1982). "Coordinated Control of a Family of Discount-Related Items." Unpublished doctoral dissertation, Department of Management Sciences, University of Waterloo, Waterloo, Ontario, Canada, Chapter 5.

Naddor, E. (1966). *Inventory Systems*. John Wiley & Sons, New York, pp. 96–102.

Page, E., and R. J. Paul (1976). "Multi-Product Inventory Situations with One Restriction." *Operational Research Quarterly*, Vol. 27, No. 4i, pp. 815–834.

Sethi, S. P. (1984). "A Quantity Discount Model with Disposals." *International Journal of Production Research*, Vol. 22, No. 1, pp. 31–39.

Silver, E. A. (1976). "Establishing the Order Quantity When the Amount Received Is Uncertain." *INFOR*, Vol. 14, No. 1, pp. 32–39.

Silver, E. A. (1979). "The Use of Programmable Calculators in Inventory Management." *Production and Inventory Management*, Vol. 20, No. 4, pp. 64–75.

Thompson, H. (1975). "Inventory Management and Capital Budgeting: A Pedogogical Note." *Decision Sciences*, Vol. 6, 1975, pp. 383–398.

Trippi, R., and D. Lewin (1979). "A Present Value Formulation of the Classical EOQ Problem." *Decision Sciences*, Vol. 5, pp. 30–35.

Welch, W. E. (1969). "How to Prepare Practical EOQ Tables." *Production and Inventory Management*, Vol. 10, No. 4, pp. 1–6.

Wilkinson, J., and A. Green (1972). "A Graphical Approach to Price Break Analysis-2." *Operational Research Quarterly*, Vol. 23, No. 3, pp. 385–394.

CHAPTER 6

Individual-Item Decision Rules for the Case of a Time-Varying Demand Pattern

In Chapter 5 we developed the economic order quantity (and various modifications of it) by essentially assuming a *level, deterministic* demand rate. In the current chapter we now relax this assumption and allow the average demand rate to vary with time, thus encompassing a broader range of practical situations, including:

1. Multiechelon assembly operations where a firm schedule of finished products exploded back through the various assembly stages leads to production requirements at these earlier levels, which are relatively deterministic but almost always vary appreciably with time. (This is a topic to which we return in Chapter 16 under the heading of Material Requirements Planning.)
2. Production to contract, where the contract requires that certain quantities have to be delivered to the customer on specified dates.
3. Items having a seasonal demand pattern. (Artificial seasonality can be induced by pricing or promotion actions.)
4. Replacement parts for an item that is being phased out of operation. Here, the demand rate drops off with time. (In some cases, particularly toward the end of its life, such an item is better treated by the Class C procedures to be discussed in Chapter 9.)
5. More generally, items with known trends in demand that are expected to continue.
6. Parts for preventive maintenance where the maintenance schedule is accurately known.

In Section 6.1 we point out how much more complex the analysis becomes when we allow the demand rate to vary with time. Section 6.2 is concerned with the choice that we have among three different approaches, namely: (1) straightforward use of the economic order quantity (even though one of the key assumptions on which it is based is violated); (2) an exact optimal procedure; and (3) an approximate heuristic method. In Section 6.3 the assumptions common to all three approaches are laid out as well as a numerical example to be used for illustrative purposes throughout Sections 6.4 to 6.7. Further details on each of the three approaches are presented in Sections 6.4, 6.5, and 6.6, including a discussion of when to use each method. Two other approaches, sometimes used in practice, are briefly treated in Section 6.7. Then, in Section 6.8, we again focus our attention on aggregate considerations by means of the exchange curve concept.

6.1 THE COMPLEXITY OF TIME-VARYING DEMAND

When the demand rate varies with time we can no longer assume that the best strategy is to always use the same replenishment quantity; in fact, this will seldom be the case (a similar difficulty arose in Chapter 5 when economic factors changed with time, such as conditions of inflation or a special opportunity to buy). An exact analysis becomes very complicated because the diagram of inventory level versus time, even for a constant replenishment quantity, is no longer the simple repeating sawtooth pattern that we saw in Figure 5.1 of Chapter 5. This prevents us from using simple average costs over a typical unit period as was possible in the EOQ derivation. Instead, we now have to use the demand information over a finite period, extending from the present, when determining the appropriate value of the current replenishment quantity. This period is known as the *planning horizon* and its length can have a substantial effect on the total relevant costs of the selected strategy. Moreover, all other factors being equal, we would prefer to have the planning horizon as short as possible because the farther into the future we look for demand information, the less accurate it is likely to be.

It should, however, be kept in mind that in actual applications a rolling-schedule procedure is almost always used. Specifically, although replenishment quantities may be computed over the entire planning horizon, *only the imminent decision is implemented*. Then, at the time of the next decision, new demand information is appended to maintain a constant length of horizon.

As indicated by the examples of time-varying demand discussed earlier, the demand can be either continuous with time or can occur only at discrete equispaced points in time. The former represents a stream of small-sized demands where the arrival rate varies with time, whereas the latter corresponds to something such as weekly shipments where a large demand quantity is satisfied at one time. The decision system that we propose is not affected by whether the demand is continuous or discrete with respect to time; all that will be needed is the total demand in each basic period. A common case that can be handled is where the demand rate stays constant throughout a period, only changing from one period to another. An illustration is shown in Figure 6.1. As discussed in Chapter 4, demand forecasts are usually developed in such a form, for example, a rate in January, another rate in February, and so on.

Another element of the problem that is important in selecting appropriate replenishment quantities is whether replenishments must be scheduled at specified discrete points in time (for example, replenishments can only be scheduled at intervals that are integer multiples of a week) or whether they can be scheduled at any point in continuous time. Considering a single item in isolation, the second case is probably more appropriate if the demand pattern is continuous with time. However, to ease scheduling coordination problems in multi-item situations, it usually makes sense to limit the opportunity times for replenishment of each item. Furthermore, if the demand pattern is such that all of the requirements for each period must be available at the beginning of that period, it is appropriate to restrict replenishment opportunities to the beginnings of periods. This latter assumption will be made in developing the logic of the decision system that we propose. (The case where replenishments can take place at any time has been treated by Silver and Meal, 1969.)

Still another factor that can materially influence the logic in selecting replenishment quantities is the duration of the demand pattern. A pattern with a clearly specified end resulting from a production contract is quite different from the demand situation where no well-defined end is in sight. In the former case it is important to plan to reach the end of the pattern with a low (if not zero) level of

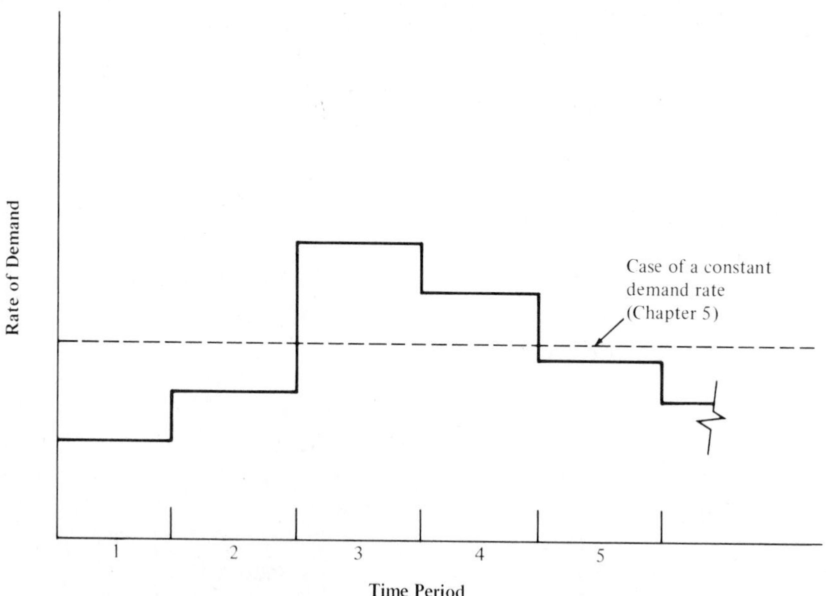

FIGURE 6.1 Demand Pattern When the Rate Stays Constant Through Each Period

inventory. In contrast, for the continuing demand situation, if we use a finite planning horizon, there is no need to force the solution to include a low inventory level at the end of the horizon. Remaining inventory can be used in the interval beyond the horizon, where demand will continue (albeit, at a possibly different rate).

6.2 THE CHOICE OF APPROACHES

There are essentially three approaches to dealing with the case of a deterministic, time-varying demand pattern.

1. *Use of the basic economic order quantity.* Here one adopts a very simple approach, namely, one uses a fixed EOQ, based on the average demand rate out to the horizon, anytime a replenishment is required. As would be expected, this approach makes sense when the variability of the demand pattern is low, that is, the constant demand rate assumption of the fixed EOQ is not significantly violated.
2. *Use of the exact best solution to a particular mathematical model of the situation.* As we will see, under a specific set of assumptions, this approach, known as the Wagner-Whitin algorithm, minimizes the total of certain costs (for reasons that will become evident later in the chapter, we purposely avoid the use of the words "total relevant costs" here).
3. *Use of an approximate or heuristic method.* The idea here is to use an approach that captures the essence of the time-varying complexity but at the same time remains relatively simple for the practitioner to understand and does not require lengthy computations.

6.3 GENERAL ASSUMPTIONS AND A NUMERICAL EXAMPLE

6.3.1 The Assumptions

There are a number of assumptions that will be made (at least implicitly) in all three of the aforementioned approaches. We now specify these rather than showing them at three separate times later in the chapter. Certain of these assumptions can be relaxed by somewhat minor modifications of the decision methodology; such modifications will be demonstrated later.

1. The demand rate is given in the form of $D(j)$ to be satisfied in period j ($j = 1, 2, \ldots, N$) where the planning horizon is at the end of period N. Of course, the demand rate may vary from one period to the next, but it is assumed known. The case of probabilistic, time-varying demand will be addressed in Chapter 8.

2. The entire requirements of each period must be available at the beginning of that period. Therefore, a replenishment arriving part-way through a period cannot be used to satisfy that period's requirements and it is cheaper, in terms of reduced carrying costs, to delay its arrival until the start of the next period. Thus, replenishments are constrained to arrive at the beginnings of periods.
3. The unit variable cost does not depend on the replenishment quantity; in particular, there are no discounts in either the unit purchase cost or the unit transportation cost.
4. The cost factors do not change appreciably with time; in particular, inflation is at a low level.
5. The item is treated entirely independently of other items, that is, benefits from joint review or replenishment do not exist or are ignored.
6. The replenishment lead time is known with certainty (a special case being zero duration) so that delivery can be timed to occur right at the beginning of a period.
7. No shortages are allowed.
8. The entire order quantity is delivered at the same time.
9. For simplicity of exposition it is assumed that the carrying cost is only applicable to inventory that is carried over from one period to the next. It should be emphasized that all three approaches can easily handle the situation where carrying charges are included on the material during the period in which it is used to satisfy the demand requirements but, for practical purposes, this is an unnecessary complication.

Reference to Section 5.1 of Chapter 5 reveals that, except for 1, 2, and 9, these assumptions are identical with those required in the derivation of the basic economic order quantity.

Because of the assumption of deterministic demand, it is clear, from assumptions 2, 6, and 7 that an appropriate method of selecting replenishment quantities should lead to the arrival of replenishments only at the beginning of periods when the inventory level is exactly zero.

6.3.2 A Numerical Example

The MIDAS International plant in Germany uses the following simple decision rule for ascertaining production run quantities: "Each time a production run is made, a quantity sufficient to satisfy the total demand in the next three months is produced." For the seasonal product PSF-007, a 25 cm by 30 cm lithographic film, MIDAS Canada is the only customer of MIDAS International. The basic unit of the product is a box of 50 sheets of film. MIDAS Canada requirements by month (shifted to take account of shipping time) in the upcoming year are:

Month	Sequential Number	Requirements (boxes)
January	1	10
February	2	62
March	3	12
April	4	130
May	5	154
June	6	129
July	7	88
August	8	52
September	9	124
October	10	160
November	11	238
December	12	41
		Total = 1200

It is seen that the demand pattern has two peaks, one in the late spring, the other in the autumn season.

The German plant estimates the fixed setup cost (A) per replenishment to be approximately \$54, and the carrying charge (r) has been set by management at 0.02 \$/\$/month. The unit variable cost (v) of the film is \$20/box.

The production planning department of MIDAS International would like to establish the size of the first production run (that needed by January 1) and also estimate the timing and sizes of future production quantities. The word "estimate" is used because MIDAS Canada could conceivably revise its requirements, particularly those late in the year, but still giving adequate time to permit adjustment of the later portions of the production schedule.

Use of the company's "three month" decision rule leads to the replenishment schedule and associated costs shown in Table 6.1. There are four replenishments covering the 12 months out to the horizon.The total relevant costs are \$663.20. The average month-ending inventory is 1118/12 or 93.17 boxes. Therefore, the turnover ratio is 1200/93.17 or 12.9.

TABLE 6.1 Results of Using the Company's "Three Month" Rule on the Numerical Example

Month	1	2	3	4	5	6	7	8	9	10	11	12	Total
Starting inventory	0	74	12	0	283	129	0	176	124	0	279	41	—
Replenishment	84	—	—	413	—	—	264	—	—	439	—	—	1200
Requirements	10	62	12	130	154	129	88	52	124	160	238	41	1200
Ending inventory	74	12	0	283	129	0	176	124	0	279	41	0	1118

Total replenishment costs = 4 × \$54 = \$216.00
Total carrying costs = 1118 box-months × \$20/box × 0.02 \$/\$/month = \$447.20
Total replenishment plus carrying costs = \$663.20

6.4 USE OF A FIXED ECONOMIC ORDER QUANTITY

When the demand rate is approximately constant we have advocated, in Chapter 5, the use of the basic economic order quantity. One possible approach to the case of a time-varying rate is to simply ignore the time variability, thus continuing to use the economic order quantity. (An alternative, closely related, approach is to use a fixed time supply equal to the EOQ time supply, T_{EOQ}. This approach will be discussed further in Section 6.7.) To be more precise, the *average* demand rate ($\bar{D}$) out to the horizon (N periods), or to whatever point our forecast information extends, is evaluated and the economic order quantity

$$\text{EOQ} = \sqrt{\frac{2A\bar{D}}{vr}}$$

is used anytime a replenishment is needed. Actually $\bar{D}$ can simply be based on a relatively infrequent estimate of the average demand per period and need not necessarily be reevaluated at the time of each replenishment decision. To account for the discrete opportunities to replenish, at the time of a replenishment, the EOQ should be adjusted to exactly satisfy the requirements of an integer number of periods. A simple way to do this is to keep accumulating periods of requirements until the closest total to the EOQ is found.

To illustrate, for our numerical example,

$$\bar{D} = \frac{\text{Total requirements}}{12 \text{ months}} = 100 \text{ boxes/month}$$

Therefore,

$$\text{EOQ} = \sqrt{\frac{2 \times \$54 \times 100 \text{ boxes/month}}{\$20/\text{box} \times 0.02\ \$/\$/\text{month}}}$$

Consider the selection of the replenishment quantity at the beginning of January. The following table is helpful:

	January	February	March	April
Requirements	10	62	12	130
Cumulative requirements to end of month	10	72	84	214

TABLE 6.2 Results of Using the Fixed EOQ Approach on the Numerical Example

Month	1	2	3	4	5	6	7	8	9	10	11	12	Total
Starting inventory	0	204	142	130	0	0	0	52	0	0	0	0	—
Replenishment	214	—	—	—	154	129	140	—	124	160	238	41	1200
Requirements	10	62	12	130	154	129	88	52	124	160	238	41	1200
Ending inventory	204	142	130	0	0	0	52	0	0	0	0	0	528

Total replenishment costs = 8 × \$54 = \$432.00

Total carrying costs = 528 box-months × \$20/box × 0.02 \$/\$/month = \$211.20

Total replenishment plus carrying costs = \$643.20

The EOQ of 164 boxes lies between 84 and 214, and 214 is closer to 164 than is 84. Therefore, the first replenishment quantity is 214 boxes, lasting through the end of April. The detailed results of applying the fixed EOQ approach to the numerical example are as shown in Table 6.2. It is seen from Tables 6.1 and 6.2 that the fixed EOQ approach, compared to the company's "three month" rule, reduces the total of replenishment and carrying costs from \$663.20 to \$643.20 or some 3.0 percent, a rather small saving. The turnover ratio has been increased from 12.9 to 1,200 × 12/528 or 27.3, but the replenishment costs have also increased.

6.5 THE WAGNER-WHITIN METHOD: AN "OPTIMAL" SOLUTION UNDER AN ADDITIONAL ASSUMPTION

Wagner and Whitin (1958), in a classic article, developed an algorithm that guarantees an optimal (in terms of minimizing the total costs of replenishment and carrying inventory) selection of replenishment quantities under the set of assumptions that were listed in Section 6.3.1 as well as one additional assumption that *may* be needed—namely, that either the demand pattern terminates at the horizon or else the ending inventory must be prespecified.

6.5.1 The Algorithm

The algorithm is an application of dynamic programming, a mathematical procedure for solving sequential decision problems.[1] The computational effort,

[1]The problem here is a sequential decision problem because the outcome of the replenishment quantity decision at one point has effects on the possible replenishment actions that can be taken at later decision times; for example, whether or not we should replenish at the beginning of March depends very much on the size of the replenishment quantity at the beginning of February. Vidal (1970) provides an equivalent linear programming formulation and an associated efficient solution procedure.

often prohibitive in dynamic programming formulations, is significantly reduced because of the use of two key properties (derived by Wagner and Whitin) which the optimal solution must satisfy:

Property 1 A replenishment only takes place when the inventory level is zero (already discussed in Section 6.3).

Property 2 There is an upper limit to how far before a period j we would include its requirements, $D(j)$, in a replenishment quantity. Eventually, the carrying costs become so high that it is less expensive to have a replenishment arrive at the start of period j instead of including its requirements in a replenishment from many periods earlier.

Suppose we define $F(t)$ as the total costs of the *best* replenishment strategy that satisfies the demand requirements in periods $1, 2, \ldots, t$. To illustrate the procedure for finding $F(t)$ and the associated replenishments, we again use the example of Table 6.1. Recall that the demand pattern is

Month	Sequential Number	Requirements (boxes)
January	1	10
February	2	62
March	3	12
April	4	130
May	5	154
June	6	129
July	7	88
August	8	52
September	9	124
October	10	160
November	11	238
December	12	41
		Total = 1200

$F(1)$ is the total costs of a replenishment of size 10 at the start of January, simply the setup cost A or \$54.

To determine $F(2)$, we have two possible options to consider:

Option 1 Replenish 10 boxes at the start of January and 62 boxes at the start of February.

Option 2 Replenish enough (72 boxes) at the start of January to cover the requirements of both January and February.

Costs of Option 1 = (Costs of best plan from the start to the end of January) + (Costs of a replenishment at the start of February to meet February's requirements)

$= F(1) + A$

$= \$54 + \$54$

$= \$108$

Costs of Option 2 = (Setup cost for January replenishment) + (Carrying costs for February's requirements)

$= \$54 + 62 \text{ boxes} \times \$0.40/\text{box/month} \times 1 \text{ month}$

$= \$54 + \$24.60$

$= \$78.60$

The cost of the second option is less than that of the first. Therefore, the best choice to satisfy the requirements of January and February is Option 2 and $F(2) = \$78.60$.

To satisfy requirements through to the end of March there are three options, namely, where we position the *last* replenishment:

Option 1 Cover to the end of February in the best possible fashion and replenish 12 boxes at the start of March.

Option 2 Cover to the end of January in the best possible fashion and replenish 74 boxes at the start of February.

Option 3 Have a single replenishment of 84 boxes at the start of January.

Costs of Option 1 $= F(2) + A$

$= \$78.60 + \$54$

$= \$132.60$

Costs of Option 2 $= F(1) + A +$ (Carrying costs for March's requirements)

$= \$54 + \$54 + (12 \times 0.40 \times 1)$

$= \$112.80$

Costs of Option 3 $= A +$ (Carrying costs for February's requirements) + (Carrying costs for March's requirements)

$= \$54 + (62 \times 0.40 \times 1) + (12 \times 0.40 \times 2)$

$= \$88.40$

Therefore, Option 3, a single replenishment at the start of January, is best in terms of meeting requirements through to the end of March.

We continue forward in this fashion until we complete period N (here $N = 12$). For any specific month t there are t possible options to evaluate. It is important to note that the method, as just described, requires an ending point where it is known that the inventory level is to be at zero or some other specified value.

To illustrate the effect of property 2 discussed at the beginning of this section, consider the options open to us in terms of meeting requirements through to the end of July (month 7). The discussion in the previous paragraph would indicate that we must evaluate seven options. However, consider the requirements of 88 boxes in the month of July. The carrying costs associated with these requirements, if they were included in a replenishment at the beginning of June, would be

$$88 \text{ boxes} \times \$0.40/\text{box/month} \times 1 \text{ month or } \$35.20$$

Similarly, if these requirements were instead included in a replenishment at the beginning of May, the carrying costs associated with the 88 units would be

$$88 \text{ boxes} \times \$0.40/\text{box/month} \times 2 \text{ months or } \$70.40$$

which is larger than \$54, the fixed cost of a replenishment. Therefore, the best solution could never have the requirements of July included in a replenishment at the beginning of May or earlier. It would be less expensive to have a replenishment arrive at the beginning of July. Thus, we need consider only two options—namely, having the last replenishment at the start of either June or July.

If one is interested in computing the size of only the first replenishment quantity, then it may not be necessary to go all the way out to the horizon (month N). Use of property 2 shows that, if for a period j the requirements are so large that

$$D(j)vr > A$$

that is

$$D(j) > A/vr$$

then the optimal solution will have a replenishment at the beginning of period j; that is, the inventory *must* go to zero at the start of period j. Therefore, the earliest j where this happens can be used as an horizon for the calculation of the first replenishment. In the numerical example,

$$A/vr = \frac{\$54}{\$20/\text{box} \times 0.02\ \$/\$/\text{month}} = 135 \text{ box-months}$$

It is seen from the demand pattern that the earliest month with $D(j) > 135$ is May. Therefore, the end of April can be considered as an horizon in computing the replenishment quantity needed at the beginning of January. It should be emphasized that there may be no month out to the horizon where this happens.

The details of the best strategy for the whole 12-month period are shown in Table 6.3. There are seven replenishments and the total costs amount to

TABLE 6.3 Results of Using the Wagner-Whitin Algorithm or the Silver-Meal Heuristic on the Numerical Example

Month	1	2	3	4	5	6	7	8	9	10	11	12	Total
Starting inventory	0	74	12	0	0	129	0	52	0	0	0	41	—
Replenishment	84	—	—	130	283	—	140	—	124	160	279	—	1200
Requirements	10	62	12	130	154	129	88	52	124	160	238	41	1200
Ending inventory	74	12	0	0	129	0	52	0	0	0	41	0	308

Total replenishment costs = 7 × \$54 = \$378.00
Total carrying costs = 308 box-months × \$20/box × 0.02 \$/\$/month = \$123.20
Total replenishment plus carrying costs = \$501.20

\$501.20. Comparison with Tables 6.1 and 6.2 shows that the Wagner-Whitin algorithm produces total costs some 24.4 percent lower than those of the company's three-month rule and some 22.1 percent lower than those of a fixed EOQ strategy. Furthermore, the turnover ratio has been increased to 1200 × 12/308 or 46.8.

6.5.2 Potential Drawbacks of the Algorithm

As mentioned earlier, the Wagner-Whitin algorithm is guaranteed to provide a set of replenishment quantities that minimize the sum of replenishment plus carrying costs out to a specified horizon. (In fact, a generalized form permits including backordering as well as replenishment costs that depend on the period in which the replenishment occurs.) However, the algorithm has received extremely limited acceptance in practice. The following are the primary reasons for this lack of acceptance:

1. The relatively complex nature of the algorithm that makes its understanding difficult for the practitioner.
2. The considerable computational effort required for each item handled by the algorithm, substantially more than for the fixed EOQ method or for the heuristic to be discussed in the next section.
3. The possible need for a well-defined ending point for the demand pattern. (This would be artificial for the typical inventoried item where termination of demand is not expected in the near future.) As shown above, such an ending point is not needed when there is at least one period whose requirements exceed A/vr. Moreover, all information out to the end point may be needed for computing even the initial replenishment quantity. In this connection considerable research effort (see for example, Blackburn and Kunreuther, 1974; Eppen et al., 1969; Kunreuther and Morton, 1973, 1974; and Lundin and Morton, 1975) has been devoted to ascertaining the minimum required length of the planning horizon to ensure the selection of the optimal value of the initial replenishment.

4. The necessary assumption that replenishments can be made only at discrete intervals (namely, at the beginning of each of the periods). This assumption can be relaxed by subdividing the periods; however, the computational requirements of the algorithm go up rapidly with the number of periods considered. (In contrast, the other two methods are easily modified to account for continuous opportunities to replenish.)

When one takes account of total relevant costs, particularly including system control costs, it is not at all surprising that the algorithm has received such limited acceptability. We do *not* advocate its use for B items (Let us not lose sight of the fact that in this chapter we are still talking about this class of items as opposed to Class A items, where for the latter considerably more control expense is justified because of the higher potential savings per item.) Instead, it is appropriate to resort to simpler heuristic methods that result in reduced control costs that more than offset any extra replenishment or carrying costs that their use may incur.

6.6 THE SILVER-MEAL HEURISTIC—A RECOMMENDED APPROACH FOR A SIGNIFICANTLY VARIABLE DEMAND PATTERN

As indicated by the results in the previous two sections, the Wagner-Whitin approach does substantially better than a fixed economic order quantity, at least for the illustrative numerical example. However, as mentioned in Section 6.5.2, the Wagner-Whitin approach has serious drawbacks from the practitioner's standpoint. Therefore, the natural question to ask is "Is there a simpler approach that will capture most of the potential savings in the total of replenishment and carrying costs?" A number of individuals (see, for example, Aucamp and Fogarty, 1982; De Matteis and Mendoza, 1968; Gorham, 1968; Groff, 1979; Karni, 1981; Quaye, 1979; and Silver and Meal, 1973) have suggested various decision rules, some of which have been widely used in practice. In particular, Silver and Meal (1973) have developed a simple variation of the basic EOQ, which, as we will find, accomplishes exactly what we desire. Moreover, in numerous test examples the Silver-Meal heuristic has performed extremely well when compared with the other rules encountered in the literature. Two of these other heuristics will be discussed in Section 6.7.

As mentioned earlier, the fixed EOQ approach should perform suitably when the demand pattern varies very little with time. For this reason we advocate use of the somewhat more complicated Silver-Meal heuristic only when the pattern is significantly variable. An operational definition of "significantly variable" will be given in Section 6.6.4.

6.6.1 The Criterion Used for Selecting a Replenishment Quantity

The heuristic selects the replenishment quantity in order to replicate a property that the basic economic order quantity possesses when the demand rate is constant with time, namely, the *total relevant costs per unit time for the duration of the replenishment quantity are minimized*. If a replenishment arrives at the beginning of the first period and it covers requirements through to the end of the Tth period, then the criterion function can be written as follows:

$$\frac{(\text{Setup cost}) + (\text{Total carrying costs to end of period } T)}{T}$$

This is a reasonable criterion and it has the desirable feature of not including, in the present replenishment, a large requirement well in the future (inclusion of such a requirement would make the "costs per unit time" measure too high). It is not difficult to develop numerical examples in which use of the criterion does not lead to the overall optimal solution, particularly for the case where the demand pattern has a well-defined ending point. Fortunately, this is not a major drawback because our primary concern is with demand patterns that do not have a clearly defined ending point in the near future. (This follows from our basic definition of Class B items.)

6.6.2 The Essence of the Heuristic

Because we are constrained to replenishing at the beginnings of periods, the best strategy must involve replenishment quantities that last for an integer number of periods. Consequently, we can think of the decision variable for a particular replenishment as being the time T that the replenishment will last, with T constrained to integer values. The replenishment quantity Q, associated with a particular value of T, is

$$Q = \sum_{j=1}^{T} D(j) \tag{6.1}$$

provided we set the time origin so that the replenishment is needed and arrives at the beginning of period 1. According to the chosen criterion, we wish to pick the T value that minimizes the total relevant costs per unit time of replenishment and carrying inventory over the time period T.

Let the total relevant costs associated with a replenishment that lasts for T periods be denoted by TRC(T). These costs are composed of the fixed replenishment cost A and the inventory carrying costs. We wish to select T to minimize the total relevant costs per unit time, TRCUT(T), where

$$\text{TRCUT}(T) = \frac{\text{TRC}(T)}{T} = \frac{A + \text{carrying costs}}{T} \tag{6.2}$$

If $T = 1$, there are no carrying costs (we only replenish enough to cover the requirements of period 1), that is,

$$\text{TRCUT}(1) = \frac{A}{1} = A$$

If the setup cost A is large, this may be unattractive when compared with including the second period's requirements in the replenishment, that is, using $T = 2$.

With $T = 2$ the carrying costs are $D(2)vr$, the cost of carrying the requirements $D(2)$ for one period. Therefore,

$$\text{TRCUT}(2) = \frac{A + D(2)vr}{2}$$

Now the setup cost is apportioned across two periods, but a carrying cost is incurred.

With $T = 3$ we still carry $D(2)$ for one period, but now we also carry $D(3)$ for two periods. Thus,

$$\text{TRCUT}(3) = \frac{A + D(2)vr + 2D(3)vr}{3}$$

In this case the setup charge is apportioned across three periods, but this may not be attractive because of the added carrying costs.

The basic idea of the heuristic is to evaluate TRCUT(T) for increasing values[2] of T until, for the first time,

$$\text{TRCUT}(T + 1) > \text{TRCUT}(T)$$

that is, the total relevant costs per unit time start increasing. When this happens the associated T is selected as the number of periods that the replenishment should cover. The corresponding replenishment quantity Q is given by Eq. 6.1.

As evidenced by Figure 6.2, this method guarantees only a local minimum in the total relevant costs per unit time, *for the current replenishment*. It is possible that still larger values of T would yield still lower costs per unit time since we stop testing with the first increase in costs per unit time. We could protect against this eventuality by computing the ratio for a few more values of T, but the likelihood of improvement in most real cases is small. Further-

[2]When some of the D's are zeros, we proceed as follows. Suppose $D(j) > 0$, $D(j + 1) = 0$, and $D(j + 2) > 0$. We evaluate TRCUT(j), then jump to TRCUT($j + 2$).

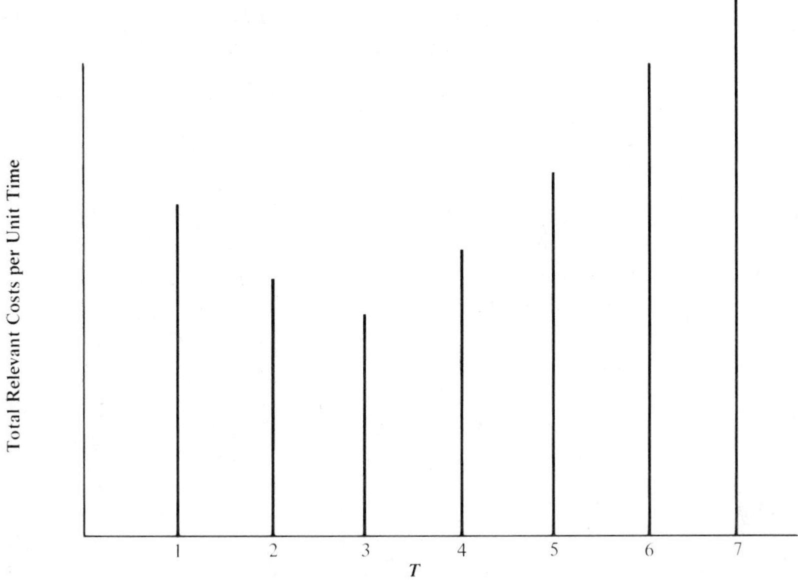

Case a — True Minimum Selected

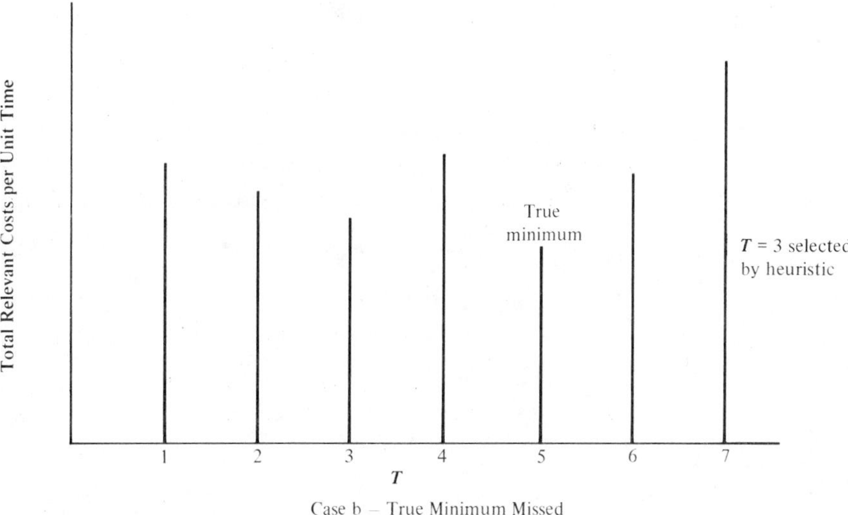

Case b — True Minimum Missed

FIGURE 6.2 Graphical Portrayal of the Selection of T in the Silver-Meal Heuristic

more, let us not lose sight of the fact that "costs per unit time for the first replenishment" is only a surrogate criterion.

It is conceivable that the TRCUT(T) may continue to decrease all the way out to $T = N$. This says that it is appropriate to cover all requirements out to the horizon with the current replenishment. In such a case, it may be appropriate to cover an even longer period, but the heuristic is unable to provide the answer without forecast information beyond period N.

Except for the unusual situation just described, the performance of the heuristic, in contrast with the Wagner-Whitin algorithm, does not crucially depend on the N value chosen. It tends to use demand data of only the first few periods, an attractive property when one recognizes that the deterministic demand assumption becomes less reasonable as one projects further into the future.

The calculations in the heuristic can be simplified somewhat if one normalizes total relevant costs per unit time by dividing by vr. The general result for T periods is, from Eq. 6.2,

$$\text{NTRCUT}(T) = \frac{\text{TRCUT}(T)}{vr} = \frac{A/vr + \sum_{j=1}^{T} (j-1)D(j)}{T} \tag{6.3}$$

Note that A, v, and r appear only in the form of a ratio, A/vr; that is, only the value of the ratio and not the individual values of A, v, and r are crucial in the selection of T. Such is also the case in the Wagner-Whitin algorithm and in the basic EOQ. The latter is obvious in that

$$\text{EOQ} = \sqrt{\frac{2AD}{vr}} = \sqrt{2D}\sqrt{\frac{A}{vr}}$$

To illustrate the application of the heuristic, let us again use the numerical example of Section 6.3. To refresh the reader's memory the values of A, v, and r and the first part of the requirements pattern are as follows:

$$A = \$54 \qquad v = \$20/\text{box} \qquad r = 0.02\$/\$/\text{month}$$

Month j	1	2	3	4	5	6 ...
Requirements $D(j)$	10	62	12	130	154	129 ...

The calculations for the first replenishment quantity (assuming that the inventory is zero at the beginning of month 1) are shown in Table 6.4. The heuristic selects a T value of 3 with an associated Q, using Eq. 6.1, of

$$\begin{aligned} Q &= D(1) + D(2) + D(3) \\ &= 10 + 62 + 12 \\ &= 84 \text{ boxes} \end{aligned}$$

TABLE 6.4 Computations for the First Replenishment Quantity Using the Silver-Meal Heuristic

T	A	$D(2)vr$	$2D(3)vr$	$3D(4)vr$	Row Sum	Cum. Sum	Cum. Sum $\div T$
1	54				54.00	54.00	54.00
2		62(20)(0.02)			24.80	78.80	39.40
3			2(12)(0.4)[a]		9.60	88.40	29.47
4				3(130)(0.4)	156.00	244.40	61.10

[a] $vr = 20(0.02) = 0.4$.

The table illustrates that the computations are simply multiplications, additions, divisions, and comparisons of numbers. Woolsey (1983) has developed a nomogram that simplifies the calculations even further.

It turns out for this numerical example (and for a substantial portion of all others tested) that this simple heuristic gives the same solution as the Wagner-Whitin algorithm. Thus, the solution has already been shown in Table 6.3.

6.6.3 Performance of the Heuristic

We know, from Section 5.2 of Chapter 5, that the basic economic order quantity is optimal under a set of assumptions which includes that the demand rate is constant and deterministic. As discussed earlier in the present chapter, when the demand rate varies with time, there is no simply implementable "optimal" procedure. The justification for the use of the Silver-Meal heuristic must be made on a combination of simplicity and reasonable cost performance. The simplicity of the method has already been demonstrated.

The discrete version of the heuristic has been tested against the Wagner-Whitin algorithm, the basic economic order quantity, and other heuristics on a wide range of examples. In these tests we reach the same conclusion—namely, that in almost all cases where the Wagner-Whitin method significantly outperforms the fixed EOQ, so does the Silver-Meal heuristic. Moreover, in these examples, the average cost penalty for using the heuristic instead of the "optimal" Wagner-Whitin algorithm has been less than 1 percent; in many cases there is no penalty whatsoever. Finally, tests in a rolling-horizon environment (see, for example, Blackburn and Millen, 1980) have revealed that frequently the heuristic actually *outperforms* the dynamic programming algorithm (because the latter now gives the optimal solution to the wrong problem).

6.6.4 When to Use the Heuristic

The heuristic, although quite simple, is still more involved than the determination of the basic economic order quantity. We know that the latter is the best replenishment quantity to use when there is no variability in the demand rate.

In fact, the variability of the demand pattern should exceed some threshold value before it makes sense to use the heuristic.

A useful measure of the variability of a demand pattern is the variability coefficient. This statistic, denoted by VC, is given by

$$VC = \frac{\text{Variance of demand per period}}{\text{Square of average demand per period}}$$

As shown in the Appendix of this chapter, this simplies to

$$VC = \frac{N \sum_{j=1}^{N} [D(j)]^2}{[\sum_{j=1}^{N} D(j)]^2} - 1 \tag{6.4}$$

where N is the number of periods of demand forecasts readily available. The aforementioned tests have shown that a threshold value of VC appears to be in the neighborhood of 0.2, that is,

If $VC < 0.2$, use a simple EOQ involving $\bar{D}$ as the demand estimate.

If $VC \geqslant 0.2$, use the Silver-Meal heuristic.

For the numerical example discussed in this chapter, Eq. 6.4 gives

$$VC = \frac{12(171{,}094)}{(1200)^2} - 1 = 0.426$$

which is greater than the threshold value indicating that the heuristic, rather than the EOQ, should be used. (Recall from Tables 6.2 and 6.3 that the heuristic produced total relevant costs 22.1 percent below those resulting from use of the EOQ.)

In addition, one should worry about the absolute importance of the item, in terms of the potential savings in replenishment and carrying costs. A useful surrogate for this quantity is the total of these costs per unit time under use of the EOQ *in the EOQ cost model* (we know that the EOQ model is, strictly speaking, only an approximation for the case of time-varying demand, but it is simple to use), namely,

$$\sqrt{2A\bar{D}vr}$$

If this quantity was very small, one would not be justified in departing from the simple EOQ decision rule. However, in this chapter we are concerned with B items, defined to be those with intermediate values of $\bar{D}v$. Thus, by definition, for such items the above test quantity will be large enough to ensure that we should not blindly remain with the basic EOQ when the demand rate varies enough.

A word of caution is in order. There are two situations where use of the heuristic can lead to significant cost penalties

1. When the demand pattern drops rapidly with time over several periods.
2. When there are a large number of periods having no demand.

Silver and Miltenburg (1984) have suggested modifications of the heuristic to cope with these circumstances.

Finally, if the Wagner-Whitin procedure is to be used at all, its use should be restricted to A items having highly variable demand patterns with a definite specified termination of the demand pattern at the horizon (such as in a fixed period contract).

6.6.5 Sensitivity to Errors in Parameters

In Section 5.3 of Chapter 5 it was illustrated that, for the case of the basic economic order quantity, the total cost curve is quite shallow in the neighborhood of the best order quantity. Thus, even substantial deviations of the order quantity away from its best value, tend to produce small percentage cost penalties. One case of such deviations is errors in the parameter (cost or demand) values. We concluded that the costs were relatively insensitive to errors in the input parameters for the case of the EOQ formulation.

Fortunately, tests have revealed that a similar phenomenon exists for the Silver-Meal heuristic. The results of one such test are shown in Figure 6.3. The basic data used (taken from Kaimann, 1969) were:

$$A/vr = 150$$

Period	1	2	3	4	5	6	7	8	9	10	11	12
Requirements	10	10	15	20	70	180	250	270	230	40	0	10

A/vr was deliberately changed from its correct value. For this incorrect value of A/vr the Silver-Meal heuristic was used to compute the replenishment quantities. The true value of A/vr was then employed to compute the costs associated with this sequence of replenishments. These costs were compared with those of the replenishment pattern resulting from using the correct value of A/vr. This was repeated for a number of different percentage errors in A/vr. To illustrate, in Figure 6.3 it is seen that if A/vr is erroneously set at a value 40 percent too high (that is, at a value of 210 instead of the correct level of 150), then the cost penalty is less than 2 percent. The plot is not a smooth curve (as was the case in Figure 5.3 of Chapter 5) because here the replenishment opportunities are discrete in nature. Nonetheless, in all cases tested, the percentage cost penalties, even for reasonable-sized errors in A/vr, were quite small.

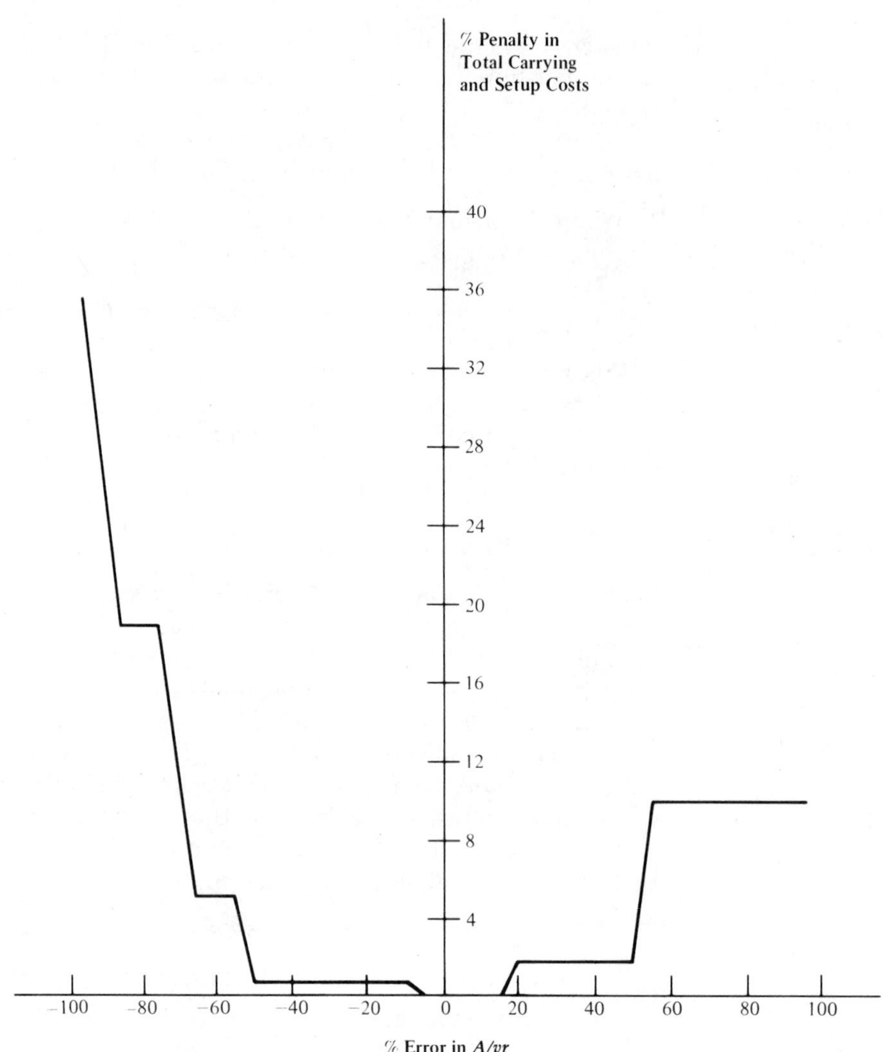

FIGURE 6.3 Illustration of Insensitivity of Heuristic Results to Errors in Cost Parameters

6.6.6 Handling of Quantity Discounts

An important extension of the heuristic is to permit inclusion of quantity discounts. As in Chapter 5 we illustrate for the case of an all-units fractional discount d if $Q \geqslant Q_b$. The presence of a discount removes the validity of one of the key properties of a solution first mentioned in Section 6.5—namely, that replenishments are received only when the inventory level is 0. Now it may indeed be appropriate to order exactly Q_b, which need not cover precisely an integer number of periods of requirements.

A revised heuristic, suggested by Lamarre and Baier (1981) after experimentation with many numerical examples, involves the evaluation of T_b, the number (not necessarily an integer) of periods of requirements covered by the breakpoint quantity Q_b. The costs per unit time for the use of T_b are given by

$$\text{TRCUT}(T_b) = \frac{A}{[T_b]} + \frac{vr\sum_{j=1}^{[T_b]}(j-1)D(j) + vr[T_b][Q_b - \sum_{j=1}^{[T_b]} D(j)] - Q_b vd}{T_b} \tag{6.5}$$

where $[T_b]$ is the integer portion of T_b (for example, if $T_b = 3.2$, then $[T_b] = 3$).

Integer values of T (that is, 1, 2, . . .) are also costed out using

$$\text{TRCUT}(T) = \begin{cases} \dfrac{A + vr\sum_{j=1}^{T}(j-1)D(j)}{T} & T < T_b \\[2ex] \dfrac{A + vr\sum_{j=1}^{T}(j-1)D(j) - vd\sum_{j=1}^{T} D(j)}{T} & T > T_b \end{cases} \tag{6.6}$$

Either T_b or the minimizing integer value of T is used, depending on whether Eq. 6.5 gives a lower value than Eq. 6.6 when the best integer T is used in the latter.

6.6.7 Reducing System Nervousness

In a rolling-horizon environment, as new demand information becomes available, the timing and sizes of future replenishments may be altered. Frequent alterations of this type may be unattractive from an operational standpoint. Carlson et al. (1979) and Kropp et al. (1983) have introduced the idea of a penalty cost for changing a previously established schedule and have shown how to incorporate this idea into the Silver-Meal heuristic. As a by-product, this modification permits the handling of the situation where the setup cost varies from period to period.

6.7 TWO OTHER HEURISTICS USED IN PRACTICE

We now briefly cover two other heuristics, primarily because they have been used by practitioners. However, as mentioned earlier, the Silver-Meal heuristic, on a large number of tests, has compared very favorably with them. Moreover, we believe that the criterion (of minimization of costs per unit time), on which the Silver-Meal method is based, is more appealing than the logic underlying these other methods.

6.71 The Economic Order Quantity Expressed as a Time Supply

One approach described earlier (in Section 6.4) was to use a fixed order quantity, based on using the average demand rate $\bar{D}$ in the EOQ equation. Empirically (see, for example, Brown, 1977), where there is significant variability in the demand pattern, better cost performance has been obtained by proceeding slightly differently. The EOQ is expressed as a time supply using $\bar{D}$, namely;

$$T_{\text{EOQ}} = \frac{\text{EOQ}}{\bar{D}} = \sqrt{\frac{2A}{\bar{D}vr}} \tag{6.7}$$

rounded to the nearest integer greater than zero. Then, any replenishment of the item is made large enough to cover exactly the requirements of this integer number of periods. Another name for this approach is the *periodic order quantity*.

For the numerical example of Section 6.3.2, Eq. 6.7 gives

$$T_{\text{EOQ}} = \sqrt{\frac{2(54)}{(100)(20)(0.02)}} = 1.64$$

which rounds to 2. Repeated use of a 2-period time supply in the example gives total costs of $553.60 as compared with $501.20 using the Silver-Meal heuristic.

6.7.2 Part-Period Balancing

The basic criterion used here is to select the number of periods covered by the replenishment such that the total carrying costs are made as close as possible to the setup cost, A. (Exact equality is usually not possible because of the discrete nature of the decision variable, T.) To illustrate, for the MIDAS numerical example of Section 6.3.2 we have

$A = \$54 \qquad v = \$20/\text{box} \qquad r = 0.02\ \$/\$/\text{month}$

Month j	1	2	3	4	5	6 ...
Requirements $D(j)$	10	62	12	130	154	129 ...

The calculations for the first replenishment quantity (assuming that the inventory is zero at the beginning of month 1) are:

T	Carrying Costs
1	0
2	$D(2)vr = \$24.80 < \$54$
3	$24.80 + 2D(3)vr = \$34.40 < \$54$
4	$\$34.40 + 3D(4)vr = \$190.40 > \$54$

\$34.40 is closer to \$54 (the A value) than is \$190.40. Therefore, a T value of 3 is selected for the first replenishment. Repeated use of this procedure gives replenishments of sizes 84, 284, 217, 176, 398, and 41 at the start of periods 1, 4, 6, 8, 10, and 12, respectively, with total costs of \$600—again well above the \$501.20 found by the Silver-Meal heuristic.

Refinements of the part-period balancing method, requiring more computational effort, have been developed (see De Matteis and Mendoza, 1968).

6.8 AGGREGATE EXCHANGE CURVES

As has been discussed earlier in the book, certain parameter values, such as r or A/r, may be selected implicitly by top management's specification of a reasonable operating situation from an aggregate standpoint. In Chapter 5, for the case of the basic economic order quantity, it was relatively easy to develop an exchange curve because of the analytic relationships between (1) total cycle stock and A/r (see Eq. 5.27) and (2) total number of replenishments per unit time and A/r (see Eq. 5.28).

For the case of time-varying demand no such simple results exist because of the discrete nature of the decision variable T, the number of periods of requirements to be included in a replenishment. Therefore, in this case, in order to develop an exchange curve, we must proceed as follows.

A representative sample of items is selected from the population of items under consideration. As will be discussed in a general way in Chapter 17, the exact sample size to select depends on the number and characteristics of items in the population that are to be controlled by the Silver-Meal heuristic (that is, have a variability coefficient exceeding 0.2).

A value of A/r is selected. Then, for each item in the sample the Silver-Meal heuristic is used to determine the replenishment quantities over a reasonable time period such as 12 months. This implies a certain number of replenishments and an average inventory level (in dollars) for the item. Summing these quantities across the items of the sample produces the total number of replenishments and the total average inventory of the sample. These figures must be appropriately scaled up to correspond with the total group of items to be controlled by the Silver-Meal procedure. This must be repeated for several values of A/r to develop the tradeoff curve.

An additional point is worth mentioning here. One often wants an exchange curve for all of the items in the population. In such a case, the results for the Silver-Meal items must be added to those for the items to be replenished according to the basic economic order quantity (Section 5.9 of Chapter 5) to produce one composite curve as a function of A/r.

6.9 SUMMARY

In this chapter we have provided a decision system for coping with the relaxation of another of the key assumptions inherent in the use of the basic economic order quantity. The system permits the practioner to deal, in a realistic way, with *time-varying* demand patterns. The Silver-Meal heuristic, through extensive testing, has been found to be robust. A guideline has been provided as to when one should consider the EOQ-based approaches as no longer being valid.

Time-varying demand patterns will play a crucial role in the Material Requirements Planning framework to be discussed in Chapter 16. In addition, an extension of the Silver-Meal heuristic to permit multiple items within a capacitated production context will be discussed in Chapter 15.

In the next chapter we return to the context of an essentially level demand pattern but, for the first time, incorporate uncertainty in the demand rate. In Chapter 8 brief mention will be made of the treatment of the combination of time-varying *and* uncertain demand.

APPENDIX TO CHAPTER 6
AN EXPRESSION FOR THE VARIABILITY COEFFICIENT

The variability coefficient VC is defined as

$$VC = \frac{\text{Variance of demand per period}}{\text{Square of average demand per period}} \tag{6.8}$$

Here the demand per period can be thought of as a discrete variable taking on the values $D(1), D(2), \ldots, D(N)$, each with probability $1/N$. Then we have that the average demand per period

$$\begin{aligned} \bar{D} \text{ or } E(D) &= \frac{1}{N}[D(1) + D(2) + \cdots + D(N)] \\ &= \frac{1}{N}\sum_{j=1}^{N} D(j) \end{aligned} \tag{6.9}$$

and the variance of demand per period

$$\begin{aligned} \text{Var}(D) &= \frac{1}{N}[D(1)]^2 + \frac{1}{N}[D(2)]^2 + \cdots + \frac{1}{N}[D(N)]^2 - [E(D)]^2 \\ &= \frac{1}{N}\sum_{j=1}^{N}[D(j)]^2 - [E(D)]^2 \end{aligned} \tag{6.10}$$

Substitution of Eqs. 6.9 and 6.10 into Eq. 6.8 gives

$$\begin{aligned} VC &= \frac{\frac{1}{N}\sum_{j=1}^{N}[D(j)]^2 - [E(D)]^2}{[E(D)]^2} \\ &= \frac{\frac{1}{N}\sum_{j=1}^{N}[D(j)]^2}{\frac{1}{N^2}\left[\sum_{j=1}^{N} D(j)\right]^2} - 1 \\ &= \frac{N\sum_{j=1}^{N}[D(j)]^2}{\left[\sum_{j=1}^{N} D(j)\right]^2} - 1 \end{aligned}$$

PROBLEMS

6.1 A sale of polarizing filters is held twice annually by MIDAS. The demand pattern for a particular size of filter for the past year is as follows:

Jan.	Feb.	Mar.	Apr.	May	June
21	29	24	86	31	38
July	Aug.	Sept.	Oct.	Nov.	Dec.
45	39	31	78	29	32

It is anticipated that demand for the next year will follow this pattern; hence these figures are being used as the "best estimates" of forthcoming sales. Demand will also continue in future years. The cost of these filters is \$8.65, ordering costs are approximately \$35, and the carrying cost is 0.24 \$/\$/yr.

Calculate the variability coefficient and select the appropriate order quantities.

6.2 The demand pattern for another type of MIDAS filter is:

Jan.	Feb.	Mar.	Apr.	May	June
18	31	23	95	29	37
July	Aug.	Sept.	Oct.	Nov.	Dec.
50	39	30	88	22	36

These filters cost the company \$4.75 each; ordering and carrying costs are as in Problem 6.1. The variability coefficient equals 0.33. Use the Silver-Meal heuristic to determine the sizes and timing of replenishments of stock.

6.3 In this chapter for the case of deterministic time-varying demand we developed the Silver-Meal heuristic. It selects a value of T which minimizes the relevant costs per unit time over the duration (T) of the replenishment.

The result we developed was to select the integer T to minimize

$$\frac{A + vr \sum_{j=1}^{T} (j-1)D(j)}{T} \tag{1}$$

Another heuristic proposed in the literature is the so-called "least unit cost" method. In it a value of T is selected to minimize the *relevant costs per unit* included in the replenishment quantity.

a. Develop an expression similar to Eq. 1 that the best (according to this criterion) T value must satisfy.

b. For the following item having zero inventory at the beginning of period 1 develop the magnitude of the *first* replenishment *only*:

Item characteristics:

$$A = \$50 \qquad v = \$2\text{/unit}$$

$$r = 0.05 \ \$/\$/\text{period}$$

Period j	1	2	3	4	5	6	7
$D(j)$	200	300	500	500	400	400	300

c. A marked difference between this method and that of Silver-Meal exists in the dependence on $D(1)$. Briefly discuss. In particular, suppose $D(1)$ was much larger than any of the other $D(j)$'s. What effect would this have on the best T for

1. Silver-Meal?

2. Least unit cost?

6.4 Consider an item with the following properties:

$$A = \$20 \qquad v = \$2\text{/unit} \qquad r = 0.24 \ \$/\$/\text{yr}$$

At time 0 the inventory has dropped to zero and a replenishment (with negligible lead time) must be made. The demand pattern for the next 12 months is:

Month j	1	2	3	4	5	6
Demand (units) $D(j)$	50	70	100	120	110	100
Month j	7	8	9	10	11	12
Demand (units) $D(j)$	100	80	120	70	60	40

All the requirements of each month must be available at the beginning of the month. Replenishments are restricted to the beginnings of the months. No shortages are allowed. Using each of the following methods, develop the pattern of replenishments to cover the 12 months and the associated total costs of each pattern (do *not* bother to count the costs of carrying $D(j)$ during its period of consumption, namely, period j). In each case, the size of the last replenishment should be selected to end month 12 with no inventory.

a. Fixed economic order quantity (rounded to the nearest integer number of months of supply; that is, each time the EOQ, based on the average demand through the entire 12 months, is adjusted so that it will last for exactly an integer number of months).

b. A fixed time supply (an integer number of periods) based on the EOQ expressed as a time supply, using the average demand rate for the 12 months.

c. On each replenishment, selection of Q (or, equivalently, the integer T), which minimizes the costs *per unit of quantity* ordered to cover demand though T.

d. The Silver-Meal heuristic.

e. One replenishment at the start of month 1 to cover all the requirements to the end of month 12.

f. A replenishment at the beginning of every month.

Hint: For each case, it would be helpful to develop a table with at least the following columns: (1)Month, (2) Replenishment Quantity, (3) Starting Inventory, (4) Demand, (5) Ending Inventory.

6.5 Consider an item with the following deterministic, time-varying demand pattern:

Week	1	2	3	4	5	6
Demand	50	80	180	80	0	0

Week	7	8	9	10	11	12
Demand	180	150	10	100	180	130

Suppose that the pattern terminates at week 12. Let other relevant characteristics of the item be:

Inventory carrying cost per week (incurred only on units carried over from one week to the next) is \$0.20/unit.

Fixed cost per replenishment is \$30.

Initial inventory and replenishment lead time are both zero.

Perform an analysis similar to that of Problem 6.4 (of course, substituting "week" for "month").

6.6 Consider an item with the following declining demand pattern:

Period	1	2	3	4	5	6	7	8	9	10
Demand	600	420	294	206	145	101	71	50	35	25

Period	11	12	13	14	15	16	17	18	19	20
Demand	17	12	9	6	5	3	2	2	1	1

There is no further demand after period 20.

$$A = \$50 \qquad v = \$2.50/\text{unit}$$

$$r = 0.02/\text{period}$$

Perform an analysis similar to that of Problem 6.4.

6.7 Discuss the implied logic underlying Eq. 6.5.

6.8 A Calgary-based company (Piedmont Pipelines) has been awarded a contract to lay a long stretch of pipeline. The planned schedule for the laying of pipe can be considered to be accurately known for the duration of the project (18 months). Because of weather conditions and the availability of labor, the rate of placement of pipe is not constant throughout the project. The supplier of the pipe offers a discount structure for purchases. Outline an analysis that would assist Piedmont in deciding on the purchase schedule for the piping.

6.9 Consider a population of items having essentially deterministic but time-varying demand patterns. Suppose that one was interested in developing an exchange curve of total cycle stock (in dollars) versus total number of replenishments per year as a function of A/r (the latter being unknown, but constant for all items). An analyst has suggested using the approach of Section 5.9 of Chapter 5 with

$$D_i = \text{annual demand for item } i$$

Discuss whether or not this is a reasonable suggestion.

6.10 Suppose you were a supplier for a single customer having a deterministic, but time-varying demand pattern. Interestingly enough, the time-varying nature is actually of benefit to you!

a. Making use of the Silver-Meal heuristic, indicate how you would decide on the maximum discount that you would be willing to give the customer in return for him maintaining his current pattern instead of providing a perfectly level demand pattern. Assume that replenishments can take place only at the beginning of periods.

b. Illustrate for the numerical example of Problem 6.5. Suppose that the current selling price is \$60/unit.

REFERENCES

Aucamp, D., and D. Fogarty (1982). "Lot Sizing in MRP." *Proceedings of the 25th International Conference of the American Production and Inventory Control Society*, pp. 1–4.

Berry, W. L. (1972). "Lot Sizing Procedures for Requirements Planning Systems: A Framework for Analysis." *Production and Inventory Management*, Vol. 13, No. 2, pp. 19–34.

Blackburn, J., and H. Kunreuther (1974). "Planning and Forecast Horizons for the Dynamic Lot Size Model with Backlogging." *Management Science*, Vol. 21, No. 3, pp. 215–255.

Blackburn, J., and R. Millen (1979a). "Selecting a Lot-Sizing Technique for a Single-Level Assembly Process: Part I—Analytical Results." *Production and Inventory Management*, Vol. 20, No. 3, pp. 49–57.

Blackburn, J., and R. Millen (1979b). "Selecting a Lot-Sizing Technique for a Single-Level Assembly Process: Part II—Empirical Results." *Production and Inventory Management*, Vol. 20, No. 4, pp. 41–52.

Blackburn, J., and R. Millen (1980). "Heuristic Lot-Sizing Performance in a Rolling-Schedule Environment." *Decision Sciences*, Vol. 11, No. 4, pp. 691–701.

Brosseau, L. A. (1982). "An Inventory Replenishment Policy for the Case of a Linear Decreasing Trend in Demand." *INFOR*, Vol. 20, No. 3, pp. 252–257.

Brown, R. G. (1977). *Materials Management Systems*, Wiley-Interscience, New York, p. 235.

Carlson, R., J. V. Jucker, and D. Kropp (1979). "Less Nervous MRP Systems: A Dynamic Economic Lot-Sizing Approach." *Management Science*, Vol. 25, No. 8, pp. 754–761.

De Matteis, J. J., and A. G. Mendoza (1968). "An Economic Lot Sizing Technique." *IBM Systems Journal*, Vol. 7, pp. 30–46.

Diegel, A. (1966). "A Linear Approach to the Dynamic Inventory Problem." *Management Science*, Vol. 12, No. 7, pp. 530–540.

Donaldson, W. A. (1977). "Inventory Replenishment Policy for a Linear Trend in Demand—An Analytical Solution." *Operational Research Quarterly*, Vol. 28, No. 3ii, pp. 663–670.

Eppen, G. D., F. J. Gould, and B. P. Pashigian (1969). "Extensions of the Planning Horizon Theorem in the Dynamic Lot Size Model." *Management Science*, Vol. 15, No. 5, pp. 268–277.

Gorham, T. (1968). "Dynamic Order Quantities." *Production and Inventory Management*, Vol. 9, No. 1, pp. 75–79.

Groff, G. (1979). "A Lot-Sizing Rule for Time-Phased Component Demand." *Production and Inventory Management*, Vol. 20, No. 1, pp. 47–53.

Kaimann, R. A. (1969). "E.O.Q. vs. Dynamic Programming—Which One to Use for Inventory Ordering?" *Production and Inventory Management*, Vol.10, No. 4, pp. 66–74.

Karni, R. (1981). "Maximum Part-Period Gain (MPG)—A Lot Sizing Procedure for Unconstrained and Constrained Requirements Planning Systems." *Production and Inventory Management*, Vol. 22, No. 2, pp. 91–98.

Kicks, P., and W. A. Donaldson (1980). "Irregular Demand: Assessing a Rough and Ready Lot Size Formula." *Journal of the Operational Research Society*, Vol. 31, No. 8, pp. 725–732.

Kropp, D., R. Carlson, and J. Jucker (1983). "Heuristic Lot-Sizing Approaches for Dealing with MRP System Nervousness." *Decision Sciences*, Vol. 14, No. 2, pp. 156–186.

Kunreuther, H., and T. Morton (1973). "Planning Horizons for Production Smoothing with Deterministic Demands: I." *Management Science*, Vol. 20, No. 1, pp. 110–125.

Kunreuther, H., and T. Morton (1974). "Planning Horizons for Production Smoothing with Deterministic Demands: II." *Management Science*, Vol. 20, No. 7, pp. 1037–1046.

Lamarre, R., and H. Baier (1981). "Lot Sizing under Time Varying Demand and All Units Discount." Paper presented at the Joint Conference of the Canadian Operational Research Society, the Operations Research Society of America and the Institute of Management Sciences, Toronto, Canada.

Lundin, R., and T. Morton (1975). "Planning Horizons for the Dynamic Lot Size Model: Zabel vs. Protective Procedures and Computational Results." *Operations Research*, Vol. 23, No. 4, pp. 711–734.

Quaye, G. (1979). "A Heuristic Procedure to the Economic Lot Size Problem." *IMSOR Report No.15*, Technical University of Denmark, Lyngby, Denmark.

Silver, E. A., and H. C. Meal (1969). "A Simple Modification of the EOQ for the Case of a Varying Demand Rate." *Production and Inventory Management*, Vol. 10, No. 4, pp. 52–65.

Silver, E. A., and H. C. Meal (1973). "A Heuristic for Selecting Lot Size Requirements for the Case of a Deterministic Time-Varying Demand Rate and Discrete Opportunities for Replenishment." *Production and Inventory Management*, Vol. 14, No. 2, pp. 64–74.

Silver, E. A., and G. J. Miltenburg (1984). "Two Modifications of the Silver-Meal Lot-Sizing Heuristic." *INFOR*, Vol. 22, No. 1, pp. 56–69.

Vidal, R. V. V. (1970). *Operations Research in Production Planning*, IMSOR, Technical University of Denmark, Lyngby, Denmark, pp. 95–99.

Wagner, H. M., and T. M. Whitin (1958). "Dynamic Version of the Economic Lot Size Model." *Management Science*, Vol. 5, pp. 89–96.

Woolsey, R. E. D. (1983). "Greening's Q & D for Varying Forecasted Demand." Part of unpublished plenary talk to the National Conference of the Canadian Operational Research Society, Winnipeg, Canada.

CHAPTER 7

Decision Systems for Individual Items Under Probabilistic Demand

In the preceding two chapters, which dealt with the determination of replenishment quantities, the decision rules resulted from analyses that assumed deterministic demand patterns. In several places we showed that the relevant costs associated with the selection of order quantities were relatively insensitive to inaccuracies in the estimates of the various factors involved. However, the costs of insufficient capacity in the short run—that is, the costs associated with shortages or with averting them—were not included in the analyses. When demand is no longer assumed deterministic, these costs assume a much greater importance. Clearly, the assumption of deterministic demand is inappropriate in many production and distribution situations. Therefore, the current chapter is devoted to the theme of how to develop control systems to cope with the more realistic case of probabilistic demand. We restrict our attention to the case (comparable to Chapter 5) where the *average* demand remains approximately constant with time. The much more difficult combination of probabilistic demand with a time-varying average will be discussed in Chapter 8.

The introduction of uncertainty in the demand pattern significantly complicates the inventory situation from a conceptual standpoint. This, together with the plethora of possible shortage costing methods or customer service measures, has made the understanding and acceptance of decision rules for coping with probabilistic demand far less frequent than is merited by the importance of the problem. It is safe to say (as will be illustrated in Section 7.9.1 of this chapter) that in most organizations an appropriate reallocation of buffer (or safety) stocks (which are kept to meet unexpected fluctuations in demand) can lead to a significant improvement in the service provided to customers.

It should be emphasized that in this and several succeeding chapters we are still dealing with a single-stage problem. When one is concerned with a multiechelon situation, a control system different from those proposed here is usually in order. One such control system is referred to as a Material Requirements Planning system. We have more to say on this topic in Chapters 12 and 16.

We begin in Section 7.1 with a careful discussion of some important issues and terminology relevant to the case of probabilistic demand. In Section 7.2 the important dichotomy of continuous versus periodic review is discussed. This is followed in Section 7.3 by an explanation of the four most common types of control systems. Section 7.4 is concerned with the many different ways of measuring service or costing shortages that may be relevant to any particular stocking situation. Section 7.5 deals with an illustrative selection of the reorder point for one type of continuous review system (order-point, order-quantity system) and one commonly used measure of service. Next, in Section 7.6, we present a detailed treatment of the order-point, order-quantity system, showing the decision rules for a wide range of methods of measuring service and costing shortages. Section 7.7 is more briefly devoted to another commonly used control system—namely, the periodic review, order-up-to-level system. This is followed, in Section 7.8, by a discussion of how to deal with appreciable variability in the replenishment lead time. Finally, Section 7.9 is concerned with aggregate considerations, in particular, exchange curves displaying total buffer stock plotted against two aggregate measures of service as a function of a policy variable, the latter being the numerical value of a particular service level or shortage cost.

7.1 SOME IMPORTANT ISSUES AND TERMINOLOGY

7.1.1 Different Definitions of Stock Level

When demand is probabilistic, it is useful to conceptually categorize inventories as follows:

1. **On-hand stock** This is stock that is physically on the shelf; it can never be negative. This quantity is relevant in determining whether a particular customer demand is satisfied directly from the shelf.
2. **Net stock** = (On hand) − (Backorders) (7.1)
   This quantity can become negative (namely, if there are backorders). It is used in some mathematical derivations and is also seen to be a component of the following important definition.
3. **Inventory position** (sometimes also called the *available stock*[1]). The inventory position is defined by the relation

$$\text{Inventory position} = (\text{On hand}) + (\text{On order}) - (\text{Backorders}) - (\text{Committed}) \tag{7.2}$$

[1]We have chosen to not use the words "available stock" because of the incorrect connotation that such stock is immediately available for satisfying customer demands.

The on-order stock is that stock which has been requisitioned but not yet received by the stocking point under consideration. The inclusion of the "committed" quantity in Eq. 7.2 is based on not being able to borrow from such stock for other purposes in the short run. If a commitment is made farther than a replenishment lead time in advance of use, such borrowing may be possible. As we will see, the inventory position is a key quantity in deciding on when to replenish.

4. **Safety stock** The safety (or buffer) stock is defined as the average level of the net stock just before a replenishment arrives. If we planned to just run out, on the average, at the moment when the replenishment arrived, the safety stock would be zero. A positive safety stock provides a cushion or buffer against larger-than-average demand during the effective replenishment lead time. The numerical value of the safety stock depends, as we will see, on what happens to demands when there is a stockout.

7.1.2 Backorders versus Lost Sales

Obviously of importance in inventory control is what happens to a customer's order when an item is temporarily out of stock. There are two extreme cases:

1. *Complete backordering.* Any demand, when out of stock, is backordered and filled as soon as an adequate sized replenishment arrives. This situation corresponds to a captive market, common in government organizations (particularly the military) and at the wholesale-retail link of some distribution systems (for example, exclusive dealerships).
2. *Complete lost sales.* Any demand when out of stock is lost; the customer goes elsewhere to satisfy his or her need. This situation is most common at the retail-consumer link. For example, a person is unlikely to backorder a demand for a loaf of bread.

In most practical situations one finds a combination of these two extremes, whereas most inventory models have been developed for one or the other of the extremes. Nevertheless, most of these models serve as reasonable approximations because the decisions which they yield tend to be relatively insensitive to the degree of backordering possible in a particular situation. This is primarily a consequence of the common use in practice of high customer service levels; high service levels imply infrequent stockout occasions.

We now show that the numerical value of the safety stock depends on the degree to which backorders or lost sales occur. Consider a particular replenishment lead time in which a stockout occurs. Under complete backordering, if demand occurs during the stockout, the net stock will be negative just before the next replenishment arrives. On the other hand, if all demands that occur when one is out of stock are lost, then the net stock will remain at the zero level throughout the stockout period. In other words, in a cycle when a stockout occurs, the value of the net stock just before the replenishment arrives depends on whether backorders can occur. Because safety stock is defined to be the *average net stock* just before a replenishment arrives, its numerical value is thus influenced by whether backordering is possible under the actual circumstances.

7.1.3 Three Key Questions To Be Answered by a Control System under Probabilistic Demand

The fundamental purpose of a replenishment control system is to provide answers to the following three questions:

1. How often should the inventory status be determined?
2. When should a replenishment order be placed?
3. How large should the replenishment order be?

Under conditions of *deterministic* demand (discussed in the previous two chapters), the first question is trivial because knowing the inventory status at any one point allows us to calculate it at all points in time (at least out to a reasonable horizon). Furthermore, under deterministic demand the second question is answered by placing an order such that it arrives precisely when the inventory level hits some prescribed value (usually set at zero). Again, under deterministic demand, use of the economic order quantity, one of its variations, or one of the procedures discussed in Chapter 6 provides the answer to the third question.

Under probabilistic demand the answers are more difficult to obtain. Regarding the first question, it takes resources (labor, computer time, etc.) to determine the inventory status. On the other hand, the less frequently the status is determined, the longer is the period over which the system must protect against unforeseen variations in demand in order to provide desired customer service. The answer to the second question rests on a tradeoff between the costs of ordering somewhat early (hence, carrying extra stock) and the costs (implicit or explicit) of providing inadequate customer service. The factors relevant in answering the third question are similar to those discussed in the derivation of the basic economic order quantity, except that under some service criteria, specified by management, there is an interaction in that the answer to the second question, "When to replenish?" may be affected by the replenishment quantity used.

7.2 CONTINUOUS VERSUS PERIODIC REVIEW

The answer to the question "How often should the inventory status be determined?" specifies the review interval (R) which is the time that elapses between two consecutive moments at which we know the stock level. An extreme case is where there is continuous review; that is, the stock status is always known. In reality, continuous surveillance is usually not required; instead, each transaction (shipment, receipt, demand, etc.) triggers an immediate updating of the status. Consequently, this type of control is often called *transactions reporting*. Transactions reporting need not be computerized as evidenced by the hundreds of manual stock card systems (for example, "Kardex" or "VISI-Record") that have been used successfully over the years. On the other hand, point-of-sale, data collection systems (involving electronic scanners), which permit transactions reporting, are having a profound impact at the retail level. With periodic review, as the name implies, the stock status is determined only every R time units; between the moments of review there may be considerable uncertainty as to the value of the stock level.

We now comment on the advantages and disadvantages of continuous and periodic review. Items may be produced on the same piece of equipment, purchased from the same supplier, or shipped in the same transportation mode. In any of these situations coordination of replenishments may be attractive. In such a case periodic review is particularly appealing in that all items in a coordinated group can be given the same review interval (for example, all items purchased from a particular supplier might be scheduled for review every Thursday). Periodic review also allows a reasonable prediction of the level of the workload on the staff involved in issuing replenishment orders. In contrast, under continuous review a replenishment decision can be made at practically any moment in time; hence the load is less predictable. A rhythmic, rather than random, pattern is usually appealing to the staff.

Another disadvantage of continuous review is that it is generally more expensive in terms of reviewing costs and reviewing errors. This is particularly true for fast-moving items where there are many transactions per unit of time. However, the aforementioned point-of-sale, data collection systems have dramatically reduced reviewing costs and errors. Moreover, for extremely slow-moving items very little costs are incurred by continuous review because updates are only made when a transaction occurs. On the other hand, we have the anomalous condition that periodic review may be more effective than continuous review in detecting spoilage (or pilferage) of such slow-moving items in that periodic review forces an occasional review of the situation, whereas, in transactions recording no automatic review will take place without a transaction occurring.

The major advantage of continuous review is that, to provide the same level of customer service, it requires less safety stock (hence, lower carrying costs) than does periodic review. This is because the period over which safety protection is required is longer under periodic review (the stock level has the opportunity to drop appreciably between review instants without any reordering action being possible in the interim).

7.3 FOUR TYPES OF CONTROL SYSTEMS

Recall that, in designing an inventory control system, we are really providing answers to the three questions:

1. How often should the inventory status be determined?
2. When should a replenishment order be placed?
3. How large should the replenishment order be?

There are a number of possible control systems. The physical operation of the four most common ones will be described in the next subsection. This will be followed by a brief discussion of the advantages and disadvantages of each of the systems.

7.3.1 Physical Operation

Order-Point, Order-Quantity[2] (*s*, *Q*) System

This system involves continuous review (that is, $R = 0$). A fixed quantity Q is ordered whenever the inventory position drops to the reorder point s or lower. Note that the inventory position, and not the net stock, is used to trigger an order. The inventory position, because it includes the on-order stock, takes proper account of the material requested but not yet received from the supplier. In contrast, if net stock was used for ordering purposes, we might unnecessarily place another order today even though a large shipment was due in tomorrow. This system is often called a two-bin system because one physical form of implementation is to have two bins for storage of an item. As long as units remain in the first bin, demand is satisfied from it. The amount in the second bin corresponds to the order point. Hence, when this second bin is opened, a replenishment is triggered. When the replenishment arrives, the second bin is refilled and the remainder is put into the first bin. It should be noted that the physical two-bin system will operate properly only when no more than one replenishment order is outstanding at any point in time. Thus, to use the system, it may be necessary to adjust Q upward so that it is appreciably larger than the average demand during a lead time.

Order-Point, Order-Up-to-Level (*s*, *S*) System

This system again involves continuous review and a replenishment is made whenever the inventory position drops to the order point s or lower. However, in contrast to the (s, Q) system, here a variable replenishment quantity is used, enough being ordered to raise the inventory position to the order-up-to-level S. If all demand transactions are unit-sized, the two systems are identical because the replenishment requisition will always be made when the inventory position

[2] The notation to be used is: s = order point; Q = order quantity; S = order-up-to-level.

is exactly at s; that is, in this case, $S = s + Q$. As soon as the transactions can be larger than unit size the replenishment quantity in the (s, S) system becomes variable. Figures 7.1a and 7.1b illustrate the difference in the behavior of the two systems. The (s, S) system is frequently referred to as a min-max system because the inventory position, except for a possible momentary drop below the reorder point, is always between a minimum value of s and a maximum value of S. An illustration of a min-max system is provided in MIDAS Case D.

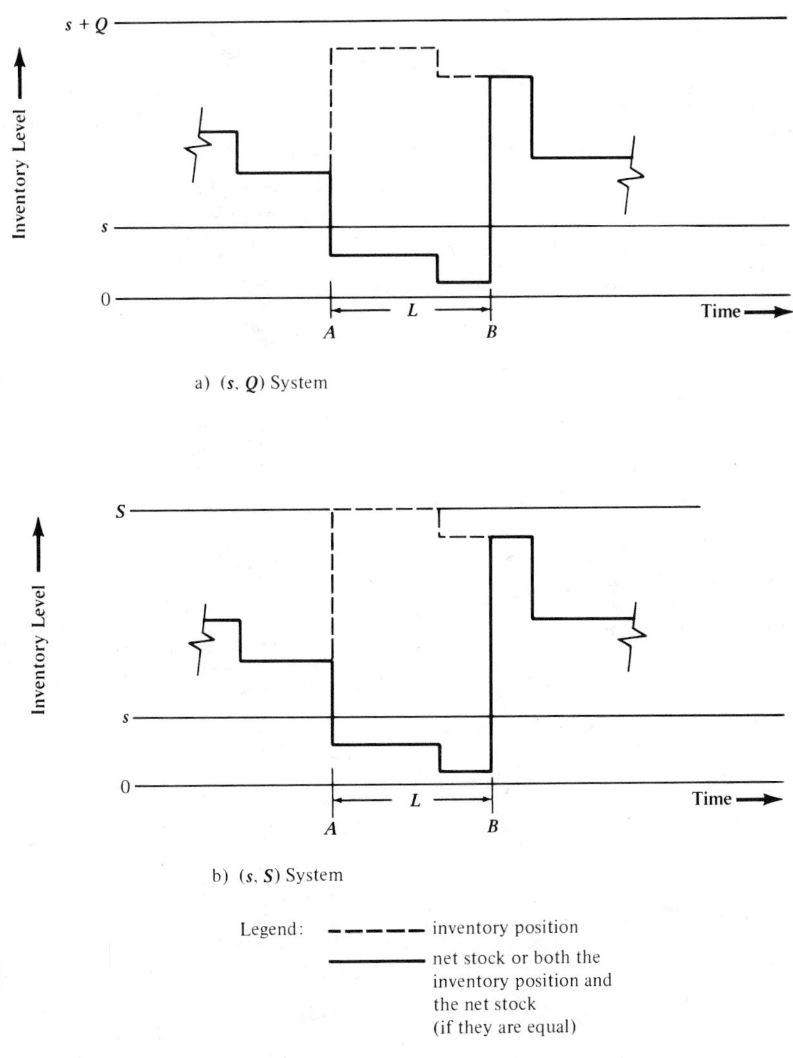

FIGURE 7.1 Two Types of Continuous Review Systems

Periodic-Review, Order-Up-to-Level (R, S) System

This system, also known as a replenishment cycle system, is in common use, particularly in companies not utilizing computer control. The control procedure is that every R units of time (that is, at each review instant) enough is ordered to raise the inventory position to the level S. A typical behavior of this type of system is shown in Figure 7.2.

(R, s, S) System

This is a combination of (s, S) and (R, S) systems. The idea is that every R units of time we check the inventory position. If it is at or below the reorder point s, we order enough to raise it to S. If the position is above s, nothing is done until at least the next review instant. The (s, S) system is the special case where $R = 0$, and the (R, S) is the special case where $s = S - 1$. Alternatively, one can think of the (R, s, S) system as a periodic version of the (s, S) system. Also, the (R, S) situation can be viewed as a periodic implementation of (s, S) with $s = S - 1$.

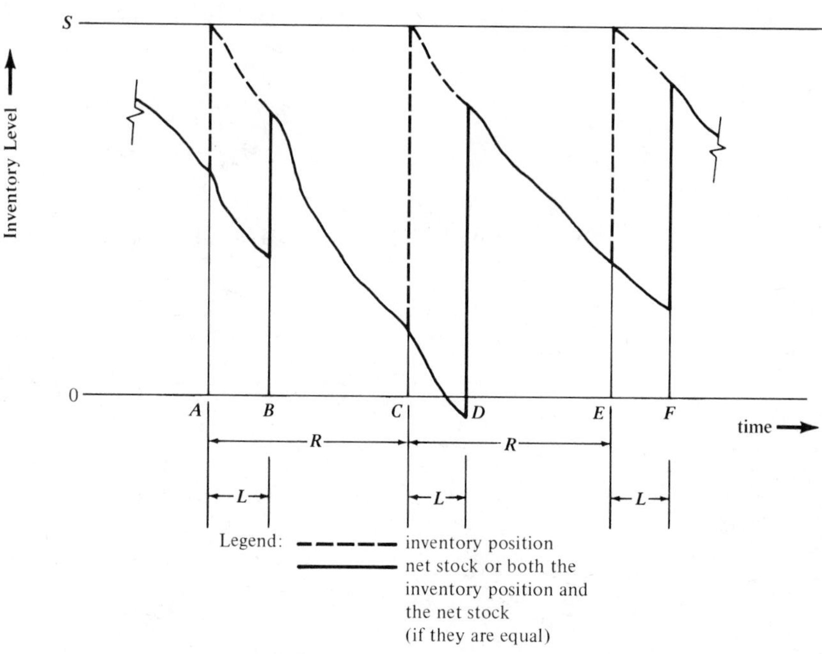

FIGURE 7.2 The (R, S) System

7.3.2 Advantages and Disadvantages

Our discussion will be rather general in that the advantages and disadvantages are dependent on the specific environment in which the systems are to be implemented.

(s, Q) System

This is a simple system, particularly in the two-bin form, for the stock clerk to understand. A fixed order quantity also has advantages in terms of less likelihood of error and also predictability of production requirements on the part of the supplier. One disadvantage of an (s, Q) system is that in its unmodified form it may not be able to effectively cope with the situation where individual transactions are of appreciable magnitude; in particular, if the transaction that triggers the replenishment in an (s, Q) system is large enough, then a replenishment of size Q won't even raise the inventory position above the reorder point (a numerical illustration would involve a Q value of 10 together with a demand transaction of size 15 occurring when the position is just 1 unit above s). Of course, in such a situation one could instead order an integer multiple of Q where the integer was large enough to raise the inventory position above s.

(s, S) System

The best (s, S) system can be shown to have total costs of replenishment, carrying inventory, and shortage no larger than those of the best (s, Q) system. However, the computational effort to find the *best* (s, S) pair is prohibitive except perhaps where we are dealing with an item where the potential savings in the aforementioned costs are appreciable (that is, an A item). It is interesting that (s, S) systems are frequently encountered in practice. However, the values of the control parameters are usually set in a rather arbitrary fashion. (See, for example, MIDAS Case D.) For B items (and even most A items) mathematical optimality does not make sense; instead, we need a fairly simple way of obtaining *reasonable* values of s and S. This will be discussed further in the next chapter, which deals with A items. A possible disadvantage of the (s, S) system is the danger of errors in requisitioning, among other operations, caused by the variable order quantity.

(R, S) System

Because of the periodic review property, this system is much preferred to order point systems in terms of coordinating the replenishments of related items. In addition, the (R, S) system offers a regular opportunity (every R units of time) to adjust the order-up-to-level S, a desirable property if the demand pattern is changing with time. The main disadvantge of the (R, S) system is that the carrying costs are higher here than in continuous review systems.

(R, s, S) System

It has been shown (see, for example, Scarf, 1960) that, under quite general assumptions concerning the demand pattern and the cost factors involved, the best (R, s, S) system produces a lower total of replenishment, carrying, and shortage costs than does any other form of system. However, the computational effort to obtain the *best* values of the three control parameters is prohibitive, certainly for class B items. Therefore, for such items, simplified methods must be used to find *reasonable* values (again, a topic we discuss in the next chapter). This system is also more difficult for a clerk to understand than some of the previously mentioned systems. (R, s, S) systems are found in practice where R is selected largely for convenience (for example, 1 day) even when point-of-sale equipment permits continuous review of the inventory position.

7.4 CHOICE AMONG CRITERIA FOR ESTABLISHING SAFETY STOCKS OF INDIVIDUAL ITEMS

When demand (or delivery capability) is probabilistic, there is a definite chance of not being able to satisfy some of the demand on a routine basis directly out of stock. If demand is unusually large, emergency actions are required to avoid a stockout situation. On the other hand, if demand is lower than anticipated, the replenishment arrives earlier than needed; hence excess inventory is carried. Managers possess differing attitudes concerning the balancing of these two types of risks. There are five possible methods of modeling these attitudes to arrive at appropriate decision rules:

1. *Safety Stocks Established Through the Use of a Common Factor* This approach, in its usual form, involves the use of a *common* time supply as the safety stock of each item. Although more easily understood than most of the other procedures to be discussed, we will find that there is a logical flaw in the use of this type of criterion.

2. *Safety Stocks Based on the Costing of Shortages* This approach involves specifying (explicitly or implicitly) a way of costing a shortage once one knows certain characteristics of the shortage (for example, the total number of transactions backordered). An illustration is provided by the MIDAS context where "air freight at a cost of approximately \$2.50 per kilogram was sometimes used to meet the demand from an important large customer." There are many alternative ways of costing a shortage; several will be illustrated shortly. Within a specific organizational context it is important, as discussed in Chapter 3, to include only the appropriate, relevant costs. Once these are determined (see, for example, Chang and Niland, 1967; Herron, 1983; and Oral et al., 1972), then the safety stock of an item is established to keep the expected total of shortage and carrying costs as low as possible.

3. *Safety Stocks Based on Service Considerations* Recognizing the severe difficulties associated with costing shortages, an alternative approach is to introduce a control parameter known as the *service level.* This becomes a constraint in establishing the safety stock of an item; for example, one might minimize the carrying costs of an item subject to satisfying, routinely from stock, 95 percent of all demands. Again, there is considerable choice in the selection of a service measure. In fact, often in practice, an inventory manager, when queried, may say that company policy is to provide a certain level of service (for example, 95 percent) and yet not be able to articulate exactly what is meant by service. Later we illustrate a number of the more common service measures.

4. *Safety Stocks Based on the Effects of Disservice on Future Demand* This approach to modeling the effects of shortages is to explicitly make future demand a function of the service now provided. Although this philosophy is conceptually appealing, it is very difficult to ascertain the appropriate functional form to use. However, Peters and Waterman (1982) have reported that "excellent" companies almost universally have *implicitly* used this idea in implementing extremely high levels of service (as well as quality). Other relevant references include Eilon (1965) and Schwartz (1966).

5. *Safety Stocks Based on Aggregate Considerations* The idea of this general approach is to establish the safety stocks of individual items, using up a given available budget, to provide the best possible *aggregate* service across a population of items. Equivalently, one selects the individual safety stocks to keep the total investment in stocks as low as possible while meeting a desired aggregate service level.

Unfortunately, there are no hard and fast rules for selecting the appropriate approach and/or measure of service. Which to use depends on the environment of the particular company under consideration as well as management's attitude toward balancing the aforementioned two types of risks. Later we will see equivalences between certain service measures and methods of costing shortages (a further reference on this topic is Oral, 1981). Moreover, it is quite possible that different *types* of shortage penalties or service measures are appropriate for different classes of items within the *same* organization. Relevant factors in deciding on a service measure or method of costing shortages include:

1. The nature of the competition for the product being demanded.
2. The nature of the customers (both in-house and out of house) involved—for example, parts for assemblies versus parts for spare usage.
3. The amount of substitutability of products (that is, standardized versus customized products).
4. Are the products purchased or manufactured?
5. How the company actually reacts to an impending shortage—for example, does it expedite?

Our treatment in this section is not meant to be exhaustive; instead, we wish to present the more common measures used in establishing safety stocks. Because of the wide variety of options for establishing safety stocks, it was deemed desirable to prepare the summary guide, which is shown in Table 7.1. As elsewhere in this text, we caution the reader against getting carried away with precision in prescribing the numerical value of a shortage cost or service level.

TABLE 7.1 Summary of Different Methods of Selecting the Safety Stocks in Control Systems under Probabilistic Demand

Criterion	Discussed in Section	Sections in Which Decision Rules for (s, Q) System Can Be Found[a]
Equal time supplies	7.4.1	—
Fixed safety factor	7.4.1	7.6.4
Cost (B_1) per stockout occasion	7.4.2	7.6.5
Fractional charge (B_2) per unit short	7.4.2	7.6.6
Fractional charge (B_3) per unit short per unit time	7.4.2	7.6.7
Specified probability (P_1) of no stockout per replenishment cycle	7.4.3	7.6.8
Specified fraction (P_2) of demand to be satisfied directly from shelf	7.4.3	7.6.9
Specified ready rate (P_3)	7.4.3	—
Specified average time (TBS) between stockout occasions	7.4.3	7.6.10
Minimization of expected total stockout occasions per year (ETSOPY) subject to a specified total safety stock	7.4.4	7.6.11
Minimization of expected total value short per year (ETVSPY) subject to a specified total safety stock	7.4.4	7.6.12

[a]As will be shown in Section 7.7, the decision rules for (R, S) systems are easily obtained from those for (s, Q) systems.

Finally, the reader should now be aware that maximizing turnover (that is, minimizing the level of inventories), in itself, is an inadequate criterion for selecting safety stocks in that it does not take account of the impact of shortages.

7.4.1 Safety Stocks Established Through the Use of a Common Factor

We illustrate with two of the most frequently used factors.

Equal Time Supplies

This is a simple, commonly used approach. The safety stocks of a broad group of (if not all) items in an inventory population are set equal to the same time supply; for example, reorder any item when its inventory position minus the forecasted lead time demand drops to a 2-month supply or lower. This approach is seriously in error because it fails to take account of the difference in uncertainty of forecasts from item to item. The policy variable here is the common number of time periods of supply.

Equal Safety Factors

As we will see later, it is convenient to define the safety stock (SS) as the product of two factors as follows:

$$SS = k\sigma_L \tag{7.3}$$

where

k is called the safety factor

σ_L, as first defined in Chapter 4, is the standard deviation of the errors of forecasts of total demand over a period of duration L (the replenishment lead time)

The *equal-safety factors* approach uses a common value of k for a broad range of items.

7.4.2 Safety Stocks Based on the Costing of Shortages

We present three illustrative cases.

Specified Fixed Cost (B_1) per Stockout Occasion

Here, it is assumed that the only cost associated with a stockout occasion is a fixed value B_1, independent of the magnitude or duration of the stockout. One possible interpretation would be the cost of an expediting action to avert an impending stockout.

Specified Fractional Charge (B_2) per Unit Short

Here one assumes that a fraction B_2 of unit value is charged per unit short; that is, the cost per unit short of item i is $B_2 v_i$ where v_i is the unit variable cost of the item. A situation where this type of costing would be appropriate is where units short are satisfied by overtime production (with an associated per unit premium).

Specified Fractional Charge (B_3) per Unit Short per Unit Time

The assumption here is that there is a charge B_3 per dollar short (equivalently, $B_3 v$ per unit short) per unit time. An example of this type of costing would be where the item under consideration was a spare part and each unit short would result in a machine being idled (with the idle time being equal to the duration of the shortage).

7.4.3 Safety Stocks Based on Service Considerations

The following are among the more common measures of service.

Specified Probability (P_1) of No Stockout per Replenishment Cycle

Equivalently, this is the fraction of cycles in which a stockout does not occur. A stockout is defined as an occasion when the on-hand stock *drops* to the zero level. As we will see later, using a common P_1 across a group of items is equivalent to using a common safety factor k.

Specified Fraction (P_2) of Demand To Be Satisfied Routinely from the Shelf (that is, Not Lost or Backordered)

A form of service measure that has considerable appeal to practitioners (particularly where a significant portion of the replenishment lead time is unalterable; for example, a branch warehouse where the major part of the lead time is the transit time by rail car) is the specification of a certain fraction of customer demand that is to be met routinely (without backorders or lost sales). A generalization is that the fraction P_2 must be met within a specified nonzero time interval rather than instantaneously (see Problem 7.8 as well as van der Veen, 1981). It can also be shown that use of the B_3 shortage costing measure leads to a decision rule equivalent to that for the P_2 service measure, where the equivalence is given by the relation

$$P_2 = \frac{B_3}{B_3 + r} \tag{7.4}$$

with r, as earlier, being the carrying charge.

Specified Ready Rate (P_3)

The ready rate is the fraction of time during which the net stock is positive; that is, there is some stock on the shelf. The ready rate finds common application in the case of equipment used for emergency purposes (for example, military hardware). Under Poisson demand, this measure is equivalent with the P_2 measure.

Specified Average Time (TBS) Between Stockout Occasions

Equivalently, one could use the reciprocal of TBS, which represents the desired average number of stockout occasions per year. If each stockout occasion is dealt with by an expediting action, then a specific TBS value can be selected to result in a tolerable number of expediting actions.

7.4.4 Safety Stocks Based on Aggregate Considerations

Two common aggregate considerations are shown. In both cases, rather than just aggregating effects across individual items, the item-level measure can be weighted by a factor known as the *essentiality* of the item. For example, if a particular item was deemed twice as important as another in terms of being in supply, then its essentiality would be double that of the other item.

Allocation of a Given Total Safety Stock among Items to Minimize the Expected Total Stockout Occasions per Year (ETSOPY)

As will be shown in Section 4 of the Appendix of this chapter, allocating a fixed total safety stock among several items to minimize the expected total number of stockout occasions per year leads to a decision rule for selecting the safety factor of each item, which is identical with that obtained by assuming a value (the same for all items) of the fixed cost B_1 and then selecting the safety factor to keep the total of carrying and stockout costs as low as possible (the latter approach was discussed in Section 7.4.2). This allocation interpretation is probably more appealing to management.

Allocation of a Given Total Safety Stock among Items to Minimize the Expected Total Value of Shortages per Year

Once more, one can show that allocating a fixed total safety stock among a group of items to minimize the expected total value (in dollars) of shortages per year leads to a decision rule for selecting the safety factor which is identical with either

1. The one obtained by assuming a value (the same for all items) of the factor B_2 and then selecting the safety factor for each item to minimize the total of carrying and shortage costs.
2. The one obtained by specifying the same average time (TBS) between stockout occasions for every item in the group.

Again, this aggregate view of allocating a limited resource may be considerably more appealing to management than the micro detail of attempting to explicitly ascertain a B_2 value from cost considerations or the somewhat arbitrary specification of a TBS value.

7.5 ILLUSTRATIVE DETERMINATION OF THE REORDER POINT *s* IN A CONTINUOUS-REVIEW, ORDER-POINT, ORDER-QUANTITY (*s*, *Q*) SYSTEM

For illustrative purposes the service measure used in this section is the probability (P_1) of no stockout in a replenishment cycle. In Section 7.6 decision rules will be presented for a broad range of service measures and methods of costing shortages.

7.5.1 Protection Over the Replenishment Lead Time

In a continuous review system a replenishment action can be taken immediately after any demand transaction. Once we place an order a replenishment lead time (L) elapses before the order is available for satisfying customer demands. Therefore, we want to place an order when the inventory is still adequate to protect us over a replenishment lead time. If the order is placed when the inventory position is at *exactly* the reorder point s, then a stockout will not occur by the end of the lead time if and only if the total demand during the lead time is less than the reorder point. This is illustrated in Figure 7.3, where, for simplicity in presentation, we have assumed that at most one replenishment

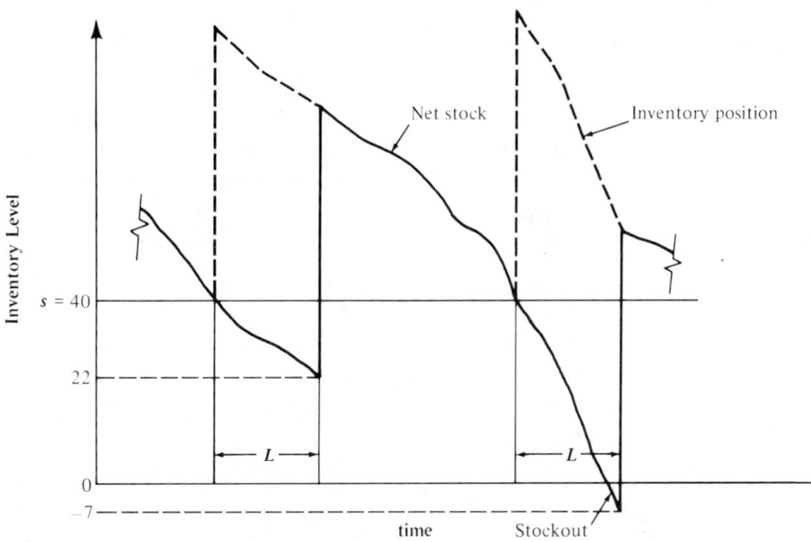

FIGURE 7.3 The Occurrence of a Stockout in an (s, Q) System

order is outstanding at any moment.[3] In the figure the reorder point is 40 units. In the first lead time shown the total demand is 18 so that the net stock just before the replenishment arrives is (40 − 18) or 22; that is, no stockout occurs. In contrast, in the second lead time the total demand is 47, resulting in a total backorder of (47 − 40) or 7 units when the replenishment arrives.

Note that above we assumed that the replenishment action is taken when the stock level is exactly at the reorder point s. Even for the situation of continuous review, this may not necessarily be the case. To illustrate, suppose at a certain moment the stock level for the item in Figure 7.3 was 42 units and a demand transaction of 5 units occurred. This would immediately drive the inventory level to 37 units, which is an undershoot of the reorder point by 3 units. It is evident that, strictly speaking, no stockout occurs if and only if the sum of the undershoot and the total demand in the replenishment lead time is less than the reorder point. Except where explicitly noted otherwise, we make the simplifying assumption that the undershoots are small enough to be neglected.

[3]The situation when two or more orders are simultaneously outsanding is somewhat more difficult to explain. Each order is initiated when the inventory position drops to the level s or lower. The level of the on-hand (or net) stock does not influence the placing of a new order. Certainly, however, a low on-hand level may initiate an expediting action on an outstanding order to avoid an impending stockout.

7.5.2 Empirical Analysis Using Actual Historical Lead Time Demand Data

MIDAS' product XSC-023 is a 10-liter set of X-ray developing chemicals. The demand for this item is not seasonal and does not have a significant trend. The actual demands observed in the last 10 lead times have been 64, 51, 48, 32, 93, 21, 47, 57, 41, and 46 units (sets) in that order. Suppose that management has specified that inventories be kept as low as possible subject to not having a stockout more frequently than once in every ten cycles (that is, $P_1 = 0.90$).

Certainly one method of establishing the reorder point would be as follows: The historical demand data, arranged slightly differently, are shown in Table 7.2. Based on these data, if any reorder point of 65 units or higher was used, only one stockout would have occurred in the ten lead times. Therefore, *assuming the historical pattern is representative of future conditions*, a reorder point of 65 units would be used.

There are three potential weaknesses of this simple procedure:

1. Normally one is interested in high service levels, that is, a small chance of a stockout during a single replenishment cycle, subject, of course, to a reasonable cost of carrying the necessary safety stock. Therefore, we would usually prefer to have information about the demand in a considerable number of historical lead times to avoid guessing about the infrequent *outliers* against which we are trying to provide adequate protection.
2. The method cannot easily cope with the situation where the basic demand rate is changing appreciably with time. For example, if the demands in the lead times in the numerical example had instead been seen in the following chronological order: 21, 32, 41, 47, 46, 48, 51, 64, 57, 93—that is, more or less increasing with time—then, unlike earlier, we would certainly not be willing to say that these values are equally likely to occur in the next lead time. Instead, we would expect a lead time demand in the higher portion of the range.

TABLE 7.2 Observed Historical Lead Time Demands for the Developing Chemicals Item

Lead Time Demand	Number of Occurrences at or above This Value	Fraction of Occurrences at or above this Value
93	1	1/10 = 0.1
64	2	0.2
57	3	0.3
51	4	0.4
48	5	0.5
47	6	0.6
46	7	0.7
41	8	0.8
32	9	0.9
21	10	1.0

3. If for some reason the replenishment lead time was altered (for example, by negotiation with the supplier), the histogram of total demand during the old lead time (for example, 3 months) would be of limited value in estimating the probabilities of various total demands in the new lead time (for example, 2 months).

To help overcome these weaknesses, it is helpful to fit a member of a family of probability distributions to the available data. This will be done in the next section using the so-called normal probability distribution.

7.6 DECISION RULES FOR CONTINUOUS-REVIEW, ORDER-POINT, ORDER-QUANTITY (s, Q) CONTROL SYSTEMS

As discussed in Section 7.4, there is a wide choice of criteria for establishing safety stocks. The choice of a criterion is a strategic decision, to be executed on a relatively infrequent basis and involving senior management directly (the exchange curves of Section 7.9 will be helpful in this regard). Once a criterion (and the implied associated decision rule) is chosen, there is then the tactical issue of the selection of a value of the associated policy variable (for example, the numerical value of P_2 for that particular service measure).

Besides the above choice of a suitable criterion, there is also a choice of the probability distribution of lead time demand (or forecast errors). As discussed in Section 4.6.5 of Chapter 4, from a pragmatic standpoint, we recommend, at least for most B items, the use of a normal distribution of forecast errors. In Section 7.6.13 we discuss the use of other theoretical distributions.

The assumptions, the notation, the general approach to the selection of the reorder point, and the portion of the derivation of the rules common to all criteria will be presented prior to showing the individual decision rules. Further details of some of the derivations can be found in the Appendix of this chapter.

7.6.1 Common Assumptions and Notation

There are a number of assumptions that hold independent of the method of costing shortages or measuring service. These include:

1. Although demand is probabilistic, the *average* demand rate changes very little with time. Although this assumption may appear somewhat unrealistic, let us not lose sight of the fact that the decision rules can be used adaptively (that is, the parameters are updated with the passage of time).

2. A replenishment order of size Q is placed when the inventory position is exactly at the order point s. This assumption is tantamount to assuming that all demand transactions are of unit size or else that the undershoots of the order

point are of negligible magnitude compared with the total lead time demand. (In Chapter 8 we will consider a situation where the undershoots are not neglected.)

3. If two or more replenishment orders for the same item are simultaneously outstanding, then they must be received in the same order in which they were placed; that is, crossing of orders is not permitted. A special case satisfying this assumption is where the replenishment lead time is a constant.

4. Unit shortage costs (explicit or implicit) are so high that a practical operating procedure will always result in the average level of backorders being negligibly small when compared with the average level of the on-hand stock.

5. Forecast errors have a normal distribution with no bias (that is, the average value of the error is zero) and a *known* standard deviation σ_L for forecasts over a lead time L. In actual fact, as discussed in Chapter 4, the forecast system only provides us with an estimate $\hat{\sigma}_L$ of σ_L. However, extensive simulation studies by Ehrhardt (1979) have revealed that performance is not seriously degraded by using $\hat{\sigma}_L$ instead of σ_L (see also Problem 7.5). Appendix B, at the end of the book, is devoted to a discussion of the normal distribution, and a graphical representation of a typical distribution is shown in Figure 7.4.

6. Where a value of Q is needed, it is assumed to have been predetermined. In most situations, the effects of the two decision variables, s and Q, are not independent; that is, the best value of Q depends on the s value, and vice versa. However, as will be shown in Chapter 8, where a closer look will be taken at the simultaneous determination of the two control parameters, the assumption of Q being predetermined without knowledge of s makes very good practical sense, particularly for B items.

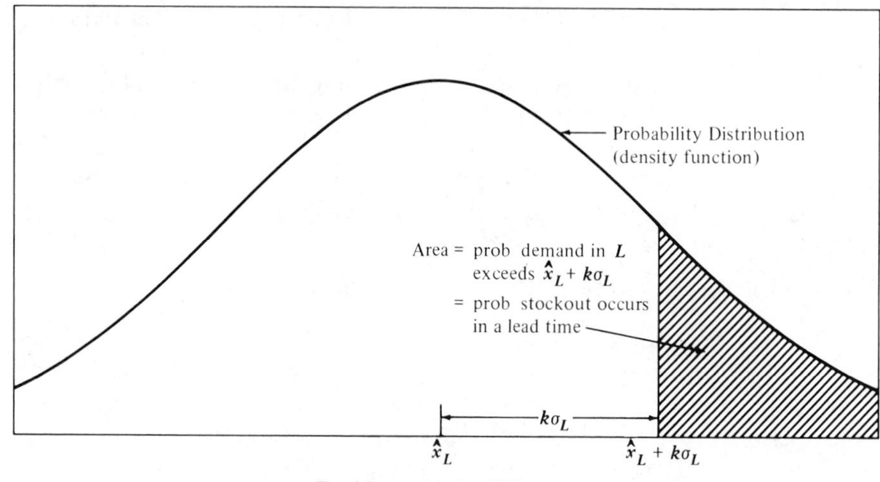

FIGURE 7.4 Normally Distributed Forecast Errors

7. The costs of the control system do not depend on the specific value of s selected.

Common notation includes:

D = demand rate in units/year

$$G_u(k) = \int_k^\infty (u_0 - k) \frac{1}{\sqrt{2\pi}} \exp(-u_0^2/2)\, du_0$$

a special function of the unit normal (mean 0, standard deviation 1) variable[4]

k = safety factor

L = replenishment lead time, in years

$p_{u\geq}(k)$ = probability that a unit normal (mean 0, standard deviation 1) variable takes on a value of k or larger.[4] (A graphical interpretation of $p_{u\geq}(k)$ is shown in Figure 7.4)

Q = prespecified order quantity, in units

r = inventory carrying charge, in \$/\$/year

s = order point, in units

SS = safety stock, in units

v = unit variable cost, in \$/unit

$\hat{x}_L$ = forecast (or expected) demand over a replenishment lead time, in units

σ_L = standard deviation of errors of forecasts over a replenishment lead time, in units

7.6.2 General Approach to Establishing the Value of s

In Section 7.5.2 we set about directly determining the required reorder point s. Here it will turn out to be more appropriate to work indirectly using the following relationships

$$\text{Reorder point, } s = \hat{x}_L + (\text{Safety stock}) \tag{7.5}$$

[4] $G_u(k)$ or $p_{u\geq}(k)$ can be obtained from k, or vice versa, using a table lookup (a table of the unit normal distribution is shown in Appendix B) or a rational approximation (see, for example, p. 933 of Abramowitz and Stegun, 1965; page 93 of Brown, 1967; Herron, 1974; Page, 1977; or Parr, 1972).

and

$$\text{Safety stock} = k\sigma_L \tag{7.6}$$

where k is known as the safety factor. Determination of a k value leads directly to a value of s through use of these two relations.

The general logic used in computing the appropriate value of s (via k) is portrayed in Figure 7.5. Of particular note is the manual override. The user should definitely have the option of adjusting the reorder point to reflect factors not included in the model. However, care must be taken to not again adjust for factors for which manual adjustments were already made as part of the forecasting system (see Figure 4.1 of Chapter 4).

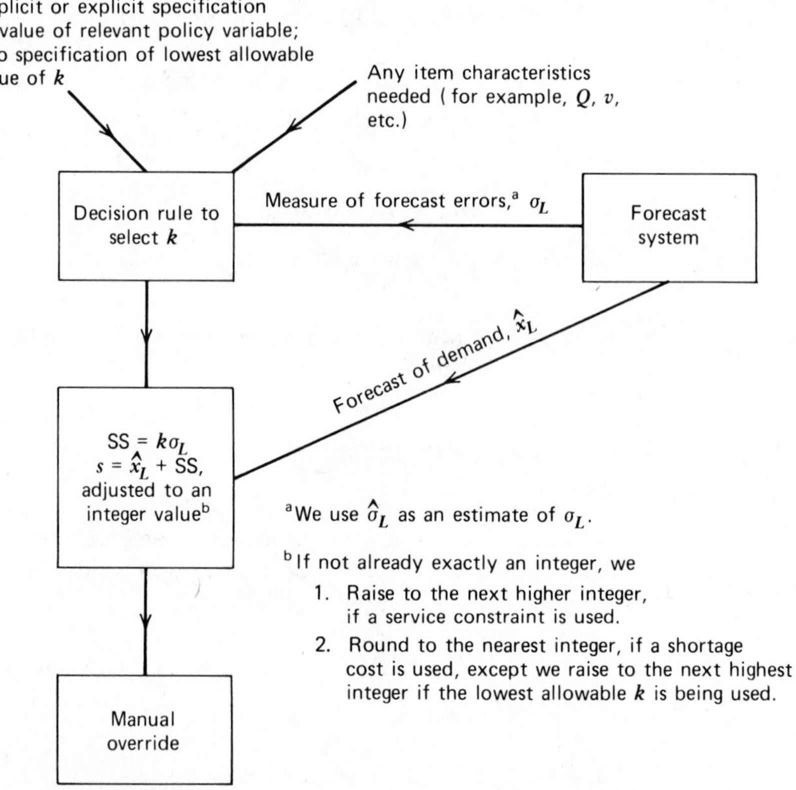

FIGURE 7.5 General Decision Logic Used in Computing the Value of s

7.6.3 Common Derivation[5]

Recall that an (s, Q) system operates in the following manner. Anytime that the inventory position drops to s or lower, a replenishment of size Q is placed. Because of the assumption of no crossing of orders, if an order is placed at some time t when the inventory position is at level s, then all previous orders outstanding at that time must have arrived prior to the moment (call it $t + L$) at which the current order arrives. Furthermore, any orders placed after the current one cannot arrive before $t + L$. In other words, all s of the inventory position at time t, and no other stock, must have reached the stocking shelf by time $t + L$. Therefore, the service impact of placing the current order when the inventory position is at the level s is determined by whether the total demand x in the replenishment lead time exceeds s (If the on-hand level happens to be very low at time t, a stockout may be incurred early in the replenishment cycle before an earlier outstanding order arrives. However, this event is independent of the current replenishment, the one at time t, and should not be considered in evaluating the consequences of using an order point s for the current order.)

If the demand (x) in the replenishment lead time has a probability density function $f_x(x_0)$ defined such that

$$f_x(x_0)dx_0 = \text{Prob }\{\text{Total demand in the lead time lies between } x_0 \text{ and } x_0 + dx_0\}$$

then the above arguments lead to the following three important results:[6]

1. Safety stock (SS) = E (Net stock just before the replenishment arrives)

$$= \int_0^\infty (s - x_0)f_x(x_0)dx_0$$

that is,

$$\text{SS} = s - \hat{x}_L \tag{7.7}$$

This has a particularly simple interpretation for the case where no more than one order is ever outstanding. In such a case Eq. 7.7 states that the average inventory level just before a replenishment arrives is equal to the inventory level when the replenishment is placed (all of this being on-hand inventory) reduced by the average demand during the lead time.

[5]The mathematical details of this subsection can be skimmed as the subsequent presentation of each decision rule will include an intuitive justification of the results. Furthermore, an alternative type of derivation (a so-called *marginal argument*), involving less complex mathematics, will be illustrated in Section 1 of the Appendix of this chapter.

[6]$E(z)$ represents the expected or mean value of the random variable z.

2. Prob {Stockout in a replenishment lead time}

$$= \text{Prob}\,\{x \geqslant s\}$$

$$= \int_s^\infty f_x(x_0)dx_0 \tag{7.8}$$

the probability that lead time demand is at least as large as the reorder point (illustrated graphically in Figure 7.4).

3. Expected shortage per replenishment cycle,

$$\text{ESPRC} = \int_s^\infty (x_0 - s)f_x(x_o)dx_0 \tag{7.9}$$

Now, recall from the basic definition of Eq. 7.1 that

$$\text{Net stock} = (\text{On hand}) - (\text{Backorders})$$

that is,

$$\text{NS} = \text{OH} - \text{BO}$$

Therefore

$$E(\text{NS}) = E(\text{OH}) - E(\text{BO}) \tag{7.10}$$

Because of the assumption of average backorders being very small relative to the average on-hand stock, we have

$$E(\text{OH}) \simeq E(\text{NS}) \tag{7.11}$$

Using Eqs. 7.7 and 7.11,

$$E(\text{OH just before a replenishment arrives}^7) \simeq \text{Safety Stock (SS)}$$
$$= s - \hat{x}_L$$

and, because each replenishment is of size Q,

$$E(\text{OH just after a replenishment arrives}) \simeq s - \hat{x}_L + Q$$

Now, the mean rate of demand is constant with time. Therefore, on the average, the OH level drops linearly during a cycle from $(s - \hat{x}_L + Q)$ right

[7]A more exact result is obtained by using

$$E(\text{OH just before a replenishment arrives}) = \int_0^s (s - x_o)\, f_x\,(x_o)\, dx_o$$

after a replenishment arrives to $(s - \hat{x}_L)$ immediately before the next replenishment arrives. Thus

$$E(\text{OH}) \simeq \frac{Q}{2} + (s - \hat{x}_L) = \frac{Q}{2} + k\sigma_L \tag{7.12}$$

where, as mentioned earlier, we have chosen to express the safety stock $(s - \hat{x}_L)$ as the multiple of two factors:

$$\text{SS} = k\sigma_L \tag{7.13}$$

A useful graphical reminder of this equation is shown in Figure 7.6.

One other common feature, independent of the service measure or shortage costing method used, is the expected number of replenishments per year. Each replenishment is of size Q and the mean rate of demand is D, as earlier. Therefore,

$$\text{Expected number of replenishments per year} = \frac{D}{Q} \tag{7.14}$$

To this point the results hold for *any* probability distribution of lead time demand (or forecast errors). To proceed further one has to specify the particular distribution. As shown in Appendix B, when forecast errors are assumed nor-

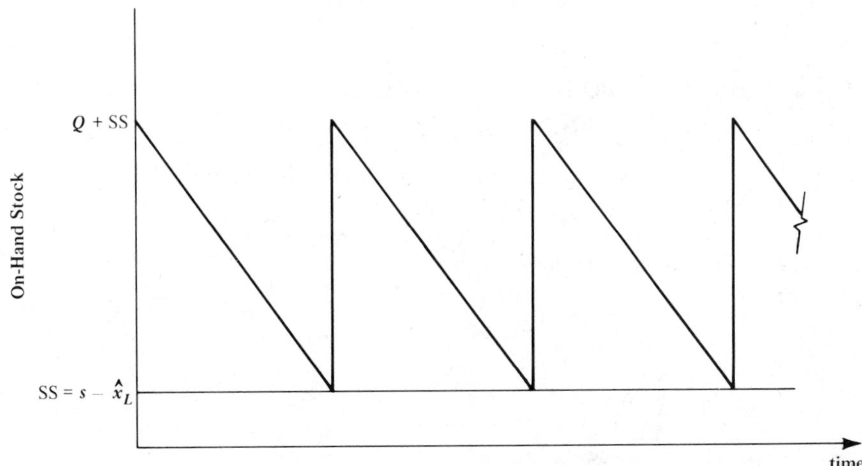

FIGURE 7.6 Average Behavior of On-Hand Stock in an (s,Q) System

mally distributed and the safety stock is expressed as in Eq. 7.13, then Eqs. 7.8 and 7.9 simplify to

$$\text{Prob \{Stockout in a replenishment lead time\}} = p_{u\geq}(k) \tag{7.15}$$

and

$$\text{ESPRC} = \sigma_L G_u(k) \tag{7.16}$$

At this point, the safety factor derivations diverge based on the particular shortage cost or service measure used. Some illustrative details can be found in the Appendix of this chapter. We now turn to the presentation of the individual decision rules. In each case we first present the rule (possibly including a graphical aid). In most cases this is followed by a numerical illustration of its use, and then by a discussion of the behavior of the rule in terms of how the safety factor k varies from item to item in a population of items. As discussed in Section 7.4 there is a wide choice of criteria for establishing safety stocks. Our treatment is only meant to be illustrative of the many possibilities.

7.6.4 Decision Rule for a Specified Safety Factor (k)

Once a k value is specified, the choice of s immediately follows from Eqs. 7.5 and 7.6:

The Rule

Step 1 Safety stock, SS = $k\sigma_L$.

Step 2 Reorder point, $s = \hat{x}_L + \text{SS}$, increased to the next higher integer (if not already *exactly* an integer).

7.6.5 Decision Rule for a Specified Cost (B_1) per Stockout Occasion

Two approaches to the derivation of the following rule are shown in Section 1 of the Appendix of this chapter.

The Rule

Step 1 Is

$$\frac{DB_1}{\sqrt{2\pi}\,Qv\sigma_L r} < 1? \tag{7.17}$$

where Q has been predetermined, presumably by one of the methods of Chapter 5, B_1 is expressed in dollars, and all the other variables (with units consistent such that the left-hand side of the equation is dimensionless) are as defined in Section 7.6.1?

Yes, then go to Step 2.

No, then continue with[8]

$$k = \sqrt{2 \ln \left(\frac{DB_1}{\sqrt{2\pi} Q v \sigma_L r} \right)} \tag{7.18}$$

If Eq. 7.18 gives a value of k lower than the minimum allowable value specified by management, then go to Step 2. Otherwise, proceed directly to Step 3.

Step 2 Set k at its lowest allowable value (specified by management).

Step 3 Reorder point $s = \hat{x}_L + k\sigma_L$, rounded to the nearest integer (except raised to next highest integer if Step 2 was used).

Numerical Illustration

Suppose an item is one of a number for which a B_1 value of \$300 has been specified. Other relevant characteristics of the item are

$$D = 200 \text{ units/yr}$$

$$Q = 80 \text{ units}$$

$$v = \$2/\text{unit}$$

$$\hat{x}_L = 50 \text{ units}$$

$$\sigma_L = 21.0 \text{ units}$$

$$r = 0.24 \text{ \$/\$/yr}$$

---

[8]An alternative to the use of Eq. 7.18 is to find by a table lookup the k value that satisfies

$$f_u(k) = \frac{Q v \sigma_L r}{DB_1} \tag{7.19}$$

where $f_u(k)$ is the probability density function of a unit normal variable evaluated at k. (See Table B.1 in Appendix B.)

Step 1

$$\frac{DB_1}{\sqrt{2\pi}\,Qv\sigma_L r} = \frac{200 \text{ units/yr} \times \$300}{\sqrt{2\pi} \times 80 \text{ units} \times \$2/\text{unit} \times 21 \text{ units} \times 0.24/\text{yr}}$$
$$= 29.7 > 1$$

Hence, from Eq. 7.18

$$k = \sqrt{2 \ln (29.7)} = 2.60$$

Step 3 (Step 2 is bypassed in this example.)

$$s = 50 + 2.60(21) = 104.6 \rightarrow 105 \text{ units}$$

The high value of B_1 has led to a rather large safety factor.

Discussion

It is seen from Eq. 7.18 that k decreases as σ_L or v goes up. Intuitively, the behavior of k with v makes sense under the assumed stockout costing mechanism. If there is only a fixed cost per stockout occasion *which is the same for all items*, then it makes sense to allocate a greater proportional safety stock to the less expensive items where an adequate level of protection is achieved with relatively little investment. Furthermore, as shown in Section 1 of the Appendix of this chapter, it follows from Eq. 7.18 that k decreases as Dv increases (this is not obvious from a quick look at the equations because both $\sigma_L v$ and Qv depend on Dv). What this means is that higher safety factors are provided to the slower-moving items.

The appearance of Q in the decision rule for finding the safety factor k indicates that a change in Q will affect the required value of the safety stock. Such effects of Q were ignored in the derivations of Chapter 5. For B items this turns out to be a reasonable approximation, as we will see in Chapter 8, where such interactions between Q and k will be more closely examined in the context of control of A items.

There is no solution to Eq. 7.18 when the condition of Eq. 7.17 is satisfied. In such a situation, as shown in the derivation in Section 1 of the Appendix, the best solution is the lowest allowable value of k.

Note that in establishing the reorder point in Step 3 we advocate rounding to the nearest integer rather than always going to the next highest integer. This is because, in contrast with service measures, here we are not bound by a service constraint.

7.6.6 Decision Rule for a Specified Fractional Charge (B_2) per Unit Short

Derivations of the following decision rule can be found in Bierman et al. (1977) and McClain and Thomas (1980).

The Rule

Step 1 Is

$$\frac{Qr}{DB_2} > 1? \tag{7.20}$$

where Q has been predetermined and the units of the variables are such that the left-hand side of the equation is dimensionless (B_2 itself is dimensionless).

Yes, then go to step 2.

No, then continue with the following. Select k so as to satisfy

$$p_{u\geq}(k) = \frac{Qr}{DB_2} \tag{7.21}$$

If use of Eq. 7.21 gives a k value lower than the minimum allowable safety factor specified by management, then go to Step 2. Otherwise, move to Step 3.

Step 2 Set k at its lowest allowable value.

Step 3 Reorder point, $s = \hat{x}_L + k\sigma_L$, rounded to the nearest integer (except raised to the next highest integer in the event that Step 2 has been used).

Graphical Aid

Figure 7.7 displays a graphical aid for solving Eq. 7.21, thus avoiding the use of a table lookup or a rational approximation.

Numerical Illustration

One of MIDAS' North American suppliers wishes to allocate a fixed amount of safety stock among a number of products to keep the total value of backorders per year as low as possible. Management feels that it is reasonable to use a B_2 value of 0.25; that is, each unit short incurs a cost equal to 25 percent of its unit value. The replenishment quantity of an item under consideration has been predetermined at 85 units. Other quantities of interest include

$\hat{x}_L = 50$ units

$\sigma_L = 10$ units

$r = 0.2$ \$/\$/yr

$D = 200$ units/yr

Step 1

$$\frac{Qr}{DB_2} = \frac{85 \text{ units} \times 0.2/\text{yr}}{200 \text{ units/yr} \times 0.25} = 0.34 < 1$$

Then, Eq. 7.21 gives

$$p_{u\geqslant}(k) = 0.34$$

From Table B.1 in Appendix B, $k \simeq 0.41$ (presumably larger than the lowest allowable value, hence we go to Step 3).

Step 3

$$s = 50 + 0.41(10) = 54.1 \rightarrow 54 \text{ units}$$

Discussion

As seen in Figure 7.7 the safety factor k increases as B_2/r increases, as one would expect. Moreover, under the use of economic order quantities, we found that Q/D decreases as Dv increases. Therefore, at least under the use of EOQ's it is seen from Eq. 7.21 that k increases as Dv increases; that is, under this decision rule, larger safety factors are given to the faster-moving items, all other things being equal.

The $p_{u\geqslant}(k)$ value represents a probability; hence there is no solution to Eq. 7.21 when the right-hand side of the equation exceeds unity; that is, when Eq. 7.20 is satisfied. It can be shown (in a manner paralleling the derivation in Section 1 of the Appendix of this chapter) that, when this happens, one should use the lowest permissible value of the safety factor.

7.6.7 Decision Rule for a Specified Fractional Charge (B_3) per Unit Short per Unit Time

As mentioned in Section 7.4.3, there is an equivalence between the B_3 costing measure and the P_2 service measure. Thus, we merely present the decision rule here, leaving further comment to the P_2 section (the derivation involves differentiating the total relevant costs with respect to k and using results in Hadley and Whitin, 1963).

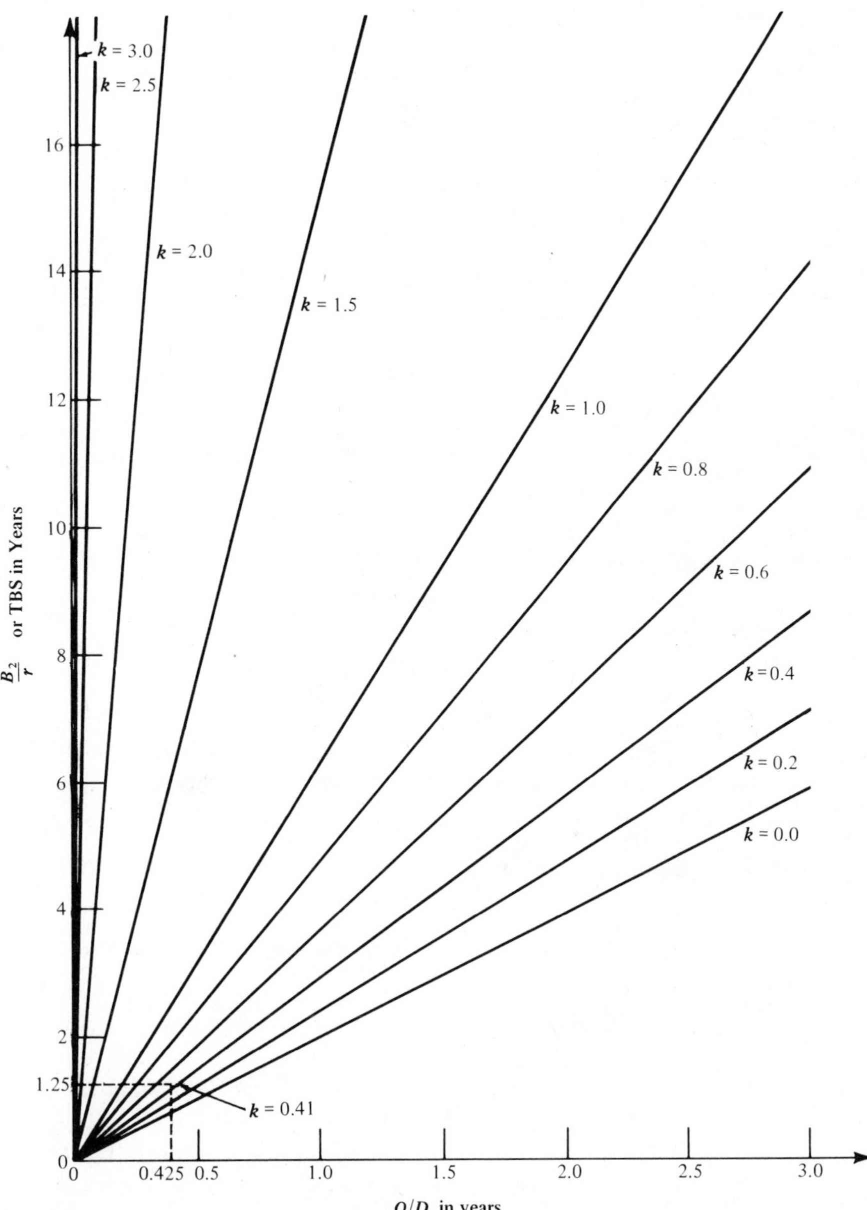

FIGURE 7.7 Graphical Aid for the B_2 Shortage Cost Measure, The TBS Service Measure, or Allocation of a Total Safety Stock to Minimize the Expected Total Value of Shortages per Year

The Rule

Step 1 Select the safety factor k that satisfies

$$G_u(k) = \frac{Q}{\sigma_L}\left(\frac{r}{B_3 + r}\right) \tag{7.22}$$

where Q has been predetermined, presumably by one of the procedures of Chapter 5 (and must be expressed in the same units as σ_L), and B_3 and r are in \$/\$/unit time.

Make sure that the k value is at least as large as the lowest allowable (management specified) value (for example, zero) of the safety factor.

Step 2 Reorder point $s = \hat{x}_L + k\sigma_L$, rounded to the nearest integer (but increased to the next highest integer if the minimum k value is used in Step 1).

7.6.8 Decision Rule for a Specified Probability (P_1) of No Stockout per Replenishment Cycle

Suppose management has specified that the probability of no stockout in a cycle should be no lower than P_1 (conversely, the probability of a stockout should be no higher than $1 - P_1$). Then we have the following simple decision rule (whose derivation is shown in Section 2 of the Appendix of this chapter).

The Rule

Step 1 Select the safety factor k to satisfy

$$p_{u\geq}(k) = 1 - P_1 \tag{7.23}$$

where

$p_{u\geq}(k)$ = Prob {Unit normal variable (mean 0, standard deviation 1) takes on a value of k or larger}, a widely tabulated function (see Table B.1 in Appendix B)

Step 2 Safety stock, SS = $k\sigma_L$.

Step 3 Reorder point, $s = \hat{x}_L$ + SS, increased to the next higher integer (if not already *exactly* an integer).

Numerical Illustration

For the developing chemicals item used in Section 7.5.2, suppose that MIDAS' forecast system had output the following values

$\hat{x}_L = 58.3$ units

$\sigma_L = 13.1$ units

Management also desires a service level of $P_1 = 0.90$.

From Eq. 7.23 we know

$$p_{u\geqslant}(k) = 0.10$$

From Table B.1 in Appendix B

$$k \simeq 1.28$$

$$\text{SS} = k\sigma_L = 1.28 \times 13.1 \text{ units}$$

$$= 16.8 \text{ units}$$

Reorder point, $s = 58.3 + 16.8 = 75.1$, say 76 units.

Discussion of the Decision Rule

From Eq. 7.23 it is seen that the safety factor k depends only on the value of P_1; in particular, it is independent of any individual-item characteristics such as the order quantity Q. Therefore, all items for which we desire the same service level, P_1, will have identical values of the safety factor k. Thus, we see an equivalence between two criteria, namely, using a specified value of k and a specified value of P_1.

From Eq. 7.23 $p_{u\geqslant}(k)$ must decrease as the desired service level (P_1) goes up. But, from Table B.1 in Appendix B, it is seen that k increases as $p_{u\geqslant}(k)$ decreases. Therefore, we have the desirable behavior of the safety factor k increasing with increasing required service level.

Because of the discrete nature of the reorder point we are not likely to be able to provide the exact level of service desired since this usually would require a noninteger value of s. Therefore, a noninteger value of s found in Eq. 7.23 is rounded up to the next higher integer with the predicted service level then being slightly higher than required.

The fact that the safety factor doesn't depend on any individual-item characteristics may cause one to reexamine the meaning of service here. Recall that service under the measure used in this section is prob {no stockout *per replenishment cycle*}. Consider two items, the first being replenished twenty times a year, the other once a year. If they both are given the same safety factor so that both have a probability of 0.10 of stockout per repenishment cycle, then we'd expect 20 × (0.10) or 2 stockouts per year for the first item and only 1 stockout every ten years (0.1 per year) for the second item. Therefore, depending on management's definition of service, we, in fact, would probably not be giving the same service on these two items. Rules based on other service measures will now be presented.

7.6.9 Decision Rule for a Specified Fraction (P_2) of Demand Satisfied Directly from Shelf

The following decision rule is derived in Section 3 of the Appendix to this chapter.

The Rule

Step 1 Select the safety factor k that satisfies[9]

$$G_u(k) = \frac{Q}{\sigma_L}(1 - P_2) \tag{7.24}$$

where Q has been predetermined, presumably by one of the procedures of Chapter 5 (and must be expressed in the same units as σ_L). The other relevant variables are defined in Section 7.6.1.

Make sure that the k value is at least as large as the lowest allowable (management specified) value of the safety factor.

Step 2 Reorder point, $s = \hat{x}_L + k\sigma_L$, increased to the next higher integer (if not already exactly an integer).

Graphical Aid

A graphical aid for solving Eq. 7.24 for k is shown in Figure 7.8. This avoids a table lookup or the use of a rational approximation. The graph actually provides a solution to the equation.

$$G_u(k) - G_u(k + Q/\sigma_L) = \frac{Q}{\sigma_L}(1 - P_2) \tag{7.26}$$

which is more accurate than Eq. 7.24, particularly for low values of Q/σ_L (see Silver, 1970).

Numerical Illustration

Consider a particular type of developing liquid distributed by MIDAS. Management has specified that 99 percent of demand is to be satisfied without backordering. A replenishment quantity of 200 gallons has been predetermined and the forecast system provides us with $\hat{x}_L = 50$ gallons and $\sigma_L = 11.4$ gallons.

---

[9]Equation 7.24 applies for the case of complete backordering. The only difference for the case of complete lost sales is that $(1 - P_2)$ is replaced by $(1 - P_2)/P_2$:

$$G_u(k) = \frac{Q}{\sigma_L}\left(\frac{1 - P_2}{P_2}\right) \tag{7.25}$$

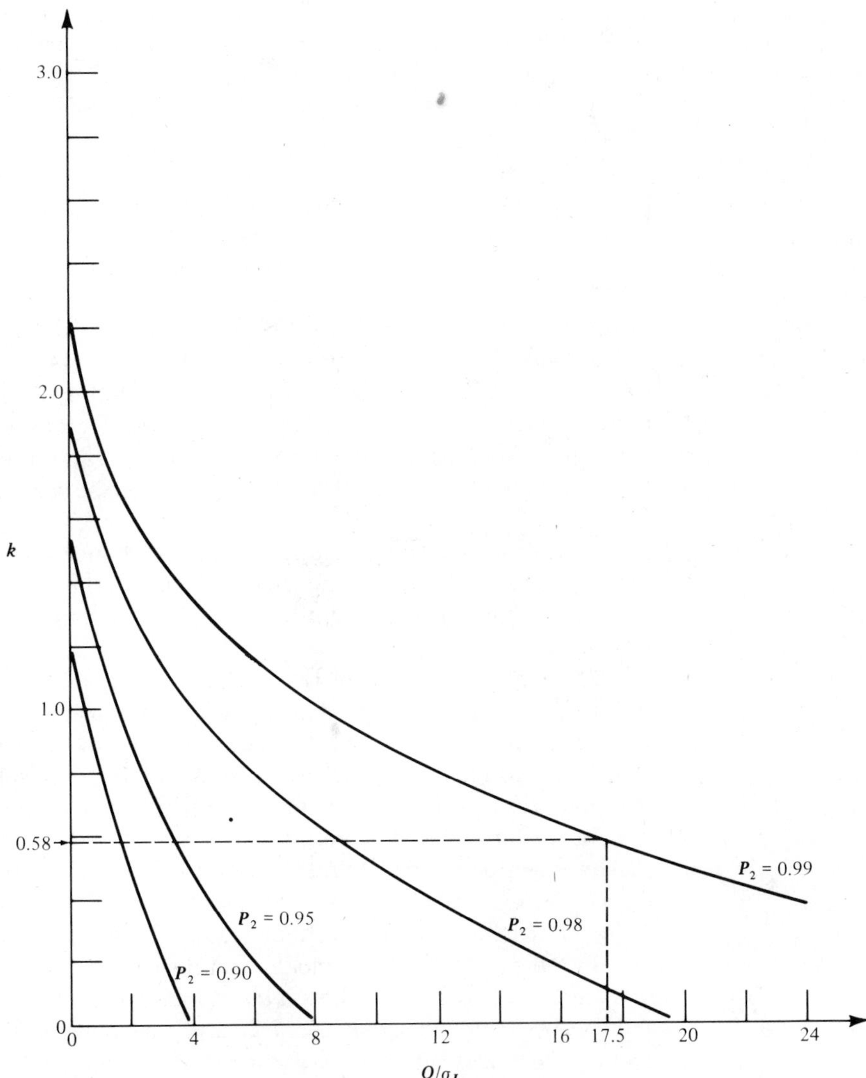

FIGURE 7.8 Graphical Aid for the P_2 Service Measure

Step 1 Equation 7.24 yields

$$G_u(k) = \frac{200}{11.4}(1 - 0.99) = 0.175$$

and Table B.1 in Appendix B gives

$$k = 0.58$$

The same result is obtained using Figure 7.8.

Step 2

$$s = 50 + 0.58(11.4) = 56.6 \rightarrow 57 \text{ gallons}$$[10]

For the case of complete lost sales (rather than backordering) use of Eq. 7.25 would lead us to the same value of the reorder point.

Discussion

Intuitively, we would expect that the required safety stock would increase if (1) Q decreased (more opportunities for stockouts), (2) σ_L increased (higher uncertainty of forecasts), or (3) P_2 increased (better service desired). If any of the above-mentioned changes take place, $G_u(k)$ decreases, but as seen from the table in Appendix B, a decrease in $G_u(k)$ implies an increase in k, that is, exactly the desired behavior. The same conclusions can be reached by examining Figure 7.8.

In addition, on the average, σ_L tends to increase with D; therefore, the increase in k with increasing σ_L says that, on the average under this decision rule, faster-moving items get higher safety factors than do the slower-moving items.

If the right-hand side of Eq. 7.24 is large enough, a negative value of k is required to produce the equality; to give a service level as *poor* as P_2, one must deliberately plan to be short on the average when a replenishment arrives. Management may find this intolerable and, instead, set a lower limit on k (for example, zero). If k is set at zero when Eq. 7.24 calls for a negative value of k, the service provided will be better than P_2.

The P_2 value is usually quite close to unity. Therefore, as evidenced by the numerical example, Eqs. 7.24 and 7.25 normally give very similar values of $G_u(k)$, that is, of k itself. In other words, the value of the safety factor is little influenced by whether the model assumes complete backordering or complete lost sales (or any mix of these two extremes).

Finally, a comparison of Eqs. 7.22 and 7.24 shows the analogy between the P_2 and B_3 measures mentioned earlier.

7.6.10 Decision Rule for a Specified Average Time (TBS) Between Stockout Occasions

The Rule

Step 1 Is

$$\frac{Q}{D(\text{TBS})} > 1? \tag{7.27}$$

[10]If the inventory can be monitored more finely than by integer gallons, the reorder point could be left at the noninteger value of 56.6.

where Q has been predetermined (presumably by the methods of Chapter 5) and the units of the variables are such that the left side is dimensionless.

Yes, then go to Step 2.

No, then continue with the following. Select the safety factor k to satisfy

$$p_{u\geqslant}(k) = \frac{Q}{D(\text{TBS})} \tag{7.28}$$

If the resulting k is lower than the minimum allowable value specified by management, then go to Step 2. Otherwise, move to Step 3.

Step 2 Set k at its lowest permitted value.

Step 3 Reorder point, $s = \hat{x}_L + k\sigma_L$ raised to the next highest integer (if not already *exactly* an integer).

Numerical Illustration

For the developing chemicals item, XSC-023, used in Sections 7.5.2 and 7.6.8, suppose that

$$\hat{x}_L = 58.3 \text{ units}$$

$$\sigma_L = 13.1 \text{ units}$$

$$D = 200 \text{ units/yr}$$

$$Q = 30 \text{ units}$$

and management specifies a desired TBS value of 2 years. Then, Eq. 7.28 gives

$$p_{u\geqslant}(k) = \frac{30}{200(2)} = 0.075$$

From Table B.1 of Appendix B, we have

$$k = 1.44$$

Then,

$$\text{SS} = 1.44 \times 13.1 = 18.9 \text{ units}$$

and,

$$s = 58.3 + 18.9 = 77.2, \text{ say } 78 \text{ units}$$

Discussion

A comparison of Eqs. 7.21 and 7.28 reveals that there is an equivalence between using the B_2 costing method and using the TBS service measure.

Specifically, we have, for equivalence, that

$$\text{TBS} = \frac{B_2}{r}$$

In fact, this equivalence was recognized in the preparation of the graphical aid of Figure 7.7. A further aid, of a tabular nature, will be discussed in connection with the control of C items in Chapter 9.

From Eq. 7.28 we see that increasing TBS leads to a lower value of $p_{u\geq}(k)$, and hence a larger value of the safety factor k, certainly an appealing behavior.

7.6.11 Decision Rule for the Allocation of a Total Safety Stock to Minimize the Expected Total Stockout Occasions per Year

As shown in Section 4 of the Appendix of this chapter, allocation of a total safety stock among a group of items to minimize the expected total stockout occasions per year leads to a decision rule identical to that under the B_1 shortage costing method. Thus, one simply has to use the procedure of Section 7.6.5, adjusting the value of B_1 until the total implied safety stock is equal to the given quantity to be allocated (conversely, when we discuss safety stock exchange curves later in this chapter, we will see that selection of an aggregate operating point on an appropriate exchange curve will imply a value of B_1 to be used).

7.6.12 Decision Rule for the Allocation of a Total Safety Stock to Minimize the Expected Total Value of Shortages per Year

In a fashion similar to that shown in Section 4 of the Appendix of this chapter, one can show that there is an equivalence between the decision rules for three different criteria:

1. Allocating a total safety stock among a group of items to minimize the expected total value of shortages per year.
2. Use of a B_2 shortage cost.
3. Use of the TBS service measure.

Thus, for the allocation criterion, one need only use the procedure of Section 7.6.6 (including the graphical aid of Figure 7.7), adjusting the value of B_2 until the total implied safety stock is equal to the given quantity to be allocated.

7.6.13 Nonnormal Forecast Errors

As mentioned earlier, for pragmatic reasons, we have shown only the case of normally distributed forecast errors in this chapter. The normal distribution often provides a good empirical fit to the observed data; it is convenient from an analytic standpoint; it is widely tabulated; and, finally, the impact of using other distributions is usually quite small (see, for example Fortuin, 1980; Naddor 1978), particularly when one recognizes the other inaccuracies present (estimates of the parameters of the distribution, estimates of cost factors, etc.). Nevertheless, as discussed in Chapter 4, the user is advised to at least test the normal distribution using data from a sample of items.

We now comment specifically on three other distributions—namely, the Gamma, the Poisson, and the Laplace. As discussed by Burgin (1975), the Gamma distribution has considerable intuitive appeal for representing the distribution of lead time demand. The distribution is not as tractable as the normal; thus considerable effort has been devoted to developing approximations and tables (see Burgin and Norman, 1976; Das, 1976b; Johnston, 1980; Taylor and Oke, 1976, 1979; Tijms, 1983; and van der Veen, 1981).

The Laplace or pseudoexponential distribution was first proposed by Presutti and Trepp (1970). It is analytically very simple to use and tests performed by Archibald et al. (1974) indicate that it is most appropriate for rather slow-moving items.

The Poisson distribution is also a candidate for slower moving items. In fact, in Chapter 8 we will illustrate its use for expensive, low-usage items.

Many other distributions of forecast errors (or lead time demand) have been proposed in the literature. We now simply provide a listing of several of them accompanied by suitable references:

1. Exponential: Brown (1977).
2. Geometric: Carlson (1982).
3. Logistic: Fortuin (1980); van Beek (1978).
4. Negative binomial: Deemer et al. (1974); Ehrhardt (1979).
5. Pearson: Kottas and Lau (1980).
6. Tukey's Lambda: Silver (1977).

7.7 DECISION RULES FOR PERIODIC-REVIEW, ORDER-UP-TO-LEVEL (*R*, *S*) CONTROL SYSTEMS

Recall that in an (R, S) system every R units of time a replenishment order is placed of sufficient magnitude to raise the inventory position to the order-up-to-level S. Fortunately, for such systems there will be no need to repeat all the detail that was necessary for (s, Q) systems in the previous section, the reason being that there is a rather remarkable, simple analogy between (R, S) and (s, Q) systems. Specifically, the (R, S) situation is exactly equivalent to the (s, Q) situation if one makes the following transformations.

(s, Q)	(R, S)
s	S
Q	DR
L	$R + L$

It therefore follows that the decision rule for determining the S value in an (R, S) system for a particular selection of shortage cost or service measure is obtained from the corresponding rule for determining s in an (s, Q) system by simply making the above three substitutions. Moreover, the graphical aids developed for the (s, Q) systems can be easily modified to handle the analogous (R, S) safety stock rules. Prior to proving the aforementioned equivalence, we will discuss the choice of R as well as the key time period involved in the selection of S.

7.7.1 The Review Interval (R)

In computing the value of S, we assume that a value of R has been predetermined. The nature of (R, S) control is such that a replenishment order is placed every R units of time. The determination of R is equivalent to the determination of an economic order quantity expressed as a time supply, except for two minor variations. First, the cost of reviewing the inventory status must be included as part of the fixed setup cost A. Second, it is clear that it would be senseless to attempt to implement certain review intervals, for example, 2.36 days; that is, R is obviously restricted to a reasonably small number of feasible discrete values.

7.7.2 The Order-Up-To-Level (S)

The key time period over which protection is required is now of duration $R + L$, instead of just a replenishment lead time L. This is illustrated in Figure 7.9 and Table 7.3 with an example where $S = 50$ units and where two consecutive orders (called X and Y) are placed at times t_0 and $t_0 + R$, respectively, and arrive at $t_0 + L$ and $t_0 + R + L$, respectively. In selecting the order-up-to-level at time t_0 we must recognize that, once we've placed order X, no other later orders (in particular Y) can be received until time $t_0 + R + L$. Therefore, the order-up-to-level at time t_0 must be sufficient to cover demand through a period of duration $R + L$. A stockout could occur in the early portion of the period (prior to $t_0 + L$) but that would be a consequece of the setting of the order-up-to-level on the order preceding order X. What is of interest to us is that a stockout will occur toward the end of the period (after time $t_0 + L$) if the total demand in an interval of length $R + L$ exceeds the order-up-to-level S. Another way of putting this is that any stockouts up to time $t_0 + L$ will not be influenced by our ordering decision at time t_0; however, this decision certainly influences the likelihood of a stockout at time $t_0 + R + L$. Of course, this does not mean that one would necessarily take no action if at time t_0 a stockout appeared likely by time $t_0 + L$. Probably,

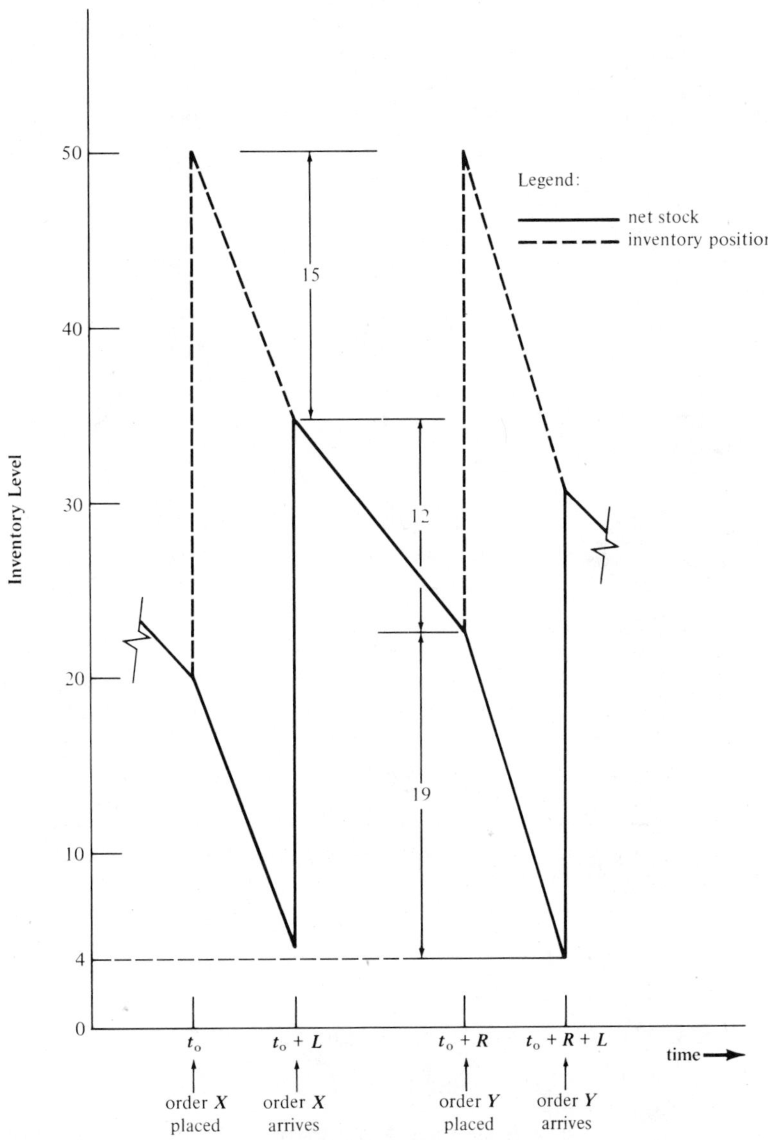

FIGURE 7.9 The Time Period of Protection in an (*R*, *S*) System

one would expedite any already outstanding order or try to get the current order (that placed at time t_0) delivered as quickly as possible. Note, however, that this still does not influence the *size* of the current order.

As mentioned above, a stockout will occur at the end of the current cycle (that is, at time $t_0 + R + L$) if the total demand in an interval of duration $R + L$ exceeds S. A little reflection shows a very close analogy with the determination of s in the continuous review system. In fact, the only difference is the duration of the time period of concern, namely, $R + L$ instead of just L.

TABLE 7.3 Illustration of Why $(R + L)$ Is the Crucial Time Interval in an (R, S) System (Illustrated for $S = 50$)

Event	Time or Interval[1]	Demand	(OH − BO)[2] Net Stock	On Order	Inventory Position
	$t_0 - \varepsilon$	—	20	—	20
Place order for 30	$t_0 - \varepsilon$ to $t_0 + \varepsilon$	—	20	30	50[a]
	$t_0 + \varepsilon$ to $t_0 + L - \varepsilon$	15[b]	5	30	35
Order of 30 arrives	$t_0 + L - \varepsilon$ to $t_0 + L + \varepsilon$	—	35	—	35
	$t_0 + L + \varepsilon$ to $t_0 + R - \varepsilon$	12[c]	23	—	23
Place order for 27	$t_0 + R - \varepsilon$ to $t_0 + R + \varepsilon$	—	23	27	50
	$t_0 + R + \varepsilon$ to $t_0 + R + L - \varepsilon$	19[d]	4[e]	27	31
Order of 27 arrives	$t_0 + R + L - \varepsilon$ to $t_0 + R + L + \varepsilon$	—	31	—	31

$$(e) = (a) - [(b) + (c) + (d)]$$

- (e): Net stock status just before a replenishment arrives at $t_0 + R + L$
- (a): Inventory position *after* order at t_0
- $[(b) + (c) + (d)]$: Total demand in t_0 to $t_0 + R + L$

[1] ε is a shorthand notation for a very small interval of time. Thus $t_0 - \varepsilon$ represents a moment just prior to time t_0, while $t_0 + \varepsilon$ represents a moment just after time t_0.
[2] (On hand) − (Backorders).

7.7.3 Common Assumptions and Notation

The assumptions include:

1. Although demand is probabilistic the *average* demand rate changes very little with time.
2. There is a negligible chance of no demand between reviews; consequently, a replenishment order is placed at every review.
3. If two or more replenishment orders for the same item are simultaneously outstanding, then they must be received in the same order in which they were placed; that is, crossing of orders is not permitted. A special case satisfying this assumption is where the replenishment lead time is a constant.

4. Unit shortage costs (explicit or implicit) are so high that a practical operating procedure will always result in the average level of backorders being negligibly small when compared with the average level of the on-hand stock.
5. Forecast errors have a normal distribution with no bias (that is, the average error is zero) and a *known* standard deviation σ_{R+L} for forecasts over a period of duration $R + L$. In fact, we only have an estimate $\hat{\sigma}_{R+L}$ (but see the discussion for the comparable assumption in Section 7.6.1).
6. The value of R is assumed to be predetermined, as was discussed in Section 7.7.1. In most situations, the effects of the two decision variables, R and S, are not independent, that is, the best value of R depends on the S value, and vice versa. However, as will be shown in Chapter 8, it is quite reasonable for practical purposes when dealing with B items to assume that R has been predetermined without knowledge of the S value.
7. The costs of the control system do not depend on the specific value of S used.

Unlike in the (s, Q) situation, the assumption of unit-sized demand transactions is not needed here.

The notation includes:

D = demand rate, in units/yr

$G_u(k) = \int_k^\infty (u_0 - k) \frac{1}{\sqrt{2\pi}} \exp(-u_0^2/2)\, du_0$, a special function of the unit normal (mean 0, standard deviation 1) variable

k = safety factor

L = replenishment lead time, in years

$p_{u\geq}(k)$ = probability that a unit normal (mean 0, standard deviation 1) variable takes on a value of k or larger

r = inventory carrying charge, in \$/\$/yr

R = prespecified review interval, expressed in years

S = order-up-to-level, in units

SS = safety stock, in units

v = unit variable cost, in \$/unit

$\hat{x}_{R+L}$ = forecast (or expected) demand over a review interval plus a replenishment lead time, in units

σ_{R+L} = standard deviation of errors of forecasts over a review interval plus a replenishment lead time, in units

7.7.4 Common Derivation

Because of assumption 2, we have

$$\text{(Number of reviews per year)} = 1/R$$

and

$$\text{(Number of replenishment orders placed per year)} = 1/R \tag{7.29}$$

In Section 7.7.2 we showed, by means of an example, that whether or not a stockout occurs in a particular cycle depends on whether or not the total demand in an interval of length $R + L$ exceeds the order-up-to-level S. We now develop the same result in a more rigorous fashion. (Reference to Figure 7.9 will be helpful.)

Consider a review instant (call it t_0) at which we place an order (call it order X) to raise the inventory position to the level S. The next order (Y) will not be placed until time $t_0 + R$. Suppose that order Y arrives L later, that is, at time $t_0 + R + L$. Because of the assumption of no crossing of orders, all previous orders, including order X, must have arrived prior to time $t_0 + R + L$. Furthermore, no orders beyond order Y could have arrived. In other words, all S of the inventory position at time t_0, and no other stock, must have reached the stocking point by a time just before $t_0 + R + L$. Therefore, the service impact of using an order-up-to-level of S in placing order X is determined by whether or not the total demand x in a review interval *plus* a replenishment lead time (that is, $R + L$) exceeds S.

If the demand (x) in $R + L$ has a probability density function $f_x(x_0)$ defined such that

$$f_x(x_0)dx_0 = \text{Prob }\{\text{Total demand in } R + L \text{ lies between } x_0 \text{ and } x_0 + dx_0\}$$

then the above reasoning leads to the following three important results[11]:

1. Safety stock (SS) = E (Net stock just before order Y arrives)

$$= \int_0^\infty (S - x_0) f_x(x_0) dx_0$$

that is,

$$\text{SS} = S - \hat{x}_{R+L} \tag{7.30}$$

[11]$E(z)$ again represents the expected or mean value of the random variable z.

2. Prob {Stockout in a replenishment cycle}

$$= \text{Prob}\,\{x \geqslant S\}$$

$$= \int_S^\infty f_x(x_0)dx_0 \tag{7.31}$$

the probability that the total demand during a review interval plus lead time is at least as large as the order-up-to-level.

3. Expected shortage per replenishment cycle, ESPRC

$$= \int_S^\infty (x_0 - S)f_x(x_0)dx_0 \tag{7.32}$$

In a manner paralleling that of Section 7.6.3, we find that

$$E(\text{OH stock just before a replenishment arrives})$$
$$\simeq \text{Safety stock(SS)}$$
$$= S - \hat{x}_{R+L}$$

Because there is a replenishment every R units of time, the average size of a replenishment is DR. Therefore,

$$E(\text{OH just after a replenishment arrives}) \simeq S - \hat{x}_{R+L} + DR$$

Now, the mean rate of demand is constant with time. Therefore, on the average, the OH level is halfway between these two extremes. Thus,

$$E(\text{OH}) \simeq S - \hat{x}_{R+L} + DR/2 \tag{7.33}$$

It is convenient to again set

$$\text{SS} = k\sigma_{R+L} \tag{7.34}$$

If forecast errors are normally distributed, then the results of Appendix B give that Eqs. 7.31 and 7.32 reduce to

$$\text{Prob}\,\{\text{Stockout in a replenishment cycle}\} = p_{u\geqslant}(k) \tag{7.35}$$

and

$$\text{ESPRC} = \sigma_{R+L}G_u(k) \tag{7.36}$$

A comparison of pairs of equations follows.

Compare	With
7.30	7.7
7.33	7.12
7.34	7.13
7.29	7.14
7.35	7.15
7.36	7.16

The comparison reveals the validity of our earlier assertion that the (R, S) situation is exactly equivalent to the (s, Q) situation if one makes the following transformations.

(s, Q)	(R, S)
s	S
Q	DR
L	$R + L$

7.8 VARIABILITY IN THE REPLENISHMENT LEAD TIME ITSELF

In all the decision systems discussed in this chapter the key variable in setting a reorder point or order-up-to-level is the total demand in an interval of length $R + L$ (which reduces to just L for the case of continuous review). So far our decisions have been based on a *known* replenishment lead time L with the only uncertain quantity being the demand *rate* during L or $R + L$. If L itself is not known with certainty, it is apparent that increased safety stock is required to protect against this additional uncertainty. It should be noted that where the pattern of variability is known, for example, seasonally varying lead times, there is no additional problem because the lead time at any given calendar time is known and the safety stock (and reorder point) can be accordingly adjusted. Where lead times are increasing in a known fashion, such as in conditions of reduced availability of raw materials, again safety stocks (and reorder points) should be appropriately adjusted.

A key component of the lead time in which uncertainty exists is the shipping time from the supplier to the stocking point under consideration. Choices among transportation modes can affect the variability, as well as the average duration, of the lead time (see Herron, 1983, and Problem 7.10).

Every reasonable effort should be made to eliminate variability in the lead time. This, of course, requires close cooperation with suppliers. In return for firm commitments well ahead of time, a reasonable supplier should be prepared to promise a more dependable lead time. The projection of firm commitments well into the future is not an easy task. We return to this point in Chapter 16 in the context of Material Requirements Planning, which offers a natural means of making such projections.

Where there is still some residual variability in the lead time, two courses of action are possible:

1. Measure actual demand over each full lead time (or review time plus lead time) and use these observations in a smoothing procedure to estimate the average demand in a lead time (or $R + L$) and its variability. This has potential drawbacks for the reasons cited in Section 7.5.2 but can still be a reasonable approach.
2. Use an *approximate* mathematical model to ascertain the standard deviation of total demand in a lead time.

This model assumes that the lead time (L) and the demand rate (D) are *independent* random variables. This is probably a reasonable approximation to reality (especially when one recognizes how complex more realistic models become!) despite the fact that, in some cases, high demand is likely to be associated with long lead times (that is, positive correlation), because of the heavy workload placed on the supplier, or low demand can be associated with long lead times (that is, negative correlation) because the supplier has to wait longer to accumulate sufficient orders for his or her desired run size. If L and D are assumed to be independent random variables, then it can be shown (see, for example, Drake, 1967) that

$$E(x) = E(L)E(D) \tag{7.37}$$

and

$$\sigma_x = \sqrt{E(L)\ \mathrm{var}\ (D) + [E(D)]^2\ \mathrm{var}\ (L)} \tag{7.38}$$

where x, with mean $E(x)$ and standard deviation σ_x is the total demand in a replenishment lead time, in units; L, with mean $E(L)$ and variance var (L), is the length of a lead time, in unit time periods; and D, with mean $E(D)$ and variance var (D), is the demand rate, in units per unit time period. Where variability in L exists, the $E(x)$ and σ_x quantities found from Eqs. 7.37 and 7.38 should be used in place of $\hat{x}_L$ and σ_L in all the decision rules of this chapter. Weeda (1982) discusses the estimation of $E(L)$ and var (L) when data are sparse.

Before showing an illustration of the use of the above model we mention that two interesting references on variable lead time are Magson (1979) and Todd (1980).

Numerical Illustration

For the developing chemicals item XSC-023, used in Section 7.6.8, let us consider two situations.

Situation 1: No Uncertainty in the Lead Time Itself (that is, var (L) = 0 in Eq. 7.38)

Suppose $E(L) = 3.5$ months

$$E(D) = 200 \text{ units/yr} = \frac{200}{12} \text{ units/month}$$

and

$$\text{var}(D) = 49 \text{ (units/month)}^2$$

Then Eqs. 7.37 and 7.38 give

$$E(x) = 58.3 \text{ units}$$

and

$$\sigma_x = 13.1 \text{ units}$$

which are the figures that were used in Section 7.6.8. There, to provide a desired probability (P_1) of no stockout per replenishment cycle equal to 0.90, we required a reorder point of 76 units.

Situation 2: Uncertainty in the Lead Time

Suppose that $E(L)$, $E(D)$, and var (D) are as above, so that $E(x)$, the expected total demand over a lead time, is still 58.3 units. However, now we assume that L itself is random, in particular

$$\text{var}(L) = 0.3844 \text{ (months)}^2$$

(The standard deviation of L is $\sqrt{\text{var}(L)}$, or 0.62 months.) Then, Eq. 7.38 gives

$$\sigma_x = \sqrt{(3.5)(49) + \left(\frac{200}{12}\right)^2 (0.3844)}$$
$$= 16.7 \text{ units}$$

Now, using the method of Section 7.6.8, we find that the reorder point must be 80 units. In other words, the uncertainty in L has increased the reorder point by 4 units. Knowing values for v and r would permit us to calculate the additional carrying costs implied by the extra 4 units. These extra costs would provide a bound on how much it would be worth to eliminate the variability in L.

7.9 EXCHANGE CURVES INVOLVING SAFETY STOCKS FOR (*s*, *Q*) SYSTEMS

As was discussed in Chapters 2 and 3, management is primarily concerned with aggregate measures of effectiveness. In Chapter 5 exchange curves were developed that showed the aggregate consequences, in terms of total cycle stock versus total number (or costs) of replenishments per year, when a particular policy (the EOQ) is used across a population of items. The curve was traced out by varying the value of the policy variable A/r. In a similar fashion exchange curves can be developed showing the aggregate consequences, in terms of total safety stock (in dollars) versus aggregate service, when a particular decision rule for establishing safety stocks (that is, reorder points) is used across a population of items. As a preparative to exchange curves, we first show, in Section 7.9.1, a simple 3-item example that illustrates the *aggregate* benefits that are usually possible in moving away from the commonly used approach of basing safety stocks (or reorder points) on equal time supplies. Exchange curves are then shown, in Section 7.9.2, for the Professional Products Division of MIDAS. As in Chapter 5, there is a policy variable for each type of decision rule. Management's selection of an aggregate operating point *implies* a value of the policy variable. Use of this implicit value in the corresponding individual-item decision rule then leads to the desired aggregate consequences. An outline of the derivation of exchange curves is presented in Section 7.9.3. We restrict attention to (s, Q) systems but, because of the analogy developed in Section 7.7, the same type of approach can be used for (R, S) systems.

Management's ability to meaningfully utilize the safety stock versus service exchange curve hinges on their capacity to think of inventories as being split into the two components of cycle stocks and safety stocks and to be able to make separate tradeoffs of cycle stocks versus replenishments and safety stocks versus aggregate service. Based on our experience, these conditions are not always met. Therefore, in Section 7.9.4 we discuss so-called composite exchange curves that show a three-way exchange of total stock (cycle plus safety, in dollars) versus number of replenishments per year versus aggregate service.

7.9.1 An Illustration of the Impact of Moving Away from Setting Reorder Points as Equal Time Supplies

It is not uncommon for organizations to use the following type of rule for setting reorder points: reorder when the inventory position has dropped to a 2-month time supply. Without going into detail, we wish to show the impact of moving away from this type of decision rule. To illustrate, let us consider three typical items produced and stocked by MIDAS International (the parent company, serving MIDAS Canada as well as other subsidiaries and direct customers in Germany, Australia, the U.S., England, etc.). Relevant characteristics of the items (three types of general-purpose photographic papers) are given in Table 7.4. The order quantities, assumed as prespecified, are as shown. The current reorder points are each based on a 2-month time supply (that is, $D/6$).

TABLE 7.4 3-Item Example

MIDAS Canada Identification	Demand Rate D (units/year)	Unit Value v ($/unit)	Lead Time L (months)	σ_L (units)	Current Order Quantity Q (units)	Current Reorder Point s (units)
PSP-001	6000	20.00	1.5	125.0	6000	1000
PSP-002	3000	10.00	1.5	187.5	1000	500
PSP-003	2400	12.00	1.5	62.5	1200	400

Assuming normally distributed forecast errors, it can be shown (by the procedure to be discussed in Section 7.9.3) that, under use of the current reorder points, the safety stocks, the expected stockout occasions per year, and the expected values short per year are as listed in columns (2), (3), and (4) of Table 7.5. If the total safety stock of $7,450 is instead allocated among the items to give equal probabilities of stockout per replenishment cycle (that is, equal P_1 values), the resulting expected stockout occasions per year and the expected values short per year are as in columns (6) and (7) of the table. The reallocation has reduced both aggregate measures of disservice by over 50 percent. The reason for this is that the current equal-time supply strategy does not take account of the fact that PSP-002's forecast is considerably more uncertain (higher σ_L) than those of the other two items. Note the shift of additional safety stock to PSP-002 under the revised strategy. The marked service improvement for PSP-002 far outweighs the slight reduction in service of the other two items caused by the transfer of some of their safety stocks to PSP-002. The type of service improvement indicated here is typical of what can be achieved in

TABLE 7.5 Numerical Example of Shifting Away from Reorder Points as Equal Time Supplies

	Equal Time Supply Reorder Points			Reorder Points Based on Equal Probabilities of Stockout per Cycle		
Item No. (1)	Safety Stock[a] (2)	Expected Stockout Occasions per Year (3)	Expected Total Value Short per Year (4)	Safety Stock (5)	Expected Stockout Occasions per Year (6)	Expected Total Value Short per Year (7)
1	$5,000	0.023	$ 21	$3,630	0.074	82
2	1,250	0.754	845	2,730	0.221	185
3	1,200	0.110	35	1,090	0.147	49
Totals	$7,450	0.887/yr	$901/yr	$7,450	0.442/yr	$316/yr

[a]Under the given strategy Safety stock (in units) $= s - \hat{x}_L = s - DL$. Then, Safety stock(in $) $= (s - DL)v$.

most actual applications of logical decision rules for computing reorder points. In fact, if one was to allocate safety stocks according to one of the criteria discussed in Section 7.4.4, instead of using the P_1 criterion, the improvements would be even larger.

7.9.2 Total Safety Stock versus Aggregate Service for the Professional Products Division of MIDAS

For most of the methods discussed in Section 7.6 two exchange curves were developed for the 823 active items in the Professional Products Division. The two sets of curves, to be found in the two parts of Figure 7.10, show:

1. Total safety stock (in dollars) versus expected total stockout occasions per year
2. Total safety stock (in dollars) versus expected total value of shortages per year

It is seen that there are two sets of curves because *aggregate* service is shown in two different ways.

For each of the decision rules the curves were generated by varying the appropriate policy variable. In all cases the exchange curves were developed assuming an (s, Q) type system and, where it was needed, the Q value was set equal to an economic order quantity (using $A = \$3.20$ and $r = 0.24$/yr, as found in Section 5.9 of Chapter 5). Two other points have been plotted in each part of Figure 7.10. These correspond to MIDAS' old and new policies (see MIDAS Case D), both of which are effectively the establishing of reorder points as time supplies.[12]

[12]Translating from Case D, the old policy sets the maximum level $(s_i + Q_i)$ of item i as a 5-month supply. Then the order point s_i is 80% of this. Therefore

$$s_i = 0.8 \frac{5\,D_i}{12} = \frac{D_i}{3}$$

and

$$Q_i = (\text{Maximum}) - (\text{Order point}) = \frac{5\,D_i}{12} - \frac{D_i}{3} = \frac{D_i}{12}$$

Under the new policy, recommended by the comptroller's office, the maximum of item i is set at

$$\frac{10 + L_i}{13} \frac{D_i}{4} \quad \text{or} \quad \frac{(10 + L_i)D_i}{52}$$

where L_i is the lead time of item i, in weeks. Again, the order point s_i is 80 percent of this. Therefore,

$$s_i = \frac{(8 + 0.8\,L_i)D_i}{52}$$

and

$$Q_i = (\text{Maximum}) - (\text{Order point}) = \frac{(2 + 0.2\,L_i)D_i}{52}$$

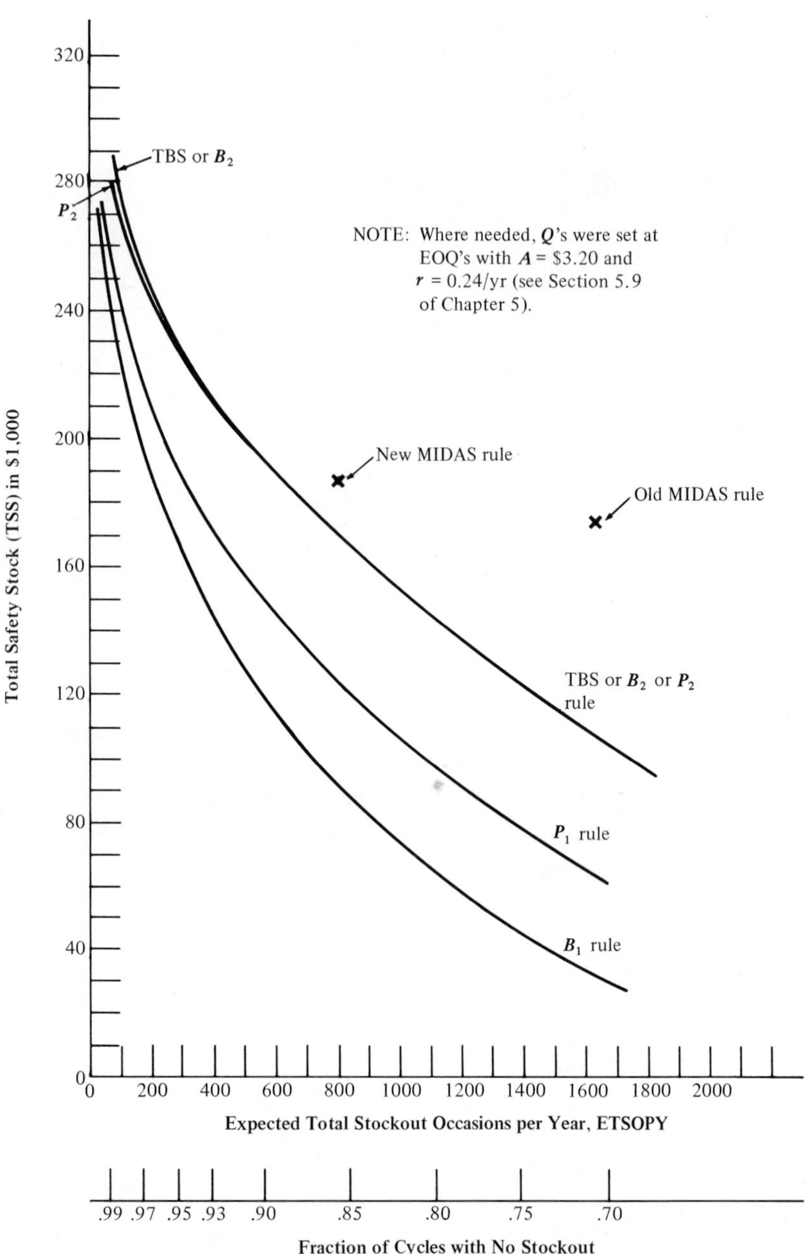

FIGURE 7.10a Exchange Curves of Safety Stock versus Expected Stockout Occasions for the Professional Products Division of MIDAS

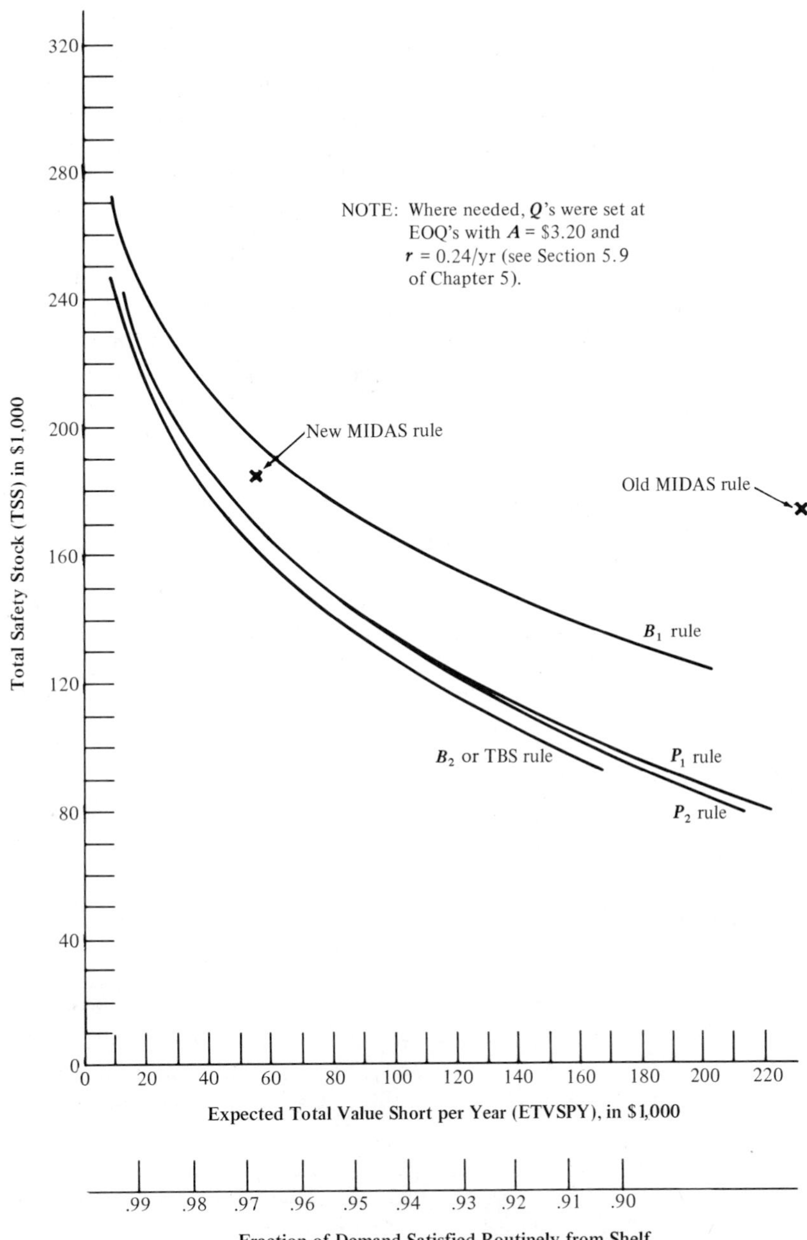

FIGURE 7.10*b* Exchange Curves of Safety Stock versus Expected Value Short for the Professional Products Division of MIDAS

Both parts of the figure show that a number of the decision rules of this chapter significantly outperform either of the MIDAS decision rules, in the sense that both the total safety stock and the expected total stockout occasions (or total value short) per year are simultaneously reduced. Under the "expected total stockout occasions per year" (Figure 7.10*a*), it is seen that no other rule does as well as the B_1 criterion. This is to be expected; as stated earlier, the B_1 decision rule is equivalent with minimizing the expected total stockout occasions per year for a given total safety stock. Similarly the B_2 or TBS rule does best in Figure 7.10*b* because of the equivalence of these rules with the rule implied by minimizing the expected total value of shortages per year for a given total safety stock. Interestingly enough, the simple P_1 (that is, equal k) rule does quite well in both graphs, that is, under either aggregate service measure. On the other hand, as expected, MIDAS' equal time supply rules do rather poorly.

7.9.3 Derivation of the Safety Stock Exchange Curves

In all cases, for a given value of the relevant policy variable, the corresponding point on each exchange curve is found in the following manner. First, the value of the safety factor[13] k_i is ascertained for each item by use of the appropriate decision rule. Then three quantities are computed for each item i:

$$\text{Safety stock (in dollars) of item } i = \text{SS}_i v_i = k_i \sigma_{Li} v_i \tag{7.39}$$

$$\text{Expected stockout occasions per year} = \frac{D_i}{Q_i} p_{u\geq}(k_i) \text{ for item } i \tag{7.40}$$

$$\text{Expected value short per year} = \frac{D_i}{Q_i} \sigma_{Li} v_i G_u(k_i) \text{ for item } i^{14} \tag{7.41}$$

Equations 7.40 and 7.41 are, of course, based on an assumption of normally distributed errors. However, one could develop comparable results for any of the other distributions discussed in Section 7.6.13.

Equation 7.40 follows from multiplying the expected number of replenish-

---

[13]The notation is the same as in Section 7.6.1 except a subscript i is used to denote that a particular item i is involved.

[14]Strictly speaking, as shown in Silver (1970), the expected value short per year for item i

$$= \frac{D_i}{Q_i} \sigma_{Li} v_i \left[G_u(k_i) - G_u\left(k_i + \frac{Q_i}{\sigma_{Li}}\right)\right]$$

The approximation of Eq. 7.41 is quite accurate as long as $Q_i/\sigma_{Li} > 1$, because then the additional term becomes negligible. When $Q_i/\sigma_{Li} < 1$, it is advisable to use the more accurate expression.

ment cycles per year (Eq. 7.14) by the probability of a stockout per cycle (Eq. 7.15). Similarly Eq. 7.41 is a result of the product of the expected number of replenishment cycles per year (Eq. 7.14) and the expected shortage per replenishment cycle, expressed in dollars (v_i times Eq. 7.16). Finally, each of the three quantities (Eqs. 7.39, 7.40, and 7.41) is summed across all items:

$$\text{Total safety stock (in dollars)} = \sum_i k_i \sigma_{Li} v_i \tag{7.42}$$

$$\text{Expected total stockout occasions per year (ETSOPY)} = \sum_i \frac{D_i}{Q_i} p_{u\geq}(k_i) \tag{7.43}$$

$$\text{Expected total value short per year (ETVSPY)} = \sum_i \frac{D_i}{Q_i} \sigma_{Li} v_i G_u(k_i) \tag{7.44}$$

The results of Eqs. 7.42 and 7.43 give a point on the first exchange curve (for example, Figure 7.10*a*) and those of Eqs. 7.42 and 7.44 give a point on the second curve (for example, Figure 7.10*b*) for the particular safety stock decision rule. Repeating the whole process for several values of the policy variable generates a set of points for each of the two curves.

In some cases it is not necessary to go through all of the calculations of Eqs. 7.42 to 7.44. To illustrate, for the case of a specified fraction (P_2) of demand to be satisfied directly off the shelf for all items,

$$\text{Expected total value short per year} = (1 - P_2) \sum_i D_i v_i$$

provided of course, that no individual k_i has to be adjusted up to a minimum allowable value (thus providing a better level of service than P_2 for that particular item).

7.9.4 Composite Exchange Curves

For any decision rule for selecting safety stocks, we can combine the EOQ exchange curve (total cycle stock versus number of replenishments per year) with either of the safety stock exchange curves (total safety stock versus aggregate service level). The result is a set of composite exchange curves showing a three-way tradeoff of total average stock versus number of replenishments per year versus aggregate service level. A separate graph is required for each combination of decision rule and aggregate service measure. For the Professional Products Division of MIDAS we have shown an illustrative set of curves (for only one aggregate service measure) in Figure 7.11. They represent the use of the P_1 decision rule and an EOQ ordering strategy.

Each curve of Figure 7.11 clearly shows the behavior, for a given aggregate service level (value of ETSOPY), of the total average stock (TAS) as the number of replenishments per year (N) varies. For a while TAS decreases as N increases;

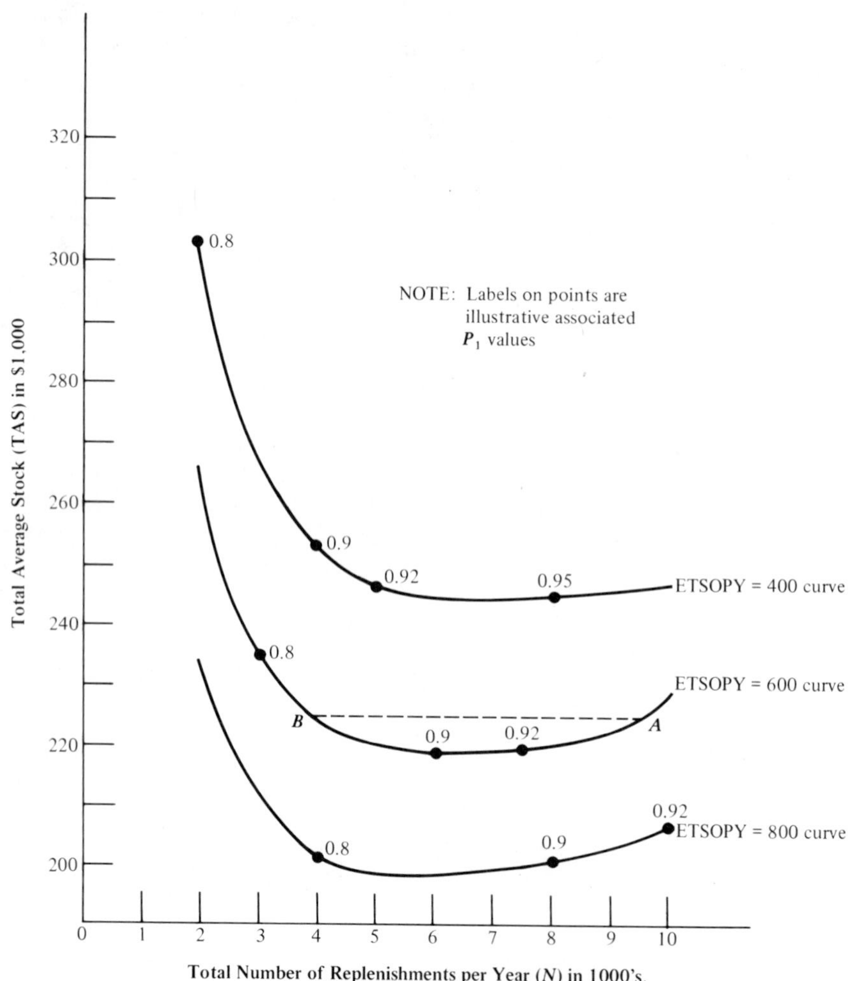

FIGURE 7.11 Composite Exchange Curves for the Professional Products Division of MIDAS Using EOQ and P_1 Decision Rules

this is a consequence of the cycle stock decreasing more quickly than the increase in the safety stock required to maintain the ETSOPY value. However, eventually as N gets larger, the increase in safety stock begins to dominate the decrease in cycle stock so that the TAS actually begins to increase. Operationally, for a given ETSOPY value, one would never operate at a point to the right of the low point of the corresponding curve (for example, point A on the middle curve). This is because there is another point (in this case B) to the left of the low point where the service and total average stock are unchanged while the replenishment load N is appreciably reduced.

Selection of a desired aggregate operating point on a composite exchange curve implies:

1. A value of A/r to be used in the economic order quantity decision rule (this is not shown directly on the graphs; instead, we show the total number of replenishments per year N. A/r can be found from N using Eq. 5.28 of Chapter 5).
2. A value of the parameter to be used in the particular safety stock decision rule under consideration (for example, P_1, TBS, B_1, etc.).

For extensions of these concepts the reader is referred to Gardner and Dannenbring (1979).

7.10 SUMMARY

In this chapter we have introduced the reader to the fundamentals of inventory control under probabilistic demand. For a variety of shortage costs and service measures, we have shown the details of two common types of decisions systems:

1. (s, Q) systems
2. (R, S) systems

The material presented included the actual decision rules, illustrative examples, graphical aids, and a discussion of each of the rules. Again, aggregate exchange curve concepts turned out to be an important aspect of the analysis.

In Chapter 8 we will address two other, somewhat more complicated control systems—namely, (s, S) and (R, s, S)—in the context of A items.

It should be apparent now to the reader that, even for the case of a single item considered in isolation at a single stocking point, it is no easy task to cope with uncertainty. It is little wonder that *very little usable theory has been developed for more complex probabilistic situations* (for example, coordinated control of related items at a single location, multiechelon control of a single item, etc.). We will have more to say on these issues in Chapters 11, 12, 15, and 16.

APPENDIX TO CHAPTER 7
SOME ILLUSTRATIVE DERIVATIONS

1. B_1 SHORTAGE COSTING

We show two different approaches: the first using total relevant costs; the second based on a marginal analysis. The latter is simpler but does not permit sensitivity analysis (in that a total cost expression is not developed).

Total Cost Approach

We develop an expression for the expected total relevant costs per year as a function of the control parameter k; let us denote this function by ETRC (k). There are three relevant components of costs: (1) replenishment, (2) carrying, and (3) stockout.

Using the result of Eq. 7.14, we have that the expected relevant replenishment costs per year are

$$C_r = AD/Q$$

As earlier, the expected carrying costs per year are

$$C_c = \bar{I}vr$$

Using Eq. 7.12, this gives

$$C_c = \left(\frac{Q}{2} + k\sigma_L\right)vr$$

The expected stockout costs C_s per year are obtained by multiplying three factors together—namely, (1) the expected number of replenishment cycles per year, (2) the probability of a stockout per cycle, and (3) the cost per stockout. Thus, using Eqs. 7.14 and 7.15, we have

$$C_s = \frac{DB_1}{Q} p_{u\geq}(k)$$

Now,

$$\text{ETRC}(k) = C_r + C_c + C_s$$

$$= AD/Q + (Q/2 + k\sigma_L)vr + \frac{DB_1}{Q} p_{u\geqslant}(k)$$

We wish to select the k value that minimizes ETRC (k). A convenient approach is to set

$$\frac{d\,\text{ETRC}(k)}{dk} = 0$$

that is,

$$\sigma_L vr + \frac{DB_1}{Q} \frac{dp_{u\geqslant}(k)}{dk} = 0 \tag{7.45}$$

But

$$\frac{dp_{u\geqslant}(k)}{dk} = -f_u(k)$$

(The derivative of the cumulative distribution function is the density function as shown in Section 3.3 of Appendix B.) Therefore, Eq. 7.45 gives

$$f_u(k) = \frac{Qv\sigma_L r}{DB_1} \tag{7.46}$$

Now the density function of the unit normal is given by

$$f_u(k) = \frac{1}{\sqrt{2\pi}} \exp(-k^2/2)$$

Therefore, Eq.7.46 gives

$$\frac{1}{\sqrt{2\pi}} \exp(-k^2/2) = \frac{Qv\sigma_L r}{DB_1} \tag{7.47}$$

which solves for

$$k = \sqrt{2 \ln \frac{DB_1}{\sqrt{2\pi}\, Qv\sigma_L r}} \tag{7.48}$$

However, one must proceed with caution. Setting the first derivative to zero does not guarantee a minimum. In fact, Eq. 7.48 will have no solution if the expression inside the square root is negative. This will occur if the argument of the logarithm is less than unity. A case where this happens is shown in part b of Figure 7.12. In such a situation the model says that the lower k is, the lower the costs are. The model assumes a linear savings in carrying costs with decreasing k. Obviously, this is not true indefinitely. The practical resolution is to set k at its lowest allowable value (usually zero).

Marginal Analysis

Let us consider the effects of increasing s by a small amount, say Δs. The extra carrying costs per year are given by

$$\text{Marginal cost/yr} = \Delta s v r \tag{7.49}$$

Savings result when, in a lead time, total demand lies exactly between s and $s + \Delta s$, so that the extra Δs has avoided a stockout. On the average there are D/Q replenishment occasions per year. Thus,

$$\begin{aligned}\text{Expected marginal savings/yr} &= \frac{D}{Q} B_1 \text{ Prob \{Demand lies in interval } s \text{ to } s + \Delta s\} \\ &= \frac{D}{Q} B_1 f_x(s) \Delta s\end{aligned} \tag{7.50}$$

Now consider a particular value of s. If the marginal cost associated with adding Δs to it exceeds the expected marginal savings, we would not want to add the Δs. In fact, we might want to go below the particular s value. On the other hand, if the expected marginal savings exceeded the marginal cost, we would definitely want to increase s by Δs. However, we might wish to continue increasing s even higher. This line of argument leads us to wanting to operate at the s value, where the marginal cost of adding Δs exactly equals the expected marginal savings. Thus, from Eqs. 7.49 and 7.50, we wish to select s so that

$$\Delta s v r = \frac{D}{Q} B_1 f_x(s) \Delta s$$

or

$$f_x(s) = \frac{Qvr}{D B_1} \tag{7.51}$$

This is a general result that holds for *any* probability distribution of lead time demand. For the normal distribution we have that

$$f_x(s) = \frac{1}{\sqrt{2\pi}\,\sigma_L} \exp\left[(s - \hat{x}_L)^2/2\,\sigma_L^2\right] \tag{7.52}$$

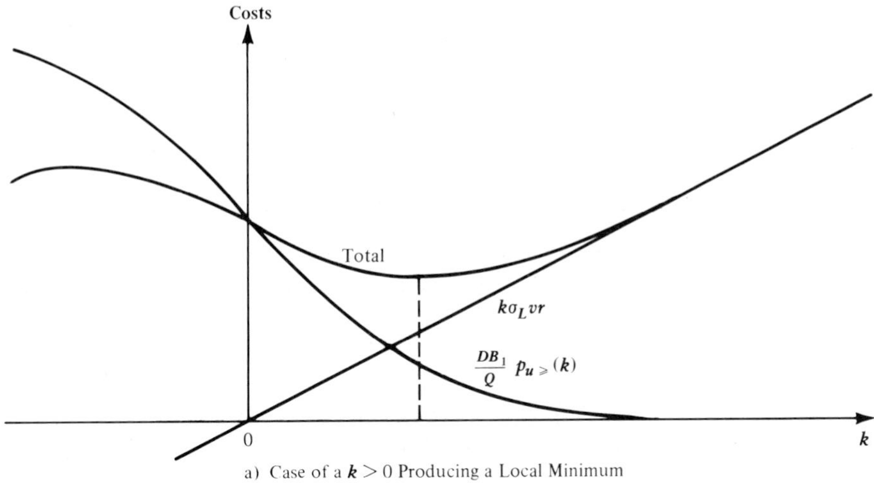

a) Case of a $k > 0$ Producing a Local Minimum

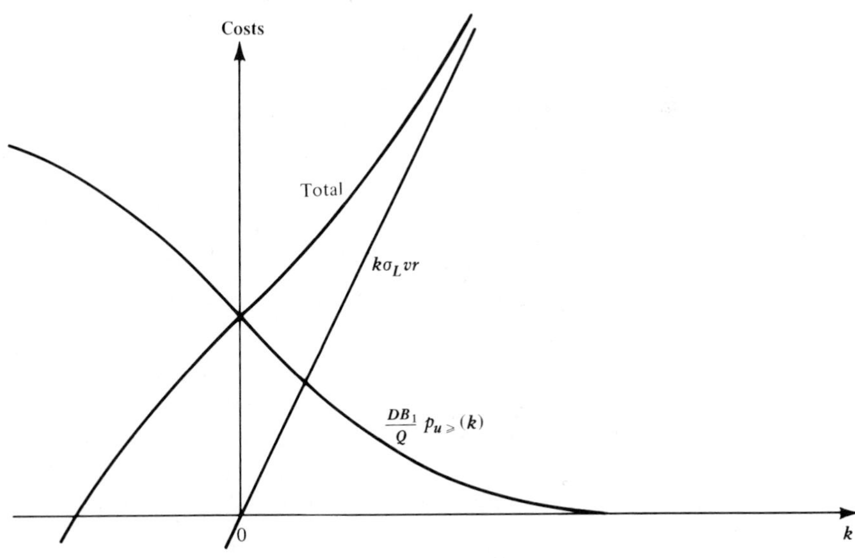

b) Case Where Lowest Possible k is Best

FIGURE 7.12 Behavior of Expected Total Relevant Costs for the Case of a Fixed Cost per Stockout

Moreover, from Eqs. 7.5 and 7.6,

$$s = \hat{x}_L + k\sigma_L \tag{7.53}$$

Substitution of Eqs. 7.52 and 7.53 into Eq. 7.51 gives the same result as Eq. 7.47.

Behavior of k as a Function of Dv

Equation 7.48 shows that k increases as $D/Qv\sigma_L$ or $Dv/Qv\sigma_L v$ increases. Now, empirically (see discussion in Chapter 4) it has been found that, *on the average,*

$$\sigma_L v \simeq c_1(Dv)^{c_2}$$

where c_1 and c_2 are constants that depend on the particular company involved but, in all known cases, c_2 lies between 0.5 and 1. Also assuming an EOQ form for Qv, we have

$$Qv = c_3\sqrt{Dv}$$

Therefore, we have that k increases as

$$\frac{Dv}{c_3\sqrt{Dv}\,c_1(Dv)^{c_2}} \quad \text{or} \quad \frac{(Dv)^{1/2 - c_2}}{c_1 c_3}$$

increases. But, because $c_2 > \frac{1}{2}$, the exponent of Dv in the above quantity is negative. Therefore, k goes down as Dv increases.

2. P_1 SERVICE MEASURE

Suppose the reorder point is expressed as the sum of the forecast demand plus safety stock, as shown in Eq. 7.5. Furthermore, suppose, as in Eq. 7.6, that the safety stock is expressed as the product of two factors

1. The safety factor k—the control parameter

2. σ_L, the standard deviation of forecast errors over a lead time

Then from Eq. 7.15 we have

$$\text{Prob \{Stockout in a lead time\}} = p_{u\geq}(k) \tag{7.54}$$

If the desired service level is P_1, then we must have

$$\text{Prob \{Stockout in a lead time\}} = 1 - P_1 \tag{7.55}$$

It follows from Eqs. 7.54 and 7.55 that we must select k to satisfy

$$p_{u\geq}(k) = 1 - P_1$$

which is Eq. 7.17.

Had we not chosen the indirect route of using Eqs. 7.5 and 7.6 we would have ended up with a more cumbersome result than Eq. 7.17, namely,

$$p_{u\geq}[(s - \hat{x}_L)/\sigma_L] = 1 - P_1$$

3. P_2 SERVICE MEASURE

Complete Backordering

Because each replenishment is of size Q, we can argue as follows:

$$\text{Fraction backordered} = \frac{\text{Expected shortage per replenishment cycle, ESPRC}}{Q}$$

Fraction of demand satisfied directly from shelf = 1 − (Fraction backordered)

Therefore, we want

$$P_2 = 1 - \frac{\text{ESPRC}}{Q} \tag{7.56}$$

Substituting from Eq. 7.16, we have

$$P_2 = 1 - \frac{\sigma_L\, G_u(k)}{Q}$$

which reduces to

$$G_u(k) = \frac{Q}{\sigma_L}(1 - P_2)$$

which is Eq. 7.24.

Complete Lost Sales

If demands when out of stock are lost instead of backordered, then the expected demand per cycle is no longer just Q, but rather is increased by the expected shortage per replenishment cycle, ESPRC. Therefore, we now have

$$\text{Fraction of demand satisfied directly from shelf} = 1 - \frac{\text{ESPRC}}{Q + \text{ESPRC}}$$

The derivation then carries through exactly as above, resulting in Eq. 7.25.

4. ALLOCATION OF A TOTAL SAFETY STOCK TO MINIMIZE THE EXPECTED TOTAL STOCKOUT OCCASIONS PER YEAR

The problem is to select the safety factors, the k_i's, to minimize

$$\sum_{i=1}^{n} \frac{D_i}{Q_i} p_{u\geq}(k_i)$$

subject to

$$\sum_{i=1}^{n} k_i \sigma_{Li} v_i = Y$$

where n is the number of items in the population and Y is the total safety stock expressed in dollars.

One method of solution is to use a Lagrange multiplier M (see Appendix A), that is, we select the k_i's to minimize

$$L(k_i\text{'s}, M) = \sum_{i=1}^{n} \frac{D_i}{Q_i} p_{u\geq}(k_i) - M\left(Y - \sum_{i=1}^{n} k_i \sigma_{Li} v_i\right)$$

This is accomplished by setting all the partial derivatives to zero. Now

$$\frac{\partial L}{\partial k_i} = -\frac{D_i}{Q_i} f_u(k_i) + M\sigma_{Li} v_i = 0$$

or

$$f_u(k_i) = M \frac{Q_i v_i \sigma_{Li}}{D_i}$$

But, this is seen to have the exact same form as Eq. 7.46 with $M \equiv r/B_1$. Therefore, selection of a particular M value implies a value of B_1. Also, of course, a given M value leads to a specific value of Y.

The economic interpretation of the Lagrange multiplier M is that it represents the marginal benefit, in terms of reduced total expected stockouts, per unit increase in the total dollar budget available for safety stocks. r is the cost to carry one dollar in safety stock for a year. B_1 is the cost associated with a stockout occasion. From a marginal viewpoint we wish to operate where

(Cost to carry last dollar of safety stock)

= (expected benefit of last dollar of safety stock)

that is,

$$r = (\text{Reduction in total expected stockouts per year}) \times (\text{Cost per stockout})$$
$$= MB_1$$

thus, $M = r/B_1$, as we found above.

PROBLEMS

7.1 Consider MIDAS item ISF-086, a type of stabilization paper. It is reasonable to assume that demand over its replenishment lead time is normally distributed with $\hat{x}_L = 20$ units and $\sigma_L = 4.2$ units.

a. For a desired service level of $P_1 = 0.90$, compute the required safety factor, safety stock, and reorder point.

b. Repeat for $P_1 = 0.95$, 0.99, and 0.995.

c. Prepare a rough sketch of safety stock versus P_1. Is the curve linear? Discuss.

7.2 Consider the developing chemicals item XSC-023 discussed in Section 7.5.2. The histogram of historical lead times was shown in Table 7.2. If this histogram is representative of probabilities of total demands in future lead times and a reorder point of 51 is used, compute

a. The various possible shortage sizes and their probabilities of occurrence.

b. The expected (or average) shortage.

c. What reorder point would you use if the average shortage was to be no larger than 5 units? What is the associated probability of a stockout?

7.3 Consider an item with $A = \$25$; $Dv = \$4000$/yr; $\sigma_L v = \$100$; $B_1 = \$30$; $r = 0.10$ \$/\$/yr.

a. Find the following:

EOQ, in dollars
k, using the B_1 criterion
Safety stock, in dollars
Annual cost of carrying safety stock
Total average stock, in dollars
Expected number of stockout occasions per year
Expected stockout costs per year

b. The cost equation used to develop the rule for the B_1 criterion is

$$\text{ETRC}(k) = k\sigma_L vr + \frac{D}{Q}B_1 p_{u\geq}(k) \qquad (1)$$

As seen in part a, the two components of Eq. 1 are not equal at the optimal k value. (This is in contrast to what we found for the EOQ analysis in Chapter 5.) Why are the two components not equal? What quantities are equal at the optimal k value?

c. By looking at the basic equations for the items requested in a, discuss how each would be affected (that is, whether it would be increased or decreased) by an increase in the r value.

7.4 Consider an item under (s, Q) control. Basic item information is as follows: $D = 40{,}000$ units/yr; $A = \$20$; $r = 0.25$ \$/\$/yr; $v = \$1.60$/unit. All demand when out of stock is backordered. The EOQ is used to establish the Q value. A service level of 0.95 (demand satisfied without backorder) is desired. The item's demand is somewhat difficult to predict and two forecasting procedures are possible.

System	Cost to Operate per Year ($/yr)	σ_L (units)
A (complex)	200	1000
B (simple)	35	2300

Which forecasting system should be used? Discuss. *Note:* Forecast errors can be assumed to be normally distributed with zero bias for both models.

7.5 Consider an item which has an *average* demand rate that does not change with time. Suppose that demands in consecutive weeks can be considered as independent, normally distributed variables. Observations of total demand in each of 15 weeks are as follows:

89, 102, 107, 146, 155, 64, 78, 122,

78, 119, 76, 80, 60, 115, and 86

a. Estimate the mean and standard deviation of demand in a 1-week period and use these values to establish the reorder point of a continuously reviewed item with $L = 1$ week. A B_2 value of 0.3 is to be used, and we have $Q = 1000$ units, $v = \$10$/unit, $r = 0.24$ \$/\$/yr, and $D = 5200$ units/yr.

b. In actual fact, the above-listed demands were randomly generated from a normal distribution with a mean of 100 units and a standard deviation of 30 units. With these true values, what is the appropriate value of the reorder point? What is the percentage cost penalty associated with using the result of part a instead?

7.6 Canadian Wheel Ltd. establishes safety stocks to provide a fraction demand satisfied directly from stock at a level of 0.94. For a basic item with an essentially level average demand, the demand rate is 1000 units/yr and an order quantity of 200 units is used. The supplier of the item ensures a *constant* lead time of 4 weeks to Canadian Wheel. The current purchase price of the item from the supplier is \$0.80/unit. Receiving and handling costs add \$0.20/unit. The supplier offers to reduce the lead time to a new constant level of 1 week, but in so doing she will increase the selling price to Canadian by \$0.05/unit. Canadian management is faced with the decision of whether or not to accept the supplier's offer.

a. Qualitatively discuss the economic tradeoff in the decision. (*Note:* Canadian would *not* increase the selling price of the item nor would they change the order quantity.)

b. Quantitatively assist management in the decision. (Assume that $\sigma_t = \sqrt{t}\,\sigma_1$ and $\sigma_4 = 100$ units where σ_4 is the standard deviation of forecast errors over the current lead time of 4 weeks. Also assume that forecast errors are normally distributed and that the carrying charge is 0.20 \$/\$/yr.)

7.7 The 4 N Company reacts to shortages at a particular branch warehouse in the following fashion: Any shortage is effectively eliminated by bringing material in from the plant by air freight at a cost of \$2.50/kg. Assume that the average demand rate of an item is essentially constant with time and that forecast errors are normally distributed. Assume that an (s, Q) system is to be used and that Q, if needed, is prespecified. To answer the following questions, introduce whatever symbols are necessary:

a. What are the expected shortage costs per cycle?

b. What are the expected shortage costs per year?

c. What are the expected total relevant costs per year associated with the safety factor k?

d. Develop an equation that the best k must satisfy.

e. If we had two items with all characteristics identical except that item 1 weighed more (on a unit basis) than item 2, how do you intuitively think that the two safety factors would compare? Verify this using the result of part d.

7.8 The Acme Company has a policy, accepted by all its customers, of being allowed up to 1 week to satisfy each demand. Acme wishes to use a P_2 service measure with a specified P_2 value. Consider an item controlled by an (s, Q) system with Q prespecified.

a. Suppose that the lead time L was equal to the grace period. Under these circumstances what s value is needed to give $P_2 = 1.00$?

b. More generally, consider an item with a desired $P_2 = 0.99$ and a Q value of 500 units. Other (possibly) relevant characteristics of the item are

$D = 1000$ units/yr (average is relatively level throughout year)
$v = \$5$/unit
$r = 0.2$ \$/\$/yr
$L = 5$ weeks
$\sigma_1 = 10$ units (for a 1-week period); $\sigma_t = \sqrt{t}\,\sigma_1$

How would you modify the logic for computing the s value to take account of the 1-week "grace" period? Illustrate with this item.

c. For the item of part b, how would you estimate the annual cost savings of having the grace period?

7.9 One of MIDAS' customers, a retail photographic-supply outlet, orders from MIDAS once every 2 weeks. For a particular item with unit value (v) of \$3 it is felt that there is a cost of \$1 for each unit demanded when out of stock. Other characteristics of the item are

$L = 1$ week (MIDAS' promised delivery time)

$r = 0.30$/yr

a. Consider a period of the year where $\hat{x}_1 = 30$ units and $\text{MAD}_1 = 6$ units (where the unit time period is 1 week). What order-up-to-level S should be used? (Assume $\sigma_t = \sqrt{t}\sigma_1$.)

b. Suppose the average demand rate changed *slowly* throughout the year. Suggest a reasonable way for the retailer to cope with this situation.

7.10 A particular company with production facilities located in Montreal has a large distribution warehouse in Vancouver. Two types of transportation are under consideration for shipping material from the plant to the remote warehouse, namely,

Option A: Send all material by railroad freight cars.

Option B: Send all material by air freight.

a. If only 1 of the 2 pure options can be used, *outline* an analysis that you would suggest to help management choose between the 2 options. Indicate the types of data that you would require.

b. *Intuitively* would it ever make sense to use both options, that is, to use rail freight for part of the shipments and air freight for the rest? *Briefly* explain why or why not.

7.11 Consider two items with the following characteristics:

Item	Unit Value (\$/unit)	D (units/yr)	$\hat{x}_L$ (units)	σ_L (units)
1	10.00	300	100	10
2	1.00	300	100	35

Suppose that the inventory controller has set the safety stock of each of these items as a 1-month time supply.

a. What are the safety stocks in units? In dollars?

b. What is the P_1 value associated with each item?

c. Reallocate the same total safety stock (in dollars) so that the two items have the same value of P_1.

d. What reduction in total safety stock is possible if both items have $P_1 = 0.95$?

7.12

a. Consider a group of n items that are each being independently controlled using an (R, S) type of system (periodic-review, order-up-to-level). Let R_i be the *prespecified* value (in months) of R for item i. Suppose that we wish to allocate a total given safety stock in dollars (call it W) among the n items to minimize the dollars of expected backorders per unit time summed across all n items. Develop the decision rule for selecting k_i, the safety factor for item i. Assume that forecast errors are normally distributed.

b. Illustrate for the following 2-item case ($r = 0.2$ \$/\$/yr; $W =$ \$1,180).

Item i	v_i (\$/unit)	A_i (\$)	D_i (units/yr)	R_i (months)
1	1.00	2.00	3000	1
2	2.00	5.00	15000	0.5

Item i	L_i (months)	σ_{R_i} (units)	σ_{L_i} (units)	$\sigma_{L_i+R_i}$ (units)
1	1	200	200	300
2	1	500	300	700

7.13 Consider three items with the following characteristics:

Item i	D_i (units/yr)	v_i (\$/unit)	Q_i (units)	σ_{L_i} (units)
1	1000	1.00	200	100
2	500	0.80	200	100
3	100	2.00	100	30

Suppose that a total safety stock of \$120 is to be allocated among the three items. Consider the following service measures (shortage costing methods):

1. Same P_1 for the 3 items
2. Same P_2 for the 3 items
3. Same B_1 for the 3 items
4. Same B_2 for the 3 items
5. Same TBS for the 3 items
6. Minimization of total expected stockout occasions per year
7. Minimization of total expected value short occasions per year
8. Equal time supply safety stocks

For each determine:

a. How the \$120 is allocated among the three items

b. ETSOPY

c. ETVOPY

Note: Assume that forecast errors are normally distributed, that the same r value is applicable to all 3 items, and that negative safety factors are not permitted.

7.14

a. At the beginning of MIDAS Case D it was pointed out that the company's stated inventory control policy was "to have zero stockouts." Is this a realistic policy to pursue? In particular, discuss the implications in terms of various types of costs.

b. "On occasion MIDAS filled an important customer order by supplying a competitor's film at below retail price." What form of shortage costing would it be appropriate to apply under such circumstances? Does this type of strategy make sense?

REFERENCES

Abramowitz, M., and I. Stegun (1965). *Handbook of Mathematical Functions*. Dover, New York.

Akinniyi, F., and E. A. Silver (1981). "Inventory Control Using a Service Constraint on the Expected Duration of Stockouts." *AIIE Transactions*, Vol. 13, No. 4, pp. 343–348.

Archibald, B., E. A. Silver, and R. Peterson (1974). "Implementation Considerations in Selecting the Probability Distribution of Lead Time Demand." *Working Paper No. 89*, Department of Management Sciences, University of Waterloo, Waterloo, Ontario, Canada.

Bierman, H., C. P. Bonini, and W. H. Hausman (1977). *Quantitative Analysis for Business Decisions*, fifth edition. Richard D. Irwin, Homewood, Illinois, pp. 460–462.

Brown, R. G. (1967). *Decision Rules for Inventory Management*. Holt, Rinehart and Winston, New York.

Brown, R. G. (1977). *Materials Management Systems*. Wiley-Interscience, New York, p. 146.

Burgin, T. (1975). "The Gamma Distribution and Inventory Control." *Operational Research Quarterly*, Vol. 26, No. 3i, pp. 507–525.

Burgin,T., and J. Norman (1976). "A Table for Determining the Probability of a Stockout and Potential Lost Sales for a Gamma Distributed Demand." *Operational Research Quarterly*, Vol. 27, No. 3ii, pp. 621–631.

Carlson, P. (1964). "On the Distribution of Lead Time Demand." *Journal of Industrial Engineering*, Vol. XV, No. 2, pp. 87–94.

Carlson, P. (1982). "An Alternative Model for Lead-Time Demand: Continuous–Review Inventory Systems." *Decision Sciences*, Vol. 13, No. 1, pp. 120–128.

Chang, Y. S., and P. Niland (1967). "A Model for Measuring Stock Depletion Costs." *Operations Research*, Vol. 15, No. 3, pp. 427–447.

Das, C. (1975). "Effect of Lead Time on Inventory: A Static Analysis." *Operational Research Quarterly*, Vol. 26, No. 2i, pp. 273–282.

Das, C. (1976a). "Explicit Formulas for the Order Size and Reorder Point in Certain Inventory Problems." *Naval Research Logistics Quarterly*, Vol. 23, No. 1, pp. 25–30.

Das, C. (1976b). "Approximate Solution to the (Q, r) Inventory Model for Gamma Lead Time Demand." *Management Science*, Vol. 22, No. 9, pp. 1043–1047.

Deemer, R., A. Kaplan, and W. K. Kruse (1974). "Application of Negative Binomial Probability to Inventory Control." *Technical Report TR74-5*, USAMC Inventory Research Office, Frankford Arsenal, Philadelphia.

Donaldson, W. (1974). "The Allocation of Inventory Items to Lot Size/Reorder Level (Q, r) and Periodic Review (T, Z) Control Systems." *Operational Research Quarterly*, Vol. 25, No. 3, pp. 481–485.

Drake, A. (1967). *Fundamentals of Applied Probability Theory*. McGraw-Hill, New York.

Ehrhardt, R. (1979). "The Power Approximation for Computing (s, S) Inventory Policies." *Management Science*, Vol. 25, No. 8, pp. 777–786.

Eilon, S. (1965). "On the Cost of Runouts in Stock Control of Perishables." *Operations Research—Verfahren II* (R. Henn, editor), pp. 65–76.

Fortuin, L. (1980). "Five Popular Probability Density Functions: A Comparison in the Field of Stock-Control Models." *Journal of the Operational Research Society*, Vol. 31, No. 10, pp. 937–942.

Foster, F., J. Rosenhead, and V. Siskind, "The Effect of the Demand Distribution in Inventory Models Combining Holding, Stockout and Re-order Costs." *Journal of Royal Statistical Society*, Series B, Vol. 33, No. 2, pp. 312–325.

Gardner, E., and D. Dannenbring (1979). "Using Optimal Policy Surfaces to Analyze Aggregate Inventory Tradeoffs." *Management Science*, Vol. 25, No. 8, pp.709–720.

Gross, D., and J. Ray (1964), "Choosing a Spare Parts Inventory Operating Procedure—Bulk Control Versus Item Control." *Journal of Industrial Engineering*, Vol. XV, No. 6, pp. 310–315.

Hadley, G., and T. Whitin (1963). *Analysis of Inventory Systems*. Prentice-Hall, Englewood Cliffs, New Jersey, Chapter 4.

Hausman, W. (1969). "Minimizing Customer Line Items Backordered in Inventory Control." *Management Science*, Vol. 15, No. 12, pp. 628–634.

Herron, D. P. (1974). "Profit Oriented Techniques for Managing Independent Demand Inventories." *Production and Inventory Management*, Vol. 15, No. 4, pp. 57–74.

Herron, D. P. (1983). "Improving Productivity in Logistics Operations." In *Applications of Management Science* (R. L. Schultz, Editor), JAI Press, Greenwich, Connecticut, pp. 49–85.

Johnston, F. R. (1980). "An Interactive Stock Control System with a Strategic Management Role." *Journal of the Operational Research Society*, Vol. 31, No. 12, pp. 1064–1084.

Kottas, J., and H. S. Lau (1980). "The Use of Versatile Distribution Families in Some Stochastic Inventory Calculations." *Journal of the Operational Research Society*, Vol. 31, No. 5, pp. 393–403.

Lau, H. S., and A. Zaki (1982). "The Sensitivity of Inventory Decisions to the Shape of Lead Time Demand Distribution." *IIE Transactions*, Vol. 1, No. 4, pp. 265–271.

Magee, J. F., and D. M. Boodman (1967). *Production Planning and Inventory Control*. McGraw-Hill, New York, Chapter 6.

Magson, D. (1979). "Stock Control When the Lead Time Cannot Be Considered Constant." *Journal of the Operational Research Society*, Vol. 30, no. 4, pp. 317–322.

McClain, J. O., and L. J. Thomas (1980). *Operations Management: Production of Goods and Services*, Prentice-Hall, Englewood Cliffs, New Jersey, pp. 286–287.

Montgomery, D., M. Bazaraa, and A. Keswani (1973). "Inventory Models with a Mixture of Backorders and Lost Sales." *Naval Research Logistics Quarterly*, Vol. 20, No. 2, pp. 255–263.

Naddor, E. (1978). "Sensitivity to Distributions in Inventory Systems." *Management Science*, Vol. 24, No.16, pp. 1769–1772.

Nahmias, S. (1979). "Simple Approximations for a Variety of Dynamic Leadtime Lost Sales Inventory Models." *Operations Research*, Vol. 27, No. 5, pp. 904–924.

Oral, M. (1981). "Improved Implementation of Inventory Control Models through Equivalent Formulations." *Journal of Operations Management*, Vol. 1, No. 4, pp. 173–181.

Oral, M., M. Salvador, A. Reisman, and B. Dean (1972). "On the Evaluation of Shortage Costs for Inventory Control of Finished Goods." *Management Science*, Vol. 18, No. 6, pp. B344–B351.

Page, E. (1977). "Approximations to the Cumulative Normal Function and Its Inverse for Use on a Pocket Calculator." *Applied Statistics*, Vol. 26, No. 1, pp. 75–76.

Parr, J. O. (1972). "Formula Approximations to Brown's Service Function." *Production and*

Inventory Management, Vol. 13, No. 1, pp. 84–86.

Peters, T. J., and R. H. Waterman, Jr. (1982). *In Search of Excellence*. Harper & Row, New York, Chapter 6.

Peterson, R., L. J. Thomas, and A. J. Loiseau (1972). "Operational Inventory Control with Stochastic, Seasonal Demand." *INFOR*, Vol. 10, No. 1, pp. 81–93.

Polyzos, P. S., and D. A. Xirokostas (1976). "An Inventory Control System with Partial Deliveries." *Operational Research Quarterly*, Vol. 27, No. 3ii, pp. 683–695.

Presutti, V., and R. Trepp (1970). "More Ado about EOQ." *Naval Research Logistics Quarterly*, Vol. 17, No. 2, pp.243–251.

Scarf, H. (1960). "The Optimality of (S, s) Policies in the Dynamic Inventory Problem." *Mathematical Methods in the Social Sciences* (K. J. Arrow, S. Karlin, and P. Suppes, Editors), Stanford University Press, Chapter 13.

Schneider, H. (1981). "Effects of Service-Levels on Order-Points or Order-Levels in Inventory Models." *International Journal of Production Research*, Vol. 19, No.6, pp. 615–631.

Schrady, D., and U. Choe (1971). "Models for Multi-Item Continuous Review Inventory Policies Subject to Constraints." *Naval Research Logistics Quarterly*, Vol. 18, No. 4, pp. 451–463.

Schroeder, R. G. (1974). "Managerial Inventory Formulations with Stockout Objectives and Fiscal Constraints." *Naval Research Logistics Quarterly*, Vol. 21, No. 3, pp. 375–388.

Schwartz, B. L. (1966). "A New Approach to Stockout Penalties." *Management Science*, Vol. 12, No. 2, pp. 538–544.

Silver, E. A. (1970). "A Modified Formula for Calculating Service under Continuous Inventory Review." *AIIE Transactions*, Vol. II, No. 3, pp. 241–245.

Silver, E. A. (1977). "A Safety Factor Approximation Based on Tukey's Lambda Distribution." *Operational Research Quarterly*, Vol. 28, No. 3ii, pp. 743–746.

Silver, E. A., and D. J. Smith (1981). "Setting Individual Item Production Rates under Significant Lead Time Conditions." *INFOR*, Vol. 19, No.1, pp. 1–19.

Snyder, R. D. (1980). "The Safety Stock Syndrome." *Journal of the Operational Research Society*, Vol. 31, No. 9, pp. 833–837.

Taylor, P. B., and K. H. Oke (1976). "Tables for Stock Control—Problems of Formulation and Computation." *Operational Research Quarterly*, Vol. 27, No. 3ii, pp. 747–758.

Taylor, P. B., and K. H. Oke (1979). "Explicit Formulae for Computing Stock-Control Levels." *Journal of the Operational Research Quarterly*, Vol. 30, No.12, pp. 1109–1118.

Tijms, H. C. (1983). "On the Numerical Calculation of the Reorder Point in (s, S) Inventory Systems with Gamma Distributed Lead Time Demand." *Research Report No. 95*, Department of Actuarial Sciences and Econometrics, Vrije Universiteit, Amsterdam, Holland.

Todd, A. W. (1980). "Lead Times—What Makes Them? What Breaks Them?" *Proceedings of the Twenty-Third Annual International Conference of the American Production and Inventory Control Society*, pp. 135–136.

van Beek, P. (1978). "An Application of the Logistic Density on a Stochastic Continuous Review Stock Control Model." *Zeitschrift für Operations Research*, Band 22, pp. B165–B173.

van der Veen, B. (1981). "Safety Stocks—An Example of Theory and Practice in OR." *European Journal of Operational Research*, Vol. 6, No. 4, pp. 367–371.

Vinson, C. (1972). "The Cost of Ignoring Lead Time Unreliability in Inventory Theory." *Decision Sciences*, Vol. 3, pp. 87–105.

Weeda, P. J. (1982). "On Reorder Level Determination in a Sparse Data Environment." Working paper, Department of Mechancial Engineering, Twente University of Technology, Enschede, The Netherlands.

PART THREE

DECISION RULES AND SYSTEMS FOR SPECIAL CLASSES OF ITEMS

In Part Two we were concerned with decision systems for the routine control of B items, that is, the bulk of the items in a typical population of stock keeping units. Now we turn our attention to special items, those at the ends of the Dv spectrum—namely, the A and C groups—as well as those items not having a well-defined continuing demand pattern (the latter having been assumed in the development of the decision systems for B items). The most important items, the A group, are handled in Chapter 8. Chapter 9 is concerned with the low-dollar movement items, the C group. Then in Chapter 10 we deal with style goods and perishable items, that is, s.k.u. that can be maintained in inventory for only relatively short periods of time. The presentation of this portion of the book continues in the same vein as Part Two; again, we are concerned primarily with decision rules for managing *individual*-item inventories.

CHAPTER 8

Decision Systems for Managing the Most Important (Class A) Inventories

In this chapter we devote our attention to the relatively small number of items classified in the A group. Section 8.1 presents a brief review of the nature of A items. This is followed, in Section 8.2, by some general guidelines for the control of such items. Then, in Section 8.3, the basic decision rules are presented for (s, Q) systems. Section 8.4 deals with a more elaborate set of decision rules which, in an (s, Q) system, take account of the service (shortage) related effects of Q in selecting its value.[1] Next, in Sections 8.5 and 8.6, we present control logic for two somewhat more complicated systems whose use may be justified for A items. Finally, the special case of intermittent demand for high unit value items is addressed in Section 8.7.

8.1 THE NATURE OF CLASS A ITEMS

Recall from Chapter 3 that class A items are defined to be those at the upper end of the spectrum of importance; that is, the total costs of replenishment, carrying stock, and shortages associated with such an item are high enough to justify a more sophisticated control system than those proposed for the less important B items in Chapters 5 to 7. This usually means a high annual dollar usage (that is, a high value of Dv). We deliberately employ the term "usage" rather than "demand" because an important class of A items are high-unit-value service parts used for maintenance activities. In addition, one or more other factors may dictate that an item be placed in the A category. For example, an item, although its sales are relatively low, may be essential to round out the product line; to

[1] Equivalently, R in an (R, S) system.

illustrate, MIDAS carries Superchrome for its prestige value. Poor customer service on such an item may have adverse effects on customers who buy large amounts of other products in the line. In essence, the important issue is a tradeoff between control system costs (such as the costs of collecting required data, performing the computations, providing action reports, etc.) and the other three categories of costs mentioned above (for simplicity, let us call this latter group "other" costs). By definition, these "other" costs for an A item will be appreciably higher than for a B item. On the other hand, *given that the same control system is used* for an A and a B item the control costs will be essentially the same for the two items. A numerical example is in order:

Consider two types of control systems: one simple, one complex. Suppose we have an A and a B item with estimated "other" costs under use of the simple system being $900/year and $70/year, respectively. It is estimated that use of the complex control system will reduce these "other" costs by 10 percent. However, the control costs of this complex system are estimated to be $40/year/item higher than those incurred in using the simple system. The following table illustrates that the complex system should be used for the A, but not for the B item.

Using Complex System

Item	Increase in Control Costs	Reduction in Other Costs	Net Increase in Costs
A	40	0.1(900) = 90	−50
B	40	0.1(70) = 7	+33

As mentioned above, the factor Dv is important in deciding on whether or not to put an item in the A category. However, the type of control to use within the A category should definitely depend on the magnitudes of the individual components, D and v. As we see later in this chapter, a high Dv resulting from a low D and a high v value (low unit sales of a high-value item) implies different control from a high Dv resulting from a high D and a low v value (high unit sales of a low-value item). To illustrate, we would certainly control the inventories of the following two items in different ways:

Item 1: Midamatic film processor, valued at $30,000, which sells at a rate of 2 per year.

Item 2: Developing chemical, valued at $2/liter, which sells at a rate of 30,000 liters per year.

8.2 GUIDELINES FOR CONTROL OF A ITEMS

In Part Two which was concerned primarily with B items, we advocated a management by exception approach; that is, most decisions would be made by routine (computerized or manual) rules. Such should *not* be the case with A items; the potential high payoff warrants frequent managerial attention to (vigilance of) the replenishment decisions of individual items. Nonetheless, decision rules, based on mathematical models, do have a place in aiding the manager. Normally these models cannot incorporate all the important factors; in such cases the manager must modify the suggested (by the model) action through the subjective incorporation of any important omitted factors. The art of management is very evident in this type of activity.

We now list a number of suggested guidelines for the control of A items; these are above and beyond what can normally be incorporated in a *usable* mathematical decision rule:

1. *Inventory records should be maintained on a perpetual* (transactions recording) *basis, particularly for the more expensive items.* This need not be through the use of a computer; the relatively small number of A items makes the use of a manual system (for example, Kardex or VISI-Record) quite attractive.

2. *Keep top management informed.* Frequent reports (for example, monthly) should be prepared for at least a portion of the A items. These should be made available to senior management for careful review.

3. *Estimate and influence demand.* This can be done in three ways.

a. Manual input to forecasts (for example, knowledge of intentions of important customers) is likely advisable.

b. Mitchell (1962) has pointed out that for expensive slow-moving items it is particularly important to ascertain the predictability of the demand. Where the demand is of a special planned nature (for example, scheduled overhaul of a piece of equipment) or where adequate warning of the need for a replacement part is given (for example, a machine part fails but can be rapidly and inexpensively repaired to last for sufficient time to requisition and receive a new part from the supplier), there is no need to carry protection stock. In fact, under such circumstances a different type of control system, Material Requirements Planning (to be discussed in Chapter 16), is in order. On the other hand, where the demand occurs without warning (that is, a random breakdown), some protective stock may be appropriate. When the unit value of an item is extremely high, it may make sense to use a pool of spare parts *shared among several companies within the same industry*. An example is in the ammonia manufacturing industry where certain spare parts are maintained in a common pool.

Forecasting demand for a *slow-moving* item is not an easy matter. Very few transactions occur over a reasonable historical period so that a purely *objective* estimate of a demand rate is usually not feasible. Instead, one must take advantage of the subjective knowledge of experts, such as design engineers in the case of spare parts for a relatively new piece of equipment. A sensitivity analysis should be undertaken; in some cases the stocking decision is not particularly sensitive to errors in estimating the demand rate.

c. One need not live with a given demand pattern. Seasonal or erratic fluctuations can sometimes be reduced by altering price structures, negotiating with customers, smoothing shipments, and so forth.

4. *Estimate and influence supply.* Again, it may not be advisable to passively accept a given pattern of supply. Negotiations (for example, establishing blanket orders and freeze periods) with suppliers may reduce the average replenishment lead time, its variability, or both. The idea of a freeze period is that the timing or size of a particular order cannot be altered within a freeze period prior to its due date. In the same vein, it is very important to coordinate A-item inventory requirements in-house with the production scheduling department.

5. *Use conservative initial provisioning.* For A that items have a very high v value and a relatively low D value the initial provisioning decision becomes particularly crucial. For such items erroneous initial overstocking (due to overestimating the usage rate) can be extremely expensive. Thus, one should probably be conservative in initial provisioning. Brown(1979) is an interesting reference on this topic.

6. *Review decision parameters frequently.* In Chapter 17 we will discuss the importance of appropriate monitoring of parameter values. Suffice it to say for now that frequent review (as often as monthly or bi-monthly), of such quantities as the order points and order quantities, is advisable for A items.

7. *Determine precise values of control quantities.* In Chapter 5 we advocated the use of tabular aids in establishing order quantities for B items. It was argued that restricting attention to a limited number of possible time supplies (for example, $\frac{1}{2}$, 1, 2, 3, 6, and 12 months) results in small cost penalties. Such is not the case for A items; the percentage penalties may still be small, but even small percentage penalties represent sizable absolute costs for such items. Therefore, order quantities of A items should be based on the most exact analysis possible.

8. *Confront shortages as opposed to setting service levels.* In Chapter 7 we pointed out that it is often very difficult to estimate the cost of shortages; an alternative suggested was to specify a desired level of customer service instead. In most cases, we do not advocate this approach for A items because of the typical management behavior in the short run in coping with potential or actual shortages of such items. One does not usually sit back passively and accept shortages of A items (nor B items, for that matter). Instead, expediting actions (both in and out of house), emergency air freight shipments, and other actions, are undertaken; that is, the shortages are avoided or eliminated quickly. Such actions, with associated costs which can be reasonably estimated, should be recognized when establishing safety stocks to prevent them. On the other hand, it should be pointed out that, in certain situations, customers are willing to wait a short time for delivery. Because A items are replenished frequently, it may be satisfactory to operate with very little on-hand stock (that is, low safety stock) and instead backorder and satisfy such demand from the next order due in very soon.

8.3 ORDER-POINT, ORDER-QUANTITY (s, Q) SYSTEMS FOR A ITEMS

In Chapter 7, for the case of B items, we argued for the almost exclusive use of the normal distribution to represent the distribution of forecast errors over a lead time. For A items, where the potential benefits of using a more accurate representation are higher, we suggest, based on extensive tests (see Archibald et al., 1974), still using the normal distribution if the average (or forecast) demand in a lead time is high enough (at least 10 units). As mentioned in the previous section, we advocate use of explicit (or implicit) costing of shortages. Therefore, decision rules such as those in Sections 7.6.5, 7.6.6, and 7.6.7 of Chapter 7 should be used. If the average,[2] $\hat{x}_L$, is below 10 units, then a discrete distribution, such as the Poisson (see the Appendix of this chapter for a discussion of some properties of the distribution), is likely more appropriate.

The Poisson distribution has but a single parameter, namely, the average demand (in this case, $\hat{x}_L$). Once $\hat{x}_L$ is specified, a value of the standard deviation of forecast errors, σ_L, follows from the Poisson relation

$$\sigma_L = \sqrt{\hat{x}_L} \tag{8.1}$$

Therefore, the Poisson is appropriate to use only when the actually observed σ_L (for the item under consideration) is quite close to $\sqrt{\hat{x}_L}$. An operational definition of quite close is within 10 percent of $\sqrt{\hat{x}_L}$. When such is not the case, somewhat more complicated discrete distributions such as the negative binomial (see Deemer et al., 1974) or a compound Poisson (see, for example, Adelson, 1966; or Feeney and Sherbrooke, 1966) should be considered. The latter class, in particular, has been observed to provide reasonable fits to empirical demand data (see, for example, Mitchell et al., 1983).

The discrete nature of the Poisson distribution (in contrast, the normal distribution deals with a continuous variable) is both a blessing and a curse. For slow-moving items, it is important to be able to deal with discrete units. On the other hand, discrete mathematics create problems in implementation, as we will soon see.

We now present rules for two different shortage costing measures. In some cases, it may also be appropriate to consider the more elaborate decision rules to be discussed in Section 8.4.

8.3.1 The B_2 Cost Measure in the Special Case of Very Slow-Moving, Expensive Items ($Q = 1$)

As mentioned above, the discrete nature of the Poisson distribution causes problems in obtaining an operational decision rule. For one important situation,

[2]In an (R, S) system $\hat{x}_L$, the average demand in a lead time, would be replaced by $\hat{x}_{R+L}$, the average demand in a review interval plus a lead time.

namely, where the replenishment quantity $Q = 1$, an analysis (based on the work of Melese et al., 1960) leads to a decision rule quite easy to implement.

First, let us see under what conditions $Q = 1$ makes sense. From Eq. 5.3 of Chapter 5 the total relevant costs, if an order quantity of size Q is used, are

$$\text{TRC}(Q) = Qvr/2 + AD/Q$$

We are indifferent between $Q = 1$ and $Q = 2$ where

$$\text{TRC}(1) = \text{TRC}(2)$$

that is,

$$vr/2 + AD = vr + AD/2$$

or

$$D = vr/A$$

For any lower value of D we prefer the use of $Q = 1$. To illustrate, for the Professional Products Division of MIDAS, we found in Chapter 5 that $A/r \simeq 13.11$. Therefore, we have

$$\text{Use } Q = 1 \qquad \text{if } D < 0.0763v$$

The line $D = 0.0763v$ is shown on Figure 8.1 as well as the boundary line for A items in MIDAS ($Dv > 6{,}000$ dollars/year). The two inequalities define a region in the figure where it is appropriate to use $Q = 1$ for A items. It is a simple matter to locate on the figure the (D, v) point corresponding to any item under consideration. The location immediately tells us if the use of $Q = 1$ is correct.

Assumptions behind the Derivation of the Decision Rule

The assumptions include:

1. Continuous-review, order-point, order-quantity system with $Q = 1$ (the remaining decision variable is the order point, s, or the order-up-to-level, $S = s + 1$).
2. Poisson demand.
3. The replenishment lead time is a constant, namely L time periods. (The results still hold if L has a probability distribution as long as we use its mean value, $E(L)$; however, the derivation is considerably more complicated in this more general case.)
4. There is complete backordering of demands when out of stock. (Karush, 1957, and Mitchell, 1962, have investigated the case of complete lost sales; the results differ very little from the complete backordering situation.)

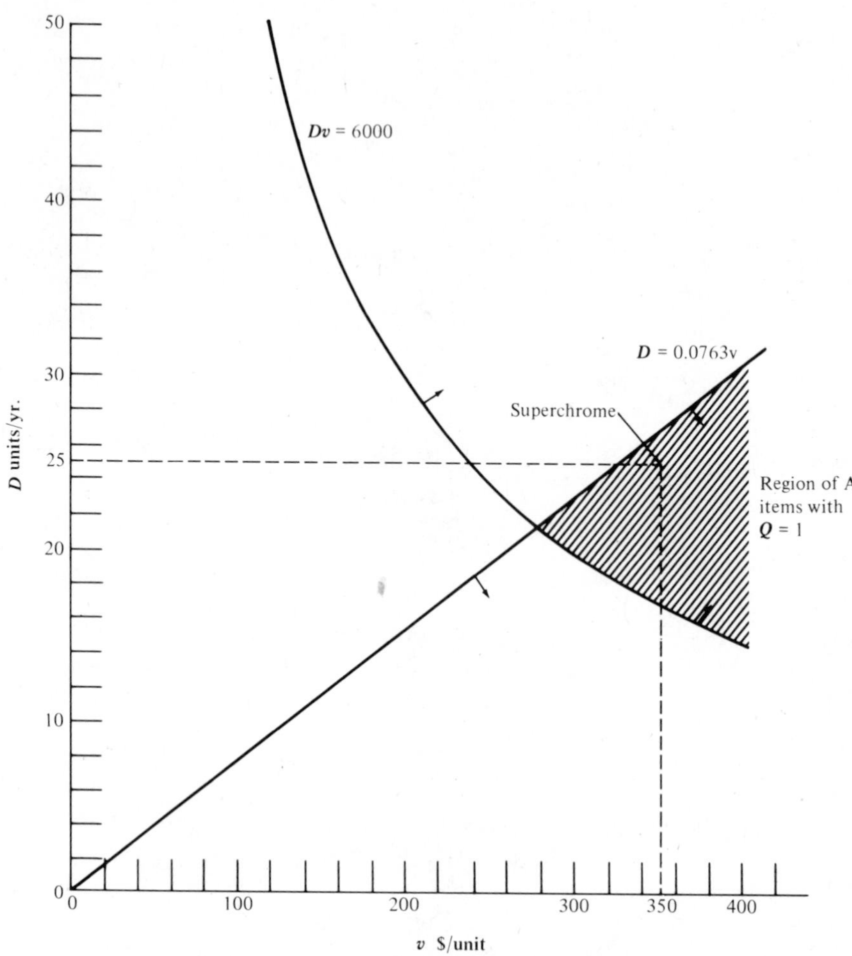

FIGURE 8.1 *A* Items with $Q = 1$ for the Professional Products Division of MIDAS

5. There is a fixed cost, B_2v, per unit backordered (that is, a fixed fraction, B_2, of the unit value is charged for each unit backordered).

Graphical Portrayal of the Decision Rule

As shown in Section 2a of the Appendix of this chapter, we are indifferent between reorder points s and $s + 1$ when

$$\frac{p_{po}(s + 1|\hat{x}_L)}{p_{po\leq}(s + 1|\hat{x}_L)} = \frac{r}{DB_2} \tag{8.2}$$

where[3]

$p_{po}(s + 1|\hat{x}_L)$ = probability that a Poisson variable with mean $\hat{x}_L$ takes on the value $s + 1$

$p_{po\leq}(s + 1|\hat{x}_L)$ = probability that a Poisson variable with mean $\hat{x}_L$ takes on a value less than or equal to $s + 1$

and, as earlier,

r = carrying charge, in \$/\$/unit time

D = demand rate, in units/unit time

B_2 = fraction of unit value charged per unit short

$\hat{x}_L$ = average (forecast) demand in a replenishment lead time

For a value of each of s and $\hat{x}_L$ Eq. 8.2 is solved for r/B_2D. For a given value of s, this is repeated for a number of values of $\hat{x}_L$ to produce a curve representing indifference between s and $s + 1$ as a function of $\hat{x}_L$ and r/B_2. This is illustrated in Figure 8.2. The computations are lengthy but they need only be done once-and-for-all to set up the curves. Note that $\hat{x}_L = DL$. These curves define regions on a graph of r/DB_2 versus $\hat{x}_L$ where we prefer one s value to others.

For a given item, values of r, D, and B_2 are used to evaluate the quantity r/DB_2. The point in Figure 8.2 corresponding to this value of r/DB_2 and the appropriate $\hat{x}_L$ indicates the best value of the order point, s, to use.

Numerical Illustration

Consider the case of Superchrome with

v = \$350/unit

D = 25 units/year

r = 0.24 \$/\$/year

L = 3 weeks = $\frac{1}{14}$ year

and B_2 is estimated to be $\frac{1}{5}$ (that is, 350/5 or \$70 per unit backordered).

[3] $p_{po}(x_0|\hat{x}_L) = \dfrac{(\hat{x}_L)^{x_0} \exp(-\hat{x}_L)}{x_0!} \qquad x_0 = 0, 1, 2, \ldots$

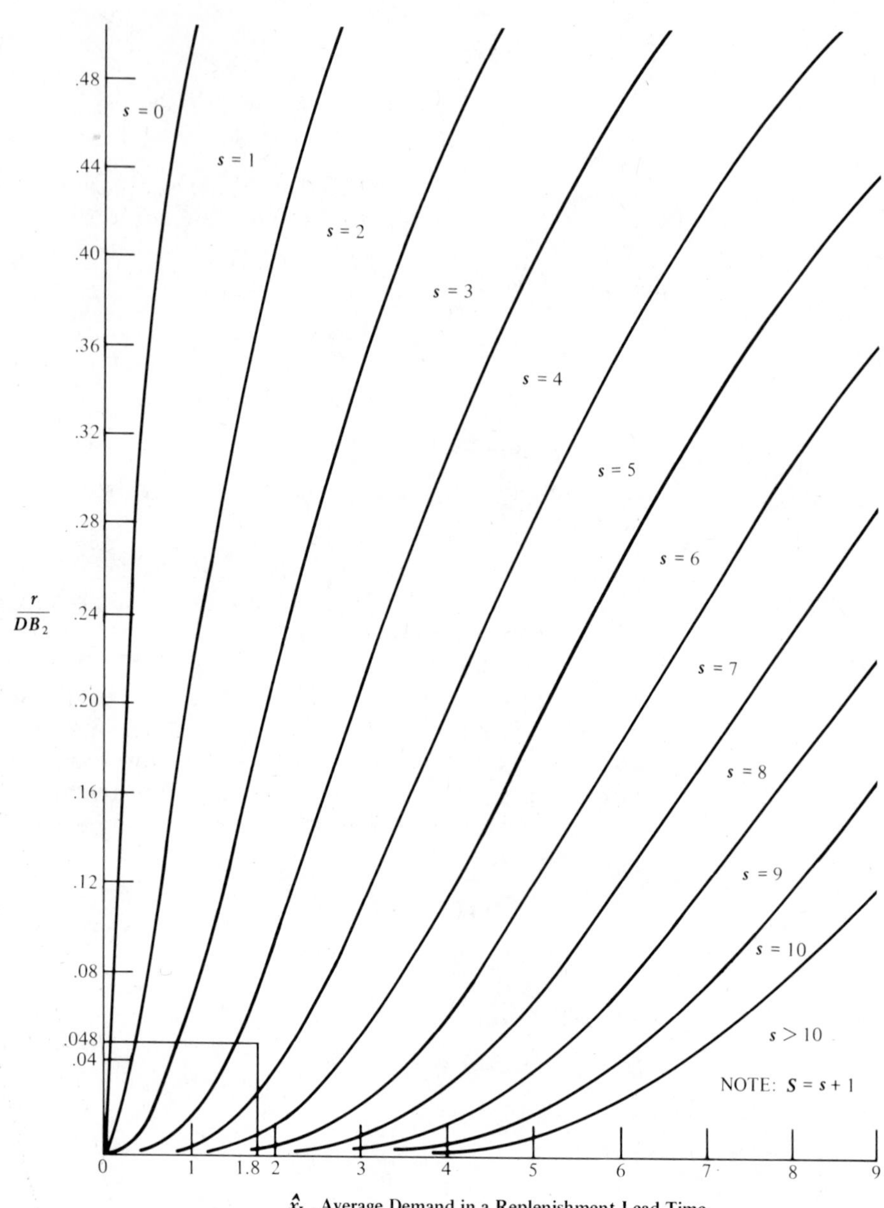

FIGURE 8.2 Indifference Curves for the Reorder Point under the B_2 Cost Measure When $Q = 1$

First, it is seen from Figure 8.1 that this is an A item with $Q = 1$ being appropriate. Now

$$\frac{r}{DB_2} = \frac{0.24}{25(\frac{1}{5})} = 0.048/\text{unit}$$

and

$$\hat{x}_L = DL = 25(\tfrac{1}{14}) \simeq 1.8 \text{ units}$$

Use of Figure 8.2 shows that the best order point is 4; that is, we order one-for-one each time a demand drops the inventory position to 4. Another way of saying this is that the inventory position should always be maintained at the level of 5.

Sensitivity to Value of B_2

A precise value of B_2 is not easy to ascertain. Fortunately, the indifference curves can be used in a different way to alleviate this difficulty. To illustrate, consider the item (Superchrome) in the above numerical illustration. Assume that D, R, and $\hat{x}_L$ are all known at the indicated values. The indifference curves identify the following regions where each s value shown is best for the given value of $\hat{x}_L$.

s Value	Range of r/DB_2	Corresponding Range of B_2
3	0.074 to 0.178	0.054 to 0.130
4	0.026 to 0.074	0.130 to 0.369
5	0.0076 to 0.026	0.369 to 1.263

These results are striking. Note the wide ranges of B_2 in which the same value of s is used. For example, as long as B_2 is anywhere between 0.130 and 0.369 the best s value is 4. Again, we see a situation where the result is insensitive to the value of one of the parameters.

8.3.2 The More General Case of $Q > 1$ and a B_2 Cost Structure

This is still the case in which a fraction of the unit cost is charged per unit short. The solution discussed above is only appropriate for $Q = 1$. When use of Figure 8.1 (or the EOQ formula) indicates that the best replenishment quantity is 2 or larger, we can no longer obtain as convenient a graphical solution, at least for the case of B_2 (a fraction of the unit value charged per unit short). An exact analysis (see Problem 8.2) leads to indifference between s and $s + 1$ where the following condition holds

$$\frac{\sum_{j=1}^{Q} p_{po}(s + j|\hat{x}_L)}{\sum_{j=1}^{Q} p_{po\leqslant}(s + j|\hat{x}_L)} = \frac{r}{DB_2} \tag{8.3}$$

where

$p_{po}(x_0|\hat{x}_L)$ is the probability that a Poisson variable with mean $\hat{x}_L$ takes on the value x_0.

$p_{po\leqslant}(x_0|\hat{x}_L)$ is the probability that the same variable takes on a value less than or equal to x_0.

Unfortunately, there are now four (instead of three) parameters in Eq. 8.3—namely, $\hat{x}_L$, s, r/DB_2, and Q. For each value of Q, a set of curves similar to Figure 8.2 (the special case of $Q = 1$) can be developed in a fashion identical to that used for Figure 8.2.

8.3.3 The Case of $Q \geqslant 1$ and a B_1 Cost Structure

In some cases it may be more appropriate to assume a fixed cost B_1 per (impending) stockout occasion as opposed to a cost per unit short. For such a case we have developed indifference curves useful for selecting the appropriate reorder point. As shown in Section 2b of the Appendix of this chapter, we are indifferent between s and $s + 1$ as reorder points when

$$\frac{p_{po}(s + 1|\hat{x}_L)}{p_{po\leqslant}(s|\hat{x}_L)} = \frac{Qvr}{DB_1} \tag{8.4}$$

where all the variables have been defined above. The indifference curves of Figure 8.3 are developed and used in the same fashion as those of Figure 8.2.

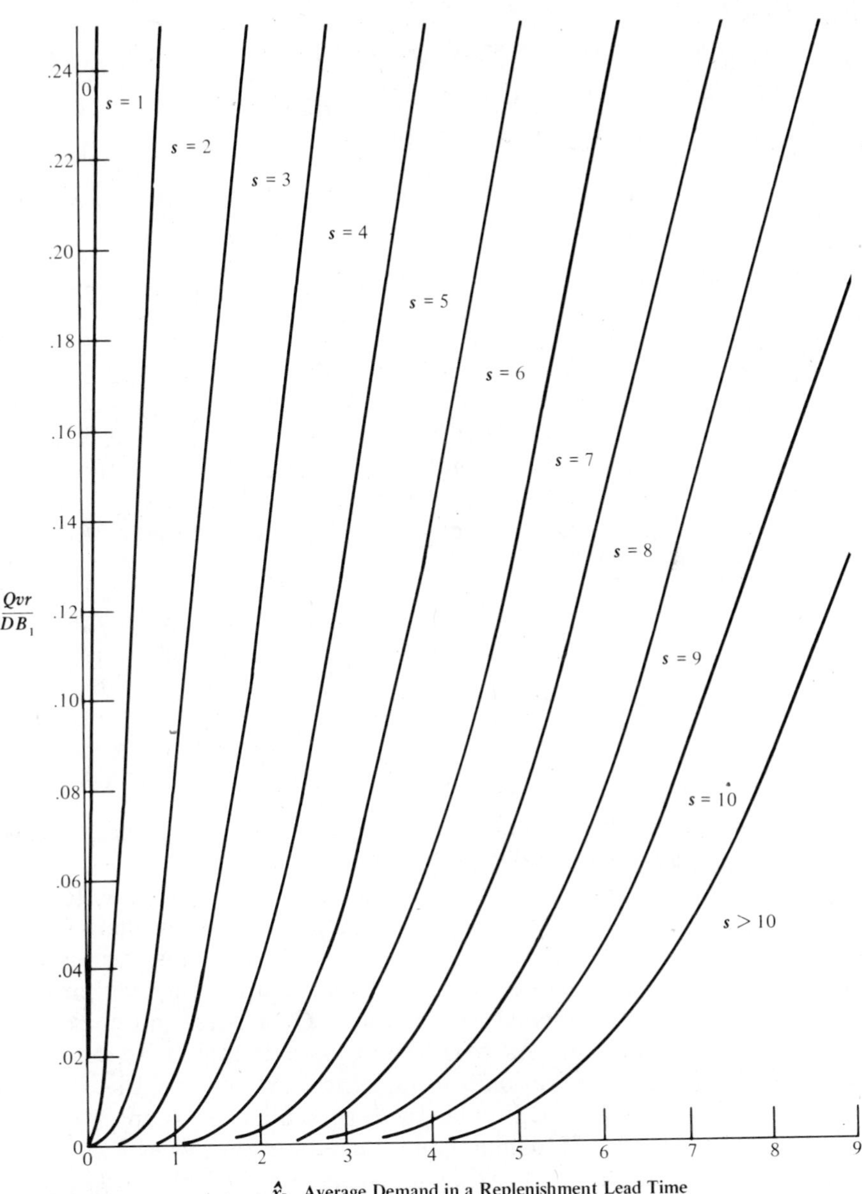

FIGURE 8.3 Indifference Curves for the Reorder Point under the B_1 Cost Measure

8.4 SIMULTANEOUS VERSUS SEQUENTIAL DETERMINATION OF TWO CONTROL PARAMETERS OF AN INDIVIDUAL ITEM

In most of our discussions in Chapter 7 there were two control parameters per item:

s and Q in an (s, Q) system

R and S in an (R, S) system

Our approach was to first determine one of the parameters—namely, Q or R; then (sequentially) find the best value of the second parameter, s or S, conditional on the value of Q or R, respectively. The derivation of the value of Q or R ignored the effect that this parameter has on the service level or shortage costs per unit time. To illustrate, consider the (s, Q) control system with a fixed cost B_1 per stockout occasion. From Section 1 of the Appendix of Chapter 7 we have

$$\text{ETRC}\ (k, Q) = AD/Q + (Q/2 + k\sigma_L)vr + \frac{DB_1}{Q}\, p_{u\geqslant}(k) \tag{8.5}$$

where, as earlier,

$$s = \hat{x}_L + k\sigma_L$$

and $p_{u\geqslant}(k)$ is a tabulated function giving the probability that a unit normal variable takes on a value of k or larger.

The approach, advocated in Chapter 7, was to first pick the Q value that minimizes the first two terms, ignoring the last term. But clearly, the selection of Q influences the shortage costs (the last term); the larger Q is, the smaller these costs become. The exact approach, of simultaneously determining k and Q, would involve finding the (k, Q) pair that minimizes the ETRC (k, Q) expression of Eq. 8.5. As we will see, this exact approach is considerably more involved from a computational standpoint. Furthermore, the order quantity is no longer the simple, well-understood economic order quantity, and hence is likely to be more difficult to implement. Fortunately, as we will show, the percentage penalty in the total of replenishment, carrying, and shortage costs using the simpler sequential approach tends to be quite small. Thus, in most situations, we were justified in advocating its use for B items. However, even small percentage savings may be attractive for A items. For this reason, we now take a closer look at the simultaneous determination of the two control parameters.

For illustrative purposes we show only one case—namely, an (s, Q) control system with a B_1 shortage cost. Similar results have been developed for a B_2 cost and for (R, S) systems (see Silver and Wilson, 1972).

The Decision Rules

The derivation is shown in Section 3a of the Appendix of this chapter. All of the underlying assumptions discussed in Section 7.6.1 of Chapter 7 still apply, except that a value of Q is no longer prespecified. The two equations in the two unknowns Q/σ_L and k (the latter being the safety factor) are

$$\frac{Q}{\sigma_L} = \frac{\text{EOQ}}{\sigma_L}\sqrt{\left[1 + \frac{B_1}{A}p_{u\geq}(k)\right]} \tag{8.6}$$

and

$$k = \sqrt{2 \ln\left[\frac{1}{2\sqrt{2\pi}}\left(\frac{B_1}{A}\right)\left(\frac{\sigma_L}{Q}\right)\left(\frac{\text{EOQ}}{\sigma_L}\right)^2\right]} \tag{8.7}$$

where

$\text{EOQ} = \sqrt{\frac{2AD}{vr}}$ is the basic economic order quantity

A = fixed cost component incurred with each replenishment

D = demand rate

v = unit variable cost of the item

r = carrying charge

σ_L = standard deviation of lead time demand

$p_{u\geq}(k)$ = a function of the unit normal variable (it is tabulated in Appendix B and a rational approximation for it is also available, as discussed earlier)

A suggested iterative solution procedure is to initially set Q = EOQ; then solve for a corresponding k value in Eq. 8.7, and then use this value in Eq.8.6 to find a new Q value, and so forth. In certain cases, Eq. 8.7 will have the square root of a negative number; in such a case, k is set at its lowest allowable value as previously discussed in Section 7.6.5 and then Q is obtained using this k value in Eq. 8.6. Because of the convex nature of the functions involved, convergence to the true simultaneous solution pair (Q and k) is ensured. For further details concerning convexity, when the solution converges, and so on, the reader should refer to Chapter 4 of Hadley and Whitin (1963) as well as Problem 8.3.

From Eq. 8.6 it is seen that the simultaneous Q is always larger than the EOQ. This makes sense when one views Eq. 8.5. The EOQ is the Q value that minimizes the sum of the first two cost components. However, at that value the last term in Eq. 8.5 is still decreasing as Q increases. Thus it pays to go somewhat above the EOQ.

Once we have ascertained that the simultaneous Q is larger than the EOQ, it follows from Eq. 8.7 that the simultaneous k is smaller than or equal to the sequential k (they may be equal because of the boundary condition of a lowest allowable k). Again, this is intuitively appealing—the larger Q value makes stockout opportunities less frequent; hence we can afford to carry less safety stock.

Numerical Illustration

For illustrative purposes suppose that MIDAS was considering the use of a B_1 shortage cost rule for certain items with a B_1 value of $32 per shortage occasion. One of these items, XSC-012, a liquid fixer, has the following characteristics:

$$D = 220 \text{ containers/yr}$$

$$v = \$12/\text{container}$$

$$\hat{x}_L = 30 \text{ containers}$$

$$\sigma_L = 10.5 \text{ containers}$$

Using the MIDAS values of $A = \$3.20$ and $r = 0.24$/yr we have that the EOQ is

$$\text{EOQ} = \sqrt{\frac{2 \times 3.20 \times 220}{12 \times 0.24}} \simeq 22$$

Therefore,

$$\text{EOQ}/\sigma_L = 22/10.5 \simeq 2.1$$

Moreover,

$$B_1/A = 32/3.20 = 10$$

With the iterative procedure, we obtain

Iteration Number	1	2	3	4	5
Q/σ_L	2.1	2.53	2.625	2.655	2.665
k	1.69	1.58	1.55	1.54	1.54

The order quantity (Q) is given by

$$Q = \sigma_L \times (\text{Final value of } Q/\sigma_L) \simeq 30 \text{ containers}$$

and the reorder point (s) by

$$s = \hat{x}_L + k\sigma_L = 30 + 1.54(10.5) \simeq 46 \text{ containers}$$

Cost Penalties

The percentage penalty in costs (excluding those of the control system) resulting from using the simpler sequential procedure in lieu of the sophisticated simultaneous approach is given by

$$\text{PCP} = \frac{[\text{ETRC(sequential parameter values)} - \text{ETRC(simultaneous parameter values)}]}{\text{ETRC(simultaneous parameter values)}} \times 100 \tag{8.8}$$

where PCP is the percentage cost penalty and the ETRC $(\cdot)$ values are expected total relevant costs (excluding system control costs) per unit time using the parameter values in the parentheses. Figure 8.4 shows PCP as a function of the two dimensionless parameters, EOQ/σ_L and B_1/A (note again the appearance of the EOQ). The curves have been terminated to the left where the simultaneous solution first gives $k = 0$.

Numerical Illustration of the Cost Penalty

For the item shown above

$$B_1/A = 10$$

and

$$\text{EOQ}/\sigma_L = 2.1$$

Use of Figure 8.4 shows that the percentage cost penalty for using the simple sequential procedure of Section 7.6.5 is

$$\text{PCP} \simeq 1.3 \text{ percent}$$

As shown in Section 3b of the Appendix of this chapter, the absolute cost penalty (ACP) in dollars is given by

$$\text{ACP} = \frac{\text{PCP}}{\text{PCP} + 100} \cdot \text{ETRC(Sequential parameter values)} \tag{8.9}$$

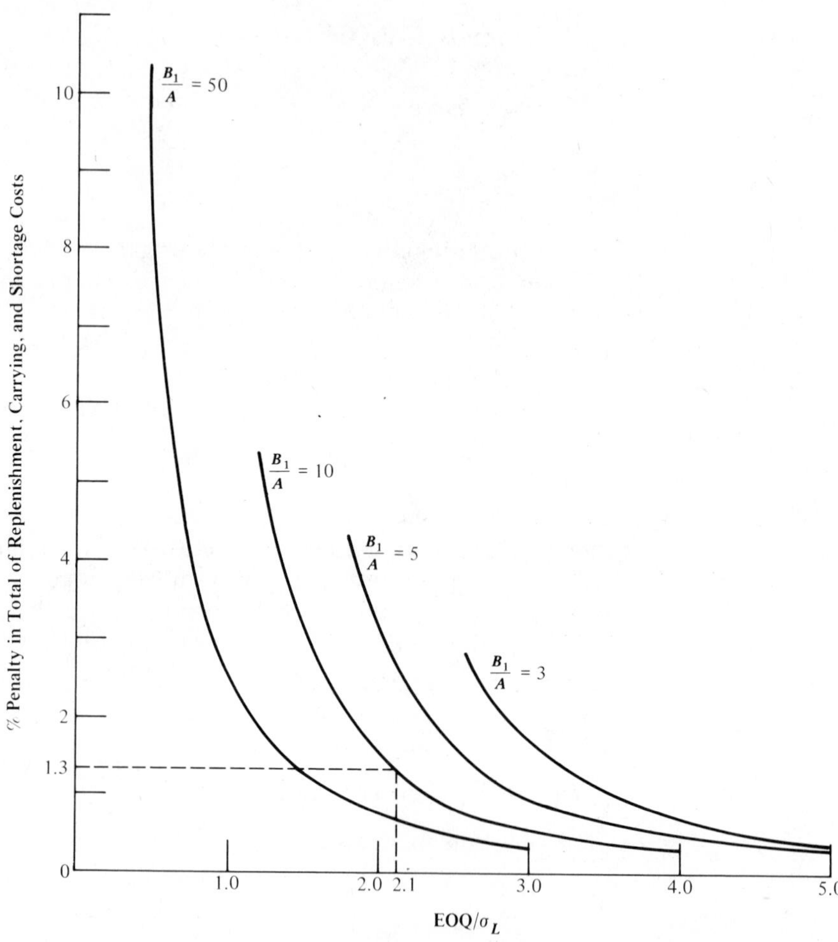

FIGURE 8.4 Percent Cost Penalty Associated with Using the Sequential Approach for an (s, Q) System for the Case of a Fixed Cost per Stockout Occasion, B_1

Now the sequential parameter values are quite easy to obtain. By the method of Section 7.6.5

$$Q = \text{EOQ} = 22$$

and k is selected to satisfy Eq. 8.7:

$$k = \sqrt{2 \ln \left[\frac{1}{2\sqrt{2\pi}} \left(\frac{B_1}{A} \right) \left(\frac{\text{EOQ}}{\sigma_L} \right) \right]}$$

$$= \sqrt{2 \ln \left[\frac{1}{2\sqrt{2\pi}} (10)(2.1) \right]}$$

$$= 1.69$$

Now

$$\text{ETRC}(k, Q) = \left(\frac{Q}{2} + k\sigma_L \right) vr + \frac{D}{Q} [A + B_1 p_{u\geq}(k)]$$

$$\text{ETRC}(1.69, 22) = \left[\frac{22}{2} + (1.69)(10.5) \right] (12.00)(0.24)$$

$$+ \frac{220}{22} [3.20 + 32(0.0455)]$$

$$= \$129.35/\text{yr}$$

Thus, from Eq. 8.9 we have

$$\text{ACP} = \frac{1.3}{1.3 + 100} (129.35)$$

$$= \$1.66/\text{yr}$$

an extremely small penalty despite the fact that the item has an annual usage of $2,640.

Further Comments

We have seen that the simultaneous approach requires an iterative solution of two complicated equations in two unknowns. (The situation is even more complicated for (R, S) systems. There we can obtain only one equation that the two unknowns must satisfy. The solution procedure is to perform a one-dimensional search on R values. For each R value the single equation implies an associated value of k. This R, k pair is then substituted in the cost equation. The R value, and associated k, giving the lowest cost are selected.) This amount of complexity should not be taken lightly when considering the possible use of a simultaneous solution. *When the simultaneous approach is used*, we would suggest the use of an implementation aid such as a nomograph or computerized routine. Implementation aids have been developed by Buckland (1970), Das (1978), Herron (1967, 1978), and Psoinos (1974). *However*, let us carefully examine the results of Figure 8.4. It is seen that the percentage cost penalty, for a fixed value of B_1/A, decreases as EOQ/σ_L increases, that is, as the variability of demand decreases relative to the EOQ. This is to be expected in that the sequential approach computes the order quantity ignoring the variability. Furthermore, the percentage penalties are quite low as long as EOQ/σ_L does not become too small.[4] Now, let us look more closely at the factor EOQ/σ_L.

$$\frac{\mathrm{EOQ}}{\sigma_L} = \sqrt{\frac{2AD}{vr\sigma_L^2}} = \sqrt{\frac{2ADv}{r(\sigma_L v)^2}} \tag{8.10}$$

As discussed in Chapter 4, some investigations have found evidence that, *on the average*, $\sigma_L v$ tends to increase with Dv in the following manner:

$$\sigma_L v \simeq c_1 (Dv)^{c_2}$$

where c_2 is greater than 0.5. Substituting this in Eq. 8.10 yields

$$\frac{\mathrm{EOQ}}{\sigma_L} \simeq \sqrt{\frac{2ADv}{rc_1^2 (Dv)^{2c_2}}} \propto (Dv)^{0.5-c_2}$$

Because c_2 is larger than 0.5, this says that, on the average, EOQ/σ_L decreases as Dv increases; that is, low values of EOQ/σ_L are more likely with A items than with B or C items. From above, this implies that the larger percentage errors in using the sequential approach are more likely to occur with A items. This, together with the fact that the absolute costs associated with A items are high, indicates that the sophisticated simultaneous procedures *may* be justified, for some A items. A corollary is that the absolute savings of a simultaneous approach are not likely to be justified for B items; hence, the suggested use of the simpler sequential approach in Chapter 7 was appropriate.

8.5 DECISION RULES FOR (*s*, *S*) SYSTEMS

Recall from Chapter 7 that in an (s, S) system we have a continuous review situation. Whenever the inventory position drops to the reorder point s or lower, an order is placed of sufficient magnitude to raise the position to the order-up-to-level S. When all transactions are of unit size then every order is of size $(S - s)$ and is placed when the inventory position is exactly at the level s. We can thus think of an order quantity

$$Q = S - s \tag{8.11}$$

and then the assumptions of an (s, Q) system (see Section 7.6.1 of Chapter 7) hold. Bartakke (1981) has reported on the use of such a system under Poisson

[4]Furthermore, Brown (1977) has suggested a pragmatic approach that eliminates the larger penalties. Specifically, if $\mathrm{EOQ} < \sigma_L$, simply use $Q = \sigma_L$ and then find k *sequentially*.

(unit-sized) demand at Sperry-Univac. *Non-unit-sized transactions are what complicate the analysis.* Furthermore, in contrast with an (R, S) system where each cycle of *fixed* length R starts with the inventory position at the level S, here we have a cycle of random length (how long it takes for the inventory position to drop from S to s or lower).

For one type of shortage costing measure (cost of B_1 per stockout occasion) and normally distributed forecast errors, we now discuss two approaches, of increasing complexity, for selecting s and S under conditions of non-unit-sized transactions. Other references on (s, S) systems include Federgruen and Zipkin (1981), Ward (1978), and Williams (1982). In addition, the related work of Tijms and Groenevelt (1982) will be discussed in Section 8.6.2. Blazer (1983a, 1983b) has also looked at a more general issue concerning an item with non-unit-sized transactions—namely, the possibility of special handling for very large demand transactions, that is, not routinely meeting such demands from stock.

Method 1: Simple Sequential Determination of s and S

Here we choose to neglect the undershoots (how far below s the inventory position is located when an order is placed). In addition, S and s are computed in a sequential fashion as follows. The Q expression of Eq. 8.11 is set equal to the economic order quantity as in Chapter 5. Then, *given this value of* Q, we find s by the procedure of Section 7.6.5 of Chapter 7. Finally, from Eq.8.11, the S value is given by

$$S = s + Q \qquad (8.12)$$

Numerical Illustration

Consider the MIDAS item XMF-014, a 1000-sheet box of 8 in. × 10 in. rapid process X-ray film. For illustrative purposes suppose that MIDAS' X-ray Film Division was considering using an (s, S) control system for this item. Relevant given characteristics of the item include

$$D = 1400 \text{ boxes/yr}$$

$$v = \$5.90/\text{box}$$

$$A = \$3.20$$

$$r = 0.24/\text{yr}$$

$$B_1 = \$150$$

$$\hat{x}_L = 270 \text{ boxes}$$

$$\sigma_L = 51.3 \text{ boxes}$$

Use of the above outlined procedure leads to

$$Q = 80 \text{ boxes}$$

$$s = 389 \text{ boxes}$$

$$S = 469 \text{ boxes}$$

Method 2: Use of Undershoot Distribution

Here we select s and S simultaneously and also attempt to take account of the nonzero undershoots. A stockout occurs if the sum of the undershoot plus the total lead time demand exceeds s. Thus, the variable in which we are interested is

$$x' = z + x$$

where z is the undershoot and x is the total lead time demand.

We know the distribution of x (assumed to be normal). The distribution of z is quite complex, depending in general on the distance $S - s$ and the probability distribution of transaction sizes. However, when $S - s$ is considerably larger than the average transaction size, then we can make use of a result developed by Karlin (1958), namely,

$$p_z(z_0) = \frac{1}{E(t)} \sum_{t_0=z_0+1}^{\infty} p_t(t_0) \tag{8.13}$$

where

$p_z(z_0)$ = probability that the undershoot is of size z_0

$p_t(t_0)$ = probability that a demand transaction is of size t_0

$E(t)$ = average transaction size

Equation 8.13 can be used to compute the mean and variance of the undershoot variable z. The results are

$$E(z) = \frac{1}{2}\left[\frac{E(t^2)}{E(t)} - 1\right]$$

and

$$\text{var}(z) = \frac{1}{12}\left\{\frac{4E(t^3)}{E(t)} - 3\left[\frac{E(t^2)}{E(t)}\right]^2 - 1\right\}$$

The two variables z and x can be assumed to be independent. Therefore

$$E(x') = E(z) + E(x) = \left[\frac{1}{2}\frac{E(t^2)}{E(t)} - 1\right] + \hat{x}_L \tag{8.14}$$

and

$$\begin{aligned} \text{var}(x') &= \text{var}(z) + \text{var}(x) \\ &= \frac{1}{12}\left\{\frac{4E(t^3)}{E(t)} - 3\left[\frac{E(t^2)}{E(t)}\right]^2 - 1\right\} + \sigma_L^2 \end{aligned} \tag{8.15}$$

For convenience, we assume that x' has a normal distribution[5] with the above shown mean and variance. With this assumption, the method, whose derivation closely parallels that shown in Section 3a of the Appendix of this chapter, is as follows:

Step 1 Select k and Q to simultaneously satisfy the following two equations:

$$Q = \text{EOQ}\sqrt{1 + \frac{B_1}{A}p_{u\geq}(k)} - E(z), \text{ rounded to an integer} \tag{8.16}$$

and

$$k = \sqrt{2\ln\left[\frac{1}{2\sqrt{2\pi}}\left(\frac{B_1}{A}\right)\frac{(\text{EOQ})^2}{(Q + E(z))\sigma_{x'}}\right]} \tag{8.17}$$

where

$p_{u\geq}(k)$ = probability that a unit normal variable takes on a value greater than or equal to k

$$\text{EOQ} = \sqrt{\frac{2AD}{vr}}$$

$$\sigma_{x'} = \sqrt{\text{var}(x')}$$

[5] x is normally distributed but z is certainly not, in that Eq. 8.13 reveals that $p_z(z_0)$ is monotonically decreasing with z_0. Hence, the assumption of $(z + x)$ having a normal distribution is only an approximation.

Step 2

$$s = E(x') + k\sigma_{x'}, \text{ rounded to the nearest integer.}$$

Step 3

$$S = s + Q$$

Numerical Illustration

We use the same item, XMF-014. Now, of course, we need a probability distribution of transaction sizes [or, alternatively, the first three moments $E(t)$, $E(t^2)$, and $E(t^3)$]. Suppose for illustrative purposes that the distribution is

t_0	1	2	3	6	12	24	36	72
$p_t(t_0)$	0.25	0.05	0.05	0.1	0.25	0.15	0.1	0.05

Then

$$E(t) = \sum_{t_0} t_0 p_t(t_0) = 14.9$$

$$E(t^2) = \sum_{t_0} t_0^2 p_t(t_0) = 515.7$$

$$E(t^3) = \sum_{t_0} t_0^3 p_t(t_0) = 25857.2$$

From Eqs. 8.14 and 8.15

$$\begin{aligned} E(x') &= \frac{1}{2}\left(\frac{515.7}{14.9} - 1\right) + 270 \\ &= 16.81 + 270 \\ &= 286.81 \end{aligned}$$

$$\begin{aligned} \text{var}\,(x') &= \frac{1}{12}\left\{\frac{4(25857.2)}{14.9} - 3\left(\frac{515.7}{14.9}\right)^2 - 1\right\} + (51.3)^2 \\ &= 278.90 + 2631.69 \\ &= 2910.59 \end{aligned}$$

Step 1 Equations 8.16 and 8.17 give that k and Q must satisfy

$$Q = 79.5\sqrt{1 + 46.875 p_{u\geq}(k)} - 16.81$$

and

$$k = \sqrt{2 \ln \left[\frac{1}{2\sqrt{2\pi}} (46.875) \frac{(79.5)^2}{(Q + 16.81)(53.95)} \right]}$$

The solution is

$$Q = 87 \text{ boxes}$$
$$k = 2.17$$

Step 2

$$s = 286.81 + 2.17\sqrt{2910.59}$$
$$= 404 \text{ boxes}$$

Step 3

$$S = 404 + 87 = 491 \text{ boxes}$$

Comparison of the Methods

It is interesting to compare the results of the two methods for the numerical illustration of item XMF-014. Archibald (1976) has developed a search procedure that finds the optimal (s, S) pair for an arbitrary discrete distribution of transaction sizes and also gives the expected total relevant costs for any (s, S) pair used (see also Archibald and Silver, 1978). Utilizing his procedure we found the results shown in Table 8.1. It is seen that Method 2, which takes account of the undershoot effects, leads to a solution negligibly close to the optimum. Note that, even with the significant departure from unit-sized transactions shown in the numerical illustration, the simplistic approach (Method 1) of Chapter 7 still

TABLE 8.1 Illustrative Comparison of the Two Methods of Finding Values of s and S, Item XMF-014

Method	Description	s	S	ETRC ($/yr)	Percent Above Best Value
1	Sequential, ignoring undershoot	389	469	350.82	3.5
2	Simultaneous and using undershoot	404	491	339.01	0.0
	Optimal solution	406	493	339.00	—

gives a cost penalty of only 3.5 percent. Based on results of this type, we suggest use of the simpler procedures of Chapter 7 unless the demand is erratic in nature (defined in Chapter 4 as when $\hat{\sigma}_1$ exceeds the demand level a, where both are measured over a unit time period). When the latter holds, one should use Method 2 or one of the more advanced procedures referenced earlier.

8.6 DECISION RULES FOR (*R*, *s*, *S*) SYSTEMS

As mentioned in Chapter 7, it has been shown that, under quite general conditions, the system that minimizes the total of review, replenishment, carrying, and shortage costs will be a member of the (R, s, S) family. However, the determination of the *exact* best values of the three parameters is extremely difficult. The problem results partly from the fact that undershoots of the reorder point s are present even if all transactions are unit-sized. This is because we only observe the inventory level every R units of time. Another aspect of the difficulty (see Wagner et al., 1965) is that, if as earlier we set $Q = S - s$, then the optimal value of Q is not a unimodal function of the demand rate; that is, as the demand rate increases, the optimal Q may first increase, then decrease, and so forth. Because of the complexity of exact analyses we again advocate and illustrate the use of heuristic approaches. Some are simple enough that they could also be used for the control of B items; hence, in Section 8.6.2 we demonstrate the use of a service constraint that would normally not be employed for A items.

8.6.1 Decision Rule for a Specified Fractional Charge (B_3) per Unit Short at the End of Each Period[6]

We present a heuristic method, known as the *Revised Power Approximation.* The original Power Approximation was suggested by Ehrhardt (1979) and the revision was proposed by Mosier (1981) (an alternative, interesting approach has been developed by Naddor, 1975).

The Revised Power Approximation involves determining values of the two control parameters $Q = S - s$ and s. We first show the Approximation and then briefly discuss its nature and its derivation.

The Revised Power Approximation Decision Rules

Step 1 Compute

$$Q_p = 1.30\hat{x}_R^{0.494}\left(\frac{A}{vr}\right)^{0.506}\left(1+\frac{\sigma_{R+L}^2}{\hat{x}_R^2}\right)^{0.116} \tag{8.18}$$

[6]Also the carrying charge r, as in Chapter 6, is based on the period-ending inventory (in dollars).

and

$$s_p = 0.973\hat{x}_{R+L} + \sigma_{R+L}\left(\frac{0.183}{z} + 1.063 - 2.192z\right) \tag{8.19}$$

where

$$z = \sqrt{\frac{Q_p r}{\sigma_{R+L} B_3}} \tag{8.20}$$

$$\hat{x}_R = DR$$

$$\hat{x}_{R+L} = D(R + L)$$

with B_3 in \$/\$ short at the end of a review interval; r in \$/\$/review interval; D in units/year; and R and L in years.

Step 2 If $Q_p/\hat{x}_R > 1.5$, then let[7]

$$s = s_p \tag{8.21}$$

$$S = s_p + Q_p \tag{8.22}$$

Otherwise, go to Step 3.

Step 3 Compute

$$S_0 = \hat{x}_{R+L} + k\sigma_{R+L} \tag{8.23}$$

where k satisfies

$$p_{u\geqslant}(k) = \frac{r}{B_3 + r} \tag{8.24}$$

Then[7]

$$s = \text{minimum}\ \{s_p, S_0\} \tag{8.25}$$

$$S = \text{minimum}\ \{s_p + Q_p, S_0\} \tag{8.26}$$

Numerical Illustration

Consider a particular item having $R = 1/2$ month and $L = 1$ month. Other relevant characteristics are $D = 1200$ units/yr, $A = \$25$, $v = \$2$/unit, $r = 0.24$ \$/\$/yr, $B_3 = 0.2$ \$/\$ short/period, and $\sigma_{R+L} = 60$ units.

[7]If demands are integer valued, then s and S are rounded to the nearest integer. There may also be a management-specified minimum value of s.

Step 1

$$\hat{x}_R = RD = \frac{1}{24}(1200) = 50 \text{ units}$$

$$\hat{x}_{R+L} = (R + L)D = 150 \text{ units}$$

$$r = \frac{0.24}{24} = 0.01 \text{ \$/\$/review interval}$$

Then from Eq. 8.18 we have

$$Q_p = 1.30\,(50)^{0.494}\,[25/(2.00)(0.01)]^{0.506}\,[1 + (60)^2/(50)^2]$$
$$\simeq 808 \text{ units}$$

Next, Eq. 8.20 gives

$$z = \sqrt{\frac{(808)(0.01)}{(60)(0.20)}} = 0.821$$

Then, use of Eq. 8.19 leads to

$$s_p = 0.973(150) + 60\left[\frac{0.183}{0.821} + 1.063 - 2.192(0.821)\right]$$
$$\simeq 115 \text{ units}$$

Step 2

$$Q_p/\hat{x}_R = 650/50 > 1.5$$

Therefore, from Eqs. 8.21 and 8.22 we have

$$s = 115 \text{ units}$$
$$S = 115 + 808 = 923 \text{ units}$$

Discussion

The rules were derived in the following fashion. Roberts (1962) had developed analytic forms for Q and s that hold for large values of A and B_3. Somewhat more general forms of the same nature were assumed containing a number of parameter values; for example,

$$Q_p = a\hat{x}_R^{1-b}\left(\frac{A}{vr}\right)^b\left(1+\frac{\sigma_{R+L}^2}{\hat{x}_R^2}\right)^c \tag{8.27}$$

where a, b, and c are parameters.

Optimal values of $Q = S - s$ and s were found (by a laborious procedure not practical for routine operational use) for a wide range of representative problems and the values of the parameters (for example, a, b, and c in Eq. 8.27) were determined by a regression fit to these optimal results. In the case of Q_p, this led to Eq. 8.18. Equations 8.19 and 8.20 were found in much the same way.

Step 3 is necessary because, when $Q_p/\hat{x}_R$ is small enough, Roberts' limiting policy is no longer appropriate; in effect, we are reduced to an order every review interval, that is, an (R, S) system. Equation 8.24 can be derived in the same fashion as Eq.7.21 of Section 7.6.6 of Chapter 7, except using the more accurate representation for the expected on-hand stock footnoted in Section 7.6.3.

Note that as $\sigma_{R+L} \to 0$ Eq. 8.18 gives a result close to the basic economic order quantity. Extensive tests by Ehrhardt (1979) and Mosier (1981) have shown that the approximation performs extremely well in most circumstances.

8.6.2 Decision Rule for a Specified Fraction (P_2) of Demand Satisfied Directly from Shelf

Again a heuristic procedure (due to Tijms and Groenevelt, 1982) is presented which, incidentally, can be adapted for use within the (s, S) context of Section 8.5, as well as for the P_1 and TBS service measures. Schneider (1978, 1981) used a somewhat different approach to derive the same results. We show the decision rule followed by a numerical illustration; then provide a brief discussion concerning the rule. The underlying assumptions are basically the same as those presented in Section 7.7.3 for (R, S) systems except, of course, now an order is placed at a review instant only if the inventory position is at or below s. We show illustrative details only for the case of normally distributed demand, which is appropriate to use as long as $(CV)_{R+L} \leq 0.5$ where $(CV)_{R+L} = \sigma_{R+L}/\hat{x}_{R+L}$ is the coefficient of variation of demand over $R + L$. When CV exceeds 0.5 a gamma distribution provides better results (see Tijms and Groenevelt, 1982; Tijms, 1983) in that, with such a high value of CV, a normal distribution would lead to a significant probability of negative demands.

Decision Rule

Select s to satisfy

$$\sigma_{R+L}^2 J_u\left(\frac{s-\hat{x}_{R+L}}{\sigma_{R+L}}\right) - \sigma_L^2 J_u\left(\frac{s-\hat{x}_L}{\sigma_L}\right) = 2(1-P_2)\hat{x}_R\left[S-s+\frac{\sigma_R^2+\hat{x}_R^2}{2\hat{x}_R}\right] \tag{8.28}$$

where

$S - s$ is assumed predetermined (for example, by EOQ considerations)

$\hat{x}_t$ = expected demand in a period of duration t

σ_t = standard deviation of errors of forecasts of total demand over a period of duration t

$J_u(k) = \int_k^\infty (u_0 - k)^2 f_u(u_0)du_0$ = another special function of the unit normal distribution.

Note that, as shown by Hadley and Whitin (1963),

$$J_u(k) = (1 + k^2)p_{u\geq}(k) - kf_u(k) \tag{8.29}$$

so that $J_u(k)$ can be evaluated using Table B.1 of Appendix B. In fact, one could develop, once and for all, an extra column for $J_u(k)$ in the table.

Equation 8.28 requires, in general, a trial-and-error type solution. However, in the event that the desired service level is high enough ($P_2 \geq 0.9$), the demand pattern is relatively smooth and R is not too small compared with L; then the second term on the left side of Eq. 8.28 can be ignored. Thus, if we set

$$s = \hat{x}_{R+L} + k\sigma_{R+L} \tag{8.30}$$

the decision rule reduces to selecting k so as to satisfy

$$\sigma_{R+L}^2 J_u(k) = 2(1-P_2)\hat{x}_R\left[S-s+\frac{\sigma_R^2+\hat{x}_R^2}{2\hat{x}_R}\right] \tag{8.31}$$

If a table of $J_u(k)$ versus k is available, then finding the appropriate k poses no difficulty. Alternatively, one can use rational functions to find k from $J_u(k)$ as suggested by Schneider (1981).

Numerical Illustration

We illustrate a situation where the simpler Eq. 8.31 can be used. Suppose a MIDAS customer in Montreal is controlling a particular item on a periodic basis with $R = 2$ weeks and the lead time $L = 1$ week. Assume that $S - s$ has been preestablished as 100 units. The forecast update period is 2 weeks and current estimates are $\hat{x}_1 = 50$ units and $\sigma_1 = 15$ units. Suppose that $P_2 = 0.95$.

First, we evaluate

$$\hat{x}_R = \hat{x}_1 = 50 \text{ units}$$

$$\hat{x}_{R+L} = \hat{x}_{3/2} = 75 \text{ units}$$

$$\sigma_R = \sigma_1 = 15 \text{ units}$$

$$\sigma_{R+L} = \sigma_{3/2} = \sqrt{3/2}\,\sigma_1 = 18.4 \text{ units}$$

$$(CV)_{R+L} = \frac{\sigma_{R+L}}{x_{R+L}} = \frac{18.4}{75} = 0.25 < 0.5$$

Thus, an assumption of normally distributed demand is reasonable.

From Eq. 8.31 we have

$$(18.4)^2 J_u(k) = 2(1 - 0.95)50\left[100 + \frac{(15)^2 + (50)^2}{2(50)}\right]$$

or

$$J_u(k) = 0.402$$

Using Eq. 8.29 we find, by trial-and-error, that

$$k \simeq 0.134$$

Thus, from Eq. 8.30 the reorder point is given by

$$\begin{aligned} s &= 75 + 0.134(18.4) \\ &\simeq 77.5 \text{ or } 78 \text{ units} \end{aligned}$$

Finally,

$$S = s + (S - s) = 78 + 100 = 178 \text{ units}$$

Incidentally use of the more complicated Eq. 8.28 produces the same results in this example.

Discussion

To derive the decision rule, one uses, as in Chapter 7,

$$1 - P_2 = \frac{\text{Expected shortage per replenishment cycle}}{\text{Expected replenishment size}} \tag{8.32}$$

As in Method 2 of Section 8.5, the key random variable is the total of the undershoot z (of the reorder point) and the demand x in a lead time. The denominator of Eq. 8.32 leads to the term in square brackets in Eq. 8.28. The numerator in Eq. 8.32 is developed based on

$$\int_s^\infty (x' - s)\, f_{x'}(x_0')dx_0'$$

where $x' = z + x$. The result, after lengthy calculus, turns out to be the left side of Eq. 8.28, divided by $2x_R$.

8.6.3 Coping with Nonstationarity

As discussed in Chapter 6, the average demand rate may vary appreciably with time. Presumably this should have an impact on the choice of control parameters such as s and S. An *exact* analysis of time-varying *and* probabilistic demand is far too complicated for routine use in practice. Therefore, again we adopt heuristic approaches. Incidentally, although we are talking about nonstationarity with respect to (R, s, S) systems, many of the concepts are applicable for other control systems. More will be said on this topic under implementation issues in Chapter 17.

If the average demand rate changes with time, then the values of R, s, and S should also change with time. From a pragmatic standpoint frequent changes in R, the review interval, are awkward to implement. Thus, changes in R, *if made at all*, should be very infrequent. One appealing approach to adjusting s and S with time is to compute the values of s and S in a particular period t using demand (forecast) information over the immediately following interval of duration $R + L$, *but still using an underlying steady state model*. This is equivalent, in the terminology of Chapter 6, to using a rolling horizon of length $R + L$. Tests by Kaufman (1977) have revealed that this simple approach performs quite well. Silver (1978) uses much the same idea but allows the demand rate to vary *within* the current horizon. This is accomplished by using safety stock considerations to decide when to place an order, followed by the *deterministic* Silver-Meal heuristic to select the size of the then current replenishment. Ashkin (1981) and Bookbinder and Tan (1983) also address this problem.

A complexity to be faced, even in the simple procedures mentioned above, is the estimation of $\sigma_{t,t+R+L}$, the standard deviation of forecast errors for a forecast, made in period t, of demand over the next $R + L$ periods. Unlike in earlier discussions, we *cannot* make the assumption that $\sigma_{t,t+R+L} = \sigma_{R+L}$. Where the average demand rate changes with time, it is certain that σ will also vary. A pragmatic approach to the estimation of $\sigma_{t,t+R+L}$ is to use an aggregate relationship, first mentioned in conjunction with estimating σ's of new items in Section 4.9.1 of Chapter 4, of the form

$$\sigma_{t,t+R+L} = c_1 \, \hat{x}^{c_2}_{t,t+R+L} \tag{8.33}$$

where $\hat{x}_{t,t+R+L}$ is the forecast, made in period t, of total demand over the next $R + L$ periods, and c_1 and c_2 are constants estimated for a population of items (as discussed in Chapter 4).

A somewhat simpler, but less accurate, approach is suggested by Krupp (1982).

8.7 CONTROLLING THE INVENTORIES OF INTERMITTENT DEMAND ITEMS

In Section 4.9.2 we argued for a special type of forecasting for this kind of item, specifically separating out as two variables (1) the time (n) between demand transactions and (2) the sizes (z) of the transactions. In particular, we advocated estimating $\hat{n}$ (the average number of periods between transactions), $\hat{z}$ (the average size of a transaction), and MAD(z). Now, in selecting values of control variables, such as s, we must take account of the intermittent nature of the demands; specifically, there may now be a significant chance of no demand at all during a lead time. Problem 8.8 deals with the case of an (s, Q) system. Where intermittent demand is *known* well ahead of time, it is more appropriate to use a decision rule based on a deterministic, time-varying demand pattern (see Chapter 6). Ekanayake et al. (1977) discuss this type of issue within a case study context.

8.8 SUMMARY

In this chapter we have dealt with the most important class of items, namely A items. In general, procedures, more elaborate than those in earlier chapters, have been suggested. Where analytic models cannot incorporate all important factors and still be solvable by deductive reasoning, it may very well be worthwhile in the case of A items to resort to simulation methods which are much broader in applicability but more expensive to use. (See Section 3.7 of Chapter 3.)

In the next chapter we turn to the opposite end of the spectrum, namely C items. However, in later chapters where we deal with coordination among items, A and B items will again play a prominent role. For example, expensive spare parts, discussed in the current chapter, will appear again under the repairable inventory models to be covered in Chapter 12.

APPENDIX TO CHAPTER 8
THE POISSON DISTRIBUTION AND SOME DERIVATIONS

1. THE POISSON DISTRIBUTION

An extensive reference is the book by Haight (1967).

Probability Mass Function

A Poisson variable is an example of a discrete random variable. Its probability mass function (p.m.f.) is given by

$$p_x(x_0) = \text{Prob}\,\{x = x_0\} = \frac{a^{x_0}\exp(-a)}{x_0!} \qquad x_0 = 0, 1, 2, \ldots$$

where a is the single parameter of the distribution. The graphical plot rises to a peak, then drops off except for very low values of a where the peak is at $x_0 = 0$.

Moments

One can show (see, for example, Drake, 1967) that

$$1.\ E(x) = \sum_{x_0=0}^{\infty} x_0 p_x(x_0) = a$$

that is, the parameter a is the mean of the distribution.

$$2.\ \sigma_x^2 = \sum_{x_0=0}^{\infty} [x_0 - E(x)]^2 p_x(x_0) = a$$

Hence, the standard deviation σ_x is given by

$$\sigma_x = \sqrt{a}$$

2. INDIFFERENCE CURVES FOR POISSON DEMAND

a. The Case of $Q = 1$ and a B_2 Penalty

Suppose an order-up-to-level S is used, or equivalently, an order for one unit is placed when the inventory position drops to the level $S - 1$. In this system the inventory position is effectively always at the level S. All outstanding orders at a time t must arrive by time $t + L$ and no order placed after t can arrive by $t + L$. Therefore, the net (on-hand minus backorders) stock at time $t + L$ must be equal to the inventory position at time t minus any demand in t to $t + L$; that is,

$$(\text{Net stock at time } t + L) = S - (\text{demand in } L)$$

or

$$p_{NS}(n_0) = \text{Prob}\,\{x = S - n_0\} \tag{8.34}$$

where

$p_{NS}(n_0)$ = probability that the net stock at a random point in time takes on the value n_0

x = total demand in the replenishment lead time

The expected on-hand inventory ($\bar{I}$) is the expected *positive* net stock, that is,

$$\begin{aligned}\bar{I} &= \sum_{n_0=0}^{S} n_0 p_{NS}(n_0) \\ &= \sum_{n_0=0}^{S} n_0 p_x(S - n_0)\end{aligned}$$

where

$p_x(x_0)$ = probability that total time demand is x_0

Substituting, $j = S - n_0$, we have

$$\bar{I} = \sum_{j=0}^{S} (S - j) p_x(j)$$

Furthermore, with Poisson demand, the probability that a particular demand requires backordering is equal to the probability that the net stock is zero or less; that is,

$$\text{Prob}\,\{\text{a demand is not satisfied}\} = p_{NS\leqslant}(0)$$

Using, Eq. 8.35 we have

$$\text{Prob}\,\{\text{a demand is not satisfied}\} = p_{x\geqslant}(S)$$

The expected shortage costs per unit time (C_s) are

$$\begin{aligned} C_s &= (\text{Cost per shortage}) \times (\text{Expected demand per unit time}) \\ &\quad \times \text{Prob}\,\{\text{a demand is not satisfied}\} \\ &= B_2 v D p_{x\geq}(S) \end{aligned}$$

Expected total relevant costs per unit time, as a function of S, are

$$\begin{aligned} \text{ETRC}(S) &= \bar{I}vr + C_s \\ &= vr \sum_{j=0}^{S} (S - j)p_x(j) + B_2 v D p_{x\geq}(S) \end{aligned}$$

A convenient method of solution is the use of indifference curves. These are obtained by equating ETRC(S) to ETRC($S + 1$) for a given value of S. In general, this gives, after simplication,

$$\frac{p_x(S)}{p_{x\leq}(S)} = \frac{r}{DB_2} \tag{8.35}$$

However, because $Q = 1$, we have that

$$s = S - 1$$

Therefore, Eq. 8.35 can be written as

$$\frac{p_x(s+1)}{p_{x\leq}(s+1)} = \frac{r}{DB_2}$$

Equation 8.2 follows by recognizing that the lead time demand (x) has a Poisson distribution with mean $\hat{x}_L$.

b. The Case of a B_1 Cost Penalty

We assume that the cost B_1 is incurred only if the demand in the lead time *exceeds* the reorder point s. The expected total relevant costs per unit time associated with using a reorder point s are

$$\text{ETRC}(s) = vr \sum_{x_0=0}^{s} (s - x_0)p_x(x_0) + \frac{D}{Q} B_1 p_{x>}(s)$$

Equating ETRC(s) = ETRC($s + 1$) for indifference between s and $s + 1$ leads to

$$\frac{p_x(s+1)}{p_{x\leq}(s)} = \frac{Qvr}{DB_1}$$

Again, Eq. 8.4 follows by recognizing that the lead time demand (x) has a Poisson distribution with mean $\hat{x}_L$.

3. SIMULTANEOUS SOLUTIONS FOR TWO CONTROL PARAMETERS

a. (s, Q) System with B_1 Cost Penalty

We let

$$s = \hat{x}_L + k\sigma_L$$

From Eq. 8.5 the expected total relevant costs per unit time under use of a safety factor k and an order quantity Q are given by

$$\text{ETRC}(k, Q) = AD/Q + (Q/2 + k\sigma_L)vr + \frac{DB_1}{Q} p_{u\geqslant}(k)$$

To reduce the number of separate parameters that have to be considered, we normalize by multiplying both sides by the constant term $2/vr\sigma_L$. We refer to the result as the normalized total relevant costs, NTRC(k, Q). Thus,

$$\text{NTRC}(k, Q) = \frac{2AD}{vrQ\sigma_L} + \frac{Q}{\sigma_L} + 2k + \frac{2AD}{vrQ\sigma_L}\frac{B_1}{A} p_{u\geqslant}(k)$$

Recall that

$$\text{EOQ} = \sqrt{\frac{2AD}{vr}}$$

Therefore,

$$\text{NTRC}(k, Q) = \left(\frac{\text{EOQ}}{\sigma_L}\right)^2 \frac{\sigma_L}{Q}\left[1 + \frac{B_1}{A} p_{u\geqslant}(k)\right] + \frac{Q}{\sigma_L} + 2k$$

A necessary condition (unless we are at a boundary) for the minimization of a function of two variables is that the partial derivative with respect to each variable be set to zero.

$$\frac{\partial \text{NTRC}(k, Q)}{\partial Q} = -\left(\frac{\text{EOQ}}{\sigma_L}\right)^2 \frac{\sigma_L}{Q^2}\left[1 + \frac{B_1}{A} p_{u\geqslant}(k)\right] + \frac{1}{\sigma_L} = 0$$

or

$$\frac{Q}{\sigma_L} = \frac{\text{EOQ}}{\sigma_L}\sqrt{\left[1 + \frac{B_1}{A} p_{u\geq}(k)\right]}$$

$$\frac{\partial \text{NTRC}(k, Q)}{\partial k} = 2 - \left(\frac{\text{EOQ}}{\sigma_L}\right)^2 \frac{\sigma_L}{Q} \frac{B_1}{A} f_u(k) = 0$$

or

$$f_u(k) = 2 \frac{A}{B_1} \frac{Q}{\sigma_L}\left(\frac{\sigma_L}{\text{EOQ}}\right)^2$$

that is,

$$\frac{1}{\sqrt{2\pi}} \exp\left(-k^2/2\right) = 2 \frac{A}{B_1} \frac{Q}{\sigma_L}\left(\frac{\sigma_L}{\text{EOQ}}\right)^2$$

This simplifies to Eq. 8.7.

Note: We have used the fact, proved in Appendix B, that

$$\frac{dp_{u\geq}(k)}{dk} = -\, f_u(k)$$

b. Absolute Cost Penalty (ACP) for Using Sequential Approach

From Eq. 8.8 we have that the *percentage* cost penalty (PCP) for using the sequential approach is

$$\text{PCP} = \frac{\begin{array}{c}[\text{ETRC (sequential parameter values)} \\ -\ \text{ETRC (simultaneous parameter values)}]\end{array}}{\text{ETRC (simultaneous parameter values)}} \times 100 \tag{8.36}$$

Now, the absolute cost penalty (ACP) is defined as

$$\begin{aligned}\text{ACP} = {} & \text{ETRC(sequential parameter values)} \\ & - \text{ETRC(simultaneous parameter values)}\end{aligned} \tag{8.37}$$

Therefore,

$$\begin{aligned}&\text{ETRC(simultaneous parameter values)} \\ &\quad = \text{ETRC(sequential parameter values)} - \text{ACP}\end{aligned} \tag{8.38}$$

Substitution of Eqs. 8.37 and 8.38 into Eq. 8.36 gives

$$\mathrm{PCP} = \frac{100(\mathrm{ACP})}{\mathrm{ETRC(sequential\ parameter\ values)} - \mathrm{ACP}}$$

This can be solved for ACP to give

$$\mathrm{ACP} = \frac{\mathrm{PCP}}{\mathrm{PCP} + 100} \cdot \mathrm{ETRC(sequential\ parameter\ values)}$$

PROBLEMS

8.1 Consider an (s, Q) system of control for a single item and with normally distributed forecast errors.

a. Find an expression that k must satisfy *given a Q value* if we wish to have an expected number of stockout occasions per year equal to N.

b. Derive the two simultaneous equations which Q and k must satisfy if we wish to minimize the total expected costs of replenishment and carrying inventory subject to the expected number of stockout occasions per year being N.

c. For the following example develop Q, k, and the associated total relevant costs per year for two strategies:

1. Q = EOQ and corresponding k.
2. Simultaneous best (Q, k) pair.

Item characteristics:

$A = \$5 \qquad v = \$2/\text{unit}$
$r = 0.16/\text{yr} \qquad D = 1000 \text{ units/yr}$
$\sigma_L = 80 \text{ units} \qquad N = 0.5/\text{yr}$

8.2 In an (s, Q) system it can be shown that the inventory position has a uniform distribution with probability $1/Q$ at each of the integers $s+1, s+2, \ldots, s+Q-1, s+Q$.

a. Using this result show, for Poisson demand and the B_2 shortage cost measure, that

$$\text{ETRC}(s) = vr \sum_{j=1}^{Q} \frac{1}{Q} \sum_{x_0=0}^{s+j} (s + j - x_0) p_{po}(x_0|\hat{x}_L) + B_2 vD \sum_{j=1}^{Q} \frac{1}{Q} \sum_{x_0=s+j}^{\infty} p_{po}(x_0|\hat{x}_L)$$

b. Show that indifference between s and $s+1$ exists when

$$\frac{\sum_{j=1}^{Q} p_{po}(s + j|\hat{x}_L)}{\sum_{j=1}^{Q} p_{po\leq}(s + j|\hat{x}_L)} = \frac{r}{DB_2}$$

(*Note:* $p_{po}(x_0|\hat{x}_L)$ is the p.m.f. of a Poisson variable with mean $\hat{x}_L$.)

8.3 Ceiling Drug is concerned about the inventory control of an important item. Currently they are using an (s, Q) system where Q is the EOQ and the safety factor k is selected based on a B_2v shortage costing method. Relevant parameter values are estimated to be:

$D = 2500 \text{ units/yr} \qquad B_2 = 0.6$
$v = \$10/\text{unit} \qquad \hat{x}_L = 500 \text{ units}$
$A = \$5 \qquad \sigma_L = 100 \text{ units}$
$r = 0.25/\text{yr}$

a. What are the Q and s values currently in use?

b. Determine the simultaneous best values of Q and s.

c. What is the percent penalty (in the total of replenishment, carrying, and shortage costs) of using the simpler sequential approach?

8.4 Consider a situation where the lowest allowable k value is 0. The B_1 shortage costing method is appropriate.

a. On a plot of k versus Q/σ_L sketch each of Eqs. 8.6 and 8.7. (Hint: For each evaluate $dk/d(Q/\sigma_L)$. Also look at the behavior of each for limiting values of k and Q/σ_L).

b. Attempt to ascertain under precisely what conditions there will be no simultaneous solution of the two equations.

c. Verify, using Eq. 8.5, that under such circumstances the cost-minimizing solution is to set $k = 0$ and

$$Q/\sigma_L = \text{EOQ}/\sigma_L\sqrt{1 + 0.5B_1/A}$$

8.5 In relation to an (s, Q) inventory control system an operations analyst has made the following observation:

Suppose we determine Q from the EOQ; then find the safety factor from the "fraction demand satisfied routinely from shelf" criterion. Suppose that through explicit cost considerations we estimate r to be a particular value r_1. Now if we deliberately set r at a lower value r_2 when determining Q and s, we can reduce actual total relevant costs.

a. Could the analyst be telling the truth? Attempt to develop an analytic proof.

b. Illustrate with an item having the following characteristics:

$Dv = \$4{,}000/\text{yr}$ $\quad \sigma_L v = \$500$
$A = \$100$ $\quad P_2 = 0.975$
$r_1 = 0.2/\text{yr}$

8.6 Company X has an A item which it controls by an (s, S) system. The item has only a few customers. According to the (s, S) policy, if a large order drives the inventory position to or below s, enough is ordered to raise the position to S. Discuss the implicit cost tradeoff that the company is making in still raising the position to S even after a large demand has just occurred.

8.7

a. Consider an item for which an (R, s, S) system is used. The review interval is 1 week. Other characteristics include

$L = 2$ weeks $\quad r = 0.26$ \$/\$/yr
$D = 800$ units/yr $\quad B_3 = 0.30$ \$/\$ short/week
$A = \$20$ $\quad \sigma_{R+L} = 14.2$ units
$v = \$1.50$/unit

Using the Revised Power Approximation, find the appropriate values of s and S. (Assume that there are exactly 52 weeks per year.)

b. Repeat for another item with the same characteristics except $v = \$150$/unit.

8.8 The Acme Company stocks an item where the demand (x) during the lead time has the following probability distribution:

$$\text{Prob}(x = 0) = 0.2$$

$f_x(x_0|x > 0)$ is normal with mean 40 units and standard deviation 8 units. In other words, nonzero demands are normally distributed.

a. If an (s, Q) system of control is used with $Q = 100$ units and the desired fraction of demand satisfied from shelf is 0.98, what value of s should be used?

b. What is the associated value of the safety stock?

8.9 An oil distribution depot supplies customers by road tanker. The depot itself is supplied by a unit[8] train with 24 cars, each with a capacity of 75 tons. At the depot three different products are stored in eight 1000 ton tanks. At present three tanks are used for product A, three tanks for product B, and two tanks for product C.

Analysis of demand records shows that the average weekly demand for product A is 600 tons with standard deviation 400 tons, average weekly demand for product B is 500 tons with standard deviation 300 tons, and average weekly demand for product C is 400 tons with standard deviation 200 tons. Any seasonal effects can be ignored.

The stock level of each product is reported by the depot to the refinery every Monday

[8]The word "unit" means that all 24 cars must go on each voyage of the train.

morning. The distribution office then has to decide whether to replenish the depot the following Friday and, if so, how many cars of the train should be filled with each product. The cost of operating the train is not reduced if any cars are empty and is approximately $3,000 per trip. If a product runs out at the depot, then the road tankers have to be diverted from that depot to another depot at considerably higher cost.

a. How does the limited capacity tankage at the depot affect the applicability of standard inventory control models?

b. Are there any other features of the problem that make standard inventory control models difficult to apply?

c. *Without doing any detailed numerical calculations*, indicate the type of inventory control guidelines that you could propose for the distribution office.

d. *Briefly* indicate what other (if any) types of data you would need. Also, what type of solution procedure (for finding precise values of control parameters within the general control guidelines of part c) do you think would be needed?

8.10 MIDAS Case D included a discussion on how the Inventory Control Manager placed orders for very expensive items. Comment on

a. "He tried to order only enough items to meet actual sales for the one-month period, one lead time period ahead," in particular the choice of a one-month period.

b. "To meet unexpected demand he usually ordered 10 to 20 percent more than the number of units he was able to identify through purchase orders or commitments."

REFERENCES

Adelson, R. M. (1966). "Compound Poisson Distributions." *Operational Research Quarterly*, Vol. 17, No. 1, pp. 73–75.

Archibald, B. (1976). "Continuous Review (*s*, *S*) Policies for Discrete, Compound Poisson, Demand Processes." Unpublished Ph.D. dissertation, Department of Management Sciences, University of Waterloo, Waterloo, Ontario, Canada.

Archibald, B., and E. A. Silver (1978). "(*s*, *S*) Policies under Continuous Review and Discrete Compound Poisson Demands." *Management Science*, Vol. 24, No. 9, pp. 899–909.

Archibald, B., E. A. Silver, and R. Peterson (1974). "Selecting the Probability Distribution of Demand in a Replenishment Lead Time." *Working Paper No. 89*, Department of Management Sciences, University of Waterloo, Waterloo, Ontario, Canada.

Ashkin, R. G. (1981). "A Procedure for Production Lot Sizing, with Probabilistic Dynamic Demand." *AIIE Transactions*, Vol. 13, No. 2, pp. 132–137.

Bartakke, M. N. (1981). "A Method of Spare Parts Inventory Planning." *OMEGA*, Vol. 9, No. 1, pp. 51–59.

Blazer, D. (1983a). "Operating Characteristics for an Inventory Model That Special Handles Extreme Value Demands." *Technical Report No. 21*, School of Business Administration and Curriculum in Operations Research and Systems Analysis, University of North Carolina at Chapel Hill, North Carolina.

Blazer, D. (1983b). "Implementation Strategy for an Inventory Filtering Rule." *Technical Report No. 25*, School of Business Administration and Curriculum in Operations Research and Systems Analysis, University of North Carolina at Chapel Hill, North Carolina.

Bookbinder, J. H., and J. Y. Tan (1983). "Strategies and a Heuristic for the Probabilistic Lot-Sizing Problem with Service-Level Constraints." *Working Paper*, Department of Management Sciences, University of Waterloo, Waterloo, Ontario, Canada.

Brown, R. G. (1977). *Materials Management Systems*. Wiley-Interscience, New York, pp. 217–221.

Brown, R. G. (1979). "Initial Provisioning of Service Parts." *Working Memorandum 145*, Materials Management Systems, Inc., Norwich, Vermont.

Buchan, J. and E. Koenigsberg. *Scientific Inventory Management*. Prentice-Hall, Englewood Cliffs, New Jersey, pp. 349–353.

Buckland, J. C. L. (1970). "A Nomogram for Stock Control." *Operational Research Quarterly*, Vol. 20, No. 4 pp. 445–450.

Burton, R., and S. Jaquette (1973). "The Initial Provisioning Decision for Insurance Type Items." *Naval Research Logistics Quarterly*, Vol. 20, No. 1, pp. 123–146.

Croston, J. D. (1974). "Stock Levels for Slow Moving Items." *Operational Research Quarterly*, Vol. 25, No. 1, pp. 123–130.

Das, C. (1978). "An Improved Formula for Inventory Decisions under Service and Safety Stock Constraints." *AIIE Transactions*, Vol. 10, No. 2, pp. 217–219.

Deemer, R., A. Kaplan, and W. K. Kruse (1974). "Application of Negative Binomial Probability to Inventory Control." *Technical Report TR 74-5*, USAMC Inventory Research Office, Frankford Arsenal, Philadelphia.

Drake, A. (1967). *Fundamentals of Applied Probability Theory*. McGraw-Hill, New York.

Ekanayake, R. B., J. M. Norman, E. Ritchie, P. H. Smith, B. R. Taylor, and P. Wilcox (1977). "Aspects of an Inventory Control Study." *European Journal of Operational Research*, Vol. 1, pp. 225–229.

Ehrhardt, R. (1979). "The Power Approximation for Computing (*s*, *S*) Inventory Policies." *Management Science*, Vol. 25, No. 8, pp. 777–786.

Federgruen, A., and P. Zipkin (1981). "An Efficient Algorithm for Computing Optimal (*s*, *S*) Policies." *Research Working Paper No. 458A*, Graduate School of Business, Columbia University, New York.

Feeney, G. J., and C. C. Sherbrooke (1966). "The ($S - 1$, *S*) Inventory Policy under Compound Poisson Demand." *Management Science*, Vol. 12, No. 5, pp. 391–411.

Freeland, J. R., and E. L. Porteus (1980). "Evaluating the Effectiveness of a New Method for Computing Approximately Optimal (*s*, *S*) Inventory Policies." *Operations Research*, Vol. 28, No. 2, pp. 353–363.

Gross, D., and J. Ince (1975). "A Comparison and Evaluation of Approximate Continuous Review Inventory Models." *International Journal of Production Research*, Vol. 13, No. 1, pp. 9–23.

Hadley, G., and T. Whitin (1963). *Analysis of Inventory Systems*. Prentice-Hall, Englewood Cliffs, New Jersey.

Haight, F. A. (1967). *Handbook of the Poisson Distribution*. John Wiley & Sons, New York.

Herron, D. P. (1967). "Inventory Management for Minimum Cost." *Management Science*, Vol. 14, No. 4, pp. B219–B235.

Herron, D. P. (1978). "A Comparison of Techniques for Multi-Item Inventory Analysis." *Production and Inventory Management*, Vol. 19, No. 1, pp. 103–115.

Hollier, R. (1980). "The Distribution of Spare Parts." *International Journal of Production Research*, Vol. 18, No. 6, pp. 665–675.

Karlin, S. (1958). "The Application of Renewal Theory to the Study of Inventory Policies." In *Studies in the Mathematical Theory of Inventory and Production* (K. Arrow, S. Karlin and H. Scarf, Editors), Stanford University Press, Stanford, California, Chapter 15.

Karush, W. (1957). "A Queueing Model for an Inventory Problem." *Operations Research*, Vol. 5, No. 5, pp. 693–703.

Kaufman, R. (1977). "(*s*, *S*) Inventory Policies in a Nonstationary Demand Environment." *Technical Report No. 11*, School of Business Administration and Curriculum in Operations Research and Systems Analysis, University of North Carolina at Chapel Hill, North Carolina.

Krupp, J. (1982). "Effective Safety Stock Planning." *Production and Inventory Management*, Vol. 23, No. 3, pp. 35–46.

Lampkin, W. (1967). "A Review of Inventory Control Theory." *The Production Engineer*, Vol. 46, No. 2, pp. 57–66.

Mayer, R. R. (1965). "The Interrelationship between Lot Sizes and Safety Stocks in Inventory Control." *Journal of Industrial Engineering*, Vol. XVI, No. 4, pp. 268–274.

Melese, M., Barache, Comes, Elina, and Hestaux (1960). "La Gestion des Stocks de Pieces de Rechange dans la Siderurgie" ("Inventory Control of Spare Parts in the French Steel Industry"). *Proceedings of the Second International Conference on Operational Research*, English Universities Press, pp. 309–323.

Mitchell, C. R., R. A. Rappold, and W. B. Faulkner (1983). "An Analysis of Air Force EOQ Data with an Application to Reorder Point Calculation." *Management Science*, Vol. 29, No. 4, pp. 440–446.

Mitchell, G. H. (1962). "Problems of Controlling Slow-Moving Engineering Spares." *Operational Research Quarterly*, Vol. 13, No. 1, pp. 23–39.

Mosier, C. (1981). "Revised (*s*, *S*) Power Approximation." *Technical Report No. 18*, School of Business Administration and Curriculum in Operations Research and Systems Analysis, University of North Carolina at Chapel Hill, North Carolina.

Naddor, E. (1975). "Optimal and Heuristic Decisions in Single- and Multi-Item Inventory Systems." *Management Science*, Vol. 21, No. 11, pp. 1234–1249.

Nemhauser, G. (1966). "A Note on Lot Sizes and Safety Stock Level." *Journal of Industrial Engineering*, Vol. XVII, No. 7, pp. 389–390.

Psoinos, D. (1974). "On the Joint Calculation of Safety Stocks and Replenishment Order Quantities." *Operational Research Quarterly*, Vol. 25, No. 1, pp. 173–177.

Roberts, D. (1962). "Approximations to Optimal Policies in a Dynamic Inventory Model." In *Studies in Applied Probability and Management Science* (K. Arrow, S. Karlin, and H. Scarf, Editors), Stanford University Press, Stanford, California, pp. 207–229.

Schneider, H. (1978). "Methods for Determining the Re-order Point of an (*s*, *S*) Ordering Policy When a Service Level Is Specified." *Journal of the Operational Research Society*, Vol. 29, No. 12, pp 1181–1193.

Schneider, H. (1981). "Effect of Service-Levels on Order-Points or Order-Levels in Inventory Models." *International Journal of Production Research*, Vol. 19, No. 6, pp. 615–631.

Silver, E. A. (1978). "Inventory Control under a Probabilistic, Time-Varying Demand Pattern." *AIIE Transactions*, Vol. 10, No. 4, pp. 371–379.

Silver, E. A., and T. G. Wilson (1972). "Cost Penalties of Simplified Procedures for Selecting Reorder Points and Order Quantities." *Proceedings of the Fifteenth Annual International Conference of the American Production and Inventory Control Society*, pp. 219–234.

Simpson, V. (1976). "A Noniterative Approximation to the Optimal EOQ with Service and Nonnegative Safety Stock Constraints." *AIIE Transactions*, Vol. 8, No. 1, pp. 155–157.

Snyder, R. (1974). "Computation of (*S*, *s*) Ordering Policy Parameters." *Management Science*, Vol. 21, No. 2, pp. 223–229.

Tijms, H. C. (1983). "On the Numerical Calculation of the Reorder Point in (*s*, *S*) Inventory Systems with Gamma Distributed Lead Time Demand." *Research Report No. 95*, Department of Actuarial Sciences and Econometrics, Vrije Universiteit, Amsterdam.

Tijms, H. C., and H. Groenevelt (1982). "Simple Approximations for the Reorder Point in Periodic and Continuous Review (*s*, *S*) Inventory Systems with Service Level Constraints." *Research Report No. 92*, Department of Actuarial Sciences and Econometrics, Vrije Universiteit, Amsterdam.

Vazsonyi, A. (1960). "Comments on a Paper by Karush." *Operations Research*, Vol. 8, No. 3, pp. 418–420.

Wagner, H. M., M. O'Hagan, and B. Lundh (1965). "An Empirical Study of Exactly and Approximately Optimal Inventory Policies." *Management Science*, Vol. 11, No. 7, pp. 690–723.

Ward, J. B. (1978). "Determining Reorder Points when Demand Is Lumpy." *Management Science*, Vol. 24, No.6, pp. 623–632.

Williams, T. M. (1982). "Reorder Levels for Lumpy Demand." *Journal of the Operational Research Society*, Vol. 33, No. 2, pp. 185–189.

CHAPTER 9

Decision Systems for Managing Routine (Class C) Inventories

The C category or so-called "cats and dogs" usually represents an appreciable percentage of the total number of distinct s.k.u., but a very small fraction of the total dollar investment in the inventory of a typical company. Each such item taken singly is relatively unimportant, but, because of their large numbers, appropriate simple control procedures must be utilized. In this chapter we discuss such methods. Section 9.1 spells out in greater detail the nature of C items and the primary objectives in designing methods for controlling them. In Section 9.2 we propose control procedures for C items having relatively steady demand. Specifically, we consider, in order, the type of inventory records to use, the selection of the reorder quantity (or reorder interval), and the choice of the reorder point (or order-up-to-level). Next, in Section 9.3 we treat the case of items with significantly declining usage patterns, that is, approaching the termination of usage. Section 9.4 is concerned with the important issue of removing totally (or relatively) inactive items from the organization's inventory. Finally, in Section 9.5 we address the related question of whether demands for a particular item should be purchased (made) to order or met from stock.

9.1 THE NATURE OF C ITEMS

The categorization of items for control purposes was first discussed in Chapter 3. To refresh the reader's memory we repeat some of the important points here.

The primary factor which indicates that an item should be placed in the C category is a low dollar usage (Dv value). The exact cut-off value between the B and C categories should be selected so that somewhere on the order of 30 to 50 percent of all the items are classified in the C category. (For the MIDAS Professional Products Division a cut-off value of \$240/yr was selected, resulting in a somewhat low 26.1 percent of all the items being in the C category.) A low Dv value alone is not sufficient to dictate that an item should be placed in the C category. The real requirement is that the annual total of replenishment, carrying, and shortage costs be quite low under any reasonable control strategy. Normally, Dv is a useful surrogate for this total. However, a low-dollar-usage item may have potentially severe shortage penalties associated with it. Some typical examples come to mind:

1. A slow-moving product that rounds out a service line provided to an important customer—shortages on this item can cause severe reductions in the usage of several faster-moving items.
2. A product that is the "pride and joy" of the president because he was instrumental in its development—here there is a high "implicit" cost associated with a shortage.
3. The authors vividly remember the case of an electronics manufacturer whose limited manufacturing area was clogged with five expensive pieces of custom-made equipment, each the size of two large refrigerators, because the company had once again run out of the plastic control knobs worth 7 cents each.

For a true C type item the low total of replenishment, carrying, and shortage costs implies that, regardless of the type of control system used, we cannot achieve a sizable *absolute* savings in these costs. Therefore, the guiding principle should be to use simple procedures that keep the control costs per s.k.u. quite low; that is, we wish to keep the labor and paperwork per item to a minimum. Equipment that permits electronic capture of data at the point of sale clearly reduces control costs. However, it is our opinion that some organizations are overusing this capability.

9.2 CONTROL OF C ITEMS HAVING STEADY DEMAND

Here we deal with items having a relatively low importance but where the demand rate is not changing appreciably with time. Moreover, we assume that it makes sense to actually stock the C items under consideration. In Section 9.5 we address the more fundamental question of stocking an item versus making or buying it to each customer order.

9.2.1 Inventory Records

As a consequence of the primary objective mentioned above, in most cases it may be most appropriate to not maintain any inventory record of a C item, but instead simply rely on an administrative mechanism for reordering such as placing an order when the last box in a bin is opened. If an inventory record is maintained, it should certainly not require the recording of each transaction (except for the possible use of electronic point-of-sale data capture); instead, a rather long review interval, such as six months, should be considered. Of course, for demand estimation and order control purposes a record should be kept of the dates of placement and receipt of replenishment orders.

Stated another way, we are saying that there are two choices in relation to the selection of a review interval for a C item:

1. Periodic review with a relatively long interval.
2. Continuous review but with a mechanism for triggering orders that requires neither a physical stock count nor the updating (in a ledger) of the stock status—an example is a two-bin system of control.

9.2.2 Selecting the Reorder Quantity (or Reorder Interval)

Stated bluntly, the frills of the economic order quantity, Silver-Meal heuristic, and so on, are completely unwarranted for Class C items. Instead, one should make use of a simple offshoot of the basic EOQ developed in Chapter 5, namely, that one of at most a few possible time supplies should be assigned to each class C item. The time supply to use should be based as much on shelf life and obsolescence considerations as on the setup, unit cost, and carrying charge factors. It is usually reasonable to use a single value of the ratio A/r for all C items (one convenient way of estimating this value is through the exchange curve notions of Chapter 5). To illustrate, consider the MIDAS situation. The value of r was found to be 0.24/year and a reasonable average value of A is \$3.20. Furthermore, for C items management has decided that only three possible time supplies—namely, 6, 12, and 18 months—are worth considering. Using the approach suggested in Section 5.4.2 of Chapter 5, we develop the particularly simple decision rule shown in Table 9.1. D would not be estimated through a forecasting system but rather through knowledge of the starting and ending inventories over a convenient time period. For example, one could proceed as follows in a two-bin (s,Q) system. Consider two consecutive orders A and B. Let A be *received* at time t_A and B be *placed* at time t_B. Let I_A be the inventory level just *before* A is received (a typically low level, hence easy to count). Then we have

TABLE 9.1 Suggested Reorder Time Supplies for MIDAS C Items with Steady Demand

For Annual Dollar Movement (Dv) in This Range (\$/yr)	Use This Number of Months of Supply
$53 \leq Dv$	6
$18 \leq Dv < 53$	12
$Dv < 18$	18

$$\text{Demand rate} \simeq \frac{I_A + Q - s}{t_B - t_A} \tag{9.1}$$

Of course, if pilferage losses are significant, an overly high estimate of the demand rate would result. Needless to say, rather than taking account of these losses, the preferable approach is to reduce the losses themselves.

9.2.3 Selecting the Reorder Point (or Order-up-to-Level)

One could choose any of the criteria, discussed in Chapter 7, for selecting the safety factor. However, we advocate the use of a specific criterion—namely, "selecting the safety factor to provide a specified expected time, TBS, between stockout occasions," which we have found to be particularly appealing to management in most C item contexts. This appears to be a method of expressing their risk aversion with which they feel comfortable. Thinking in terms of an average time between stockouts is apparently more straightforward than dealing with probabilities or fractions. Quite often many C items are involved in a single customer order. Therefore, to assure a reasonable chance of satisfying the complete customer order, a very high level of service must be used for each C item. Therefore, large values of TBS (for example, 5 years to 100 years) are not unreasonable when one recognizes the small added expense of carrying a high safety stock. The decision rule for the TBS criterion (see Section 7.6.10 of Chapter 7) is to select the safety factor k to satisfy[1]

$$p_{u\geq}(k) = \frac{Q}{D(\text{TBS})} \tag{9.2}$$

where

$p_{u\geq}(k)$ = Prob {Unit normal variable (mean 0, standard deviation 1) takes on a value of k or larger}

is a widely tabulated function (see Table B.1 in Appendix B). Then we set the reorder point[2]

$$s = \hat{x}_L + k\sigma_L \tag{9.3}$$

[1]In Eq. 9.2 a negative k results if $Q/D(\text{TBS}) > 0.5$. This is very unlikely to occur if TBS is large, as suggested earlier. In any event management should specify a minimum allowable value of k.

[2]If a periodic review, order-up-to-level (R, S) system is to be used, then throughout this section the decision rules should be modified as follows:

1. Replace L by $R + L$
2. Repace Q/D by R
3. Replace s by S

where[3]

$$\hat{x}_L = DL \tag{9.4}$$

is the expected demand (in units) in the replenishment lead time of length L (years), and σ_L is the estimate of the standard deviation (in units) of forecast errors over L (we return shortly to a discussion of how σ_L is estimated).

Now at this stage the alert reader surely must be wondering, "Who needs all this aggravation, especially for C items?" Such a viewpoint is indeed correct. Equation 9.2 holds for general values of Q/D and TBS. In the context of any company only a few values of each of these two parameters would be specified. For these few combinations, the equations could be used once-and-for-all to develop a simple table. We illustrate this for the MIDAS case in Table 9.2 using the earlier selected Q/D values of 6, 12, and 18 months and also management-specified values of 10, 20, and 50 years for TBS.

Once k is selected, then the reorder point follows from Eq. 9.3. However, for this purpose an estimate of σ_L is required. One point is certain: σ_L should *not* be developed from observing forecast errors of the specific C item under consideration. Instead, we suggest the use of either of the following methods of developing an estimate of σ_L:

1. Use an aggregate relationship of the form[4]

$$\sigma_L = c_1(D/12)^{c_2}L^c \tag{9.5}$$

where L is expressed in months and D is in units/year.

TABLE 9.2 Table to Select Safety Factor, k, for MIDAS Situation

TBS Value (years)	Order Quantity Expressed as a Time Supply in Months ($12Q/D$)		
	6	12	18
10	1.64	1.23	1.04
20	1.96	1.64	1.44
50	2.33	2.05	1.88

[3]Note: $\hat{x}_L$ is not an output of the forecast system (as mentioned earlier, we are advocating not forecasting C items). D is estimated as discussed in the preceding subsection.

[4]As discussed in Chapter 4, c_1,c_2, and c are parameters estimated from a sample of items from the population under consideration; in the case of MIDAS their values were found to be:

$c_1 = 1.3 \qquad c_2 = 0.65 \qquad c = 0.5$

2. Assume that the lead time demand of a C item is approximately Poisson distributed. For such a distribution (see the Appendix of Chapter 8) we have the simple relation

$$\sigma_L = \sqrt{\hat{x}_L} = \sqrt{DL} \tag{9.6}$$

Numerical Illustration

Consider item XSC-037, a slow-moving X-ray developing chemical, with $D = 48$ units/year, $L = 2$ months, an order quantity time supply of 12 months, and a specified TBS of 20 years.

$$\hat{x}_L = DL = 48 \text{ units/year} \times 1/6 \text{ year} = 8 \text{ units}$$

From Table 9.2 we read that the safety factor k should be set at 1.64. Suppose we make the Poisson assumption. Then Eq. 9.6 gives

$$\sigma_L \simeq \sqrt{8} = 2.83 \text{ units}$$

From Eq. 9.3 we have that the reorder point is

$$s = 8 + 1.64(2.83) = 12.6, \text{ say } 13 \text{ units}$$

9.2.4 The Two-Bin System Revisited

In Section 7.3 of Chapter 7 we described a particularly simple physical form of an (s, Q) system—namely, what is called a two-bin system. To review, in a two-bin system the on-hand inventory is segregated into two distinct sections (generically called bins). The capacity of one of the bins (called the reserve bin) is set equal to the reorder point. Demands are satisfied from the other bin until its stock is depleted. When it becomes necessary to open the reserve bin this is a signal to place a replenishment order. When the order arrives the reserve bin is refilled and sealed. The remainder of the order is placed in the other bin.

The authors have seen some rather clever forms of the bins concept. Examples include:

1. The use of "baggies" in the case of small electronic components.
2. Color coding of the end of an appropriate bar in steel stacked in a distribution warehouse.

To facilitate proper initiation of an order a bin reserve tag should be attached to the reserve bin such that when the latter is opened the clerk now has the tag which serves as a reminder to report the opening of the bin. In fact, in many cases, the tag itself can be used as an order form. At the very least, dates and order quantities can be recorded on it (permitting an estimate of D when it is needed).

Obviously, for satisfactory performance of such a system it is imperative that a tag be promptly submitted to purchasing (or production scheduling) whenever a reserve bin is opened. Supervisors, assemblers, sales personnel and others must be motivated to follow this procedure while they meet their own objectives in the rush of daily activities.

9.2.5 A Simple Form of the (R, S) System

Smith (1978) reports that the J. C. Penney organization developed a simple form of the (R, S) system, known as the Semiautomatic Stock Control System, that is particularly effective for control of C (as well as B) items in a retail environment. Here is how it operates for any particular item, illustrated for a weekly review interval and a lead time less than R.

Periodically (likely less often than every review period, for example, each quarter-year) management specifies a desired value of S and at *only* that time the on-hand stock is counted and an order is placed to raise the inventory position to S (that is, the on-hand plus the order quantity must equal S). Then, at each regular review instant (here each week), the computer simply orders enough to replace sales since the last review; that is, the only record that must be maintained is the total sales in the current review interval. Problem 9.3 deals with how a desired increase or decrease in S would be implemented.

Numerical Illustration

Consider an item where the desired value of S is 35 units and a physical stock count reveals that the on-hand is 26 units (with nothing on order). Then an order for 9 units would be placed. Suppose that the sales prior to the next review (ordering time) were 12 units. As a result, the next order would simply be for 12 units.

9.2.6 Grouping of Items

In some cases it may be advantageous to group C items for control purposes. In particular, if a group of items (including some from the A and B categories) are provided by the same supplier, or produced in-house on the same equipment, then coordinated control (to be discussed in Chapter 11) may very well be in order to reduce replenishment costs; that is, when one item in the group needs reordering, several others should likely be included in the order. This is particularly appealing for a C item; by including it in an order initiated by another item, we avoid incurring a full setup cost (A) for the replenishment of the C item.

Coordination does not rule out the use of a two-bin system of control for the individual C item. Instead, reserve tags of opened reserve bins are held centrally between designated periodic times at which the group under consideration is ordered. Of course, the reserve stock must be appropriately scaled up to provide protection over a length of time equal to the sum of the periodic ordering interval plus the replenishment lead time.

9.3 CONTROL OF ITEMS WITH DECLINING DEMAND PATTERNS

Here we are dealing with items nearing the end of their usage lifetimes (the end of the Product Life Cycle that was discussed in Section 2.3 of Chapter 2). In effect, the ideas are applicable beyond just C items. In particular, high-unit-value service parts (that is, B and A items) eventually enter a period of declining requirements in that the parent population is ultimately phased out.

9.3.1 Establishing the Timing and Sizes of Replenishments under Deterministic Demand

Brosseau (1982) has studied the special, but important, case where the demand rate is dropping *linearly* with time. The optimal strategy turns out to be a function of only a single parameter

$$M = \frac{Ab^2}{vra^3} \tag{9.7}$$

where

$$x_t = a - bt \tag{9.8}$$

is the demand pattern and the other parameters are as defined earlier. Note that M gets larger as a/b decreases—that is, as we get closer to the end of the demand pattern.

Brosseau, as a function of M, ascertains

1. How many replenishments to make.
2. The timing of the replenishments (as fractions of the horizon a/b).

These results are shown in the form of a simple table. However, more important, he shows that a very simple procedure, based again on the EOQ, produces negligible cost penalties. Specifically, one uses the basic EOQ, based on the *current* demand rate and expressed as a time supply, as long as $M < 0.075$, and a single last replenishment equal to the total remaining requirements ($a^2/2b$) when $M \geq 0.075$. The cutoff value of 0.075 turns out to be approximately the value of M where we are indifferent between 1 and 2 replenishments *in the optimal solution.*

Smith (1977) and Brown (1977) have found similar results for other types of declining demand patterns (including a continuous analogue of the geometric pattern described in Section 4.9.4 of Chapter 4)—namely, that use of the EOQ, until it implies an order quantity almost as large as the total remaining requirements, produces excellent results. We operationalize these results by suggesting the use of the EOQ as long as the total remaining requirements are at least 1.3 EOQ. If not, simply use one last replenishment to cover the remaining requirements. One can show that the 1.3 factor is equivalent to Brosseau's cutoff M value for the case of linearly decreasing demand.

9.3.2 The Sizing of the Final Replenishment under Probabilistic Demand

When demand is declining, but probabilistic in nature, the choice of the size of one last replenishment involves a tradeoff between (1) the costs of insufficient inventory (reordering, expediting, shortages, etc.) if the total remaining demand exceeds the inventory position after the order is placed, and (2) the costs of overacquisition if the total remaining demand is less than the inventory position. Again, the first category of costs is typically very difficult to establish, so management may resort to the use of a desired service level, which, in turn, is likely to be largely dictated by industry norms (for example, meeting 95 percent of all requests for spare parts during a 10-year period after the last sale of a new unit). We present a decision rule based on satisfying a certain fraction of the remaining demand. The derivation is outlined in Section 1 of the Appendix of this chapter. Fortuin (1980) has treated other service measures.

Decision Rule

Select the order-up-to-level[5] S where

$$S = \hat{y} + k\sigma_y \tag{9.9}$$

with $\hat{y}$ being the forecasted total remaining demand,[6] σ_y the standard deviation of the total remaining demand (one way to estimate σ_y would be by using the procedure of Brown, 1981, referenced in Section 4.9.4 of Chapter 4), and the safety factor k satisfying

---

[5] S = (Current inventory position) + (Order quantity).

[6] For the deterministic linear model of Eq. 9.8,

$$\hat{y} = \frac{a^2}{2b} \tag{9.10}$$

For the geometrically decaying pattern of Eq. 4.82 of Chapter 4, namely

$$x_t = f^t x_0 = f^t a$$

we have, from Eq. 4.84 of Chapter 4,

$$\hat{y} = \frac{fa}{1 - f} \tag{9.11}$$

$$G_u(k) = \frac{\hat{y}(1 - P_2)}{\sigma_y} \tag{9.12}$$

where $G_u(k)$ is again the special function of the unit normal distribution tabulated in Table B.1 of Appendix B.

Numerical Illustration

An automotive manufacturer is concerned with the size of the last replenishment of a spare part for a particular make of automobile that was discontinued some 3 years back. A fit to recent historical monthly usage indicates that a geometrically decaying pattern is appropriate with

$$\hat{y} = 83.1 \text{ units}$$

$$\sigma_y = 16.8 \text{ units}$$

Suppose that it is management's decision to select an S value for the last replenishment so that 95 percent of the remaining demand for the spare part will be met by S. (This does not mean that the other 5 percent would be lost; instead, cost-incurring actions, such as parts conversion, may be taken to satisfy the remaining demand.)

By using Eq. 9.12, we obtain

$$G_u(k) = \frac{83.1}{16.8}(1 - 0.95) = 0.2473$$

Then, from Table B.1 of Appendix B,

$$k \simeq 0.35$$

Hence, from Eq. 9.9

$$S = 83.1 + 0.35\,(16.8)$$

$$\simeq 89 \text{ units}$$

9.4 REDUCING EXCESS INVENTORIES

When a study of the inventory control situation of a company is undertaken it is not uncommon to find a significant percentage of the stocked items that have had absolutely no sales (or internal usage) in the last one or more years of time. Dyer (1973b) reports that for the distribution industry the percentage of stocked items that have had no usage in the previous 52 weeks has been found to lie anywhere from 16 to 47 percent. We refer to these s.k.u. as dead items.

Of course, any remaining stock of a dead item is, by definition, excess stock. In addition, there are often many slow-moving items where stock levels are excessive. The reasons for excess inventories can be grouped into two categories. First are errors associated with replenishments, that is, having purchased or produced too much of an item. These include production overruns, unjustified quantity purchases, errors in the transmission of an order request (for example, 1000 units instead of a desired 100 units), and inaccurate inventory records (for example, location errors, "hording" of parts, etc.). The second class of reasons relates to overestimating the demand rate. Included in here are inaccurate forecasts, deliberate changes in sales/marketing efforts, technological obsolescence (such as through an engineering change), and customer cancellations.

Whatever the cause(s) of excess stocks, it is important to be able to (1) identify the associated items and (2) decide on what remedial action(s) to take. Of course, ideally one would like to be able to anticipate the drop in usage of an item and take appropriate action(s) to avoid being caught with a large surplus stock. It should be noted that this general problem area is likely to increase in importance as the rate of technological change increases, causing the life cycle of the typical product to shorten.

9.4.1 Review of the Distribution by Value

Again, we make use of a simple, but powerful, tool of analysis—the Distribution by Value (DBV) list. Recall from an earlier discussion (see Table 1.4 in Chapter 1) that the DBV is a listing of items in decreasing order of annual dollar usage (Dv value). At the bottom of the table listing will be all of the items that had no sales (or internal usage) over the period from which D was estimated (normally the most recent full year). Furthermore, moving up the table, we immediately encounter the items that have had very low usage.

To establish the DBV, values of D_i and v_i are required for each item i. If, at the same time, a reading on the inventory level I_i of item i can be obtained, then a very useful additional table can be developed as follows.

For each item the expected time at which the current stock level will be depleted, also called the "coverage," is computed by the formula,

$$CO = \frac{12I}{D} \tag{9.13}$$

where

CO = coverage, in months

I = on-hand inventory, in units

D = expected usage rate, in units/year

The items are then shown in a table (see Table 9.3) in decreasing order of coverage. Also shown is the inventory (in dollars) of each item and the cumula-

TABLE 9.3 Items Listed by Coverage

Rank Order	Cumulative Percent of Items	Item Identification	I (units)	D (units/ year)	v (\$/unit)	CO (months)	Iv (\$)	Cumulative Inventory In Dollars	Cumulative Inventory As Percent of Total
1	0.5	—	150	0	1.80	Infinite	270	270	3.4[a]
2	1.0	—	60	0	0.50	Infinite	30	300	3.8
3	1.5	—	10	0	1.10	Infinite	11	311	4.0
4	2.0	—	5	0	3.20	Infinite	16	327	4.2
5	2.5	—	53	2	1.00	318	53	380	4.8
6	3.0	—	40	3	0.90	160	36	416	5.3
7	3.5	—	64	12	2.00	64	128	544	6.9
8	4.0	—	180	37	0.35	58.4	63	607	7.7
.	.	.	.	.	.	.	.	.	.
.	.	.	.	.	.	.	.	.	.
.	.	.	.	.	.	.	.	.	.
								7,861	100.0
199	99.5	—	2	1,000	1.00	0.024	2.00	7,863	100.0
200	100.0	—	0	463	0.20	0	0	7,863	100.0

[a]3.4 = (270/7,863) × 100.

tive percentage of the total inventory as one proceeds down the table. In Table 9.3 (involving a population of 200 items with a total inventory valued at \$7,863), it is seen that 4.2 percent of the total inventory is tied up in stock of zero-movers and some 6.9 percent is included in items having a coverage of 5 years (60 months) or more. Such information would be of use to management in deciding on the seriousness of the overstock situation and on what remedial course(s) of action to take.

Individual item usage values (D_i's) are needed to construct the Distribution by Value table. Where these are not readily available a practical alternative is to simply tour the storage facilities applying a so-called *dust test:* any stock that looks overly dusty (or its equivalent) is a candidate for identification as a dead or very slow-moving item.

9.4.2 A Rule for the Disposal Decision

By disposing of some stock, we now achieve benefits of salvage revenue (possibly negative) and reduced inventory carrying costs. On the other hand, we will have to replenish at an earlier time compared to if no stock disposal was made. With regard to inventory carrying costs one should recognize that often the most costly aspect of excess inventory is that it is taking up significant space in a storage area of limited capacity. In addition, there is often a nuisance cost associated with stock that has physically deteriorated. Examples include the presence of rats and vermin, excessive rusting, and so forth. The authors recall the case of manufactured, large, metal piping that was stored in an open yard.

One particular item, left standing for a number of years, had slowly sunk into the mud with each spring thaw until it stabilized in a semisubmerged state. Excavation equipment, with associated high-usage cost, was required to remove the dead stock in order to free up the space that it was occupying.

The derivation, presented in Section 2 of the Appendix of this chapter, is based on a deterministic level demand pattern. Alternative decision rules could be developed (1) for a declining, but still deterministic, demand pattern or (2) for probabilistic demand; the latter case closely parallels the selection of S for the terminal replenishment (see Section 9.3.2).

Let W be the amount of stock to dispose. Then W is given by

$$W = I - \text{EOQ} - \frac{D(v-g)}{vr} \tag{9.14}$$

where I is the current inventory level of the item

$$\text{EOQ} = \sqrt{\frac{2AD}{vr}}$$

as earlier, and g is the unit salvage value (g can be negative if there is a net cost per unit associated with disposing of stock). Note that when $v = g$, that is, the salvage value is equal to the full unit variable cost, Eq. 9.14 says that $I - W$ (which is the amount to leave in stock) is equal to the EOQ; that is, when we get our full money back, it is best to put the stock into the same situation as just *after* the receipt of an EOQ.

Numerical Illustration

The manager of the hardware division of a retail outlet has discovered that the stock level of a particular item is 1200 units, not 200 units as he had expected. Thus, he feels that some of the stock should be disposed of by means of a sale at 2/3 of unit cost (that is, $g = (2/3)v$). He estimates the following values for other characteristics of the item:

$D = 400$ units/yr

$A = \$20$

$v = \$3.00$/unit

$r = 0.25$ \$/\$/yr

Equation 9.14 implies that the disposal amount should be

$$\begin{aligned} W &= 1200 - \sqrt{\frac{2(20)(400)}{(3.00)(0.25)}} - \frac{400(3.00 - 2.00)}{(3.00)(0.25)} \\ &= 521 \text{ units} \end{aligned}$$

9.4.3 Options for Disposing of Excess Stock

Possible courses of action for disposing of excess stock include the following.

1. *Returns to suppliers at a unit value likely lower than the initial acquisition cost.* A good example is that of a college bookstore returning extra copies of a book to the publishing company's distributor.

2. *Shipment of the material to another location.* Where an item is stocked at more than one location it may have negligible demand at one location but still experience a significant demand elsewhere. The transfer of stock not only frees up space at the "first" location, but it also helps avoid the costly setup (or acquisition) costs associated with satisfying the likely infrequent demands at the other location(s).

3. *Mark-downs or special sales.* The unit price is reduced sufficiently to generate appreciable demand for the product; an example would be the reduced price of wrapping paper or decorations immediately following the Christmas season.

4. *Use for other purposes.* For example, in the case of components or raw materials, consider their use, possibly requiring some rework, in different final products.

5. *Use of stock for promotional purposes.* Excess stock may be converted to a revenue generator by providing free samples of it when customers purchase other products; for example, an appliance store with an overstock situation of an inexpensive table lamp might offer it free as a bonus to each customer buying a color television set. The extreme case of this action is donation of the stock to some charitable cause.

6. *Auctions.* These should not be overlooked as a possible means of salvaging some value from excess stock.

7. *Disposal for scrap value.* The best course of action may be to sell the material directly to a scrapdealer, a common transaction when there is a significant metallic component of the item.

Whatever the course of action that is selected, the excess stock will not disappear overnight. Therefore, it is important to lay out an approximate timetable for disposal and to ensure subsequently that appropriate followup effort is provided.

9.5 STOCKING VERSUS NOT STOCKING AN ITEM

Many items with extremely low sales may be minor variations of faster moving products. In such a case, it can be attractive to eliminate the slow-moving special versions. Of course, decisions of this type, as well as those where there is no substitute product, go beyond the area of production planning and inventory management. Marketing considerations, including customer relations (for example, the slow-mover may be carried as a service item for an important customer), are obviously relevant. Furthermore, the appropriate course of action may not be to discontinue selling the item, but rather to make or buy it to order as opposed to stocking it, an issue addressed in the following material.

Given that we have decided to satisfy customer demands for a given s.k.u. the question we now face is: *Should we make a special purchase from the supplier (or production run) to satisfy each individual customer-demand transaction or should we purchase (or produce) to stock?* It should be emphasized that this question is not just restricted to C items. As we will see, a low demand rate tends to favor nonstocking, but there are a number of other factors that also influence the decision.

Earlier in the book we have seen that, *given that an item is stocked*, its total relevant costs per year are quite insensitive to the precise settings of the control variables (for example, the reorder point and the order quantity). Interestingly enough, more substantial savings can often be achieved through the appropriate answer to the question of whether or not the item should even be stocked.

9.5.1 The Relevant Factors

For simplicity, we talk in terms of a purchased item; the concepts are readily adaptable to the in-house production context. There are a number of factors that can influence the decision to stock or not stock the item. These include:

1. The system cost (file maintenance, forecasting, etc.) per unit time of stocking an item.
2. The unit variable cost of the item both when it is bought for stock and when it is purchased to meet each demand transaction: a more favorable price may be achieved by the regular larger buys associated with stocking. In addition, a premium per unit may be necessary if the nonstocking purchases are made from a competitor.
3. The cost of a temporary backorder associated with each demand in the nonstocking situation.
4. The fixed setup cost associated with each repenishment in both contexts. An account should be taken of possible coordination with other items, in that setup costs are reduced by such coordination.
5. The carrying charge (including the effects of obsolescence) which, together with the unit variable cost, determines the cost of carrying each unit of inventory per unit time.
6. The frequency and magnitudes of demand transactions.
7. The replenishment lead time.

9.5.2 A Simple Decision Rule

A general model to handle all of the above factors would be, because of its complexity, of limited value to the typical practitioner. Therefore, in this subsection we present a simple rule (based on work by Popp, 1965), valid under specific assumptions. Even when these assumptions are violated the rule should still be useful as a guideline. In any event, in the next subsection some extensions will be discussed. Recently, Valadares Tavares and Tadeu Almeida (1983) have presented an even simpler decision rule under somewhat more restrictive assumptions (Poisson demand and a choice solely between stocking 1 unit versus no stocking).

Assumptions

1. The unit variable cost is the same under stocking and nonstocking.
2. The fixed setup cost is the same under stocking and nonstocking.
3. In deriving the decision rule to decide on whether to stock the item or not we allow the order quantity to be a noninteger (of course, if the item was actually stocked and demands were in integer units, we would use an integer value for the order quantity).
4. The replenishment lead time is negligible; consequently, there is no backordering cost.

The Decision Rule[7]

Do *not* stock the item if *either* of the following two conditions holds (otherwise stock the item):

$$c_s > A/E(i) \tag{9.15}$$

or

$$E(t)vr > \frac{E(i)}{2A}\left[\frac{A}{E(i)} - c_s\right]^2 \tag{9.16}$$

where

c_s = system cost, in dollars per unit time, of having the item stocked

A = fixed setup cost, in dollars, associated with a replenishment

$E(i)$ = expected (or average) interval (or time) between demand transactions

$E(t)$ = expected (or average) size of a demand transaction in units

v = unit variable cost of the item, in \$/unit

r = carrying charge, in \$/\$/unit time

[7]The derivation of this rule is given in Section 3 of the Appendix of this chapter.

A graphical representation of the decision rule is shown in Figure 9.1. For a given c_s value we use the associated curve. If the $E(t)vr$ and $A/E(i)$ values are such that the corresponding point falls to the left or above the curve, the item should not be stocked. If, on the other hand, the point falls to the right or below the curve, then the item should be stocked using the economic order quantity

$$\text{EOQ} = \sqrt{\frac{2AD}{vr}} \tag{9.17}$$

where

$$D = E(t)/E(i) \tag{9.18}$$

is the demand rate, in units per unit time.

The behavior of the rule (best illustrated by Figure 9.1) as a function of the factors involved makes intuitive sense. As the setup cost A goes up we move to the right in the graph, thus tending to the stocking situation. In the same way, as the expected time between transactions decreases we move to the region where stocking is preferred. Considering the vertical axis, as v or r increase, we tend to the nonstocking situation; it becomes too expensive to carry the item in inventory. It is seen that as c_s increases we are less likely to prefer stocking of the item. Finally, the larger the expected transaction size $E(t)$, the more likely we are to be in the region of nonstocking. Larger transaction sizes tend to support nonstocking in that now the individual special orders satisfy a relatively large demand.

Numerical Illustration

MIDAS Canada has been purchasing a specialty film item PDF-088 from a competitor each time that a customer demand has been encountered. The manager of purchasing feels that it would be attractive to make less frequent, larger purchases. Relevant parameter values have been estimated as follows:

$$v = \$4.70/\text{roll}$$

$$E(t) = 1.4 \text{ rolls}$$

$$E(i) = 10 \text{ weeks or } 10/52 \text{ yr}$$

$$A = \$2.50$$

$$r = 0.24 \ \$/\$/\text{yr}$$

$$c_s = 0.20 \ \$/\text{yr}$$

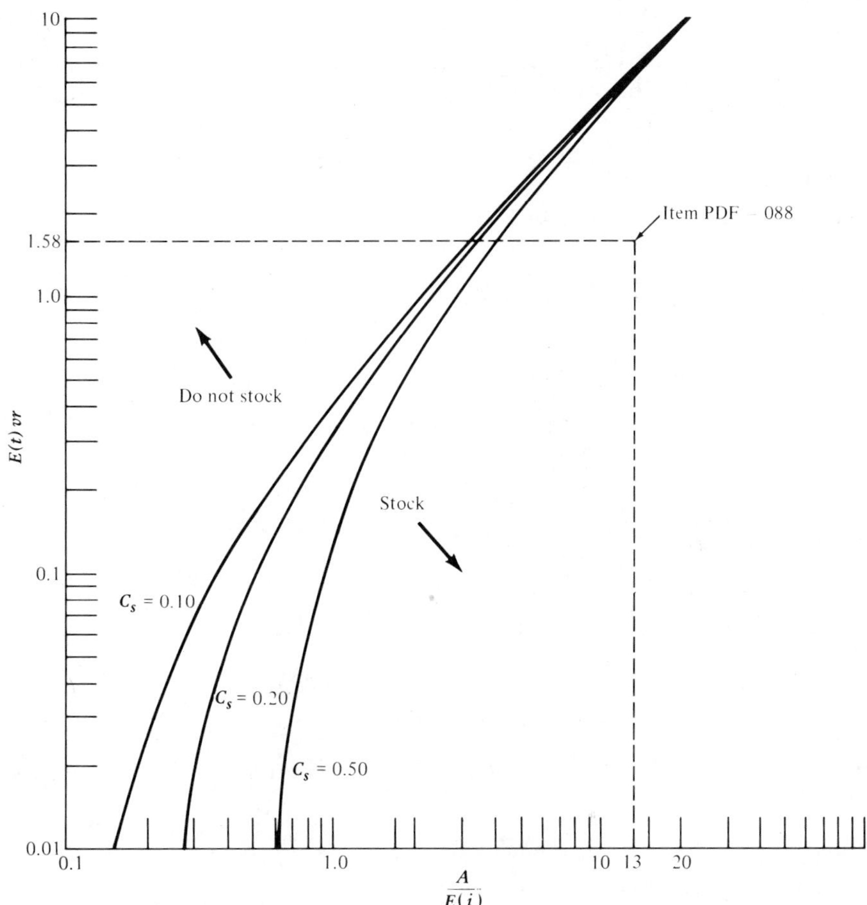

FIGURE 9.1 A Rule for the Stock–No Stock Decision

We have

$$E(t)vr = (1.4)(4.70)(0.24) = 1.58 \text{ \$/yr}$$

$$A/E(i) = 2.50/10/52 = 13.00 \text{ \$/yr}$$

Use of Eqs. 9.15 and 9.16 or Figure 9.1 reveals that the item should indeed be purchased for stock with the best order quantity, from Eqs. 9.17 and 9.18, being 6 rolls.

9.5.3 Some Extensions

It is rather straightforward (see Problem 9.6) to generalize the decision rule of the previous subsection to allow the unit variable cost and the fixed setup cost to each depend on whether or not the item is purchased for stock. In place of Eqs. 9.15 and 9.16, we can develop the following.

Do *not* stock the item if *either* of the following conditions hold (otherwise stock the item):

$$c_s > \frac{A_{ns}}{E(i)} + \frac{E(t)}{E(i)}(v_{ns} - v_s) \tag{9.19}$$

or

$$E(t)v_s r > \frac{E(i)}{2A_s}\left[\frac{A_{ns}}{E(i)} + \frac{E(t)}{E(i)}(v_{ns} - v_s) - c_s\right]^2 \tag{9.20}$$

where

v_s = unit variable cost, in \$/unit, if the item is stocked

v_{ns} = unit variable cost, in \$/unit, if the item is not stocked

A_s = fixed setup cost, in dollars, if the item is stocked

A_{ns} = fixed setup cost, in dollars, if the item is not stocked (the cost of backordering and extra paperwork would be included in A_{ns})

and all the other variables are as defined after Eqs. 9.15 and 9.16.

Croston (1974) has developed a decision rule, including a graphical aid, for the case of a periodic review, order-up-to-level (R, S) system. His model assumes a negligible replenishment lead time, at most one demand transaction in each review interval, and a normal distribution of transaction sizes. Shorrock (1978) has developed a tabular aid for the stock/no stock decision.

It should be emphasized that the two quantities, $E(t)$ and $E(i)$, needed in Eqs. 9.15 and 9.16 or Eqs. 9.19 and 9.20 would be estimated from rather sparse data—sparse because of the low usage nature of the items under consideration. The statistical fluctuations of such limited data could cause an item, whose underlying parameters had really not changed, to pass the stocking test one year and fail it in the next. Johnson (1962) has proposed the useful idea of two threshold values, one to discontinue stocking an item, the other to institute stocking. The intermediate or buffer area helps prevent an item from flipping back and forth between stocking and nonstocking as time passes.

9.6 SUMMARY

In this chapter we have discussed procedures for controlling the inventories of the large number of items with low annual dollar usage. Simplicity of control was stressed because of the low annual total of replenishment, carrying, and shortage costs associated with such items. Said another way, if the total of replenishment, carrying, and shortage costs for an item is on the order of but a few dollars per year, we must use for that item a control system that costs only pennies per year.

A final point worth mentioning is that with C items, in particular, the best method of control may be ascertained from the warehouse supervisor or production foreman who knows, for example, that a lot size of 10 units fits conveniently into a storage bin or into the usual production schedule. Using a decision rule that provides a different quantity (with a likely trivial annual difference in costs) is hardly worth the risk of alienating the warehouse supervisor or foreman.

APPENDIX TO CHAPTER 9
SOME DERIVATIONS

1. THE DECISION RULE FOR THE SIZE OF THE LAST REPLENISHMENT

We are interested in the total remaining demand y for the item; y is a random variable. We approximate its mean value $E(y)$ by the total demand $\hat{y}$ implied by the *deterministic* representation of the declining demand rate as a function of time (see Eqs. 9.10 and 9.11). In addition, we make the plausible assumption that y has a normal distribution (although the derivation could be modified to handle any other desired distribution) with standard deviation σ_y. Then, closely paralleling the P_2 service derivation in Section 3 of the Appendix to Chapter 7, we have that the expected shortage over the lifetime

$$ES = \sigma_y G_u(k)$$

and we want

$$\frac{ES}{\hat{y}} = 1 - P_2$$

so that

$$G_u(k) = \frac{\hat{y}(1 - P_2)}{\sigma_y}$$

2. THE DECISION RULE FOR DISPOSAL OF STOCK

Assuming a deterministic demand pattern (rate D), the situation is conceptually identical with that of a special opportunity to procure at a reduced unit cost (see Section 5.8.5 of Chapter 5). Let I be the current inventory level and W be the disposal amount. Then, as in Section 5.8.5, we look at costs out to time I/D—that is, when the current inventory would be depleted if no disposal took place. Under the option of no disposal, the costs would be

$$C_{ND} = \frac{I^2 vr}{2D}$$

If we dispose of W, then the remaining stock will run out at time $(I - W)/D$. Assuming an EOQ strategy after that, the relevent costs of the disposal decision out to time I/D are approximately

$$C_D = -gW + \left(\frac{I - W}{D}\right)\left(\frac{I - W}{2}\right) vr + \frac{W}{D}(\sqrt{2ADvr} + Dv)$$

As in Section 5.8.5 we select W to maximize $C_{ND} - C_D$. Using calculus, this leads to the decision rule of Eq. 9.14.

3. THE DECISION RULE FOR STOCKING VERSUS NOT STOCKING

The demand rate per unit time D is given by

$$D = E(t)/E(i) \tag{9.21}$$

Ignoring the minor effects of the non-unit-sized transactions, we have the same setting as in the derivation of the economic order quantity (Section 5.2 of Chapter 5). Therefore, from Eq. 5.4 of Chapter 5 and Eq. 9.21 the best order quantity, if the item is stocked, is

$$\text{EOQ} = \sqrt{\frac{2AE(t)}{vrE(i)}}$$

Moreover, from Eq. 5.5 of Chapter 5 and including the c_s system cost, the best total relevant costs per unit time, if the item is stocked, are

$$\text{TRC}_s(\text{EOQ}) = \sqrt{2AE(t)vr/E(i)} + c_s \tag{9.22}$$

If the item is not stocked, there is a cost A associated with each transaction which occurs, on the average, every $E(i)$ units of time. Therefore, the total relevant costs per unit time, if the item is not stocked are

$$\text{TRC}_{ns} = A/E(i) \tag{9.23}$$

Clearly, if c_s itself is larger than $A/E(i)$, then $\text{TRC}_{ns} < \text{TRC}_s$. This gives the condition of Eq. 9.15. More generally, requiring

$$\text{TRC}_{ns} < \text{TRC}_s$$

and using Eqs. 9.22 and 9.23, leads to

$$A/E(i) < \sqrt{2AE(t)vr/E(i)} + c_s$$

or

$$2AE(t)vr/E(i) > \left[\frac{A}{E(i)} - c_s\right]^2$$

that is,

$$E(t)vr > \frac{E(i)}{2A}\left[\frac{A}{E(i)} - c_s\right]^2$$

PROBLEMS

9.1 Consider a MIDAS item with the following characteristics

$v = \$0.40/\text{unit}$

$D = 50 \text{ units/yr}$

$L = 3 \text{ months}$

In establishing a value of σ it is reasonable to assume that demand for the item is adequately approximated by a Poisson process. For an (s, Q) control system

a. Find the appropriate Q value using Table 9.1.

b. Find the s value assuming a desired TBS of 20 years and using Table 9.2.

9.2 Suppose for the item in Problem 9.1 we instead decided to use an (R, S) system of control. What should be the values of R and S?

9.3 Suppose that in a retail outlet an item was being controlled by the Semiautomatic Stock Control System described in Section 9.2.5 and that an S value of 35 units had been in use.

a. Due to changing conditions, management now feels that it is appropriate to increase S to 40 units. Exactly what, if anything, has to be done to ensure that the system uses $S = 40$ from now on?

b. Repeat part a for a decrease of S from 35 to 28 units.

9.4 The Fly-by-Night Airlines has been phasing out one of the older types of aircraft that has been a mainstay of its illustrious fleet. Consequently, it has been observed that the associated usage of a glue used for maintenance of this type of aircraft has been "dropping off" linearly with time. The current level and trend of usage are estimated to be 110 liters/yr and minus 45 liters /yr/yr. Other characteristics of the glue include $A = \$25$, $v = \$4.50/\text{liter}$, and $r = 0.3$ \$/\$/yr.

a. If it is now time to replenish (that is, there is no inventory left), what order quantity should be used?

b. If the usage rate continues to drop off at the same linear rate, what should be the size of the *next* replenishment?

9.5 Dr. Hunsen Bunnydew of Puppet Laboratories, Inc. had asked his assistant Test Tube to order in some beakers. Poor Test Tube made a mistake in placing the order, and the lab now has a 20-year supply! Hunsen has informed Test Tube that he must dispose of an appropriate number of beakers. Test Tube's friend, Zongo, has arranged for another medical laboratory to purchase any quantity that Puppet offers, but at \$0.50/beaker which is 1/3 of what Test Tube paid for each of them. Using the following information come to Test Tube's aid by suggesting an appropriate amount to sell off.

$A = \$15$

$r = 0.2 \text{ \$/\$/yr}$

$D = 500 \text{ beakers/yr}$

9.6 Develop Eqs. 9.19 and 9.20.

9.7 For the speciality film item discussed in Section 9.5.2, how large would c_s have to be to make it unattractive to stock the item?

9.8 A C item is often purchased from the same supplier as a B or A item. Suppose that such is the case and, based on an EOQ analysis for the B (or A) item involved, an order is placed for the B (or A) item every 2 months. Assume that demand for the C item is essentially constant with time at a rate of 18 units/yr. Assume that the item has a unit value of

$3/unit. The *additional* fixed cost of including the C item in an order of the B (or A) item is $1.20. The carrying charge is 0.24/yr. It is reasonable to restrict attention to ordering the C item in a quantity that will last for 2 months, 4 months, 6 months, and so on (that is, an integer multiple of the time supply of the other item). Which of these time supplies is preferred?

9.9 Suppose you have been hired as an inventory control consultant by a client having thousands of inventoried items. The client feels that there is merit in each of the (R, S) and two-bin (s, Q) systems of control and is willing to have some C items under each of the two types of control. Using whatever symbols you feel are appropriate, develop as simple a decision rule as possible for deciding on which type of control to use for each specific item.

9.10 In the first part of MIDAS Case D a description was presented of the Inventory Control Manager's method of dealing with slow-moving items. Review his method, suggesting possible improvements.

REFERENCES

Brosseau, L. J. (1982). "An Inventory Replenishment Policy for the Case of a Linear Decreasing Trend in Demand." *INFOR*, Vol. 20, No. 2, pp. 252–257.

Brown, R. G. (1977). *Materials Management Systems.* Wiley-Interscience, New York, pp. 259–261.

Brown, R. G. (1981). "Confidence in All-Time Supply Forecasts." *Working Memorandum 181*, Materials Management Systems, Inc., Norwich, Vermont.

Croston, J. D. (1974). "Stock Levels for Slow-Moving Items." *Operational Research Quarterly*, Vol. 25, No. 1, pp. 123–130.

Dyer, D. (1973a). "To Stock or Not to Stock? That is the Question." *Modern Distribution Management*, Vol. 7, No. 5, pp. 3–7.

Dyer, D. (1973b). "Manufacturers! Dead Items Are Killing You." *Modern Distribution Management*, Vol. 7, No. 16, pp. 3–6.

Fortuin, L. (1980). "The All-Time Requirement of Spare Parts for Service after Sales—Theoretical Analysis and Practical Results." *International Journal of Operations & Production Management*, Vol. 1, No.1, pp. 59–70.

Hart, A. (1973). "Determination of Excess Stock Quantities." *Management Science*, Vol. 19, No. 12, pp. 1444–1451.

Johnson, J. (1962). "On Stock Selection at Spare Parts Stores Sections." *Naval Research Logistics Quarterly*, Vol. 9, No. 1, pp. 49–59.

Popp, W. (1965). "Simple and Combined Inventory Policies, Production to Stock or to Order." *Management Science*, Vol. 11, No. 9, pp. 868–873.

Shorrock, B. (1978). "Some Key Problems in Controlling Component Stocks." *Journal of the Operational Research Society*, Vol. 29, No. 7, pp. 683–689.

Smith, B. T. (1978). *Focus Forecasting: Computer Techniques for Inventory Control.* CBI Publishing Company, Inc., Boston, Massachusetts.

Smith, P. H. (1977). "Optimal Production Policies for Items with Decreasing Demand." *European Journal of Operational Research*, Vol. 1, pp. 355–367.

Valadares Tavares, L., and L. Tadeu Almeida (1983). "A Binary Decision Model for the Stock Control of Very Slow Moving Items." *Journal of the Operational Research Society*, Vol. 34, No. 3, pp. 249–252.

CHAPTER 10

Decision Rules for Style Goods and Perishable Items

The developments in Chapters 5 to 9 were all based on the assumption of a demand pattern for an item continuing well into the future (possibly on a time-varying basis)—that is, "a going concern" with the opportunity to store inventory from one selling period to the next. In the present chapter we remove this ability to indefinitely store inventory. The inability to carry inventory for a long time may be the result of perishability or obsolescence. Decision situations where this type of framework is relevant include:

1. The newsboy: How many copies of a particular issue of a newspaper to stock?
2. The Christmas tree vendor: How many trees should be purchased to put on sale?
3. The cafeteria manager: How many hot meals of a particular type should be prepared prior to the arrival of customers?
4. The supermarket manager: How much meat or fresh produce should be purchased for a particular day of the week?
5. The administrator of a regional blood bank: How many donations of blood should be sought and how should they be distributed among hospitals?
6. The supplies manager in a remote region (for example, medical and welfare work in northern Canada): What quantity of supplies should be brought in by boat prior to the long winter freeze-up?
7. The farmer: What quantity of a particular crop should be planted in a specific season?
8. The toy manufacturer: A particular product shows significant potential sales as a "fad" item. How many units should be produced on the one major production run to be made?
9. The garment manufacturer: What quantity of a particular style good should be produced prior to the short selling season?

In the simplest situation inventory cannot be carried forward at all from one period to the next. In this context the decoupling property of a single period being relevant for each replenishment decision significantly simplifies the analysis in contrast with the earlier, more general, case where inventory is storable from one period to the next and, hence, the effects of a replenishment action can last for several periods and thus can interact with later replenishment actions. If we refer to the lifetime of an item as the length of time until it becomes obsolete or perishes, then the analysis becomes much more complicated as the lifetime increases.

In Section 10.1 we spell out in more detail the characteristics (and associated complexity) of the general style goods problem. The models presented in Sections 10.2 through 10.4 deal with progressively more realistic, but more complicated, versions of the problem. In Section 10.2 we are concerned with the case of a single product with but one replenishment (procurement or production) opportunity. This is followed in Section 10.3 by the important generalization to more than one product, thus permitting the aggregate viewpoint first emphasized in Chapter 2. Again, an exchange curve is a key by-product of the analysis. Next, in Section 10.4 we provide some brief comments concerning the situation where there are several production periods with capacity restrictions prior to the selling season. Section 10.5 deals with some other issues relevant to the control of style goods. The chapter is completed by a discussion in Section10.6 concerning items subject to perishability.

10.1 THE STYLE GOODS PROBLEM

The main features of the style goods problem are:

1. There is a relatively short (no longer than 3 or 4 months) selling season with a well-defined beginning and end.
2. Buyers (at the stocking point) or producers have to commit themselves to a large extent, in terms of how much of each stock keeping unit to order or produce, prior to the start of the selling season.
3. There may be one or more opportunities for replenishment after the initial order is placed. Such replenishment actions may be taken prior to the selling season (if the forecast of demand has risen appreciably) or during the early part of the selling season itself (if actual demand to date indicates that the original forecast was considerably low).
4. Forecasts prior to the season include considerable uncertainty stemming from the long period of inactivity (no sales) between seasons. During this inactive period, the economic conditions or style considerations may have changed appreciably. Consequently, forecast revisions tend to be heavily influenced by firm orders or sales to date in the current season, far more than in the case of reasonably stable items (as discussed in Chapter 4).

5. When the total demand in the season exceeds the stock made available, there are associated underage costs. These may simply be lost profit if the sales are foregone. On the other hand, they may represent the added costs of expediting (for example, a special order by air freight) or acquiring the material from a competitor at a high unit value.
6. When the total demand in the season turns out to be less than the stock made available, overage costs result. The unit salvage value of leftover inventory at the end of a season is likely to be quite low (well below the unit acquisition cost). It is quite expensive to carry stock over to the next season; moreover, there is no guarantee that such leftover stock will even sell at that time. Markdowns (that is, reduced selling prices) or transfers (between locations) may be used to avoid leftover stock. (Incidentally, the style goods situation can be thought of as a special case of perishability where there is not physical deterioration but, instead, a marked deterioration in the economic value of the goods as of a particular point in time.)
7. Style goods products are often substitutable. Depending on how finely one defines a "style," a stockout in one s.k.u. does not necessarily mean a lost sale, because the demand may be satisfied by another product.
8. Sales of style goods are usually influenced by promotional activities, and space allocation in the store, among other things.

In the simplest form of the style goods problem, wherein we ignore the last two points made above as well as markdowns and transfers, the remaining decision variables are the timing and magnitudes of the replenishment quantities. To illustrate the complexity of even this simplified version, one need only refer to the work of Wadsworth (1959) who considered the case of a style good sold in a fall season with raw material acquisition required in the spring, summer production of unlimited capacity, and a limited amount of fall production (after the total season demand is known exactly) being possible but at a higher unit cost than the summer production. The complex nature of Wadsworth's solution to this problem indicates that an *exact* analysis of a more realistic style goods problem is out of the question. For this reason, as elsewhere in this book, we advocate the use of heuristic methods designed to generate *reasonable* solutions.

10.2 THE SIMPLEST CASE: THE UNCONSTRAINED, SINGLE-ITEM, NEWSBOY PROBLEM

10.2.1 Determination of the Best Order Quantity

Let us consider the situation faced by the owner of a newstand. Each day he has to decide on the number of copies of a particular paper to stock. There is an underage cost c_u, associated with each demand that he cannot meet and an overage cost, c_o, associated with each copy that he is not able to sell. Suppose the underage cost was exactly equal to the overage cost. Then it seems intuitively reasonable that he would want to select the number (Q) of copies to purchase such that there was a 50 percent chance of the total demand being below Q and a 50 percent chance of it being above Q. But what about the case where $c_u = 2c_o$ or $c_u = 3c_o$? It turns out that his decision rule should be to select the Q^* value that satisfies

$$p_{x<}(Q^*) = \frac{c_u}{c_u + c_o} \tag{10.1}$$

where $p_{x<}(x_0)$ is the probability that the total demand x is less than the value x_0.

Notice that when $c_u = c_0$ Eq. 10.1 gives

$$p_{x<}(Q^*) = 0.5$$

which is the intuitive result discussed above.

When $c_u = 2c_o$, we have from Eq. 10.1

$$p_{x<}(Q^*) = \frac{2c_o}{2c_o + c_o} = \frac{2}{3}$$

that is, he should select the order quantity such that the probability of the total demand being smaller than the order quantity is $\frac{2}{3}$.

Now let us reflect on how Eq. 10.1 is developed. The simplest derivation is a marginal analysis, as first used in Section 1 of the Appendix to Chapter 7. The argument proceeds as follows.

Consider the Qth unit purchased. It will be sold if, and only if, the total demand x equals or exceeds Q; otherwise, an overage cost will be incurred for this Qth unit. However, if the demand equals or exceeds Q, we have avoided an underage cost by having the Qth unit available. In other words, we have

Specific Cost Element	Probability That the Specific Cost Element Is Incurred (or Avoided) by the Acquisition of the Qth Unit	Expected Value of the Specific Cost Element Associated with the Qth Unit (product of previous two columns)
Overage, c_o	Prob {Demand is less than Q} $= p_{x<}(Q)$	$c_o p_{x<}(Q)$
Underage, c_u	Prob {Demand is greater than or equal to Q} $= 1 - p_{x<}(Q)$	$c_u[1 - p_{x<}(Q)]$

Consider a particular Qth unit. If the expected overage cost associated with acquiring it exceeded the expected saving in underage costs, we would not want to acquire that unit. In fact, we might not want to acquire the $(Q - 1)$st, the $(Q - 2)$nd, and so forth. On the other hand, if the expected saving in underage costs exceeded the expected overage cost associated with acquiring the Qth unit, we would want to acquire it. However, we might also wish to acquire the $(Q + 1)$st, the $(Q + 2)$nd, etc. The last unit (Q^*) we would want to acquire is that one where the expected overage cost incurred exactly equalled the expected underage cost saved; that is, Q^* must satisfy

$$c_o p_{x<}(Q^*) = c_u[1 - p_{x<}(Q^*)]$$

or

$$p_{x<}(Q^*) = \frac{c_u}{c_u + c_o}$$

which is Eq. 10.1

The solution of Eq. 10.1 is shown graphically in Figure 10.1 where we have plotted the cumulative distribution of demand, $p_{x<}(x_0)$. One locates the value of $c_u/(c_u + c_o)$ on the vertical axis, comes across horizontally to the curve, then

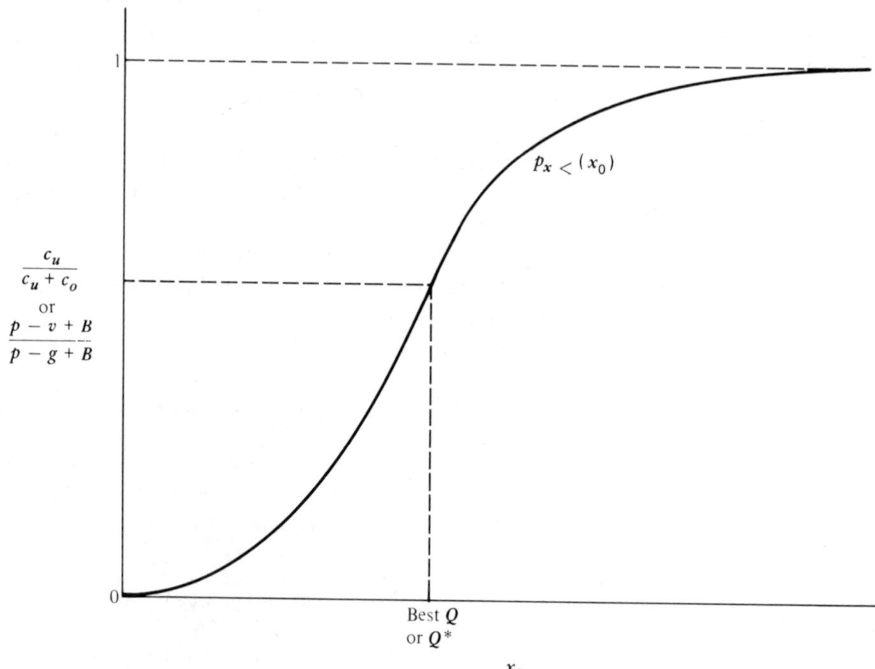

FIGURE 10.1 Graphical Solution of the Newsboy Problem

down vertically to read the corresponding x_0 which is the Q^* value. There is always a solution because the fraction lies between zero and unity, which is the range covered by the cumulative distribution.

We have just seen that the marginal cost analysis approach leads to the decision rule of Eq. 10.1 in a rather straightforward fashion. However, it does not give us an expression for evaluating the expected costs when any particular Q value is used. The alternative approach of minimizing total cost does, but the analysis is considerably more complicated.

10.2.2 An Equivalent Result Obtained through Profit Maximization

The above discussion has centered on cost minimization. Instead, let us now approach the problem from a profit maximization standpoint. Let

v = acquisition cost, in dollars/unit

p = revenue per sale (that is, the selling price), in dollars/unit

B (or B_2v) = penalty for not satisfying demand, in dollars/unit (B_2, as in Chapter 7, is the fraction of unit value that is charged per unit of demand unsatisfied)

g = salvage value, in dollars/unit

As earlier, we let

Q = quantity to be stocked, in units

and $p_{x<}(x_0)$ represent the cumulative distribution of total demand, the probability that total demand x takes on a value less than x_0.

Then, as shown in Section 1a of the Appendix of this chapter, the decision rule is to select the Q^* that satisfies

$$p_{x<}(Q^*) = \frac{p - v + B}{p - g + B} \tag{10.2}$$

This result is identical with that of Eq. 10.1 when we realize that the cost of underage is given by

$$c_u = p - v + B$$

and the cost of overage is

$$c_o = v - g$$

Because the cumulative distribution function is nondecreasing as its argument increases, we can make the following intuitively appealing deductions from Eq. 10.2.

1. If the sales price, cost per unit short, or salvage value increases, the best Q increases.
2. If the acquisition cost per unit increases, the best Q decreases.

10.2.3 The Case of Normally Distributed Demand

The result of Eq. 10.1 or 10.2 is applicable for any distribution of total demand. Again, it is worthwhile, as in Chapter 7, to look at the special case of normally distributed demand. First, such a distribution tends to be applicable in a significant number of situations. Second, as we will see, sensitivity analysis (effects of incorrectly specifying the order quantity Q) can be performed rather easily when demand is normal, in contrast with the case of a general probability distribution.

Suppose the demand x is normally distributed with a mean of $\hat{x}$ and a standard deviation of σ_x and we define

$$k = \frac{Q - \hat{x}}{\sigma_x} \tag{10.3}$$

This is analogous to what we did in Chapter 7. Then, as shown in Section 1b of the Appendix of this chapter, the decision rule of Eq. 10.2 transforms to

$$\text{Select } k \text{ such that} \qquad p_{u\geq}(k) = \frac{v - g}{p - g + B} \tag{10.4}$$

where $p_{u\geq}(k)$ is the probability that a unit normal variable takes on a value of k or larger; this is a widely tabulated function (see, for example, Table B.1 of Appendix B) first introduced in Chapter 7. Then, from Eq. 10.3, set

$$Q = \hat{x} + k\sigma_x \tag{10.5}$$

Furthermore, in this case, as shown in the Appendix of this chapter, we obtain a relatively simple expression for expected profit as a function of Q, namely,

$$E[P(Q)] = (p - g)\hat{x} - (v - g)Q - (p - g + B)\sigma_x G_u\left(\frac{Q - \hat{x}}{\sigma_x}\right) \tag{10.6}$$

where $G_u(u_0)$ is a tabulated function of the unit normal variable (see Table B.1 of Appendix B) first introduced in Chapter 7; in fact, Schlaifer (1961) defines the $G_u(\cdot)$ function through consideration of a problem of this type.

Numerical Illustration

MIDAS supplies several products to the federal government through a "National Standing Offer Contract" until March 31, 1986. Unfortunately from MIDAS' standpoint, such a contract does not specify a fixed amount of each product. The case of product PMF-198 poses a serious problem. This product, which is sold to the government only, is 50-meter rolls of 60-cm-wide lithographic film. For technological reasons the plant in Germany is discontinuing the product as of June 15, 1985. The issue is one of deciding on how many rolls to buy before the line is discontinued. The selling price is \$50.30 per roll whereas the unit cost to MIDAS is \$35.10. Should the need arise the product could be bought from competitors at a retail price of approximately \$60 per roll. Any material not sold to the government could be disposed of at a special price of \$25 per roll.

Through an analysis of historical buying behavior of the government on this and similar products, MIDAS' inventory manager is willing to assume that the total demand through March 31, 1986 is approximately normally distributed with a mean of 900 rolls and a standard deviation of 122 rolls.[1]

Using our notation

$$p = \$50.30/\text{roll}$$

$$v = \$35.10/\text{roll}$$

$$g = \$25.00/\text{roll}$$

$$B = (\$60.00 - 50.30) \text{ or } \$9.70/\text{roll}$$

---

[1]One way of arriving at an estimate of the standard deviation would be to specify the probability that total demand exceeded a certain value (other than the mean); for example, prob $(x \geq 1100) = 0.05$ leads to the standard deviation of 122 rolls. For x normally distributed,

$$\text{Prob}\,(x \geq 1100) = p_{u\geq}\left(\frac{1100 - \hat{x}}{\sigma_x}\right) = p_{u\geq}\left(\frac{200}{\sigma_x}\right)$$

But from the table in Appendix B

$$p_{u\geq}(1.645) = 0.05$$

Therefore,

$$\frac{200}{\sigma_x} = 1.645$$

or

$$\sigma_x = 122$$

From Eq. 10.4 we want

$$p_{u\geq}(k) = \frac{35.10 - 25}{50.30 - 25 + 9.70} = 0.288$$

From the table in Appendix B, we have

$$k = 0.56$$

Therefore, Eq. 10.5 gives

$$Q = 900 + 0.56(122) = 968.3, \text{ say } 968 \text{ rolls}$$

Use of Eq. 10.6 gives the expected profit for various values of Q; the results are shown in Table 10.1. It is interesting to note that by following the temptation of ordering the expected demand—namely, $Q = 900$—we would be led to a 2.0 percent reduction in expected profit.

10.2.4 The Case of a Fixed Charge to Place the Order

Where there is a high enough fixed setup cost to place any size order, the best strategy may be to not order anything at all. The decision would be based on comparing the cost of not ordering at all with the expected profit (ignoring the fixed cost as we did earlier) under use of the Q^* value:

If $E[P(Q^*)] > A - B\hat{x}$, order Q^*.

If $E[P(Q^*)] < A - B\hat{x}$, order nothing.

In general, $E[P(Q^*)]$ is quite difficult to evaluate. In the case of normally distributed demand Eq. 10.6 is of considerable help in this direction.

TABLE 10.1 Sensitivity of Expected Profit to Q Value Selected in Film Example

Q	Percent Deviation from Best Q (namely, 968)	$E[P(Q)]$	Percent of Best Possible Profit
700	27.7	8,670	71.0
800	17.4	10,690	87.5
900	7.0	11,980	98.0
930	3.9	12,150	99.4
968	0	12,220	100.0
1000	3.3	12,170	99.6
1030	6.4	12,050	98.6
1100	13.6	11,570	94.7
1200	24.0	10,640	87.1

10.2.5 The Case of Discrete Demand

Strictly speaking, when we are dealing with discrete (integer) units of demand and purchase quantity, it is unlikely that there is an integer Q value that exactly satisfies Eq. 10.1 or Eq. 10.2. To illustrate, suppose we have an item where

$$\frac{c_u}{c_u + c_0} = 0.68$$

and the probability distribution of demand is as shown in the second row of the following table (the third row is derived from the second row):

Number of units, x_0	1	2	3	4	5	Total
$p_x(x_0) = \text{prob}\ (x = x_0)$	0.2	0.3	0.2	0.2	0.1	1
$p_{x<}(x_0) = \text{prob}\ (x < x_0)$	0	0.2	0.5	0.7	0.9	—

It is seen from the third row that there is no Q that would give $p_{x<}(Q) = 0.68$; the nearest values are $p_{x<}(3) = 0.5$ and $p_{x<}(4) = 0.7$. As shown in Section 1c of the Appendix of this chapter, when discrete units are used, the best value of Q is the smallest Q value that satisfies

$$p_{x\leqslant}(Q) > \frac{c_u}{c_u + c_o} = \frac{p - v + B}{p - g + B} \tag{10.7}$$

Numerical Illustration

Consider the case of a Mennonite farmer who raises cattle and sells the beef at the weekly farmer's market in Kitchener-Waterloo, Ontario. He is particularly concerned about a specific expensive cut of meat. He sells it in a uniform size of 5 kg at a price of \$30. He wants to know how many 5-kg units to take to market. Demand is not known with certainty; all that he has available are frequency counts of the total 5-kg units demanded in each of the last 20 market sessions. These are chronologically as follows: 1, 3, 3, 2, 2, 5, 1, 2, 4, 4, 2, 3, 4, 1, 5, 2, 2, 3, 1, and 4. Frequency counts of how many 1's, how many 2's, etc., occurred in the 20 weeks are shown in the second row of Table 10.2. The third row is a set of estimates of the probabilities of the various sized demands based on the assumption that the historical occurrences are representative of the probabilities. For example, in 6 out of 20 weeks the total demand has been 2 units; therefore, the probability of a total demand of 2 units is approximately 6/20 or 0.3.

The farmer stores the processed beef in a freezer on his farm. He estimates the value of a 5-kg unit to be \$19 after he removes it from the freezer and gets it to the market. Once the beef is brought to market he chooses not to take it home and refreeze it. Therefore, any leftover beef at the market he sells to a local butcher at a discount price of \$15 per 5-kg unit. Finally, other than the foregone

TABLE 10.2 Demand Distribution for Farmer's Meat Example

1. Demand in a session x_0	1	2	3	4	5	Total
2. Frequency count $N(x_0)$	4	6	4	4	2	20
3. $p_x(x_0) \simeq \dfrac{N(x_0)}{20}$	0.2	0.3	0.2	0.2	0.1	1.0
4. $p_{x\leq}(x_0)$	0.2	0.5	0.7	0.9	1.0	—

profit, he feels that there is no additional cost (for example, loss of goodwill) associated with not satisfying a demand.

According to our notation

$$p = \$30/\text{unit}$$
$$v = \$19/\text{unit}$$
$$B = 0$$
$$g = \$15/\text{unit}$$

Therefore,

$$\frac{p - v + B}{p - g + B} = \frac{30 - 19 + 0}{30 - 15 + 0} = 0.734$$

Use of the fourth row of Table 10.2, together with the decision rule of Eq. 10.7, shows that he should bring four 5-kg units to market. It is interesting to note that the average or expected demand is

$$\begin{aligned}\hat{x} &= \sum_{x_0} x_o p_x(x_0) = (1)(0.2) + 2(0.3) + 3(0.2) + 4(0.2) + 5(0.1)\\ &= 2.7 \text{ units}\end{aligned}$$

Therefore, because of the economics, the best strategy is to take (4 − 2.7) or 1.3 units above the average demand.

10.3 THE SINGLE-PERIOD, CONSTRAINED, MULTI-ITEM SITUATION

Now we consider the situation of more than one type of stock keeping unit to be stocked for a single period's demand. It should be emphasized that the model to be developed here is based on the assumption of independent demands for the various products. However, there is a space or budget constraint on the group of items. Examples include the following.

1. Several different newspapers sharing a limited space or budget in a corner newsstand.
2. A buyer for a style goods department of a retail outlet who has a budget limitation for a group of items.
3. The provisioning of supplies or spare parts on a spacecraft, submarine, or the like, prior to a long mission without the possibility of resupply.
4. The repair kit taken by a maintenance crew on a routine visit to an operating facility.

We illustrate the solution procedure for the case of a restriction on the total dollar value of the units stocked. First, some notation is required. Let

n = number of different items (s.k.u.'s) involved (numbered 1, 2, 3, . . . , n)

${}_ip_{x<}(x_0)$ = prob{total demand for item i is less than x_0}

v_i = acquisition cost of item i, in \$/unit

p_i = selling price of item i, in \$/unit

B_i = penalty for not satisfying demand of item i, in \$/unit

g_i = salvage value of item i, in \$/unit

W = budget available for allocation among the stocks of the n items, in dollars

Suppose that a manager wishes to use up the total budget[2] in such a way as to maximize the total expected profit of the n items. As shown in Section 2 of the Appendix of this chapter, a convenient way to solve this problem is through the use of a Lagrange multiplier. The resulting decision procedure is:[3]

---

[2]We are assuming that the total budget is to be allocated. If such is not necessarily the case, each item i's unconstrained optimal Q_i^* should be ascertained independently using Eq. 10.2. If the total $\Sigma Q_i^* v_i < W$, then the Q_i^*'s should be used. If not, the constrained approach must be used to find the Q_i's.

[3]If the constraint is, instead, of a production nature such that no more than W units can be produced, then the decision procedure is modified in two ways:

1. Equation 10.8 is changed to

$$ {}_ip_{x<}(Q_i) = \frac{p_i - v_i - M + B_i}{p_i - g_i + B_i} \tag{10.9}$$

2. In Step 3 we compare

$$\sum_{i=1}^{n} Qi$$

with W.

Step 1 Select an initial positive value of the multiplier, M.

Step 2 Determine each Q_i ($i = 1, 2, 3, \ldots, n$) to satisfy

$$ {}_ip_{x<}(Q_i) = \frac{p_i - (M+1)v_i + B_i}{p_i - g_i + B_i} \qquad \text{and} \qquad Q_i \geqslant 0 \tag{10.8}$$

Step 3 Compare

$$\sum_{i=1}^{n} Q_i v_i$$

with W.

If $\Sigma\, Q_i v_i \simeq W$, we're through.
If $\Sigma\, Q_i v_i < W$, return to Step 2 with a smaller value of M.
If $\Sigma\, Q_i v_i > W$, return to Step 2 with a larger value of M.

The multiplier has an interesting economic interpretation; it is the value (in terms of increased total expected profit) of adding one more dollar to the available budget, W.

It is important to recognize that as different values of M are used, one is actually tracing out an exchange curve of total expected profit versus total allowed budget (investment in stock) as illustrated in Figure 10.2, which is an exchange curve for the numerical illustration to be presented momentarily.

The above formulation assumes that the individual-item stocking decisions have *independent* effects on the objective function to be maximized or minimized. Smith et al. (1980) have addressed the following more complicated situation. Consider the kit of spare parts stocked by a repair crew visiting an off-site location. A particular repair job may require more than one spare part. An appropriate measure of effectiveness is now the fraction of jobs completed without stockout, as opposed to the fraction of needed individual spare parts that are provided. In addition, Mamer and Smith (1982) extend the analysis to the situation where part demands are no longer independent.

Numerical Illustration

Suppose MIDAS was faced with decisions on four items rather than just the one illustrated in Section 10.2.3. The manager is willing to accept that in each case total demand is normally distributed. For the case of normally distributed demand, Eq. 10.8 becomes

$$ p_{u\geqslant}(k_i) = \frac{(M+1)v_i - g_i}{p_i - g_i + B_i} \tag{10.10}$$

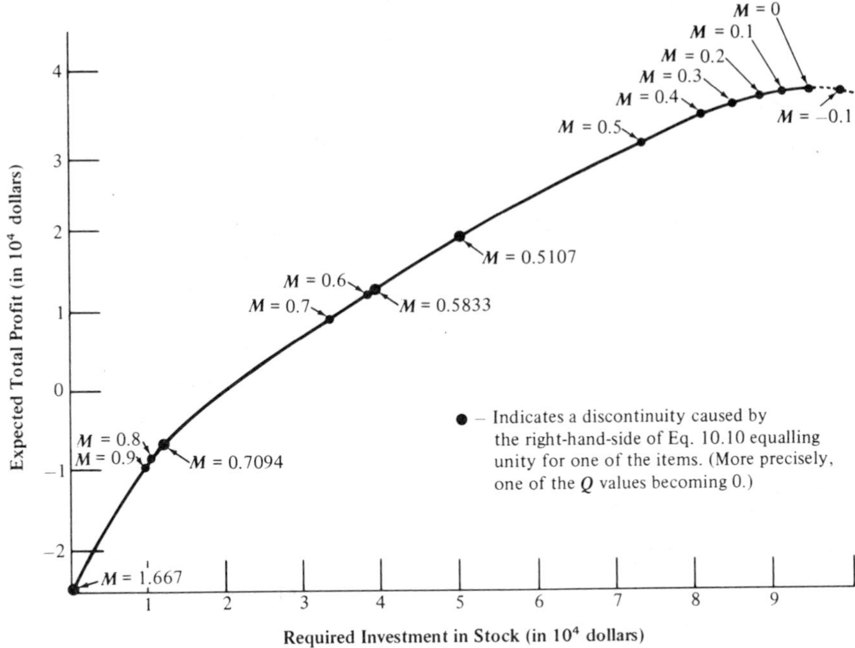

FIGURE 10.2 Exchange Curve for the Multi-item, Single-Period Situation

where, as earlier, $p_{u\geq}(k_i)$ is the probability that a unit normal variable takes on a value of k_i or larger (tabulated in Appendix B) and

$$Q_i = \max (0, \hat{x}_i + k_i\sigma_i) \tag{10.11}$$

where

$\hat{x}$ = forecast demand for item i

σ_i = standard deviation of the demand for item i (here we have simplified the notation somewhat to avoid a subsubscript)

The relevant parameter values are estimated to be as shown in the top six rows of Table 10.3. The manager has a budget of $70,000 to allocate among these four items. She would like to know how to do this. She is also quite interested in the profit impact if the budget is changed somewhat. The calculations for several values of the multiplier M are shown in the lower part of Table 10.3 and the results are shown graphically in Figure 10.2. It is seen that the expected total profit is approximately $28,800 when the proposed budget of $70,000 is used. However, increasing the budget could lead to a substantial improvement in the total profit, a useful piece of information for top management. The dotted

TABLE 10.3 Numerical Illustration of Multi-Item, Single-Period Problem

	Item 1	Item 2	Item 3	Item 4	Total
p_i \$/unit	50.30	40.00	32.00	6.10	—
v_i \$/unit	35.10	15.00	28.00	4.80	—
g_i \$/unit	25.00	12.50	15.10	2.00	—
B_i \$/unit	9.70	0	10.30	1.50	—
$\hat{x}$ units	900	800	1,200	2,300	—
σ_i units	122	200	170	200	—
Using $M = 0$ (that is, no budget restriction):					
Q_i from Eqs. 10.10 and 10.11	968	1,066	1,211	2,300	—
$E[P(Q_i)]$ from Eq. 10.6	12,220	19,100	2,960	2,540	\$36,820
$Q_i v_i$ \$	33,977	15,990	33,908	11,040	\$94,915
Using $M = 0.4$:					
Q_i	840	900	995	2,101	—
$E[P(Q_i)]$	11,340	18,660	1,610	2,340	\$33,950
$Q_i v_i$	29,484	13,500	27,864	10,085	\$80,933
Using $M = 0.6$:					
Q_i	750	842	0[a]	0[a]	—
$E[P(Q_i)]$	9,720	18,230	−12,360	−3,450	\$12,140
$Q_i v_i$	26,325	12,630	0	0	\$38,955
Using $M = 0.5093$[b]:					
Q_i	797	866	695	1,995	—
$E[P(Q_i)]$	10,660	18,430	−2,420	2,110	\$28,780
$Q_i v_i$	27,992	12,990	19,460	9,577	\$70,019

[a]The right-hand side of Eq. 10.10 exceeds unity, implying that k_i (or equivalently Q_i) should be set at its lowest possible value. The lowest value for Q_i is zero from Eq. 10.11.

[b]By trial and error, it was found that this value of M was required to produce a total used budget of approximately \$70,000.

part (on the far right) of the curve shows that the total expected profit would start to decrease if the budget was too high and *one was required to invest the whole amount in stocks of the four items* (a negative value of M applies in this region). In actuality, once a budget of approximately \$94,900 was reached, no further investment would be made as this is the budget needed for the best solution with no budget restriction (the case of $M = 0$).

10.4 MORE THAN ONE PERIOD IN WHICH TO PREPARE FOR THE SELLING SEASON

Particularly in a production context (for example, style goods in the garment industry) there may be an extended length of time (divided, for convenience, into several time periods) in which replenishment commitments are made before the actual selling season begins. There are likely to be production constraints on the total amounts that can be acquired in each time period. Furthermore, forecasts of total demand are almost certain to change during these preseason periods, perhaps as a consequence of firm customer orders being received. We would like to be able to modify the decision rule of the previous section to cope with these new complexities effectively.

For multiperiod production/inventory problems, Ignall and Veinott (1969) have developed conditions under which a relatively simple policy, known as a *myopic policy*, is optimal for the sequence of periods. A myopic policy is one that selects the production quantities for the current period to minimize expected costs *in the current period alone*. Obviously, a myopic policy is much simpler to compute than is a more general multiperiod policy. However, the multiperiod style goods problem discussed above does not satisfy the conditions for which a myopic policy is optimal.

Furthermore, Hausman and Peterson (1972) have shown that an "optimal" solution to the problem is out of the question. However, they have proposed two heuristic decision rules that appear to perform quite well, at least on the numerical examples tested. The heuristics are closely related to the single-period procedure of Section 10.3, but allowance is made for production capability in all remaining periods. Another related reference is Crowston et al. (1973).

10.5 OTHER ISSUES RELEVANT TO THE CONTROL OF STYLE GOODS

In this section we provide the highlights of other investigations that have been conducted relevant to the control of style goods. The interested reader is encouraged to seek out the details in the referenced literature.

10.5.1 Updating of Forecasts

This topic has been treated in Chapter 4, but we now reexamine those aspects of particular relevance to the style goods problem. In a multiperiod problem opportunities exist to update forecasts. Several alternative methods exist including:

1. *Exploitation of the properties of the forecasts made by decision makers.* Hausman (1969) has found that under certain circumstances ratios of successive forecasts turn out to be independent variables with a specific form of probability distribution.

2. *Taking advantage of the observation that sales at the retail level tend to be proportional to inventory displayed.* Wolfe (1968), in particular, has used this approach to revise forecasts based on demands observed early in the selling period.

3. *Simple extrapolation methods using a particular mathematical form for the cumulative sales as a function of time.* Hertz and Schaffir (1960) assume a normal-shaped cumulative curve. More recently, Gilding and Lock (1980), in the context of a furniture manufacturer, have dealt with the case of an artificial seasonality induced by sales promotions and have found that a Gompertz curve provides a reasonable fit to cumulative sales:

$$Y_{\text{ult}} = \ln Y_t + ae^{-bt} \tag{10.12}$$

where

Y_{ult} represents the ultimate (total) sales of the item

Y_t cumulative sales as of time t

and

a and b are constants.

4. *Bayesian procedures.* In the Bayesian approach one or more parameters of the probability distribution of demand are assumed unknown. Prior knowledge is encoded in the form of probability distributions over the possible values of these parameters. As demands are observed in the early part of the season, these probability distributions are appropriately modified to take account of the additional information. References include Chang and Fyffe (1971), Murray and Silver (1966), and Riter (1967).

10.5.2 Reorders and Markdowns

Wolfe (1968), using the aforementioned assumption about sales being proportional to the inventory level, develops methods of determining each of the following:

1. The expected time T_F to sell a fraction F of the initial inventory if a fraction f has been sold by time t $(f < F)$. A style can be tentatively identified as a fast-mover (with associated possible reorder) or slow-mover (with associated possible markdown) depending on the value of T_F for a particular selected F value.
2. The associated order-up-to-level if a reorder is to be placed at a specific time.
3. The timing of a markdown as a function of the fraction of initial inventory sold to date, the current price, the markdown price, the salvage value of leftover material, and the *assumed known* ratio of the sales rate after the markdown to that before it.

Carlson (1982a, 1982b) also develops a pragmatic approach to deciding on reorders and markdowns in a retail fashion context.

10.6 INVENTORY CONTROL OF PERISHABLE ITEMS

In earlier parts of the book we have not *explicitly* dealt with perishability, other than possibly through a rather crude adjustment of the inventory carrying charge. In recent years considerable work has been done on a more explicit treatment of perishability in inventory control. An extensive review is provided by Nahmias (1982).

Perishability refers to the physical deterioration of units of a product. Demand continues for further units of the item. In contrast, when obsolescence occurs, there is negligible further demand for the s.k.u. involved.

Perishable items can be divided into two categories dependent on the lifetime of a unit of the item. There are those items with a fixed lifetime; in this case, the utility of each unit stays essentially constant for a *fixed* period of time, then drops appreciably (perhaps decreed by law). In contrast, there are items where the lifetime is a random variable. Furthermore, in the latter case, the utility can decrease throughout the lifetime in a fashion that may or may not depend on the age of the unit involved (examples include fresh produce, certain types of volatile chemicals, drugs, etc.).

In the subsequent discussion we treat only the first category above—an item with a fixed known lifetime, with constant utility during the life and zero utility thereafter. This case (and a major portion of the research that has been carried out on the control of perishable items) is motivated by the problem of blood banking (see extensive bibliographies in Elston, 1970; Prastacos, 1979).

10.6.1 The Optimal Policy for an Item Having a Constant Utility during Its Known Lifetime of m Periods

A number of authors referenced in the aforementioned Nahmias (1982) review paper, have treated this type of problem. However, we choose to follow the approach suggested by Nahmias himself in his comprehensive research program.

Assumptions made include:

1. A periodic review system is used.
2. All orders are placed at the beginnings of periods, and the replenishment lead time is negligible.
3. All stock arrives in a "new" state.
4. Demands in successive periods are independent random variables with the same known probability distribution.

5. Inventory is depleted according to a first-in-first-out (FIFO) policy; that is, the oldest inventory is used first. FIFO is an optimal issuing policy over a wide range of assumptions, particularly where the issuing organization has *complete* control over the issuing actions. However, where the customer makes the selection (for example, in retail food distribution where the expiration date is shown on each unit), a last-in-first-out (LIFO) policy is likely to be observed. For further discussion of issuing policies, see Albright (1976) and Pierskalla and Roach (1972).
6. If a unit has not been used by the time it has been on-hand for m periods, then it deteriorates (is outdated) and must be discarded.
7. There is complete backordering of unsatisifed demand (the case of complete lost sales can also be handled).
8. Costs (all assumed linear) include acquisition, holding, shortages, and outdates (again a somewhat more general cost structure can be handled). *Note that there is no fixed cost (A) associated with a replenishment.*

At the beginning of each period we know the numbers of units on hand of each age. It is convenient to let x_i = number of units on hand that will end their lifetime (outdate) exactly i periods in the future. Thus, a vector

$$\mathbf{x} = (x_{m-1}, x_{m-2}, \ldots, x_2, x_1)$$

represents the state of the system at the start of a period (prior to the placement of an order). We let y represent the amount of new units to be ordered. The problem is to develop a decision rule for y as a function of $\mathbf{x}$, the demand distribution, and all the unit costs. Incidentally, under the above set of assumptions the special case of $m = 1$ reduces to the newsboy problem treated in Section 10.2.

Nahmias (1975b) shows that the optimal policy is of the form:

$$\begin{aligned} &\text{If } \mathbf{x} \text{ is such that } \sum_{i=1}^{m-1} x_i \leq x_c, \text{ then order } y(\mathbf{x}). \\ &\text{If } \mathbf{x} \text{ is such that } \sum_{i=1}^{m-1} x_i > x_c, \text{ then } y = 0. \end{aligned} \tag{10.13}$$

where the critical level x_c depends on the unit costs and the probability distribution of demand.

Thus, whether or not to order and how much to order both depend on the vector $\mathbf{x}$ (which has $m - 1$ components). To make matters worse, the computation of $y(\mathbf{x})$ is extremely complex. A primary reason for this is the complicated way in which the vector state of the process changes from period to period. Any units in state i (that is, x_i) at the start of a particular period that are not used to satisfy demand in that period will move into state $i - 1$ at the start of the next period (that is, will become the x_{i-1} value at that time). Unfortunately, how many (call the number z_i) of the x_i units are used to satisfy demand in the single period depends not only on the demand value d but also on the values of $x_1, x_2, \ldots, x_{i-1}$—namely, as follows (using the FIFO assumption):

$$z_i = \begin{cases} 0 & \text{if } d \leq \sum_{j=1}^{i-1} x_j \\ d - \sum_{j=1}^{i-1} x_j & \text{if } \sum_{j=1}^{i-1} x_j < d \leq \sum_{j=1}^{i} x_j \\ x_i & \text{if } \sum_{j=1}^{i} x_j < d \end{cases} \tag{10.14}$$

Thus, the x_{i-1} value at the start of the next period (which is the current x_i minus the z_i value) depends in a complicated way on d and all of $x_1, x_2, \ldots, x_i$ in the current period.

Intuitively appealing properties of the optimal solution include the following:

1. Perishability decreases the size of the best order quantity in comparison with the nonperishable case, and the difference is largest for low values of starting inventory.
2. If the initial stock of inventory of any specific age level is increased by one unit, the best order quantity decreases, but by less than a whole unit. Moreover, the order quantity is more sensitive to changes in newer inventory.

When there is a significant setup cost A, the form of the optimal policy is even more complicated than the above (see Nahmias, 1978).

10.6.2 A Heuristic Policy for an Item Having a Constant Utility during Its Known Lifetime of *m* Periods

The unwieldy nature of the optimal solution (both in terms of being able to compute the solution as well as the recordkeeping necessary to know the current age distribution of the stock) identifies the need for a simpler, heuristic inventory control policy. Nahmias (1975a), using simulation, looked at three plausible heuristics and found a "single critical number" policy to be preferable from the combined viewpoint of simplicity and low-cost performance.

A "single critical number" policy operates as follows. We collapse the state of the system into a single dimension, using

$$x = \sum_{i=1}^{m-1} x_i \tag{10.15}$$

that is, the total on-hand inventory, regardless of its age. Then, the order quantity y is given by

$$y = \begin{cases} x_c' - x & x < x_c' \\ 0 & \text{otherwise} \end{cases} \tag{10.16}$$

where x_c' is the critical number (order-up-to-level). This type of policy is appealing for at least three reasons. First, the rule used to decide on whether to order anything at all, namely,

$$\sum_{i=1}^{m-1} x_i < x_c'$$

is of essentially the same form as in the optimal policy (see Eq. 10.13). Second, for nonperishable items earlier in the book one of our basic control systems was an (R, S) system, which is precisely what the heuristic is advocating. Third, a fixed order-up-to-level represents a relatively easy policy to implement.

Having decided to pursue a "single critical number" policy, our worries would not necessarily be over. Again, primarily because of the complex nature of the change in inventory status from period to period, it is very difficult to find the optimal "single critical number" policy. Fortunately, Nahmias (1976) has, if you like, developed a heuristic within a heuristic—namely, a simple myopic approach for finding a single critical number close to the optimal one. The word myopic, meaning near-sighted, implies that the critical number (the order-up-to-level) is selected only taking account of the approximate costs in the very next period, neglecting costs beyond that point. For small values of m (namely, $m = 2$ and 3), where it is possible (although extremely time-consuming) to compute the optimal policy, he has found that use of the much simpler, myopic, single critical number policy results in an average cost penalty of less than 1 percent—an extremely encouraging result. However, even for normally distributed demand, the heuristic decision rule requires a trial-and-error solution of an equation involving three separate $p_{u\geq}(\cdot)$ functions and thus involves considerably more computational effort than other decision rules presented earlier.

10.7 SUMMARY

In this chapter we have presented some decision logic for coping with items subject to obsolescence or perishability. In the style goods version of the problem, the logic exploited the property of not being able (for economic reasons) to carry stock over from one selling season to the next. With this chapter we have completed our coverage of *individual-item* inventory management.

APPENDIX TO CHAPTER 10
DERIVATIONS

1. BASIC NEWSBOY RESULTS

a. Profit Maximization

Each unit purchased costs v, each unit sold produces a revenue of p, each unit disposed as salvage gives a revenue of g, and there is an additional cost B associated with each unit of demand not satisfied. If a quantity Q is stocked and a demand x_0 occurs, the profit is

$$P(Q, x_0) = \begin{cases} -Qv + px_0 + g(Q - x_0) & \text{if } x_0 \leqslant Q \quad (10.17) \\ -Qv + pQ - B(x_0 - Q) & \text{if } x_0 \geqslant Q \quad (10.18) \end{cases}$$

The expected value of the profit, as a function of Q, is given by

$$E[P(Q)] = \int_0^\infty P(Q, x_0) f_x(x_0) dx_0$$

By substituting from Eqs. 10.17 and 10.18, we obtain

$$\begin{aligned} E[P(Q)] &= \int_0^Q [-Qv + px_0 + g(Q - x_0)] f_x(x_0) dx_0 \\ &\quad + \int_Q^\infty [-Qv + pQ - B(x_0 - Q)] f_x(x_0) dx_0 \\ &= -Qv \int_0^\infty f_x(x_0) dx_0 + (p - g) \int_0^Q x_0 f_x(x_0) dx_0 \\ &\quad + gQ \int_0^Q f_x(x_0) dx_0 - B \int_Q^\infty x_0 f_x(x_0) dx_0 \\ &\quad + (p + B)Q \int_Q^\infty f_x(x_0) dx_0 \end{aligned} \qquad (10.19)$$

To find the maximizing value of Q, we set

$$\frac{dE[P(Q)]}{dQ} = 0 \qquad (10.20)$$

In doing this we make use of the following theorem of calculus (for a proof see, for example, Sokolnikoff and Redheffer, 1958):

Theorem: Consider a definite integral, denoted by $I(x)$, which is a function of a variable x in two ways. First, the integrand $f(x, y)$ is a function of x (and the variable y which is integrated). Second, both of the limits denoted by $y_1(x)$ and $y_2(x)$ are functions of x. Mathematically we have

$$I(x) = \int_{y_1(x)}^{y_2(x)} f(x, y)dy$$

Then, the derivative is given by

$$\frac{dI(x)}{dx} = \int_{y_1(x)}^{y_2(x)} \frac{\partial f(x, y)}{\partial x} dy + f(x, y_2)\frac{dy_2(x)}{dx} - f(x, y_1)\frac{dy_1(x)}{dx} \tag{10.21}$$

Use of Equations 10.19, 10.20, and 10.21, and also recognizing that

$$\int_0^\infty f_x(x_0)dx_0 = 1$$

gives

$$-v + (p - g)Qf_x(Q) + g\int_0^Q f_x(x_0)dx_0 + gQf_x(Q)$$
$$+ BQf_x(Q) + (p + B)\int_Q^\infty f_x(x_0)dx_0 - (p + B)Qf_x(Q) = 0$$

Several terms cancel to give

$$-v + g\int_0^Q f_x(x_0)dx_0 + (p + B)\int_Q^\infty f_x(x_0)dx_0 = 0$$
$$-v + gp_{x<}(Q) + (p + B)[1 - p_{x<}(Q)] = 0$$

or

$$p_{x<}(Q) = \frac{p - v + B}{p - g + B} \tag{10.22}$$

In addition, one can show that the second derivative

$$\frac{d^2E[P(Q)]}{dQ^2}$$

is negative, thus ensuring that we have found a profit maximizing (and not minimizing) value of Q.

b. Normally Distributed Demand

If we set

$$k = \frac{Q - x}{\sigma_x} \tag{10.23}$$

then, as shown in Section B.5 of Appendix B, Eq. 10.22 simplifies to

$$p_{u<}(k) = \frac{p - v + B}{p - g + B} \tag{10.24}$$

where

$$p_{u<}(k) = \mathit{Prob}\,\{\text{a unit normal variable takes on a value less than } k\}$$

Using the fact that

$$p_{u\geqslant}(k) = 1 - p_{u<}(k)$$

Eq. 10.24 reduces to

$$p_{u\geqslant}(k) = \frac{v - g}{p - g + B}$$

Next, we wish to show the simplification in Eq. 10.19, which results for the case of normally distributed demand. To do this we need to recognize that, under the use of Eq. 10.23, it is shown in Section B.5 of Appendix B that

1. $\displaystyle\int_Q^\infty f_x(x_0)dx_0 = p_{u\geqslant}(k)$

2. $\displaystyle\int_Q^\infty x_0 f_x(x_0 dx_0 = \int_Q^\infty (x_0 - Q) f_x(x_0)dx_0 + Q\int_Q^\infty f_x(x_0)dx_0$

$$= \sigma_x G_u(k) + Qp_{u\geqslant}(k)$$

3. $\displaystyle\int_0^Q x_0 f_x(x_0)dx_0 = \int_0^\infty x_0 f_x(x_0)dx_0 - \int_Q^\infty x_0 f_x(x_0)dx_0$

$$\simeq \hat{x} - \sigma_x G_u(k) - Qp_{u\geqslant}(k)$$

Therefore, Eq. 10.19 becomes

$$\begin{aligned} E[P(Q)] = & - Qv + (p - g)[\hat{x} - \sigma_x G_u(k) - Qp_{u\geq}(k)] \\ & + gQ[1 - p_{u\geq}(k)] - B[\sigma_x G_u(k) + Qp_{u\geq}(k)] \\ & + (p + B)Qp_{u\geq}(k) \end{aligned}$$

or

$$E[P(Q)] = (p - g)\hat{x} - (v - g)Q - (p - g + B)\sigma_x G_u(k)$$

c. Discrete Case

The expected total cost in the discrete case is

$$\text{ETC}(Q) = \sum_{x_0=0}^{Q-1} c_o(Q - x_0)p_x(x_0) + \sum_{x_0=Q}^{\infty} c_u(x_0 - Q)p_x(x_0) \tag{10.25}$$

where

$$p_x(x_0) = \text{Prob}\ \{x = x_0\}$$

Let

$$\Delta\text{ETC}(Q) = \text{ETC}(Q + 1) - \text{ETC}(Q) \tag{10.26}$$

Then, $\Delta\text{ETC}(Q)$ is the change in expected total cost when we switch from Q to $Q + 1$. For a convex cost function (the case here) the best Q (or one of the best Q values) will be the lowest Q where $\Delta\text{ETC}(Q)$ is greater than zero. Therefore, we select the smallest Q for which

$$\Delta\text{ETC}(Q) > 0$$

Substituting from Eqs. 10.25 and 10.26 leads, after considerable simplification, to Eq. 10.7.

2. THE CONSTRAINED MULTI-ITEM SITUATION

The problem is to select the Q_i's $(i = 1, 2, \ldots, n)$ to maximize

$$\sum_{i=1}^{n} E[P(Q_i)]$$

subject to

$$\sum_{i=1}^{n} Q_i v_i = W \tag{10.27}$$

where, from Eq. 10.19

$$E[P(Q_i)] = -Q_i v_i + \int_0^{Q_i} [p_i x_0 + g_i(Q_i - x_0)]_i f_x(x_0) dx_0$$
$$+ \int_{Q_i}^{\infty} [p_i Q_i - B_i(x_0 - Q_i)]_i f_x(x_0) dx_0 \qquad (10.28)$$

and

$${}_i f_x(x_0) dx_0 = \text{Prob \{Total demand for product } i \text{ lies between } x_0 \text{ and } x_0 + dx_0\}$$

The Lagrangian approach (see Appendix A) is to select the multiplier M and Q_i's to maximize

$$L(Q_i\text{'s}, M) = \sum_{i=1}^{n} E[P(Q_i)] - M\left[\sum_{i=1}^{n} Q_i v_i - W\right] \qquad (10.29)$$

This is accomplished by setting partial derivatives to zero.

$$\frac{\partial L}{\partial M} = 0$$

simply produces Eq. 10.27. Substituting Eq. 10.28 into Eq. 10.29, we have

$$L(Q_i\text{'s}, M) = \sum_{i=1}^{n} (-Q_i v_i + I_1 + I_2) - M\left[\sum_{i=1}^{n} Q_i v_i - W\right] \qquad (10.30)$$

where I_1 and I_2 are the two integrals in Eq. 10.28. The key point is that I_1 and I_2 do not involve the v_i's.

Now Eq. 10.30 can be rewritten as

$$L(Q_i\text{'s}, M) = \sum_{i=1}^{n} [-Q_i(M+1)v_i + I_1 + I_2] + MW$$

The expression in square brackets is the same as $E[P(Q_i)]$, except that v_i is replaced by $(M + 1)v_i$. Therefore, when we set

$$\frac{\partial L}{\partial Q_i} = 0$$

we obtain the same result as the independent Q^* for item i except that v_i is replaced by $(M + 1)v_i$; that is, select Q_i to satisfy

$$ {}_ip_{x<}(Q_i) = \frac{p_i - (M + 1)v_i + B_i}{p_i - g_i + B_i} \tag{10.31} $$

A given value of M implies a value for each Q_i which in turn implies a value of

$$ \sum_{i=1}^{n} Q_i v_i $$

Equation 10.31 shows that the higher the value of M, the lower must be ${}_ip_{x<}(Q_i)$—that is, the lower must be Q_i.

PROBLEMS

10.1 Alexander Norman owns several retail fur stores in a large North American city. In the spring of each year he must decide on the number of each type of fur coat to order from his manufacturing supplier for the upcoming winter season. For a particular muskrat line his cost per coat is \$150 and the retail selling price is \$210. He estimates an average sales of 100 coats but with considerable uncertainty, which he is willing to express as a uniform distribution between 75 and 125. Any coat not sold at the end of the winter can be disposed of at cost (\$150) to a discount house. However, Norman feels that on any such coat he has lost money because of the capital tied up in the inventory for the whole season. He estimates a loss of \$0.15 for every dollar tied up in a coat that must be sold off at the end of the season.

a. How many coats should he order?

b. One of the factors contributing to the uncertainty in sales is the unknown level of retail luxury tax on coats that will be established by the government early in the fall. Norman has connections in the government and manages to learn the tax level prior to his buying decision. This changes his probability distribution to a normal form with a mean of 110 and a standard deviation of 15. Now what is the best order quantity? How much was the inside information concerning the tax worth to him?

10.2 Consider the situation where tooling is set up to make a major piece of equipment and spare parts can be made relatively inexpensively. After this one production run of the product and its spares, the dyes, etc., will be discarded. Discuss the relationship between the problem of how many spares to run and the single-period problem.

10.3 Neighborhood Hardware Ltd. acts as a central buying agent and distributor for a large number of retail hardware outlets in Canada. The product line is divided into six major categories, with a different buyer being responsible for each single category. One category is miscellaneous equipment for outdoor work around the home. The buyer for this group, Mr. Harry Lock, seeks assistance from a recently hired analyst, J. D. Smith, in the computer division of the company. In particular, he is concerned with the acquisition of a particular type of small snowblower that must be ordered several months before the winter. Smith, after considerable discussions with Lock, has the latter's agreement with the following data:

Unit acquisition cost is \$60.00/unit.

Selling price is \$100.00/unit.

Any units unsold at the end of the winter will be marked down to \$51/unit, ensuring a complete clearance and thus avoiding the prohibitive expense of storage until the next season. The probability distribution of regular demand is estimated to be:

Hundreds of units, j_0	3	4	5	6	7	8
$p_j(j_0)$	0.1	0.1	0.4	0.2	0.1	0.1

a. What is the expected demand?

b. What is the standard deviation of demand?

c. To maximize expected profit, how many units should Smith (using a discrete demand model) tell Lock to acquire?

d. What is the expected profit under the strategy of part c?

e. Suppose Smith instead decides to fit a normal distribution, having the same mean and standard deviation, to the above discrete distribution. With this normal model, what is the recommended order quantity, rounded to the nearest hundred units?

f. If the discrete distribution is the true one, what cost penalty is incurred by the use of the somewhat simpler normal model?

10.4 Suppose the supplier in Problem 10.3 offers a discount such that the unit cost is \$55 if an order of at least 750 units is placed? Should Neighborhood take advantage of this offer?

10.5 In reality, Mr. Lock of Neighborhood Hardware has to order three different snowblowers from the same supplier. He tells the analyst, Smith, that he'll go along with his normal model (whatever that is!) but, in no event, will he allocate more than \$70,000 for the acquisition of snowblowers. In addition to item SB-1, described in Problem 10.3, characteristics of the other two items are:

Item	Unit Acquisition Cost (\$/unit)	Selling Price (\$/unit)	Clearance Price (\$/unit)
SB-2	80	110	70
SB-3	130	200	120

	Demand	
Item	Mean (units)	Standard Deviation (units)
SB-2	300	50
SB-3	200	40

a. What should Smith suggest as the order quantities of the three items?

b. What would be the approximate change in expected profit if Lock agreed to a \$5,000 increase in the budget allocated for snowblowers?

Note: Assume in this problem that there are no quantity discounts available.

10.6 The Calgary Herald has a policy of not permitting returns from hotels and stores on unsold newspapers. To compensate for this fact, they have lowered the value of v somewhat.

a. From the standpoint of a particular store, how would you evaluate the effect of a change from v_1, g_1 to $v_2, 0$ where $g_1 > 0$ and $v_2 < v_1$?

b. Discuss the rationale for the Herald's policy.

10.7 Professor Leo Libin, an expert in inventory theory, feels that his wife is considering the preparation of far too much food for an upcoming family get-together. He feels that the newsboy formulation is relevant to this situation.

a. What kinds of data (objective or subjective) should he collect?

b. His wife says that certain types of leftovers can be put in the freezer. Briefly indicate what impact this has on the analysis.

10.8 Consider a company with N warehouses and a certain amount (W units) of stock of a particular s.k.u. to allocate among the warehouses. The next allocation will not be made until one period from now. Let

$_if_x(x_0)$ = probability density of demand in a period for warehouse $i (i = 1, 2, \ldots, N)$

Develop a rule for allocating the W units of stock under each of the following costing assumptions (treated separately).

a. A cost H_i incurred at warehouse i if any shortage occurs.

b. A cost B_i is charged per unit short at warehouse i.

10.9 Consider a perishable item with a unit acquisition cost v, a fixed ordering cost A, a known demand rate D, and a carrying charge r. The perishability is reflected in the following behavior of the selling price p as a function of the age t of a unit:

$$p(t) = p - bt \qquad 0 < t < SL$$

where

b = positive constant

SL = shelf life

Any units of age SL are disposed of at a unit value of g, which is less than both v and $p - b(SL)$. Set up a decision rule for finding the profit maximizing value of the order quantity Q.

10.10 Consider a sporting goods company that carries ski equipment in stores across Canada. Because of unusual weather conditions one year, near the end of the ski season, the company finds itself with a surplus of ski equipment in the West and with not enough on hand in the East to meet the demand. At a meeting of marketing managers a person from the East requests that the surplus goods in the West be rush-shipped to the East. On the other hand, a Western manager suggests a discount sale there to get rid of the stock. In an effort to resolve the conflict the President asks the Management Sciences Group to analyze the problem and report back with a recommended decision within one week. *Briefly* outline an analysis you would undertake, including the types of data that would be required. Also, if possible, suggest another alternative (that is, differing from the two suggested by the marketing managers).

REFERENCES

Albright, S. C. (1976). "Optimal Stock Depletion Policies with Stochastic Lives." *Management Science*, Vol. 22, No. 8, pp. 852–857.

Brodheim, E., C. Derman, and G. P. Prastacas (1975). "On the Evaluation of a Class of Inventory Policies for Perishable Products such as Whole Blood." *Management Science*, Vol. 21, No.11, pp. 1320–1325.

Burton, J., and S. Morgan (1982). "The Multi-Period Newsboy Problem." *Working Paper 5-82-01*, College of Business Administration, Drexel University, Philadelphia.

Carlson, P. C. (1982a). "A System for the Control of Retail Fashion Inventories." *Proceedings of the Spring National Conference*, Institute of Industrial Engineers, New Orleans, pp. 505–510.

Carlson, P. C. (1982b). "Fashion Retailing: Orders, Reorders and Markdowns." *Proceedings of the Fall National Conference*, Institute of Industrial Engineers, Cincinnati, pp. 315–321.

Chang, S. H., and D. E. Fyffe (1971). "Estimation of Forecast Errors for Seasonal Style-Goods Sales." *Management Science*, Vol. 18, No. 2, pp. B89–B96.

Cohen, M. A., and D. Pekelman (1978). "LIFO Inventory Systems." *Management Science*, Vol. 24, No. 11, pp. 1150–1162.

Crowston, W. B., W. H. Hausman, and W. R. Kampe II (1973). "Multistage Production for Stochastic Seasonal Demand." *Management Science*, Vol. 19, No. 8, pp. 924–935.

Elston, R. (1970). "Blood Bank Inventories." *CRC Critical Reviews in Clinical Laboratory Science*, Vol. 1, pp. 528–548.

Emmons, H. (1968). "A Replenishment Model for Radioactive Nuclide Generators." *Management Science*, Vol. 14, No. 5, pp. 263–274.

Friedman, Y., and Y. Hoch (1978). "A Dynamic Lot-Size Model with Inventory Deterioration." *INFOR*, Vol. 16, No. 2, pp. 183–188.

Fries, B. (1975). "Optimal Ordering Policy for a Perishable Commodity with Fixed Lifetime." *Operations Research*, Vol. 23, No. 1, pp. 46–61.

Gilding, D. B., and C. Lock (1980). "Determination of Stock for Sale Promotions." *Journal of the Operational Research Society*. Vol. 31, No. 4, pp. 311–318.

Goyal, S. (1973). "Optimal Decision Rules for Producing Greeting Cards." *Operational Research Quarterly*, Vol. 24, No. 3, pp. 391–401.

Graves, S. C. (1982). "The Application of Queueing Theory to Continuous Perishable Inventory Systems." *Management Science*, Vol. 28, No. 4, pp. 400–406.

Hartung, P. (1972). "A Simple Style Goods Inventory Model." *Management Science*, Vol. 19, No. 12, pp. 1452–1458.

Hausman, W. H. (1969). "Sequential Decision Problems: A Model to Exploit Existing Forecasters." *Management Science*, Vol. 16, No. 2, pp. 93–111.

Hausman, W. H., and R. Peterson (1972). "Multiproduct Production Scheduling for Style Goods with Limited Capacity, Forecast Revisions and Terminal Delivery." *Management Science*, Vol. 18, No. 7, pp. 370–383.

Hausman, W. H., and R. St. G. Sides (1973). "Mail-order Demands for Style Goods: Theory and Data Analysis." *Management Science*, Vol. 20, No. 2, pp. 191–202.

Hertz, D. B., and K. H. Schaffir (1960). "A Forecasting Method for Management of Seasonal Style-Goods Inventories." *Operations Research*, Vol. 8, No. 1, pp. 45–52.

Ignall, E., and A. Veinott (1969). "Optimality of Myopic Inventory Policies for Several Substitute Products." *Management Science*, Vol. 15, No. 5, pp. 284–304.

Mamer, J., and S. A. Smith (1982). "Optimizing Field Repair Kits Based on Job Completion Rate." *Management Science*, Vol. 28, No. 11, pp. 1328–1333.

Murray, G. R., Jr., and E. A. Silver (1966). "A Bayesian Analysis of the Style Goods Inventory Problem." *Management Science*, Vol. 12, No. 11, pp. 785–797.

Nahmias, S. (1975a). "A Comparison of Alternative Approximations for Ordering Perishable Inventory." *INFOR*, Vol. 13, No. 2, pp. 175–184.

Nahmias, S. (1975b). "Optimal Ordering Policies for Perishable Inventory-II." *Operations Research*, Vol. 23, No. 4, pp. 735–749.

Nahmias, S. (1976). "Myopic Approximations for the Perishable Inventory Problem." *Management Science*, Vol. 22, No. 9, pp. 1002–1008.

Nahmias, S. (1978). "The Fixed Charge Perishable Inventory Problem." *Operations Research*, Vol. 26, No. 3, pp. 464–481.

Nahmias, S. (1982). "Perishable Inventory Theory: A Review." *Operations Research*, Vol. 30, No. 4, pp. 680–708.

Nahmias, S., and S. Wang (1979). "A Heuristic Lot-Size Reorder Point Model for Decaying Inventories." *Management Science*, Vol. 25, No. 1, pp. 90–97.

Pierskalla, W., and C. Roach (1972). "Optimal Issuing Policies for Perishable Inventory." *Management Science*, Vol. 18, No. 11, pp. 603–614.

Prastacos, G. P. (1979). "Blood Management Systems: An Overview of Theory and Practice." *Working Paper 79-09-04*, Department of Decision Sciences, The University of Pennsylvania, Philadelpha.

Riter, C. (1967). "The Merchandising Decision under Uncertainty." *Journal of Marketing*, Vol. 31, pp. 44–47.

Schlaifer, R. (1961). *Introduction to Statistics for Business Decisions.* McGraw-Hill, New York, p. 320.

Shah, Y., and M. Jaiswal (1977). "A Periodic Review Model for an Inventory System with Deteriorating Items." *International Journal of Production Research*, Vol. 15, pp. 179–190.

Smith, S. A., J. C. Chambers, E. Schlifer (1980). "Optimal Inventories Based on Job Completion Rate for Repairs Requiring Multiple Items." *Management Science*, Vol. 26, No. 8, pp. 849–852.

Sokolnikoff, I. S., and R. M. Redheffer (1958). *Mathematics of Physics and Modern Engineering*. McGraw-Hill, New York, pp. 261–262.

Tadikamalla, P. R. (1978). "An EOQ Model for Items with Gamma Distributed Deterioration." *AIIE Transactions*, Vol. 10, No. 1, pp. 100–103.

Wadsworth, G. P. (1959). "Probability." Chapter 1 in *Notes on Operations Research*. Technology Press, Cambridge, Massachusetts, pp. 26–29.

Weiss, H. J. (1980). "Optimal Ordering Policies for Continuous Review, Perishable Inventory Models." *Operations Research*, Vol. 28, No. 2, pp. 365–374.

Wolfe, H. B. (1968). "A Model for Control of Style Merchandise." *Industrial Management Review*. Vol. 9, No.2, pp. 69–82.

PART FOUR
COORDINATION OF ITEMS IN NONPRODUCTION CONTEXTS

In Parts Two and Three we have been concerned with the control of individual items. The rules and systems developed have treated the individual items in isolation, the one exception being where we were concerned with aggregate consequences of a particular decision rule. Examples of the latter were all the exchange curve considerations and situations (such as the multi-item, single-period problem of Chapter 10) where there was a constraint on the total value of the order quantities. In Part Four we now turn to explicit consideration of coordinated control, but in nonproduction situations. There are two important contexts where such coordination often leads to substantial cost savings.

First, in Chapter 11 we deal with a single stocking point context (as in Chapters 5 to 10) but now consider coordination of replenishments of a group of items to reduce costs. Such coordination makes sense if one of the following conditions occurs:

1. Several items are purchased from the same supplier.
2. Several items share the same mode of transportation. (An analogous production situation is the case where several items are produced on the same piece of equipment and setup costs depend on the sequencing of the items.)

Chapter 12 deals with multiechelon inventory situations—the second context where coordination can lead to appreciable cost savings. Material is stored at more than one geographical location with one or more central stores feeding the stock to branch locations, and so on. It is clear that decisions concerning the same item at different locations should not be made independently.

Because of these coordination issues, *exact analyses* are an order of magnitude more complex than those of earlier chapters. Therefore, we are frequently forced to resort to heuristic decision rules. In Chapters 15 and 16 we address coordination issues within production environments.

CHAPTER 11

Coordinated Replenishments at a Single Stocking Point

In this chapter we address an important situation in which it makes sense to coordinate the control of different stock keeping units. Specifically, the items are all stocked at the same location and they share a common supplier or mode of transportation.[1] Conceptually, the items to be coordinated could be the same item at different, *parallel* locations. We emphasize the word parallel because coordination in a multiechelon (serial) situation (one location feeding stock into another) is quite different. The latter situation will be addressed in Chapter 12.

As we will see in Section 11.1, there are several possible advantages in coordinating the replenishments of a group of items at the same stocking location. The potential disadvantages will also be discussed. In Section 11.2, for the case of deterministic demand, the economic order quantity analysis of Chapter 5 (which there assumed *independent* control of items) is extended to the situation where there is a major fixed (setup) cost associated with a replenishment of a family of coordinated items and a minor fixed (setup) cost for each item involved in the particular replenishment. Section 11.3 extends the quantity discount arguments of Chapter 5 to the case where the discount is based on the magnitude of the total replenishment of a group of items—for example, a freight rate reduction if a carload size replenishment is achieved. Then, in Section 11.4 we discuss the complexity of the situation in which items are to be coordinated but demand is probabilistic. Subsequently, two pragmatic control systems are presented. First, in Section 11.5 we deal with the case where group quantity discounts are not relevant. A so-called "can-order" system is described. It is of a

[1]There is a closely related production situation—namely, where the items share a common production facility. In the latter case, to which we will return in Chapter 15, there is the added complexity of a finite productive capacity to be shared each period.

continuous review nature. When the inventory of any item of a coordinated group drops low enough, a replenishment is triggered. Whether or not each other item is included in the replenishment is dictated by how low its inventory level happens to be at that moment. Then, in Section 11.6 we deal with the situation where group discounts are of paramount importance so that, when a group order is placed, we normally strive to achieve a certain overall size (or dollar value) of order.

It should be noted that in the literature the terminology "joint replenishment" is sometimes used in lieu of "coordinated replenishment."

11.1 ADVANTAGES AND DISADVANTAGES OF COORDINATION

There are a number of reasons for coordinating items when making replenishment decisions. These include the following.

1. *Savings on unit purchase costs.* When a group of items is ordered from the same vendor, a quantity discount in purchase cost may be realized if the total order is greater than some breakpoint quantity. It may be uneconomical to order this much of a single item, but it could certainly make sense to coordinate several items to achieve a total order size as large as the breakpoint. An example of such a situation would be the acquisition by a distributor of a line of steel products from a particular manufacturer. In some cases a vendor-imposed minimum order quantity may dictate the same sort of joint consideration.

2. *Savings on unit transportation costs.* The discussion is basically the same as above. Now a grouping of individual item orders may be advisable to achieve a quantity such as a carload. A good example, observed by the authors is the shipment of cereal products from a supplier to the regional warehouses of a supermarket chain. The MIDAS situation (Case A) provides another example—several items from the parent company in Germany are simultaneously shipped to Canada in the same container.

3. *Savings on ordering costs.* In some cases where the fixed (setup) cost of placing a replenishment order is high, it might make sense to put several items on a single order to reduce the annual total of these fixed costs. (This is particularly relevant where the replenishment is by in-house production. In such a case the major component of the fixed ordering cost is the manufacturing setup cost. An illustration would be in the bottling of beer products. There are major changeover costs in converting the production line from one quality of beer to another. In contrast, the costs of changing from one container type to another are rather minor.)

4. *Ease of scheduling.* Coordinated handling of a vendor group can facilitate scheduling of buyer time, receiving (and inspection) workload, and so forth. In fact, we have found that, by and large, managers and purchasing agents alike tend to think and deal in terms of vendors or suppliers rather than individual s.k.u.

On the other hand, there are possible disadvantages of using coordinated replenishment procedures. These include the following:

1. *An increase in the average inventory level.* When items are coordinated some will be reordered earlier than if they were treated independently.
2. *An increase in system control costs.* By the very nature of the problem, coordinated control is more complex than independent control of individual items. Therefore, under coordinated control review costs, computation costs, and so on, are likely to be higher.
3. *Reduced flexibility.* Not being able to work with items independently reduces our flexibility in dealing with unusual situations. One possible result is reduced stability of customer service on an individual-item basis.

11.2 THE DETERMINISTIC CASE: SELECTION OF REPLENISHMENT QUANTITIES IN A FAMILY OF ITEMS

In this section we consider the case (discussed above) where there is a family of coordinated items defined in the following manner. There is a major setup cost (A) associated with a replenishment of the family. In the procurement context this is the fixed (or header) cost of placing an order, independent of the number of distinct items involved in the order. (In the production environment this is the changeover cost associated with converting the facility from the production of some other family to production within the family of interest.) Then there is a minor setup cost (a_i) associated with including item i in a replenishment of the family. In the procurement context a_i is often called the line cost, the cost of adding one more item or line to the requisition. (From a production standpoint a_i represents the relatively minor cost of switching to production of item i from production of some other item within the same family.)

11.2.1 Assumptions

All of the assumptions behind the derivation of the economic order quantity (Section 5.1 of Chapter 5) are retained except that now coordination of items is allowed in an effort to reduce setup costs. We recapitulate the assumptions:

1. The demand rate of each item is constant and deterministic (this deterministic assumption will be relaxed in Sections 11.4 to 11.6).[2]

[2]The situation of *time-varying* but deterministic demand patterns (as was the case in Chapter 6) has been analyzed by Kao (1979) and Lambrecht et al. (1979). In particular, the latter present a heuristic procedure that efficiently determines the timing and sizes of replenishments of the various items involved.

2. The replenishment quantity of an item need not be an integral number of units (the extension to integral units is as discussed for a single item in Chapter 5).
3. The unit variable cost of any of the items does not depend on the replenishment quantity; in particular, there are no discounts in either the unit purchase cost or the unit transportation cost (we will relax this assumption in Section 11.3).
4. The replenishment lead time is of zero duration (the extension to a fixed, known, nonzero duration, independent of the magnitude of the replenishment, is straightforward).
5. No shortages are allowed. (Sections 11.4 and 11.6 will deal with the situation where shortages can occur.)
6. The entire order quantity is delivered at the same time.

11.2.2 The Decision Rule

In the independent EOQ analysis of Chapter 5 we showed that the EOQ expressed as a time supply was given by

$$T_{\mathrm{EOQ}} = \sqrt{\frac{2A}{Dvr}}$$

Note that T_{EOQ} increases as the ratio A/Dv increases. Within our present context this indicates than an item i with a high setup cost a_i and a low dollar usage rate $D_i v_i$ should probably be replenished less frequently (higher time supply) than an item j having a low a_j and a high $D_j v_j$. Because of the assumptions of deterministic demand, no shortages permitted, and instantaneous delivery, it makes sense to include an item in a replenishment only when its inventory drops to the zero level. Therefore, a reasonable type of policy to consider is the use of a time interval (T) between replenishments of the family and a set of m_i's where m_i, an integer, is the number of T intervals that the replenishment quantity of item i will last; that is, item i will be included in every m_ith replenishment of the family.[3] For example, if $m_{17} = 3$, this says that item 17 will only be included in every third replenishment of the family, with a replenishment quantity sufficient to last a time interval of duration $3T$ (each time it will be replenished just as its stock hits the zero level). We wish to select the values of T and the m_i's to keep the total relevant costs as low as possible.

[3]Jackson et al. (1983) have developed an efficient procedure for the more restrictive situation where $m_i = 1, 2, 4, 8$, etc. (that is, a multiple of 2) and T itself is also such a multiple of some basic time period (such as a day or a week). This type of restriction is commonly found in practice. Moreover, Jackson et al. have shown that their solution is, at most, 6 percent more costly than the "optimal" solution to the problem. We do not present the details here since their solution is more difficult conceptually than is ours.

As shown in the Appendix of this chapter, the integer m_i's must be selected to minimize

$$\left(A + \sum_{i=1}^{n} \frac{a_i}{m_i}\right) \sum_{i=1}^{n} m_i D_i v_i \tag{11.1}$$

where

A = major setup cost for the family, in dollars

a_i = minor setup cost for item i, in dollars

D_i = demand rate of item i, in units/unit time

v_i = unit variable cost of item i, in \$/unit

n = number of items in the family (the items are numbered 1, 2, 3, . . . , $n - 1$, n).

Also, once the best m_i's are known, the corresponding appropriate value of T is given by

$$T^*(m_i\text{'s}) = \sqrt{\frac{2(A + \Sigma\, a_i/m_i)}{r \Sigma m_i D_i v_i}} \tag{11.2}$$

It is worth noting that r does not appear in Eq. 11.1; that is, the best values of the m_i's do not depend on the carrying charge.

Goyal (1974), among others (see the reference list at the end of this chapter), has proposed a search procedure for finding the best set of m_i's. We suggest, instead, the use of the following much simpler (noniterative) procedure which is derived in the Appendix of this chapter:

Step 1 Number the items such that

$$\frac{a_i}{D_i v_i}$$

is smallest for item 1. Set $m_1 = 1$.

Step 2 Evaluate

$$m_i = \sqrt{\frac{a_i}{D_i v_i} \frac{D_1 v_1}{A + a_1}} \tag{11.3}$$

rounded to the nearest integer greater than zero.

Step 3 Evaluate T^* using the m_i's of Step 2 in Eq. 11.2.

Step 4 Determine

$$Q_i v_i = m_i D_i v_i T^* \qquad i = 1, 2, \ldots, n \tag{11.4}$$

In numerous tests (see Silver, 1975) this procedure has produced results at or near the best possible solution.

11.2.3 A Graphical Aid

The square root computations of Eq. 11.3 can be avoided through the use of a simple graphical aid. Because of the rounding rule of Eq. 11.3, we are indifferent between the integer values m_i and $m_i + 1$ when

$$\sqrt{\frac{a_i}{D_i v_i} \frac{D_1 v_1}{A + a_1}}$$

is halfway between m_i and $m_i + 1$; that is

$$m_i + \tfrac{1}{2} = \sqrt{\frac{a_i}{D_i v_i} \frac{D_1 v_1}{A + a_1}}$$

This leads to

$$\frac{a_i}{D_i v_i} = (m_i + \tfrac{1}{2})^2 \frac{A + a_1}{D_1 v_1}$$

which is a straight line in a plot of $a_i/D_i v_i$ versus $(A + a_1)/D_1 v_1$. Thus, the indifference curves are a set of straight lines as shown in Figure 11.1.[4] Multiplication of both of $a_i/D_i v_i$ and $(A + a_1)/D_1 v_1$ by the same constant does not affect the solution of Eq. 11.3. This provides us with considerable flexibility in using the graph (for example, if both ratios are extremely small, we can multiple each by the same large number and only then ascertain the location on the graph of the corresponding point).

[4]A somewhat more rigorous (rather than simply rounding) argument (see Silver,1976) leads to indifference between m_i and $m_i + 1$ where

$$\frac{a_i}{D_i v_i} = m_i(m_i + 1) \frac{A + a_1}{D_1 v_1}$$

which again gives straight lines (albeit with slopes slightly differing from those found above) on Figure 11.1. The cost effects of this more sophisticated version are likely to be minimal.

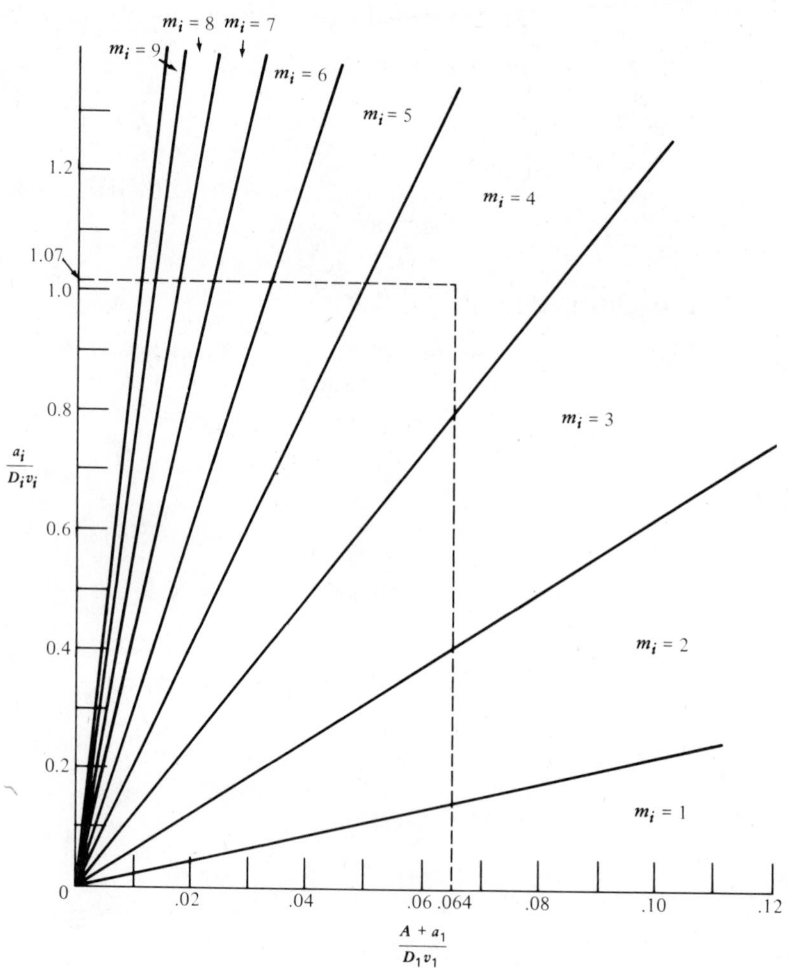

FIGURE 11.1 Implementation Aid for the Determination of the m_i's

Numerical Illustration

The MIDAS International plant (in West Germany) uses the same machinery to place three different developing liquids into assorted container sizes. One of these liquids (known as product XSC in MIDAS Canada) is packaged in four different sized containers—namely 1, 5, 10, and 50 liters. The major setup cost to convert to this type of liquid is estimated to be \$40. It costs \$15 to switch from one container size to another. The demand rates of this family of items are shown in Table 11.1. The carrying charge has been established as 0.24 \$/\$/year. Moreover, there is substantial excess capacity in the packaging operation, so it is reasonable to ignore capacity considerations.

TABLE 11.1 The MIDAS Family of Items Problem
$A = \$40$, $a_i = \$15$ (independent of i), $r = 0.24$ \$/\$/yr

Item i Description	1[a] 10 liters	2 1 liter	3 5 liters	4 50 liters
D_iv_i(\$/yr)	86,000	12,500	1,400	3,000
m_i	1	1	4	3
		$T^* = 0.0762$ yr		
Q_iv_i(\$)	6,550	950	430	690

[a]As discussed in the decision logic the items have been numbered such that item 1 has the smallest value of a_i/D_iv_i. (Here the largest value of D_iv_i because all the a_i's are the same.)

Use of Step 2 of the decision rule gives

$$m_2 = \sqrt{\frac{15}{12{,}500}\,\frac{86{,}000}{55}} = 1.37 \rightarrow 1$$

$$m_3 = \sqrt{\frac{15}{1{,}400}\,\frac{86{,}000}{55}} = 4.09 \rightarrow 4$$

$$m_4 = \sqrt{\frac{15}{3{,}000}\,\frac{86{,}000}{55}} = 2.80 \rightarrow 3$$

These entries are shown in Table 11.1.

Then Step 3 gives

$$T^* = \sqrt{\frac{2(40 + \frac{15}{1} + \frac{15}{1} + \frac{15}{4} + \frac{15}{3})}{0.24[1(86{,}000) + 1(12{,}500) + 4(1{,}400) + 3(3{,}000)]}}$$
$$= 0.0762 \text{ yr} \simeq 4 \text{ weeks}$$

With Step 4, we obtain the run quantities

$$Q_1v_1 = (1)(86{,}000)(0.0762) = \$6{,}550$$ (run quantity in dollars of 10-liter container)

$$Q_2v_2 = (1)(12{,}500)(0.0762) \simeq \$950$$

$$Q_3v_3 = (4)(1{,}400)(0.0762) \simeq \$430$$

$$Q_4v_4 = (3)(3{,}000)(0.0762) \simeq \$690$$

To convert these run quantities to units, we would have to divide by the v_i values.

To illustrate the use of the graphical aid consider item 3:

$$\frac{a_3}{D_3 v_3} = \frac{15}{1{,}400} = 0.0107$$

and

$$\frac{A + a_1}{D_1 v_1} = \frac{55}{86{,}000} = 0.000640$$

We multiply both ratios by 100; the resulting point is shown in Figure 11.1. The associated m_3 is seen to be 4 which, of course, agrees with the result found above through direct use of Eq. 11.3.

11.2.4 A Bound on the Cost Penalty of the Heuristic Solution

By definition, a heuristic solution is not guaranteed to give a solution with a low cost penalty. Fortunately for this problem, it is possible, as shown in the Appendix of this chapter, to find a simple lower bound for the cost of the best (T, m_i's) policy, namely,

$$\text{TRC}_{\text{bound}} = \sqrt{2(A + a_1)D_1 v_1 r} + \sum_{j=2}^{n} \sqrt{2a_j D_j v_j r} \tag{11.5}$$

There is an interesting interpretation of the bound when one remembers that an optimal policy must have item 1 included in every replenishment of the family. The first term is the total relevant cost per unit time of an EOQ strategy (see Eq. 5.5 of Chapter 5) for item 1 considered alone, if one associates the full cost $A + a_1$ with each replenishment of item 1. The second term represents a summation of the total relevant costs per unit time of an EOQ strategy of each of the other items, where a cost of only a_j is associated with a replenishment of item j ($j \neq 1$).

For our numerical illustration, the value of this bound works out to be \$2054.15/yr. As shown in the Appendix of this chapter, the cost of *any* (T, m_i's) solution is given by

$$\text{TRC}(T, m_i\text{'s}) = \frac{A + \sum_{i=1}^{n} a_i/m_i}{T} + \sum_{i=1}^{n} \frac{D_i m_i T v_i r}{2} \tag{11.6}$$

The solution developed by the heuristic has a cost of \$2067.65/yr (evaluated by substituting the *integer* m_i values, found by the heuristic, into Eq. 11.6). The bound clearly indicates that the heuristic solution is very close to (if not right at) the optimum for the particular example.

11.3 THE DETERMINISTIC CASE WITH GROUP DISCOUNTS

As mentioned earlier, unit price or freight rate discounts may be offered on the total dollar value or the total volume of a replenishment made up of several items (for example, the use of containers for MIDAS shipments from Germany to Canada). Consequently, the inventory control manager would like to ascertain when to take advantage of such a discount. Therefore, knowing the discount structure, the major setup cost (A) of a group of items, the item characteristics (a_i's, D_i's, and v_i's), and the carrying charge (r), we want to develop decision logic for selecting the appropriate individual order quantities, which imply a group quantity and, hence, whether or not a particular discount is achieved. We mention that sometimes discount structures are designed for much smaller customers than the organization under consideration. In such cases discounts can be achieved by individual-item orders so that the more complex coordinated control is not necessarily needed.

As in the case of a single item, treated in Chapter 5, taking advantage of an offered discount reduces the replenishment costs (both the fixed and unit costs) but increases the inventory carrying costs. At first glance, it would appear that the analysis for multiple items should not be much more difficult than that for a single item. Such would be the case if every item was included in every replenishment. However, we know from the preceding section that an $m_i > 1$ is likely for an item having a high value of a_i/D_iv_i; that is, such items should not necessarily be included in every replenishment, even to help achieve a quantity discount level. Therefore, it is conceivable that the best strategy might be one where on certain replenishments a discount was achieved, while on others it was not (even though all demand rates are assumed known and at constant levels). The analysis of such a strategy would be quite complex because the replenishment cycles would no longer all be of the same duration, T (the ones where quantity discounts were achieved would be longer than the others). Rather than attempting to explicitly model such complex possibilities we suggest the following reasonable compromise solution (illustrated for the case of a single possible discount based on the total replenishment size, in units).

Our approach parallels that used in Section 5.5 of Chapter 5. We consider three possible solutions. The first (and if it is feasible, it is the best to use) is where a coordinated analysis, assuming a quantity discount, leads to total replenishment quantities which are *always* sufficient to achieve the discount. The second case is where the best result is achieved right at the breakpoint. Finally, the third possibility is the coordinated solution without a quantity discount. Therefore, first, the method of Section 11.2 is used to ascertain the m_i's and T, assuming that the discount is achieved. The *smallest*[5] replenishment quantity is computed and compared with the breakpoint quantity (Q_b) required. If it exceeds Q_b, we use the m_i's and T developed. If it is less than Q_b, then we must compare the cost of the best solution without a discount to the cost of the solution where the smallest replenishment quantity is right at the breakpoint. Whichever of these has the lower cost is then the solution to use. The details are as follows:

Step 1 Compute the m_i's and T as in Section 11.2 but assuming that each

$$v_i = v_{oi}(1 - d)$$

where

v_{oi} = basic unit cost of item i without a discount

d = fractional discount when the *total* replenishment equals or exceeds the breakpoint quantity Q_b

It should be noted that the set of m_i's does not depend on the size of the discount as long as the unit cost of each item is reduced by the same percentage discount (which is typically the case). This can be seen from Eq. 11.3, where, if we use $v_i = v_{oi}(1 - d)$ for all i, the $(1 - d)$ terms in the numerator and denominator cancel.

Compute the size of the smallest family replenishment

$$Q_{sm} = (\text{Summation of order quantities of all items having } m_i = 1) \tag{11.7}$$

If $Q_{sm} \geq Q_b$, use the m_i's, T, and Q_i's found above. If not, we proceed to Step 2.

Step 2 We scale up the family cycle time T (found in Step 1) until the smallest replenishment size equals the quantity breakpoint. This is achieved at

$$T_b = \frac{Q_b}{(\text{Summation of } D_i\text{'s of all items having } m_i = 1)} \tag{11.8}$$

[5]What we are assuming here is that if a discount is to be achieved, it must be achieved by every replenishment; that is, we are ignoring the more complex possibility of achieving a discount on only some of the replenishments. The smallest replenishments are those where only the items with $m_i = 1$ are included.

The m_i's found in Step 1 are maintained. The cost of this breakpoint solution is evaluated using the following total relevant cost expression:

$$\mathrm{TRC}(T_b, m_i\text{'s}) = (1-d)\sum_{i=1}^{n} D_i v_{oi} + \frac{A + \sum_{i=1}^{n} \frac{a_i}{m_i}}{T_b} + \frac{r(1-d)T_b}{2}\sum_{i=1}^{n} m_i D_i v_{oi} \tag{11.9}$$

Step 3 The procedure of Section 11.2 is used to find the m_i's, T, and Q_i's without a discount (as mentioned earlier, the best m_i's here must be the same as those found in Step 1). As shown in the Appendix to this chapter, the total relevant costs of this solution are given by a somewhat simpler expression than Eq. 11.9, namely,

$$\mathrm{TRC}(\text{best } T \text{ and } m_i\text{'s}) = \sum_{i=1}^{n} D_i v_{oi} + \sqrt{2\left(A + \sum_{i=1}^{n} \frac{a_i}{m_i}\right) r \sum_{i=1}^{n} m_i D_i v_{oi}} \tag{11.10}$$

Step 4 The TRC values found in Steps 2 and 3 are compared. The m_i's, T, and Q_i's associated with the lower of these are to be used. If the solution right at the breakpoint is used, care must be taken (because of the likely required integer nature of the Q's) to ensure that the breakpoint is actually achieved. Adjustment of one or more Q values to the next higher integers may be necessary.

Prior to showing a numerical illustration of the above procedure, we make a few remarks related to the work of Schneider (1982), which was developed in the context of the food distribution industry. Specifically, he incorporates the idea of a modular order quantity (MOQ) for each item. Then, anytime the item is ordered, the size of the order must be an integer multiple of MOQ. Furthermore, recognizing that demand is probabilistic, he presents an approximation for the average inventory level of each item as a function of MOQ, the item's demand rate, and the vendor order quantity (the breakpoint). This permits the selection of the best MOQ for each possible breakpoint so that the various breakpoint solutions can be costed out.

Numerical Illustration

Consider three parts, EDS-031, EDS-032, and EDS-033, used in the assembly of the MIDAS Stabilization Processor. These three products are purchased from the same domestic supplier who offers a discount of 5 percent if the value of the total replenishment quantity is at least \$600. We use \$1.50 as the basic cost of placing an order with one item involved. The inclusion of each additonal item costs \$0.50. It therefore follows that

$$A = \$1.50 - \$0.50 = \$1.00$$

and

$$a_i = \$0.50 \qquad \text{for all } i$$

An r value of 0.24 \$/\$/yr is to be used and the D_i's and v_{oi}'s are shown in columns 1 and 2 of Table 11.2.

Following the above procedure Step 1 produces the results shown in columns 4 through 6 of Table 11.2. It is seen from Eq. 11.7 that

$$Q_{\text{sm}} \text{ in dollars} = 275 + 110 = \$385$$

TABLE 11.2 MIDAS Example with Group Quantity Discount $A = \$1$, $a_i = a = \$0.50$, $r = 0.24$ \$/\$/yr.

Results of Step 1

Item i	Code	D_i (units/yr) (1)	v_{oi} (\$/unit) (2)	D_iv_{oi} (\$/yr) (3)	m_i (4)	T (yr) (5)	Q_iv_{oi} (\$) (6)
1	EDS-001	12,000	0.50	6,000	1		275 } 385
2	EDS-002	8,000	0.30	2,400	1	0.0459	110 }
3	EDS-003	700	0.10	70	5		16
				8,470			

385 < 600 Therefore go to Step 2

Final Solution

$T = 0.0715$ yr

Item i	m_i	Q_i (units)	Q_iv_i (\$)
1	1	858	429.00 } \$600.60
2	1	572	171.60 }
3	5	250	25.00

which is below the quantity breakpoint of \$600. Therefore, we proceed to Step 2. Use of Eq. 11.8, suitably modified because the breakpoint is expressed in dollars, gives

$$T_b = \frac{\$600}{\$6{,}000/\text{yr} + \$2{,}400/\text{yr}}$$
$$= 0.07143 \text{ yr}$$

The cost of the breakpoint solution is from Eq. 11.9:

$$\text{TRC}(T_b, m_i\text{'s}) = 0.95(8{,}470) + \frac{1.00 + 0.50 + 0.50 + 0.10}{0.07143}$$
$$+ \frac{0.24(0.95)}{2}(0.07143)(6{,}000 + 2{,}400 + 350)$$
$$= 8{,}047 + 29 + 71$$
$$= \$8{,}147/\text{yr}$$

In Step 3 we know that the set of best m_i's is $m_1 = m_2 = 1$ and $m_3 = 5$ (from Step 1). Using Eq. 11.10 we have

$$\text{TRC(best } T \text{ and } m_i\text{'s)} = 8{,}470 + \sqrt{2(2.10)0.24(8{,}750)}$$
$$= 8{,}470 + 94$$
$$= \$8{,}564/\text{yr} > \$8{,}147/\text{yr}$$

Therefore, we should use the solution of Step 2—namely, that which assures that the smallest replenishment quantity is at the breakpoint. This is achieved by using[6]

$T = 0.0715$ yr

$Q_1 = 858$ units (D_1T) every group replenishment

$Q_2 = 572$ units (D_2T) every group replenishment

$Q_3 = 250$ units ($5D_3T$) every fifth group replenishment

It is seen that a sizable saving of (8,654 − 8,147) or \$417/yr is achieved by taking the discount.

[6]The T and Q values have been adjusted slightly upwards to ensure that $Q_1v_{01} + Q_2v_{02}$ is at least as large as the breakpoint value of \$600.

11.4 COMPLEXITIES INTRODUCED BY PROBABILISTIC DEMAND

Probabilistic demand greatly complicates the decision problem in a coordinated control context. Several questions must be answered:

1. How often do we review the status of items? (That is, the choice of the review interval, R.)
2. When do we reorder the group?
3. How much do we order? (In particular, whether or not to achieve a discount quantity on a particular order.)
4. How do we allocate the total order among the individual items?

Because of the coordination, it no longer follows that an item will always be at its reorder point when it is included in a replenishment. Usually, it will be above in that some other item in the family will have triggered the order. This complicates matters in two ways. First, it is now more difficult to ascertain the average inventory level of an item. Second, and more serious, the service implications of any particular reorder point are much more difficult to evaluate than in the case of individual-item control.

In the next two sections we present an overview of two important types of coordinated control systems under probabilistic demand.

11.5 THE CASE OF NO QUANTITY DISCOUNTS: CAN-ORDER SYSTEMS

Can-order systems are specifically geared to the situation where savings in setup costs are of primary concern (for example, where several products are run on the same piece of equipment) as opposed to achieving a specified total replenishment size (for quantity discount purposes).

11.5.1 The Physical Operation of an (S, c, s) System

Balintfy (1964) was the first to propose the use of an (S, c, s) system, a special type of continuous review system for controlling coordinated items. In such a system, whenever item i's inventory position drops to s_i (called its must-order point) or lower, it triggers a replenishment action that raises item i's level to its order-up-to-level S_i. At the same time any other item j (within the associated family) with its inventory positon at or below its can-order point c_j is included in the replenishment. If item j is included, a quantity is ordered sufficient to raise its level to S_j. The idea of having a can-order point is to allow an item j, whose inventory position is low enough (at c_j or lower), to be included in the order triggered by item i, thus eliminating an extra major setup cost that would likely occur in the near future when item j reaches its must-order point. On the other hand, inclusion of item j in the order is not worthwhile if its inventory position is high enough above its must-order point (that is, above c_j). The behavior of a typical item under such a system of control is shown in Figure 11.2.

Ignall (1969) has shown that an (S, c, s) policy does not necessarily minimize the sum of replenishment, inventory carrying, and shortage costs. However, the policy that would minimize these costs would be considerably more complex than the (S, c, s) strategy. Therefore, when one properly takes account of the system control costs, it is felt that an (S, c, s) approach achieves a solution that is close to the best attainable.

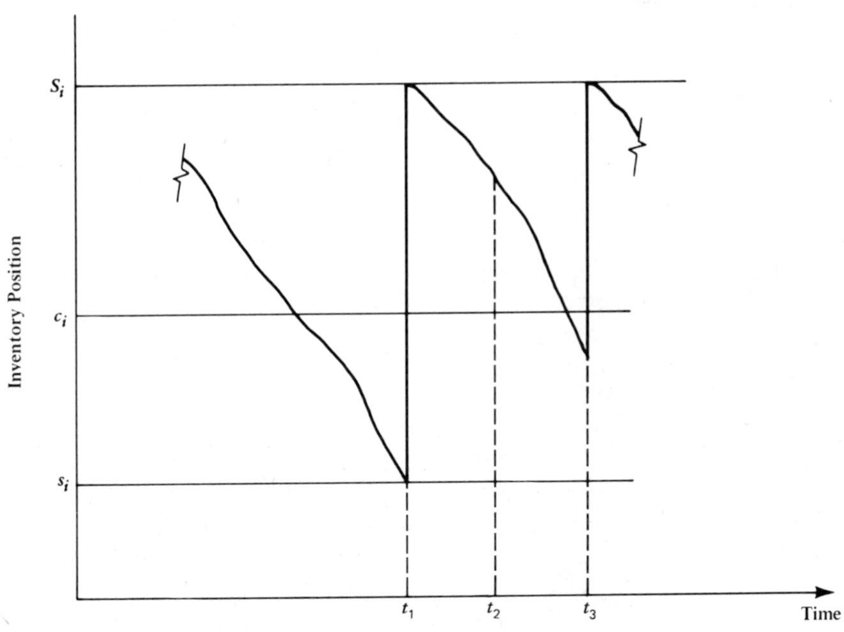

At time t_1 this item triggers a replenishment.

At time t_2 some other item in the group triggers a replenishment, but this item is not included because its inventory position is above its can-order point.

At time t_3 some other item in the group triggers a replenishment in which this item is now included.

FIGURE 11.2 Behavior of an Item under (S, c, s) Control

11.5.2 A Suggested Procedure for Computing Values of the Control Parameters

Further details on the procedure to be discussed are available in Silver (1974) and Silver and Massard (1980). The derivation is based on a set of assumptions, the most severe of which are the following.

1. The replenishment lead time is of constant known length. Furthermore, its length does not depend on which subset of the items of the family are involved in the replenishment.

2. Demand for each item is of a Poisson nature where, of course, each item can have a different demand rate. The Poisson distribution is an approximation to reality, most appropriate for the case of many small customers. The assumption of Poisson arrivals of individual customer transactions is reasonable. However, transactions of greater than unit size would result in what is known as a compound Poisson distribution of demand. (An extension of the procedure to handle this more general case is provided by Thompstone and Silver, 1975; and Silver, 1981. In addition, Federgruen et al. 1984, have developed an alternative approach based on a Markov process model of the coordinated control situation).

3. From the viewpoint of any particular item the sequence of group replenishments triggered by *other* items can be approximated by a Poisson process (quite reasonable as long as n is not too small).

For each item i there are three quantities (S_i, c_i, and s_i) to specify—that is, if the family has 10 items, there are 30 interrelated control variables that must be given values. In Chapters 5 to 7 we advocated first determining Q (or R) and then finding s (or S) conditional on the specified value of Q (or R) rather than attempting to simultaneously select the (s, Q) or (R, S) pair. Again, here a sequential approach is used. The S's and c's are found, using a simple graphical procedure for the case of a negligible replenishment lead time (each s is zero in this case); then, conditional on these S and c values, one finds the lowest s_i that satisfies a prespecified service constraint for the particular item i. As earlier, we know that the S's, c's, and s's so obtained will not strictly minimize the sum of replenishment and carrying costs. However, the cost penalty is likely to be low, and we are willing to absorb it in order to have a computationally feasible scheme for evaluating the control parameters.

Finding S and c (for $L = 0$)

The graphical aid was developed through the following reasoning. The expected cost per unit time for item i, denoted by EC_i, is first expressed analytically. The best S_i for a given c_i is then determined by setting the partial derivative of EC_i with respect to S_i equal to 0. We denote this quantity by $\hat{S}(c)$ and it is given by (we suppress the subscript i)

$$\hat{S}(c) = \max \left\{ c, c - \frac{\rho(1-\rho^c)}{1-\rho} + \sqrt{\frac{2\lambda(a+\rho^c A)}{vr} + \frac{2c\rho^{c+1}}{1-\rho} - \frac{\rho(1-\rho^c)(1+\rho^{c+1})}{(1-\rho)^2}} \right\} \tag{11.11}$$

where

λ_i = Poisson demand rate for the item (i)

$$\rho_i = \frac{\lambda_i}{\lambda_i + \mu_i} \tag{11.12}$$

with μ_i being the rate at which group replenishments are triggered by all items other than item i.

When $\hat{S}(c)$ is substituted back into EC_i, one obtains $E\hat{C}_i(c)$—the minimum cost per unit time for item i when c is used. Indifference between the use of c or $c + 1$ is achieved by equating $E\hat{C}_i(c)$ and $E\hat{C}_i(c + 1)$. The results are extremely complicated but can be expressed in functional form as

$$f(a/A, c, \rho, \text{EOQ}) = 0 \tag{11.13}$$

where

$$\text{EOQ} = \sqrt{\frac{2A\lambda}{vr}} \tag{11.14}$$

For a given value of c Eq. 11.13 represents an indifference surface in a three-dimensional space of a/A, ρ, and EOQ. For practical purposes, one can use a set of two-dimensional plots of EOQ versus ρ, one for each of several reasonable values of a/A. An illustration is shown in Figure 11.3 for $a/A = 0.1$. The apparent discontinuity at $\rho = 0.85$ is simply a consequence of the change of the scale of ρ at that point (introduced to permit coverage of a broader range of ρ values on the single graph).

To use the indifference curves for any particular item i, we need to know the value of ρ_i which depends on μ_i. The latter is a function of the S's and c's of all the other items. Fortunately, it turns out that total costs are very insensitive to the value of ρ. Thus we are able to use a crude estimate of ρ, based on assuming *independent* control of all other items in the family. In such a case

$$\mu_i = \sum_{j \neq i} \sqrt{\frac{\lambda_j v_j r}{2(A + a_j)}} \tag{11.15}$$

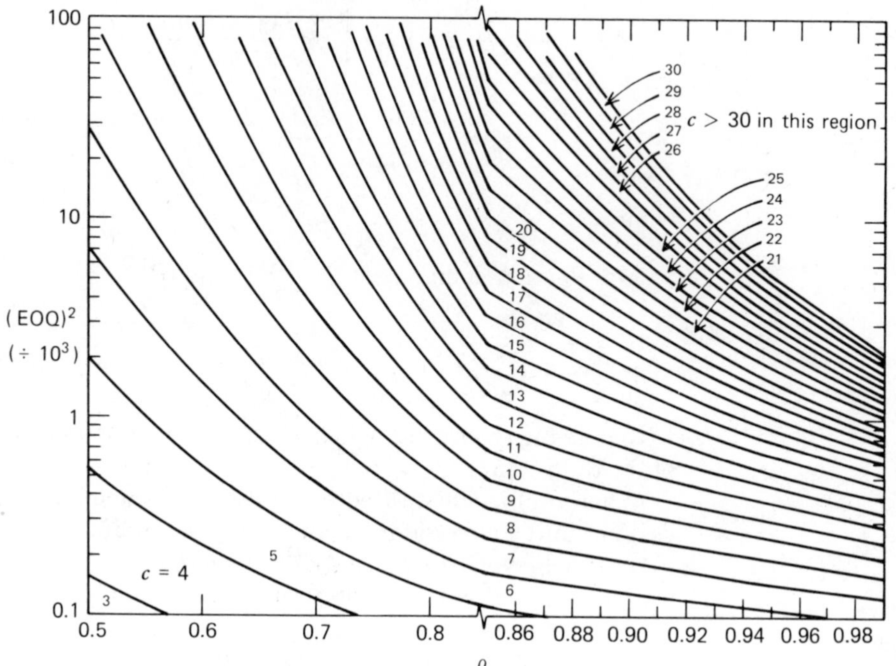

FIGURE 11.3 Indifference Curves to find the Best c for $a/A = 0.1$

where the square root expression gives the number of independent EOQ replenishments of item j per unit time.

Once the appropriate c value is found, from using the indifference curves, then the associated S follows from Eq. 11.11.

Numerical Illustration Consider a family of three items with $A = \$25$, $a = \$2.50$, $r = 0.25$ \$/\$/yr, and item characteristics as shown in columns 1 to 3 of Table 11.3. Let us determine the c and S for item 3. First, from Eq. 11.15 and the entries in column 4 of the table, we have $\mu_3 = 1.381$. Then Eq. 11.12 gives us

$$\rho_3 = \frac{15}{15 + 1.381} = 0.916$$

Now, for item 3, Eq. 11.14 gives $(\text{EOQ})^2 = 1500$. From Figure 11.3, $c_3 \simeq 17$. Finally, Eq. 11.11 results in $S_3 = 30$.

TABLE 11.3 Numerical Illustration of the Use of Indifference Curves

Item j (1)	λ_j (units/yr) (2)	v_j (\$/unit) (3)	$\sqrt{\dfrac{\lambda_j v_j r}{2(A + a_j)}}$ (4)
1	11	10.00	0.707
2	20	5.00	0.674
3	15	2.00	0.369

The Case of $L > 0$

As argued earlier, when the lead time (denoted by L) becomes nonzero, we use a sequential approach of finding the s value *given* the S and c values found from the case of negligible lead time ($L = 0$). More precisely we use

Case of Negligible Lead Time	**Case of Significant Lead Time**
$S(\text{for } L = 0)$	$S(\text{for } L = 0) + s$
$c(\text{for } L = 0)$	$c(\text{for } L = 0) + s$
$s = 0$	s

We illustrate for the P_1 (probability of no stockout per repenishment cycle) service measure. Unlike in independent control (Chapter 7) where we assumed that an item was always at its reorder point (s) when it was ordered, here an item's inventory position can lie anywhere between c and s when it is included in an order. Using the Poisson nature of demands for item i and group replenishments triggered by *other* items, one can show that we wish to select the smallest value of s such that (suppressing the subscript i notation)

$$(1/\rho)^c p_{po\leqslant}(s + c|\lambda L) - p_{po}(s + 1|\lambda L) - \rho^{s+1} \sum_{x_0=s+2}^{s+c} p_{po}(x_0|\lambda L)\,(1/\rho)^{x_0} \geqslant P_1/\rho^c \tag{11.16}$$

where

$p_{po}(x_0|\lambda L)$ = Prob {Poisson variable with parameter λL takes on a value equal to x_0}

$p_{po\leqslant}(x_0|\lambda L)$ = Prob {Poisson variable with parameter λL takes on a value less than or equal to x_0}

Condition 11.16 has been programmed on an HP-97 calculator.

Numerical Illustration In our three-item example, suppose that a lead time of 3 months (that is, $L = 0.25$ years) is appropriate and a P_1 value of 0.95 is desired. We consider the determination of the must-order point s for item 3. From the earlier results we know that

$$S_3\,(L = 0) = 30 \qquad c_3\,(L = 0) = 17 \qquad \rho_3 = 0.916$$

Use of condition 11.16 gives $s = 5$. It is seen that the final parameter settings for item 3 are thus

$$S_3 = 35 \qquad c_3 = 22 \qquad s_3 = 5$$

Performance of the Procedure

On a wide range of test examples the procedure produced average cost savings of close to 15 percent when compared with independent control of individual items. In examples involving only two items (the only value of n where it is practical to find the *optimal* solution) the procedure gave an average cost penalty of only 0.1 percent above the optimal solution, a reassuring performance.

11.5.3 General Effects of (S, c, s) Control

Besides the significant cost savings described above, other findings include

1. The cost savings increase as the a/A ratio decreases—certainly intuitively appealing.
2. The cost savings improve as n increases; the more items there are in the group, the more attractive coordinated replenishment becomes.
3. The *percent* cost savings tend to diminish as the required service level increases (a large safety stock dominates either type of control).
4. Coordination tends to substantially lower the order-up-to-levels (the S's). This is because under coordination the average setup cost associated with the replenishment of an item tends to be lower; thus we need not order as much each time we replenish.
5. Coordination, to a lesser extent, lowers the must-order points (the s's). Under coordination, an item i is often reordered when its inventory level is substantially above s_i; hence s_i can be lowered (compared with the case of independent control) while still providing adequate service.
6. The major impact of coordination is on the lower dollar usage items.

11.6 PROBABILISTIC DEMAND AND QUANTITY DISCOUNTS

In contrast with the situation in the previous section, now it is attractive to achieve a specified group order size. One obvious example is where a discount is offered if the group order size exceeds some level. Another relevant situation is one in which several products are shipped on a periodic basis to a remote location (for example, a regional warehouse) in a single truck, rail car, or boat. In either case one wishes to answer the four questions posed in Section 11.4.

The situation is even more complicated than that in Section 11.5 because we now have the added facet of economies of scale. We provide an overview of a system developed by Miltenburg (1982) that is adapted to use on a microcomputer. His system, in a set of tests, has outperformed the more widely known IMPACT and INFOREM systems (see IBM, 1971, 1972, 1978; Kleijnen and Rens, 1978; and Schneider, 1979). Other interesting references on coordinated control are Johnston (1980) and Low and Waddington (1967). Figure 11.4 should be helpful in understanding the following discussion of Miltenburg's system.

Block 1 in Figure 11.4 indicates that either continuous or periodic review can be used. In a coordinated situation (particularly the transportation setting described earlier) one would typically use a convenient periodic review interval such as a day or a week.

As indicated in Block 2, a reorder point system is used. At a review instant, if the inventory position of any item in the family is at or below its reorder point, then a group replenishment is triggered. The setting of the reorder points will be discussed later.

The choice of an appropriate group replenishment (Block 5), of course, depends on the current inventory status of each item (Block 3) and what quantity discounts are currently available (Block 4). In this decision one could use the methodology of Section 11.2; however, it is based on a steady state model and does not take into account the current inventory situation. Thus, instead, the more appropriate decision logic of the "special opportunity to buy" situation (Section 5.8.5 of Chapter 5) is used to evaluate the various possible group replenishment sizes.

Once an overall replenishment size is selected, it must be allocated (Block 6) among the individual items. This is done to maximize the time until the next replenishment. After any given allocation we then have the individual stock levels being depleted by demands. The first to hit its reorder point triggers a new group order at the next review instant. Because of the probabilistic nature of the demand, the time until the next reorder is a random variable. Miltenburg models the demands for separate items as independent, diffusion processes (a diffusion process, besides being mathematically convenient, has the attractive property of implying that the total demand over any particular interval of time has a normal distribution).

Just as in Section 11.5, often an item will be reordered when it is *above* its reorder point. This is because some other item in the family will trigger the replenishment. The excess stock above the reorder point is known as *residual stock*. Account must be taken of such residual stock because it provides safety stock above and beyond the usual safety stock built into the reorder point. Unfortunately, the probability distribution of the residual stock of an item depends on the inventory positions of *all* of the items after the allocation is made. Thus, after every allocation these distributions must be evaluated and

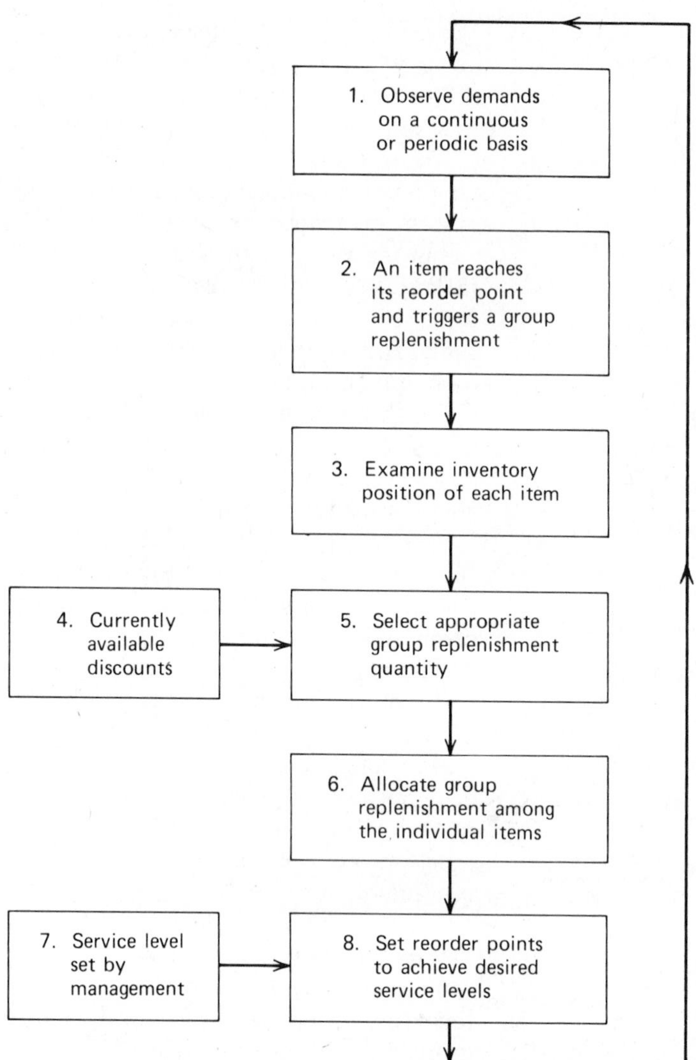

FIGURE 11.4 Components of a Coordinated Control System with Quantity Discounts and Probabilistic Demand

used to establish the reorder points (Block 8) in order to provide a desired service level (Block 7). As in Section 7.7.2 of Chapter 7, the appropriate period over which protection is required is of duration $R + L$. To illustrate the complexity of the situation, if x denotes the demand in $R + L$, z the residual stock of an item, and s the reorder point of the item, then the probability of a stockout by the end of $R + L$ is

$$\text{Prob}\,\{\text{Stockout}\} = \text{Prob}\,\{x \geqslant s + z\}$$

$$= \int_{z_0=-\infty}^{\infty} f_z(z_0)dz_0 \int_{x=s+z_0}^{\infty} f_x(x_0)dx_0 \tag{11.17}$$

where $f_x(x_0)$ and $f_z(z_0)$ are the probability density functions of x and z, respectively.

For the case of period review, Miltenburg has found that a normal distribution provides a reasonable fit to the distribution of residual stock. In contrast, for the case of continuous review, a more appropriate fit is achieved by a spike at 0 and a truncated normal distribution above it (see Problem 11.9). As mentioned earlier, $f_x(x_0)$ is a normal distribution.

11.7 SUMMARY

In this chapter we first showed the details of coordinated control under deterministic demand, both with and without quantity discounts. Then we developed an appreciation of the complexity of the probabilistic demand situation. For the latter we discussed two quite different types of coordinated control.

We will have more to say about coordination of items in production contexts, particularly in the process industry environment of Chapter 15 where there typically is a bottleneck operation whose capacity must be shared among a group of items.

In the next chapter we turn to another, probably more important, type of coordination—namely, where the same item is stored at more than one location with stock flowing from one location to another.

APPENDIX TO CHAPTER 11
DERIVATION OF RESULTS IN SECTION 11.2

If a time interval T between replenishments of the family and a set of m_i's are used, where m_i, an integer, is the number of T intervals that the replenishment quantity of item i will last, then this replenishment quantity (Q_i) is given by

$$Q_i = D_i m_i T \tag{11.18}$$

The typical saw-tooth diagram of inventory is applicable so that the average inventory of item i ($\bar{I}_i$) is

$$\bar{I}_i = \frac{Q_i}{2} = \frac{D_i m_i T}{2}$$

A group setup cost (A) is incurred every T units of time, whereas the cost a_i is incurred only once in every $m_i T$ units of time. Therefore, the total relevant costs per unit time are given by

$$\text{TRC}(T, m_i\text{'s}) = \frac{A + \sum_{i=1}^{n} a_i/m_i}{T} + \sum_{i=1}^{n} \frac{D_i m_i T v_i r}{2} \tag{11.19}$$

Setting

$$\frac{\partial \text{TRC}}{\partial T} = 0$$

gives the best T for the particular set of m_i's; that is,

$$-\frac{A + \sum_i a_i/m_i}{T^2} + \frac{r}{2} \sum_i m_i D_i v_i = 0$$

or

$$T^*(m_i\text{'s}) = \sqrt{\frac{2(A + \Sigma\, a_i/m_i)}{r\, \Sigma\, m_i D_i v_i}} \tag{11.20}$$

which is Eq. 11.2.

Substitution of Eq. 11.20 back into Eq. 11.19 gives the best cost for a given set of m_i's:

$$\text{TRC}^*(m_i\text{'s}) = \frac{A + \Sigma\, a_i/m_i}{\sqrt{\dfrac{2(A + \Sigma\, a_i/m_i)}{r\,\Sigma\, m_i D_i v_i}}} + \sqrt{\frac{2(A + \Sigma\, a_i/m_i}{r\,\Sigma\, m_i D_i v_i}}\;\frac{r\,\Sigma\, m_i D_i v_i}{2}$$

which simplifies to

$$\text{TRC}^*(m_i\text{'s}) = \sqrt{2(A + \Sigma\, a_i/m_i) r\,\Sigma\, m_i D_i v_i} \tag{11.21}$$

(This equation was used to directly produce Eq. 11.10.)

We wish to select the m_i's to minimize TRC*(m_i's). From an inspection of Eq. 11.21 this is achieved by selecting the m_i's to minimize

$$F(m_i\text{'s}) = (A + \Sigma\, a_i/m_i)\,\Sigma\, m_i D_i v_i \tag{11.22}$$

The minimization of Eq. 11.22 is no simple matter because of two facts: (1) the m_i's interact (that is, the effects of one m_i value depend on the values of the other m_i's) and (2) the m_i's must be integers (see Schweitzer and Silver, 1983).

If we choose to ignore the integer constraints on the m_i's and set partial derivatives of $F(m_i$'s) equal to zero (necessary conditions for a minimum), then

$$\frac{\partial F(m_i\text{'s})}{\partial m_j} = -\frac{a_j}{m_j^2}\sum_i m_i D_i v_i + D_j v_j\left(A + \sum a_i/m_i\right) = 0$$

or

$$m_j^2 = \frac{a_j\,\Sigma\, m_i D_i v_i}{D_j v_j (A + \Sigma\, a_i/m_i)} \qquad j = 1, 2, \ldots, n \tag{11.23}$$

For $j \neq k$, we have

$$m_k^2 = \frac{a_k}{D_k v_k}\;\frac{\Sigma\, m_i D_i v_i}{(A + \Sigma\, a_i/m_i)}$$

Dividing gives

$$\frac{m_j^2}{m_k^2} = \frac{a_j}{D_j v_j}\;\frac{D_k v_k}{a_k}$$

or

$$\frac{m_j}{m_k} = \sqrt{\frac{a_j}{D_j v_j} \frac{D_k v_k}{a_k}} \qquad j \neq k$$

It is seen that if

$$\frac{a_j}{D_j v_j} < \frac{a_k}{D_k v_k}$$

then (the continuous solution) m_j is less than (the continuous solution) m_k. Therefore, the item i having the smallest value of $a_i/D_i v_i$ should have the lowest value of m_i—namely, 1. It is reasonable to assume that this will hold even when the m_j's are restricted to being integers; of course, in this case, more than one item could have $m_j = 1$.

If the items are numbered such that item 1 has the smallest value of $a_i/D_i v_i$, then

$$m_1 = 1 \tag{11.24}$$

and, from Eq. 11.23,

$$m_j = \sqrt{\frac{a_j}{D_j v_j}} \sqrt{\frac{\Sigma\, m_i D_i v_i}{(A + \Sigma\, a_i/m_i)}} \qquad j = 2, 3, \ldots, n \tag{11.25}$$

Suppose that there is a solution to these equations which results in

$$\sqrt{\frac{\Sigma\, m_i D_i v_i}{(A + \Sigma\, a_i/m_i)}} = C \tag{11.26}$$

Then, from Eq. 11.25, we have

$$m_j = C \sqrt{\frac{a_j}{D_j v_j}} \qquad j = 2, 3, \ldots, n \tag{11.27}$$

Therefore,

$$\begin{aligned} \sum_{i=1}^{n} m_i D_i v_i &= D_1 v_1 + \sum_{i=2}^{n} C \sqrt{\frac{a_i}{D_i v_i}} D_i v_i \\ &= D_1 v_1 + C \sum_{i=2}^{n} \sqrt{a_i D_i v_i} \end{aligned} \tag{11.28}$$

Similarly

$$\sum_{i=1}^{n} a_i/m_i = a_1 + \frac{1}{C} \sum_{i=2}^{n} \sqrt{a_i D_i v_i} \tag{11.29}$$

Substituting Eqs. 11.28 and 11.29 back into the left-hand side of Eq. 11.26 and squaring, we obtain

$$\frac{D_1 v_1 + C \sum_{i=2}^{n} \sqrt{a_i D_i v_i}}{A + a_1 + \frac{1}{C} \sum_{i=2}^{n} \sqrt{a_i D_i v_i}} = C^2$$

Cross-multiplication gives

$$D_1 v_1 + C \sum_{i=2}^{n} \sqrt{a_i D_i v_i} = C^2(A + a_1) + C \sum_{i=2}^{n} \sqrt{a_i D_i v_i}$$

or

$$C = \sqrt{\frac{D_1 v_1}{A + a_1}}$$

Substitution of this expression back into Eq. 11.27 gives

$$m_j = \sqrt{\frac{a_j}{D_j v_j} \frac{D_1 v_1}{A + a_1}} \qquad j = 2, 3, \ldots, n \tag{11.30}$$

which is Eq. 11.3.

To find a bound on the *best* possible solution we substitute $m_i = 1$ and the generally *noninteger* m_j's of Eq. 11.30 into Eq. 11.21. This leads, after considerable algebra, to the result of Eq. 11.5.

PROBLEMS

11.1 Consider a family of four items with the following characteristics:

$A = \$100 \qquad r = 0.2/\text{yr}$

Item i	D_iv_i ($/yr)	a_i ($)
1	100,000	5
2	20,000	5
3	1,000	21.5
4	300	5

a. Use the procedure of Section 11.2.2 to find appropriate values of the family cycle time T and the integer m_i's.

b. Suppose that we restricted attention to the case where every item is included in each replenishment of the family. What does this say about the m_i's? Now find the best value of T.

c. Using Eq. 11.19 (in this Appendix), find the cost difference in the answers to parts a and b.

11.2 The Ptomaine Tavern, a famous fast lunch spot near an institute of higher learning, procures three basic cooking ingredients from the same supplier. H. Fishman, one of the co-owners, estimates that the fixed cost associated with placing an order is $10. In addition, there is a fixed "aggravation" charge of $1 for each s.k.u. included in the order. Usage of each of the three ingredients is relatively stable with time. The usages and basic unit values are as follows:

Item *ID*	Usage Rate (units/wk)	Unit Value ($/unit)
CO-1	300	1.00
CO-2	80	0.50
CO-3	10	0.40

a. If a coordinated replenishment strategy is to be used, what should be the values of the m_i's?

b. When pressed by a consulting analyst for a value of the carrying charge r (needed to compute the family cycle time T), Fishman replies: "I don't know from nothing concerning a carrying charge! All I know is that I'm satisfied with placing an order every two weeks." How would you use this answer to impute an approximate value of r? Discuss why it is likely to be only an approximation.

c. What quantities of the three items should the Tavern order?

d. Suppose that the supplier offers Ptomaine a 3 percent discount on any order totaling at least $1,350 in value (before the discount). Fishman's partner, L. Talks, likes the idea of saving on the purchase price. Fishman is not so sure about the advisability of tieing up so much money in inventory. Should Ptomaine take advantage of the quantity discount offer?

11.3 Suppose you wished to estimate the annual costs of treating the members of a family independently in setting up run quantities. Under independent treatment some major setups would be avoided, simply by the chance happening of two items of the same family being run one right after the other. How would you estimate the fraction of setups where this would happen?

11.4 A certain large manufacturing company has just hired a new member of its industrial engineering department, a Ms. V. G. Rickson. Rickson, knowing all about coordinated control, selects a family of two items with the following properties:

Item i	D_i (units/yr)	v_i ($/unit)
1	10,000	0.50
2	1,000	0.40

From accounting records and discussions with operating personnel, she estimates that $A = \$5$, $a_1 = \$1$, $a_2 = \$4$, and $r = 0.2/\text{yr}$.

a. She computes the best values of T, m_1, and m_2. What are these values?

b. The production supervisor, Mr. C. W. Donrath, is skeptical of the value of coordination and argues that independent control is less costly, at least for this family of two items. Is he correct?

11.5 For the A, a_i's deterministic demand context, consider a special coordinated strategy—namely, where all $m_i = 1$.

a. Determine the optimal value of T.

b. Determine the associated minimum total relevant costs per unit time.

c. Find the best independent and coordinated (the latter with all $m_i = 1$ as above) strategies for each of the following two examples:

Example 1

$A = \$10 \quad r = 0.2/\text{yr}$

Item i	D_i (units/yr)	v_i ($/unit)	a_i ($)
1	800	1	2
2	400	0.5	4

Example 2

$A = \$10 \quad r = 0.2/\text{yr}$

Item i	D_i (units/yr)	v_i ($/unit)	a_i ($)
1	900	1	2
2	20	0.5	4

d. Determine as simple a relationship as possible that must be satisfied in order for the above special case of coordinated control (every $m_i = 1$) to be preferable to completely independent control. Ignore any system costs in your analysis. Normalize where possible to reduce the number of parameters.

11.6 The Steady-Milver Corporation produces ball bearings. It has a family of three items which, run consecutively, do not take much time for changeovers. The characteristics of the items are as follows:

Item i	ID	D_i (units/yr)	Raw Material ($/unit)
1	BB1	2,000	2.50
2	BB2	1,000	2.50
3	BB3	500	1.60

Item i	Value Added ($/unit)	Value after Production v_i ($/unit)	a_i ($)
1	0.50	3.00	5
2	0.50	3.00	2
3	0.40	2.00	1

The initial setup cost for the family is $30. Management has agreed on an r value of 0.10 $/$/yr. Production rates are substantially larger than the demand rates.

a. What are the preferred run quantities of the three items?

b. Raw material for product BB1 is acquired from a supplier distinct from that for the other two products. Suppose that the BB1 supplier offers an 8 percent discount on all units if an order of 700 or more is placed. Should Steady-Milver take the discount offer?

11.7 For the three-item example of Section 11.5.2 find:

a. s and c for item 2 when $L = 0$.

b. S, c, and s for item 2 when $L = 0.25$ yr and $P_1 = 0.95$.

11.8 Brown (1967) has suggested a procedure for allocating a total order (of size W dollars) among a group of n items ($i = 1, 2, \ldots, n$). A particular time interval (perhaps until the next order arrives) of duration T is considered. The allocation is made so that the probability that item i runs out during T is proportional to the fraction of the group's sales that item i contributes. (Brown shows that this procedure, at least approximately, minimizes the total stock remaining at the end of the interval.) Suppose that it is reasonable to assume that demand in period T for item i is normally distributed with mean $\hat{x}_i$ and standard deviation σ_{Ti}.

a. Introducing whatever symbols are necessary, develop a routine for allocating the order among the items according to the above criterion.

b. Illustrate for the following 3 item example, in which $W = \$900$:

Item i	$\hat{x}_i$ (units)	σ_{Ti} (units)	v_i (\$/unit)	Initial (before allocation) Inventory I_i (units)
1	100	40	1.00	50
2	300	70	2.00	100
3	250	100	1.20	250

c. Repeat part b but with

$$I_1 = 250 \qquad I_2 = 150 \qquad I_3 = 0$$

11.9 In Miltenburg's coordinated control system recall that we denoted the residual stock of a particular item by the symbol z, and in the case of periodic review it turned out to be reasonable to approximate its distribution by a normal distribution with mean μ_z and standard deviation σ_z.

a. Why is there a spike at $z = 0$ in the continuous review case but not in the periodic review case? Also, why can z be negative in the periodic review situation?

b. Using Eq. 11.17 and assuming that the demand x during $R + L$ is normally distributed with mean $\hat{x}_{R+L}$ and standard deviation σ_{R+L}, find as simple an expression as possible that the reorder point s must satisfy to ensure a probability of no stockout equal to P_1.

Hint: Use the following result proved by Miltenburg (1982).

$$\int_{-\infty}^{\infty} \frac{1}{\sqrt{2\pi}\sigma_z} \exp[-(z_0-\mu_z)^2/2\sigma_z^2]\, p_{u\geq}\left(\frac{s + z_0 - \hat{x}_{R+L}}{\sigma_{R+L}}\right) dz_0 = p_{u\geq}\left(\frac{s + \mu_z - \hat{x}_{R+L}}{c\sigma_{R+L}}\right)$$

where

$$c = \sqrt{1 + \sigma_z^2/\sigma_{R+L}^2}$$

c. Find s for the case where $P_1 = 0.96$, $\mu_z = 5.0$, $\sigma_z = 2.3$, $\hat{x}_{R+L} = 12.0$, and $\sigma_{R+L} = 4.2$. What s value would be used if the residual stock was ignored?

REFERENCES

Andres, F., and H. Emmons (1975). "A Multiproduct Inventory System with Interactive Set-up Costs." *Management Science*, Vol. 21, No. 9, pp. 1055–1063.

Balintfy, J. L. (1964). "On a Basic Class of Multi-Item Inventory Problems." *Management Science*, Vol. 10, No. 2, pp. 287–297.

Brown, R. G. (1967). *Decision Rules for Inventory Management*. Holt, Rinehart and Winston, New York, Chapter 20.

Cahen, J. F. (1972). "Stock Policy in Case of Simultaneous Ordering." *International Journal of Production Research*. Vol. 10, No. 4, pp. 301–312.

Chern, C. M. (1974). "A Multi-Product Joint Ordering Model with Dependent Set-Up Cost." *Management Science*, Vol. 20, No. 7, pp. 1081–1091.

Curry, G. L., R. W. Skeith, and R. G. Harper (1970). "A Multi-product Dependent Inventory Model." *AIIE Transactions*, Vol. II, No. 3, pp. 263–267.

Federgruen, A., H. Groenevelt, and H. C. Tijms (1984). "Coordinated Replenishments in a Multi-Item Inventory System with Compound Poisson Demands." *Management Science*, Vol. 30, No. 3, pp. 344–357.

Fogarty, D., and T. Hoffman (1980). "Joint Replenishments—Lot Sizes." *Scandanavian Journal of Materials Administration*, Vol. 6, No. 3, pp. 48–71.

Goyal, S. K. (1974). "Determination of Optimum Packaging Frequency of Items Jointly Replenished." *Management Science*, Vol. 21, No. 4, pp. 436–443.

IBM Corporation (1971). *Wholesale IMPACT—Advanced Principles and Implementation Reference Manual*, Second Edition, GE20-0174-1, White Plains, New York.

IBM Corporation (1972). *Basic Principles of Wholesale IMPACT—Inventory Management Program and Control Techniques*, Second Edition, GE20-8105-1, White Plains, New York.

IBM Corporation (1978). *INFOREM ALLOCATION: Program Description/Operations Manual*, SB21-2324-0, White Plains, New York.

Ignall, E. (1969). "Optimal Continuous Review Policies for Two Product Inventory Systems with Joint Set-up Costs." *Management Science*, Vol. 15, No. 5, pp. 278–283.

Jackson, P., W. Maxwell, and J. Muckstadt (1983). "The Joint Replenishment Problem with a Powers of Two Restriction." *Technical Report No. 579*, School of Operations Research and Industrial Engineering, Cornell University, Ithaca, New York.

Johnston, F. R. (1980). "An Interactive Stock Control System with a Strategic Management Role." *Journal of the Operational Research Society*, Vol. 31, No. 12, pp. 1069–1084.

Kao, E. (1979). "A Multi-Product Dynamic Lot-Size Model with Individual and Joint Set-up Costs." *Operations Research*, Vol. 27, No. 2, pp. 279–289.

Kaspi, M., and M. J. Rosenblatt (1983). "An Improvement of Silver's Algorithm for the Joint Replenishment Problem." *IIE Transactions*, Vol. 15, No. 3, pp. 264–267.

Kleijnen, J. P. C., and Rens, P. J. (1978). "IMPACT Revisited: A Critical Analysis of IBM's Inventory Package 'IMPACT.'" *Production and Inventory Management*, Vol. 19, No. 1, pp. 71–90.

Lambrecht, M. R., H. Vanderveken, and J. Vander Eecken (1979). "On the Joint Replenishment Problem under Deterministic Time Varying Demand Patterns." *Report No.*

7907, Department of Applied Economics, Katholieke Universiteit, Leuven, Belgium.

Low, R., and J. Waddington (1967). "The Determination of the Optimum Joint Replenishment Policy for a Group of Discount–Connected Stock Lines." *Operational Research Quarterly*, Vol. 18, No. 4, pp. 443–462.

Maher, M., J. Gittins, and R. Morgan (1973). "An Analysis of a Multi-Line Re-Order System Using a Can-Order Policy." *Management Science*, Vol. 19, No. 7, pp. 800–808.

Miltenburg, G. J. (1982). "The Co-ordinated Control of a Family of Discount-Related Items." Unpublished Doctoral Dissertation, Department of Management Sciences, University of Waterloo, Waterloo, Ontario, Canada.

Naddor, E. (1975). "Optimal and Heuristic Decisions in Single and Multi-Item Inventory Systems." *Management Science*, Vol. 21, No. 11, pp. 1234–1249.

Schneider, H. (1979). "The Service Level in Inventory Control Systems." *Engineering Process Economics*, Vol. 4, pp. 341–348.

Schneider, M. J. (1982). "Optimization of Purchasing from a Multi-item Vendor." Paper presented at EURO V and the 25th International Conference of the Institute of Management Sciences, Lausanne, Switzerland.

Schweitzer, P. J., and E. A. Silver (1983). "Mathematical Pitfalls in the One Machine Multiproduct Economic Lot Scheduling Problem." *Operations Research*, Vol. 31, No. 2, pp. 401–405.

Silver, E. A. (1974). "A Control System for Coordinated Inventory Replenishment." *International Journal of Production Research*, Vol. 12, No. 6, pp. 647–671.

Silver, E. A. (1975). "Modifying the Economic Order Quantity (EOQ) to Handle Coordinated Replenishments of Two or More Items." *Production and Inventory Management*, Vol. 16, No. 3, pp. 26–38.

Silver, E. A. (1976). "A Simple Method of Determining Order Quantities in Joint Replenishments under Deterministic Demand." *Management Science*, Vol. 22, No. 12, pp. 1351–1361.

Silver, E. A. (1981). "Establishing Reorder Points in the (S, c, s) Coordinated Control System under Compound Poisson Demand." *International Journal of Production Research*, Vol. 19, No. 6, pp. 743–750.

Silver, E. A., and N. Massard (1980). "Setting of Parameter Values in Coordinated Inventory Control by Means of Graphical and Hand Calculator Methods." *Proceedings of the First International Symposium on Inventories*, Akademia Kiado, Budapest, Hungary, pp. 553–566.

Thompstone, R. M., and E. A. Silver (1975). "A Coordinated Inventory Control System for Compound Poisson Demand and Zero Lead Time." *International Journal of Production Research*, Vol. 13, No. 6, pp. 581–602.

CHAPTER 12

Planning and Control in Multiechelon Inventory Situations

In this chapter we deal with another important situation, different from that of Chapter 11, where it is appropriate to coordinate the control of different stock keeping units. Specifically, we look at the case of an item being stocked at more than one location with resupply being made between at least some of the locations. A three-echelon illustration is shown in Figure 12.1. Retail outlets (the first echelon) are replenished from branch warehouses (the second echelon) which are supplied from a central warehouse (the third echelon). The latter, in turn, is replenished from outside sources. In such a situation coordinated control makes sense in that, for example, replenishment decisions at the branches impinge as demand on the central warehouse. We say that the demand at the central warehouse is dependent on the demand (and stocking decisions) at the branches. More generally, we refer to this as a dependent demand situation in contrast with earlier chapters of the book where demands for different stock keeping units were considered as being independent.

Multistage manufacturing situations (raw materials, components, subassemblies, assemblies) are conceptually very similar to multiechelon inventory systems. However, within the current chapter we restrict attention to pure inventory (distribution) situations. Specifically, we ignore any finite replenishment capacities that are usually present in the production context. Nevertheless, some of the results of this chapter can be applied, with due caution, within production environments and, in fact, were developed with that type of application in mind. In addition, we will return in Chapter 16 to a detailed treatment of multistage manufacturing systems in which the aforementioned concept of dependent demand will play a crucial role.

In Section 12.1 we deal with the conceptually easiest situation of deterministic demand. Nevertheless, particularly when the demand rate varies with time, exact analyses quickly become quite complicated. Section 12.2 introduces the complexities of probabilistic demand in a multiechelon framework. Then, in

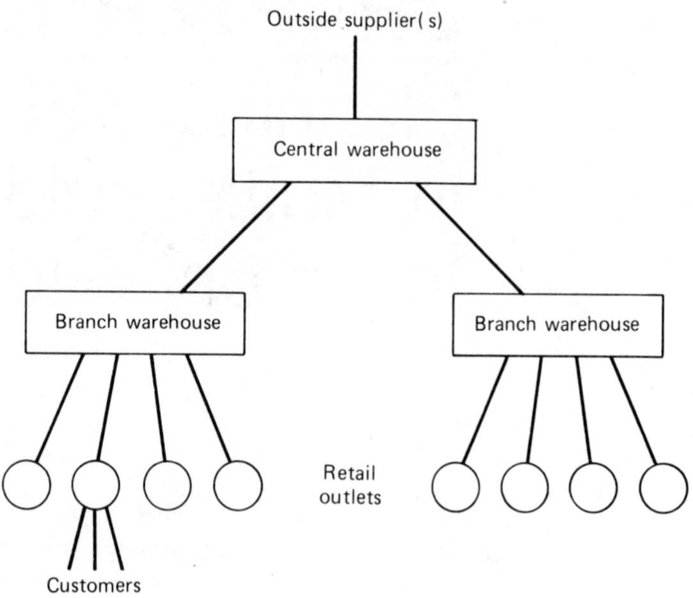

FIGURE 12.1 A Multiechelon Inventory Situation

Section 12.3 we describe what is known as a *base stock control system* in which a limited amount of coordination is achieved. Subsequently, in Section 12.4, PUSH systems are presented; these systems involve highly centralized coordination. Some additional results under probabilistic demand are discussed in Section 12.5. Next, in Section 12.6, for the first time, we deal with the so-called *repairables situation*. Specifically, now not all units demanded are consumed, but rather some units are returned, perhaps in a damaged state. As a result, *both* repair and purchase decisions must be made. Finally, some strategic issues, related to multiechelon inventories, are raised in Section 12.7.

12.1 CASES INVOLVING DETERMINISTIC DEMAND

In this section we deal with the *relatively* simple situation in which the external demand rates are known with certainty. This is admittedly an idealization, but initially is important to study for two reasons. First, the models will reveal the basic interactions among replenishment quantities at the different echelons. Second, as in earlier chapters, we choose, where possible, the pragmatic route of developing replenishment strategies based on deterministic demand, and then, conditional on these results, establishing safety stocks to provide appropriate protection against uncertainties. We also assume that replenishment lead times are known.

12.1.1 Sequential Stocking Points with Level Demand

Consider the simplest of multiechelon situations, namely, where the stocking points are serially connected—for example, 1 central warehouse, 1 branch warehouse, and 1 retail outlet. A more interesting production interpretation is depicted in Figure 12.2 where an item progresses serially through a series of operations, none of which are of an assembly or splitting nature; that is, each operation has only one predecessor and only one successor operation. In fact, for exposition purposes, we restrict ourselves to the most simple case of but two operations, denoted by primary (p) and finishing (f). Primary could correspond to simply the purchase of raw material.

Let us introduce some preliminary notation:

D = deterministic, constant demand rate for the finished product, in units/unit time (normally one year)

A_p = fixed (setup) cost associated with a replenishment at the primary stage, in dollars

A_f = fixed (setup) cost associated with a replenishment at the finishing stage, in dollars

v_p = unit variable cost or value (raw material plus processing) of the item immediately *after* the primary operation, in \$/unit

v_f = unit variable cost or value (raw material plus processing) of the item immediately *after* the finishing operation, in \$/unit

r = carrying charge, the cost of having one dollar of the item tied up in inventory for a unit time interval, that is, the dimensions are \$/\$/unit time

Q_p = replenishment quantity at the primary stage, in units

Q_f = replenishment quantity at the finishing stage, in units

The two controllable (or decision) variables are the replenishment sizes Q_p and Q_f. Figure 12.3 shows the behavior of the two levels of inventory with the passage of time for the particular case where $Q_p = 3Q_f$. A little reflection shows that (at least for the case of deterministic demand) it never would make sense to

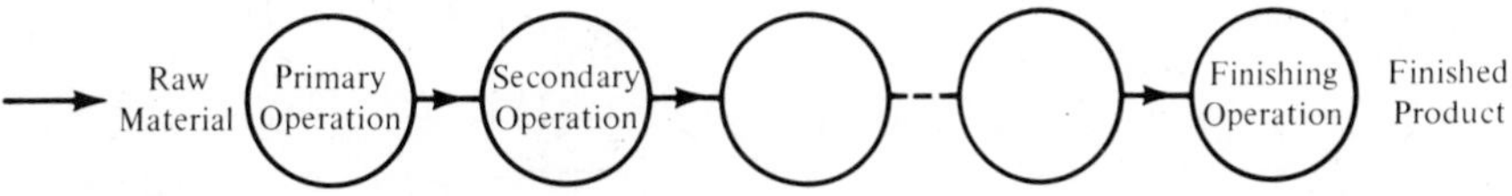

FIGURE 12.2 A Serial Production Process

have Q_p anything but an integer multiple of Q_f. Therefore, we can think of two alternative decision variables Q_f and n where

$$Q_p = nQ_f \qquad n = 1, 2, 3, \ldots \tag{12.1}$$

that is, n is a positive integer.

Note that from Figure 12.3 the inventory at the primary operation does not follow the usual sawtooth pattern even though the end usage is deterministic and constant with time. The reason is that the withdrawals from the primary inventory are of size Q_f. One could carry out an analysis using the conventional

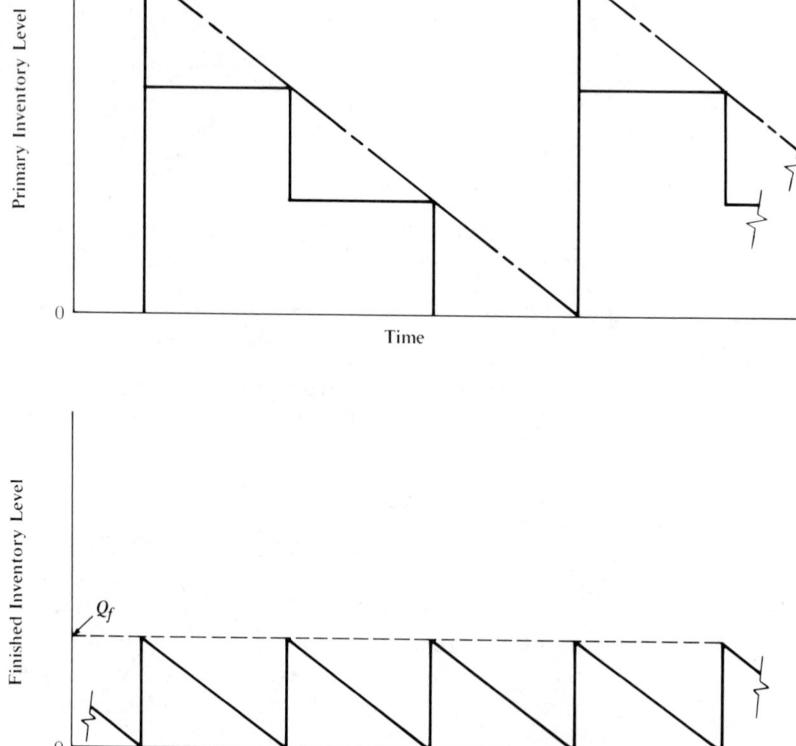

FIGURE 12.3 Behavior of the Inventory Levels in a Deterministic Two-Stage Process

definitions of inventories, but the determination of average inventory levels becomes complicated. Instead, it is easier to use a different concept, known as *echelon stock*, first introduced by Clark and Scarf (1960). They define the echelon stock of echelon j (in a general multiechelon system) as the number of units in the system that are at, or have passed through, echelon j but have as yet not been specifically committed to outside customers (when backorders are permitted the echelon stock can be negative). With this definition and uniform end-item demand each echelon stock has a sawtooth pattern with time as illustrated in Figure 12.3; thus, it is simple to compute the average value of an echelon stock. However, we cannot simply multiply each average echelon stock by the standard vr term and sum to obtain total inventory carrying costs. The reason is that the same physical units of stock can appear in more than one echelon inventory; for example, in our two-stage process the actual finished inventory is counted in both the finished echelon inventory *and* the primary echelon inventory. The way around this dilemma is to value any specific echelon inventory at only the value *added* at that particular echelon. (Problem 12.2 is concerned with showing that this is equivalent to using the usual definitions of inventory levels and stock valuations.) Thus, in our two-stage example the primary echelon inventory is valued at $v_p' = v_p$, while the finished echelon inventory is valued at only $v_f' = v_f - v_p$. More generally, in a production assembly context the echelon valuation v_i' at a particular stage i is given by

$$v_i' = v_i - \Sigma\, v_j \tag{12.2}$$

where the summation is over all
immediate predecessors, j

Returning to our two-stage serial situation, the total relevant (setup plus carrying) costs per unit time are given by

$$\text{TRC}\,(Q_p, Q_f) = \frac{A_pD}{Q_p} + \bar{I}_p'v_p'r + \frac{A_fD}{Q_f} + \bar{I}_f'v_f'r \tag{12.3}$$

where

$\bar{I}_p'$ = average value of the primary *echelon* inventory, in units

$\bar{I}_f'$ = average value of the finishing *echelon* inventory, in units

Substituting from Eq. 12.1 and noting that the echelon stocks follow sawtooth patterns,

$$\begin{aligned}\text{TRC}\,(n, Q_f) &= \frac{A_pD}{nQ_f} + n\,\frac{Q_fv_p'r}{2} + \frac{A_fD}{Q_f} + \frac{Q_fv_f'r}{2}\\ &= \frac{D}{Q_f}\left(A_f + \frac{A_p}{n}\right) + \frac{Q_fr}{2}\,(nv_p' + v_f')\end{aligned} \tag{12.4}$$

We must find the values of n (an integer) and Q_f that minimize this expression. As proved in the Appendix of this chapter, this is achieved by the following procedure.

Step 1 Compute

$$n^* = \sqrt{\frac{A_p v_f'}{A_f v_p'}} \tag{12.5}$$

If n^* is exactly an integer, go to Step 4 with $n = n^*$. Also, if $n^* < 1$, go to Step 4 with $n = 1$. Otherwise, proceed to Step 2.

Step 2 Ascertain the two integer values, n_1 and n_2, that surround n^*.

Step 3 Evaluate

$$F(n_1) = \left[A_f + \frac{A_p}{n_1}\right][n_1 v_p' + v_f']$$

and

$$F(n_2) = \left[A_f + \frac{A_p}{n_2}\right][n_2 v_p' + v_f'] \tag{12.6}$$

If $F(n_1) \leq F(n_2)$, use $n = n_1$.
If $F(n_1) > F(n_2)$, use $n = n_2$.

Step 4 Evaluate

$$Q_f = \sqrt{\frac{2\left[A_f + \frac{A_p}{n}\right]D}{[n v_p' + v_f']r}} \tag{12.7}$$

Step 5 Calculate

$$Q_p = nQ_f$$

Numerical Illustration of the Logic

Let us consider a particular liquid developer, product XSC-444, which MIDAS buys in bulk, then breaks down and repackages. The demand for this item can be assumed to be essentially deterministic and level at a rate of 1,000 liters per year. The unit value of the bulk material (v_p' or v_p) is \$1/liter, while the value added by the transforming (break and package) operation $v_f' = (v_f - v_p)$ is \$4/liter. The fixed component of the purchase charge (A_p) is \$10, while the setup cost for the break and repackage operation (A_f) is $15. Finally, the estimated carrying charge is 0.24 $/$/yr.

Step 1

$$n^* = \sqrt{\frac{(10)(4)}{(15)(1)}}$$
$$= 1.66$$

Step 2

$$n_1 = 1$$
$$n_2 = 2$$

Step 3

$$F(1) = [15 + \tfrac{10}{1}][1 + 4] = 125$$
$$F(2) = [15 + \tfrac{10}{2}][(2)(1) + 4] = 120$$

that is, $F(1) > F(2)$.
Thus, use $n = 2$.

Step 4

$$Q_f = \sqrt{\frac{2[15 + \frac{10}{2}]1{,}000}{[(2)(1) + 4]0.24}} \simeq 167 \text{ liters}$$

Step 5

$$Q_p = (2)(167) = 334 \text{ liters}$$

In words, we purchase 334 liters[1] at a time; one-half of these or 167 liters are immediately broken and repackaged. When these 167 (finished) liters are depleted, a second break and repackage run of 167 liters is made. When these are depleted, we start a new cycle by again purchasing 334 liters of raw material.

[1]Of course, it may make sense to round this quantity to a convenient shipment size such as 350 liters. In such a case, Q_f would also be adjusted (to 175 liters).

12.1.2 Other Results for the Case of Level Demand

For the serial situation described in the previous subsection Szendrovits (1975) has proposed a different type of control procedure—namely, where the *same* lot size is used at all operations but subbatches can be moved between operations. This allows an overlap between operations, hence reduces the manufacturing cycle time. He shows that, under certain conditions, this type of control procedure can outperform that proposed in the preceding subsection.

A number of authors have looked at systems more general in nature than the previously described serial situation. Schwarz (1973) deals with what he calls a one-warehouse, n-retailer situation (depicted in Fig. 12.4 for $n = 4$). For $n \geq 3$ he shows that the form of the optimal policy can be very complex; in particular, requiring that the order quantity at one or more of the locations vary with time even though all relevant demand and cost factors are time-invariant. He rightfully argues for restricting attention to a simpler class of strategies (where each location's order quantity does not change with time) and develops an effective heuristic for finding quite good solutions.

Schwarz and Schrage (1975) adopt essentially the same approach for another type of deterministic situation—namely, "pure" assembly[2] (each node feeds into, at most, one other node; a simple illustration is portrayed in Figure 12.5). They make use of a "myopic" strategy where each node and its successor are treated in isolation by much the same procedure as for the two-stage serial case discussed in the preceding section. Graves and Schwarz (1977) do a similar type of analysis for arborescent systems (just the opposite of a "pure" assembly system; now each node has, at most, one node feeding *into* it).

Williams (1981, 1983) treats the general situation of an assembly network feeding into an arborescent system (assembly production followed by distribution). Maxwell and Muckstadt (1983) address the same problem but impose several restrictions (based on practical considerations) on the nature of the policy to be used, specifically:

1. The policy is nested—that is, a replenishment cannot occur at an operation unless one also occurs at immediate successor operations.
2. The policy is stationary—that is, the time between replenishments at each stage is a constant.
3. A base planning period (for example, a shift, day, week, etc.) exists, and all reorder intervals must be an *integer* multiple of this base period.
4. The time between replenishments at any particular stage must be 1 or 2 or 4 or 8 or . . . times the interval between replenishments at any immediately following stage. This is the "multiple of 2" restriction first encountered in Section 11.2.2 of Chapter 11.

---

[2]The term *assembly* implies a production context. However, the procedures discussed here ignore any capacity constraints.

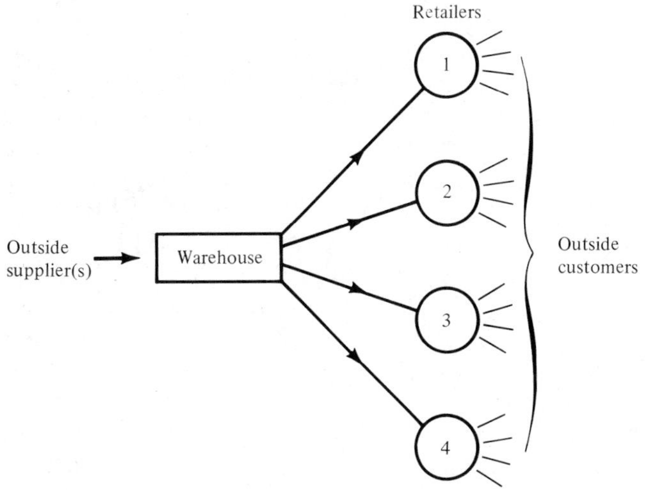

FIGURE 12.4 A One-Warehouse, Four-Retailer System

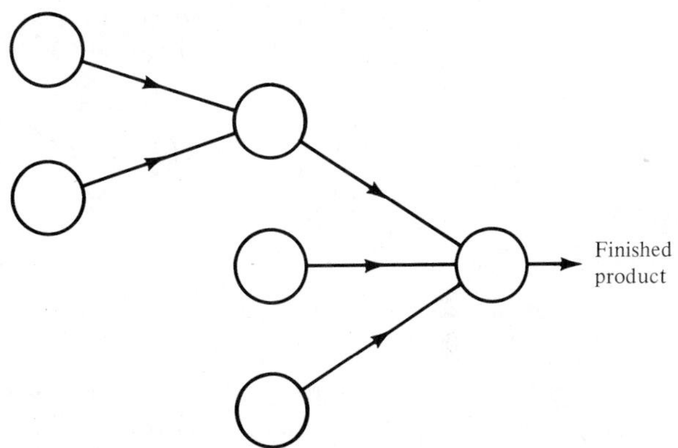

FIGURE 12.5 A "Pure" Assembly System

The resulting mathematical formulation results in a large, nonlinear, integer programming problem, but the authors suggest an efficient, specialized solution procedure.

12.1.3 Multiechelon Stocking Points with Time-Varying Demand

Here we return to the demand situation assumed in Chapter 6, namely, where end-item usage is known *but varies from period to period* [$D(j)$ in period j]. Also carrying costs are incurred only on period-ending inventories. However, now we have a multiechelon assembly or distribution system. Several authors have analyzed this type of situation (see, for example, Lambrecht et al., 1981; Graves, 1981), but our discussion is based on the work of Blackburn and Millen (1982) specifically for an assembly structure. Moreover, for illustrative purposes, we concentrate on the simple two-stage serial process used in Section 12.1.1. (The more general case can be found in the Blackburn and Millen reference.)

One approach would be simply to use one of the procedures of Chapter 6 sequentially echelon by echelon. For example, the Silver-Meal heuristic could be utilized to schedule replenishments of the finished item. This would imply a pattern of requirements for the primary material which would then be used as input to the Silver-Meal heuristic to plan the replenishments of the primary item.[3] Although this approach is simple, it ignores the cost interdependency of the two echelons. Specifically, in choosing the replenishment strategy at the finishing stage the method does not take account of the cost implications at the primary level.

Recognizing the above deficiency, we wish to develop a procedure that can still be applied sequentially (to keep implementation costs at a reasonable level) but that captures the essence of the cost interdependencies. An examination of the *level* demand case provides considerable insight. In particular, we repeat Eq. 12.4 here:

$$\text{TRC}(Q_p, Q_f) = \frac{D}{Q_f}\left(A_f + \frac{A_p}{n}\right) + \frac{Q_f r}{2}(nv_p' + v_f') \tag{12.8}$$

where

$$Q_p = nQ_f \tag{12.9}$$

Equation 12.8 is analogous with a *single* echelon problem (the selection of Q_f) if the *adjusted* fixed cost of a replenishment is

$$\hat{A}_f = A_f + \frac{A_p}{n} \tag{12.10}$$

and the *adjusted* unit variable cost of the item is

$$\hat{v}_f = nv_p' + v_f' \tag{12.11}$$

Note that the term A_p/n reflects that there is a primary setup at only every nth finishing setup. We can select Q_f (see Eq. 12.7), including properly taking

[3]Because of batching at the finishing stage, the resulting requirements pattern at the primary level is likely to contain a number of periods with no demand. As mentioned in Section 6.6.4 of Chapter 6, the *unmodified* Silver-Meal heuristic should be used with caution under such circumstances.

account of the cost impact at the primary stage, if we have a good pre-estimate of n. One could use Steps 1 to 3 of the algorithm in Section 12.1.1, but Blackburn and Millen have found that simply using Eq. 12.5 and ensuring that n is at least unity works well (particularly in more complex, assembly structures). Thus we have

$$n = \max\left[\sqrt{\frac{A_p v'_f}{A_f v'_p}}, 1\right] \tag{12.12}$$

Returning to the time-varying demand situation we compute n using Eq. 12.12; then employ the n value to obtain adjusted setup and unit variable costs for the finishing operation according to Eqs. 12.10 and 12.11. Then the Silver-Meal heuristic can be applied to the finishing operation using $\hat{A}_f$ and $\hat{v}_f$. The resulting replenishments again imply a requirements pattern for the primary operation. Subsequently, the Silver-Meal (or another suitable), lot-sizing procedure is used at the primary stage with A_p and v_p. Problem 12.4 presents a numerical example.

Numerical Illustration

To illustrate the computation of $\hat{A}_f$ and $\hat{v}_f$, consider a two-stage process where $A_p = \$30$, $A_f = \$20$, $v_p = \$2$/unit, and $v_f = \$7$/unit. First, from Eq. 12.2 we have

$$v'_f = v_f - v_p = \$5/\text{unit}$$

$$v'_p = v_p = \$2/\text{unit}$$

Then, using Eq. 12.12, we obtain

$$n = \max\left[\sqrt{\frac{(30)(5)}{(20)(2)}}, 1\right]$$

$$= \max\,[1.94, 1]$$

$$n = 1.94$$

Finally, Eqs. 12.10 and 12.11 give us

$$\hat{A}_f = 20 + \frac{30}{1.94} = \$35.46$$

and

$$\hat{v}_f = 5.00 + 1.94(2.00) = \$8.88/\text{unit}$$

12.2 THE COMPLEXITIES OF PROBABILISTIC DEMAND

Probabilistic demand raises several new issues and creates extreme modeling complexities in a multiechelon inventory situation. For discussion purposes we examine the relatively simple three-echelon distribution system depicted in Figure 12.6.

The replenishment lead times between adjacent levels (in each case *assuming that the feeding level has adequate stock*) are as follows:

Branch to retailer—1 week

Central to branch—1 week

Supplier to central—3 weeks

Straightforward use of the methods of Chapters 5 through 7 would dictate that each stocking level (retailer, branch warehouse, and central warehouse) would *independently* make replenishment decisions based on its own

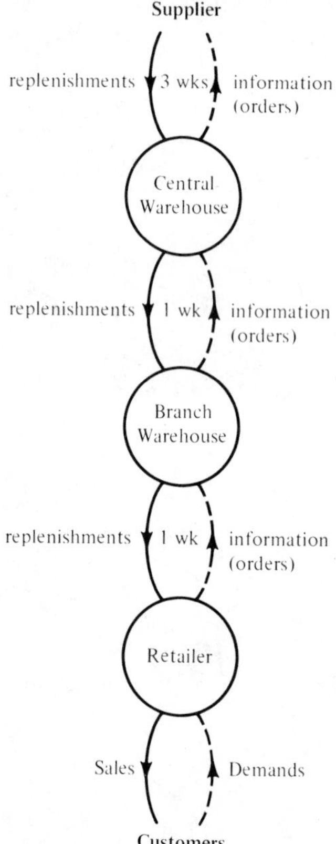

FIGURE 12.6 A Multiechelon Situation with Single-Stage Information Flow

1. Cost factors and service considerations
2. Predicted demand—presumably forecasts based on historical demand that it has observed *from the next stocking point down the line*
3. Replenishment lead time from the next stocking point up the line

Such a system has two serious flaws. First, as discussed in Section 12.1, it ignores the cost implications at one echelon of using certain ordering logic at another level. Second, even if end-customer demand is fairly smooth, the orders placed farther and farther up the line become progressively larger and less frequent; for example, the central warehouse is now faced with a "demand" pattern made up of infrequent transactions equal in size to the replenishment orders generated at the branch warehouse.[4] Under an order point type system of control, the central warehouse would thus have to carry a large safety stock to protect against these infrequent demands, even when end-item usage possessed relatively little variability.

Other complicating factors include

1. How does one define service in a multiechelon situation? Normally, service is measured only at the lowest echelon. A stockout at one of the higher echelons has only a secondary effect on service—namely, it *may* elongate the lead time for a lower echelon, which ultimately may cause customer disservice. It is seen that safety stock at a particular echelon has effects on stockouts at *other* echelons. Thus, one has to be careful to avoid unnecessary duplication of safety stocks.
2. Suppose that the branch warehouse places orders of size Q_b on the central warehouse. What happens when such an order is placed and the on-hand stock at the central location is less than Q_b? Is a partial shipment made or does the system wait until the entire order can be shipped?
3. What about the possibility of an emergency shipment directly from the central warehouse to the retailer?
4. If we go to a more comprehensive centralized control system, prompt and reliable communication of demands and stock situations at the various locations is needed. Moreover, the number of interdependent decision variables increases rapidly, implying heavy computational needs.
5. In more complicated multiechelon structures transshipments between points at the same echelon may be possible, for example, between retailers if there was more than one retail outlet in Figure 12.6.
6. Again, for more complicated structures when one central facility supplies several different stocking points (at the next echelon), the central facility is

[4]The mathematical complications are evident when one realizes that a Poisson demand process (the simplest from a mathematical standpoint) at the retail level is converted to an Erlang process at the branch warehouse.

likely to adopt a rationing policy when it faces multiple requests with insufficient stock to meet them all (the PUSH system of Section 12.5 will specifically address this issue).

Despite all of the above complexities, it is indeed still worthwhile to use multiechelon control procedures. In particular, Muckstadt and Thomas (1980) show substantial benefits in a military supply context, and Lawrence (1977) does the same for a commercial distribution system.

12.3 THE BASE STOCK CONTROL SYSTEM

In the previous section we pointed out the problems associated with each echelon deciding when to reorder based only on demand from the next lower echelon. The base stock system is a response to these difficulties. The key change is to make end-item demand information available for decision making at *all* stocking points as illustrated in Figure 12.7. This necessitates the use of an effective communication system, for example, a remote input computer linkage. *Each stocking point makes replenishments based on actual end-item customer demands* rather than on replenishment orders from the next level downstream. With this modification the procedures of Chapters 5 through 7 are now more appropriate to use. In particular, the most common type of base stock system is one where an order point and an order-up-to-level are used for each stocking point, that is, an (s, S) system. For each stocking point treated independently an order quantity (Q) is established (using end-item demand forecasts) by one of the methods of Chapters 5 and 6. Next, a reorder point s is established by one of the procedures of Chapter 7, using end-item demand forecasts over the replenishment lead time appropriate to the level under consideration[5] (for example, the central warehouse would use a lead time of 3 weeks). Then *the order-up-to-level S, also called the base stock level*, is determined through the relation

$$S = s + Q \tag{12.13}$$

In terms of physical operation, the echelon inventory position at each level is monitored according to the following relation:

$$\text{Echelon inventory position} = (\text{Echelon stock}) + (\text{On order}) \tag{12.14}$$

where, as defined earlier, the echelon stock of echelon j is the number of units in the system that are at, or have passed through, echelon j but have as yet not been specifically committed to outside customers.

The "on-order" term in Eq. 12.14 refers to an order placed by echelon j on the

[5]Usually potential stockouts at the next higher echelon, which would increase the lead time, are ignored.

next *higher* echelon. To illustrate, suppose that at a point in time the physical stocks of our example (Figure 12.7) are:

Branch warehouse—50 units

Retail outlet—20 units

Furthermore, suppose that 5 units of known customer demand have not yet been satisfied. Moreover, assume that there is no order outstanding from the branch on the central warehouse and that 10 units are in transit between the branch and the retail outlet. Then, the inventory position for the branch level would be

$$\text{Inventory position} = (50 + 10 + 20 - 5) + (0) = 75 \text{ units}$$

Once the echelon inventory position is known (after each transaction or on a periodic basis; in the latter case the replenishment lead time for safety stock calculations at each level must be increased by the review interval), it is

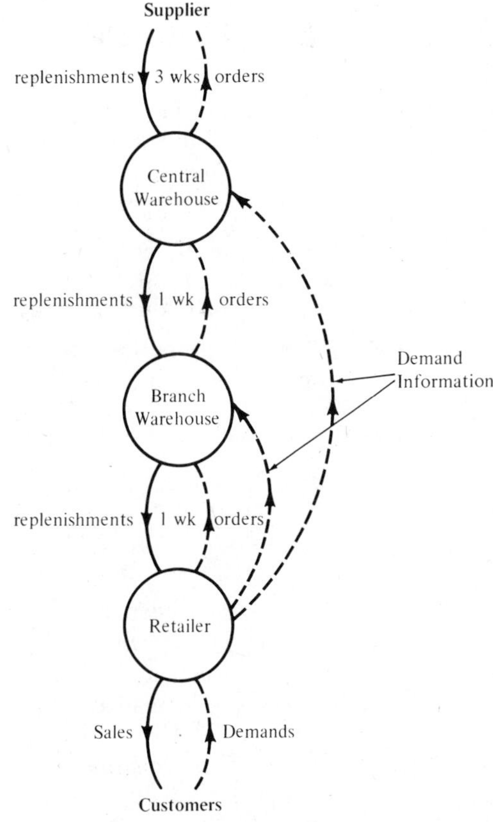

FIGURE 12.7 Information and Stock Flow in a Base Stock System

compared with the reorder point s. Whenever it is at or lower than s, enough is ordered (from the preceding level) to raise the position to the base stock level S.

To repeat, ordering decisions at any stocking point in the base stock system are made as a result of *end-item* demand, not orders from the next level downstream. There is much less variability in the former than in the latter; hence significantly lower safety stocks (reduced carrying costs) are achieved by the base stock system.

The Serial Situation

For the special case of a serial system (such as in Figure 12.1) De Bodt and Graves (1983) have proposed a procedure, for computing the replenishment quantities and reorder points, *that explicitly takes account* of the effects of the stock at one echelon on the lead time at the next lower echelon. Again, for illustrative purposes and consistency with Section 12.1, we restrict our description to the case of two stages and call them "primary" and "finishing."

The assumptions underlying the decision rules include:

1. External demand occurs only at the finishing stage and it is a stationary process. Conceptually, the method can certainly be applied to a process that changes slowly with time where we have estimates of the mean and standard deviation of demand over suitable durations of time; in fact, this is how we present the logic (including assuming normally distributed forecast errors).
2. There is a deterministic replenishment lead time associated with each stage (L_p and L_f). Furthermore, the lead time L_f only begins when there is sufficient primary stock available to fulfill a finishing replenishment.
3. The policy used is of the (s, Q) form, that is, continuous review with four parameters:

   s_p = reorder point (based on the echelon inventory position) at the primary stage

   Q_p = order quantity at the primary stage

   s_f = reorder point at the finishing stage

   Q_f = order quantity at the finishing point

   Furthermore, for our purposes we assume that Q_f and $Q_p = nQ_f$ have been *predetermined* by the procedure of Section 12.1.1. (De Bodt and Graves suggest an iterative scheme to *simultaneously* find the Q's and s's similar to what was shown in Section 8.4 of Chapter 8.)

The decision rules for choosing s_f and s_p are:

1. Select s_f such that

$$s_f = \hat{x}_{L_f} + k_f \, \sigma_{L_f} \tag{12.15}$$

where

$\hat{x}_{L_f}$ = expected (forecast) demand over a finishing lead time

σ_{L_f} = standard deviation of forecast errors over the same interval

k_f = finishing safety factor, which satisfies

$$p_{u\geq}(k_f) = \frac{Q_f(v_f - v_p)r}{B_2 v_f D} \qquad (12.16)$$

with D being the annual demand rate for the item and r the carrying charge in \$/\$/year.

2. Select s_p such that

$$s_p = \hat{x}_{L_p+L_f} + k_p \sigma_{L_p+L_f} \qquad (12.17)$$

where

$\hat{x}_{L_p+L_f}$ = expected demand over a primary lead time, plus a finishing lead time

$\sigma_{L_p+L_f}$ = standard deviation of forecast errors over the same interval

k_p = primary safety factor, which satisfies

$$p_{u\geq}(k_p) = \frac{Q_f[v_f + (n-1)v_p]r}{B_2 v_f D} \qquad (12.18)$$

The v expressions in the numerators of Eqs. 12.16 and 12.18 are equivalent with echelon valuations. The $L_p + L_f$ combination occurs in Eq. 12.17 because on every nth replenishment at the finishing stage we have an associated primary replenishment and the latter should be initiated when there is sufficient echelon stock to protect against shortages over a period of length $L_p + L_f$ (recall assumption 2). The derivation (see De Bodt and Graves, 1983) uses echelon stocks and hinges on distinguishing this special replenishment from the other $n - 1$ finishing replenishments. Note that the right-hand side of Eq. 12.16 is always smaller than that of Eq. 12.18. Hence, the safety factor at the finishing stage is always larger than the safety factor at the primary level.

Numerical Illustration

We use the same example as in Section 12.1.1, the liquid developer, product XSC-044, which MIDAS buys in bulk (primary operation), then breaks down and repackages (finishing stage). Suppose that the purchasing lead time is 6 weeks and the lead time for the finishing operation is 1 week. Also, assume that forecast errors are normally distributed with the σ for 1 week being 6.4 units. From Section 12.1.1 we know that the annual demand rate is 1000 liters, v_p = \$1/liter, v_f = \$5/liter, r = 0.24 \$/\$/yr, n = 2, and Q_f = 167 liters. Finally, suppose that the fractional charge per unit short, B_2, is set at 0.35.

From Eq. 12.16 we obtain

$$p_{u\geq}(k_f) = \frac{(167)(5.00 - 1.00)(0.24)}{(0.35)(5.00)(1000)}$$
$$= 0.0916$$

Then, Table B.1 in Appendix B gives

$$k_f = 1.33$$

Consequently, from Eq.12.15

$$s_f = \frac{1}{52}(1000) + 1.33\,(6.4)$$
$$= 27.7, \text{ say 28 liters}$$

From Eq. 12.18

$$p_{u\geq}(k_p) = \frac{(167)[5.00 + (2 - 1)(1.00)]0.24}{(0.35)(5.00)(1000)}$$
$$= 0.1374$$

Thus, we have

$$k_p = 1.09$$

and, using Eq. 12.17,

$$s_p = \frac{7}{52}(1000) + 1.09\sqrt{7}\,(6.4)$$
$$= 153.1, \text{ say 153 liters}$$

To summarize, we place a purchase order for 334 liters of bulk material when the *echelon* inventory position of bulk material drops to153 liters or lower. Also, when the inventory position of the repackaged material drops to 28 liters or lower, we initiate the breaking and repackaging of 167 liters of bulk material.

12.4 SPECIALIZED RESULTS UNDER PROBABILISTIC DEMAND

In this section, we briefly comment on some useful results that have been obtained for certain special cases of multiechelon structures under probabilistic control.

12.4.1 Central Warehouse with n Regional Warehouses

Rosenbaum (1981a, 1981b) discusses an inventory control system developed for Eastman Kodak Company. (An analysis of a somewhat similar situation for Philips' Industries is provided by van Beek, 1981.) Each item is stocked at a central warehouse that replenishes regional warehouses. The latter, in turn, satisfy customer demands. An (R, S) type of control system is used at the central warehouse where there is a manufacturing replenishment lead time L_c. At each regional warehouse i an (s_i, EOQ$_i$) system of control is utilized, where there is a replenishment lead time L_i, *assuming that there is sufficient stock at the central warehouse.*

Ignoring the interaction of the two echelons, one could use the decision rule of Section 7.6.9 of Chapter 7 to select S in order to meet directly from stock at the central warehouse a certain fraction P_{2c} of the orders from the branch warehouses. Moreover, each s_i could be selected to satisfy directly from stock a certain (hypothetical) fraction HP_{2i} of the customer demands at regional warehouse i, *assuming that there is always sufficient stock at the central warehouse.* Because of stockouts at the central warehouse the use of S and s_i will give an actual service level AP_{2i} which will be lower than HP_{2i}. Through extensive experimentation Rosenbaum develops a procedure for estimating AP_{2i} as a function of P_{2c} and HP_{2i}. This, in turn, permits dealing with a more important problem—namely, the achieving of a desired actual service level AP_{2r} (assumed the same at all regional warehouses) while using the minimum amount of total system (central and branches) safety stock for the item under consideration. This is accomplished as follows. For any given value of P_{2c} the above estimation procedure allows us to find the required HP_{2i} for each branch warehouse i in order to achieve the desired AP_{2r}. The P_{2c} and HP_{2i} values, in turn, provide us with the various safety stocks. A search is carried out on P_{2c} values until the sum of these safety stocks is minimized.

12.4.2 Economic Incentives to Centralize Stocks

In the following we parallel the presentation of Schwarz (1981). Consider n retail outlets ($i = 1, 2, \ldots, n$). Using an independent or decentralized (s_i, EOQ$_i$) strategy for each and assuming, for simplicity, the same safety factor k at each location (equivalently, equal P_1 service levels), we have that the expected total relevant costs for the system are

$$\text{ETRC (decentralized)} = \sum_{i=1}^{n} \text{ETRC}_i$$

$$= \sum_{i=1}^{n} [\sqrt{2A_iD_ivr} + k\sigma_ivr]$$

Assuming the ordering cost A_i is the same (A) at all locations, this becomes

$$\text{ETRC (decentralized)} = \sqrt{2Avr} \sum_{i=1}^{n} \sqrt{D_i} + kvr \sum_{i=1}^{n} \sigma_i \tag{12.19}$$

Suppose, instead that the stocking was done at a single centralized location. Then the expected total relevant costs are

$$\text{ETRC (centralized)} = \sqrt{2AD_cvr} + kvr\sigma_c \tag{12.20}$$

where

$$D_c = \sum_{i=1}^{n} D_i$$

hence

$$\sqrt{D_c} \leq \sum_{i=1}^{n} \sqrt{D_i} \tag{12.21}$$

and σ_c is the standard deviation of total demand.

It can be shown that

$$\sigma_c \leq \sum_{i=1}^{n} \sigma_i \tag{12.22}$$

This result is known, in the finance literature, as the *portfolio effect*. It results from the fact that higher than average demands at some locations will be simultaneously offset by lower than average demands at some other locations.

Using conditions 12.21 and 12.22, it follows from Eq.12.19 and 12.20 that

$$\text{ETRC (centralized)} \leq \text{ETRC (decentralized)}$$

Furthermore, the difference can be quite substantial (see Problem 12.8).

Eppen and Schrage (1981) apply the above concepts to a two-echelon situation—namely, a central depot and n regional warehouses. However, there is limited or no stocking at the depot. The depot simply acts as a broker (and possible transshipment point) to achieve economies of scale from a purchasing standpoint (for example, quantity discounts) and also permits benefits from the portfolio effect. Eppen and Schrage examine a depot policy of ordering from the supplier and making allocations to the warehouses every m periods of time. The choice of the m value is closely related to the choice of an EOQ time supply. The result for the system order-up-to-level also bears a close resemblance to the newsboy problem results of Chapter 10.

Above we mentioned the idea of allocating a system stock among the various warehouses. This is a key concept in PUSH systems, the topic of the next section.

12.5 PUSH CONTROL SYSTEMS

The base stock system, discussed in Section 12.3, permitted better use of customer demand information to decide on replenishments. However, it was still predicated on each location *pulling* (ordering) stock from the next higher echelon. In contrast, PUSH systems, as the name implies, are based on centralized control with a *push* of stocks down to the lower echelons based on a *system-wide* viewpoint. The rationale is that this broad viewpoint and the elimination of "surprise" large replenishment orders should reduce the costs to achieve a given customer service level or improve the service level for a given total stock investment. Brown(1982) has played a central role in "pushing" the use of this type of system.

12.5.1 Operation of a PUSH System

For simplicity in explanation, we deal with a two-echelon system. The top echelon is a central warehouse supplied by a manufacturing facility or an outside vendor. The lower echelon encompasses a number of branch warehouses meeting customer demands. The central warehouse can also have its own direct customers. The PUSH concept can certainly be applied to systems having three or more echelons. For example, one of the authors was involved in a consulting study for a major international supplier of automotive parts where the three echelons were a central warehouse, regional distribution centers, and retail outlets.

The block diagram of Figure 12.8 should be helpful with respect to the following discussion. We begin in Block 1 with a review (on a periodic basis, typically daily or weekly) of the stock status of every s.k.u. (recall that the same item at two different locations is considered as two distinct s.k.u.). The first point to query (Block 2) is whether or not a system replenishment from the supplier is ready for shipment (this replenishment would have been initiated a system or central lead time, L_c, earlier). If indeed there is such a replenishment,

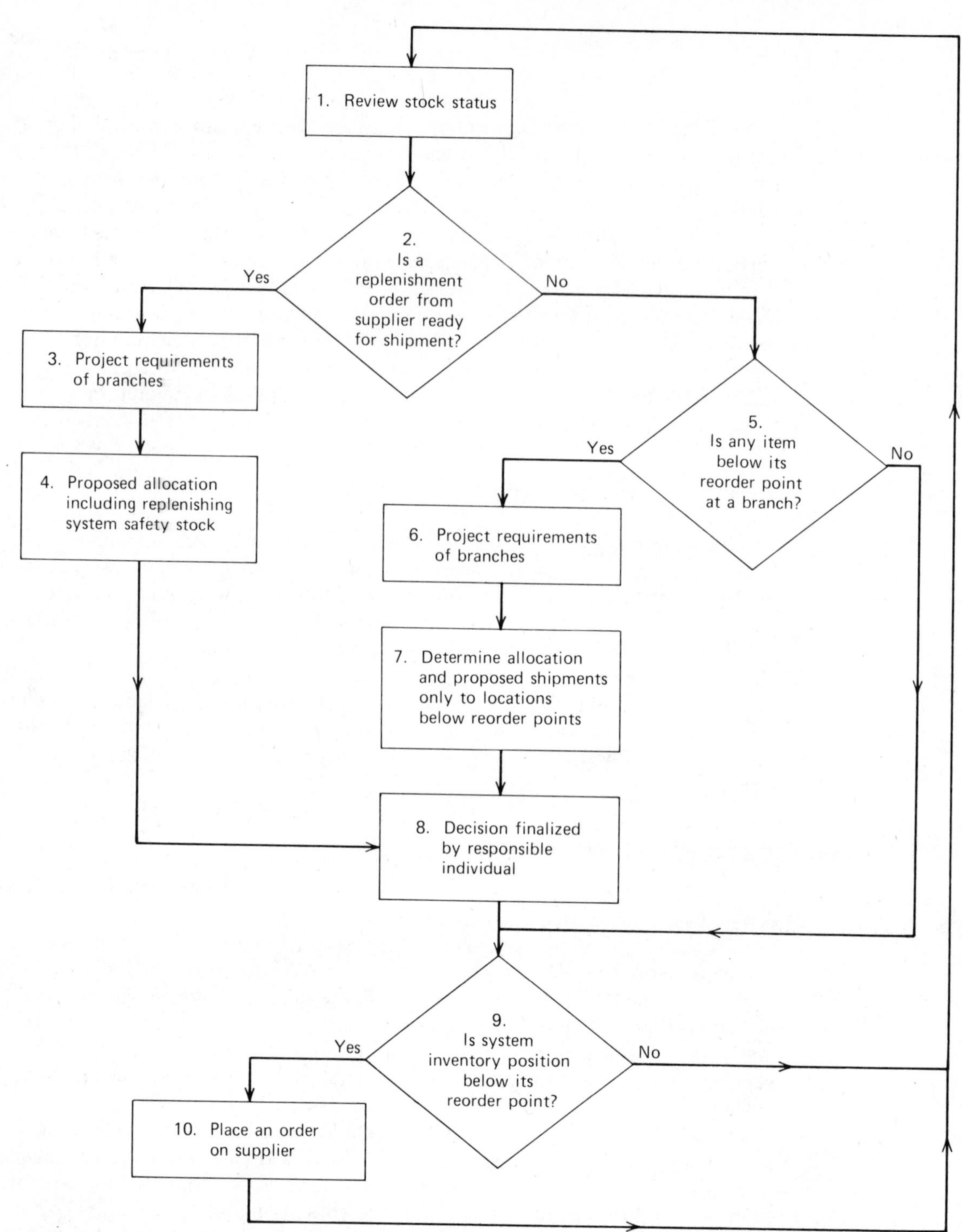

FIGURE 12.8 A PUSH Control System

then we must next (Block 3) project the net requirements at each branch warehouse of the item involved.[6] At a particular branch the time series (period by period) of net requirements is obtained in two steps. First, the gross requirements (ignoring the inventory position) are projected based on firm customer orders and forecasted demand. Then, the on-hand and on-order (in transit or firmly committed to the branch) inventories are taken into account, properly reducing the gross requirements to what are called the *net requirements*. In addition, the requirements must be offset (moved forward) in time by the shipping time to the branch involved to portray properly the timing of the needs as viewed by the shipping point. Furthermore, net requirements may be computed above a desired safety stock level. The concept of evaluating net requirements will be central to Material Requirements Planning, a manufacturing environment control system that will be discussed in detail (including examples of net requirements planning) in Chapter 16.

The replenishment quantity is then allocated (Block 4). First, we ensure that adequate stock is maintained at the central warehouse; normally, this is the so-called *system safety stock*. The system safety stock is selected to balance the costs of carrying this stock versus having to expedite replenishments from the supplier—the latter action to ensure that the central warehouse does not run out of stock. The variability of *total system* demand in a central lead time (L_c) is an important factor and the decision rule of Section 7.6.5 of Chapter 7 can be used to select the safety factor. The centrally held stock is useful for responding to future (prior to the arrival of the next system replenishment) needs of the branches (see Section 12.4.2). The rest of the replenishment order is allocated and shipped to the branches where it is reasonable to ensure that the time supply above the reorder point is the same for each branch. (A branch reorder point is based on its replenishment lead time from the central warehouse, *assuming that there is adequate stock at the latter location*. The branch safety factor can be based on, for example, providing a desired customer service level.) Incidentally, to avoid double-handling one can arrange shipments direct from the supplier to the branches.

In the event that at a review time there is not a replenishment order ready for shipment, we next (Block 5) investigate the inventory position of each item at each branch. If any s.k.u. (item at a branch) is below its reorder point, then (Block 6) the net requirements of that item at each branch are projected (as previously discussed with respect to Block 3). An allocation (Block 7) *on paper* is made of the current *system* stock of the item involved (the stock is divided into what is called *fair shares* for the various locations). Shipments (or transshipments) are *proposed* for only the item-branch combinations below their reorder points. (We will comment in Section 12.5.2 on the choice of an allocation

[6]For simplicity we discuss the case of a single item in the replenishment. The logic is directly extendable to the more general case of multiple items in a single order.

scheme.) Restrictions, such as minimum and maximum quantities to be shipped or convenient quantities (for example, whole pallets), can easily be incorporated. Moreover, the space and weight requirements of the proposed quantities can be portrayed on a computer terminal, perhaps summarized by destination and required shipping date (this is of prime importance in terms of utilizing bulk freight methods).

Next (Block 8), the shipping schedule is finalized by an individual, such as a materials manager or distribution planner, who has the ultimate responsibility for the decisions made. That individual may very well make changes, such as shipping some units early to fill up a freight car, ordering in an extra truck, and so forth.

The next step in the logic at a review point is to check (Block 9) the need for a system replenishment. (Specifically, is the *system* inventory position at or below the system reorder point?) Any such order is initiated (Block 10), possibly using coordinated control logic (such as that of Section 5.8.5 of Chapter 5). This then completes the procedure at an instant of review; the process is repeated after the passage of a review interval.

The PUSH system goes beyond the base stock system (Section 12.3) in two important ways. First, one tends to project *actual* requirements at any particular branch well into the future rather than just using a forecasting procedure. Second, the allocation decision is based on the *system* stock level and *all* of the projections. The methodology of Distribution Requirements Planning (DRP), to be discussed in Chapter 16, is similar to that of a PUSH system in the sense that actual requirements are projected at each branch. The important difference is that the lot sizes in DRP are established locally by the branches themselves (this is analogous to the suboptimal, sequential, independent treatment of echelons as discussed in Section 12.1).

12.5.2 Some Comments and Guidelines

We present a number of comments and suggested guidelines with regard to PUSH systems.

1. There is currently no simple way of *analytically* predicting the customer service level as a function of the branch and system safety factors. This is because the underlying stochastic process is extremely complicated. To illustrate, consider a case of but two branches, numbered 1 and 2. Suppose that we are at a review point where several reviews have already occurred since the last system replenishment. Recall that a follow-up shipment is made to a branch only if its inventory position drops to or below its reorder point. Thus, for example, the current inventory position at Branch 1 and the current system inventory position depend in a complicated way on the equence of demands that have taken place at both of Branches 1 and 2 in that at an earlier review one or both may have triggered an allocation.

2. Brown (1975, 1982) has conducted a number of simulation experiments to test different methods of allocation of system stock among the central and branch warehouses. His results suggest the following guidelines:

- **a.** Hold the system safety stock centrally (*centrally* can mean at the branch having the highest usage of the particular item).
- **b.** Where there is adequate system stock, allocate to raise branch stocks to equal time supplies above their reorder points.
- **c.** When the total system stock is less than the sum of the branch reorder points, allocate to cover the expected lead time demand plus a common fraction of each branch's safety stock.

3. The concept of expediting to avoid shortages of system stock works well as long as there are not too many expediting actions needed. The parameter B_1 (the implicit cost of an expediting action) can be adjusted to give a reasonable *aggregate* expediting workload.

4. Effective operation of a PUSH system depends on having accurate and timely information on the stock status at all locations (as well as in-transit). It is important to ensure that such an information retrieval system is properly operating *prior* to implementing a PUSH system.

5. Rather than immediately trying to include detailed rules for transshipping options, it is best to introduce these gradually as experience is gained with a system involving simpler logic.

6. The introduction of a PUSH system will almost always require organizational adjustments. The authority and responsibilities of different individuals will change. For example, branch managers will no longer be responsible for the timing and sizes of replenishments. Their primary responsibilities will now be to ensure timely transmission of accurate data on stock status and to provide forecast information (the latter likely on an override basis as discussed in Chapter 4). Considerable educational effort is needed as well as the assurance that performance evaluation is properly geared to the new responsibilities. Sawchuk (1981) provides further comments on these issues based on the implementation of a PUSH system in the Norton company.

7. The decision rules should be viewed only as an aid to the decision maker. There are important factors, not included in the underlying models, that must be incorporated manually prior to finalizing the allocation and shipping decisions.

12.6 CONTROL PROCEDURES FOR THE CASE OF REPAIRABLE ITEMS

Thus far, we have restricted our attention to consumable items. Now we turn to units that can be repaired. Examples include vehicles, telephones, military equipment, computers, copying machines, and so on.

The analysis of a repairable item situation is considerably more complicated than that of a consumable item. Normally, in a repair situation the number of units demanded is not balanced completely by the return of repairable units. Thus, in addition to repairs, one must also purchase some new units from time to time. Consequently, even at a single location, there are five decision variables: (1) how often to review the stock status, (2) when to repair returned units, (3) how many to repair at a time (4) when to order new units, and (5) how many to order.

12.6.1 A Repairable Item at a Single Location

In this subsection we deal with the case of a single stocking location. However, in a repair context it can be considered as a special case of a two-echelon system (see Figure 12.9). Returned units go to echelon 2 where they are repaired and then become available as servicable units at echelon 1.

Deterministic Usage and Returns

For the case where the usage (demand) rate is a constant D units/yr, a fixed fraction f of units are returned in a repairable state, and lead times are known. Schrady (1967) has developed the following decision rules for selecting the best values of the repair and purchase lot sizes (Q_R and Q_p, respectively):

$$Q_R^* = \sqrt{\frac{2A_R D}{(v_R + v_S)r}} \tag{12.23}$$

and

$$Q_P^* = \sqrt{\frac{2A_P D(1 - f)}{[v_R f + v_S(1 - f)]r}} \tag{12.24}$$

where

A_R = fixed (setup) cost per repair replenishment, in dollars

A_p = fixed (setup) cost per purchase replenishment, in dollars

v_R = unit variable cost of units *that need repair*, in \$/unit

v_S = unit variable cost of units that are in a serviceable state, in \$/unit

r = carrying charge, in \$/\$/yr

We will not present the details of the derivation. It is based on the use of Figure 12.10, which shows the behavior of the two types of inventory with the passage of time. A typical cycle repeats each time that a purchase lot size (Q_p) arrives. No repairs are undertaken while the Q_p is being consumed. There is an integer number (n) of lots Q_R repaired each cycle ($n = 4$ in Figure 12.10). Thus, there must be a specific relationship between Q_p, Q_R and n that can be developed as

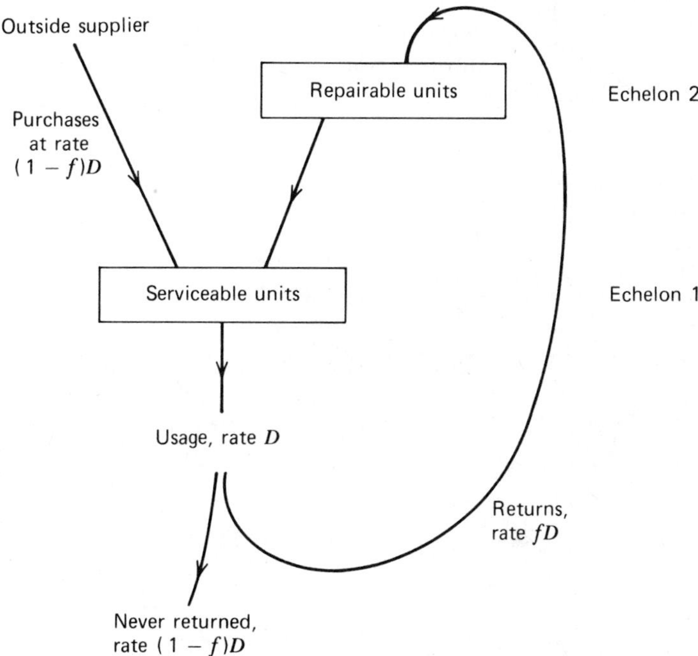

FIGURE 12.9 Repairable Units at a Single Location

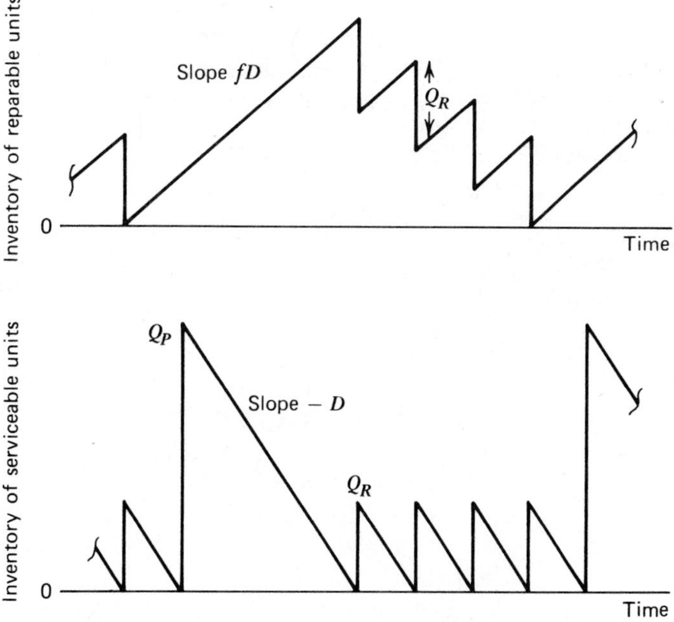

FIGURE 12.10 Deterministic Repairable Inventory Model

follows. In each cycle, $Q_p + nQ_R$ units are issued. A fraction f of these are returned for repair. The inflow of repairables must equal the outflow of repaired units. Thus,

$$f(Q_P + nQ_R) = nQ_R$$

or

$$Q_P = \frac{nQ_R(1 - f)}{f} \tag{12.25}$$

Problem 12.9 affords a numerical illustration of the procedure.

Nahmias and Rivera (1979) have extended the above model in two respects. First, they permit a finite rate buildup of the repaired units. Second, they take account of limited storage space.

Probabilistic Usage and Returns

Muckstadt and Isaac (1981) report on a model developed in connection with a manufacturer of reprographic equipment. As above, there is a single location with two types of inventory: serviceable and repairable. However, now demands for serviceable units and returns of repairable units occur probabilistically, specifically, according to *independent* Poisson processes with rates D and fD, respectively. In addition, repairs are done on a continuous, first come-first served, basis (for example, at a local machine shop). Any demands for serviceable units, when none are available, are backordered at a cost B_3v_S per unit short per unit time. Purchases of new stock from outside involve a known lead time L_p. With respect to purchase decisions a continuous review (s, Q) system is used; specifically, when the inventory position drops to s or lower, a quantity Q is purchased. The inventory position is defined by

$$\begin{aligned}\text{Inventory position} &= (\text{On-hand serviceables}) - (\text{Backorders})\\ &\quad + (\text{Units in repair}) + (\text{Units on order})\end{aligned} \tag{12.26}$$

The authors use a Markov model, together with a normal approximation of net inventory (on-hand serviceables minus backorders), to obtain reasonably simple results for the best (s, Q) pair. The results, as expected, depend on the nature of the service and waiting processes in the repair facility.

Muckstadt and Isaac also discuss an extension of their model to a two-echelon context. Other references on probabilistic models of single-location repair situations include Gajdalo (1973), Heyman (1978), Nahmias (1981a), and Simpson (1978).

12.6.2 Allocation of Stock among Assemblies and Repairable Subassemblies

Consider a complex piece of equipment (an assembly) that is made up of a number of subassemblies, which in turn have components, and so forth. (The levels in this hierarchy are often called *indenture levels.*) An example would be an aircraft with engines, guidance system, and so forth. The equipment breaks down from time to time, such breakdowns being caused by the failure of specific components. Having estimates of the failure rates of the various components, the cost of each component or subassembly, and detection and repair time distributions, an important problem is to ascertain how to allocate a budget among spare components, subassemblies, and complete assemblies to maximize the availability of operable complete units or, alternatively, to minimize the inventory investment to achieve a desired service level.

A more complex version of the above problem has been studied, almost exclusively, in military supply contexts. The added complexity is that there is a multiechelon structure of stocking points and repair facilities. Now, in addition to choosing how many of each s.k.u. to have in stock, one must also ascertain where the units should be kept.

The multiechelon structure introduces a type of complexity as discussed earlier—namely, that the stock level at a specific echelon has an indirect effect on service further down the system in that stockouts at the specific echelon (for example, a central warehouse) will increase the effective lead time for the next lower echelon (regional warehouse). However, because of the indenture hierarchy, we have a further complexity, specifically that components cannot be treated independently, since any specific piece of equipment requires a particular set of components. Recognizing these complexities, it is not surprising that simple mathematical results are not forthcoming and the applications have been restricted primarily to large-scale military systems.

We next briefly review some of the key developments in this general problem area. Interested readers are encouraged to pursue the reference readings cited. In particular, comprehensive reviews are provided by Demmy and Presutti (1981) and Nahmias (1981b).

1. Sherbrooke (1968), in his METRIC model, considers a two-echelon system structure, but does not deal with the indenture issue. There are a set of bases and a central depot. Each location in the system may possess a supply of serviceable spare parts and a repair capability for converting repairable units into serviceable items. (In each case, all that is needed is the mean repair time. In addition, the repair times are assumed independent, which is equivalent to assuming unlimited capacity at each repair facility. Graves (1982) addresses a relaxation of this latter assumption.) Demand at each base for each item follows a compound Poisson distribution. The inventory policy followed for each item at each location is a continuous review $(S - 1, S)$ policy; that is, the inventory position is always kept at the same order-up-to-level S (where, of course, S varies among item-location pairs). As discussed in Section 8.3.1 of Chapter 8, an $(S - 1, S)$ policy is most appropriate for expensive, slow-moving items. This type of policy substantially simplifies the mathematical analysis, in that the net inventory of any item at any base, at a random point in time, is the difference between the particular S and the demand in a mean repair time, where the demand has a compound Poisson distribution. Furthermore, no lateral transfers are permitted between bases. Now if there are n bases, we wish to select values of S_{i0}, S_{i1}, $S_{i2}, \ldots, S_{in}$ for each item i where S_{ij} $(j = 1, 2, \ldots, n)$ is the inventory position of item i at base j and S_{i0} is the position at the depot. There is a budget constraint on the total value of the spares, and the objective used is the minimization of the total expected number of units backordered at the bases. Fox and Landi (1970) show that a Lagrangian minimization approach (see Appendix A at the end of the book) can substantially reduce the computational effort, and Muckstadt (1978) expands on this idea.

2. Muckstadt's (1973) MOD-METRIC model addresses a two-indenture version of the above situation. The two indentures are line replaceable units (LRUs) that may be removed and replaced in the field and shop replaceable units (SRUs) that are components or subassemblies of LRUs that must be removed or replaced in the repair shops. An $(S - 1, S)$ policy is again employed. The objective is to allocate a total budget among spares to minimize the total expected LRU base-level backorders. The heuristic solution procedure works as follows. The available budget W is divided into two components W_1 and W_2. W_1, using METRIC, is allocated among the SRUs in order to minimize the expected LRU repair delays summed over all bases. The resulting allocation determines average resupply time for each LRU at each base. Knowing these, METRIC is again used to allocate W_2 among the LRUs to minimize the expected LRU base-level backorders. These steps are repeated for various values of W_1 and W_2 (summing to W), and the best partition is used. Muckstadt (1976a, 1976b) also reports on extensions to more than two echelons.

3. Clark (1978) addresses the same multiechelon, multi-indenture situation with $(S - 1, S)$ policies and compound Poisson demand, as does the aforementioned MOD-METRIC model. However, he uses a somewhat different criterion—namely, maximizing the availablity of equipment at the bases where availability is defined as the fraction of time the equipment is operational. A somewhat different marginal solution procedure is also used. Finally, Clark also gives some suggestions on how to deal with the more general (s, S) policy where $s \neq S - 1$.

4. The LMI Procurement Model (1978) essentially combines the classical series-reliability model (a complete system does not operate unless all of its component systems operate) with the basic METRIC assumptions for individual-item, two-echelon situations. The objective is to establish procurement quantities that maximize the expected number of operational pieces of equipment (complete systems), subject to a given budget constraint. A marginal analysis solution procedure is again used. (Starting with no units procured, we keep increasing procurement quantities one unit at a time, always picking the unit that has the largest incremental effect on the objective function.)

5. Hausman and Scudder (1982) use a simulation model to test various rules for scheduling repair operations in a shop supporting a multi-item inventory system with an indentured product structure. In contrast with all of the models discussed earlier, here repair times need not be assumed independent.

12.7 SOME STRATEGIC ISSUES

There are a number of important strategic issues related to multiechelon inventory structures that top management faces. Strategic matters were addressed in a general sense in Chapter 2 and more will be said on this topic, primarily in production contexts, in Chapter 13. For now we briefly mention some strategic questions with an indication of how the operational/tactical decison models of this chapter would be of use in addressing them. An important related reference is Wagner (1980).

1. *What warehouses (and other stocking points) are needed and what should be their sizes?* Customer service argues for having numerous stocking points close to customers. However, this leads to duplication of effort, extra carrying costs, and possible extra transportation costs (a few regional warehouses can permit bulk shipping). The required inventory capacities and related costs of different options can be evaluated by the procedures of this chapter.

2. *What mode(s) and frequencies of transportation should be used?* Different modes imply different average lead times and different variabilities of lead times. Less frequent shipments permit economies of scale but adversely affect customer service and required safety stocks (in that the review interval R is increased). Moreover, there is an interrelationship with the previous issue in that the capacity of a warehouse depends on the frequency of shipments.

3. *Which items should be stocked and at which locations?* Using the methods of this chapter, we can evaluate the inventory-related costs of any specific choice of locations for the stocking of a particular item. In Section 9.5 of Chapter 9 we dealt with the choice of stock versus no-stock for the case of a single possible location. Again, there is an interaction with the first issue; the locations of warehouses and their sizes restrict our options here. Brown (1982) has proposed a common-sense rule for deciding where to stock each item. We discuss his approach for the case of three echelons (central warehouse, regional warehouse, and retail outlets). Estimate the number of customer demand transactions per year for each item (this is less than D unless all transactions are of unit size). A relatively small percentage of the items should be stocked at all locations—namely, those items having the most transactions. The items having very few transactions should be stored, if at all, only at the central location. The intermediate group of items can be placed at the central and regional warehouses.

4. *Which s.k.u. should be repaired as opposed to being treated as completely consumable?* The models of Section 12.6 permit us to evaluate the inventory-related costs of the different options. Obviously of importance are relative unit costs of repair and acquisiton, but equally crucial are the availability of sufficient repair capacity, the lead times involved, and the reliability of repair and delivery of new units.

5. *What is the impact of centralized versus decentralized control?* As discussed in Section 12.3 the centralized control required in PUSH systems has ramifications well beyond the typical costs considered in inventory control models, particularly from the standpoint of organizational behavior.

12.8 SUMMARY

With this chapter we have dealt with the difficult multiechelon situation in which there is a dependency of demand among s.k.u. Exact analyses, particularly in the case of probabilistic demand, quickly become intractable. Thus, again the use of heuristic methods has been advocated.

This completes our treatment of "pure" inventory situations. Beginning with Chapter 13 we address production contexts. Chapter 16 will deal with the production analog of a multiechelon situation.

APPENDIX TO CHAPTER 12
DERIVATION OF THE LOGIC FOR COMPUTING THE BEST REPLENISHMENT QUANTITIES IN A DETERMINISTIC, TWO-STAGE PROCESS

We wish to select n (an integer) and Q_f in order to minimize

$$\text{TRC}(n, Q_f) = \frac{D}{Q_f}\left(A_f + \frac{A_p}{n}\right) + \frac{Q_f r}{2}(nv_p' + v_f') \tag{12.27}$$

A convenient approach is to first set the partial derivative of TRC with respect to Q_f equal to zero and solve for the associated $Q_f^*(n)$, which is the best Q_f given the particular n value:

$$\frac{\partial \text{TRC}}{\partial Q_f} = -\frac{D}{Q_f^2}\left(A_f + \frac{A_p}{n}\right) + \frac{r}{2}(nv_p' + v_f')$$

which solves for

$$Q_f^*(n) = \sqrt{\frac{2\left[A_f + \frac{A_p}{n}\right]D}{(nv_p' + v_f')r}} \tag{12.28}$$

This expression is then substituted back into Eq. 12.27 to give TRC*(n), the lowest cost possible for the given value of n. The resulting equation is

$$\text{TRC}^*(n) = \sqrt{2\left[A_f + \frac{A_p}{n}\right]D(nv_p' + v_f')r}$$

Finally, we must find the integer value of n that minimizes TRC* (n). First, we recognize that the n that minimizes the simpler expression

$$F(n) = \left[A_f + \frac{A_p}{n}\right](nv_p' + v_f') \tag{12.29}$$

will also minimize TRC* (n).

A convenient way to find the minimizing n value is to first set

$$\frac{dF(n)}{dn} = 0$$

which gives

$$(nv_p' + v_f')\left[-\frac{A_p}{n^2}\right] + \left[A_f + \frac{A_p}{n}\right] v_p' = 0$$

This solves for

$$n^* = \sqrt{\frac{A_p\, v_f'}{A_f v_p'}} \tag{12.30}$$

which in general will not be an integer. The next step is to ascertain $F(n_1)$ and $F(n_2)$ from Eq. 12.29 where n_1 and n_2 are the two integers surrounding the n^* of Eq. 12.30. Whichever gives the lower value of F is the appropriate n to use. Finally, the corresponding Q_f and Q_p values are found by using this n in Eqs. 12.28 and 12.1, respectively.

PROBLEMS

12.1 Consider a two-stage serial process where the second stage is a rather minor operation adding little extra value to the product. To be more specific, suppose we have an item with these characteristics:

$D = 1000$ units/yr	$v_p = \$5$/unit
$v_f = \$6$/unit	$r = 0.24$/yr
$A_p = \$20$	$A_f = \$10$

Use the procedure of Section 12.1.1 to obtain Q_p, Q_f, and n. Do your results make intuitive sense?

12.2 For the situation of Section 12.1.3,

a. Verify that the average actual *(not echelon)* inventory at the primary stage is

$$\bar{I}_p = \left(\frac{n-1}{2n}\right) Q_p$$

b. Show that $\bar{I}_p v_p + \bar{I}_f v_f = \bar{I}'_p v'_p + \bar{I}'_f v'_f$

12.3 Starting with the result of Eq. 12.29 (in the Appendix of this chapter), find an expression, involving A_f, A_p, v'_p, v'_f, and n, that must be satisfied for indifference between n and $n + 1$. Sketch the curves (for different n values) with suitable horizontal and vertical axes.

12.4 Consider the MIDAS International example that was used throughout Chapter 6. Suppose that the production process actually involves two stages (call them primary and finishing). The relevant cost parameters are $A_p = \$24$, $A_f = \$30$, $v_p = \$15$/box, $v_f = \$20$/box, and $r = 0.02$ \$/\$/month. Note that $A_p + A_f = \$54$—the A value that was used, with $v = \$20$/unit, in Chapter 6. Thus, implicitly in Chapter 6 we assumed that any replenishment at the primary stage was immediately processed through the finishing stage (with no primary inventory being retained). For simplicity, we use only the first 8 months of the requirements pattern, repeated as follows:

Month	1	2	3	4	5	6	7	8
Requirements in boxes (for finished product)	10	62	12	130	154	129	88	52

a. Use the sequential, unmodified, Silver-Meal approach to determine the patterns of replenishments. To be specific, first use the Silver-Meal at the finishing stage with $A = \$30$ and $v = \$20$/box to get the pattern of replenishments at the finishing stage. These replenishments become the requirements pattern for the primary stage. Use these, with $A = \$24$ and $v = \$15$/box, to find the replenishments at the primary stage. Finally, cost out the overall solution.

b. Use the Blackburn-Millen approach to establish the replenishments. In particular, Eqs. 12.10 to 12.12 are used to establish $\hat{A}_f$ and $\hat{v}_f$ for the Silver-Meal heuristic at the finishing stage. Again, cost out the overall solution and compare with part a.

12.5 Using Eqs. 12.10 to 12.12 prove that

$$\frac{\hat{A}_f}{\hat{v}_f} > \frac{A_f}{v_f}$$

hence that there will tend to be more batching at the finishing stage under the Blackburn-Millen procedure than under the straight sequential approach.

12.6 A famous remote lodge in the Canadian Rocky Mountains uses a fuel oil for cooking and heating purposes. The lodge is accessible by a four-wheel drive truck on a rough forestry road. The fuel is stored in bulk in a large tank where the forestry road intersects with the main highway. On each trip the truck can carry 3000 liters of fuel and the main tank holds 18,000 liters. The usage of the fuel at the lodge is rather uncertain, particularly because of weather conditions. However, in a specific season of interest, data indicate that for a 1-day period usage can be assumed to be normally distributed with $\hat{x}_1 = 450$ liters and $\sigma_1 = 125$ liters. The capacity for storage at the lodge is 4000 liters and deliveries of 15,000 liters are made by tanker-truck to the tank on the highway. The unit cost of the fuel delivered to the main tank is \$0.15/liter and the value added through the loading, trucking up the forestry road, and unloading is estimated to be \$0.04/liter. A lead time of 2 days is involved to replenish the lodge's supply (assuming there is fuel in the main tank) and the lead time is 12 days for a replenishment of the main tank. When a stockout occurs at the lodge, propane can be used but at a cost of \$0.28/liter. Assume a carrying charge of 0.26 \$/\$/yr.

a. What should be the reorder points for the lodge and for the main tank?

b. Discuss some complexities ignored.

12.7 In the procedure, described in Section 12.3, for selecting the base stock level in a general, multiechelon situation, what implicit assumption is made about the availability of stock at the next (further removed from the customer) level? Can you suggest a correction factor that might allow relaxation of this assumption.

12.8 For the situation of Section 12.4.2, suppose that $D_i = D$ and $\sigma_i = \sigma$ $(i = 1, 2, \ldots, n)$ and that there is no correlation among forecast errors at different locations. Under such circumstances determine ETRC (centralized) ÷ ETRC (decentralized) as a function of n, and evaluate for $n = 2$, 4, and 9.

12.9 Max Berman is responsible for ensuring that the furnishings at the Calgary Corral (a sports stadium) are maintained in proper working order. One item causing him problems is a type of portable chair used at ringside for the weekly Stampede Wrestling. On the average, 5 chairs are severely damaged at each wrestling show (it seems that they are effective weapons used by Wildman Woodward for slowing down aggressive opponents). Seventy percent of damaged chairs have to be thrown out and replaced by new ones at a unit variable cost of \$20/chair. The other 30 percent can be repaired at an average cost of \$7/chair. The repairman estimates a setup cost of \$10 to get his tools organized, etc., to repair 1 or more chairs. The fixed cost associated with an order for new chairs is approximately \$15 and the carrying charge for inventories of chairs is 0.26 \$/\$/yr.

a. How many damaged chairs should Berman have repaired at one time?

b. How many new chairs should be purchased together?

c. How often, on the average, would each type of replenishment take place?

12.16 $p_{u \geq k_f} = \frac{(3000)(.04)(.005)}{.09(450 \times 7)}$ $k_f = 2.86$

12.15 $s_f = 2 \times 450 + 2.86\sqrt{2} \times 125$

12.18 $p_{u \geq k_p} = \frac{[(3000)(.19 + 4(.15))]\ .005}{.09(450 \times 7)} = .418$

$s_p = 14 \times 450 + 1.73\sqrt{14}(125)$

REFERENCES

Afentakis, P. (1981). "A Class of Heuristic Algorithms for Lot-Sizing in Multistage Systems." *Working Paper 20-81-82*, Graduate School of Industrial Administration, Carnegie-Mellon University, Pittsburgh, Pennsylvania.

Axsäter, S., and P. Lundell (1979). "Multi-Stage Lot Sizing in a Case with Initial Inventories." *Methods of Operations Research*, Vol. 38, Verlagsgruppe Athenaum/Hain/Scriptor/Hanstein, Konigstein, West Germany, pp. 237–251.

Blackburn, J., and R. Millen (1981). "Guidelines for Lot-Sizing Selection in Multi-Echelon Requirements Planning Systems." In *The Economics and Management of Inventories*, Part B (A. Chikan, Editor), Akademiai Kiado,Budapest, pp. 57–66.

Blackburn, J., and R. Millen (1982). "Improved Heuristics for Multi-Stage Requirements Planning Systems." *Management Science*, Vol. 28, No. 1, pp. 44–56.

Brown, R. G. (1975). "Comparison among Allocation Techniques." *Working Memorandum 84*, Materials Management Systems, Inc., Norwich, Vermont.

Brown, R. G. (1982). *Advanced Service Parts Inventory Control.* Materials Management Systems, Inc., Norwich, Vermont, Chapters 12 and 14.

Clark, A. J. (1972). "An Informal Survey of Multi-Echelon Inventory Theory." *Naval Research Logistics Quarterly*, Vol. 19, No. 4, pp. 621–650.

Clark, A. J. (1978). "Logistic Support Economic Evaluation (LSEE): Optimal Operational Availability Inventory Model." *R-7806*, CACI Inc., Federal Systems and Logistics Division, Arlington, Virginia.

Clark, A. J. (1981). "Experiences with a Multi-Indentured Multi-Echelon Inventory Model." In *Multi-Level Production/Inventory Control Systems: Theory and Practice* (L. B. Schwarz, Editor), Vol. 16, Studies in the Management Sciences, North-Holland, Amsterdam, pp. 299–330.

Clark, A. J., and H. Scarf (1960). "Optimal Policies for a Multi-Echelon Inventory Problem." *Management Science*, Vol. 6, No. 4, pp. 475–490.

Connors, M., C. Coray, C. Cuccaro,W. Green, D. Low, and H. Markowitz (1972). "The Distribution System Simulator." *Management Science*, Vol. 18, No. 8, pp. B425–B453.

Crowston, W., M. Wagner, and A. Henshaw (1972). "A Comparison of Exact and Heuristic Routines for Lot-Size Determination in Multi-Stage Assembly Systems." *AIIE Transactions*, Vol. 4, No. 4, pp. 313–317.

Crowston, W., M. Wagner, and J. Williams (1973). "Economic Lot Size Determination in Multi-Stage Assembly Systems." *Management Science*, Vol. 19, No. 5, pp. 517–527.

De Bodt, M., and S.C. Graves (1983)."Continuous-Review Policies for a Multi-Echelon Inventory Problem with Stochastic Demand." *Working Paper 1441-83*, Alfred P. Sloan School of Management, Massachusetts Institute of Technology, Cambridge, Massachusetts.

Demmy, W. S., and V. J. Presutti (1981). "Multi-Echelon Inventory Theory in the Air Force Logistics Command." In *Multi-Level Production/Inventory Control Systems: Theory and Practice* (L. B. Schwarz, Editor), Vol. 16, Studies in the Management Sciences, North-Holland, Amsterdam, pp. 279–297.

Ehrhardt, R. A., C. R. Schultz, and H. M. Wagner (1981)."(s, S) Policies for a Wholesale Inventory System." In *Multi-Level Production/Inventory Control Systems: Theory and Practice* (L. B. Schwarz, Editor), Vol. 16, Studies in the Management Sciences, North-Holland, Amsterdam, pp.145–161.

Eppen, G. D. (1979). "Effects of Centralization on Expected Costs in a Multi-Location Newsboy Problem." *Management Science*, Vol. 25, No. 5, pp. 498–501.

Eppen, G., and L. Schrage (1981). "Centralized Ordering Policies in a Multi-Warehouse System with Lead Times and Random Demand." In *Multi-Level Production/Inventory Control Systems: Theory and Practice* (L. B. Schwarz, Editor), Vol. 16, Studies in the Management Sciences, North-Holland, Amsterdam, pp. 51–67.

Fox, B., and M. Landi (1970). "Searching for the Multiplier in One-Constraint Optimization Problems." *Operations Research*, Vol. 18, No. 2, pp. 253–262.

Gajdalo, S. (1973). "Heuristics for Computing Variable Safety Levels/Economic Order Quantities for Repairable Items." *AD 760528*, AMC Inventory Research Office, Institute of Logistics Research, U.S. Army Logistics Management Center, Fort Lee, Virginia.

Geoffrion, A. M. (1976). "Better Distribution Planning with Computer Models." *Harvard Business Review*, Vol. 52, No. 4, pp. 92–99.

Graves, S. C. (1981). "Multi-Stage Lot Sizing: An Iterative Procedure." In *Multi-Level Production/Inventory Control Systems: Theory and Practice* (L. B. Schwarz, Editor), Vol. 16, Studies in the Management Sciences, North-Holland, Amsterdam, pp. 95–110.

Graves, S. C. (1982). "A Multi-Echelon Inventory Model for a Low Demand Repairable Item." *Working Paper No. 1299-82*, Sloan School of Management, Massachussets Institute of Technology, Cambridge, Massachusetts.

Graves, S., and L. Schwarz (1977). "Single Cycle Continuous Review Policies for Arborescent Production/Inventory Systems." *Management Science*, Vol. 23, No. 5, pp. 529–540.

Haber, S., and R. Sitgreaves (1975). "An Optimal Inventory Model for the Intermediate Echelon When Repair Is Possible." *Management Science*, Vol. 21, No. 6, pp. 638–648.

Hausman, W. H., and G. D. Scudder (1982). "Priority Scheduling Rules for Repairable Inventory Systems." *Management Science*, Vol. 28, No. 11, pp. 1215–1232.

Heyman, D. P. (1978). "Return Policies for an Inventory System with Positive and Negative Demands." *Naval Research Logistics Quarterly*, Vol. 25, pp. 581–596.

Kaplan, A. (1973). "A Stock Redistribution Model." *Naval Research Logistics Quarterly*, Vol. 20, No. 2, pp. 231–239.

Kaplan, A., and R. Deemer (1971). "Stock Allocation in a Multi-Echelon System." *Final Report*, Inventory Research Office, Institute for Logistics Research, U.S. Army Logistics Management Center, Fort Lee, Virginia.

Lambrecht, M. R., J. Vander Eecken, and H. Vanderveken (1981). "Review of Optimal and Heuristic Methods for a Class of Facilities in Series Dynamic Lot-Size Problems." In *Multi-Level Production/Inventory Control Systems: Theory and Practice* (L. B. Schwarz, Editor), Vol. 16, Studies in the Management Sciences, North-Holland, Amsterdam, pp. 69–94.

Lawrence, M. (1977). "An Integrated Inventory Control System." *INTERFACES*, Vol. 7, No. 2, pp. 55–62.

Logistics Management Institute (1978). *LMI Availability System: Procurement Model*, Washington, D.C.

Maxwell, W. L., and J. A. Muckstadt (1983). "Establishing Consistent and Realistic Reorder Intervals in Production-Distribution Systems." *Technical Report No. 561*, School of Industrial Engineering and Operations Research, Cornell University, Ithaca, New York.

McLaren, B. J. (1976). "A Study of Multi-Stage Level Lot-Sizing Techniques for Material Requirements Planning Systems." Unpublished Doctoral Dissertation, Purdue University, West Lafayette, Indiana.

Miller, B. L. (1974). "Dispatching from Depot Repair in a Recoverable Item Inventory System: On the Optimality of a Heuristic Rule." *Management Science*, Vol. 21, No. 3, pp. 316–325.

Muckstadt, J. A. (1973). "A Model for a Multi-Item, Multi-Echelon, Multi-Indenture Inventory System." *Management Science*, Vol. 20, No. 4, pp. 472–481.

Muckstadt, J. A. (1976a). "Consolidated Support Model (CSM): A Three-Echelon, Multi-Item Model for Recoverable Items," R-1928-PR, The RAND Corporation, Santa Monica, California.

Muckstadt, J. A. (1976b). "NAVMET: A Four-Echelon Model for Determining the Optimal Quantity and Distribution of Navy Spare Aircraft Engines." *Technical Report No. 263*, School of Operations Research and Industrial Engineerng, Cornell Universty, Ithaca, New York.

Muckstadt, J. A. (1978). "Some Approximations in Multi-Item, Multi-Echelon, Inventory Systems for Recoverable Items." *Naval Research Logistics Quarterly*, Vol. 25, No. 3, pp. 377–394.

Muckstadt, J. A., and L. J. Thomas (1980). "Are Multi-Echelon Inventory Methods Worth Implementing in Systems with Low-Demand-Rate Items?" *Management Science*, Vol. 26, No. 5, pp. 483–494.

Muckstadt, J. A., and M. H. Isaac (1981). "An Analysis of Single Item Inventory Systems with Returns." *Naval Research Logistics Quarterly*, Vol. 28, No. 2, pp. 237–254.

Nahmias, S. (1981a). "Approximation Techniques for Several Stochastic Inventory Models." *Computers & Operations Research*, Vol. 8, No.3, pp. 141–158.

Nahmias, S. (1981b). "Managing Repairable Item Inventory Systems: A Review." In *Multi-Level Production/Inventory Control Systems: Theory and Practice* (L. B. Schwarz, Editor), Vol. 16, Studies in the Management Sciences, North-Holland, Amsterdam, pp. 253–277.

Nahmias, S. and H. Rivera (1979). "A Deterministic Model for a Repairable Item Inventory System with a Finite Repair Rate." *International Journal of Production Research*, Vol. 17, No. 3, pp. 215–221.

New, C. (1974). "Lot-Sizing in Multi-Level Requirements Planning Systems." *Production and Inventory Management*, Vol. 15, No. 4, pp. 57–71.

Pinkus, C. E., D. Gross, and R. M. Soland (1973). "Optimal Design of a Multiactivity, Multifacility System by Branch and Bound." *Operations Research*, Vol. 21, No. 1, pp. 270–283.

Porter, R. (1972). "Management of Multiple Warehouse Systems." *Automation*, pp. 52–56.

Rhodes, P., and S. Wilson (1972). "A Decentralized Inventory Control System for Distribution Warehouses." *Production and Inventory Management*, Vol. 13, No. 4, pp. 73–93.

Rosenbaum, B. A. (1981a). "Inventory Placement in a Two-Echelon Inventory System: An Application." In *Multi-Level Production/Inventory Control Systems: Theory and Practice* (L. B. Schwarz, Editor), Vol. 16, Studies in the Management Sciences, North-Holland, Amsterdam, pp. 195–207.

Rosenbaum, B. A. (1981b). "Service Level Relationships in a Multi-Echelon Inventory System." *Management Science*, Vol. 27, No. 8, pp. 926–945.

Sawchuk, P. A. (1981). "Installing a 'PUSH' Distribution System." *Proceedings of the 24th Annual International Conference of the American Production and Inventory Control Society*, pp. 279–281.

Schrady, D. A. (1967). "A Deterministic Inventory Model for Repairable Items." *Naval Research Logistics Quarterly*, Vol. 14, pp. 391–398.

Schwarz, L. (1973). "A Simple Continuous Review, Deterministic, One-Warehouse, *N*-Retailer, Inventory Problem." *Management Science*, Vol. 19, No. 5, pp. 555–566.

Schwarz, L. B. (1981). "Physical Distribution: The Analysis of Inventory and Location." *AIIE Transactions*, Vol. 13, No. 2, pp. 138–150.

Schwarz, L., and L. Schrage (1975). "Optimal and System Myopic Policies for Multi-Echelon Production/Inventory Assembly Systems." *Management Science*, Vol. 21, No. 11, pp. 1285–1294.

Schwarz, L. B., and L. Schrage (1978). "On Echelon Holding Costs." *Management Science*, Vol. 24, No. 8, pp. 865–866.

Sherbrooke,C. C. (1968). "METRIC: A Multi-Echelon Technique for Recoverable Item Control." *Operations Research*, Vol. 16, No. 1, pp. 122–141.

Sherbrooke, C. C. (1971). "An Evaluator for the Number of Operationally Ready Aircraft in a Multilevel Supply System." *Operations Research*, Vol. 19, No. 3, pp. 618–635.

Simon, R. M. (1971). "Stationary Properties of a Two Echelon Inventory Model for Low Demand Items." *Operations Research*, Vol. 19, No. 3, pp. 761–777.

Simpson, V. P. (1978). "Optimum Solution Structure for a Repairable Inventory Problem." *Operations Research*, Vol. 26, No. 2, pp. 270–281.

Szendrovits, A. Z. (1975). "Manufacturing Cycle Time Determination for a Multi-Stage Economic Production Quantity Model." *Management Science*, Vol. 22, No. 3, pp. 298–308.

van Beek, P. (1981). "Modelling and Analysis of a Multi-Echelon Inventory System: A Case Study." *European Journal of Operational Research*, Vol. 6, pp. 380–385.

Wagner, H. M. (1980). "Research Portfolio for Inventory Management and Production Planning Systems." *Operations Research*, Vol. 28, No. 3, Part 1, pp. 445–475.

Williams, J. F. (1974). "Multi-Echelon Production Scheduling When Demand Is Stochastic." *Management Science*, Vol. 20, No. 9, pp. 1253–1263.

Williams, J. F. (1981). "Heuristic Techniques for Simultaneous Scheduling of Production and Distribution in Multi-Echelon Structures: Theory and Empirical Considerations." *Management Science*, Vol. 27, No. 3, pp. 336–352.

Williams, J. F. (1983). "A Hybrid Algorithm for Simultaneous Scheduling of Production and Distribution in Multi-Echelon Structures." *Management Science*, Vol. 29, No. 1, pp. 77–92.

Zacks, S. (1970). "A Two-Echelon Multi-Station Inventory Model for Naval Applications." *Naval Research Logistics Quarterly*, Vol. 17, No. 1, pp. 79–85.

PART FIVE

DECISION SYSTEMS FOR THE PRODUCTION CONTEXT

In this section of the book we turn to the details of decision making in a production environment where one has to face two additional complexities. First, there are capacity constraints at individual work centers; such capacity must be shared among the individual s.k.u. processed at the specific centers. Second, items are intimately related in that raw materials are converted into final products through continuous processes (of a chemical nature) or through fabrication/assembly. Thus, coordination of decisions concerning individual s.k.u. is mandatory.

In Chapter 13 we provide a broad overview of decision making in production situations. A decision framework is presented that encompasses strategic (long-range), tactical (medium-range), and operational (short-range) concerns.

Chapter 14 addresses medium-range aggregate production planning. This encompasses the selection of work force levels and aggregate production rates, typically month by month out to a horizon of approximately one year. Particular emphasis is given to some of the nonmathematical aspects of aggregate planning.

In Chapters 15 and 16 we turn to the shorter range decisions of scheduling and control: Capacity-oriented (bottleneck) process industry situations are considered in Chapter 15. In contrast Chapter 16 deals with fabrication/assembly situations where the overriding concern is with proper coordination of materials and effective use of labor. Specifically, the details of two important systems are presented—namely, Material Requirements Planning and Just-in-Time Manufacturing.

CHAPTER 13

An Overall Framework for Decision Making in Production Situations

In this relatively short chapter we present a framework that we believe is quite useful for managerial decision making in production situations. Although a single framework is developed, there are important differences in detail with respect to two broad types of production contexts. Thus, Section 13.1 provides a summary statement of the dichotomy, developed in Chapter 2, between capacity-oriented process industries and materials/labor-oriented fabrication/assembly industries. In Section 13.2 we discuss the proposed decision-making framework. It recognizes a natural hierarchy of production decision making, and Section 13.3 describes options available to deal with the hierarchy of decisions.

13.1 THE DICHOTOMY BETWEEN CAPACITY-ORIENTED PROCESS INDUSTRIES AND MATERIALS/LABOR-ORIENTED FABRICATION/ASSEMBLY INDUSTRIES

In Chapter 2[1] an examination of the following points led us to a useful dichotomy.

1. The concept of the product life cycle.
2. Characteristics of process versus fabrication/assembly industries.
3. The product-process matrix.
4. The relative ease of associating raw material and part requirements with a schedule of end products.

---

[1]The reader is encouraged to review Sections 2.3 to 2.5 of Chapter 2.

The dichotomy we identified existed between the capacity-oriented process industries and the materials/labor-oriented industries.

The key differences between the two categories of industries, from a production planning and control standpoint, are summarized in Table 13.1. The production planning and control systems, appropriate for the two settings, should reflect these differences. In particular, *in the capacity-oriented process situation a paramount consideration should be the coordination of items at a singe bottleneck operation, to achieve as high a capacity utilization as possible. In contrast, in the materials/labor-oriented fabrication/assembly context, the primary concern should be the appropriate coordination of raw materials, components, and so forth, across multiple stages of the production operations.*

13.2 A FRAMEWORK FOR PRODUCTION DECISION MAKING

In this section we first step back from the production function and view managerial decision making from a broader perspective, identifying a hierarchy of interconnected decisions. Next, we recall another type of interrelationship

TABLE 13.1 Summary of Key Differences between Capacity-Oriented Process Industries and Materials/Labor-Oriented Fabrication/Assembly Industries

	Type of Industry	
Characteristic	Capacity-Oriented Process	Materials/Labor-Oriented Fabrication/Assembly
Orientation in planning	Capacity	Materials/labor
Nature of production layout	Flow	Job shop
Definition of production capacity (via bottleneck operation)	Easy	Difficult
Production geared more to	Stock	Order
Natural grouping of products (that is, coordination needed)	Likely	Unlikely
Aggregate planning[a]	Important and easier	Less important and more difficult
Provision for scheduled downtime	More likely	Less likely
Number of raw materials	Lower	Higher
Labor/plant ratio	Lower	Higher
Variability of yield	Lower	Higher

[a]Setting overall output rates and work force sizes (for example, on a monthly basis).

among production decisions at the operational level—namely, the flow of materials between stages in a multistage process. These two types of interrelationships then lead us to a proposed framework for decision making within production contexts.

13.2.1 A Review of Anthony's Hierarchy of Managerial Decisions

Anthony (1965) proposed that managerial activities fall into three broad categories, whose names have been somewhat modified over the years (see, for example, Hax, 1976) to become *strategic planning, tactical planning,* and *operational control.*

In Section 2.1 of Chapter 2, we briefly discussed strategic planning within an overall corporate strategy. A key point was the need for decision making in the production/inventory area to be consistent with that in other functional areas of the organization. Strategic planning is clearly of long-range scope and is a

TABLE 13.2 Summary of Anthony's Hierarchy Applied to the Production Function

Category of Activity	Strategic	Tactical	Operational
General types of decisions	Plans for acquisition of resources	Plans for utilization of resources	Detailed execution of schedules
Managerial level	Top	Middle	Low
Time horizon	Long (2+ years)	6 to 18 months	Short range
Level of detail	Very aggregated	Aggregated	Very detailed
Degree of uncertainty	High	Medium	Low
Examples of variables under control of management	Products to sell; sizes and locations of facilities; nature of equipment (for example, general purpose versus specialized); long-term raw material and energy contracts; labor skills needed; nature of production planning and inventory management decision systems	Operating hours of plants; work force sizes; inventory levels; subcontracting levels; output rates; transportation modes used	What to produce (procure), when, on what machine (from which vendor), in what quantity, and in what order; order processing and followup; material control

responsibility of senior management. Tactical planning is a medium-range activity involving middle and top management, concerned with the effective use of existing resources within a given market situation. Finally, operational control involves short-range actions, typically executed by lower levels of management and nonmanagerial personnel, to carry out the day-to-day activities of the organization efficiently.

We now expand on the discussion of the three levels of activities, tailoring our discussion for the production context. The reader should find the summary in Table 13.2 of assistance.

Strategic (or long-range) decisions of relevance to the production area (but with important interactions with other functional areas) include which products are to be produced (and on which of the dimensions of cost, quality, reliability, and flexibility will the company compete), where facilities are to be located, the nature of the production equipment, and long-range choices concerning raw materials, energy, and labor skills. However, in this book our emphasis is on the development of decision systems, where we are already largely constrained by other strategic decisions made earlier. Chapter 2 included a discussion of the strategic choice between alternative decision systems for production planning and inventory management.

Tactical (medium-range) plans, with a planning horizon from six months to two years into the future, take the basic physical production capacity constraints and projected demand pattern established by a long-range plan and ration available resources to meet demand as effectively and as profitably as possible. Even though basic production capacity is essentially fixed by long-range considerations, production capacity can be increased or decreased within limits in the medium term. One can decide to vary one or more of the following: the size of the workforce, the amount of overtime worked, the number of shifts worked, the rate of production, the amount of inventory, the shipping modes used, and possibly the amount of subcontracting utilized by the company. These plans, in turn, constrain but provide stability to what can be done at the operational level.

Operational (short-term) activities provide the day-to-day flexibility needed to meet customer requirements on a daily basis within the guidelines established by the more aggregate plans discussed above. Short-range operating schedules take the orders directly from customers, or as generated by the inventory decision system, and plan in detail how the products should be processed through a plant. Detailed schedules are drawn up for one week, then one day, and finally one shift in advance. They involve the assignment of products to machines, the sequencing and routing of orders through the plant, the determination of replenishment quantities for each and every stock keeping unit, and so on.

13.2.2 Integration at the Operational Level

There is a second type of integration of decisions that is important in the context of multistage production operations. Specifically, at the operational level we must ensure that there is proper coordination of the input streams of the various raw materials, components, subassemblies, and so forth. In addition, as already evidenced in Chapter 12, there should be a coordination of actions back through all the stages of distribution to the interface with production.

13.2.3 The Framework

We now present a single general framework for planning and control within a production environment. It embraces Anthony's hierarchy of decisions as well as the above-mentioned integration at the operational level. The earlier emphasized differences between capacity-oriented process industries and materials/labor-oriented fabrication/assembly industries will lead to a different importance being assigned to specific components of the decision structure. The framework essentially encompasses what is called Closed Loop, Material Requirements Planning[2] (see, for example, Wight, 1981), a system developed primarily for fabrication/assembly industries,[3] but the framework is flexible enough to accommodate process situations (see Taylor et al., 1981). Frequent references will be made to Figure 13.1 in the following discussion. We restrict our attention to the tactical (medium-range) and operational (short-range) levels. Furthermore, where a chapter number is indicated in the text in connection with a particular block of the diagram, further coverage of that block will be provided (or has been provided) in the designated chapter.

We begin with medium-range aggregate production planning (Block 1 and Chapter 14). Here one is primarily concerned with establishing production rates, work force sizes, and inventory levels for something on the order of 6 to 24 months into the future. The time block used is generally 1 month, and the planning is done on an aggregate basis for families of items (produced on the same equipment)—that is, not on an individual-item basis. This stage of planning assumes extreme importance for capacity-oriented process industries for two reasons. First, it is designed to properly utilize capacity. Second, because of the typical similarity of the products and the flow nature of the production line, it is relatively easy to aggregate and subsequently disaggregate in the shorter range planning. This is usually not the case in fabrication/assembly environments. Finally, in capacity-oriented situations the aggregate planning must properly take into account planned maintenance downtime.

[2]A more complete system, known as *Manufacturing Resources Planning* (or MRP II), converts a number of the outputs of production planning and control into financial terms—for example, inventories in dollars, labor budget, shipping budget, standard hours of output in dollars, vendor dollar commitments, and so forth. For further details see Wight (1981).

[3]The discussion in the remainder of this chapter will *not* deal explicitly with the Just-in-Time Manufacturing system that was developed specifically for the case of very high volume, repetitive fabrication/assembly. This was discussed in Section 2.7 of Chapter 2 and will be treated further in Section 16.7 of Chapter 16.

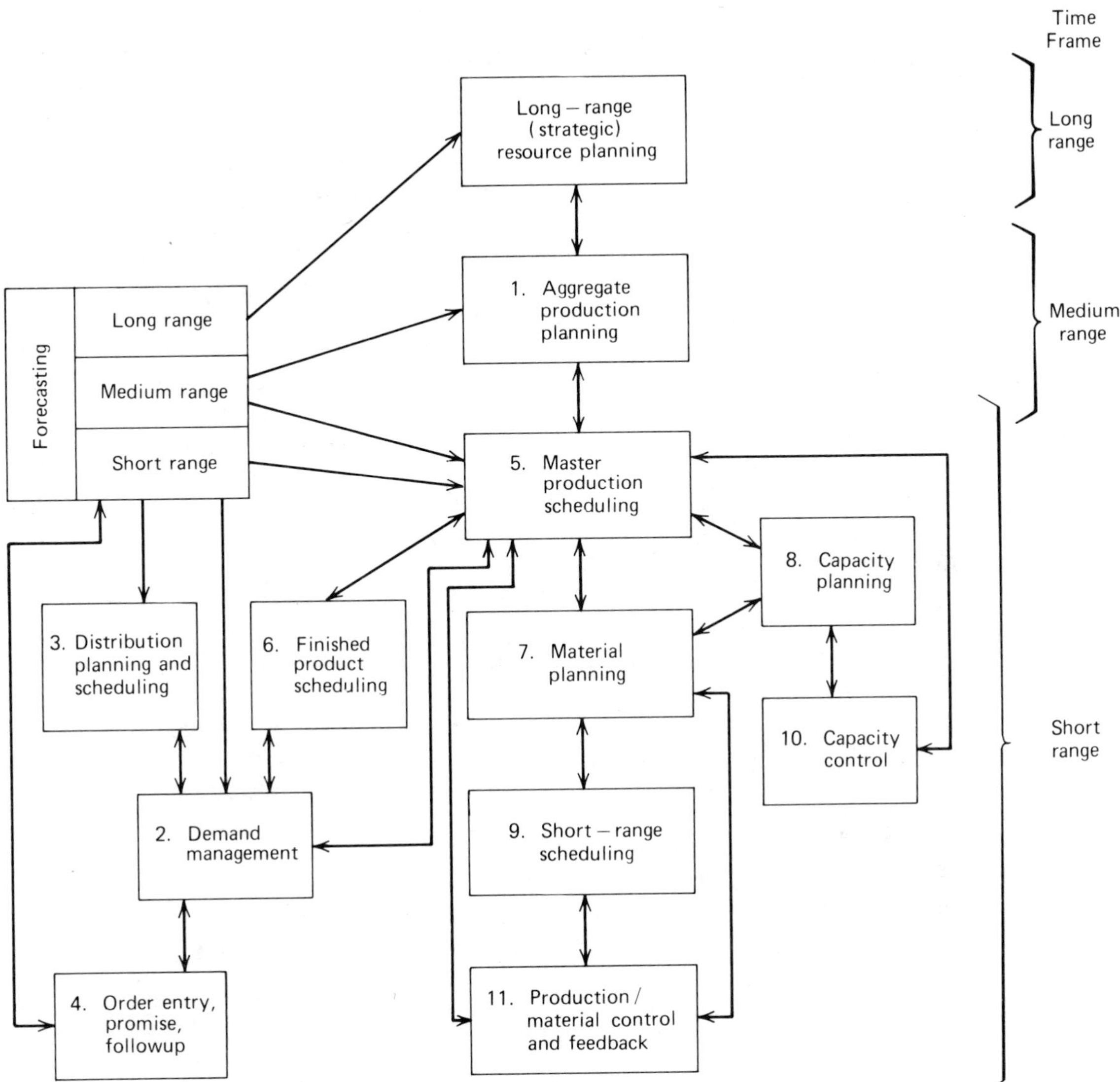

FIGURE 13.1 A Production Decision Making Framework

We next turn to demand management (Block 2). This function coordinates demand requirements and supply information emanating from five different sources. Obviously, one source is the forecasting module, which tends to be of greater importance in process industries where there is usually a significant amount of production to stock. Distribution planning and scheduling (Block 3 and Chapter 12) represent a second component of the framework that interacts with demand management. They include possible interplant transfers and international distribution. Another input to demand management emanates from order entry, promise, and followup (Block 4). In order entry actual customer orders are received and short-range forecasts of *remaining* demand in the current period must be accordingly modified. Order promise involves making a firm delivery commitment, based on material and capacity availability. These two ideas are illustrated in Figure 13.2 (adapted from the Boise Cascade control system described in Bolander et al., 1981). Followup involves activities such as customer notification, lot identification, and so forth.

The central component of the whole framework is master production scheduling (Block 5 and Chapter 15). It serves as the primary interface between marketing and production, and essentially drives all of the shorter run operations (see Collins and Whybark, 1982). In essence, the master production schedule takes the aggregate production plan (with its implied constraints) and disaggregates it into a production schedule of specific products to be produced in particular time periods at each manufacturing facility. Normally the time periods are smaller (weeks or days) than those used in the aggregate plan. The master schedule must be realistic; among other things it is used to provide customer delivery dates. We repeat that the overriding concern in a capacity-oriented, process situation is to use up the available capacity at the bottleneck operation. Thus, the master scheduling would normally be done at that stage. In a fabrication/assembly environment the choice of where to master schedule is less obvious. Sometimes it is convenient to master schedule the finished products themselves. However, where there are many combinations of options in a finished product, it may be preferable to master schedule at the subassembly or at other, intermediate product levels. The same idea applies when myriad packages are used for the same basic product (see Sanderson, 1981). An important issue is how far into the future one must prepare a master schedule. Each item that can appear on the master schedule will have a cumulative lead time (to purchase its raw materials, process them into components, etc.). The longest of these cumulative lead times is the minimum planning horizon for the master schedule.

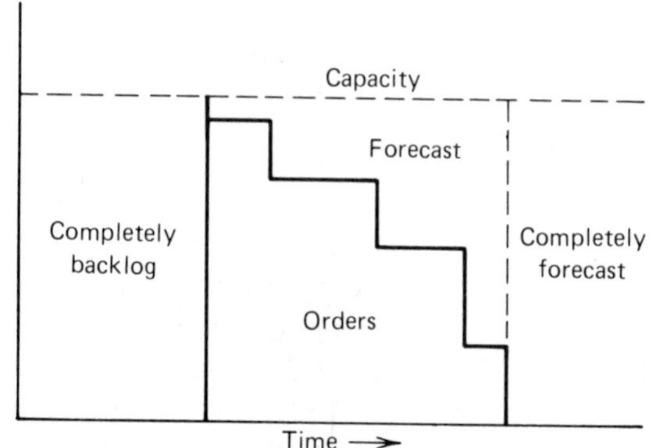

FIGURE 13.2 Order Backlog and Forecasts

Ideally, one would like to establish the master schedule while still keeping total relevant costs as low as possible. This is a feasible goal to achieve in a bottleneck process situation (Chapter15). However, in a fabrication/assembly context, the bottleneck and the flow patterns change with the product mix. Furthermore, there are likely to be many more short-range changes because of alterations in customer orders, machine breakdowns, material supply difficulties, and so on. Thus in fabrication/assembly situations one strives, essentially by trial and error, for a *feasible* solution that is flexible and *reasonable* from a cost standpoint (Chapter 16). Moreover, in such an environment the master schedule is likely to be more heavily influenced by "horse-trading" among marketing, production, and finance than is the case in process situations.

As mentioned above, frequent updates of input information are likely. To prevent extreme instability of plans, organizations usually use the concept of *time fences*. For example, no order can be changed, without presidential approval, within the last two days prior to its production time; changes within one week of scheduled production require sign-off by the vice-president of manufacturing, and any reasonable change can be instituted beyond a production lead time.

The master production schedule can be effectively used in a "what-if" mode to determine the consequences of proposed tactical actions, for example, to determine the production/inventory impact of a special sales campaign proposed by marketing. Also, the "what-if" mode can be used to provide input for longer range resources planning.

There are a number of excellent references on master production scheduling, in particular Berry et al. (1979) and Wight (1981, pp. 165–180).

Finished product scheduling (Block 6) is relevant when the master scheduling is *not* done at the finished product stage. In this case, items must be scheduled for processing from the master schedule level to the finished products stage. For example, the master scheduling may be done to stock with bulk products. Then, final packaging could be scheduled to firm customer orders as they develop. Finished product scheduling, in turn, is likely to activate shipping schedules (an indirect link to Block 3 is shown in Figure 13.1 via demand management). Finished product scheduling is sometimes called *final assembly scheduling*, but, as seen above, the finishing operations need not involve assembly.

Material planning (Block 7 and Chapter 16) explodes the master production schedule into implied, detailed production/procurement schedules (timing and quantities) of all components and raw materials. This is a complicated, crucial task in fabrication/assembly contexts where there can be literally thousands of s.k.u. involved. In contrast, in most process situations material planning is a relatively straightforward undertaking.

Capacity planning (Block 8 and Chapter 16) really occurs at two stages in time in fabrication/assembly environments. First, there is what is called a *rough-cut capacity check* that is done during preparation of the master production schedule. The purpose is to make a rough check on the feasibility of the master schedule (against labor availability, raw materials, and limiting pieces of equipment) *before carrying out the details of material planning*. Then, once the material planning is undertaken, detailed calculations afford a more accurate check on the feasibility of the plan. In capacity-oriented situations feasibility constraints may be directly built into a mathematical model that permits scheduling of the bottleneck operation. Where capacity planning reveals serious capacity problems, this type of information should be relayed back to the higher level aggregate production planning (this direct link is not shown in Figure 13.1). Capacity planning can also be of considerable assistance to suppliers in that a projection of order workload can help reduce a supplier's lead time and costs of production.

Once a feasible master production schedule is established, we turn to short-range scheduling (Block 9). Again, this is a relatively simple task in most process industry settings, whereas it involves much more detail in materials/labor-oriented circumstances. Here we are concerned with the final scheduling of production, likely narrowed down to a finer time detail than was used in the master schedule. Orders are released to production (in-house) and suppliers (purchasing) and indicate, *based on the master production schedule and the associated material plan*, which items should be replenished and their associated due dates. This can include the rescheduling of open (tentative) orders. Within house, dispatch lists are typically used on a daily basis first thing in the morning. These *suggest* the sequence in which jobs are to be run on each machine on the shop floor. We emphasize the word "suggest," since the shop foreman knows the hidden agenda that can never be factored into a priority-setting model; for example, Helen simply dislikes running certain types of jobs, particularly on a Monday morning. There is a large literature on sequencing decision rules; see, for example, Andersson et al. (1981), Buffa and Miller (1979), Eilon (1978), Graves (1981), and Johnson and Montgomery (1974). Material planning and short-range scheduling involve the use of lead times (including queueing time at work centers) that must be reestimated as shop conditions change.

Capacity control (Block 10) monitors the level of output, compares it to planned levels, and executes short-term corrective actions if substantial (defined by control limits) deviations are observed. An output control report is a useful device; it shows the actual output, the planned output, and the actual input for each work center. The input is needed because it may reveal that a center's output is down simply because it was starved for input. The possible short-term actions include use of overtime, transfer of people between work centers, alternative routings of jobs, and so forth.

Finally, the whole system will not operate effectively without the detailed production/material control and feedback function (Block 11). First, there must be well-defined responsibility (involving signing authority) for key short-range actions such as the accepting of dispatch lists. Production status and inventory records must be punctually and accurately updated. Prompt feedback on deviations from the plan must be provided. Possible deviations include changes in customer orders and forecasts, manufacturing problems (machine breakdowns, quality difficulties with a particular batch, lower than average yield, etc.), vendor problems (quality, can't meet promise dates, etc.), inventory inaccuracies (identified by stock counts), engineering changes, and so on. More generally, feedback and corrective actions on any perceived problems are to be actively encouraged (the concept of quality circles). Other short-run control functions include the measurement of yield, scrap, energy utilization, and productivity as well as possible records for product traceability.

13.3 OPTIONS IN DEALING WITH THE HIERARCHY OF DECISIONS

In Section 13.2.1 a hierarchy of three levels (strategic, tactical, and operational) of managerial decision making was presented. The purpose of the current section is to identify briefly three different possible approaches for coping with this hierarchy. In discussing these approaches we keep in mind the following managerial objectives with respect to production planning, scheduling, and control (partly adapted from Meal et al., 1982):

1. Effective determination of required production resources.
2. Efficient *planned* use of these resources at the tactical level of aggregate planning.
3. Efficient *actual* use of the resources at the operational stage.
4. Plans at the operational level that stay within the aggregate constraints implied by the output of the tactical level—that is, short-term behavior that, *in the aggregate*, is consistent with tactical plans.
5. Realistic planning system for the organization—specifically, having a planning procedure that fits the organizational structure and is practical to implement.

13.3.1 Monolithic Modeling Approach

Several authors (see, for example, Dzielinski and Gomory, 1965, Lasdon and Terjung, 1971; Newsom, 1975), in response to objectives 2, 3, and 4 above, have proposed one large (monolithic) mathematical programming model of the *combined tactical* production planning and *operational* scheduling problem. Quite aside from severe computational and input data requirements (for example, detailed *individual*-product demand information projected out to the reasonably long horizon needed for aggregate planning), this approach does not normally provide an appropriate response to the fifth objective, except perhaps in a very simple, capacity-oriented flow situation with highly centralized control.

13.3.2 Explicit Hierarchical Planning

A second approach, first proposed by Hax and Meal (1975) is known as *hierarchical production planning*. (See also Meal, 1984.) Specifically, two separate decision stages are adopted for the tactical and operational phases, recognizing the way that most organizations are structured. Consistent with the framework of Figure 13.1, an aggregated model is used to assist middle and senior management with the tactical production planning. Then, *explicitly* subject to the constraints imposed by the aggregate plan, a lower level of management, with the aid of a more detailed model, develops the shorter range production and procurement schedules for individual items. Thus, such a so-called hierarchical decision system permits effective coordination throughout the organizational structure, establishing consistent subgoals at each level that become progressively more specific as they approach the actual day of manufacture. Moreover, appropriate managerial levels now address only questions of prime interest to them. For example, as pointed out by Jönsson (1983), individual-item scheduling details should not be of concern to senior management who need more of an aggregate perspective. Clearly, this framework directly addresses the objective of having a system that is consistent with the structure of most organizations. The tradeoff is that *tangible* costs may be increased somewhat because of the sequential nature of the decision making. However, consistent with our earlier findings on individual-item decision rules, it would appear that effectively developed hierarchical (sequential) procedures can do almost as well, from a tangible cost standpoint, as do monolithic approaches, particularly when there is a well-defined bottleneck operation (as in many process situations).

13.3.3 Implicit Hierarchical Planning

Many organizations, with structures that permit hierarchical planning, do their planning with very little, if any, formal interconnections (of a costing or constraint nature) between the tactical and operational levels. Thus, hierarchical planning is done only on an implicit basis. This is particularly so in organizations that carry out materials/labor-oriented fabrication/assembly production. This has been the case until quite recently with most installations of Material Requirements Planning, where the primary emphasis has been on deterministic models of detailed, short-run production and procurement schedules. Problems with capacity constraints have been handled on a trial-and-error basis without much prescriptive advice. The rationale is that in most fabrication/assembly situations it is very difficult to define aggregate capacity in the first place, and that the capacity is flexible, in any event, in the short run. Thus, modeling efforts, involving precise capacities, at the tactical level are questionable exercises in this environment.

13.4 SUMMARY

In this chapter we have provided a general framework for decision making within a production environment. In Chapter 14 we elaborate on the tactical, aggregate production planning phase. Then, in Chapters 15 and 16, two approaches for coping with the details of operational scheduling and control will be presented. Although we present Material Requirements Planning in Chapter 16, distinct from the explicit hierarchical planning framework of Chapter 15, we believe, as do other authors (see, for example, Andersson et al., 1981; Bitran et al., 1980; Meal, 1978; Meal et al., 1982), that the hierarchical framework, perhaps in a somewhat more flexible mode, is quite appropriate in fabrication/assembly organizations. Furthermore, we hasten to emphasize that no single approach to production planning, scheduling, and control is appropriate for all situations and that what we present are not the only possibilities. Specifically, for a fabrication/assembly environment other approaches, involving mathematical models that more explicitly deal with costs, have been suggested by Brown et al. (1981), Maxwell and Muckstadt (1981), and Maxwell et al. (1982). In addition, Goldratt (1980), in his procedure known as OPT, explicitly recognizes capacity restrictions in selecting batch sizes, in setting priorities, and in the final scheduling of products in order to maximize the throughput of a plant.

PROBLEMS

13.1 Select a local process industry and illustrate the production planning, scheduling, and control activities through the use of the individual blocks of Figure 13.1.

13.2 Repeat Problem 1 but for a fabrication/assembly situation.

13.3 Using Figure 13.1, indicate major interactions with other functional areas of the firm and identify in which blocks they take place.

13.4 In Section 2.4.3 of Chapter 2 mention was made of by-products in process situations.

a. Give an example other than the one in the text.

b. Discuss why lot sizing and inventory management are complicated by by-products. Illustrate for the case of a single major product, a single by-product, and deterministic level demand.

13.5 Compare the decision processes in the framework in Figure 13.1 to the one given in Figure 13.3 for Rolls-Royce Motors.

a. Are they substantially the same? If not, what are the main differences?

b. Should top and middle management get involved in short-range decision making? If not, why not? If yes, how should they contribute?

13.6 From the literature select an approach, different from Anthony's, to grouping management activities. What are the main differences between your selection and Anthony's structure? Do they matter?

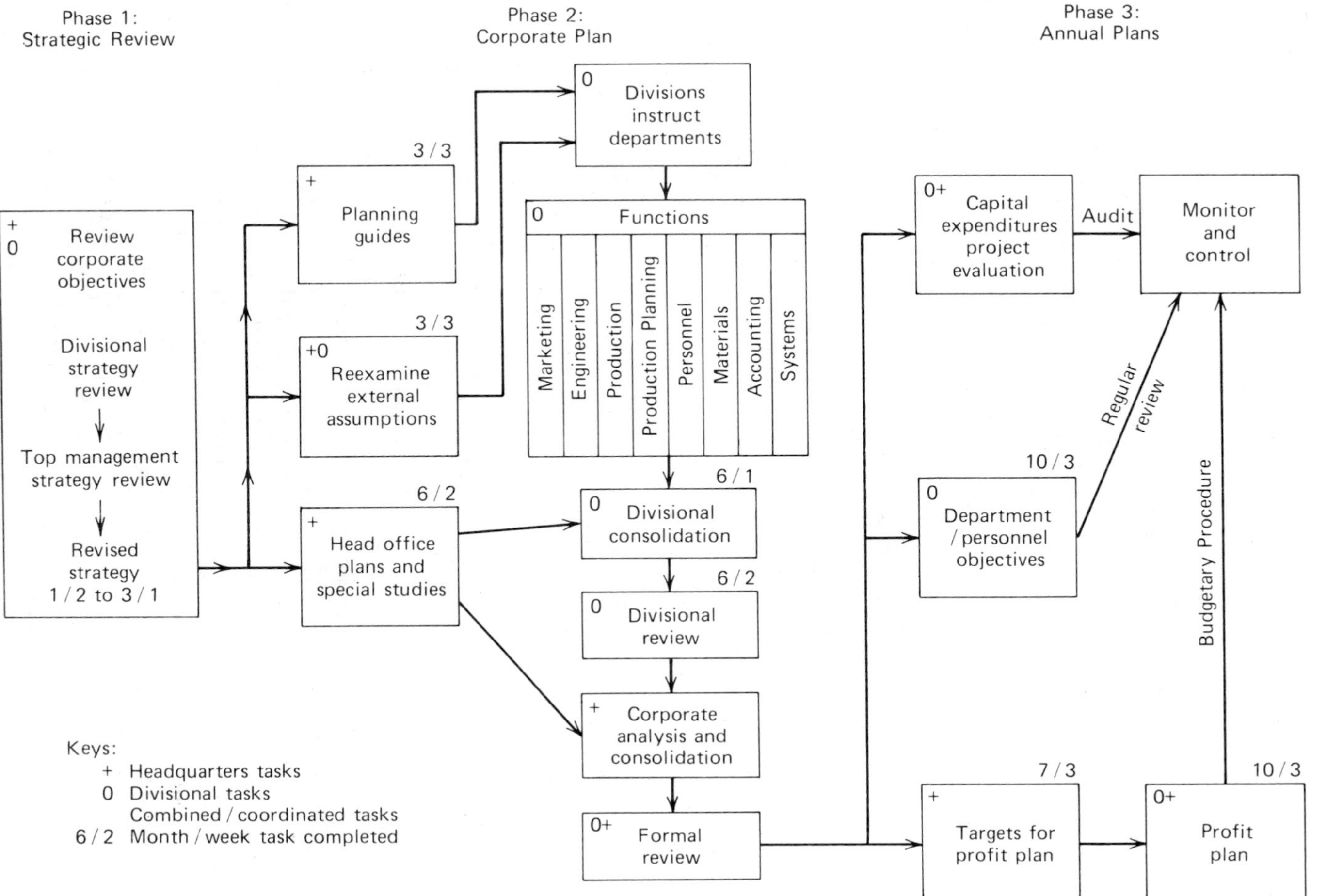

FIGURE 13.3 The Limited Strategic Planning Process of Rolls-Royce Motors. Source: R. Young, "Corporate Planning at Rolls Royce Motors Limited," *Long Range Planning*, April 1977, p. 7. Reprinted with permission. Copyright © 1977, Pergamon Press Ltd.

REFERENCES

Andersson, H., S. Axsäter, and H. Jönsson (1981). "Hierarchical Material Requirements Planning." *International Journal of Production Research*, Vol. 19, No. 1, pp. 45–57.

Anthony, R. N. (1965). *Planning and Control Systems: A Framework for Analysis*. Harvard University Graduate School of Business Administration, Boston, Massachusetts.

Axsäter, S. (1976). "Coordinating Control of Production—Inventory Systems." *International Journal of Production Research*, Vol. 14, No. 6, pp. 669–688.

Berry, W. L., T. E. Vollman, and D. C. Whybark (1979). *Master Production Scheduling: Principles and Practice*. American Production and Inventory Control Society, Washington, D.C.

Bitran, G. B., E. A. Haas, and A. C. Hax (1980). "Hierarchical Production Planning: A Two Stage System." *Technical Report No. 179*, Operations Research Center, Massachusetts Institute of Technology, Cambridge, Massachusetts.

Bolander, S. F., R. C. Heard, S. M. Seward, and S. G. Taylor (1981). *Manufacturing Planning and Control in Process Industries*. American Production and Inventory Control Society, Falls Church, Virginia.

Bromberg, H. (1979). "Converting the Forecast to the Master Production Schedule." *Proceedings of the 22nd Annual International Conference of the American Production and Inventory Control Society*, pp. 123–125.

Brown, G. G., A. Geoffrion, and G. Bradley (1981). "Production and Sales Planning with Limited Shared Tooling at the Key Operation." *Management Science*, Vol. 27, No. 3, pp. 247–259.

Buffa, E. S., and J. G. Miller (1979). *Production—Inventory Systems: Planning and Control*, Third Edition, Richard D. Irwin, Inc., Homewood, Illinois, Chapters 10 and 11.

Collins, R. S., and D. C. Whybark (1982). "Coordinating Manufacturing and Distribution Activities." *Working Paper 1*, IMEDE Management Development Institute, Lausanne, Switzerland.

Dzielinski, B. P., and R. E. Gomory (1965). "Optimal Programming of Lot Sizes, Inventory and Labor Allocations." *Management Science*, Vol. 11, No. 9, pp. 874–890.

Eilon, S. (1978). "Production Scheduling." In *OR '78* (K. B. Haley, Editor). North-Holland, Amsterdam, pp. 1–30.

Everdell, R. (1972). "Master Scheduling: Its New Importance in the Management of Materials." *Modern Materials Handling*, pp. 33–40.

Goldratt, E. (1980). "Optimized Production Timetable: A Revolutionary Program for Industry." *Proceedings of the 23rd Annual International Conference of the American Production and Inventory Control Society*, pp. 172–176.

Graves, S. C. (1981). "A Review of Production Scheduling." *Operations Research*, Vol. 29, No. 4, pp. 646–675.

Hanson, S. (1973). "The Synergistic Effects of Master Scheduling." *Production and Inventory Management*, Vol. 14, No. 3, pp. 75–77.

Hax, A. C. (1976). "The Design of Large Scale Logistics Systems: A Survey and an Approach." In *Modern Trends in Logistics Research* (W. H. Marlow, Editor). The M.I.T. Press, Cambridge, Massachusetts.

Hax, A. C., and H. C. Meal (1975). "Hierarchical Integration of Production Planning and Scheduling." In *Logistics* (M. A. Geisler, Editor), Studies in Management Sciences, Vol. 1, North-Holland, Amsterdam and American Elsevier, New York, pp. 53–69.

Johnson, L. A., and D. C. Montgomery (1974). *Operations Research in Production Planning, Scheduling and Inventory Control*. John Wiley & Sons, New York, Chapter 5.

Jönsson, H. (1983). "Simulation Studies of Hierarchical Systems in Production and Inventory Control." *Dissertation No. 91*, Department of Production Economics, Linköping Institute of Technology, Linköping, Sweden, pp. 193–194.

Lasdon, L. S., and R. C. Terjung (1971). "An Efficient Algorithm for Multi-Item Scheduling." *Operations Research*, Vol. 19, No. 4, pp. 946–969.

Maxwell, W., and J. A. Muckstadt (1981). "Coordination of Production Schedules with Shipping Schedules." In *Multi-Level Production/Inventory Control Systems* (L. B. Schwarz, Editor), Volume 16, Studies in the Management Sciences, North-Holland, Amsterdam, pp. 127–143.

Maxwell, W., J. A. Muckstadt, L. J. Thomas, and J. Vander Eecken (1982). "A Modeling Framework for Planning and Control of Production in Discrete Parts Manufacturing and Assembly Systems." *Working Paper*, School of Operations Research and Industrial Engineering, Cornell University, Ithaca, New York.

Meal, H. C. (1978). "A Study of Multi-Stage Production Planning." In *Studies in Operations Management* (A. C. Hax, Editor), North Holland Publishing Co., Amsterdam.

Meal, H. C. (1984). "Putting Production Decisions Where They Belong." *Harvard Business Review*, Vol. 62, No. 2, pp. 102–111.

Meal, H. C., M. H. Wachter, and D. C. Whybark (1982). "Material Requirements Planning and Hierarchical Planning Systems." *Working Paper 2*, IMEDE Management Development Institute, Lausanne, Switzerland.

Newsom, E. F. P. (1975). "Multi-Item Lot Size Scheduling by Heuristic. Part II: With Variable Resources." *Management Science*, Vol. 21, No. 10, pp. 1194–1203.

Sanderson, G. A. (1981). "Reverse/Balance Scheduling." *Proceedings of the 24th Annual International Conference of the American Production and Inventory Control Society*, pp. 76–79.

Taylor, S. G., S. M. Seward, S. F. Bolander, and R. C. Heard (1981). "Process Industry Production and Inventory Planning Framework: A Summary." *Production and Inventory Management*, Vol. 22, No.1, pp. 15–32.

Wight, O. (1981). *MRP II: Unlocking America's Productivity Potential*. Oliver Wight Limited Publications, Inc., Brattleboro, Vermont.

Case E

MIDAS CANADA CORPORATION*

The Assembly Department in 1984 consisted of a total of 17 employees and a manager who was responsible for scheduling the day-to-day assembly of Midamatics and Stabilization Processors, the installation of Takashi Camera Systems, the repairs of all three types of equipment, and the breaking and packaging of bulk shipments of processing chemicals. He also helped out on the assembly lines during emergencies.

In preparing by hand the overall Master Plan for his department, the Assembly Manager stated that his goal was to provide employment for all 17 employees at an approximately constant rate throughout the year, subject to some policy constraints. He was not allowed to carry finished Midamatics or Takashi Camera Systems in inventory and he was to avoid working overtime whenever possible. On the basis of the Master Plan, more detailed daily schedules were prepared by him once a week and revised daily. The Assembly Manager described his job as follows:

Recently I read an article in the Harvard Business Review** *which rather nicely described what I do. The author used an analogy from space. A space rocket, if it is to hit the moon, must be launched within a "window" of a few hours and miles per hour. The limits on the window at launching are much rougher than they are at the other end, when the rocket nears the moon; if the launch falls outside the window, the target will be missed. This is exactly what I try to do. My objective is to plan for an actual daily work load in the department two and three months from now which will fall within the limits of the workforce capability that will be available to me at that time.*

THE SCHEDULING COMMITTEE

A Master Plan for the coming year was prepared during the latter part of December and revised normally only once in July. The Scheduling Committee consisted of the Sales Manager of the Equipment Division, the Inventory Control Manager, the Comptroller, and the President, the latter acting as chairman. The Assembly De-

*The MIDAS cases describe actual decision systems that are based on the consulting experiences of the authors. They do not describe the situation at any single company, but are in fact a compendium of actual situations that have been compressed into the environment of a single firm and industry for illustrative purposes. The cases are not intended as presentations of either effective or ineffective ways of handling administrative problems.

**See W. K. Holstein(1968). "Production Planning and Control Integrated." *Harvard Business Review*, May–June, 1968, p. 125.

partment Manager acted as secretary and prepared draft Master Plans for the Committee's consideration and approval.

The scheduling process started with a consideration of projected sales estimates for each of the next 12 months initiated by the respective sales managers and reviewed by the Inventory Control Manager. Usually only estimates that deviated by more than 10 percent from last year's experience were challenged by the Committee and had to be defended by the originators who were often asked to prepare written presentations of their reasons. Once a consensus was reached, these sales forecasts became the basis for all subsequent planning in the Assembly Department (see Table 1).

THE MASTER PLAN

1. Determination of Workforce Size

The Assembly Department Manager converted the forecasts in Table 1 into equivalent labor hours as shown in Table 2. He allowed 100 hours for the assembly of Midamatics, 4 hours for the assembly of Processors, and 32 hours for each expected installation of a Takashi camera system. The conversion factors were based on experience gained over the years. Actual times varied from these average figures depending on circumstances and somewhat on the exact specification of the equipment involved. On the same basis he allowed two minutes per kilogram or decaliter

TABLE 1. MIDAS Canada Corporation: 1985 Sales Forecasts

Month	Midamatics (units)	Stabilization Processors (units)	Install. (units)	Repairs (hr)	Bulk (kg)	Bulk (dkl)[a]
January	0	40	0	800	800	560
February	8	60	0	600	2,400	1,680
March	5	120	1	300	1,600	1,120
April	10	240	2	200	1,400	980
May	15	300	2	200	1,800	1,260
June	7	100	0	500	1,600	1,120
July	2	100	0	500	1,000	700
August	5	100	0	500	1,200	840
September	10	200	1	300	2,400	1,680
October	15	300	1	300	2,000	1,400
November	20	400	3	200	3,000	2,100
December	3	40	0	600	800	560
Totals	100	2,000	10	5,000	20,000	14,000

[a]1 dkl = 1 decaliter = 10 liters.

TABLE 2 MIDAS Canada Corporation: 1985 Manpower Forecasts (in man-hours)

Month	Midamatics (1)	Stabilization Processors (2)	Install. (3)	Repairs (4)	Bulk (5)	Totals (6)
January	0	160	0	800	45	1,005
February	800	240	0	600	136	1,776
March	500	480	32	300	91	1,403
April	1,000	960	64	200	79	2,303
May	1,500	1,200	64	200	102	3,066
June	700	400	0	500	91	1,691
July	200	400	0	500	57	1,157
August	500	400	0	500	68	1,468
September	1,000	800	32	300	136	2,268
October	1,500	1,200	32	300	113	3,145
November	2,000	1,600	96	200	170	4,066
December	300	160	0	600	45	1,105
Totals	10,000	8,000	320	5,000	1,133	24,453

of chemical that was repackaged into smaller quantities. The Assembly Manager stated:

I can make no defense of these factors other than saying that they have worked in the past. We haven't done any studies to actually check them. Over the years we have come to accept these factors as being reasonable. For example, we feel that it is not worth our while to differentiate between kilograms and decaliter units of chemicals packed—so we add the expected sales quantities for liquids and solids together and treat them as one and the same from an overall planning point of view.

The next step was the determination of how large a total workforce would be required. Each employee received 2 weeks holidays in July when the Assembly Department was shut down. In addition, 5 statutory holidays were granted to the nonunionized employees who normally worked a 35-hour week. On this basis the Assembly Manager calculated that the 245 working days available in 1985 would be distributed as given in columns 1 and 2 of Table 3. During January, the available 21 working days were equivalent to 8.6 percent (column 2, Table 3) of the 245 working days of capacity available for the whole year. Theoretically speaking, if the Assembly Manager hired exactly enough employees to produce the forecasted 24,453 man-hours of required output, then 8.6 percent of the production would have to be carried out in January.

Column 3 of Table 3 lists the percent of total expected sales, as given in Table 2, that must be met each month. For example, in January, 1005 man-hours were being forecast as being required (column 6, Table 2) which amounted to 4.1 percent (column 3, Table 3) of expected annual sales of 24,453.

TABLE 3 MIDAS Canada Corporation: 1985 Stabilized Monthly Production Rates

Month	No. of Working Days (1)	Percent of Production Capacity (%) (2)	Expected Sales Rate (%) (3)	Planned Production Capacity (%) (4)	Available Slack (%) (5)
January	21	8.6	4.1	10.2	6.1
February	20	8.2	7.4	9.8	2.4
March	22	9.0	5.7	10.7	5.0
April	22	9.0	9.4	10.7	1.3
May	22	9.0	12.5	10.7	−1.8
June	21	8.6	6.9	10.2	3.3
July	13	5.3	4.7	6.3	1.6
August	21	8.6	6.0	10.2	4.2
September	22	9.0	9.3	10.7	1.4
October	21	8.6	12.9	10.2	−2.7
November	21	8.6	16.6	10.2	−6.4
December	19	7.8	4.5	9.3	4.8
Totals	245	100.3[a]	100.0	119.2	19.2

[a]This column does not add up to 100.0 percent because of rounding inaccuracies.

Conceivably a theoretical minimum of only 14.26 employees would be required to handle the expected annual workload of 24,453 man-hours:

$$\frac{24{,}453 \text{ man-hours}}{7 \text{ hr/day} \times 245 \text{ days/man}} = 14.26$$

The Assembly Manager normally proposed the hiring of approximately 20 percent more employees than the theoretical minimum, in this case 17 men, to provide for flexibility in his planning. The workforce of 17 represented, in terms of total annual man-hours, 119.2 percent of expected annual demand:

$$\frac{17 \text{ men} \times 7 \text{ hr/day} \times 245 \text{ days/man} \times 100}{24{,}453 \text{ hours}} = 119.2\%$$

That is, in terms of workforce capacity, 19.2 percent of overcapacity or slack was available for scheduling the production of the six product lines and for meeting unforeseen contingencies. The 119.2 percent of planned capacity was distributed by month as given in column 4 of Table 3. For example, the planned production capacity for January with 17 men was calculated to be 10.2 percent of expected annual demand:

$$\frac{17 \text{ men} \times 7 \text{ hr/day} \times 21 \text{ days}}{24{,}453 \text{ man-hours}} \times 100 = 10.2\%$$

As a result (10.2 − 4.1) or 6.1 percent of slack was available for production planning in January (column 5, Table 3).

2. *Planning the Production of Major Product Lines*

The Scheduling Committee had in 1984, once again, debated the wisdom of hiring a workforce that could produce 20 percent more output than forecasted sales. They reluctantly approved the Assembly Manager's proposal only after the latter had explained that historically he had found it necessary "to allow for 1 to 3 percent slack per month in order to have some flexibility to meet unexpected deviations from forecasted sales patterns, schedule disruptions brought about by the unavailability of materials, machine breakdowns, illness in the workforce. . . ." He also stated that he had found it difficult to completely smooth out all seasonal fluctuation in expected sales and to compile weekly and daily schedules within the constraints of a Master Plan unless this amount of slack was available to him.

It was company policy not to carry any finished Midamatics or Takashi Camera systems in inventory. Therefore, the Assembly Manager first allocated exactly the amount of capacity required per month to produce the forecasted units as in Table 4.

TABLE 4 MIDAS Canada Corporation: 1985 Master Plan, Phase I (All Figures in Percent of Total Forecasted Sales of 24,453)

	Midamatics		Takashi		Total		
Month	Exp. Sales (1)	Cap. Alloc. (2)	Exp. Sales (3)	Cap. Alloc. (4)	Cap. Alloc. (5)	Planned Capacity (6)	Available Slack (7)
January	0	0	0	0	0	10.2	10.2
February	3.3	3.3	0	0	3.3	9.8	6.5
March	2.0	2.0	0.1	0.1	2.1	10.7	8.6
April	4.1	4.1	0.3	0.3	4.4	10.7	6.3
May	6.1	6.1	0.3	0.3	6.4	10.7	4.3
June	2.9	2.9	0	0	2.9	10.2	7.3
July	0.8	0.8	0	0	0.8	6.3	5.5
August	2.0	2.0	0	0	2.0	10.2	8.2
September	4.1	4.1	0.1	0.1	4.2	10.7	6.5
October	6.1	6.1	0.1	0.1	6.2	10.2	4.0
November	8.2	8.2	0.4	0.4	8.6	10.2	1.6
December	1.2	1.2	0	0	1.2	9.3	8.1
Totals	40.8	40.8	1.3	1.3	42.1	119.2	77.1

All allocations were made in terms of percent of total forecasted 1985 sales of 24,453 man-hours.*

In Phase II of developing the Master Plan the Assembly Manager allocated some of the "Available Slack" (column 7, Table 4) to the breaking of bulk and to repairs. From experience, the Assembly Manager had found it not worthwhile to plan more than six months ahead. He felt that the extra effort needed produced minimal benefits because of the many changes that usually occurred during a six-month period. Therefore, in December he prepared a plan that did not extend beyond June 30, by which time a new revised schedule would have been prepared by the Scheduling Committee for the second half of the year.

The easiest thing to smooth was the breaking of bulk shipments of chemicals. The Inventory Control Manager agreed to combine the forecasted orders for chemicals for January, February, and March, a total of 1.2 percent of annual sales, for disassembly in January (see Table 5, columns 5 and 6). Similarly, the expected orders for April, May, and June (1.1%) were also grouped for disassembly in March. The Comptroller approved these temporary increases of total dollar investment in production smoothing inventories.

With the cooperation of his sales personnel the Equipment Division Manager agreed to compile a list of customers whose equipment could be serviced in January rather than in the month predicted according to column 3 of Table 5. The list would include both customers who would likely need repairs or who had maintenance contracts that stipulated service in either February or March and who agreed to receiving repair service earlier. In this manner the Assembly Manager hoped to shift the repair work load as indicated in Table 5, column 4.

The final step, Phase III, in the development of the Master Plan consisted of the smoothing of the assembly rate of MIDAS Stabilization Processors. This always proved to be a contentious issue and often required the intervention of the Presi-

TABLE 5 MIDAS Canada Corporation: 1985 Master Plan, Phase II (All Figures in Percent of Total Forecasted Sales of 24,453)

			Repairs		Bulk				
Month	Midamatics Cap. Alloc. (1)	Takashi Cap. Alloc. (2)	Exp. Sales (3)	Cap. Alloc. (4)	Exp. Sales (5)	Cap. Alloc. (6)	Total Cap. Alloc. (7)	Planned Capacity (8)	Available Slack (9)
January	0	0	3.3	5.3	0.2	1.2	6.5	10.2	3.7
February	3.3	0	2.5	1.5	0.6	0	4.8	9.8	5.0
March	2.0	0.1	1.2	0.6	0.4	1.1	3.8	10.7	6.9
April	4.1	0.3	0.8	0.8	0.3	0	5.2	10.7	5.5
May	6.1	0.3	0.8	0.4	0.4	0	6.8	10.7	3.9
June	2.9	0	2.0	2.0	0.4	0	4.9	10.2	5.3

*The production smoothing system, which the Assembly Manager used, had been installed at MIDAS Canada by a management consulting firm from New York City in 1978.

dent for resolution. In 1985, for example, the Assembly Manager proposed the capacity allocation outlined in column 6 of Table 6. This proposed production schedule would result in the production smoothing inventories calculated in the sixth column of Table 7.

The Comptroller objected vigorously to this last aspect of the proposed plan. The Assembly Manager responded by pointing out that it was company policy not to carry any finished goods inventory in Midamatics and to install Takashi Camera Systems on demand. As a result, he pointed out, he had no other option but to smooth the assembly rate of Processors if the overall production rate was to be stabilized.

TABLE 6 MIDAS Canada Corporation: 1985 Master Plan, Phase III (All Figures in Percent of Total Forecasted Sales of 24,453)

Month	Midamatics Cap. Alloc. (1)	Takashi Cap. Alloc. (2)	Repair Cap. Alloc. (3)	Bulk Cap. Alloc. (4)	Processor Exp. Sales (5)	Processor Cap. Alloc. (6)	Total Cap. Alloc. (7)	Planned Cap. (8)	Available Slack (9)
January	0	0	5.3	1.2	0.7	1.2	7.7	10.2	2.5
February	3.3	0	1.5	0	1.0	2.5	7.3	9.8	2.5
March	2.0	0.1	0.6	1.1	2.0	4.4	8.2	10.7	2.5
April	4.1	0.3	0.8	0	3.9	3.0	8.2	10.7	2.5
May	6.1	0.3	0.4	0	4.9	1.9	8.7	10.7	2.0
June	2.9	0	2.0	0	1.6	2.3	7.2	10.2	3.0

TABLE 7 MIDAS Canada Corporation: 1985 Production Smoothing Inventories for Stabilization Processors

Month	Exp. Sales (1)	Prod. Rate (2)	Cum. Sales (3)	Cum. Prod. (4)	Invent. (%) (5)	Invent.[a] (units) (6)
December	—	—	—	—	—	10
January	0.7	1.2	0.7	1.2	0.5	41
February	1.0	2.5	1.7	3.7	2.0	132
March	2.0	4.4	3.7	8.1	4.4	279
April	3.9	3.0	7.6	11.1	3.5	224
May	4.9	1.9	12.5	13.0	0.5	41
June	1.6	2.3	14.1	15.3	1.2	83

[a]All of columns 1 to 5 are in percentages of annual sales expressed in hours. To convert inventory from percentages to units, the following calculation is necessary. For example in January:

$$\text{Ending inventory} = \frac{24{,}453 \text{ hr/yr} \times 0.005}{4 \text{ hr/unit}} + 10 = 41 \text{ units}$$

The 10 units added on in the above equation refer to the amount of inventory on hand at the beginning of January.

The Committee then discussed the possible merits of keeping limited numbers of subassemblies of Midamatics and Processors in inventory in order to give more options and flexibility to the Assembly Manager. The advisability of carrying some Takashi equipment in inventory, as proposed by the Vice-President of Sales, was rejected on the basis that the limited amount of sales did not justify the stocking of any inventories. The Assembly Manager commented, saying

My major concern is providing flexibility for the months ahead so that I can avoid getting myself into a bind and having to use overtime because I do not have enough experienced skilled repair staff or installers when needed. I do have some additional flexibility that is not reflected in the Master Plan. The warehouse can lend me a worker now and then to help out, and I, of course, in turn help them out when I can. Sometimes I get sales personnel to part ship, or to delay their sale by a month or so.

The Assembly Manager then expressed concern about whether he could schedule his work load daily within the constraints of the Master Plan so as to meet the daily shipment requirements of each of the sales divisions. In particular, he was unsure about the mix of assemblers, repair staff, and installers that should constitute the 17 employees for the year ahead.

Since no other proposals were put forward, the President suggested that the Master Plan, as proposed by the Assembly Manager, be accepted. (See Tables 8 and 9.)

TABLE 8 MIDAS Canada Corporation: The 1985 Master Plan (As of December 31, 1984)[a]

	Midamatics	Stabilization Processor		Takashi Install.	Repairs		Bulk		Totals			Total Production	
	Exp. Sales (1)	Exp. Sales (2)	Alloc. Cap. (3)	Exp. Sales (4)	Exp. Sales (5)	Alloc. Cap. (6)	Exp. Sales (7)	Alloc. Cap. (8)	Exp. Sales (9)	Planned Prod'n. (10)	Cap. (11)	Available Slack (12)	Planned Slack (13)
January	0	0.7	1.2	0	3.3	5.3	0.2	1.2	4.2	7.7	10.2	6.0	2.5
February	3.3	1.0	2.5	0	2.5	1.5	0.6	0	7.4	7.3	9.8	2.4	2.5
March	2.0	2.0	4.4	0.1	1.2	0.6	0.4	1.1	5.7	8.2	10.7	5.0	2.5
April	4.1	3.9	3.0	0.3	0.8	0.8	0.3	0	9.4	8.2	10.7	1.3	2.5
May	6.1	4.9	1.9	0.3	0.8	0.4	0.4	0	12.5	8.7	10.7	−1.8	2.0
June	2.9	1.6	2.3	0	2.0	2.0	0.4	0	6.9	7.2	10.2	3.3	3.0
July	0.8	1.6	—	0	2.0	—	0.2	—	4.6	—	6.3	1.7	—
August	2.0	1.6	—	0	2.0	—	0.3	—	5.9	—	10.2	4.3	—
September	4.1	3.3	—	0.1	1.2	—	0.6	—	9.3	—	10.7	1.4	—
October	6.1	4.9	—	0.1	1.2	—	0.5	—	12.8	—	10.2	−2.6	—
November	8.2	6.5	—	0.4	0.8	—	0.7	—	16.6	—	10.2	−6.4	—
December	1.2	0.7	—	0	2.5	—	0.2	—	4.6	—	9.3	4.7	—
Totals	40.8	32.7		1.3	20.3		4.8		99.9		119.2		

[a]Note that because of rounding errors some of the figures in the Tables do not match exactly. For example, columns 3 and 5, Table 3, should be identical to columns 9 and 12 of Table 8, respectively.

TABLE 9 MIDAS Canada Corporation: 1985 Production Smoothing Inventories for the Assembly Department

	December	January	February	March	April	May	June
Midamatics (units)[a]	0	0	0	0	0	0	0
Processors (units)[b]	10	41	132	279	224	41	83
Takashi (units)[a]	0	0	0	0	0	0	0
Repairs (hours)[c]	0	489	244	98	98	0	0
Bulk (kg + dkl)[d]	0	7336	2934	8069	5869	2934	0

[a]As a matter of policy no Midamatics were allowed to be carried in inventory as a means of production smoothing.

[b]Includes total inventory of Processors. Ten were left in inventory at end of 1984.

[c]"Inventory" here indicated the number of hours of repair business that sales staff were asked to solicit over and above that which was expected to result during the normal course of events during that month. It was assumed that the amount of business solicited in this manner would reduce next month's expected repairs accordingly. This amounted to a planned maintenance program that resulted from a desire to smooth workload.

[d]Only inventory over and above normal stocks that resulted from production smoothing is listed here.

CHAPTER 14

Medium-Range Aggregate Production Planning

Within the framework of Figure 13.1 of Chapter 13, we now deal with the medium-range, tactical problem of establishing aggregate production rates, workforce sizes, inventory levels, and, possibly, shipping rates. We present an evaluative overview of a selection of approaches to dealing with this problem. Table 14.1 provides a summary of the approaches to be discussed.

While a rich selection of decision systems that could be used in corporate planning exists, modeling has progressed much faster than application in practice. More careful consideration needs to be given to the *process and strategy* of introducing aggregate planning technology. There is a need in most organizations to demonstrate to management that the aggregate planning problem can be structured rationally and resolved with the assistance of relatively simple, yet powerful, concepts and models. Moreover, many analysts do not seem to be aware of the current low level of implemented aggregate planning theory. This is why we will emphasize in our overview the implementability and practicality of existing methodology.

In Section 14.1 we elaborate on the aggregate planning problem. Next, in Section14.2 the relevant costs are discussed. Section 14.3 deals with the choice of the planning horizon and appropriate ending conditions. Then, in Sections 14.4 to 14.9 we describe various methods for coping with the aggregate production planning problem.

14.1 THE AGGREGATE PLANNING PROBLEM

The aggregate production planning problem, in its most general form as treated by analysts to date, can be stated as follows: Given a set of (usually monthly) forecasts of demand for a *single* product, or for some measure of output that is

TABLE 14.1 A Classification of Selected Aggregate Production Planning Methods and Models

Classification	Type of Model/Method	Type of Cost Structure	Discussed In
A. Feasible solution methods	1. Barter	General/not explicit	14.4.1
	2. Graphical/tabular	Linear/discrete	14.4.2
B. Mathematically optimal models	3. Transportation models	Linear/continuous	14.5
	4. Linear programming models	Linear/continuous	14.6
	5. Linear decision rules	Linear/quadratic/continuous	14.10
C. Heuristic decision procedures	6. Simulation search procedures	General/explicit	14.7
	7. Management coefficients	Not explicit	14.9.1
	8. Projected capacity utilization ratios	Not explicit	14.9.2
	9. Parametric production planning	Quadratic/not specified	14.10

common across several products, what should be specified for each period in terms of:[1]

1. Size of the workforce W_t
2. Rate of production P_t
3. Quantity shipped[2] S_t

The problem is usually resolved *analytically* by minimizing the expected total costs over a given planning interval (6 to 24 months). The cost components include:

1. Cost of regular payroll and overtime
2. Cost of changing the production rate from one period to the next (including such items as costs of layoffs, hiring, training, learning, etc.)

[1]One other decision variable in some situations is the amount of subcontracting utilized, which we are implicitly ignoring here.

[2]Note that we use the shipments S_t, as opposed to the demand D_t, because in general it is not profitable to always try to meet *all* demands on time. Specifically, in practice it is usually true that

$$S_t \neq D_t \qquad \text{for some } t \tag{14.1}$$

That is, the quantity shipped is not identical to the quantity demanded in every period, nor should it be, as has been pointed out by Peterson (1971).

3. Cost of carrying inventory

4. Cost of insufficient capacity in the short run

In the above definition only three decision variables need to be determined: the required workforce size W_t (number of workers in month t); the required production rate per period P_t (units of product produced in month t); and the number of units S_t to be shipped in month t. The resulting inventory at the end of month t, I_t, can then be determined as follows:

$$I_t = I_{t-1} + P_t - S_t \tag{14.2}$$

The workforce variable W_t does not appear directly in Eq. 14.2 because any set level of W_t in turn determines the possible range of values that P_t can assume. That is, the size of the workforce is always *one* of the important determinants of the feasible rate of production per period.

Equation 14.2 is for the case of production to stock. An analogous result for the situation of production to order is the following (assuming that shipments are sent out as soon as possible):

$$B_t = B_{t-1} - P_t + D_t \tag{14.3}$$

where

B_t = backlog at the end of period t

D_t = actual (or forecasted) demand in period t

It would appear at first glance that production smoothing (that is, stabilizing the work load) is not possible in a make-to-order situation. However, see Problem 14.3, which is based on the work of Cruickshanks et al. (1984).

Returning to the make-to-stock situation, note that the solution to the problem posed is greatly simplified *if average demand over the planning interval is expected to be constant*. Under such a circumstance there would be no need to consider changing the level of the production rate, nor the size of the workforce, nor the planned quantity to be shipped from period to period.[3] One would need only carry sufficient inventory (safety stock) to balance the risk of running out using one of the many methods described in Chapter 7. The appropriate size of regular payroll would be given by:

$$W_t = \frac{\text{Average demand rate per period}}{\text{Productivity per worker}} \tag{14.4}$$

[3]We are also assuming implicitly that there are no problems in receiving a constant supply of raw materials and labor at a fixed wage rate. If the supply of raw materials or labor is seasonal, then these statements need to be modified.

We would have to consider using overtime only to replenish safety stock on occasion or if Eq. 14.4 resulted in a noninteger number of workers so that it might be worthwhile to round down and make up the shortfall through working overtime.

The complexity in the aggregate production planning problem therefore arises from the fact that in most situations demand per period is not constant but varies from month to month according to some *known* (seasonal) pattern. Only then do the following questions need to be answered:[3]

1. Should inventory investment be used to absorb the fluctuation in demand over the planning period by accumulating inventories during slack periods to meet demand in peak periods?
2. Why not absorb the fluctuations in demand by varying the size of the workforce by hiring or laying off workers?
3. Why not keep the size of the workforce constant and absorb fluctuations in demand by changing the rate of production per period by working shorter or longer hours as necessary, including the payment of overtime?
4. In process industries and where capacity exceeds average demand over a long period, should periodic shutdowns be used or should the plant be throttled (run at less than full capacity)? Taylor (1980) discusses this situation (see also Problem 14.4).
5. Why not keep the size of the workforce constant and meet the fluctuation in demand though planned backlogs or by subcontracting excess demand?
6. Is it always profitable to meet all fluctuations in demand or should some orders not be accepted?

To develop decision models to analyze these questions, a number of logical conditions and data requirements have to be met. First, as is obvious from the above, management must be able to forecast reasonably accurately the *fluctuating* demand over an appropriately long planning interval (horizon). The degree to which the different models that we will discuss are affected by forecast errors will vary, but they will all require that a reasonable forecast of demand be made (for example, by using the regression methods referred to in Chapter 4).

Second, to apply any of the *analytical* approaches, management must be able to develop a single overall *surrogate* measure of output and sales for all the different products to be scheduled by an aggregate production plan. This can prove to be quite difficult in practice, particularly when one realizes that disaggregation of the aggregate results is subsequently needed for the shorter range, operational, scheduling actions (see, for example, Axsäter, 1981; Axsäter et al., 1983; Boskma, 1982; Bitran et al., 1981). Some examples of units used in past applications include gallons of paint or beer, man-hours of assembly labor, machine hours in some job shop situations, cases of cans packed by a cannery, and dollars of sales, where each dollar of sales represented approximately the same amount of productive effort to be allocated.

---

[3]See footnote on page 533.

Third, to use an *analytical* approach, management must be able to identify and measure the costs associated with the various options raised above (these costs are discussed in greater detail in the next section). In actual fact, there are important intangibles that must also be included in deciding on whether to use a particular decision system (for example, the willingness of management to use a specific model as a decision aid, the effects on public image or public relations of frequent layoffs of employees, etc.).

Prior to discussing costs we mention the importance of taking a broad look at the aggregate planning problem, particularly questioning some of the "givens." For example, if there is a highly seasonal demand pattern, can inducements be given to customers to reduce the seasonal variations? Is there a possibility of expanding the product line to include items with a counterbalancing seasonal pattern (for example, snowblowers and lawnmowers)? Also, can the capacity be expanded by sharing equipment with other organizations whose needs occur during a different period of the year? An interesting reference on these kinds of issues is Galbraith (1969).

14.2 THE COSTS INVOLVED

There are essentially six categories of costs involved in the aggregate planning problem:

1. **Regular time costs.** The cost of producing a unit of output during regular working hours, including direct and indirect labor, materials, and manufacturing expenses.
2. **Overtime costs.** The costs associated with using manpower beyond normal working hours.
3. **Production-rate change costs.** The expenses incurred in altering the production rate substantially from one period to the next.
4. **Inventory associated costs.** The costs (both out of pocket and lost opportunity) associated with carrying inventory.
5. **Costs of insufficient capacity in the short run.** The costs incurred when demands occur while an item is out of stock. Such costs can be a result of backordering, lost sales revenue, and loss of goodwill. Also included in this category are the costs of actions initiated to prevent shortages—for example, split lots and expediting.
6. **Control system costs.** The costs associated with operating the control system. They include the costs of acquiring the data required by analytical decision rules, the costs of computational effort exerted per time period, and any implementation costs that depend on the particular control system chosen.

As Vergin (1980) has pointed out, *percentage* cost comparisons among alternative procedures should only include controllable variable costs and not fixed costs that are independent of the policy used.

14.2.1 Costs of Regular Time Production

A typical relation of cost versus production rate is shown in Figure 14.1. Usually some form of monotonic increasing behavior is assumed (that is, the costs associated with any production rate must be at least as high as those associated with any lower production rate). The near vertical rises in Figure 14.1 occur because additional pieces of equipment are required at increasingly higher rates of production. The shape of the cost curve may also depend on the particular time period under consideration.

A major portion of regular-time production costs in Figure 14.1 is the regular-time wage bill paid to the full-time workforce. When such costs are identified separately, they are usually assumed to increase linearly with the size of the workforce, as shown in Figure 14.2. It is becoming more difficult in practice to reduce the size of the workforce from one month to the next because of social pressures, public opinion, and union contracts. As a result, W_t, the size of the workforce, in many situations is in effect a constant and not a decision variable that can be altered at will. Under such a circumstance, the regular wage bill becomes a fixed cost, as shown by the dotted line in Figure 14.2, and the size of the intercept "C" on Figure 14.1 would have to be adjusted upward accordingly.

14.2.2 Overtime Costs

The general graphical form of overtime costs is illustrated in Figure 14.3. The production rate is at first increased beyond the regular-time capacity at little extra cost. This is because only the bottleneck operations need to run on overtime. However, with continued increases in the production rate, more and more

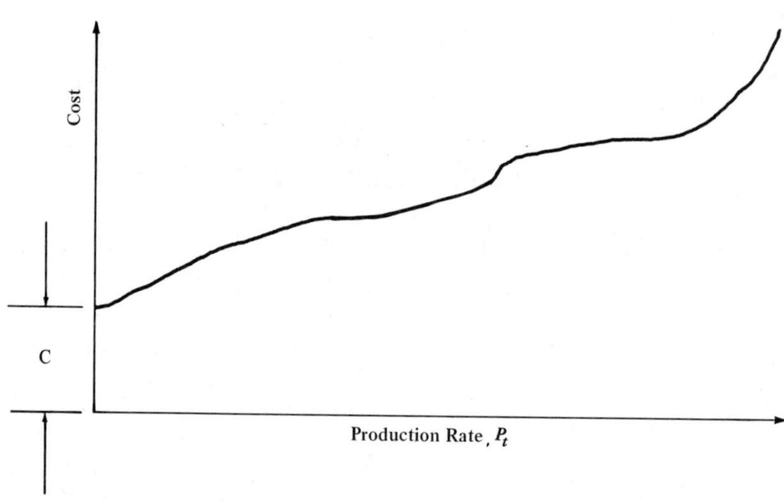

FIGURE 14.1 Typical Costs of Regular Time Production

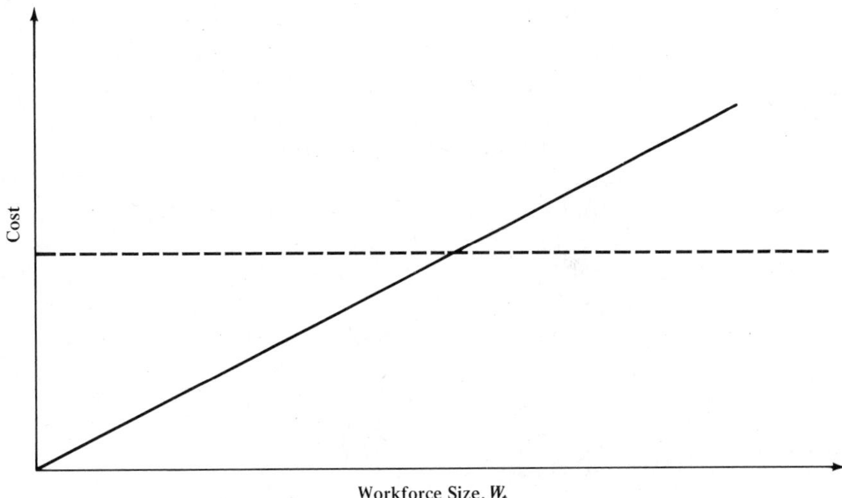

FIGURE 14.2 Typical Costs of Regular Time Labor

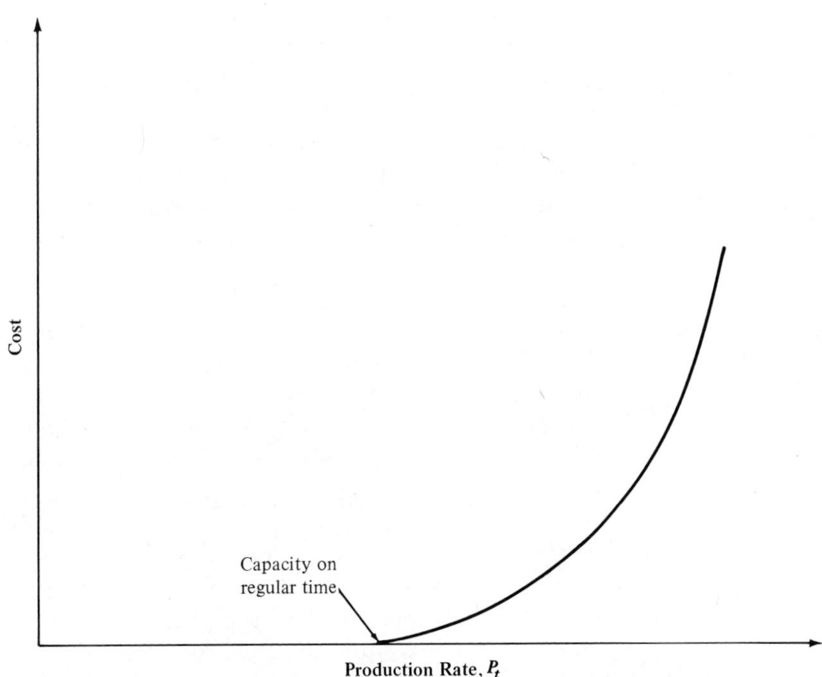

FIGURE 14.3 Typical Shape of Overtime Costs for a Given Work Force Size

of the operation must be run at overtime premium rates. The overtime cost curve rises sharply at higher levels of overtime because the efficiency with which workers produce, when asked to work longer and longer hours, starts to decrease at some point, resulting in lower productivity per man-hour worked. It is clear that a single overtime cost curve versus production rate is appropriate only for a fixed size of workforce; that is, there really is a whole set of curves for different workforce sizes. There is also a different curve for every t (when workforce is held constant) if workers are asked to work overtime day after day. Such *cumulative tiredness* results in curves with increasing slopes for every consecutive t worked on overtime. The curve in Figure 14.3 is not always as smooth as shown. Discontinuities are common.

14.2.3 Costs of Changing the Production Rate

These costs consist primarily of production rate changes brought on by changes in the size of the workforce. Such changes incur costs of training, reorganization, terminal pay, loss of morale, and decreased interim productivity. Decreased productivity results in part from the learning process when new labor or equipment must be started up. Another source of changeover costs is a common union requirement that specifies that, when an individual is laid off, that person's job can revert to any other union member according to seniority. As a result, the layoff of a few workers can result in "bumping," a series of shifts in job responsibilities.

A typical behavior of the costs as a function of the change in rates is shown in Figure 14.4. Two points are worth mentioning. First, the curve is usually asymmetric about the vertical axis; that is, a unit increase does not necessarily cost the same as a unit decrease. Second, ideally there should be a separate curve for each starting rate P_{t-1}. This is because a change from 90 percent to 95 percent of production capacity has an appreciably different cost than going from 30 percent to 35 percent.

Some decision models do not include a cost for changing production rates. Instead, they may specify that the change from one period to the next can be no greater than a certain value, or simply that the rate itself must stay within certain bounds. A special case is where no change is permitted from period to period—the policy of a level workforce that has been adopted by some organizations. Examples, as reported by Bolander et al. (1981), are the Clairol Products Division of Bristol Meyers and the Champion Spark Plug Company.

As we will see, the inclusion/exclusion of an explicit cost of changing the production rate becomes an important issue in the evaluation of alternative analytical models. In particular, this type of cost is very difficult to explicitly determine (see Welam, 1978).

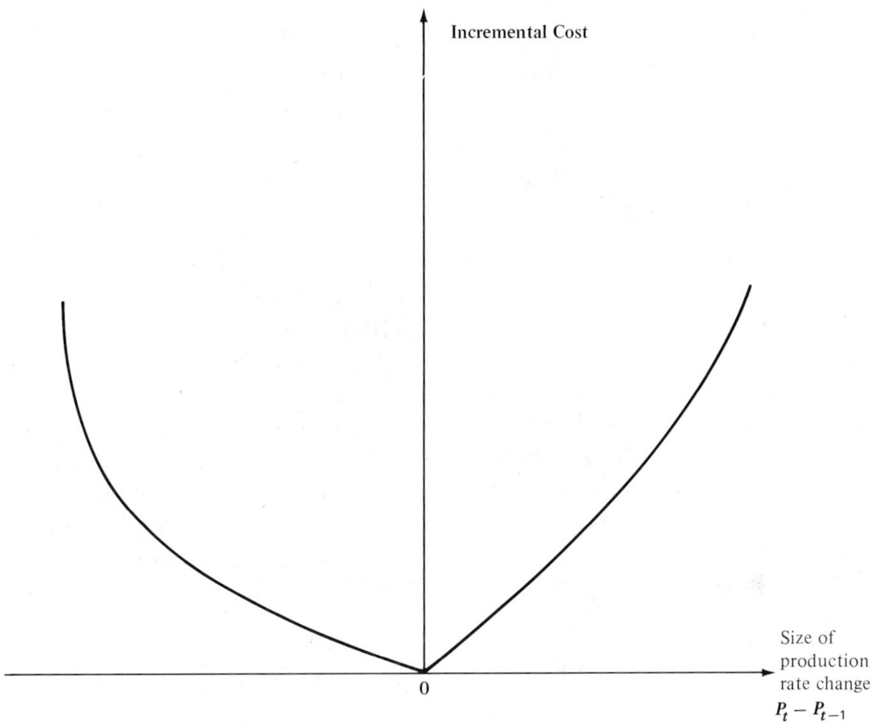

FIGURE 14.4 Costs of Production Rate Changes

14.2.4 Inventory Associated Costs

As discussed in Chapter 3, there is a cost associated with tieing up funds invested in inventory. The standard approach is to say that the costs for T periods are given by

$$\begin{aligned} \text{Costs for } T \text{ periods} &= \bar{I}_1 vr + \bar{I}_2 vr + \cdots + \bar{I}_T vr \\ &= vr \sum_{t=1}^{T} \bar{I}_t \end{aligned} \tag{14.5}$$

where

$\bar{I}_t$ = average inventory (in aggregate units) in period t, often approximated by the starting or ending inventory

v = unit variable cost of the aggregate unit used[4]

r = carrying charge in \$/\$/period (possibly determined implicitly through the use of exchange curves)

14.2.5 Costs of Insufficient Capacity in the Short Run

When an unplanned shortage actually occurs, the costs can be expressed in a number of different ways; which method to use is a function of the environment of the particular stocking point under consideration. Also relevant are costs associated with actions undertaken to avoid shortages. These types of costs, discussed in more detail in Chapter 7, are generally quite difficult to estimate.

Some aggregate planning models look at the combined costs of inventory and insufficient short-run capacity in a slightly different and more aggregate fashion. From fundamental economic arguments, which we presented in Chapter 5, the best inventory level in period t can be shown to be proportional to the square root of D_t, where D_t is the forecasted demand for period t. Over a narrow range any square root function can be approximated reasonably well by a straight line; that is,

$$\text{Optimal inventory in period } t \simeq a + bD_t \tag{14.6}$$

where a and b are constants.

Deviations from the optimal inventory result in extra costs. Too high an inventory results in excessive carrying costs; too low an inventory leads to inordinate shortage costs. For a given value of D_t, the typical curve of costs versus inventory is shown in Figure 14.5. There is actually a whole set of such curves, one for each value of D_t, the current aggregate rate of demand. See Holt et al. (1960) for a complete discussion.

14.3 THE PLANNING HORIZON

The planning horizon refers to how far into the future one uses information (particularly demand forecasts) in making the current decisions. This concept was first introduced in Chapter 6 with respect to individual item lot sizing, but it is equally applicable in aggregate production planning. *If the demand pattern (and other factors) were known with certainty*, then the quality of the decision making would never decrease as the planning horizon was increased. However,

[4]At any point the actual value of the inventory will depend on the mix of individual items present. The variable v represents the unit value of an *average* mix. This suggests that, if possible, the aggregate unit should be selected so that it represents roughly the same dollar value of each of the underlying individual s.k.u.

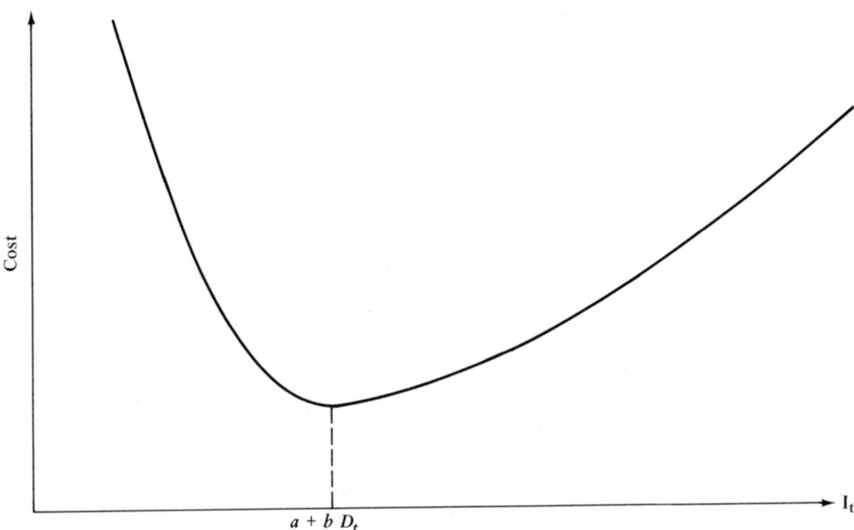

FIGURE 14.5 Inventory and Shortage Costs

demand forecasts become less accurate the further into the future we make projections. Considerable testing has revealed that, in a seasonal demand situation, the horizon should be such as to extend beyond the next seasonal peak. To keep the number of decision variables manageable, an effective device is to vary the length of the individual periods within the horizon—for example, by using a 12-month horizon composed of six 1-month periods, followed by two 3-month intervals (see Boskma, 1982). Perhaps more important is the use of a reasonable desired ending inventory situation to reflect the on-going nature of the business beyond the artificial horizon (see Baker and Peterson, 1979; McClain and Thomas, 1977).

As in Chapter 6 it is also important to recognize that implementation, because of future uncertainties, is almost always on a rolling horizon basis. Specifically, if the planning horizon is of length T periods, only the first period results of the aggregate planning model are implemented. Then, at the end of the first period, a new (rolling) horizon of T periods is used to establish new results, and so on.

The notion of a frozen period is often also relevant. In particular, if planning is done at the beginning of January, the first period where changes can be made may be February (or even later); that is, the previous decisions for January (or even longer) may be frozen. This is usually the case where scarce, highly skilled labor is involved or where the production process itself involves long delays in bringing about a change in the output rate.

14.4 FEASIBLE SOLUTION METHODS

14.4.1 General Comments

Most *feasible solution methods* make only a limited effort toward achieving some form of explicit tradeoff among the competing costs discussed earlier. The apparent overriding objective for these approaches is the achievement of *any* feasible allocation of available resources that guarantees that daily orders will be met.

Each group within an organization approaches the determination of appropriate inventory investment (and thereby production smoothing and workforce balancing) with somewhat different motives. Top management, along with financial managers, are pleased if inventory investment can be successfully kept at a "minimum." Operating management prefers long production runs, smooth production and workforce levels, and thereby also fluctuating inventory investment. Marketing managers usually elect for a larger inventory investment, but are less concerned with the length of production runs than with having most finished items available on demand off the shelf.

Feasible solution methods attempt to strike a compromise position among the various desires of the parties involved. Many companies have a scheduling committee, consisting of all the senior managers affected by an aggregate production plan, which considers various alternatives and agrees on a feasible set of tradeoffs. Frequently, a compromise is achieved through a bargaining (barter process). "You support my production plan for our division in England and I will support your request in Argentina."[5]

An approach often used in industry is to take last year's plan and adjust it slightly to meet this year's conditions. The danger in doing this lies in the implicit assumption that any previous plan was close to optimal; by pursuing such a course, management takes the risk of getting locked into a series of poor plans.

In many situations a graphic or tabular approach, such as that to be discussed in the next subsection, can be used to focus attention on the key tradeoffs to be made in aggregate production planning. Harrison (1976) has advocated the use of a deterministic simulation program that traces the likely pattern of physical effects (for example, inventory level, workforce level, and capacity utilization) versus time of a given aggregate strategy, without the introduction of any cost parameters in the explicit model. Duersch and Wheeler (1981) have operationalized this concept in an interactive computer mode.

[5]Donald B. McCaskill former Executive Vice-President of Warner-Lambert Company, as quoted in "Management Science in Canada," *Management Science*, Vol. 20, No. 4, December 1973, Special Edition (edited by Rein Peterson, David W. Conrath, and C. T. L. Janssen), p. 571.

14.4.2 An Example of a Graphic-Tabular Method[6]

The most useful and rudimentary analytical extensions of bartering are of a graphic-tabular nature. Such procedures, while not mathematically optimal, always guarantee a feasible solution. Such methods are surprisingly effective and difficult to improve on.

Consider the forecasted demand pattern in Table 14.2 and its plot as cumulative demand in Figure 14.6. The straight line $a-e$ represents a level (constant) production plan of 30 hours of production per month, which meets the *expected* cumulative forecast of 360 production hours for the 12 month period.[7] Other cumulative production plan lines can be drawn on Figure 14.6 (for example, $a-b-c-d-e$) that may be more desirable because they cost less or because they take better account of the uncertainty of the forecasts.

The dotted lines above and below the solid black line $0-g-f$ represent the maximum and minimum forecasted cumulative sales that could reasonably occur. For example, by the end of month 6, cumulative sales could be as much as 240 production hours or as little as 120 production hours, rather than the expected 180 hours forecasted, which will be used as the basis for planning.[8] In Table 14.3, part of the relevant information from the graph is presented in tabular form for the case of a constant production plan.

Note from Figure 14.6 and Table 14.3 that, *if sales materialize as expected, then a constant production plan is feasible*, although during months 8 to 10 inclusive, inventory would be drawn down to zero. (In Figure 14.6 we have assumed that 30 hours of production were in inventory at the begining of period zero. The same 30 hours of production are available at the end of the 12-month planning horizon.) Any cumulative production plan that ends up at point f or higher on Figure 14.6 without violating any exogenous constraints would be *feasible*. This is a very powerful and useful result, quite easily achieved graphi-

TABLE 14.2 Cumulative Forecasts (In Production Hours)

Period t	Forecast Demand D_t	Cumulative Demand
1. September–October	30	30
2. November–December	30	60
3. January–February	120	180
4. March–April	90	270
5. May–June	60	330
6. July–August	30	360

[6]References include Close (1968) and Gordon (1966).

[7]The single surrogate measure of output in which all variables are measured is assumed to be production hours. A single hour of production may require several man-hours to achieve.

[8]In practice a number of possible future scenarios, such as those of Figure 14.6, are usually explored.

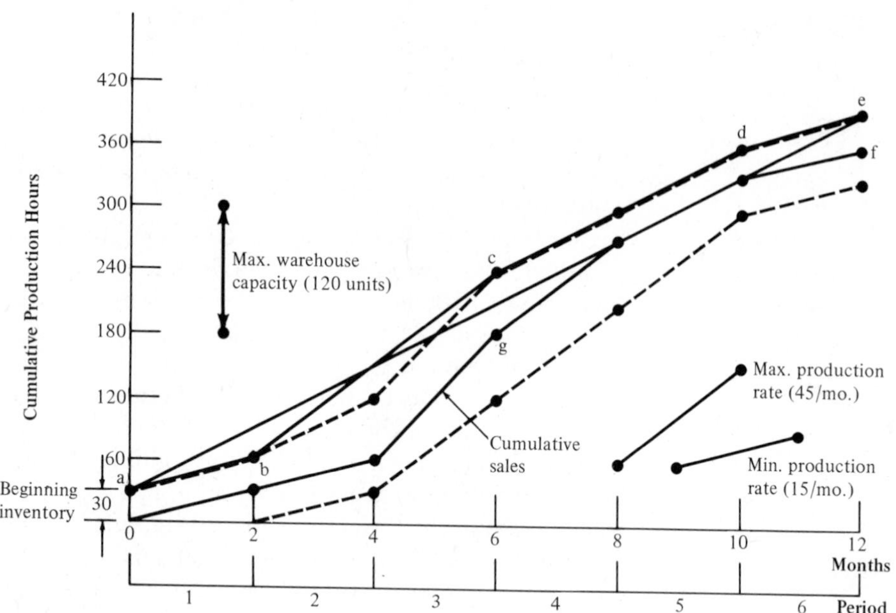

FIGURE 14.6 Graphs of Cumulative Forecasts and Alternative Production Plans

TABLE 14.3 Constant Production Plan (30 Hours of Production/Month)

End of Period	Cum. Avail.	Expected Cum. Demand	Expected Invent.	Max. Cum. Demand	Min. Invent.	Min. Cum. Demand	Max. Invent.
1	90	30	60	60	30	0	90
2	150	60	90	120	30	30	120
3	210	180	30	240	−30	120	90
4	270	270	0	300	−30	210	60
5	330	330	0	360	−30	300	30
6	390	360	30	390	0	330	60

cally! The selection of a low-cost, feasible production plan graphically, from among the infinite numbers possible, will be somewhat more difficult, as we will see.

In Figure 14.6 any vertical distance between a cumulative sales line and a cumulative production line represents the amount of inventory on hand at that time. For example, at the end of month 2 we *expect* to have 60 hours of production on hand. At the end of month 8, if sales are *higher* than expected, we could be 30 production hours short. On the other hand, if *lower* than expected sales materialize, then we could have a maximum of 120 hours of production on hand at the end of month 4. The possibility of running out of inventory in months 8 to 10 inclusive could render the constant production plan infeasible. Company policy could dictate that such a possibility should not be tolerated in any production plan considered. In addition, there is usually a maximum level of inventory that is allowed by management policy. This could represent either the maximum space available in the warehouse for storage or alternatively the maximum investment risk that management is willing to undertake. (In Figure 14.6 warehouse capacity is assumed to be 120 production hours.) Such constraints are called *exogenous*; that is, such constraints are imposed externally on the decision problem.[9]

Other exogenous constraints are possible. For example, in Figure 14.6 we have assumed that the manufacturing facility can support a maximum production rate of 45 production hours/month and that management is unwilling to take the chance of losing key personnel which a production rate of less than 15 production hours/month would entail.

All exogenous constraints are shown graphically in Figure 14.6 and can be used graphically as follows. When drawing alternate *feasible* production plans in Figure 14.6, the slopes of production lines drawn must always lie between the maximum (45 production hours/month) and minimum (15 production hours/month) extremes allowed. Furthermore, the vertical distance between any cumulative production plan and any cumulative sales forecast must be *greater* than zero and less than 120 production hours (because of top management policy). Under these exogeneous constraints the constant production plan is *infeasible*, as is clear from Table 14.3. On the other hand, the other production plan $a-b-c-d-e$ on Figure 14.6 and summarized in Table 14.4 is feasible.

To this point we have not considered costs in our discussion of the production plans that are possible. This would in practice be the next level of sophistication that is attempted. By assuming the data in Table 14.5, the *expected* cost of production plan $a-b-c-d-e$ can be computed as in Table 14.6.

TABLE 14.4 Production Plan $a-b-c-d-e$

End of Period	Cum. Avail.	Expected Cum. Demand	Expected Invent.	Max. Cum. Demand	Min. Invent.	Min. Cum. Demand	Max. Invent.
1	60	30	30	60	0	0	60
2	150	60	90	120	30	30	120
3	240	180	60	240	0	120	120
4	300	270	30	300	0	210	90
5	360	330	30	360	0	300	60
6	390	360	30	390	0	330	60

[9] To keep the exposition simple we have assumed that the cumulative production lines are achievable with certainty. Note that it is possible under this procedure to draw on Figure 14.6 dotted cumulative production lines above and below the expected production line to represent any uncertainty involved.

TABLE 14.5 Cost Structure and Initial Conditions

Cost of regular time (R/T) labor = $200/production hour
Cost of overtime (O/T) labor = $300/production hour
Cost of hiring = $120/production hour
Cost of firing = $70/production hour
Cost of carrying inventory = $40/production hour/2-month period
Initial inventory = 30 production hours
Initial workforce = 30 production hours/2-month period

TABLE 14.6 Expected Cost of Production Plan $a-b-c-d-e$

	Workforce				Production		Expected	
t	W_{t-1}	Hired	Fired	W_t	R/T	O/T	D_t	I_t
0	—	—	—	(30)	—	—	—	(30)
1	30	0	0	30	30	0	30	30
2	30	60	0	90	90	0	30	90
3	90	0	0	90	90	0	120	60
4	90	0	30	60	60	0	90	30
5	60	0	0	60	60	0	60	30
6	60		30	30	30	0	30	30
Totals	—	60	60	360	360	0	360	270
Costs	—	$7,200	$4,200	$72,000	—	0	—	$10,800
Total cost = $94,200								

Having found one feasible production plan and its expected cost, there remains the task of trying to find a better feasible production plan that is lower in cost to that in Table 14.6. This could involve a further ad hoc trial-and-error search or alternatively one could introduce an analytic technique as discussed in the next section.

Before proceeding, let us summarize the steps that are required in using the graphic-tabular procedure we have been discussing:

1. Plot the cumulative expected forecasts and the attendant maximum and minimum extremes on a graph (as in Figure 14.6).
2. Consider first a plan involving a constant production rate (that is, $a-e$ on Figure 14.6) which involves *zero changeover costs*. Check to see if a constant production plan is feasible, given exogenous constraints. Determine the total cost of this plan.
3. Consider next a plan tailored to match the forecast fluctuations as exactly as *feasible* (that is, $a-b-c-d-e$ on Figure 14.6). This will result in a plan with *minimum inventory holding costs*. Determine the total cost of this plan as in Table 14.6.

4. After examining the plans derived in Steps 2 and 3, investigate plans intermediate in position.[10] These plans should attempt to tradeoff inventory holding (and shortage) costs versus changeover, regular-time, and overtime costs. The Land algorithm, discussed in the next section, which calculates the *optimal* allocation of exogenously determined production capacity, may be useful at this stage. For each plan devised, determine the total cost.
5. Select the feasible plan found by the steps above that is considered to be most desirable by a scheduling committee or its equivalent. (Total cost, we hope, would be one of the relevant criteria.)

Note that the best one can hope for is to design a mathematically near-optimal plan by this procedure. One shortcoming of our heuristic method is that it does not usually yield mathematically optimal tradeoffs between the costs of regular-time and overtime production, carrying costs, and changeover costs. What is worse, one is never quite sure how near or far from a mathematical optimum any particular plan is. Close (1968) claims that experienced production planners can, by trial and error, design feasible production plans that are surprisingly close to the mathematically optimal tradeoffs possible. This appears to be the case because (as we saw in Chapter 5) the total cost equation of most inventory decision models tends to be u-shaped, with a shallow bottom around the optimal point. It is, of course, possible that mathematical optimality is an irrelevant criterion to the managers on a scheduling committee who strive to "optimize" far more complex objectives.

14.5 THE LAND ALGORITHM

A simple optimization technique, which could be used to help deal with the problem discussed in this chapter, was originally proposed by Bowman (1956). In this section we examine another form of this special linear programming (transportation) model, proposed by Beale and Morton (1958) and Land (1958). Land's algorithm is suitable for manual computations, as are the closely related procedures developed by Rand (1974) and Posner and Szwarc (1983). The transportation optimization methodology, as we will see, has many features that make it quite practical. These features, we believe, have not received their rightful recognition by analysts, nor acceptance by managers.

What a transportation optimization technique adds to a graphic-tabular procedure, such as we have been discussing, is summarized by the diagram of Figure 14.7. That is, for a set of exogenously determined ad hoc inputs (chosen by a decision maker using his or her own biases, insights, and creativity), a

[10]Note that plans $a-e$ and $a-b-c-d-e$ in Figure 14.6 do not bound the large number of alternatives possible. That is, the optimal plan does not necessarily lie on a line drawn between them. Nevertheless, the two graphs from Steps 2 and 3 usually greatly delimit the number of alternatives one would want to consider evaluating.

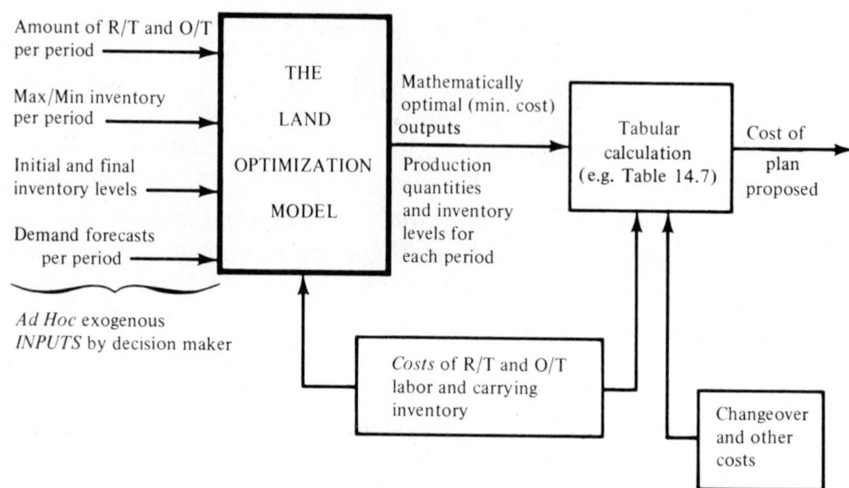

FIGURE 14.7 Aggregate Planning Involving the Land Algorithm

mathematically optimal production plan is routinely calculated. We first present the Land algorithm verbally. The underlying mathematical model will be shown in a later subsection.

14.5.1 The Algorithm

The transportation tableau, as suggested by Land, for manually[11] solving the aggregate planning problem that we have been discussing, is given in Table 14.7. Columns 1 and 2 are self-explanatory. The I_{max} variable is the maximum inventory (90 production hours) that may be carried from one period to the next and is the upper limit allowed to the sum of the figures for any single period in column 8 (Bowman's original model did not incorporate maximum inventory constraints). The beginning inventory of 30 production hours is subtracted from the 120 production hours of warehouse capacity because it is expected that at least this amount will always be on hand at the end of each period, and it is also the amount of inventory that is expected to be on hand at the end of period 6.

Column 3 lists the two sources of production available in period 1: regular time (1, 1) and overtime (1, 2). The cost of each source in column 4 is derived from Table 14.5. In column 5 a rank is assigned to each source, starting with the least expensive source. Column 6 records the capacity available from each source for each period. These capacity figures have to be determined exogenously by the decision maker. In Table 14.7 the regular-time capacity was set at 60 production hours/period based on insights garnered by the authors from the constant production plan we examined in Table 14.3. In particular, by allowing overtime

[11]While we show the use of the Land algorithm and the graphic-tabular methodology in a manual mode, there is, of course, no reason why it cannot be computerized using visual displays.

TABLE 14.7 The Land Algorithm Applied to the Aggregate Planning Problem

$I_{\max} = 120 - 30 = 90$

Period (1)	(2)	Source (3)		Cost at t (4)	Rank (5)	Capacity: Avail. at t (6)	Capacity: Used in t (7)	Capacity: Avail. in $t+1$ (8)	Cost at $t+1$ (9)
1	September–October	1	1	200	1	60	30	30	240
	$D_1 = 30$	1	2	300	2	18		18	340
2	November–December	2	1	200	1	60	30	30	240
	$D_2 = 30$	2	2	300	3	18		18	340
		1	1	240	2	30		30	280
		1	2	340	4	18		12[a]	380
3	January–February	3	1	200	1	60	60	0	—
	$D_3 = 120$	3	2	300	4	18		18	340
		2	1	240	2	30	30	0	—
		2	2	340	5	18		18	380
		1	1	280	3	30	30	0	—
		1	2	380	6	12		12	420
4	March–April	4	1	200	1	60	60	0	—
	$D_4 = 90$	4	2	300	2	18	18	0	—
		3	2	340	3	18	12	6	380
		2	2	380	4	18		18	420
		1	2	420	5	12		12	460
5	May–June	5	1	200	1	60	60	0	—
	$D_5 = 60$	5	2	300	2	18		18	340
		3	2	380	3	6		6	420
		2	2	420	4	18		18	460
		1	2	460	5	12		12	500
6	July–August	6	1	200	1	30	30	0	—
	$D_6 = 30$	6	2	300	2	9		9	340
		5	2	340	3	18		18	400
		3	2	420	4	6		6	460
		2	2	460	5	18		18	500
		1	2	500	6	12		12	540

[a]Reduced from 18 to 12 to satisfy the inventory capacity constraint.

to a maximum of 30 percent of regular-time capacity, the undesirable (infeasible) zero expected inventory position calculated in Table 14.3 could now be overcome. The 30 production hour regular-time capacity for period 6 was chosen to make the ending condition of period 6 the same as that at the beginning of period 1. (Equivalently, one could inflate the demand in period 6 by 30 units instead of reducing the capacity by 30 units.)

In column 7 are recorded the actual amounts of production scheduled in each period. The Land algorithm instructs us to use the sources available in column 6 in order of rank given in column 5 until the forecasted requirements in column 2 (D_i) have been met. The remaining capacity is then available for use in $t + 1$ (column 8) as long as the total capacity carried forward in any one period is less than 90 production hours (I_{max}).

For example, in period 3 expected demand is $D_3 = 120$. The least expensive source is (3, 1). The total capacity of 60 production hours is used up leaving none for period 4 (column 8). The next lowest cost source is (2, 1), and all of its capacity of 30 production hours is scheduled. (This means that 30 production hours of regular time are scheduled in period 2 to meet demand in period 3.) The remaining 30 man-hours of expected demand are then scheduled using the third lowest cost source (1, 1), regular-time production in period 1 carried forward in inventory for two periods for use in period 3.

From column 7 of Table 14.7 we can derive the production plan given in Table 14.8. Note that the production quantities for each period *cannot* be read directly from Table 14.7.

The production plan in Table 14.8 is not feasible since there is a chance that in period 3, if sales are higher than expected, we could run out of inventory. (That is, safety stock is less than the 60 shown on Figure 14.6.) To overcome this deficiency, we must increase the inventory level at the end of period 3 by 18 production hours. From Table 14.7 we see that this increase in inventory can be best achieved by producing 6 man-hours on (3, 2), because at the end of period 6 there were only that many man-hours left in this source, and the remaining 12 man-hours on (2, 2). To make the ending inventory at the end of period 6 equal to 30, we must compensate for these increases in inventory by reducing the production in period 4 from source (4, 2) to zero, from 18. Such minor adjustments will often be necessary with the Land algorithm when applied in our context. Note that these minor adjustments did not alter the mathematical optimality of the solution we had achieved in Table 14.7. These minor adjustments do not appear in Tables 14.7 and 14.8, but are included in the cost calculations of Table 14.9.

TABLE 14.8 Production Plan Derived in Table 14.7

Period	R/T Production	O/T Production	Expected Demand	Expected Inventory	Max. Demand	Min. Inventory	Min. Demand	Max. Inventory
0	—	—	—	30	—	30	—	30
1	30 + 30 = 60	0	30	60	60	30	0	90
2	30 + 30 = 60	0	30	90	60	30	30	120
3	60	12	120	42	120	−18	90	102
4	60	18	90	30	60	0	90	90
5	60	0	60	30	60	0	90	60
6	30	0	30	30	30	0	30	60

TABLE 14.9 Expected Cost of Adjusted Production Plan

Period	Workforce				Production		Expected	
t	W_{t-1}	Hired	Fired	W_t	R/T	O/T	D_t	I_t
0	—	—	—	(30)	—	—	—	(30)
1	30	30	0	60	60	0	30	60
2	60	0	0	60	60	12	30	102
3	60	0	0	60	60	18	120	60
4	60	0	0	60	60	0	90	30
5	60	0	0	60	60	0	60	30
6	60	0	30	30	30	0	30	30
Totals	—	30	30	330	330	30	360	312
Cost	—	$3,600	$2,100	$66,000	—	$9,000	—	$12,480
Total cost = $93,180								

14.5.2 Comments Concerning the Algorithm

Note that the total cost of the plan in Table 14.9 is only 1 percent lower than plan $a-b-c-d-e$ (see Table 14.6). That is, the graphic-tabular procedure seems to have yielded a reasonably good plan right off the bat. Close (1968) reports similar kinds of findings in his research. Under two different cost structures his plans were within 3 and 0.4 percent of mathematically optimal solutions, which require considerably more effort and time to compile. Such small gains are of little practical significance since most cost data are probably not accurate within 3 percent, and forecast errors can wipe out most or all of such small differences.

We must, of course, be careful not to overgeneralize on the basis of a simple example. One reason that we were able to quickly derive a good solution is the fact that the cost and demand structure made it relatively easy to make the tradeoffs required. Basically, the example required only the trading off of hiring/firing costs, costs of regular production, and the costs of carrying an appropriate level of inventories. We felt that *the cost of overtime was so prohibitive that it never really entered into consideration in our graphic phase*[12] *(yet some overtime was used in the final Land solution).*

If the tradeoffs had not been so obvious, and if other variables in addition had to be considered, it would have been much more difficult to derive a good solution. Under such circumstances the Land algorithm would have proven to be much more valuable than it actually was in the example we considered. This is one of the basic advantages of any algorithm that results in a mathematically

[12]Perhaps this is one of the reasons that many managers intuitively are reluctant in practice to plan for the use of overtime in their aggregate schedules.

optimal solution. It can make tradeoffs between more variables, and more efficiently, compared to a heuristic procedure that depends on analysts to make the necessary tradeoffs using their own judgment.

Moreover, the example does not really reveal another extremely important feature of the Land algorithm. Specifically, management can specify different resource patterns (in particular, patterns of workforce size with time) and, for each, the algorithm gives the minimum total of regular-time, overtime, and inventory carrying costs. The importance of this capability is captured by the following quotation from Welam (1978) who adopts much the same philosophy:

> *The costs of laying off and hiring workers can often be so complex as to defy meaningful explicit analytic representation . . . we shall develop a man-machine interactive model for evaluating a wide spectrum of workforce policies, from those with no hirings or firings at all to those with no restrictions at all on hiring and firing. The manager must decide where in this spectrum the right trade-off is achieved between tangible production and inventory costs and the largely intangible costs of hiring and firing. Estimating costs of direct labor, overtime, carrying inventory, and being out of stock is not trivial, but compared with quantitatively estimating hiring and layoff costs, it is still relatively straightforward. We therefore propose a man-machine interactive aggregate planning model where the "machine part" contains a rigorous analytic description of tangible production and inventory costs, and where the "man part" deals with the more difficult hiring and firing costs by stipulating a set of workforce constraints which must be observed during the machine optimization. Man can call upon the machine to generate an optimal solution relative to any specific set of constraints, e.g., no hiring or firing permitted at all. He can also trace the behavior of total tangible cost as a function of the number of workers hired or fired in specific periods and superimpose this function on his own mental image of the concomitant hiring and firing cost function. . . . Hiring and firing costs are not explicitly modelled; a manager's judgmental estimates are relied upon to arrive at a proper trade-off between these largely intangible costs and the more tangible production smoothing costs which have been included in the machine optimization model.*

Essentially the same approach is suggested by Rhodes (1977) in a paint industry application.

In some aggregate planning situations it may not be possible to have a single aggregate product but rather two or more distinct classes of products. *In the event that every inventory constraint can be specified separately for each class,* then the Land algorithm can be slightly modified to deal with this more general problem. Specifically, let the units of each class be defined so that each uses up unit production capacity (demands and unit variable costs must be accordingly modified). Let v_j denote the unit variable cost of inventory of class j and suppose that the classes are numbered so that $v_j \geqslant v_k$ for $j < k$. Let n be the number of items. Then we proceed, period by period, as in Table 14.7 where, for any particular period, we completely satisfy the demands of class 1, then class 2, . . . , class n.

A deterministic model, such as that underlying the Land algorithm or linear programming (to be discussed in Section 14.6), can be adopted to accommodate uncertainties in demand. In particular, required safety stocks can be established period by period (as in Chapter 7), recognizing the uncertainty of forecasts and the costs of carrying safety stock and of having stockouts.

14.5.3 The Underlying Mathematical Model

The mathematical model considered by Land can be stated as:

$$\text{Min } C_{\text{TOT}} = \sum_{i=1}^{T} \sum_{j=1}^{k} \sum_{t=1}^{T} c_{ijt} p_{ijt} + \sum_{t=1}^{T} I_t v r_t$$

Subject to:

$$0 \leq p_{ijt} \leq P_{ijt} \qquad (t = 1, 2, \ldots, T;\ i = 1, 2, \ldots, T;\ j = 1, 2, \ldots, k)$$

$$\sum_{t} p_{ijt} \leq P_{ij} \qquad (i = 1, 2, \ldots, T;\ j = 1, 2, \ldots, k)$$

$$0 \leq I_t \leq I_{t\,\max} \qquad (t = 1, 2, \ldots, T)$$

$$(I_0, I_T \text{ specified outside model})$$

$$\mathrm{I}_{i-1} + \sum_{t=1}^{\mathrm{T}} \sum_{j=1}^{\mathrm{k}} p_{ijt} - D_i = I_t \qquad (i = 1, 2, \ldots, T)$$

where

T = length of the planning horizon

p_{ijt} = amount produced in source (for example, shift) j of period i to satisfy demand in period t

c_{ijt} = production cost per unit of p_{ijt} (normally c_{ijt} would not depend on t)

D_t = requirements (demand) in period t

P_{ijt} = capacity limit on each p_{ijt}

P_{ij} = production capacity in source j of period i

I_t = inventory at the end of period t

$I_{t\,\max}$ = capacity limit on I_t

r_t = charge per unit carried in inventory at the end of period t

v = unit variable cost of the aggregate unit used

14.6 LINEAR PROGRAMMING MODELS

Linear programming (LP) models can be tailored to suit the particular cost and decision structure faced by most companies. This accounts in part for the relatively large number of formulations in existence. Many complex mathematical programming models, including both linear and integer (fixed) cost components, have been proposed. For example, see those by Hanssmann and Hess (1969) and Haehling von Lanzenauer (1970). The Land transportation model, discussed in the preceding section, is a special case of linear programming.

Because of the large variety of possible formulations, we start by listing the common assumptions made by most formulations and then present a relatively simple specific model, one which is similar to those that have been implemented in practice.

Most practicable linear programs are structured as follows:

1. Demand is taken as deterministic and known

$$D_t \text{ in period } t \qquad (t = 1, 2, \ldots, T)$$

2. The costs of regular-time production in period t are usually described by piecewise linear or convex functions as shown in Figure 14.8 (convex merely means that the slopes of the linear segments become larger and larger; that is, the marginal cost is increasing).
3. The cost of changes in the production rate is usually taken to be piecewise linear as shown in Figure 14.9. Note that the cost function need not be symmetrical about the vertical axis. An alternate approach in some linear programming formulations is not to assign costs for changes in production

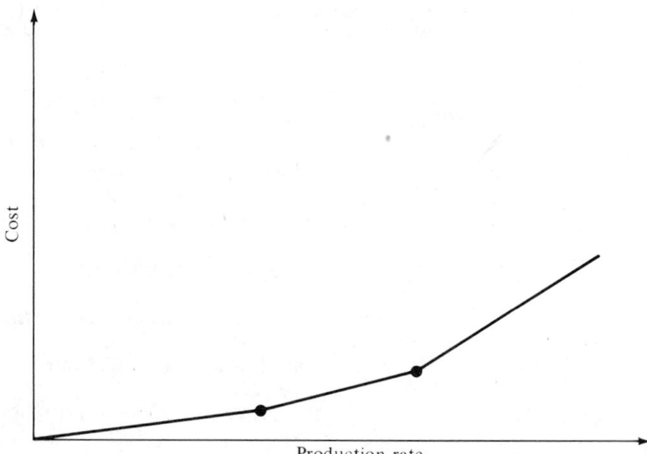

FIGURE 14.8 The Cost of Regular Time Production in General Linear Programming Models

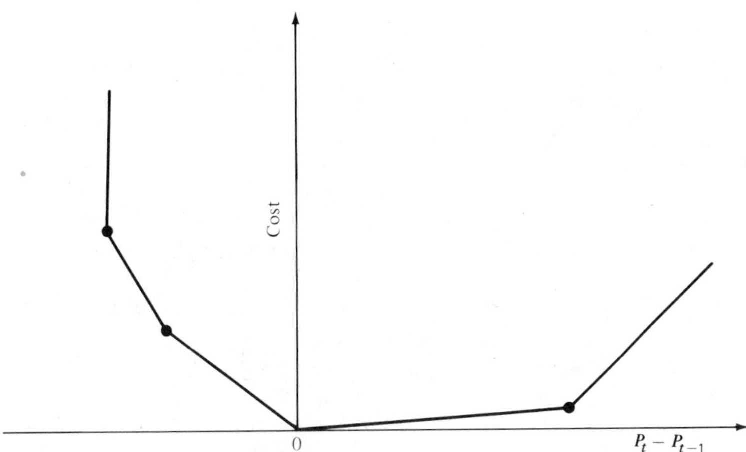

FIGURE 14.9 Costs of Changes in the Production Rate in General Linear Programming Models

rates at all, but rather to limit the size of the change or, alternatively, to simply put upper and lower bounds on the allowable production rates in any particular period.

4. Upper and lower bounds on production rates are usually specified. A similar statement holds for the inventory levels.
5. The inventory carrying cost can be different for each period.
6. It is usually assumed that there is a single production facility serving a given market.
7. In most formulations, backorders or lost sales are not permitted.

One of the most important characteristics of linear programming models is that many constraints can be directly incorporated in the problem formulation. Also many product categories can be included in the formulation rather than having to define a single, overall surrogate measure of production.

These characteristics are illustrated in the following LP model:

Minimize:

$$C_{\text{TOT}} = \sum_{t=1}^{T} \sum_{i=1}^{n} [c_{i1}I_{it} + c_{i2}W_{it} + c_{i3}W'_{it} + c_{i4}H_{it} + c_{i5}F_{it}]$$

Subject to

$$\left.\begin{aligned} I_{it} &= I_{i,t-1} + W_{it} + W'_{it} - D_{it} \\ W_{it} &= W_{i,t-1} + H_{it} - F_{it} \end{aligned}\right\} \begin{aligned} i &= 1, \ldots, n \\ t &= 1, \ldots, T \end{aligned} \tag{14.7}$$

$$W'_{it} \leq a_{it}W_{it}$$

and

$$I_{it}, W_{it}, W'_{it}, H_{it}, F_{it}, D_{it} \geqslant 0 \qquad \text{for all} \quad i, \; t.$$

where

n = number of product groups

T = length of the planning horizon

I_{it} = inventory of product group i at end of t

W_{it} = workforce level (expressed as a regular-time production rate) of product group i at the end of t

W'_{it} = amount of overtime of product group i during t

a_{it} = maximum fraction overtime allowed for group i in t

H_{it} = amount of hiring for product group i in t

F_{it} = amount of firing for product group i in t

D_{it} = forecasted requirements (demand) for group i in t

and the c's are unit cost coefficients

While this may look complicated, the basic ideas expressed in the total cost objective function are quite simple. The total cost is the sum of the costs of carrying inventory, regular workforce, overtime, and hiring and firing for each product group i during each period t. These decision variables are constrained by three equations. The inventory at the end of t (I_{it}) is equal to the inventory in the previous period, plus the amount of product produced on regular time (W_{it}), plus the amount of product produced on overtime (W_{it}), less the amount of product shipped to meet requirements (D_{it}). The second constraint specifies that the regular-time workforce in this period must be equal to that in the previous period plus the amount hired less the amount fired. (H_{it} and F_{it} will never both be greater than zero at the same time.) The third constraint sets available overtime in any period equal to or less than a fraction a_{it} of the regular-time workforce capacity. The last line of Eq. 14.7 states that all decision variables must be positive or zero.

Note the similarity of the objective function in Eq. 14.7 to the way we evaluated costs in the graphic-tabular method in Section 14.4. But compared to the graphic-tabular methods the LP model in Eq. 14.7 yields an optimal rather than near-optimal solution. It also determines the size of the workforce W_{it} directly by including changeover costs in the objective function rather than requiring a manager to specify it exogenously as was the case in the earlier models.

In Eq. 14.7 no constraints are placed on the maximum or minimum levels of inventory, workforce, or production, nor are backorders allowed. Note that these could be introduced without difficulty by defining additional constraint equations. However, each additional constraint specified, as well as each additional product group chosen for individual attention, increases the computational effort required.

In Section 14.1 we discussed the difficulties in choosing appropriate groups of items to aggregate. The above LP formulation now provides some insight. Members of the same aggregate product group should share similar seasonal patterns (D_{it}), production costs (c_{i2}, c_{i3}), carrying costs (c_{i1}), and hiring/firing costs (c_{i4}, c_{i5}). Obviously, to reduce the number of equations needed, some severe compromises have to be made in defining product families.

14.6.1 Strengths and Weaknesses

One of the basic weaknesses of linear programming approaches (and most other aggregate planning techniques) is the assumption of deterministic demand. In most applications there is considerable uncertainty in the forecasts of demand. However, tests have been done by Dzielinski et al. (1963), using a deterministic model under stochastic conditions, that indicated that under many situations the deterministic model can perform favorably, particularly when one recognizes that the solution is adapted as new forecast information becomes available (that is, a rolling-horizon implementation is used).

Another shortcoming of linear programming models is the requirement of linear cost functions. However, the possibility of piecewise linearity improves the validity (at a cost of additional computational effort).

An important benefit of a linear programming model is the potential use of the dual solution to obtain the implicit costs of constraints such as maximum allowable inventory levels. Also, parametric methods allow a simple determination of the production plan for conditions somewhat different from those for which the primary solution is obtained. This last property is useful for two purposes: first, for sensitivity analysis on the estimated cost parameters; second, as a means of measuring the effects of slight changes in one or more of the uncertain conditions.

One could argue that another restriction of linear programming is that there must be a single measure of effectiveness (normally total costs). In actual fact, a generalization, known as *goal programming*, permits the use of multiple objectives, which, however, must be prioritized. A chemical industry example is provided by Sanderson (1978) where the objectives include:

1. Minimize the quantity of by-products burnt as fuel.
2. Minimize the unplanned purchases of materials.
3. Minimize the intersite movements of materials.
4. Minimize the variation in production levels between time periods.
5. Minimize the deviation of stocks from preferred levels.
6. Minimize the deviation of production from preferred levels.

See also Lockett and Muhlemann (1978).

14.6.2 The Inclusion of Integer Variables in Linear Programming Formulations

One or more integer variables are required to include a setup cost or any other type of concave cost in a LP model. (*Concave* means that the *marginal* cost is decreasing.) The reason for the integer variable in the case of the setup cost is because of the discontinuity in the cost function. When production is zero, the cost is zero; however, a very small production quantity incurs the entire setup cost.

The need for the integer variable in the case of the concave function is not as obvious. To illustrate the need, let us look at a simple example.

Consider a product whose concave production costs are as follows:

Rate Range (Pieces/Period)	Cost per Additional Piece Produced
0–10	2
11 and higher	1

The basic linear programming model would select production units only from the 11 and higher range because they are less expensive than those in the 0 to 10 range. Of course, this is physically impossible. An integer variable is needed to force the use of all of the 0 to 10 range before any production can be taken from the next higher range. The integer variable takes on only the value 0 or 1. The 11 and higher range can only be used when the integer variable is 1. The logic is arranged such that it is 1 only when the entire 0 to 10 range is used.

The presence of integer variables drastically increases the computational time. While thousands of continuous decision variables can be handled in a regular linear program, only problems with considerably less integer variables can be solved in a reasonable length of time with existing solution algorithms.

14.7 SIMULATION SEARCH PROCEDURES

Vergin (1966) observed that in many cases the current state of the art does not allow the analytical solution of a mathematical decision model that is representative of the situation faced in practice by a manager. Therefore, he argued, it is better to model the actual cost functions very accurately in mathematical or tabular form, so that functions more complex than those allowed in such approaches as linear programming could be solved. For a horizon of T months, in general terms, in the case of the aggregate scheduling decision:

$$C_{\text{TOT}} = f(W_1, P_1, W_2, P_2, \ldots, W_T, P_T) \tag{14.8}$$

As in any simulation, the approach is to vary the variables (for example, the workforce sizes and production rates) systematically until a reasonable (and, we hope, near optimal) solution is obtained. Normally, a computer is required to make the approach feasible, even under the assumption of no uncertainty in the forecasts of demand.

The most comprehensive computerized search methodology, known as *Search Decision Rules (SDR)*, has been developed by Taubert (1968). He defined C_{TOT} as a function of $(W_t, P_t, W_{t-1}, I_{t-1}, D_t;\ t = 1, 2, \ldots, 12)$ and then identified the factors within C_{TOT} by the following vectors:

$$\begin{aligned} \{D\} &= \{\text{Decision vector} = P_t, W_t;\ t = 1, 2, \ldots, 12\} \\ \{S\} &= \{\text{Stage vector} = W_{t-1}, I_{t-1};\ t = 1, 2, \ldots, 12\} \\ \{P\} &= \{\text{Parameter vector} = \text{Cost coefficients at time } t \text{ and } D_t; \\ &\quad\ t = 1, 2, \ldots, 12\} \end{aligned} \tag{14.9}$$

His decision vector contains 24 (or $2T$) independent decision variables, the desired output of SDR methodology. The stage vector transmits information about the *state* of the system from time $t - 1$ to t. The parameter vector contains the forecasts and the cost coefficients *that could be different from stage to stage.*

SDR searches directly for decision vectors that reduce C_{TOT}. Computer search routines attempt to optimize all stages simultaneously generating 24 trial decisions per iteration. The search procedure terminates when successive iterations result in small reductions in C_{TOT}.

The appropriate procedure for generating alternative values of the decision vector $\{D\}$ is not obvious. The generation technique chosen determines the total time to arrive at a near-optimal C_{TOT}, or whether a near-optimal C_{TOT} is even achieved. We refer the reader to the references at the end of the paper by Taubert (1968) for a detailed discussion of computer search techniques.

Taubert, using SDR, was able to achieve results that were very close to those realized by other mathematically optimal methods. Similar results have been obtained by a number of other researchers. (See, for example, Lee and Khumawala, 1974; Mellichamp and Love, 1978). In their book, Buffa and Miller (1979) summarize the advantages and disadvantages of SDR methodology as follows.

SDR Advantages

1. Permits realistic modeling free from many restrictive assumptions, such as closed-form mathematical expressions, linear/quadratic cost functions, and so on.
2. Permits a variation in mathematical structure from stage to stage (heterogeneous stages), so that anticipated system changes such as the introduction of new products or production equipment, reorganizations, wage increases, etc., can be considered.
3. Provides the operating manager with a set of current and projected decisions.
4. Permits optimized disaggregate decision making.

5. Lends itself to evolutionary cost model development and provides solutions at desired points in the iterative process.
6. Facilitates sensitivity analysis and provides sensitivity data while the search routine is converging on a solution.
7. Easily handles cash flow discounting, nonlinear utility functions, multiple objective functions, and complex constraints.
8. Offers the potential of solving many otherwise impossible operations planning problems.
9. The methodology is general and can be applied to single or multistage decision problems that are not related to aggregate planning. For example, determining the optimal capital structure of a firm given a forecast of interest rates, stock performance, etc., or determining a least cost allocation of manpower to activities defined by a critical path network.

SDR Disadvantages

1. Optimization using computer search routines is an art and it is currently impossible to state, a priori, which search routine will give the best performance on a particular objective function.
2. Decisions made by this methodology may not, and in general will not, represent the absolute global optimum.
3. Response surface dimensionality appears to be a limiting factor (in terms of computational effort required).[13]

14.8 PLANNING FOR ADJUSTMENTS RECOGNIZING UNCERTAINTY

Earlier we have argued that one way to cope with uncertainty is to use a rolling-horizon implementation. An alternative methodology has been proposed by Hanssmann (1962) and Magee and Boodman (1967). Specifically, an *initial* solution is developed (by some procedure such as linear programming) for a horizon of T periods. This initial solution implies target (or planned) inventory and production levels through time. Since actual demands differ from the forecasted values, we may wish to adjust the individual production rates from their original planned levels rather than reusing the original algorithm at each period with a rolling horizon of T periods.

Let P_t be the production rate actually used in period t and P_t^* be the originally planned (or target) production rate for period t. Suppose that there is a lead time of L periods to initiate a change in production rate (that is, any change in the production rate for period $t + L + 1$ must be initiated at the end of period t). Then a simple, plausible decision rule is to schedule a production rate P_{t+L+1}

[13]A potential tool for a drastic reduction in computational time is the branch-and-bound technique (see, for example, Wagner, 1975).

equal to the originally planned rate, P^*_{t+L+1}, plus an adjustment equal to a fraction f of the projected inventory discrepancy at the end of period $t + L$. That is,

$$P_{t+L+1} = P^*_{t+L+1} + f[I^*_t - I_t - \sum_{j=1}^{L} (P_{t+j} - P^*_{t+j})] \tag{14.10}$$

where

I_t = *actual* inventory level at the end of period t

I^*_t = *target* inventory level at the end of period t *resulting from the original plan*

The summation term in Eq. 14.10 represents the additional change in the inventory level that will occur during the lead time L as a result of prior adjustments in $P_{t+1}, P_{t+2}, \ldots, P_{t+L}$.

Obviously, the behavior of the decision rule depends on the choice of f. As f increases, the changes in the production rate will tend to be larger, but the buffer inventory required to protect against the demand uncertainty will decrease. *Under the restrictive assumption of stationary demand* (that is, an *average* demand level that does not change with time) *and independent forecast errors* from period to period, one can show (see Johnson and Montgomery, 1974; Magee and Boodman, 1967) that

$$E[|\Delta P|] \simeq 0.8 \sqrt{\frac{2f}{2-f}}\, \sigma_\varepsilon \tag{14.11}$$

and

$$\sigma_{\text{ID}} \simeq \sqrt{\frac{1 + L(2f - f^2)}{2f - f^2}}\, \sigma_\varepsilon \tag{14.12}$$

where

$\Delta P = P_t - P_{t-1}$ = change in the production rate from period to period (with stationary demand ΔP would be 0 if there were no forecast errors)

$E[|\Delta P|]$ = expected (or average) absolute change in the production rate

σ_{ID} = standard deviation of the inventory discrepancy $I_t - I^*_T$

σ_ε = standard deviation of errors of forecasts over a unit time period

The above analysis assumes that any (continuous) production rate can be used. In fact, there may only be a few discrete possible production rates—for example, high (H), normal (N), and low (L). In such a case a plausible strategy (first suggested by Orr, 1962, and subsequently developed by Elmaleh and Eilon, 1974, and Mellichamp and Love, 1978), *still under a stationary demand pattern*, is to use three inventory levels $a > c > b$ and to set the production rate in period $t + 1$ as follows:

$$P_{t+1} = \begin{cases} H & \text{if } I_t \text{ drops below } b \\ N & \text{if } I_t \text{ crosses } c \\ L & \text{if } I_t \text{ rises above } a \\ P_t & \text{otherwise} \end{cases} \tag{14.13}$$

The values of a, b, and c are found by some form of search procedure.

Lambrecht et al. (1982) have shown that the decision rule of Eq. 14.13 can lead to sizable cost penalties when the demand pattern is no longer stationary (that is, the average rate changes appreciably with time). Furthermore, they suggest a heuristic modification to cope with this more realistic situation—namely, recomputing the a, b, and c values when the average demand over the next n periods deviates by more than x percent from the average demand over the interval used to last compute the parameter values. The quantities n and x now become two additional controllable parameters of the policy.

14.9 MODELING THE BEHAVIOR OF MANAGERS

In Sections 14.6 and 14.7 we examined models that attempted to capture the important tradeoffs required by an aggregate scheduling decision through *explicit* specification of relatively complex mathematical formulations. These modeling strategies confront analysts and managers with other difficulties that result from their limited ability to measure the more esoteric costs required and the difficulties that result from having to derive solutions to more complex mathematical formulations. In the previous section we moved to a somewhat simpler type of strategy that does not necessarily require the *explicit* specification of cost parameters (management can directly set the values of the control parameters, for example, the a, b, and c values in Eq. 14.13). Continuing in this direction, we now discuss a different philosophy of modeling based on *implicit* cost measurement; in particular, we identify key costs and other factors by interviewing managers and observing their actual decision-making behavior. Specifically, we comment on two distinct approaches of this general nature.

14.9.1 Management Coefficients Models

Based on his consulting experiences Bowman (1963) suggested that

> *Managerial decisions might be improved more by making them more consistent from one time to another than by approaches purporting to give "optimal solutions" to explicit models . . . especially for problems where intangibles (run-out costs, delay penalties) must otherwise be estimated or assumed.*

Bowman justified this philosophy by observing that experienced managers are generally quite aware of the criteria and cost factors that influence decisions they must make. Over many repetitive decisions their decision behavior is unbiased; that is, on the average, they make the correct response to the decision environment they face. However, their behavior is probably more erratic than it should be. Spurious influences such as emergency phone calls from superiors, suppliers, and customers can produce deviations from normal (average) behavior when not warranted. Therefore, Bowman argued, why not adopt an approach to modeling that tries to keep a manager closer to his average decison behavior by dampening out most of these erratic reactions. Bowman named his methodology/philosophy the *Management Coefficients Model.* Kunreuther (1969) and Gordon (1966), among others, have reported applications of this approach.

The Management Coefficients approach utilizes standard multiple regression methodology to fit decision rules to historical data on actual managerial decision behavior. By fitting a regression line, the analyst attempts to capture the average historical relationship between cues in the environment and management's responses. Erratic behavior (the residuals) is "dampened" by minimizing least squares.

The first step is to select a form of relationship between the decision variable(s) and the historical data on environmental variables. For example, in the production smoothing and workforce balancing situation, Bowman chose:

$$P_t = aP_{t-1} + b_1D_t + b_2D_{t+1} + c \tag{14.14}$$

That is, the production rate (P_t) in period t is assumed to be *linearly* related to the production rate in the previous period (P_{t-1}) and the estimated orders in periods $t(D_t)$ and $t + 1(D_{t+1})$. There should, of course, be no other reason, except the logic of the relationships involved, to limit such regressions (in general) to linear forms.

Having fit a management coefficients regression equation, the analyst can now describe to management how they would have normally (on the average) reacted in the past to any forecasted pattern of future orders, given existing on-hand inventories and prevailing production rates. Presumably this would cause decision makers to consider more carefully and justify any contemplated deviation from a conventional response to cues in the environment based on their actions in the past.

Tests with actual company data have shown that costs can be significantly reduced through the use of the Management Coefficients approach.[14] A serious drawback of the procedure is the essentially subjective selection of the form of the rule. It very easily can be selected incorrectly. Implicit in Bowman's approach is the assumption that past decisions are a good basis for future actions. A historical orientation could prevent a manager from quickly adapting to new conditions in a rapidly changing competitive environment.

Kunreuther (1969) has proposed general criteria that must be satisfied if a Management Coefficients approach is to have validity in an actual application. The criteria are similar to conditions that must hold for any least squares regression model. Kunreuther makes two recommendations. When managers have limited information regarding future sales, as when they develop their initial production estimate, then a plan based on average (past) decision behavior is very useful. However, when environmental cues provide reliable information on future sales of specific items (as when subsequent revisions are made in the Master Plan), then actual decisions are clearly superior to those suggested by an averaging rule. In such cases, variance in managerial action is beneficial rather than costly to a firm and should not be averaged out.

14.9.2 Manpower Decision Framework

Colley et al. (1977) interviewed a number of managers responsible for aggregate planning decisions and observed that these managers felt that capacity utilization in both the short and long term was of paramount importance in their decision making. Thus, two ratio factors are proposed, specifically,

$$\text{Current period ratio (CPR)} = \frac{\text{Demand for current period production}}{\text{Current period productive capacity}} \tag{14.15}$$

$$\text{Planning period ratio (PPR)} = \frac{\begin{array}{l}\text{Average monthly order backlog and}\\ \text{additional anticipated orders}\\ \text{in planning period}^{15}\end{array}}{\text{Monthly productive capacity}} \tag{14.16}$$

Ideally, one would like to have both of these ratios close to unity. Nine possible states are defined by three possible values of each of the two ratios. These values are (1) significantly below unity, (2) near unity, and (3) significantly above

[14] Strictly speaking, one cannot really compare actual company decision behavior with a management coefficients model, or with any of the other explicit models discussed in this chapter. The objective function that management may have tried to minimize with their past decisions may have been far different from any of the ones we have formulated mathematically.

[15] The planning period is the time interval out to the planning horizon.

unity. The boundaries (for example, between "significantly below" and "near" unity) are under management control. In consultation with management plausible courses of action are defined for each of the states. For example, if we were in the state

$$\text{CPR} \gg 1 \qquad \text{and} \qquad \text{PPR} \simeq 1$$

then use of some overtime would likely be appropriate. On the other hand, if both

$$\text{CPR} \gg 1 \qquad \text{and} \qquad \text{PPR} \gg 1$$

then one would probably wish to increase the size of the workforce.

14.10 SUMMARY

In this chapter we have presented a number of approaches to dealing with the aggregate production planning problem. The major insight, that we have attempted to convey, is the need to always select decision models for aggregate planning whose sophistication matches the complexity demanded by the specific situation faced in different organizations. Shycon (1974) has pointed out the fact that management scientists can get carried away in their search for generality and optimality. In Shycon's words, they "tend, at times, to over-agonize about the entire analytical process. In short, sometimes they make more of a big deal of the routines of analysis than is justified by the type of result required and the management need." We believe that aggregate planning theory is one area where management scientists have gotten somewhat carried away.

The sparse number of applications in this area is therefore in large part the result of two related reasons. First, some management scientists have tried to construct more and more complex models, which are not easy to adapt to changing real-world conditions. It is for this reason that we have not discussed certain other mathematical models and associated decision rules, such as the Linear Decision Rule (see Holt et al., 1955), which, although of conceptual value, have had little practical implementation. Second, the manager is too often isolated from the process of achieving a "solution." It is possible that every time we claim we have invented a more complex model that includes more decision variables than ever before, or when we claim that some computerized algorithms can achieve an "optimal solution" faster than ever before, we are actually progressively alienating more and more managers from ever considering using decision models for aggregate planning. Managers do not necessarily want quick and easy answers. Nor do they want to delegate too much of the analysis to an inanimate process. They may well want to agonize, to make deals and compromises, and to derive "personalized" alternative plans—even at the expense of *mathematical* optimality. Plans may be personalized in the sense that they are partly the result of historical accidents, deals, and organizational compromises in which the decision makers have a stake, or in the sense that every feasible schedule in practice will include such details as John Doe, the best tool and die maker in your plant, being on vacation in August. Thus, in summary, the aggregate plan is too important a decision to a manager for that individual *not* to spend a considerable amount of time in developing it.

PROBLEMS

14.1 Referring to Case E of the MIDAS Corporation, answer the following questions.

a. The president of MIDAS Canada suspected that the Assembly Manager was building too much slack into his Master Plan. Do you agree and what action (if any) would you recommend?

b. The Assembly Manager described how he planned to inventory "man-hours of repairs." Explain how this can be done. Do you see any problems in doing this?

c. The Master Plan is prepared only 6 months ahead. Is this advisable in this case? Under what circumstances would you recommend a longer decision horizon?

d. Provide a general critique of the aggregate planning procedure described in the case.

14.2 Given the description of the problem in Case E, how would you go about formulating the MIDAS situation in a Land transportation format? (See Table 14.7.) Do you have all the information you need?

14.3 In a production to stock situation where demand varies with time, an aggregate planning strategy is to produce to stock, using this stock to level out the required production rate through time. In a make-to-order situation one cannot directly use this strategy because of the custom nature of the demands. However, smoothing is still available through the introduction of a so-called *planning window*, which represents the amount by which the promise time exceeds the production lead time. Within such a planning window, one can smooth requirements without causing any backorders.

a. By what means could one increase the planning window?

b. Discuss the costs relevant in choosing the appropriate size of the window.

14.4 Consider a plant whose capacity, on the average, exceeds the demand rate. There are two options for balancing capacity used with the demand rate: Option 1—periodic shutdown and Option 2—throttling (running at less than full capacity).

Let

c_{sf} = semifixed operating cost, in \$/year, incurred whenever the plant is operating (independent of the operating level)

h = inventory carrying cost, in \$/unit/year

C_s = cost of shutting down and starting up, in \$

P_{max} = production rate when the plant is running at capacity, in units/year

For the case where the demand rate is level at D units/year, answer the following questions:

a. For Option 1 write an expression for the total relevant cost per year as a function of the time T between shutdowns and the production rate used P units/year.

b. Find the best value of T for a given value of P.

c. What P value(s) need(s) to be considered in the shutdown strategy? What are the total relevant costs for this(these) value(s)?

d. What is the decision rule for choosing, based on costs, between shutdown and throttling?

14.5 Clarke Manufacturing Co. makes 30 types of transformers. Sales forecasts for 1985 for type CT-OIM are as below:

Month	Demand (units)
January	600
February	500
March	700
April	900
May	1000
June	1200
July	900
August	700
September	700
October	600
November	600
December	600

A maximum of 24 transformers of this type can be produced at one time. The company works one shift of 8 hr/day. Each worker can handle only one machine at a time and produces, on the average, 2 units per 8-hour shift.

Regular-time pay is $4/hr and the overtime rate is $6/hr. cost of carrying inventory is set at 0.02 $/$/month. Costs of hiring and firing a worker are estimated at $360 and $180, respectively. Union contract stipulates that at least 14 workers have to be employed at all times. On December 31, 1984 there were 15 workers on the payroll and inventory on hand was 300 units. The desired minimum level of inventory was set at 300 units with each unit costed at $50. Normally a worker can work a maximum of 56 hours in a week. Assume each month is 20 working days in length.

Formulate the least-cost production plan for 1985 using a graphic approach. (No back-ordering is allowed, and inventory level should not go too far below 300 units.)

14.6 Starship Ltd. manufactures boats and distributes them across the United States. Part C-212 (a motor) is the most expensive single part. The table below shows the sales forecast for this part for the next 12 months.

Months	Forecast (units)
1	300
2	600
3	300
4	400
5	800
6	900
7	1600
8	1800
9	1600
10	800
11	500
12	400

Labor cost is $40 per unit at regular time and $60 per unit at overtime. Carrying cost is $2 per month per unit.

A maximum of 20 people can work at any time. The monthly output on regular time per person is 50 units. Overtime production can be up to 40 percent of regular-time production. Maximum monthly inventory is set at 1000 units. There is no constraint on the minimum number of workers per month.

a. Develop an optimal production schedule for the next 12 months. Indicate

1. Total cost of production (that is, labor and carrying costs)
2. Total production every month
3. Total number of workers required in each of the 12 months

b. Draw the cumulative production and demand curves.

14.7 In Problem 14.6, if the maximum inventory limit is raised to 1300 units, how much is the increased storage capacity worth?

14.8 Refer to Problem 14.6. If at least 12 workers have to be employed at all times, how does this constraint affect total cost?

14.9 Suppose that a *minimum* inventory level $I_{m,t}$ must be maintained at the end of period t ($t = 1, 2, \ldots, T$). How could this type of constraint be handled in the Land algorithm?

14.10 A version of the linear programming model of the aggregate scheduling problem that has been used in practice is:

Minimize:

$$C_{\text{TOT}} = \sum_{i=1}^{N} \sum_{t=1}^{T} (v_{it} P_{it} + I_{it}\, v_i r_t)$$
$$+ \sum_{t=1}^{T} (c_w W_t + c_O W'_t)$$

Subject to:

$$P_{it} + I_{i,t-1} - I_{it} = D_{it} \qquad \begin{cases} t = 1, \ldots, T \\ i = 1, \ldots, N \end{cases}$$

$$\sum_{i=1}^{N} k_i P_{it} - W_t - W'_t = 0 \qquad t = 1, \ldots, T$$

$$0 \leqslant W_t \leqslant W_{t,\max} \qquad t = 1, \ldots, T$$

$$0 \leqslant W'_t \leqslant W'_{t,\max} \qquad t = 1, \ldots, T$$

$$P_{it}, I_{it} \geqslant 0 \qquad \begin{cases} i = 1, \ldots, N \\ t = 1, \ldots, T \end{cases}$$

a. Define all symbols, giving the units of all variables as well as the point in time when they must be measured.

b. Which data must be collected or estimated?

c. Which variables must be assigned values and which variables are decision variables whose values will be determined by an LP algorithm?

14.11

a. Using Eqs. 14.11 and 14.12, prove that

1. $E[|\Delta P|]$ increases as f increases.
2. σ_{ID} decreases as f increases.

b. Outline an analysis to aid in the choice of the value of f, based on cost considerations.

14.12 For the historical data given below, fit by linear regression, suitable management coefficients equations similar to those in Eq. 14.14. Explain your reasons for selecting the number of variables in your model. Is it a good enough fit that you would recommend it for future decisions? Discuss.

Period t	D_t	S_t	W_t
1	—	—	84
2	445	445	79
3	438	426	75
4	321	356	72
5	396	388	69
6	376	373	68
7	292	331	67
8	455	416	67
9	400	386	67
10	355	363	69
11	289	338	71
12	430	427	74
13	395	475	77
14	513	496	81
15	505	503	85

Period t	P_t	I_t
1	515	302
2	447	303
3	418	295
4	390	329
5	380	321
6	371	319
7	365	353
8	377	314
9	376	308
10	376	316
11	386	364
12	386	358
13	455	337
14	482	323
15	504	325

REFERENCES

Axsäter, S. (1981). "Aggregation of Product Data for Hierarchical Production Planning." *Operations Research*, Vol. 29, No. 4, pp. 744–756.

Axsäter, S., H. Jönsson, and A. Thorstenson (1983). "Approximate Aggregation of Product Data." *Engineering Costs and Production Economics*, Vol. 7, No. 2, pp. 119–126.

Baker, K. R., and D. Peterson (1979). "An Analytic Framework for Evaluating Rolling Schedules." *Management Science*, Vol. 25, No. 4, pp. 341–351.

Beale, E. M. L., and G. Morton (1958). "Solution of a Purchase-Storage Programme: Part I." *Operational Research Quarterly*, Vol. 9, No. 3, pp. 174–187.

Bitran, G., E. Haas, and A. C. Hax (1981). "Hierarchical Production Planning: A Single Stage System." *Operations Research*, Vol. 29, No. 4, pp. 717–743.

Bolander, S. F., R. C. Heard, S. M. Seward, and S. G. Taylor (1981). *Manufacturing Planning and Control in Process Industries.* American Production and Inventory Control Society, Falls Church, Virginia.

Boskma, K. (1982). "Aggregation and the Design of Models for Medium-Term Planning of Production." *European Journal of Operational Research*, Vol. 10, pp. 244–249.

Bowman, E. H. (1956). "Production Scheduling by the Transportation Method of Linear Programming." *Operations Research*, Vol. 4, No. 1, pp. 100–103.

Bowman, E. H. (1963). "Consistency and Optimality in Managerial Decision Making." *Management Science*, Vol. 9, No. 2, pp. 310–321.

Buffa, E. S., and J. G. Miller (1979). *Production Inventory Systems: Planning and Control*, Third Edition. Richard D. Irwin, Inc., Homewood, Illinois, Chapters 5 and 6.

Close, J. F. C. (1968). "A Simplified Planning Scheme for the Manufacturer with Seasonal Demand." *The Journal of Industrial Engineering*, Vol. XIX, pp. 454–462.

Colley, J. L., R. D. Landel, and R. R. Fair (1977). *Production Operations Planning and Control.* Holden-Day, San Franciso, California, Chapter 8 and Case 17.

Cruickshanks, A. B., R. D. Drescher, and S. C. Graves (1984). "A Study of Production Smoothing in a Job Shop Environment." *Management Science*, Vol. 30, No. 3, pp. 368–380.

Duersch, R., and D. B. Wheeler (1981). "An Interactive Scheduling Model for Assembly-Line Manufacturing." *International Journal of Modelling & Simulation*, Vol. 1, No. 3, pp. 241–245.

Dzielinski, B., C. Baker, and A. Manne (1963). "Simulation Tests of Lot Size Programming." *Management Science*, Vol. 9, No. 2, pp. 229–258.

Eilon, S. (1971). "Comments on Optimal Smoothing of Shipments in Response to Orders." *Management Science*, Vol. 17, No. 9, pp. 608–609.

Eilon, S. (1975). "Five Approaches to Aggregate Production Planning." *AIIE Transactions*, Vol. 7, No. 2, pp. 118–131.

Elmaleh, J., and S. Eilon (1974). "A New Approach to Production Smoothing." *International Journal of Production Research*, Vol. 12, No. 6, pp. 673–681.

Fabian, T. (1967). "Blast Furnace Production Planning—A Linear Programming Example." *Management Science*, Vol. 14, No. 2, pp. 1–27.

Galbraith, J. (1969). "Solving Production Smoothing Problems." *Management Science*, Vol. 15, No. 12, pp. 665–674.

Gordon, J. R. M. (1966). "A Multi-Model Analysis of an Aggregate Scheduling Decision." Unpublished Doctoral Dissertation, Sloan School of Management, Massachusetts Institute of Technology, Cambridge, Massachusetts.

Haehling von Lanzenauer, C. (1970). "Production and Employment Scheduling in Multistage Production Systems." *Naval Research Logistics Quarterly*, Vol. 17, No. 2, pp. 193–198.

Hanssmann, F. (1962). *Operations Research in Production and Inventory Control*, John Wiley & Sons, New York.

Hanssmann, F., and S. W. Hess (1960). "A Linear Programming Approach to Production and Employment Scheduling." *Management Technology*, Vol. 1, No. 1, pp. 46–51.

Harrison, F. L. (1976). "Production Planning in Practice." *OMEGA*, Vol. 4, No. 4, pp. 447–454.

Hax, A. C. (1978). "Aggregate Production Planning." In *Handbook of Operations Research* (J. Moder and S. Elmaghraby, Editors), Van Nostrand Reinhold, New York.

Holt, C., F. Modigliani, J. Muth, and H. Simon (1960). *Planning Production, Inventories and Work Force*, Prentice-Hall, Englewood Cliffs, New Jersey.

Holt, C., F. Modigliani, and H. Simon (1955). "A Linear Decision Rule for Production and Employment Scheduling." *Management Science*, Vol. 2, No. 1, pp. 1–30.

Johnson, L. A., and D. C. Montgomery (1974). *Operations Research in Production Planning, Scheduling and Inventory Control*, John Wiley & Sons, New York, pp. 236–242.

Jones, C. H. (1967). "Parametric Production Planning." *Management Science*, Vol. 13, No. 11, pp. 843–866.

Khoshnevis, B., and P. M. Wolfe (1983). "An Aggregate Production Planning Model Incorporating Dynamic Productivity: Part I. Model Development." *IIE Transactions*, Vol. 15, No. 2, pp. 111–118.

Kunreuther, H. (1969). "Extensions of Bowman's Theory on Managerial Decision Making." *Management Science*, Vol. 15, No. 8, pp. B415–B439.

Lambrecht, M. R., R. Luyten, and J. Vander Eecken (1982). "The Production Switching Heuristic under Non-Stationary Demand." *Engineering Costs and Production Economics*, Vol. 7, pp. 55–61.

Land, A. H. (1958). "Solution of a Purchase-Storage Programme: Part II." *Operational Research Quarterly*, Vol. 9, No. 3, pp. 188–197.

Lee, W. B., and B. M. Khumawala (1974). "Simulation Testing of Aggregate Production Planning Models in an Implementation Methodology." *Management Science*, Vol. 20, No. 6, pp. 903–911.

Lockett, A. G., and A. P. Muhlemann (1978). "A Problem of Aggregate Scheduling—An Application of Goal Programming." *International Journal of Production Research*, Vol. 16, No. 2, pp. 127–135.

Magee, J. F., and D. M. Boodman (1967). *Production Planning and Inventory Control*, Second Edition. McGraw-Hill, New York, pp. 199–208, 361–364.

McClain, J. O., and L. J. Thomas (1977). "Horizon Effects in Aggregate Production Planning with Seasonal Demand." *Management Science*, Vol. 23, No. 7, pp. 728–736.

Mellichamp, J., and R. M. Love (1978). "Production Switching Heuristics for the Aggregate Planning Problem." *Management Science*, Vol. 24, No. 12, pp. 1242–1251.

Moskowitz, H. (1972). "The Value of Information in Aggregate Production Planning—A Behavioral Experiment." *AIIE Transactions*, Vol. 4, No. 4, pp. 290–297.

Moskowitz, H., and J. G. Miller (1975). "Information and Decision Systems for Production Planning." *Management Science*, Vol. 22, No. 3, pp. 359–370.

Orr, D. (1962). "A Random Walk Production-Inventory Policy." *Management Science*, Vol. 9, No. 1, pp. 108–122.

Peterson, R. (1971). "Optimal Smoothing of Shipments in Response to Orders." *Management Science*, Vol. 17, No. 9, pp. 597–607.

Posner, M. E., and W. Szwarc (1983). "A Transportation Type Aggregate Production Model with Backordering." *Management Science*, Vol. 29, No. 2, pp. 188–199.

Rand, G. K. (1974). "A Manual Production Scheduling Algorithm." *Operational Research Quarterly*, Vol. 25, No. 4, pp. 541–551.

Rhodes, P. (1977). "A Paint Industry Production Planning and Smoothing System." *Production and Inventory Management*, Vol. 18, No. 4, pp. 17–29.

Ritzman, L. P., L. J. Krajewski, W. L. Berry, S. H. Goodman, S. T. Hardy, and L. D. Vitt, Editors (1979). *Disaggregation Problems in Manufacturing and Service Organizations.* Martinus Nijhoff, Hingham, Massachusetts.

Sadlier, C. D. (1970). "Use of the Transportation Method of Linear Programming in Production Planning: A Case Study." *Operational Research Quarterly*, Vol. 21, No. 4, pp. 393–402.

Sanderson, I. W. (1978). "An Interactive Production Planning System in the Chemical Industry." *Journal of the Operational Research Society*, Vol. 29, No. 8, pp. 731–739.

Schwarz, L. B., and R. E. Johnson (1978). "An Appraisal of the Empirical Performance of the Linear Decision Rule for Aggregate Planning." *Management Science*, Vol. 24, No. 8, pp. 844–849.

Shycon, H. N. (1974). "Perspectives on MS Applications." *INTERFACES*, Vol. 4, No. 3, p. 23.

Taubert, W. H. (1968). "A Search Decision Rule for the Aggregate Scheduling Problem." *Management Science*, Vol. 14, No. 6, pp. 343–359.

Taylor, S. (1980). "Optimal Aggregate Production Strategies for Plants with Semifixed Operating Costs." *AIIE Transactions*, Vol. 12, No. 3, pp. 253–257.

Van de Panne, C., and P. Bosje (1962). "Sensitivity Analysis of Cost Coefficient Estimates: The Case of Linear Decision Rules for Employment and Production." *Management Science*, Vol. 9, No. 1, pp. 82–107.

Vergin, R. C. (1966). "Production Scheduling under Seasonal Demand." *Journal of Industrial Engineering*, Vol. XVII, No. 5, pp. 260–266.

Vergin, R. C. (1980). "On 'A New Look at Production Switching Heuristics for the Aggregate Planning Problem.'" *Management Science*, Vol. 26, No. 11, pp. 1185–1186.

Vidal, R. V. V. (1974). "Solving Multi-Item Production Planning Problems." *Colloquia*

Mathematica Societatis Jánas Bolyai, 12. Progress in Operations Research, Eger, Hungary.

Wagner, H. M. (1975). *Principles of Operations Research*, Second Edition. Prentice-Hall, Englewood Cliffs, New Jersey, pp. 484–493.

Welam, U. P. (1978). "An HMMS Type Interactive Model for Aggregate Planning." *Management Science*, Vol. 24, No. 5, pp. 564–575.

Zoller, K. (1971). "Optimal Disaggregation of Aggregate Production Plans." *Management Science*, Vol. 17, No. 8, pp. 553–579.

CHAPTER 15

Production Planning and Scheduling in Capacity-Oriented Process Industries

In this chapter we concentrate on industries primarily concerned with high utilization of capacity. We place an emphasis on a hierarchical planning framework first suggested by Hax and Meal (1975). Chapter 16 will address situations in which the primary concern is the operational coordination of components and raw materials. However, as first mentioned in Chapter 13, some of the ideas in the current chapter should be of use in the context of Chapter 16, and vice versa.

Section 15.1 is concerned with the Hax-Meal planning system, which includes the operational scheduling of individual items to use up capacity implied by the earlier tactical aggregate planning phase. In Section 15.2 we present some alternative approaches to dealing with the item scheduling situation. Then, Section 15.3 discusses a procedure for coping with *uncertainty* in the short run when items compete for limited capacity at a bottleneck operation.

15.1 THE HAX-MEAL HIERARCHICAL PLANNING SYSTEM

The concepts of hierarchical planning were first presented in Section 13.3.2 of Chapter 13. (The reader is encouraged to now review that material.) In the current section we initially concentrate on the original hierarchical system developed by Hax and Meal (1975); then we present some of the subsequent modifications that have appeared in the literature. Examples of other hierarchical planning systems are provided by McClain and Thomas (1980, Chapter 14) and van Beek (1977).

In summary, the philosophy underlying a hierarchical planning system is to partition the overall planning problem into procedures for decision making at strategic, tactical, and operational levels that

1. Perform reasonably well from the standpoint of overall tangible costs.
2. Are consistent; that is, lower level decisions stay within constraints imposed by higher level decisions.
3. Fit the organizational structure and are practical to implement both in terms of behavioral considerations and data/computational requirements.

In deciding on the distinct decision levels to use within a hierarchical planning system, Meal et al. (1982) identify three principles, specifically:

1. **Lead time and planning horizon.** Decisions are more likely to be placed at different hierarchical levels if they have significantly different implementation lead times or required planning horizons.
2. **Similarity.** If a number of resources or products are similar with respect to certain decisions, it may be convenient to make decisions about the *aggregate* resource or product at a higher level in the hierarchy and then some, more detailed, decisions at a lower level.
3. **Natural Locus of Decision Making.** Some decisions, such as plant investments, are decided by the board of directors while others, such as lot sizing, are made by production control personnel.

Based on the above principles, the original Hax-Meal system incorporated four hierarchical levels. The first was at the strategic level, involving capacity provision decisions and the assignment of products to specific manufacturing facilities. We do not discuss this level here but will instead concentrate on the other three levels of the system; that is, we assume that the capacity of each manufacturing facility is given as well as the set of products that are produced there. The three further levels are primarily a consequence of recognizing three different levels of detail in the product structure (which are quite common in certain types of process industries):

1. **Individual items.** This is the finest level of detail for scheduling and control purposes (what we have earlier denoted as s.k.u.). A given product may generate a large number of items differing in certain characteristics such as size, color, packaging, etc.
2. **Families.** As mentioned in Chapter 11 a family of items, in a production context, shares a common major manufacturing setup cost. There are benefits from coordinating the replenishments of such items. In chemical processes families are often called *process train units*.
3. **Types.** These are groups of families whose production quantities are to be determined *simultaneously* by an aggregate production plan. As discussed in Chapter 14, the choice of a group of families relates to the selection of the aggregate unit of measure. (Families in a group should have similar seasonal

demand patterns and approximately the same production rate as measured by inventory investment produced per unit time.[1])

The above three product levels, considered in reverse order, give the three hierarchical decision levels:

Level 1 Aggregate production planning subsystem (involves types).

Level 2 Family scheduling subsystem (allocates production quantities for each type among families belonging to that type).

Level 3 Individual-item scheduling subsystem (allocates production quantity of each family among its individual item members).

A summary of the resulting hierarchical decision system is shown in Figure 15.1. In the following material, an illustrative example will be used involving one type, three families, and ten items.

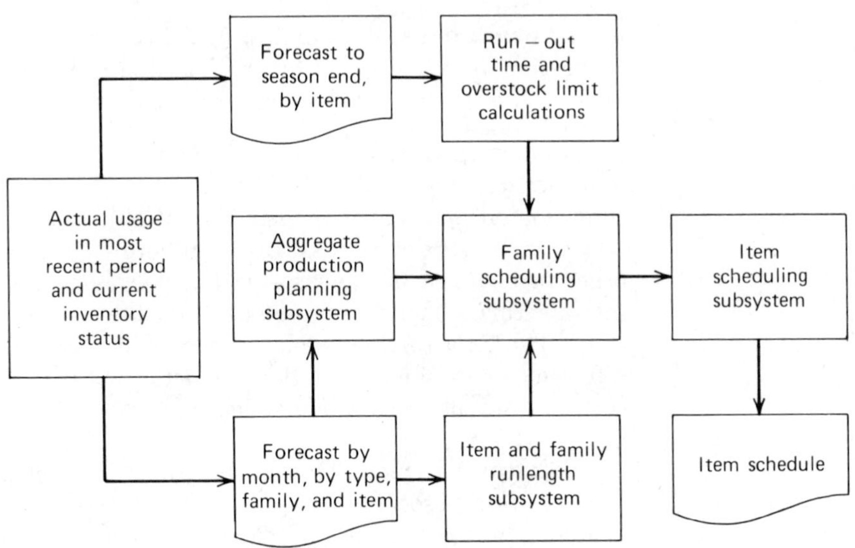

FIGURE 15.1 Summary of the Hierarchical Decision System

[1]Note that this definition of "type" simplifies the real problem. If two items within the same type have markedly different inventory investments per unit production time, then it follows logically that we would want to produce the item with the lower investment in the seasonal buildup period and the one with the higher investment in the peak demand season, thus saving on carrying costs. Moreover, the value of the inventory at any particular time would depend on the actual mix of s.k.u. and not just on the amount of production time. This would considerably complicate the modeling of the decision process.

15.1.1 The Aggregate Production Planning Subsystem

In this subsystem we address the tactical issue of selecting workforce levels, production rates, and inventories for each product type. One of the procedures discussed in Chapter 14 is used. Hax and Meal use a linear programming model; we instead will use the Land algorithm for a transportation model formulation (discussed in Section 14.5).

Suppose that the demand (requirements) for the type are as shown in Column 2 of Table 15.1. Also shown in Table 15.1 are the initial inventory, the planned workforce levels, and maximum and minimum inventory levels specified by management. Minimum inventory levels are based on the degree of uncertainty per monthly forecast, using techniques such as those discussed in Chapter 7. Production smoothing considerations also play a role in the determination of maximum/minimum levels. Note that in the example we have assumed that the company follows a policy where the regular workforce is kept at a constant level. Table 15.2 shows the details of the calculations of the Land algorithm for the first four months. This particular aggregate production schedule was computed for a decision horizon of 12 months. Table 15.3 records the summarized results for the full 12 months. However, it should be emphasized that normally the implementation would be on a rolling-horizon basis; that is, only the first month results of the aggregate model are implemented. In other

TABLE 15.1 Demand, Workforce, and Inventory Constraints (All Figures in Labor-Hours)

Month t (1)	Demand (2)	Inventory at End of t (3)	Minimum Inventory at t (4)	Maximum Inventory at t (5)	Available Regular-Time Workforce[a] (6)
0		25,000	10,000	30,000	
1	20,600		10,000	30,000	18,270
2	30,000		10,000	30,000	20,300
3	27,500		10,000	30,000	20,000
4	22,500		10,000	30,000	22,330
5	22,500		10,000	30,000	20,300
6	25,000		10,000	20,000	20,300
7	15,000		5,000	15,000	14,210
8	12,500		5,000	15,000	23,345
9	17,500		5,000	15,000	19,285
10	20,000		10,000	20,000	24,360
11	22,500		15,000	30,000	20,300
12	15,000		20,000	30,000	15,225
Totals	250,600				238,525

[a]The workforce levels in column 6 fluctuate because, although the number of workers is held constant, the number of work days per month varies from month to month.

TABLE 15.2 The Land Algorithm Applied to the Aggregate Production Planning Problem[a]

	Source	Cost	Rank	Available at t	Production at t	Available at $t+1$	Max. Inv. at End of t	Min. Inv. at End of t
Month 1:	00	—	1	15,000	15,000	0	30,000	10,000
Demand = 20,600	11	0	2	18,270	5,600	12,670		
	12	8	3	5,480	0	5,480		
Month 2:	00	—	1	0	0	0	30,000	10,000
Demand = 30,000	21	0	2	20,300	20,300	0		
	22	8	4	6,090	0	6,090		
	11	2	3	12,670	9,700	2,970		
	12	10	5	5,480	0	5,480		
Month 3:	00	—	1	0	0	0	30,000	10,000
Demand = 27,500	31	0	2	20,300	20,300	0		
	32	8	4	6,090	4,230	1,860		
	22	10	5	6,090	0	6,090		
	11	4	3	2,970	2,970	0		
	12	12	6	5,480	0	5,480		
Month 4:	00	—	1	0	0	0	30,000	10,000
Demand = 22,500	41	0	2	22,330	22,330	0		
	42	8	3	6,700	170	6,530		
	32	10	4	1,860	0	1,860		
	22	12	5	6,090	0	6,090		
	12	14	6	5,480	0	5,480		

[a]Source 00 refers to the amount of inventory available for use to meet demand during the specific period, or if not required, in subsequent periods. Note that available inventory listed under 00 does not include seasonal (anticipation) inventories previously allocated by the algorithm. Source 00 only lists inventory that has not been committed at any time t. Recall from Chapter 14 that sources 11 and 12 refer to the amount of regular time (second digit equals 1) and overtime (second digit equals 2) available in period 1, respectively, etc. Note that the variable cost of producing on regular time is assumed to be zero and on overtime $8 per labor-hour. The cost of carrying one labor-hour for one period is given as $2. Overtime is limited to 30 percent of regular-time capacity.

words, the only data conveyed to the next level of planning are the aggregated type production quantities for the first month. (See Section 14.3 for further discussion of rolling horizons.)

15.1.2 The Family Scheduling Subsystem

To set the family run quantities correctly and to preserve the aggregate schedule determined in Table 15.3, the decision system in this section must schedule

TABLE 15.3 Master Production Plan

Month	Demand	Regular-Time Production Scheduled P_t	Overtime Production Scheduled OT_t	Inventory at End of t I_t
0	—	—	—	25,000
1	20,600	18,270	0	22,670
2	30,000	20,300	0	12,970
3	27,500	20,300	4,230	10,000
4	22,500	22,330	170	10,000
5	22,500	20,300	2,200	10,000
6	25,000	20,300	4,700	10,000
7	15,000	10,000	0	5,000
8	12,500	20,715	0	13,215
9	17,500	19,285	0	15,000
10	20,000	24,360	0	19,360
11	22,500	20,300	0	17,160
12	15,000	15,225	2,615	20,000

just enough production in each of the families in the product type to use up the aggregate production time scheduled above. As we will see, the accumulated seasonal stock will be allocated in such a manner as to not incur any additional major setup costs associated with the production of each product type. At the same time, customer service standards will be met without violating individual s.k.u. overstock limits. Within these constraints any family belonging to a type can be produced. To achieve these ends a four-step procedure is recommended by Hax and Meal:

1. Determine the families in each type that must be run in the scheduling interval to meet s.k.u. service requirements.
2. Initial family run quantities are determined to minimize cycle inventory and changeover costs.
3. Then the initial family run quantities are adjusted so that all the product time scheduled to a particular type is used up.
4. At each of the above steps, individual s.k.u. overstock limits are checked.

To determine which families must be scheduled for production this month, Hax and Meal calculate the run-out time for each family using Eq. 15.1. For our example, all families with a run-out time less than one will be scheduled. This is equivalent to assuming that families are scheduled once a month and that the production lead time is negligible.[2] In general, all families i whose RT_i is less than the time left until the end of the period being scheduled must be put in the schedule for that period.

$$RT_i = \underset{\substack{\text{items } j \\ \text{belonging to family } i}}{\text{Min}} [(I_{ijt} - SS_{ijt})/D_{ijt}] \tag{15.1}$$

where

RT_i = earliest time at which the available inventory for any member of family i will reach its safety stock level

I_{ijt} = inventory of s.k.u. j in family i at the *start* of period t

SS_{ijt} = safety stock level of s.k.u. j in family i at the beginning of period t

D_{ijt} = forecast demand for s.k.u. j in family i for period t

The current status of the ten s.k.u. in our example is given in Table 15.4. From the table we can calculate, using Eq. 15.1, the expected run-out time for each of the three families involved:

RT_1 = Min [(2600 − 730)/1500, (2550 − 220)/450, (3250 − 480)/1000, (3750 − 1150)/2400, (2600 − 820)/1700] = 1.05 (from s.k.u. 5)

RT_2 = Min [(3750 − 1520)/3100, (1500 − 770)/1500, (1250 − 340)/700] = 0.49 (from s.k.u. 7)

RT_3 = Min [(1750 − 2170)/4500, (2000 − 1800)/3750] = −0.09 (from s.k.u. 9)

From the above calculations we can see that families 2 and 3 must be produced during the period being scheduled. Hax and Meal define the trial family run quantity as:

$$RQ_i = \sum_j RQ_{ij} = \sum_j \text{Min}\,[Q_{ij}, (L_{ijt} - I_{ijt})] \tag{15.3}$$

[2]When the lead time is of duration L periods (months), then, instead of Eq. 15.1, any item j in family i must now (at the start of period t) be scheduled for production of at least a quantity

$$LB_{ij} = \text{Max}\,[0, (D_{ijt} + D_{ij,t+1} + D_{ij,t+2} + \cdots + D_{ij,t+L} - I_{ijt} + SS_{ijt})] \tag{15.2}$$

If any $LB_{ij} > 0$, then family i must be scheduled for production in period $t + L$.

TABLE 15.4 Status of Items at Beginning of Month 1

Family i	s.k.u. j	Available Stock I_{ij1}	Safety Stock SS_{ij}	Forecast Month 1
1	1	2,600	730	1,500
	2	2,550	220	450
	3	3,250	480	1,000
	4	3,750	1,150	2,400
	5	2,600	820	1,700
2	6	3,750	1,520	3,100
	7	1,500	770	1,500
	8	1,250	340	700
3	9	1,750	2,170	4,500
	10	2,000	1,800	3,750
Totals		25,000	10,000	20,600

where

RQ_{ij} = trial run quantity for s.k.u. j in family i

Q_{ij} = order quantity for s.k.u. j in family i determined, for example, by the Economic Order Quantity formula in Chapter 5 or by the Silver-Meal heuristic in Chapter 6

L_{ijt} = overstock limit for s.k.u. j in family i at start of t

I_{ijt} = available stock level at the beginning of period t

Overstock L_{ijt} could be determined in a number of ways. In our expository example, we are at $t = 1$ in Table 15.3, that is, the beginning of a seasonal peak in production requirements which abate in approximately six months. Therefore, as a simple measure one could specify that at $t = 1$, L_{ijt} is equal to six months forecasted demand. Alternatively, one could attempt to use one of the single-period techniques described for style items in Chapter 10. The cost of an understock *could* be set equal to the changeover cost associated with having to make an extra run between now and the end of the season, whereas the unit cost of overstock could be set equal to the cost of carrying stock from one season to the next. This was the approach taken by Hax and Meal.[3] The determination of L_{ijt}

[3]Strictly speaking, the overstock cost is not always equal to the cost of carrying stock from one season to the next. Units not sold during a peak season do not always have to be held until the next peak; some could be used up shortly after the current peak. This means, though, that the marginal cost of an overstock increases with the size of the overstock. In the models presented in Chapter 10 we assumed that the marginal cost of an overstock was always constant. Therefore, strictly speaking, the models of Chapter 10 would need some minor modifications.

will depend on the specifics of the application being carried out. Conceptually, L_{ijt} attempts to limit individual s.k.u. and family inventory levels from getting way out of line. Table 15.5 presents the example calculations necessary for Eq. 15.3 in tabular form.

Note from Table 15.5 that the trial run quantity total for the type $\Sigma_i RQ_i$ is equal to 16,350 man-hours. For our example the trial quantity is less than the available production scheduled in Table 15.3 for month $t = 1$ (18,270 man-hours). The trial family run quantities must be increased so that this excess capacity is used up and thereby the aggregate production smoothing requirements are met. Hax and Meal recommend the following procedure to determine the final family run quantity RQ_i^*:

1. If $\Sigma_i RQ_i < (P_t + OT_t)$ then set

$$RQ_i^* = \text{Min}\left\{\sum_j (L_{ijt} - I_{ijt}),\, RQ_i + \left[(P_t + OT_t) - \sum_k RQ_k\right] f_i\right\}$$

where

$$f_i = \sum_j (L_{ijt} - I_{ijt}) / \sum_k \sum_j (L_{kjt} - I_{kjt}) \tag{15.4}$$

P_t = regular-time production capacity scheduled in period t for the type under consideration

OT_t = overtime production capacity scheduled in period t for the type under consideration

TABLE 15.5 Calculation of Trial Family Run Quantities

Family i	s.k.u. j	Available Inventory I_{ijt}	Q_{ij}	L_{ijt}	$(L_{ijt} - I_{ijt})$	Min $(Q_{ij}, L_{ijt} - I_{ijt})$
2	6	3,750	1,650	14,500	10,750	1,650
	7	1,500	1,750	7,800	6,300	1,750
	8	1,250	4,000	4,300	3,050	3,050
					Σ 20,100	RQ_2 = 6,450
3	9	1,750	6,500	21,100	19,350	6,500
	10	2,000	3,400	19,600	17,600	3,400
					Σ 36,950	RQ_3 = 9,900
						Total = 16,350 ($\Sigma_i RQ_i$)

Note: Family 1 is ignored because $RT > 1$ and, therefore, no production is necessary in the current month.

2. If $\sum_i RQ_i > (P_t + OT_t)$, then set

$$RQ_i^* = (P_t + OT_t)\, RQ_i / \sum_k RQ_k \tag{15.5}$$

Note that in Eq. 15.4, the term $RQ_i + (P_t + OT_t)f_i$ sets the *increment* to the run quantity for family i proportional to the maximum amount that can be run of that quantity (relative to the total maximum amount that can be run of the whole type). The term $\Sigma_j\,(L_{ijt} - I_{ijt})$ is simply the maximum quantity of family i that may be produced. Similarly, in Eq. 15.5, each family run quantity is scaled down proportionately.

Our example falls into the first case above and requires the use of Eq. 15.4.

For Family i = 2:

$$f_2 = \frac{20{,}100}{20{,}100 + 36{,}950} = 0.35$$

$$\begin{aligned} RQ_2^* &= \text{Min}\,\{20{,}100,\ 6450 + [(18{,}270 + 0) - 16{,}350]0.35\} \\ &= \text{Min}\,\{20{,}100,\ 7{,}122\} \\ &= 7{,}122 \end{aligned}$$

For Family i = 3:

$$f_3 = \frac{36{,}950}{20{,}100 + 36{,}950} = 0.65$$

$$\begin{aligned} RQ_3^* &= \text{Min}\,\{36{,}900,\ 9900 + [(18{,}270 + 0) - 16{,}350]0.65\} \\ &= \text{Min}\,\{36{,}900,\ 11{,}148\} \\ &= 11{,}148 \end{aligned}$$

Note that $RQ_2^* + RQ_3^*$ uses up the total production capacity determined in the aggregate production planning subsystem (that is, 18,270 man-hours as per Table 15.3; see scheduled P_t and OT_t for $t = 1$).

The $\Sigma_i RQ_i^*$ derived in the above manner will not always equal the total $(P_t + OT_t)$ available. Consider the contrived example in Table 15.6 where the

TABLE 15.6 Contrived Example

Family i	RQ_i	$(L_{ijt} - I_{ijt})$	f_i	$(RQ_i + 2200f_i)$	Min. (1) or (2)
		(1)		(2)	
1	6,000	9,000	0.56	7,232	7,232
2	3,000	5,000	0.31	3,682	3,682
3	2,000	2,100	0.13	2,286	2,100
	ΣRQ_i = 11,000	16,100	1.00	ΣRQ_i^* =	13,014

assumed $(P_t + OT_t)$ equals 13,200. Therefore, from Eq. 15.4, $RQ_i + [(P_t + OT_t) - \Sigma_k RQ_k]f_i$ reduces to $RQ_i + 2200f_1$ as given in column 2 of Table 15.6. Note that ΣRQ_i^* is less than 13,200, the available capacity (because the $L - I$ term takes effect for family 3). This means that a second iteration is necessary. That is, we must allocate the remaining capacity (13,200 − 13,014) or 186 labor-hours among families 1 and 2. We suggest the following procedure:

$$f_1' = \frac{9000}{9000 + 5000} = 0.64$$

Therefore,

$$f_2' = 0.36$$

$$RQ_1^* = \text{previous}\, RQ_1^* + 186 \times f_1'$$

$$= 7232 + 119 = 7351$$

$$RQ_2^* = 3682 + 67 = 3749$$

$$RQ_3^* = 2100 \text{ (as per Table 15.6)}$$

Now ΣRQ_i^* equals the available total capacity of 13,200. This method will always work as long as $(P_t + OT_t)$ does not exceed $\Sigma_i \Sigma_j (L_{ijt} - I_{ijt})$.

Returning to our main example (as in Table 15.5) what remains to be done now is the scheduling of individual s.k.u. within each family so that the total run quantities, RQ_i^*, are effectively utilized.

15.1.3 Individual-Item Scheduling Subsystem

Hax and Meal, in their original system, recommend the scheduling of individual s.k.u. by calculating quantities that equate the expected run-out times for all items in a family. Effectively, this keeps average inventories as low as possible in that most items will be at reasonably low levels when the family is next scheduled. Recall that the concept of equal time supplies was central in the coordinated control decision rules of Chapter 11. See Bolander et al. (1981) and Rhodes (1977) for specific applications of this concept. In trying to equate the expected run-out times, overstock limits must not be violated. It can be shown (see Problem 15.5) that equal run-out times are achieved by using

$$RQ_{ij}^* = [RQ_i^* + \Sigma_k (I_{kt} - SS_{ikt})]\, D_{ijt}/\Sigma_k D_{ikt} + SS_{ijt} - I_{ijt} \qquad (15.6)$$

where

RQ_{ij}^* = desired run quantity for the jth s.k.u. in family i

D_{ijt} = forecast demand for the jth s.k.u. in family i for period t

RQ_i^* = desired family run quantity determined from the family scheduling subsystem

Note that in Eq. 15.6, strictly speaking, SS_{ijt} and D_{ijt} are only approximations of the safety stock and demand rates in the future, made at time t. Demand is unlikely to continue at the same rate for all t; neither is a constant safety stock reasonable for all t. Therefore, Eq. 15.6 is an approximation that leads to operationally useful results. From Eq. 15.6 it follows (see Problem 15.5) that the *common* expected run-out time for each s.k.u. j in family i will be given by:

$$RT_{ij} = (RQ_{ij}^* + I_{ijt} - SS_{ijt})/D_{ijt} \tag{15.7}$$

In Table 15.7 we carry out the computation of scheduled quantities for our expository example. The common run-out times of 2.06 and 1.33 months for families 2 and 3 are given in the last column.

15.1.4 Extensions of the Original System

We briefly discuss three types of modifications that have been suggested to improve the overall performance of the Hax-Meal hierarchical planning system.

Avoiding Infeasibilities in Disaggregation

In the original Hax-Meal system, because of the aggregation at the production planning stage, it is possible to obtain a feasible solution to the aggregate problem that will *not* permit any feasible solution to the subsequent family and individual-item scheduling problems. This happens because of an imbalance among the initial inventories of the various items that make up the product type of the aggregate problem. Bitran and Hax (1977) suggest the computation of so-called *effective individual-item demands* that circumvent this difficulty. (The

TABLE 15.7 Scheduled Individual-Item Quantities and Run-Out Times

Type	Family i	Item j	Demand D_{ij}	Inventory I_{ijt}	Safety Stock SS_{ijt}	Calculated Order Quantity Q_{ij}	Scheduled RQ_{ij}^*	Run-Out Time RT_{ij}
1	2	6	3,100	3,750	1,520	1,650	4,199	2.06
		7	1,500	1,500	770	1,750	2,361	2.06
		8	700	1,250	340	4,000	533	2.06
	3	9	4,500	1,750	2,170	6,500	6,381	1.33
		10	3,750	2,000	1,800	3,400	4,767	1.33

proof is provided by Gabbay, 1976). The effective demands are determined as follows:

Let

D_{jt} = actual (or forecasted) demand for item j in period t

I_{j0} = initial (available) inventory of item j

SS_j = safety stock of item j

D'_{jt} = *effective* demand for item j in period t

Then, if $I_{j0} > SS_j$, the excess can be used to satisfy at least part of the demand for item j. Mathematically, we have

$$D'_{jt} = \text{Max}\ [0, \sum_{k=1}^{t} D_{jk} - I_{j0} + SS_j] \qquad t = 1,2, \ldots \tag{15.8}$$

Finally, the effective demand in period t for the product type is obtained by summing D'_{jt} across all items belonging to the type. These effective demands are then used in the aggregate planning procedure.

An Alternative Procedure for Selecting Family Run Quantities

The procedure of Section 15.1.2 is based on first trying to use individual-item economic order quantities. From Chapter 5 we know that the EOQ is an order quantity that strikes a balance between setup and carrying costs. However, total inventory costs for a product type are predetermined by the results of the aggregate planning stage. Thus, Bitran and Hax (1977) suggest a different family scheduling routine that allocates the aggregate production of a product type to families in an effort to minimize only the total of family setup costs. Specifically, the family run quantities, the RQ_i's, are selected to

$$\text{Minimize} \sum_i \frac{A_i D_i}{RQ_i} \tag{15.9}$$

$$\text{Subject to} \sum_i RQ_i = P_t + OT_t \tag{15.10}$$

and

$$LB_i \leq RQ_i \leq L_{it} - I_{it} \tag{15.11}$$

where

A_i = setup cost for family i

D_i = demand rate for family i

P_t and OT_t = regular-time and overtime production quantities allocated to the product type under consideration

LB_i = lower bound on the production quantity for family i (see, for example, Eq. 15.2)

L_{it} = overstock limit for family i at the start of period t, as discussed with respect to Eq. 15.3

I_{it} = inventory of family i at the start of period t

The summations in Eqs. 15.9 and 15.10 are over all families belonging to the particular product type under consideration and that require production in the period being scheduled. Equation 15.9 is an approximation to the total annual setup costs.

Bitran and Hax provide an efficient algorithm for solving the above problem. They also present a procedure for individual-item scheduling somewhat different from that described in Section 15.1.3.

The Case of Very High Setup Costs

In Hax and Meal's particular selection of hierarchical levels, setup costs are ignored in the aggregate planning decision (Section 15.1.1). Thus, an *implicit* assumption is that the choice of the aggregate plan will have a relatively minor (as a percentage of total relevant costs) impact on setup costs. Consequently, a modification has been suggested by Bitran et al. (1981) when setup costs are relatively large. Operationally, one can define "relatively large" as when the *unmodified* procedure leads to a solution (through to and including the family stage) where setup costs are larger than 10 percent of the total costs (holding, overtime, and setup). The modification proceeds essentially as follows:

Step 1. The aggregate planning problem for the product type is solved in the usual fashion (that is, ignoring setup costs).

Step 2. The family scheduling solution is obtained[4] for the period under consideration, using up the aggregate production rate determined by Step 1. At the same time, the marginal benefit (in terms of reduced setup costs) of having a larger aggregate production rate is obtained. If this is positive and there are regular production hours unallocated in the current (Step 1) solution to the aggregate problem, then additional regular hours are added to the solution until the marginal benefit is no longer positive or until all regular production time is used up.

[4]In actual fact, a Silver-Meal type algorithm is used, permitting treatment of the case of time-varying demand.

In essence, Step 2 provides a type of feedback between the two levels of the hierarchical system to compensate for having ignored setup costs at the aggregate planning stage. Graves (1982) shows a more formalized feedback linkage by means of a Lagrange multiplier formulation.

The need for a modification when setup costs are relatively high points out a fact mentioned earlier—namely, that the appropriate hierarchical decomposition is dependent on the cost structure of the particular firm as well as on its organizational structure.

15.2 OTHER DECISION RULES FOR INDIVIDUAL-ITEM SCHEDULING AT A BOTTLENECK OPERATION UNDER DETERMINISTIC DEMAND

Although the scope of this book is not intended to encompass the details of short-range scheduling and sequencing of products, in the current section we do provide a brief overview of the problem of allocating the capacity of a bottleneck operation to the production of several items. This allocation can be viewed as the master production scheduling step in the general decision framework presented in Figure 13.1 of Chapter 13.

The allocation problem is extremely complicated because of the capacity constraint and the associated necessity of avoiding interference of run times of separate items. (References on the complexity issue include Bartholdi and Rosenthal, 1979; Bitran and Yanasse, 1982, Florian et al., 1980; and Hsu, 1983). We do not necessarily have to be dealing with a family context in which there are cost economies associated with the coordination of production runs of different items. Instead, we may simply have a group of items sharing a common production facility so that coordination becomes necessary to ensure a feasible schedule.

The methods to be discussed, and most of those appearing in the literature, do not force the usage of the *total* resource allocated by the preceding aggregate planning decision, but rather treat it as an upper constraint. This is in contrast with our earlier discussion where, to ensure the appropriate buildup or depletion of aggregate stock with time, the allocated aggregate resource was completely utilized. Bishop (1979) elaborates further on this point.

15.2.1 The Case of Constant Demand and Constant Capacity

This is the simplest situation, essentially the economic order quantity context (see Section 5.1 of Chapter 5), except there are several items with differing demand rates and finite production rates, and there is, of course, a production capacity restriction. A simple selection of *independent* finite-rate economic run quantities of the separate items (see Eq. 5.17 of Chapter 5) can easily lead to an infeasible solution in that two or more items are likely to require production at the same time. Thus, some type of heuristic adjustment of such a solution is necessary. A particularly useful aid is some form of graphic portrayal of tentatively scheduled production versus time, in that a visual display permits an operator to make manual adjustments to ensure feasibility (see, for example, Duersch and Wheeler, 1981). Another useful concept, first introduced in Chapter 11, is that of a common base cycle time for the group of items produced on the facility under consideration, with each item being produced in a time supply that is an integer multiple of the base time.

A large number of publications have appeared on this problem area. Recent contributions include Boctor (1982), Delporte and Thomas (1977), Graves and Haessler (1978), McClain and Thomas (1980, pp. 343–5), Saipe (1977), Senju and Fujita (1980), and Vemuganti (1978). A particularly good survey is provided by Elmaghraby (1978).

15.2.2 The Case of Time-Varying Demand and Capacity

Here we consider the more realistic case where demand rates and production capacities vary with time (but they are still assumed to be known with certainty). Under such circumstances, as in Chapter 6, it is most common to consider discrete time intervals such as days or weeks, each with a known capacity and known individual-item demand rates. The objective is to keep the total (across all items and all periods out to some horizon) of setup and carrying costs as low as possible, subject to (1) no backlogging of demand or loss of sales and (2) no violations of production capacity constraints.

In Chapter 6, for the single-item, *uncapacitated* situation, we were able to argue that a replenishment quantity need only be placed when the inventory level is zero[5] and also that we can restrict our attention to replenishment quantities that would cover exactly an integer number of periods of requirements. This is certainly not the case with capacitated production as evidenced by the simple, single-item example shown in Table 15.8. The *only feasible* schedule is to produce at capacity (that is, 10 units) each period. Clearly, the

TABLE 15.8 Single-Item, Capacitated Example

Period t	1	2	3	4	Total
Demand D_t	7	10	9	14	40
Capacity C_t	10	10	10	10	40

[5]The discussion here assumes a negligible lead time. If there is a known lead time L, then the order should be placed L time units before the inventory level hits 0.

quantity produced in period 1 lasts for 1.3 periods and, moreover, production must take place in period 2 even though the starting inventory in that period is nonzero (3 units). Thus, the nature of the solution, *even for a single-item problem*, is considerably more complicated when production capacities are taken into account. Not surprisingly, a mathematically optimal solution is out of the question when one deals with the multi-item, time-varying, capacitated case; one must again turn to the use of a heuristic solution procedure.

We outline the nature of a heuristic procedure first developed by Dixon (1979) and also presented in Dixon and Silver (1981). Subsequent industrial applications are described by Van Wassenhove and De Bodt (1983) and Van Wassenhove and Vanderhenst (1983). The latter, in particular, use the heuristic as part of a hierarchical planning framework. The procedure is forward-looking in nature; as with the basic Silver-Meal heuristic of Chapter 6, it develops the current period's production quantities using demand information for as few periods into the future as possible (a desirable characteristic when one recognizes the increasing uncertainty in forecasts as one projects further into the future). The heuristic makes use of the Silver-Meal heuristic's basic criterion—namely, that, if item i is to be produced in period 1, then we wish to select the production time supply (T_i) as the *integer* number of periods that produces the (first local) minimum of the total relevant costs per unit time:

$$\mathrm{TRCUT}(T_i) = \frac{A_i + h_i \sum_{j=1}^{T_i} (j-1) D_{ij}}{T_i} \tag{15.12}$$

where

A_i = setup cost for item i, in \$

h_i (or $v_i r$) = holding cost for item i, in \$/unit/period

D_{ij} = demand for item i in period j, in units

However, where capacity is limited, there is competition for a scarce resource and it is quite likely that not all lot sizes to be produced in a particular period can be such that the associated TRCUT is minimized.

In order to describe how the heuristic deals with the above difficulty, we need to introduce a new variable U_i, defined as follows:

$$U_i = \frac{\mathrm{TRCUT}(T_i) - \mathrm{TRCUT}(T_i + 1)}{k_i D_{i,T_i+1}} \tag{15.13}$$

where k_i is the amount of production resource required per unit produced of item i.

It is seen that U_i represents the marginal decrease in costs per unit time of item i per unit of capacity absorbed if the time supply produced of item i is increased from T_i to $T_i + 1$. Each item requiring production in the period under consideration has its T_i first set to unity (the minimum feasible amount that must be produced). Then, the item with the largest *positive* U_i has its T_i increased to $T_i + 1$. This is continued until there is insufficient capacity to increase any of the T_i's by unity or until all U_i's are negative (the latter situation would give the *unconstrained* Silver-Meal lot sizes for each of the items).

The above procedure clearly does not violate the capacity restriction in the particular period being scheduled. However, it does not guard against another type of infeasibility. Consider the situation where in some *future* period the total demand exceeds the production capacity of that period. Then, some of the requirements of that period *must* be satisfied by production in preceding periods. This is illustrated by our earlier example of Table 15.8 where four of the units required in period 4 must be produced prior to that period. Thus, the heuristic also has a look-ahead feature built into it to ensure that as the T_i's are increased (as described in the previous paragraph), enough total production is done to prevent future infeasibilities from developing.

If the heuristic is applied to a problem having a horizon with well-defined ending conditions, then the above procedure is used to establish an initial solution of all production lots out to the horizon. In such a case the authors discuss several possible adjustments for improving on the initial solution. However, extensive testing has revealed that only one of these types of adjustments tends to be attractive in terms of potential savings without too much extra computational effort. Specifically, one should attempt to eliminate each scheduled lot by, if possible, allocating the production to periods where there is capacity available and the item under consideration is already being produced. The lot should be eliminated only if the increased carrying costs do not exceed the setup cost saved. In the more common case of a rolling-horizon implementation with an indefinite ending point, we do *not* recommend any such adjustment procedure.

There have been a number of other heuristic procedures developed for solving the capacitated, multi-item, time-varying demand problem (see, for example, Bolander and Taylor, 1983; Dogramaci et al., 1981; Eisenhut 1975; Florian and Klein, 1971; Lambert and Luss, 1982; Lambrecht and Vanderveken, 1979; and Newsom, 1975). We make special mention of a procedure presented by van Nunen and Wessels (1978) because it involves a conceptual approach very different from that of the above described heuristic. The latter builds up an initial feasible schedule with possible subsequent attempts at improvement. The van Nunen and Wessels approach is to first ignore the capacity restrictions and solve each individual item problem independently. The resulting overall solution is usually infeasible, violating one or more of the production capacities. The next step is to adjust the solution until it is feasible with as small as possible an increase in the costs. (Karni and Roll, 1982, adopt much the same approach.)

15.3 COPING WITH UNCERTAINTY IN THE SHORT RUN

As seen from Eq. 15.6 the Hax-Meal procedure copes with uncertainty in demand in two ways when scheduling individual-item run quantities: (1) safety stocks are used and (2) the current stock status is taken into account.

For the case of *stationary* (that is, an average that does not vary with time), but probabilistic, demand patterns Vergin and Lee (1978), expanding on the earlier work of Magee and Boodman (1967), use simulation to test several different decision rules for deciding when to switch production from one item to another when several items are competing for limited production capacity. They treat the case where setup costs (and times) are *not* dependent on the sequence of production. Costs considered are those of setups, carrying inventory, and shortages (the latter assumed proportional to the number of units backordered or lost).

Vergin and Lee test several possible control strategies, three of which are of particular interest to us.

Strategy 1 This method involves the use of a deterministic cycling model, a strategy first proposed by Buffa (1968). All items are produced exactly once on each cycle and the cycle is of duration T. Backorder costs are incorporated only through a deterministic model that assumes level demand and deliberate backordering to a cost-minimizing level (analogous with Problem 5.5 of Chapter 5).[6] Under such circumstances the best T value is given by

$$T = \sqrt{\frac{2\sum_{i=1}^{n} A_i}{\sum_{i=1}^{n} D_i v_i (1 - D_i/m_i)} \cdot \frac{B_3 + r}{B_3 r}} \tag{15.14}$$

with

$$Q_i = D_i T \tag{15.15}$$

where

D_i = demand rate of item i

m_i = production rate of item i

A_i = setup cost of item i

---

[6] A more appropriate model, not tested by Vergin and Lee, would incorporate

1. The possibility of some items not being produced on every cycle (see Section 11.2 of Chapter 11).
2. The calculation of safety stocks based on the standard deviation of forecast errors.

v_i = unit variable cost of item i

B_3 = cost per unit backordered of an item per unit time expressed as a fraction of its unit variable cost

r = carrying charge

Strategy 2 This strategy was suggested by Magee and Boodman. Under a deterministic model, similar to that above, but ignoring backorders, the maximum inventory level of item j, as a proportion of the total average inventory of all items, is given by

$$p_j = \frac{2D_j(1 - D_j/m_j)}{\sum_{i=1}^{n} D_i(1 - D_i/m_i)} \tag{15.16}$$

Because of the uncertainty caused by forecast errors, rather than using the Q's of Eq. 15.15 together with safety stocks, Magee and Boodman suggest short-run control in the following fashion. Production of an individual item j is continued until one of two conditions results: (1) the inventory of some other item runs out, or (2) the inventory of item j builds up to a proportion p_j of the total on-hand inventory. At this point production is shifted to the item that has the smallest remaining time supply of inventory.

Strategy 3 This strategy was developed by Vergin and Lee. If the capacity of the production facility involved exceeds the total average demand, then use of the Magee and Boodman strategy can lead to total inventory increasing indefinitely. Thus, Vergin and Lee suggest the following variation (also recognizing that the usual implementation will be on a periodic review basis). In addition to condition 2 specified in the paragraph above, production of item j is stopped if its actual inventory level reaches an established maximum value (for example, the Q_i value of Eq. 15.15 plus a suitable safety stock). Production is switched to the item having the smallest remaining time supply (recognizing that backorders represent a negative time supply), but if the level of this item is already at or above its specified maximum level, then no production occurs for at least one review period.

Extensive tests show that Strategy 3 outperforms Strategy 2 which, in turn, is much better than Strategy 1. However, it would be interesting to see the improvement in Strategy 1 that would result from the modifications suggested in footnote 6.

15.4 SUMMARY

In this chapter we have addressed the capacity-oriented situation of a bottleneck operation. The pragmatic hierarchical planning system of Hax and Meal was presented at length, followed by a discussion of other decision rules for allocating limited capacity among the competing items. In the next chapter we turn to a different type of situation—namely, where our primary concern is with the coordination of materials (raw materials, components, subassemblies, etc.) in the short run.

PROBLEMS

15.1 Formulate a linear programming model of the seasonal planning problem discussed in Section 15.1.1. How would the answer compare with that obtained by the Land algorithm? What about the relative computational efforts?

15.2 For the same company (that is, the same cost structure and maximum amount of overtime) as that in Section 15.1.1, prepare a master production plan for another plant in the context of the information given in Table 15.9.

TABLE 15.9

	Demand		Inventory at End of t		Minimum Inventory at t		Maximum Inventory at t		Available R/T	
Month	Type 1	Type 2	Type 1	Type 2	Type 1	Type 2	Type 1	Type 2	Type 1	Type 2
0			18,850	15,250						
1	18,600	9,700			8,850	3,800	25,000	10,000	11,180	8,600
2	18,000	6,740			8,850	3,000	25,000	10,000	10,660	8,200
3	16,500	6,500			8,850	3,000	25,000	8,000	11,700	9,000
4	13,500	5,000			8,850	3,000	25,000	8,000	11,700	9,000
5	13,500	4,000			8,850	3,000	25,000	8,000	11,700	9,000
6	15,000	6,000			8,850	3,000	20,000	8,000	11,180	8,600
7	9,000	8,500			4,500	3,000	15,000	10,000	6,890	5,300
8	7,500	8,500			4,500	3,000	15,000	15,000	11,180	8,600
9	10,500	10,500			4,500	5,000	20,000	20,000	11,700	9,000
10	12,000	15,000			8,850	8,000	25,000	25,000	11,180	8,600
11	13,000	20,000			10,000	10,000	30,000	20,000	11,180	8,600
12	13,500	13,800			12,000	7,000	30,000	15,000	10,140	7,800
Totals	160,600	114,240							130,390	100,300

The economic order quantities and the overstock limits are as follows:

Type	Family i	s.k.u. j	Q_{ij}	I_{ij1}
1	1	1	6,450	10,600
		2	460	2,300
		3	9,400	10,000
		4	6,600	11,000
		5	10,600	14,000
	3	9	6,500	21,100
		10	3,400	19,600
2	4	11	8,000	13,300
		12	3,850	11,400
		13	2,250	4,500
		14	3,450	6,000

15.3 Using your answer to Problem 15.2 and the procedures described in Section 15.1.2, compute the family run quantities for the plant under consideration, assuming the inventory status at the beginning of month 1, shown in Table 15.10.

TABLE 15.10

Type	Family i	s.k.u. j	Available Stock I_{ij1}	Safety Stock SS_{ij}	Forecast Month 1
1	1	1	2,100	700	2,000
		2	650	200	400
		3	1,400	500	1,200
		4	3,500	1,000	2,000
		5	200	1,200	2,500
	3	9	4,300	2,250	4,500
		10	6,700	3,000	6,000
		Subtotals	18,850	8,850	18,600
2	4	11	6,100	1,500	4,000
		12	5,700	1,400	3,500
		13	250	500	1,200
		14	3,200	400	1,000
		Subtotals	15,250	3,800	9,700

15.4 Using your results from Problems 15.2 and 15.3, as well as the procedures described in Section 15.1.3, prepare an individual-item schedule for all s.k.u. to be manufactured at the plant in month 1.

15.5 Prove that Eq. 15.6 does, indeed, give equal run-out times.

15.6 When the market turns down, the usual North American response has been to layoff workers, thus reducing capacity. Suppose instead that the same number of workers were retained. What could be done, in terms of setups and inventory levels, with the associated excess capacity? What about the same questions related to an upturn in the market?

15.7 Consider the following three-product, four-period problem:

Item i	Setup Cost A_i	Holding Cost $h_i = v_i r$	Capacity Absorption Rate k_i
1	5	.10	1
2	25	.03	1
3	75	.01	1

Item i	Demand in Period 1	2	3	4
1	0	147	0	514
2	103	179	257	197
3	231	260	874	199
Capacity	800	800	700	700

Attempt to find the timing and sizes of lots of the three items to keep costs as low as possible without any backorders, while staying within the capacity constraints. Assume, as in Section 15.2.2, that demand can be satisfied by production within the same period.

15.8 An issue of strategic importance is the level of product variety offered to customers (that is, the number and types of options offered). Discuss how the material of Section 15.2 could be useful in helping determine the capacity and cost implications of different levels of variety.

15.9 For the following three-item problem, compute the p_j's and maximum absolute inventory levels for the Vergin-Lee switching procedure discussed in Section 15.3.

Item i	D_i (units/yr)	v_i (\$/unit)	A_i (\$)	m_i (units/yr)
1	1000	10.00	20	2000
2	500	5.00	20	2000
3	200	20.00	15	2000

Assume $B_3 = 0.8$/yr and $r = 0.2$/yr.

REFERENCES

Bartholdi, J., and A. S. Rosenthal (1979). "Periodic Scheduling of a Material Handling System." *Proceedings of the IEEE Conference on Decision and Control*, pp. 548–552.

Bishop, J. (1979). "Integrating Critical Elements of Production Planning." *Harvard Business Review*, Vol. 57, No. 5, pp. 154–160.

Bitran, G. R., E. A. Haas, and A. C. Hax (1981). "Hierarchical Production Planning: A Single Stage System." *Operations Research*, Vol. 29, No. 4, pp. 717–743.

Bitran, G. R., and A. C. Hax (1977). "On the Design of Hierarchical Production Planning Systems." *Decision Sciences*, Vol. 8, No. 1, pp. 28–55.

Bitran, G. R., and H. H. Yanasse (1982). "Computational Complexity of the Capacitated Lot Size Problem." *Management Science*, Vol. 28, No. 10, pp. 1174–1186.

Boctor, F. F. (1982). "The Two-Product, Single-Machine, Static Demand, Infinite Horizon Lot Scheduling Problem." *Management Science*, Vol. 28, No. 7, pp. 798–807.

Bolander, S. F., R. C. Heard, S. M. Seward, and S. G. Taylor (1981). *Manufacturing Planning and Control in Process Industries*. American Production and Inventory Control Society, Falls Church, Virginia, p. 132.

Bolander, S., and S. Taylor (1983). "Time Phased Forward Scheduling: A Capacity Dominated Scheduling Technique." *Production and Inventory Management*, Vol. 24, No. 1, pp. 83–97.

Buffa, E. S. (1968). *Operations Management*, John Wiley & Sons, New York, pp. 490–495.

Delporte, C., and L. J. Thomas (1977). "Lot Sizing and Sequencing for *N* Products on One Facility." *Management Science*, Vol. 23, No. 10, pp. 1070–1079.

Dixon, P. S. (1979). "Multi-Item Lot-Sizing with Limited Capacity." Unpublished Doctoral Dissertation, Department of Management Sciences, University of Waterloo, Waterloo, Ontario, Canada.

Dixon, P. S., and E. A. Silver (1981). "A Heuristic Solution Procedure for the Multi-Item, Single-Level, Limited Capacity, Lot-Sizing Problem." *Journal of Operations Management*, Vol. 2, No. 1, pp. 23–40.

Dogramaci, A., J. C. Panayiotopoulos, and N. R. Adam (1981). "The Dynamic Lot-Sizing Problem for Multiple Items under Limited Capacity." *AIIE Transactions*, Vol. 13, No. 4, pp. 295–303.

Duersch, R. R., and D. B. Wheeler (1981). "An Interactive Scheduling Model for Assembly-Line Manufacturing." *International Journal of Modelling and Simulation*, Vol. 1, No. 3, pp. 241–245.

Eisenhut, P. S. (1975). "A Dynamic Lot-Sizing Algorithm with Capacity Constraints." *AIIE Transactions*, Vol. 7, No. 2, pp. 170–176.

Elmaghraby, S. (1978). "The Economic Lot Scheduling Problem (ELSP): Review and Extensions." *Management Science*, Vol. 24, No. 6, pp. 587–598.

Florian, M., and M. Klein (1971). "Deterministic Production Planning with Concave Costs and Capacity Constraints." *Management Science*, Vol. 18, No. 1, pp. 12–20.

Florian, M., J. K. Lenstra, and A. M. G. Rinnooy Kan (1980). "Deterministic Production Planning: Algorithm and Complexity." *Management Science*, Vol. 26, No. 7, pp. 669–679.

Gabbay, H. (1976). "A Hierarchical Approach to Production Planning." Unpublished Doctoral Dissertation, Operations Research Center, Massachusetts Institute of Technology, Cambridge, Massachusetts.

Geoffrion, A., and G. Graves (1976). "Scheduling Parallel Production Lines with Changeover Costs: Practical Application of a Quadratic Assignment/LP Approach." *Operations Research*, Vol. 24, No. 4, pp. 595–610.

Graves, S. C. (1981). "A Review of Production Scheduling." *Operations Research*, Vol. 29, No. 4, pp. 646–675.

Graves, S. C. (1982). "Using Lagrangian Techniques to Solve Hierarchical Production Planning Problems." *Management Science*, Vol. 28, No. 3, pp. 260–275.

Graves, S. C., and R. W. Haessler (1978). "On Production Runs for Multiple Products: The Two Product Heuristic." *Management Science*, Vol. 22, No. 11, pp. 1194–1196.

Hax, A. C., and H. C. Meal (1975). "Hierarchical Integration of Production Planning and Scheduling." In *Logistics* (M. A. Geisler, Editor), Studies in Management Sciences, Vol. 1, North-Holland, Amsterdam and American Elsevier, New York, pp. 53–69.

Hsu, W. L. (1983). "On the General Feasibility Test of Scheduling Lot Sizes for Several Products on One Machine." *Management Science*, Vol. 29, No. 1, pp. 93–105.

Karni, R., and Y. Roll (1982). "A Heuristic Algorithm for the Multi-Item Lot-Sizing Problem with Capacity Constraints." *IIE Transactions*, Vol. 14, No. 4, pp. 249–256.

Lambert, A. M., and H. Luss (1982). "Production Planning with Time-Dependent Capacity Bounds." *European Journal of Operational Research*, Vol. 9, pp. 275–280.

Lambrecht, M., and H. Vanderveken (1979). "Heuristic Procedures for the Single Operation, Multi-Item Loading Problem." *AIIE Transactions*, Vol. 11, No. 4, pp. 319–326.

Magee, J. F., and D. M. Boodman (1967). *Production Planning and Inventory Control*, Second Edition. McGraw-Hill, New York, pp. 150–152.

McClain, J. O., and L. J. Thomas (1980). *Operations Management: Production of Goods and Services*. Prentice-Hall, Englewood Cliffs, New Jersey.

Meal, H. C., M. H. Wachter, and D. C. Whybark (1982). "Material Requirements Planning in Hierarchical Planning Systems." *Working Paper 2*, IMEDE Management Development Institute, Lausanne, Switzerland.

Newsom, E. F. P. (1975). "Multi-Item Lot Size Scheduling by Heuristic Part I: With Fixed Resources." *Management Science*, Vol. 21, No. 10, pp. 1186–1193.

Rhodes, P. (1977). "A Paint Industry Production Planning and Smoothing System." *Production and Inventory Management*, Vol. 18, No. 4, pp. 17–29.

Saipe, A. (1977). "Production Runs for Multiple Products: The Two-Product Heuristic." *Management Science*, Vol. 23, No. 12, pp. 1321–1327.

Senju, S., and S. Fujita (1980). "An Applied Procedure for Determining the Economic Lot Sizes of Multiple Products." *Decision Sciences*, Vol. 11, No. 3, pp. 503–513.

van Beek, P. (1977). "An Application of Dynamic Programming and the HMMS Rule on Two-Level Production Control." *Zeitschrift für Operations Research*, Band 21, pp. B133–B141.

van Nunen, J. A. E. E., and J. Wessels (1978). "Multi-Item Lot Size Determination and Scheduling under Capacity Constraints." *European Journal of Operational Research*, Vol. 2, No. 1, pp. 36–41.

Van Wassenhove, L. N., and M. A. De Bodt (1983). "Capacitated Lot Sizing for Injection Molding: A Case Study." *Journal of the Operational Research Society*, Vol. 34, No. 6, pp. 489–501.

Van Wassenhove, L. N., and P. Vanderhenst (1983). "Planning Production in a Bottleneck Department: A Case Study." *European Journal of Operational Research*, Vol. 12, pp. 127–137.

Vemuganti, R. R. (1978). "On the Feasibility of Scheduling Lot Sizes for Two Products on One Machine." *Management Science*, Vol. 24, No. 15, pp. 1668–1673.

Vergin, R. C., and T. N. Lee (1978). "Scheduling Rules for the Multiple Product Single Machine System with Stochastic Demand." *INFOR*, Vol. 16, No. 1, pp. 64–73.

Wilson, G. T. (1978). "Seasonal Production Planning for Several Products Whose Storage Costs Differ." *Production and Inventory Management*, Vol. 19, No. 1, pp. 49–62.

Case F

MIDAS CANADA CORPORATION*

INTER-OFFICE MEMORANDUM (TRANSLATED FROM GERMAN)

To: Mr. Wolfgang Gatzke, Manager of Manufacturing, MIDAS International
From: Mr. Otto Felker, Vice-President of Operations, MIDAS International
Topic: Inventory Control in the Manufacturing of Film Processors

I have recently received feedback from two individuals. Mr. Klaus Reiner, Vice-President of Marketing, informs me that most promised due dates for customer deliveries are not being met. In fact, he states: "The only way we can get something delivered anywhere near the promised date is to expedite like crazy." At the same time, Mr. Dieter Schwaban, the Comptroller, states that raw material and in-process inventories have increased markedly in the past year. How is it possible that simultaneously customer service is decreasing while inventories are rising?

I have scanned the shift reports of a number of production foremen. Perhaps some of their typical comments may provide some insight:

We don't seem to ever know our needs in terms of components. For example, there were 50 units of the wash tank for the assembly W53688 in inventory for several months. This week, when we finally received an order release for assembling the tanks into the larger processing units, 75 of them were needed!

Production order V7145 could not be completed today. As usual, one of the five needed components was out of stock.

Production was below standard because a rush order forced us to tear down lot V7286 which was partially completed.

These order quantities and reorder points, based on mathematics, are useless! I don't care what they suggest. This week I needed components for the assembly of 30 tube and pivot assemblies and I won't need any more for several weeks as no further assemblies are planned in that period.

Didn't you state at the last scheduling meeting that we now had item inventory records on the computer and that forecasting procedures for usage of each component item had been developed? Clearly, something is wrong with the procedures.

*The MIDAS cases describe actual decision systems that are based on the consulting experiences of the authors. They do not describe the situation at any single company, but are in fact a compendium of actual situations that have been compressed into the environment of a single firm and industry for illustrative purposes. The cases are not intended as presentations of either effective or ineffective ways of handling administrative problems.

Are they appropriate for our type of manufacturing environment? In particular, I recall that Rudy Ertle, who attended an international meeting of a production and inventory control society last year, was enthusiastic about an approach (MPR, MRP, PMR or something like that) that he thought was particularly well suited for our situation. I suggest that you talk with Rudy.

CHAPTER 16

Production Planning, Scheduling, and Control in Materials/Labor-Oriented Fabrication/Assembly Situations

In the previous chapter we were primarily concerned with the effective use of capacity at a bottleneck production operation. Now we turn to a different situation—namely, one in which the overriding concern is with the coordination of materials at the various stages of the production process. The concept of dependent demand, introduced in the nonproduction, multiechelon context of Chapter 12, is vital here, in that the demand for components and raw materials is, to a large extent, determined when production schedules are established for parent items in which these materials are used. For example, in the assembly of automobiles the requirements of a certain type of engine are known accurately when the assembly schedules of automobiles, in which the engine is used, are specified.

In Section 16.1, the complexity of multistage fabrication/assembly manufacturing is discussed. Historically, in such contexts, many organizations have attempted to use the types of replenishment systems discussed earlier in the text (for example, in Chapters 5 to 7). Section 16.2 addresses the weaknesses of such an approach. Next, in Section 16.3 we review Closed Loop, Material Requirements Planning (MRP), a planning and control system encompassed in the decision framework introduced in Chapter 13. The details of the material planning, central component of this system are laid out in Section 16.4. Another key element, capacity requirements planning, is presented in Section 16.5. Section 16.6 is concerned with the conceptual extension of MRP to distribution. Finally, in Section 16.7 we comment on the production/inventory control aspects of "Just-In-Time Manufacturing" and its relationship to MRP.

16.1 THE COMPLEXITY OF MULTISTAGE FABRICATION/ASSEMBLY MANUFACTURING

Let us consider a manufacturing facility with a number of different work centers or stations. To achieve each finished product (in the form of an assembly of several components), processing through several of these centers is required. Inventories can exist in the following forms:

1. Raw materials
2. Work-in-process raw materials to component parts
3. Component parts
4. Work-in-process component parts to subassemblies
5. Subassemblies
6. Work-in-process subassemblies to assemblies
7. Assemblies

As mentioned earlier, the requirements through time of a particular component are influenced (in fact, primarily dictated) by the production schedules of the next (closer-to-the-end-items) level of components in which this element is used; that is, there are complicated interactions between the production schedules (and associated inventories) of the various level items. Furthermore, relatively smooth demand for end products can produce erratic requirements through time for a particular component because of the batching of assemblies, subassemblies, etc. This is illustrated in the example of Table 16.1, where the same subassembly *A* is used in three different assemblies. Notice that the end usage of each assembly is uniform with time, yet the requirements for subassembly *A* are

TABLE 16.1 An Illustration of Erratic Requirements for a Subassembly[a]

Time Period	1	2	3	4	5	6	7	8	9	10
Assembly *X*										
Demand	10	10	10	10	10	10	10	10	10	10
Production	30	—	—	30	—	—	30	—	—	30
Assembly *Y*										
Demand	5	5	5	5	5	5	5	5	5	5
Production	20	—	—	—	20	—	—	—	20	—
Assembly *Z*										
Demand	7	7	7	7	7	7	7	7	7	7
Production	14	—	14	—	14	—	14	—	14	—
Subassembly *A*										
Requirements	64	—	14	30	34	—	44	—	34	30

[a]Each of assemblies *X*, *Y*, *Z* requires one unit of subassembly *A*. For simplicity, we assume negligible assembly times.

highly erratic with time because the assemblies (for setup cost reasons) are made in lots covering more than a single period of demand.

An added complexity in a manufacturing environment is the frequent need for many components to achieve a single finished item. Inadequate supplies of any of the components will lead to delays as well as excess in-process stock of the other components. To make matters worse, there are capacity constraints at the work centers (only so many machine-hours of production can be achieved at a particular work center in a shift of operation).

The cost components involved include setup and value added costs at machine centers (or replenishment costs for raw materials), inventory carrying costs, production overtime costs, shortage costs, and system control costs. Ideally, given forecasts of usage of end-items by time period, one would like to establish production run (purchase) quantities through time at the various levels of manufacturing to keep the total relevant costs as low as possible, while not violating any of the constraints. The problem is not static in nature; there are likely to be many short-run changes such as alterations in customer orders, machine breakdowns, quality rejections, and so forth. With the current state of the art, an "optimal" solution to this complex problem is out of the question. Instead, the best we can hope for is a feasible solution that produces reasonable costs. This is the philosophy underlying the Closed Loop, Material Requirements Planning system to be discussed later in this chapter. However, before that discussion, we now emphasize the weaknesses of using traditional replenishment systems in a manufacturing environment.

16.2 THE WEAKNESSES OF TRADITIONAL REPLENISHMENT SYSTEMS IN A MANUFACTURING SETTING

By "traditional replenishment" we mean decision rules, discussed earlier in this book, whereby the timing and sizes of orders of each item are determined *independently*, in particular under the assumption of statistically independent demand for each item. The weaknesses of such an approach in a fabrication/assembly environment include the following.

1. There is no need to statistically forecast the requirements of a component. Once the production plans for all items in which it is used have been established, then the requirements of the component follow, as *dependent* demand, by simple arithmetic. (This is illustrated by the example of Table 16.1).

2. The procedures for establishing safety stocks are usually based on reasonably smooth demand. As discussed above (and illustrated in Table 16.1), this is usually unrealistic in the case of component items.

3. Traditional, replenishment systems are geared to replenish stocks immediately following large demands that drive inventories to low levels. Again, in an erratic demand situation, a large demand may be followed by several *known* periods of inactivity. In such a situation it makes no sense to immediately replenish the stock—unnecessary carrying costs would be incurred by such an action.

4. Where several components are needed for a single assembly, the inventories of these individual components should not be treated in isolation. To illustrate, consider the case where 20 different components are required for a particular assembly. Suppose, under *independent* control of the components, that for each component there is a 95 percent chance that it is in stock. Then the probability of being able to build a complete assembly is only $(0.95)^{20}$ or 0.36; that is, 64 percent of the time at least one of the components would be unavailable, thus delaying the completion of an assembly.

16.3 CLOSED LOOP, MATERIAL REQUIREMENTS PLANNING

This topic was already covered to a large extent in the production decision-making framework of Section 13.2.3 of Chapter 13. For convenience, Figure 16.1 is a repetition of the major portion of Figure 13.1 that is normally considered as Closed Loop, Material Requirements Planning (MRP).

Aggregate production planning (Block 1) was treated in detail in Chapter 14, but one added difficulty in a fabrication/assembly context is deciding for which work center the planning should be done, since, in the shorter run, capacity difficulties could crop up at other work centers. A similar dilemma will be mentioned with respect to master production scheduling. In the current chapter (Sections 16.4 and 16.5) we concentrate on material planning (Block 7) and capacity planning (Block 8). Other than the following brief comments on master production scheduling (Block 5) as it particularly relates to Closed Loop MRP, we do not say anything further about the other components of Figure 16.1. In this regard, the reader is encouraged to review Section 13.2.3 of Chapter 13 at this stage.

Master production scheduling is a complex task in an MRP fabrication/assembly setting. For one thing, the bottleneck work center can shift depending on the changing nature of the work load and the labor force available in the short run. Thus, what appears on the surface to be a feasible master schedule may not be so when the detailed, implied needs at other production (and procurement) stages are worked out. Thus, although some of the bottleneck scheduling decision rules of Section 15.2 of Chapter 15 may be of assistance in master scheduling, a trial-and-error component, as well as some negotiation, will almost certainly be required.

There are a number of excellent writings on MRP (see, for example, New, 1974b; Orlicky, 1975; Smith, 1978; and Wight, 1981). Moreover the American Production and Inventory Control Society has several study guides on the topic. In addition, several software packages are commercially available (see Bourke, 1980). Thus we have chosen to omit some of the finer details in our discussion.

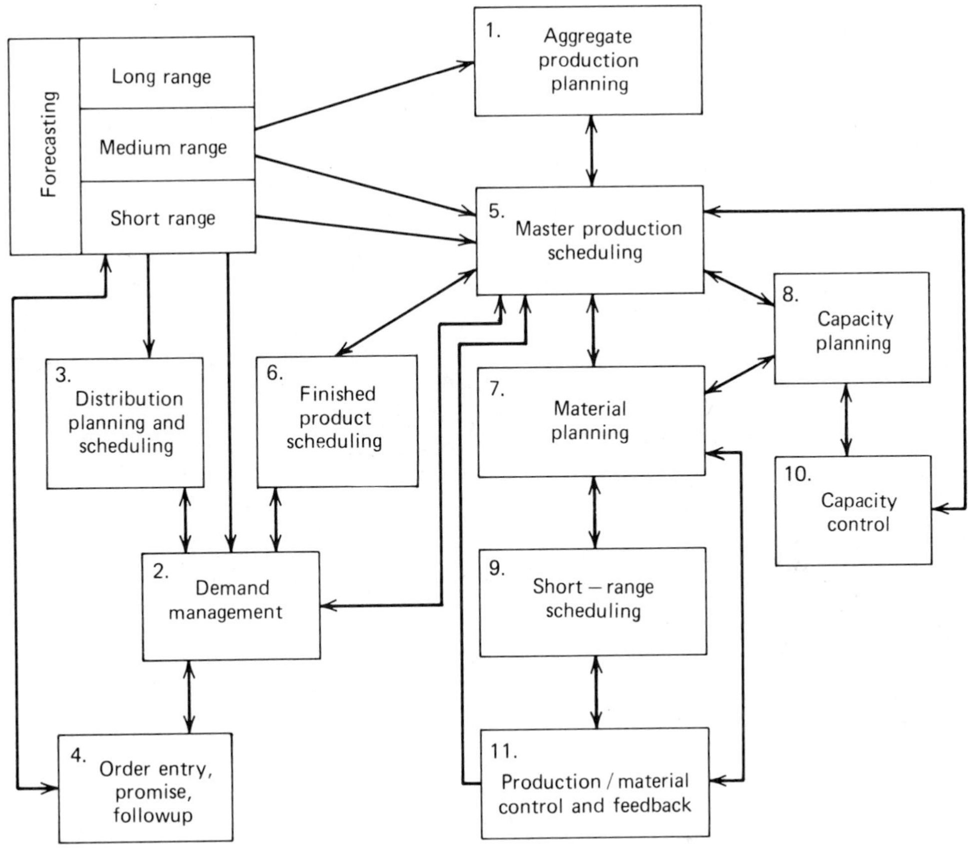

FIGURE 16.1 Closed Loop Material Requirements Planning

In summary, Closed Loop MRP is a system for generating reasonable feasible solutions to the complex problem of planning, scheduling, and controlling production/procurement in a dynamically changing, fabrication/assembly situation.

16.4 MATERIAL REQUIREMENTS PLANNING

To review from Chapter 13, material requirements planning (or simply materials planning) takes the master production schedule and explodes it into implied, detailed production/procurement schedules (timing and quantities) of all components and raw materials. This includes scheduling alterations (cancellations, adjustments in delivery dates, etc.) caused by changes in various conditions such as customer order sizes, quality difficulties, and so on. Because of the large amount of data handling involved, a computer-based system is essential. As was discussed in Chapter 13, master scheduling need not necessarily be done at the end-item level. In such a case, in addition to material requirements planning, one must use finished product scheduling for the processing stages from the master schedule level to the finished products level.

16.4.1 Some Important Terminology

Before describing the MRP approach, it is first necessary to discuss some concepts that will be utilized in our description.

Bill of Materials

To properly take account of the dependent nature of demand we must have a means of projecting the needs, in terms of components, for a production lot of a particular assembly or subassembly. The bill of materials helps us achieve this goal. In the so-called *modular form*, which we utilize, a bill of materials for a particular inventory item (termed the *parent*) shows all of its *immediate* components and their numbers per unit of the parent. This is illustrated in Figure 16.2 for the dryer roll assembly (which is itself only a rather minor component of

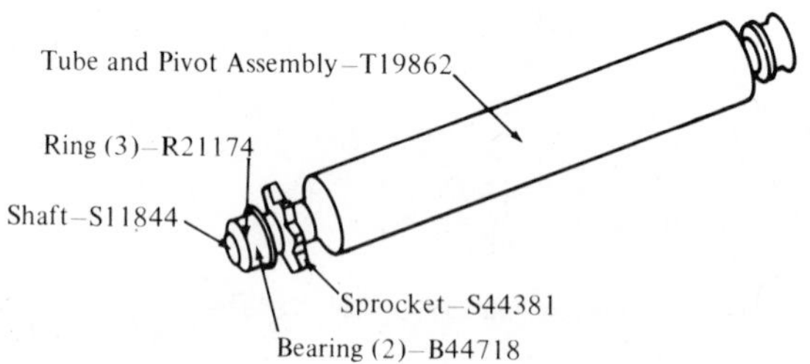

Bill of Materials:

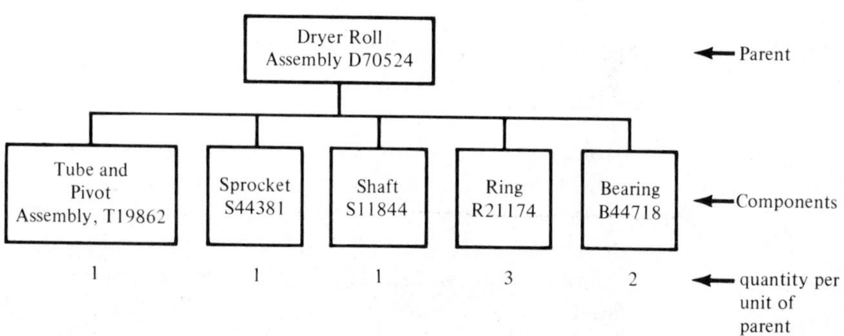

FIGURE 16.2 The Dryer Roll Assembly of an Automatic Film Processor

several options of MIDAS International's automatic film processors). The meaning of the word *immediate* becomes clear when it is seen that in Figure 16.2 we do not subdivide the tube and pivot assembly, T19862, into its components. This would be done on a separate modular bill of materials for that item.

Where there is a wide diversity of end-items (because of a number of optional choices available to the customer), one would not bother to develop a bill of materials for each end-item; instead, the first level would be that of the major subassemblies. This is completely analogous with master scheduling the major subassemblies instead of the end-items.

It will be convenient to illustrate a second common form of the bill of material after we introduce the concept of *level coding*. There are also other, less common types of bills of materials that are used for special purposes, such as phasing in an engineering replacement for an existing item (see Chapter 13 of Wight, 1981).

Level Coding

To provide a systematic framework for exploding back the implications on all components of a given master production schedule, it is convenient to use a particular method of coding the individual s.k.u. Each item (or equivalently, its bill of materials) is assigned a level code according to the following logic:

Level 0 A finished product (or end-item) not used as a component of any other product.

Level 1 The most removed (from the ultimate consumer) level of usage of the item under consideration is as a direct component of a level 0 item. At the same time, the level 1 item could also be a finished product in itself. To illustrate, consider the example of an automobile and tires. A particular type of tire could be sold as a finished product in its own right. However, if it was used as as direct component in the manufacture of one or more types of level 0 automobiles, it would be classified as a level 1 item.

Level 2 The most removed (from the ultimate consumer) level of usage is as a direct component of a level 1 item. Again, as shown by the dotted lines in Figure 16.3, a level 2 item could be used as a direct component of a level 0 item or could even itself be a finished product.

. .
. .
. .

Level n The most removed level of usage is as a direct component of a level $(n - 1)$ item, that is, as a component on a bill of materials with level code $(n - 1)$.

This coding process is continued all the way back to raw materials, which are themselves given appropriate level codes. It is seen that the level coding is equivalent with the concept of indentures used in Chapter 12 when describing multiechelon inventory systems involving repairable items.

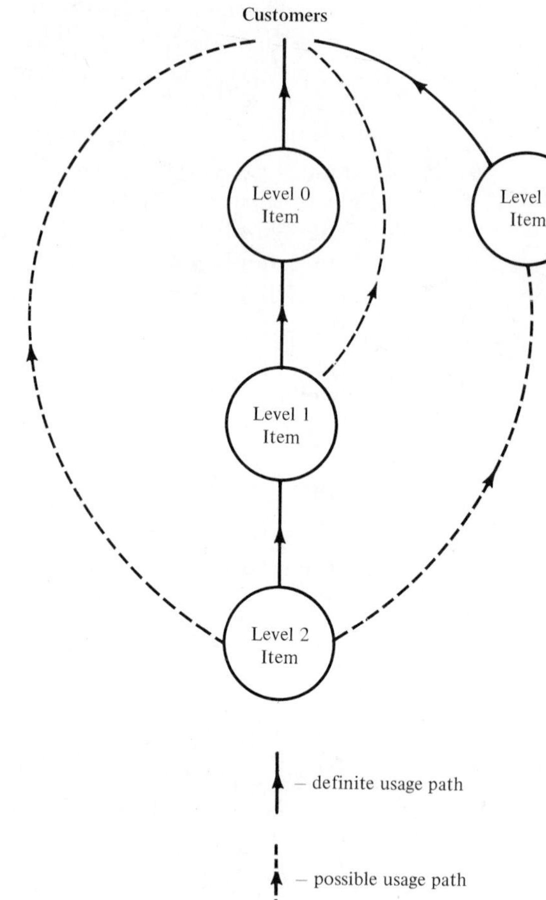

FIGURE 16.3 Level Coding

Figure 16.4 illustrates a portion (only a small fraction of the components are shown) of the coding for one particular model of MIDAS' automatic film processors. Note the position of the dryer roll assembly (of Figure 16.2) which, incidentally, is also used to satisfy direct demand as a service part.

The example of Figure 16.4 provides an opportunity to show the so-called *indented form* of a bill of materials. For the film processor example, it is illustrated in Table 16.2 (some further detail has been taken from Figure 16.2). It shows all of the components right back to raw materials, and there is a one-to-one correspondence between the indentation and the level code.

Lead Times (Offsetting)

This concept was already introduced in Section 12.5.1 of Chapter 12 when we dealt with multiechelon inventory systems. The manufacturing operation

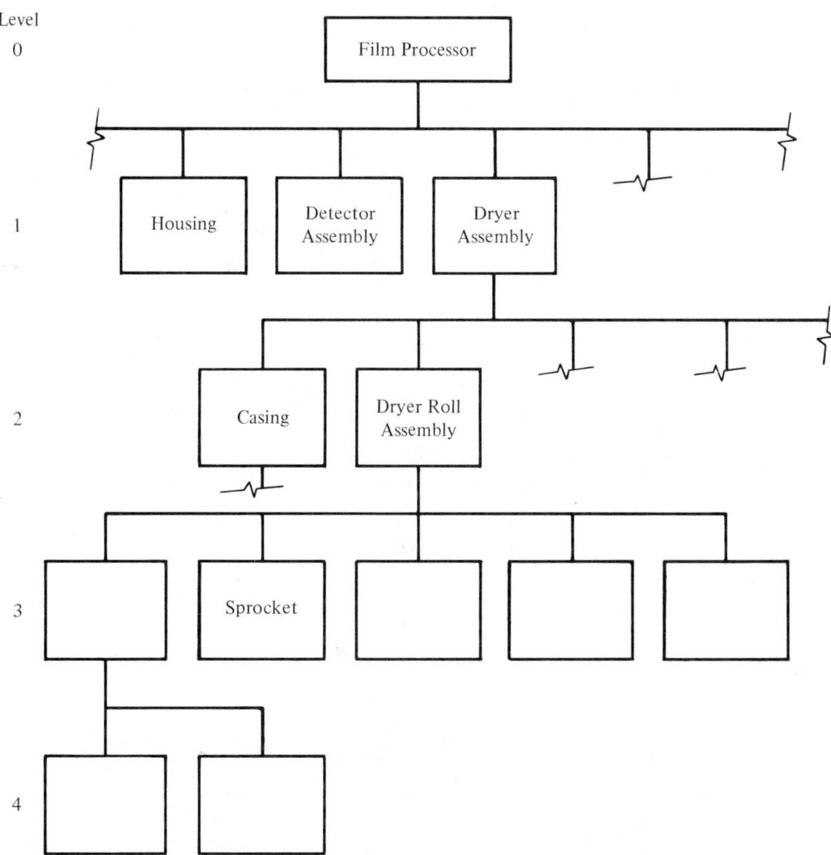

FIGURE 16.4 A Portion of the Level-by-Level Coding for a MIDAS Automatic Film Processor

represented by a particular bill of materials, for example, combining components B and C in a complicated machining activity to produce subassembly A, may require a considerable length of time, particularly when one recognizes that such operations tend to be performed on batches of items and these batches compete with other orders for the use of a particular machine. In such a case, if certain requirements of item A are specified for a particular date (the due date), then we must properly offset (or phase in time) the order release date for the machining operation; in other words, the corresponding units of parts B and C must be available at a suitably earlier time, recognizing the waiting and processing time at the particular operation. The waiting time varies with the shop load and is quite difficult to estimate on a timely basis (see Hoyt, 1978). To illustrate, suppose that the dryer assembly (Figure 16.4) operation is performed in a batch size such that approximately one week (under current shop conditions) is required from order release to completion date. Therefore, if 100 dryer assemblies were required by, for example, June 26, then 100 of the components—

TABLE 16.2 Indented Bill of Materials for the Film Processor

Part Number	Description
	Housing
	Detector assembly
	Dryer assembly
D70524	Casing
T19862	Dryer roll assembly
	Tube and pivot assembly
	x x x
	x x x
S44381	Sprocket
S11844	Shaft
R21174	Ring (3)
B44718	Bearing (2)
	x x x
	.
	.
	.
	x x x
	.
	.
	.
	x x x
	.
	.
	.

Note: The x's represent items not named in Figure 16.4.

namely, the casing, dryer roll assembly, etc.—would be needed by June 19. (In actuality one might be able to start assembling the 100 dryer units before all 100 of each of the components were available.) In the case of a raw material, the lead time (offset) is the time that elapses from when we decide to send the purchase order until the moment when the material is physically present for the first processing operation.

Routing

For each item that could appear on the master schedule, the routing shows the sequence of production operations (and associated work centers) and the standard hours for each operation. The routings are essential for the capacity planning activity to be discussed in Section 16.5.

16.4.2 Information Required for MRP

To carry out material requirements planning, the following input information is essential:

1. The master production schedule projected out to the planning horizon.
2. The inventory status of each item (including possible backorders). Accurate stock status information is essential because MRP, in contrast with traditional replenishment systems, establishes the timing of replenishments to keep inventories as low as possible; thus, errors in stock status can cause severe problems. In many companies utilizing MRP it has been found appropriate to physically hold stocks in limited access stores. Also, regular physical counts to verify records are necessary (this latter point will be discussed further in Chapter 17).
3. The timing of and quantities involved in any outstanding or planned replenishment orders.
4. Forecasts (which can be partially or entirely firm customer orders) of demand for each component, *subject to direct customer demand*, by time period out to the planning horizon.
5. All relevants bills of materials and associated level codes.
6. All routings.[1]
7. Production or procurement lead times (offsets) for each operation.
8. Possible scrap (or yield) allowances for some operations (for example, to convert item B to item A we require, because of losses, on the average, 105 units of B to obtain 100 good units of A).

As will be discussed later, additional information may be needed in order to determine the replenishment quantities (lot sizes) for any specific item.

16.4.3 The General Approach of MRP

In this subsection, to provide an overview, we present only an outline of the general approach used in MRP, purposely omitting details that we subsequently discuss in the numerical illustration in the following subsection.

MRP seeks to overcome the weaknesses of traditional replenishment systems in a manufacturing environment, the latter as discussed in Section 16.2. In particular, MRP makes specific use of the dependent nature of demands for components, and it takes account of the time-varying (erratic) nature of the requirements for components. Moreover, the inventories of different components needed for the same operation are coordinated to avoid the situation of a

[1]Routings are only needed in capacity requirements planning (to be treated in Section 16.5).

shortage of one element delaying the operation as well as tying up the other components in inventory.

MRP begins with a master production schedule that provides the timing (order release dates) and quantities of production of all end-items (level 0) on a discrete time basis (normally a 1-week period or *bucket* is used).[2] The product files (bills of materials) indicate the immediate component items and their quantities per unit of each parent item. Thus, a time series of requirements (at each order release date of the level 0 items) is generated for the level 1 items. For each level 1 item one must add to this time series of *dependent* requirements any requirements for externally generated direct independent demand (for example, as service parts). The result is a new series of requirements by time period, known as the *gross requirements*[3] of the item.

Next, for each level 1 item the existing inventory position (quantities on-hand and already on-order) are allocated against the gross requirements to produce a modified series of requirements by time period, known as the *net requirements* of the item. Figure 16.5 shows the graphic relationship among the inventory position, *cumulative* gross requirements, and *cumulative* net requirements for a situation in which there are nonzero gross requirements at the start of periods 1, 2, 4, and 5, and there is an initial on-hand inventory with a replenishment due at the start of period 3. When the dotted line is above the

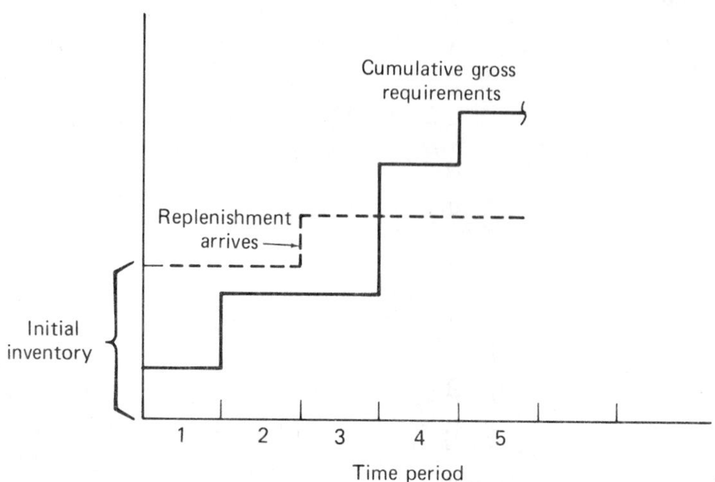

FIGURE 16.5 Cumulative Gross and Net Requirements

---

[2]MRP, in its usual computerized form, requires the handling of scheduling on a discrete time basis, the normal period being one week; that is, requirements and replenishment quantities are shown no finer than on a weekly time basis. Conceptually, as pointed out by Rhodes (1974) one could certainly handle MRP on an event (transaction) basis rather than by the somewhat artificial basis of discrete time slots.

[3]We have already used the concepts of gross and net requirements in Section 12.5.1 of Chapter 12 where we dealt with a nonproduction, multiechelon, dependent demand situation.

solid line in Figure 16.5, there are no positive net requirements; the distance between the lines represents the projected on-hand inventory.[4] However, when the solid line is above the dotted one, the distance between them gives the *cumulative* net requirements.

The next step is to provide appropriate coverage for the net requirements of the level 1 item under consideration by adjusting previously scheduled replenishment actions or by initiating new replenishment actions. In other words, net requirements are covered by planned *receipts* of replenishment lots. When these lots are backed off (offset) over the lead time, such replenishment actions are then known as planned order *releases*. Possible adjustments include:

1. Increasing (or decreasing) a replenishment quantity
2. Advancing (or delaying) the order due date
3. Canceling the order

A new action involves specification of the item involved, the order quantity, the order release date, and the order receipt date.

In selecting the timing and sizes of replenishments, we are faced with a primarily deterministic, time-varying pattern of demands, precisely the situation encountered in Chapter 6. Therefore, the Silver-Meal heuristic (the details are in Section 6.6 of Chapter 6) could certainly be used for selecting the lot sizes. However, quite often a very simple solution (which would be found by the heuristic) is appropriate—namely, to cover each net requirement with a separate replenishment quantity. This type of solution is known as a *lot-for-lot strategy*. It is appropriate when

1. The requirements pattern is very erratic; that is, the only requirements are large occasional quantities, or
2. The production operation involved has a very low setup cost, usually the case in an assembly operation.

We will have more to say about low setup costs and lot-for-lot strategies in Section 16.7. The part-period balancing heuristic (discussed in Section 6.7.2 of Chapter 6) has also been frequently used in MRP systems. Tests by De Bodt and Van Wassenhove (1983) have revealed that the basic *fixed* EOQ can perform surprisingly well when there is considerable uncertainty in the demand pattern. If an analytic procedure such as the EOQ, the Silver-Meal heuristic, or part-period balancing heuristic is used, provision must be made for manual overrides—the scheduler likely possesses information not included in the model; for example, "Georges Roy, the foreman at a particular work center, will never accept a small lot size late in a month." Further discussion on this issue is provided by Rucinski and Woodman (1977). Finally, it should be emphasized that lot-sizing decisions at the level under consideration have ramifications back through *all* the component levels. However, the usual lot-sizing procedures

[4]Equivalently, one could think of this situation as representing negative cumulative net requirements.

consider carrying and setup costs only at the level being scheduled. Thus, at best, a suboptimization is achieved and one should really use multiechelon adjustments in carrying and setup costs, as discussed in Section 12.1 of Chapter 12.

Once coverage is completed for the level 1 item, the associated bill of materials indicates which level 2 items are used as components. The order release dates and quantities of the level 1 item thus imply requirements through time of level 2 items. This is done for all level 1 items. Again, any direct external demand for a level 2 item, as well as any usage as a *direct* component of any level 0 items, must then be included to obtain the gross requirements of that item. These requirements are then netted, covered, and so on.

The above process is continued all the way back to all raw materials which, in turn, have their requirements properly covered by purchasing actions. In summary, for each item we determine gross requirements, net requirements, planned order receipts, and planned order releases. The latter, in turn, contribute to the gross requirements of the item's immediate components. Note that all items having a given level code are processed before any items on the next (higher numbered) level. It is clear that a computer is indispensable for the step-by-step explosion of requirements at the next level implied by each individual-item coverage pattern.

16.4.4 A Numerical Illustration of the MRP Procedure

We use the context of the MIDAS International automatic film processors to illustrate the MRP procedure. Reference is made to the product structure depicted in Figures 16.2 and 16.4. In particular, let us focus in on the dryer roll assembly, D70524. It is used in two different dryer assemblies (D63321 and D63322) which, in turn, appear in several different options of the end-item automatic film processors. Suppose that through the first stages of application of MRP we have arrived at the order release patterns for the two dryer assemblies shown in Table 16.3. These patterns, together with direct external demand, imply the gross requirements pattern for the dryer roll assembly, shown at the bottom of the table. The gross requirement in a period is the total number of units in the order releases of the two parents planned for that period (we can simply take the total here because precisely 1 unit of the component is needed for each unit of either parent) plus any anticipated direct external demand in the period.

Next, net requirements for item D70524 are determined by taking account of any on-hand inventory and any released or planned orders. Suppose that

1. The offset (production lead time) for this item is 1 period.
2. The current on-hand inventory is 10 units and there are no released or planned orders.

Table 16.4 shows the material requirements plan for item D70524. Row 3, the projected net inventory, gives the *cumulative* net requirements when the projected net inventory is *negative*. This is completely consistent with the earlier discussion of Figure 16.5. When there are cumulative requirements in any period (that is, the net inventory is negative), this signifies that the current plan does not adequately provide coverage for the projected needs. Thus, some change is in order.

Since there are net requirements for item D70524 in period 2, an order should be scheduled for receipt in that period. Where the lead time of item D70524 is 1 period, this order should be released in period 1. It might be attractive to order enough to also cover the requirements in later periods (particulary periods 3 and 4). In any event, at least tentative coverage should now be made for all periods

TABLE 16.3 Derivation of Gross Requirements for the Dryer Roll Assembly, D70524[a]

Source	Time Period	1	2	3	4	5	6	7	8
Parent	Dryer assembly, D63321, planned order releases	—	50	—	20	—	40	—	60
Parent	Dryer assembly, D63322, planned order releases	—	—	30	—	—	30	—	—
External	Dryer roll assembly, D70524, direct external demand (dealer requests for spare parts)	—	—	10	—	—	—	10	—
Total	Dryer roll assembly, D70524, gross requirements	—	50	40	20	—	70	10	60

[a]1 unit of D70524 is used in each of D63321 and D63322.

TABLE 16.4 Material Requirements Plan for the Dryer Roll Assembly, D70524
Lead time = 1 period
Order quantity = not fixed[a]

Time Period	0	1	2	3	4	5	6	7	8
1. Projected gross requirements	—	—	50	40	20	—	70	10	60
2. Planned order receipts	—	—	—	—	—	—	—	—	—
3. Projected net inventory[b] at end of period	10	10	−40	−80	−100	−100	−170	−180	−240
4. Planned order releases	—	—	—	—	—	—	—	—	—

[a]Provision is made to have a preestablished, fixed order quantity.

[b]Recall from Chapter 6 that

Net Inventory = (On-hand) − (Backorders)

out to the horizon (here period 8). Suppose that the setup cost for the dryer roll assembly operation is \$7.50, the *added* variable cost at this operation is \$8/unit, and the inventory carrying charge has been set at 0.005 \$/\$/period (if the period was 1 week, this would correspond to an r value of 0.26 \$/\$/yr). If the Silver-Meal heuristic was used, then the logic of Section 6.6.2 of Chapter 6 gives the production schedule (in terms of planned order receipts of assemblies of dryer rolls) shown in Row 2 of Table 16.5, which is the revised material plan for item D70524. With the 1-period lead time the corresponding schedule of order releases is shown in Row 4. Only the order in period 1 would be released, the later quantities are tentative for planning purposes. Neglecting any possible need for safety stock we now see from Row 3 that adequate coverage is provided.

To show one further level of the MRP computations consider the ring item, R21174, used in the assembly of the dryer roll, D70524 (see Figure 16.2). Part of the gross requirements for the ring are implied by the dates and quantities of the order releases for the dryer roll, D70524, shown in the last row of Table 16.5. Recognizing that three rings are required for each dryer roll assembly, the associated ring requirements are shown in the first row of Table 16.6. The rings are used in a number of other assemblies. MRP would first be used to determine

TABLE 16.5 Revised Material Requirements Plan for the Dryer Roll Assembly, D70524
Lead time = 1 period
Order quantity = not fixed

Time Period	0	1	2	3	4	5	6	7	8
1. Projected gross requirements	—	—	50	40	20	—	70	10	60
2. Planned order receipts	—	—	100	—	—	—	80	—	60
3. Projected net inventory at end of period	10	10	60	20	0	0	10	0	0
4. Planned order releases	—	100	—	—	—	80	—	60	—

TABLE 16.6 Determination of Gross Requirements for the Ring, R21174[a]

Source	Time Period	1	2	3	4	5	6	7	8
Parent	Dryer roll assembly, D70524, planned order releases	300	—	—	—	240	—	180	—
Parents	Other dryer roll assemblies, planned order releases	700	500	300	700	300	200	600	100
Total	Gross requirements of the ring	1,000	500	300	700	540	200	780	100

[a]All entries in the table are expressed in terms of rings; for example, where 3 rings are required for 1 dryer roll assembly, D70524, the order release of 100 units of D70524 in period 1 (see Table 16.5) implies 300 rings.

TABLE 16.7 Initial Material Requirements Plan for the Ring, R21174
Lead time = 3 weeks
Order quantity = not fixed

Time Period	0	1	2	3	4	5	6	7	8
1. Projected gross requirements	—	1000	500	300	700	540	200	780	100
2. Planned order receipts	—	—	1100[a]	—	—	700	—	—	—
3. Projected net inventory at end of period	1,200	200	800	500	−200	−40	−240	−1020	−1120
4. Planned order releases	—	—	700	—	—	—	—	—	—

[a]This order was released in period (−1).

the order release patterns of these other assemblies. Suppose this has already been done and the combined order releases, expressed in terms of numbers of rings required, are as shown in the second row of Table 16.6. Assuming that there is no other usage of the rings, then the last row of Table 16.6 provides the gross requirements. These entries become the gross requirements in Row 1 of Table 16.7, which is an initial material requirements plan for item R21174.

Suppose that the purchase lead time is three periods and the current inventory, material on order, and planned purchase orders are as shown in Table 16.7. Then, the resulting projected inventory is as indicated in Row 3 of the table.

In this example there are no net requirements for the first three periods. This is fortunate in that this is the procurement lead time; any net requirements in this period would have required expediting of an outstanding order or a crash new order. There are net requirements in period 4. One simple way of covering these would be to advance the due date of the second order by one period. This means that the order would be released in period 1 instead of period 2. Of course, one would almost certainly increase the size of this order or plan additional future orders to cover the substantial net requirements in the later periods.

16.4.5 The Material Requirements Plan and Its Uses

The material requirements plan provides several types of information of use to management, particularly in a dynamic environment, including alterations in customer demands, scrap output, equipment failures, and so forth. The information includes:

1. Actual and projected inventory status of every item.
2. Listing of released and planned orders by time period—this document is useful for two purposes. First, in a summary form, it is fed back to the aggregate planning stage (discussed in Chapter 14) of a hierarchical planning system. Second, it is a necessary input for detailed capacity requirements planning (to be discussed in Section 16.5).

3. Rescheduling and cancellation notices—these are particularly helpful in establishing and adjusting order priorities for both in-house production and outside procurement (Block 9 of Figure 16.1; see also Section 13.2.3 of Chapter 13 for further discussion).

Because of the typically very large number of s.k.u. in an MRP system, the material requirements plan must display information on an exception basis, that is, only for those items where an immediate action is likely necessary. Examples include:

1. An open order exists this period, but will not cover existing backorders.
2. Net requirements exist this period, but the next open order is not due until a future period.
3. An open order exists this period, but the net requirements can be met from the already existing, on-hand inventory.

16.4.6 Low-Value, Common-Usage Items

There is one exception to the rule of using MRP level-by-level explosion to ascertain the requirements of all items—namely, the case of low-value items having high-usage rates, that is, basic components of many items (for example, bolts, washers, nuts, etc.). The costs of precise physical control and the computer processing time required to ascertain the requirements are likely to be prohibitive when one recognizes the low cost of carrying safety stocks of such items. Therefore, for such items it is preferable to use one of the control systems suggested in Chapter 7—namely, a continuous-review, order-point, order-quantity system (that is, a two-bin system) or a periodic-review, order-up-to-level system. Sødahl (1981) supports this viewpoint in the automotive industry (see also Collier, 1982; Jönsson et al., 1982).

16.4.7 Pegging

Consider an item that is used as a component of several other items. Straightforward use of MRP, as discussed above, leads to gross requirements on this item that are generated from a number of sources. In some circumstances, it may be important to know which items generated which amounts of these requirements. In particular, if a shortage of the item under consideration is imminent, it would be helpful to know which subassemblies, assemblies, finished products and, ultimately, customer orders would be affected. To achieve this we proceed as follows. When the production (procurement) schedule of an item is exploded to generate gross requirements on the next (higher numbered) level items, these requirements are "pegged" with an identification of the item generating them.

It is clear that considerable file space and data processing effort are required in connection with pegging. Therefore, this procedure should be used only when the information so generated is of paramount importance.

16.4.8 Handling Changes

Our discussions so far have implicitly dealt with MRP as a process carried out once per basic time period. However, changes in various inputs are certainly not restricted to occurring only once per period. These possible changes include:

1. Changes in the master schedule or in direct external demand for components
2. Identified discrepancies in inventory records
3. Changes in machine availability (for example, breakdowns)
4. Actual completion time or quantity different from planned
5. Engineering changes in product structure (bill of materials)
6. Changes in costs, lead times, etc.

MRP must be able to effectively cope with such changes. There are two very different options available: regeneration and net change.

In the regeneration method the entire MRP process, as discussed in Sections 16.4.3 and 16.4.4, is carried out once per period (typically the period is of a one-week duration) using batch-processing computer techniques. All changes that have taken place since the previous regeneration are incorporated in the new run. In the net change approach, one does not wait until the next period to incorporate a change and replan coverage. Replanning takes place on essentially a continuous time basis. For a particular change the possible effects are limited to components of the item causing the change. Therefore, the modification of the previous schedule tends to be much more limited than under regeneration; in effect, only a partial explosion of requirements is undertaken each time a change is processed. Orlicky (1973) presents the details of how a net change system operates.

In a regenerative system, between regenerations, only the on-hand and on-order inventory levels of each item are updated according to the standard inventory transactions such as demands, receipts, quality losses, and so forth. The possible associated changes in requirements for component items are not updated until the next regeneration; hence these requirements become less reliable as the period between regenerations progresses. In contrast, these requirements (and associated priorities, etc.) are kept up to date in a net change system as changes are incorporated on a frequent basis.

Obviously this up-to-date, rapid response capability of a net change system is desirable. Furthermore, the data processing load is more evenly spread through time than in a regenerative arrangement. Primarily for the first of these reasons it appears that most users will eventually switch to a net change system. However, there are potential problems that should not be overlooked. First, net change tends to promulgate any earlier errors. Therefore, on an occasional basis a regeneration is necessary to purge the system of errors. Second, some judgment must be used in deciding on how quickly to process the different changes. Too frequent processing can lead to unnecessary instability—for example, the size of an order jumping up and down several times prior to the actual production. Finally, net change is somewhat less efficient from a data processing standpoint.

16.4.9 Coping with Uncertainty in MRP

To this point our discussions on MRP have essentially ignored the effects of uncertainty. In Chapter 7 we coped with uncertainty by the introduction of safety stocks. This is *not* the predominant approach in MRP. The usual argument is that safety stocks are not really appropriate in a dependent demand situation. Instead, one can more effectively avoid shortages and excess inventories through the adjustment of lead times, these adjustments being accomplished by expediting or, more generally, shifting priorities of shop and vendor orders.

Outright elimination of safety stocks or safety times (the latter meaning that orders are scheduled for completion slightly ahead of the requirements time) for the dependent demand items is not the final answer in MRP. Whybark and Williams (1976) provide considerable *qualitative* insight concerning four general sources of uncertainty in an MRP setting and appropriate general approaches for dealing with them. The sources of uncertainty are (1) supply timing, (2) supply quantity (for example, variable yield as discussed by New, 1982), (3) demand timing, and (4) demand quantity. Sources (2) and (4), involving quantity uncertainty, are best handled by safety stocks, whereas safety times (scheduling replenishments to arrive ahead of the *expected* need date) are more appropriate for sources (1) and (3). However, a *quantitative* analysis of exactly how much safety stock or safety time is appropriate for each item is very complicated because of the erratic, time-varying, dependent nature of the demand patterns. Summary guidelines include the possible use of the following.

1. Safety stock in items with direct external usage
2. Safety stock in items produced by a process with a significantly variable yield
3. Safety stock in items produced at a bottleneck operation
4. Safety stock in certain semifinished items used for a myriad of end-items
5. Safety time in raw materials

Further references on dealing with uncertainty in MRP include Berry and Whybark (1977), De Bodt and Van Wassenhove (1983), De Bodt et al. (1982), and Miller (1979).

16.5 CAPACITY REQUIREMENTS PLANNING

This section deals with Block 8 of Figure 16.1. Capacity Requirements Planning (CRP) determines the needed capacity through time at each work center as implied by a given or proposed master production schedule. As mentioned in Chapter 13, CRP takes place at two stages in time. First, a rough-cut CRP is sometimes used to evaluate a *tentative* master production schedule. In this regard a useful construct to employ is the *load profile*. It gives the approximate needs in terms of various resources by time period that are associated with 1 unit of a particular end-item being put in the master schedule in a base period. Such load profiles are developed for each item that could be master scheduled, but need only be done once in a lifetime for a product (except, of course, if engineering or process changes take place). The MRP system itself is used to develop these load profiles (for details, see Chapter 11 of Orlicky, 1975). The profiles are then used to project the likely resource requirements by time period of the particular trial master schedule.

The second and more common type of CRP is more detailed in nature. A master schedule is exploded through the material requirements plan (Section 16.4), producing a set of released and planned shop (and supplier) orders. Using the routings of the various items, these orders are converted to requirements (for example, in machine hours) period by period at the various work centers. In this way the required capacity for each center in each time period is determined. In the usual approach, known as *infinite loading*, capacity constraints are ignored in developing the capacity profile. In *finite loading* a master schedule is built up that stays within capacity constraints at *all* work centers (see Section 15.2 of Chapter 15 as well as Hastings et al., 1982). Figure 16.6 shows a schematic representation of the required profile, obtained by infinite loading, for a hypothetical center.

Next, the *actual* capacity through time is estimated. This is typically *not* equal to the gross capacity scheduled. Instead, account must be taken of machine breakdowns, time for minor maintenance, delays because of missing parts, and so on. An efficiency factor, expressed as

$$\text{Efficiency factor} = \frac{\text{Actual capacity}}{\text{Gross capacity}}$$

can be estimated (and updated) based on recent actual operating experience. Figure 16.6 shows an estimated actual capacity that is level through time.

The next step is to compare required with actual capacity. When the required exceeds the actual (which is the case in periods 4 and 6 of Figure 16.6), there are several possible courses of action:

1. Shift some orders into nearby periods having excess capacity (for example, in the case of Figure 16.6, perhaps some of the orders in period 4 could be moved back into period 3; however, this would have a ripple effect on the schedules of components of the moved orders).
2. Use overtime.
3. Use subcontracting.
4. Purchase some processed parts instead of raw materials.

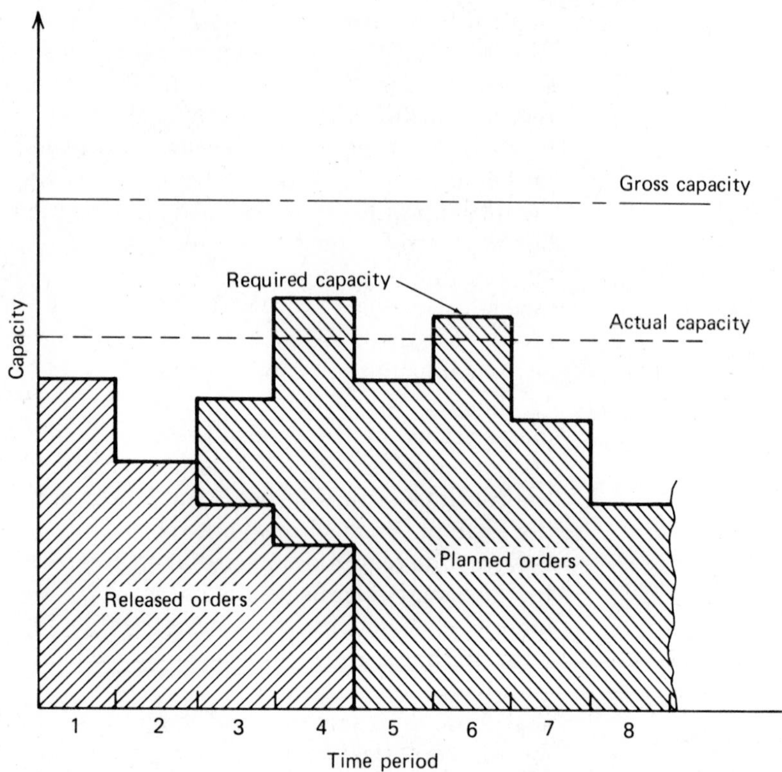

FIGURE 16.6 Required and Actual Capacity Profiles

5. Transfer personnel from underutilized areas.
6. Use alternate (less desirable) routings for certain orders.
7. If all else fails, modify the master schedule itself.

An excellent general reference on CRP is the paper by Vollmann (1973).

16.6 DISTRIBUTION REQUIREMENTS PLANNING

In Chapter 12 we examined multiechelon inventory systems and pointed out the drawbacks of using *independent* control of the same item at different locations, particularly without information flow between the different echelons. There is a very natural extension of MRP that addresses this problem; it is known as Distribution Requirements Planning (DRP). Martin (1980, 1983) has been a pioneer in the development and implementation of DRP.

To describe DRP, let us consider a relatively simple, two-echelon system with a central warehouse (perhaps adjacent to a production facility) and several branch warehouses. Also, to facilitate understanding, our discussion will concentrate on the control of a single product. Rather than using an order-point system, each branch warehouse develops a master schedule—that is, a projected replenishment pattern to satisfy the net requirements at that location. Almost certainly, forecasts of demand will first be needed to establish the gross requirements. The item located at a branch warehouse has a level code of 0 and its bill of materials is extremely simple—its only component is the same item (level code 1) at the central warehouse. The offset is the replenishment lead time between the central and the branch warehouse. Once all of the master schedules are established at the branches, the dependent demand at the central warehouse can be calculated. Any projected direct customer demand on the central warehouse can be added to the dependent demand, resulting in gross requirements, and so forth. If there is a linkage back to a manufacturing facility (plant), then the same item at the plant has a level code of 2. Thus, we see that DRP is an extension of MRP into the distribution phase of operations. A company only involved in distribution (that is, no manufacturing) can still make use of DRP, including a possible linkage back to a (manufacturing) supplier's MRP system.

When one recognizes that the replenishment lot-sizing at the separate branches should not be done independently, but rather by taking account of the system-wide stock status, then it is a very natural further step from DRP to the PUSH control system of Section 12.5 of Chapter 12 (also, see Brown, 1981).

16.7 PRODUCTION/INVENTORY CONTROL ASPECTS OF "JUST-IN-TIME" MANUFACTURING AND THEIR RELATIONSHIP TO MRP

Recall from Chapter 2 that Just-in-Time Manufacturing (JITM) is only a part of the overall approach known as *stockless production*. In this section we discuss the production/inventory control aspects of JITM and compare them with those of MRP. The reader is encouraged to review the more general discussion of stockless production in Section 2.7 of Chapter 2, particularly Section 2.7.2 which deals with the conditions necessary for its effective use.

JITM is used in a high-volume, repetitive, manufacturing setting. (In some cases, where end products are not of this type, group technology provides the opportunity to use JITM for the manufacture of component parts.) As with MRP, JITM is a PULL type system; the final assembly schedule pulls material through the preceding stations in a chain of orders, but, in contrast with MRP, only in exactly the quantities needed to support the assembly schedule, which, in turn, closely matches actual customer requirements. Each feeding work center produces only what its following (or consuming) work center uses to satisfy the assembly schedule. JITM is predicated on extremely low fixed setup or ordering costs that imply replenishment quantities of a single unit (or the smallest practical number of units, such as a standard container holding, for example, 6 units of a particular product). There is no stockroom; all in-process stock is on the production floor between the various work stations. Furthermore, this inventory is kept to a minimum. The same applies to in-process inventories between suppliers and the first production operations; frequent small shipments of raw materials are realized.

16.7.1 The Kanban (Card) and the Short-Run Operation of the System

The cards, tags, or tickets (Kanban in Japanese) represent the information system for Just-in-Time Manufacturing. Henceforth we simply refer to them as cards. They have two major functions in a JITM system: first, to provide the mechanism for the short-range implementation of the system *given a prescribed number of cards*; and second, to facilitate reduction in the work-in-process inventory through a systematic removal of cards from the system (this is part of the approach used in a JITM system to move toward the goal of stockless production).

Two types of cards are used:

1. *Move cards.* These authorize the transfer of one standard container[5] of a specific part from the outbound stockpoint of the work center where it is produced to the inbound stockpoint of the center where it is to be used. A set of move cards is issued for the exclusive use of a single s.k.u. between a specific pair of work centers.
2. *Production cards.* These authorize the production of one standard container of a specific part at a particular work center in order to replace a container just taken from the outbound stockpoint of that center. A set of production cards is issued exclusively for the production of a specific s.k.u. at a particular work center.

A card typically contains the following information:

1. The Kanban number (the identification of the specific card)
2. Part number
3. Name and description of part
4. Place where the card is used (the two associated centers in the case of a move card; a single center for a production card)
5. The number of units in the standard container

Every container at an inbound stockpoint must have a move card attached. When such a container is selected for use in production at the specific center (A in Figure 16.7), an employee detaches the move card and attaches it to an empty

[5]As discussed earlier, in JITM as low lot sizes as possible are used. Thus, a standard container could contain but a single unit of a specific item.

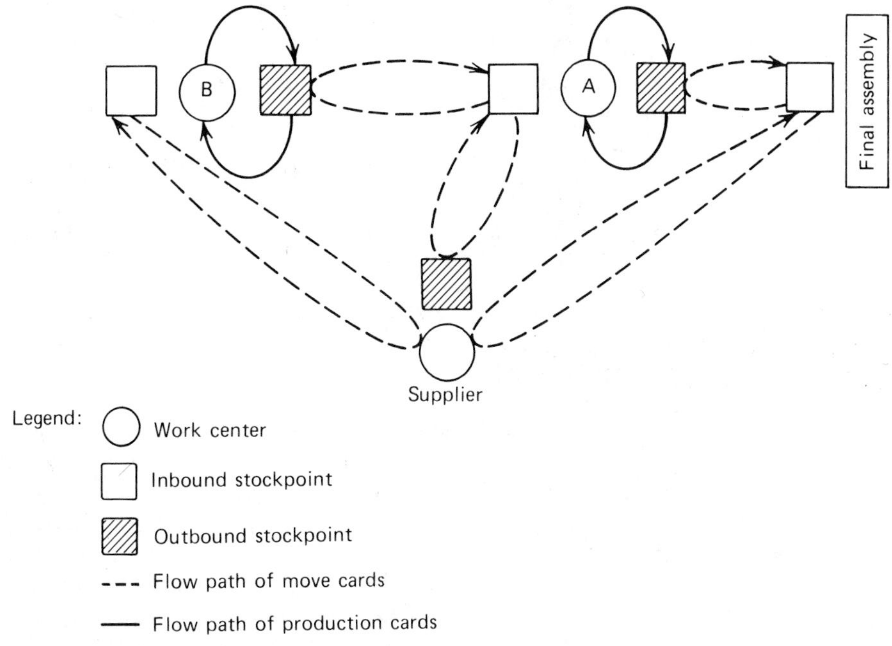

FIGURE 16.7 The Kanban Flow Paths

container (call it C1), which is then moved to the outbound stockpoint of the supplying work center (B in Figure 16.7). There the move card is detached and placed on a full container (call it C2), thus leaving the empty container C1 without any card. The production card is removed from container C2 and placed in a collection box. The full replacement container C2 (now with only a move card attached) is transferred to the consuming center (A). On a frequent basis an employee at the supplying center (B) picks up the released production cards from the collection box. For each such card a container of parts is produced. Empty containers (such as C1) are used to receive these parts, and each such filled container has a production card attached to it and is then placed in the outbound stockpoint of the center (B). The making of each container of parts requires a withdrawal from the inbound stockpoint of the supplying center (B), which initiates further upstream actions. Figure 16.7 (adopted from Hall, 1983) also shows the flow paths of the different types of cards, including move cards to and from a supplier of raw materials. Supplier shipments of containers, each holding a small number of units, necessitate a shipping procedure different from the method that has been conventionally used. Instead of infrequent large shipments involving only one or a few s.k.u., now many items are involved (in smaller quantities) in each shipment. Nellemann (1982) points out that the Japanese refer to this as the water beetle method of transport. Moreover, where a supplier is geographically remote from the production facility, the lead time can obviously be reduced through electronic transmission of a supply need as opposed to the physical shipment of a container and associated Kanban (card).

The JITM system is completely manual. For it to operate properly, strict adherence to three rules is required:

1. A standard container must always be filled with the prescribed number of parts.
2. A container must not be moved forward until authorized by the receipt of a move card.
3. A container of parts must not be produced until authorized by a detached production card.

16.7.2 The Different Stages of Planning and Control

As discussed in Section 2.7 of Chapter 2, the JITM system requires high-volume, repetitive manufacturing with a reasonably stable workload (even and consistent flow of parts) at the various production centers. Thus, where there are multiple items produced by the final assembly operation, it is necessary to develop a regular cycle among these items, at the same time ensuring the aforementioned relatively smooth workload. Some of the cycling ideas of Section 15.2 of Chapter 15 may be useful here; however, a small cycle time (on the order of a single day) is in order for two reasons: (1) to avoid an excessive buildup of stock of finished goods and (2) to keep the customer response time quite low. Only minor deviations (less than 10% or so) from a planned schedule can be tolerated without jeopardizing the effectiveness of a JITM system.

Typically, a rough-cut master schedule is developed for a horizon of anywhere from 3 months to 1 year. Replanning is done approximately 1 to 4 times per month, with the portion up to the next replanning date being firmed up. A detailed final assembly schedule, determined by actual customer orders, is set for something on the order of 1 to a few days in advance. As mentioned above, the actual flow rates and material mix should not deviate very much from the previous (replanning) stage's firmed up figures (that is, JITM is *not* an expediting system). Thus, marketing should not expect production to make large shifts in the firm schedule in response to unexpected changes in requirements. With a relatively short duration of the firm schedule (that is, a relatively short response time), this situation should be quite tolerable from marketing's perspective. Minor deviations from the plan are typically handled by means of slack deliberately left in the system (for example, overtime or extra time between shifts).

16.7.3 Comparison with MRP

There are considerable similarities between MRP and JITM. Both are PULL systems in which the assembly (or master scheduled operation) pulls requirements through the earlier stages of manufacturing and procurement. JITM can be viewed as the special case of MRP where there are very short time buckets (essentially continuous-time MRP) and where all replenishments are on a lot-for-lot basis.

This special situation permits a much simpler control system than in more general MRP. Specifically, in JITM centralized control is necessary for only the final assembly operation, whereas MRP, typically also requires the detailed, centralized control of subassemblies, components, and so forth. Thus, a computer-based system is essential in MRP, whereas manual control is the norm in JITM.

Jönsson and Olhager (1983) have conducted a simulation comparison of the two types of control systems. Their results are intuitively appealing. MRP has cost advantages over JITM *(excluding system control costs)* when demand varies highly with time and setup times are relatively large. On the other hand, JITM does very well, from a cost standpoint, for stable (repetitive) demand and relatively low setup times. Moreover, achieving reductions in setup times may be more important than the choice among the two control systems. See also Goddard (1982).

In summary, JITM is a simple, effective control system for high-volume, repetitive demand when individual setup times (costs) are quite low. In Chapter 12 and in Section 16.2 we pointed out potential weaknesses of a PULL system of control. Although JITM is a PULL system, it overcomes these weaknesses. First, because small lot sizes are used with a lot-for-lot replenishment strategy, variability in demand is *not* amplified back through the system. Moreover, the relatively level assembly schedule and very short lead times eliminate the usual need for substantial safety stocks.

16.8 SUMMARY

In this chapter we have concentrated on production/inventory planning and control in fabrication/assembly (materials/labor-oriented) situations. The emphasis has been on Closed Loop, Material Requirements Planning. Such a system is not optimal in a mathematical sense, but, when compared with the more traditional replenishment systems, it typically provides substantial benefits to management, in terms of excellent summarized information, in a complex multistage, manufacturing environment (both make-to-order and make-to-stock). Moreover, although the methods of Chapter 15 were recommended for process industries, applications of MRP in such settings have been reported (see, for example, Cohen, 1980; Kochalka, 1978). Perhaps the major benefit of MRP in a complex manufacturing setting is the ability to more quickly adapt to a rapidly changing environment. This is partly accomplished through the use of the logic in a simulation mode to provide answers to "what-if" questions.

Wight (1981, p. 75) reported, as of mid-1981, that some 8000 companies in the United States had some type of MRP system but that, at most, 5 percent of these were being used to anywhere near their capabilities. This indicates considerable difficulties in implementation. In particular, organizations have not given enough emphasis to the input of reliable information nor to the maintenance of a stable master production schedule. This is probably the result, in large part, of inadequate education and training of management, supervisors, and other staff, concerning the nature and proper operation of MRP systems. Anderson and Schroeder (1978) report implementation costs for MRP systems ranging from \$100,000 to almost \$3,000,000 (depending on company size) with a mean of over \$700,000. The tangible benefits are very difficult to quantify, but see Anderson et al. (1982) and Wight (1981, Chapter 4); the latter provides a general discussion about how to estimate the impact of MRP II on manufacturing productivity. Despite the weaknesses discussed in Section 16.2, Etienne (1983) points out that, under certain circumstances, the relative simplicity of the traditional replenishment systems may still make them attractive to use in a manufacturing environment.

Finally, in Section 16.7 we outlined the operational control aspects of Just-In-Time Manufacturing, a control system particularly appealing for highly repetitive manufacturing with relatively low setup costs.

PROBLEMS

16.1 For the product structure sketched in Figure 16.8, which of the items could be subject to independent demand? Which to dependent demand?

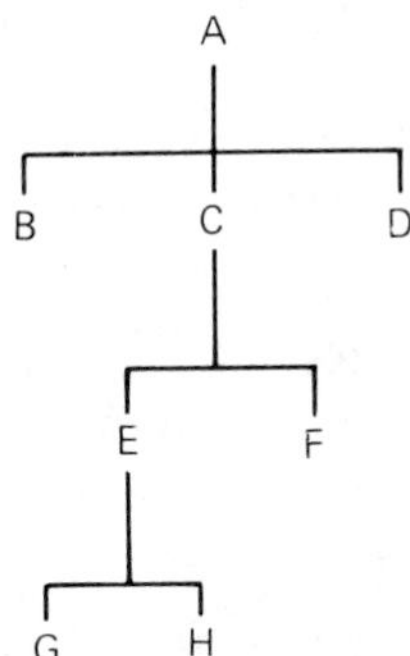

FIGURE 16.8 A Product Structure

16.2 A company assembles three distinct finished s.k.u., items F1, F2, and F3. The bills of materials for these items, their components, and quantities, are as follows:

Item F1: Composed of 1 unit of A1, A2, and A3 and 2 units of A4

Item F2: Composed of 1 unit of A1, A2, and A4

Item F3: Composed of 1 unit of A1 and A4

Item A1: Composed of 1 unit of A2 and B1

Item A2: Composed of 1 unit of A4, B1, and B2

Item A3: Composed of 1 unit of B1 and B2 and 3 units of B3

Item A4: Composed of 2 units of B3

Item B1: Composed of 1 unit of B3 and C1

Item B2: Composed of 1 unit of C1 and C2

Item B3: Composed of 1 unit of C1, C2, and C3

Items C1, C2, and C3 are purchased parts. In addition, items A1 and A2 are sold directly to customers as spare parts.

Develop a level-by-level coding for the 13 items.

16.3 Suppose that the offsets for the operations involved in Problem 16.2 are as follows:

Assembly, Fabrication, or Purchase of Item	Offset (weeks)
F1	1
F2	2
F3	1
A1	1
A2	2
A3	2
A4	3
B1	1
B2	3
B3	1
C1	2
C2	2
C3	4

Considering only F1 and its components,

a. What minimum horizon should be used for the master production schedule?

b. If the only customer order is for 10 units of item F1 in week 15 and there is no initial on-hand or on-order stock for any items, establish the procurement and production schedule for item F1 and all its components.

16.4 If a master production schedule (MPS) is overstated (that is, not realizable), briefly discuss which of the following will or will not result:

a. A material plan inconsistent with the MPS will be developed.

b. Inappropriate priorities will result on shop/vendor orders.

c. Overstated capacity requirements will be set.

d. Excessive component part inventories will be developed.

e. It will be easier to cope with large, unexpected orders.

16.5 Eastern Telecom produces switching units for telecommunication systems. They use MRP and an analyst, Maxine Schultz, is responsible for the lot-sizing of a class of s.k.u. including item C703. Based on earlier material planning, there is an on-hand inventory of 230 units of item C703 at the start of week 1, a firm order of 200 units to be delivered in week 3, and a tentative order of 290 units scheduled for delivery in week 6. This and other relevant information is portrayed in Table 16.8.

a. Compute the projected net inventory at the end of each week as well as the cumulative net requirements.

b. What is the impact on net inventory and cumulative net requirements of moving the delivery of the tentative order into week 4?

c. How does the discussion in Section 6.6.7 of Chapter 6 relate to this type of action?

16.6 Consider a particular work center A in a manufacturing environment. The gross capacity per week is 120 hours with an efficiency factor of 0.85. The projected work load for weeks 6, 7, and 8 is as shown in Table 16.9.

a. How would the entries in the "Standard Hours Required" column be obtained?

b. Sketch a graphic representation of the work load at the center.

c. What change(s) would you recommend in the schedule of orders?

TABLE 16.8 Material Plan for Item C703

Lead time = 1 period
Order quantity = not fixed

Time Period	0	1	2	3	4	5	6	7
Projected gross requirements	—	150	120	130	180	160	90	100
Planned order receipts	—	—	—	200	—	—	290	—
Projected net inventory at end of period	230							

TABLE 16.9 Workload at Center A

Week	Order No.	Standard Hours Required
6	315	41.2
	317	18.8
	314	22.5
7	322	51.5
	318	47.6
	313	27.7
	320	15.8
8	327	43.5
	325	16.7
	326	15.4

16.7 In MIDAS Case D the Inventory Control Manager described his method of separating Midamatics (and Processors) parts into two physically separate storage areas: one for assembly parts, the other for spare parts. His last comment was "I've often wondered whether there was any way of combining the inventory for both types of parts so that there would be enough safety stock to meet emergencies from either of the two sources." What suggestions would you have in this regard? Include a discussion of some of the less tangible factors.

16.8 MIDAS Case F shows that the Manager of Manufacturing, Mr. Wolfgang Gatzke, is on the firing line. Briefly indicate what suggestions you would make to him.

16.9 In a JITM system, discuss the tradeoff involved in the choice of the number of move cards for a particular part between two specific centers.

16.10 Review the operations of a local manufacturing firm and briefly discuss the applicability of

a. MRP
b. JITM

REFERENCES

Anderson, J. C., and R. G. Schroeder (1978). "A Survey of MRP Implementation and Practice." *Proceedings of the MRP Implementation Conference*, American Production and Inventory Control Society, Falls Church, Virginia.

Anderson, J. C., R. G. Schroeder, S. E. Tupy, and E. M. White (1982). "Material Requirements Planning Systems: The State of the Art." *Production and Inventory Management*, Vol. 23, No. 4, pp. 51–66.

Berry, W. L., and D. C. Whybark (1977). "Buffering against Uncertainty in Material Requirements Planning Systems." *Discussion Paper No. 82*, Division of Research, School of Business, Indiana University, West Lafayette, Indiana.

Biggs, J., S. Goodman, and S. Hardy (1977). "Lot Sizing Rules in a Hierarchical Multi-Stage Inventory System." *Production and Inventory Management*, Vol. 18, No. 1, pp. 104–116.

Billington, P., J. McClain, and L. J. Thomas (1983). "Mathematical Programming Approaches to Capacity–Constrained MRP Systems: Review, Formulation and Problem Reduction." *Management Science*, Vol. 29, No. 10, pp. 1126–1141.

Bourke, R. (1980). "Surveying the Software." *Datamation*, Vol. 26, No. 10, pp. 101–120.

Brown, R. G. (1981). "The New Push for DRP." *Inventories & Production Magazine*, July–August, pp. 25–27.

Cohen, R. L. (1980). "Case Study: Production and Inventory Control in the Chemical Process Industry." *Proceedings of the 23rd Annual International Conference of the American Production and Inventory Control Society*, pp. 153–154.

Collier, D. A. (1980). "The Interaction of Single-Stage Lot Size Models in a Material Requirements Planning System." *Production and Inventory Management*, Vol. 21, No. 4, pp. 11–20.

Collier, D. A. (1982). "Aggregate Safety Stock Levels and Component Part Commonality." *Management Science*, Vol. 28, No. 11, pp. 1296–1303.

De Bodt, M., and L. Van Wassenhove (1983). "Lot Sizes and Safety Stocks in MRP: A Case Study." *Production and Inventory Management*, Vol. 24, No. 1, pp. 1–16.

De Bodt, M., L. Van Wassenhove, and L. Gelders (1982). "Lot-Sizing and Safety Stock Decisions in an MRP-System with Demand Uncertainty." *Engineering Costs and Production Economics*, Vol. 6, pp. 67–75.

Etienne, E. C. (1983). "MRP May Not Be Right for You: At Least Not Yet." *Production and Inventory Management*, Vol. 24, No. 3, pp. 33–45.

Fox, R. E. (1982). "MRP, Kanban and OPT—What's Best?" *Proceedings of the 25th Annual International Conference of the American Production and Inventory Control Society*, pp. 482–486.

Goddard, W. E. (1982). "Kanban versus MRP II—Which is Best for You?", *Modern Materials Handling*, November 5, pp. 40–48.

Hall, R. W. (1983). *Zero Inventories*. Dow-Jones, Irwin, Homewood, Illinois.

Hastings, N., P. Marshall, and R. Willis (1982). "Schedule Based MRP: An Integrated Approach to Production Scheduling and Material Requirements Planning." *Journal of the Operational Research Society*, Vol. 22, No. 11, pp. 1021–1029.

Hoffman, W. C. (1981). "MRP II at a Paper Goods Plant—Case Study." *Proceedings of the 24th Annual International Conference of the American Production and Inventory Control Society*, pp. 226–228.

Hoyt, J. (1978). "Dynamic Lead Times That Fit Today's Dynamic Planning (QUOAT Lead Times)." *Production and Inventory Management*, Vol. 19, No. 1, pp. 63–70.

Jönsson, H., P. Lundell, and A. Thorstenson (1982). "Some Aspects on Uncertainty in a Multi-Level Inventory System." *Engineering Costs and Production Economics*, Vol. 6, pp. 141–146.

Jönsson, H., and J. Olhager (1983). "A Comparison of MRP and Kanban as Information Systems for Production and Inventory Control." *Research Report No. 92*, Department of Production Economics, Linköping Institute of Technology, Linköping, Sweden.

Kochalka, T. (1978). "MRP in a Process Industry—Why Wait?" *Production and Inventory Management*, Vol. 19, No. 4, pp. 17–20.

Martin, A. (1980). "Distribution Resource Planning (DRP II)." *Proceedings of the 23rd Annual International Conference of the American Production and Inventory Control Society*, pp. 161–165.

Martin, A. (1983). *DRP—Distribution Resource Planning: Distribution Management's Most Powerful Tool*. Prentice-Hall & Oliver Wight Ltd. Publications, Inc., Essex Junction, Vermont.

McClain, J., W. Maxwell, J. Muckstadt, L. J. Thomas, and E. Weiss (1982). "On MRP Lot Sizing." *Management Science*, Vol. 28, No. 5, pp. 582–584.

Miller, J. G. (1979). "Hedging the Master Schedule." In *Disaggregation Problems in Manufacturing and Service Organizations*, (L. P. Ritzman, L. J. Krajewski, W. L. Berry, S. H. Goodman, S. T. Hardy, and L. D. Vitt, Editors). Martinas Nijhoff, Hingham, Massachusetts, pp. 237–256.

Nakane, J., and R. W. Hall (1983). "Management Specs for Stockless Production." *Harvard Business Review*, Vol. 61, No. 3, pp. 84–91.

Nellemann, D. O. (1982). "MRP vs. Kanban? Combining the Best of the East and West." *Proceedings of the 25th Annual International Conference of the American Production and Inventory Control Society*, pp. 124–128.

New, C. (1974a). "Lot-Sizing in Multi-Level Requirements Planning Systems." *Production and Inventory Management*, Vol. 15, No. 4, pp. 57–71.

New, C. (1974b). *Requirements Planning*. Gower Press, Essex, England.

New, C. (1975). "Safety Stocks for Requirements Planning." *Production and Inventory Management*, Vol. 16, No. 2, pp. 1–18.

New, C. C. (1982). "Material Requirements Planning in High Yield Loss Manufacturing Systems." *Working Paper*, Cranfield School of Management, Cranfield, England.

Orlicky, J. A. (1973). "Net Change Material Requirements Planning." *IBM Systems Journal*, Vol. 12, No. 1, pp. 2–29.

Orlicky, J. A. (1975). *Material Requirements Planning*. McGraw-Hill, New York.

Plossl, G., and O. Wight (1971). *Material Requirements Planning by Computer*. Special Report of the American Production and Inventory Control Society, Washington, D. C.

Putnam, A. O. (1983). "MRP for Repetitive Manufacturing Shops: A Flexible KANBAN System for America." *Production and Inventory Management*, Vol. 24, No. 3, pp. 61–88.

Rhodes, P. (1974). "Lot Allocation Planning—A Fresh Approach to Material Requirements Planning." *Proceedings of the Seventeenth Annual International Conference of the American Production and Inventory Control Society*, pp. 14–19.

Rice, J. W., and T. Yashikawa (1982). "A Comparison of Kanban and MRP Concepts for the Control of Repetitive Manufacturing Systems." *Production and Inventory Management*, Vol. 23, No. 1, pp. 1–13.

Ritzman, L. P., and L. J. Krajewski (1981). "Performance Comparison Between MRP and Reorder Point Systems." *Working Paper 81–89*, College of Administrative Science, The Ohio State University, Columbus, Ohio.

Rosling, K. A. (1977). "Three Essays on Batch Production and Optimization." PROFIL 3, Production-Economic Research, Linköping Institute of Technology, Linköping, Sweden.

Rucinski, D., and F. Woodman (1977). "Use of the Firm Planned Order." *Production and Inventory Management*, Vol. 18, No. 4, pp. 30–44.

Smith, D. J. (1978). "Material Requirements Planning." In *Studies in Operations Management* (A. C. Hax, Editor), North Holland, Amsterdam.

Sødahl, L. (1981). "How Do You Master Schedule Half a Million Product Variants?" *Proceedings of the 24th Annual International Conference of the American Production and Inventory Control Society*, pp. 70–72.

Steinberg, E., and H. A. Napier (1980). "Optimal Multi-Level Lot Sizing for Requirements Planning Systems." *Management Science*, Vol. 26, No. 12, pp. 1258–1271.

Vollman, T. (1973). "Capacity Planning: The Missing Link." *Production and Inventory Management*, Vol. 14, No. 1, pp. 61–74.

Whybark, D. C., and J. C. Williams (1976). "Material Requirements Planning Under Uncertainty." *Decision Sciences*, Vol. 7, No. 4, pp. 595–606.

Wight, O. (1981). *MRP II: Unlocking America's Productivity Potential.* Oliver Wight Limited Publications, Inc., Brattleboro, Vermont.

PART SIX

SYNTHESIS

The two chapters in this, the last, part of the book could logically follow the introductory Chapters 1, 2, and 3 in Part One. An attempt is made to pull together the major themes presented in the book, with the intention of providing the reader with an increased perspective regarding the extensive, complex topics we have examined in much detail.

Chapter 17 emphasizes the important issues with respect to the effective implementation of decision systems. We also address how to estimate a priori the costs and benefits of a proposed new system.

The potential need for, and design of, the computerization of production/inventory decision systems is the topic of Chapter 18. The chapter ends with a summary dealing with the entire book.

CHAPTER 17

Planning, Implementation, Control, and Evaluation

Many books on management science modeling have discussed implementation considerations as if they were the last step in a sequential process consisting of goal specification, problem definition, model construction-solution and testing, and implementation strategy. While implementation of production/inventory decision systems, per se, is discussed in this, one of the last chapters, it is important to recall that throughout the book we have rejected the conventional (sequential) approach. Instead, we have presented the building of decision systems as a process of organizational intervention, whereby a model builder disrupts existing managerial decision processes in attempting to improve on the quality of decisions being made. By intervening, a management scientist accepts a great responsibility—that of ensuring that the daily routines in the client's organization are carried on, at least as well as before, during the period of transition to the newly designed decision procedures and subsequently during the new steady state that will ensue. Acceptance of such a responsibility implies that implementation considerations have to dominate all phases of the design of an operational decision system. In particular, successfully implemented innovations require careful planning, and once in place must be maintained, evaluated, and adapted, *ad infinitum*, through an effective monitoring and control system.

In Section 17.1 we present some general comments concerning the human aspects of implementation. Then Section 17.2 deals with the overall planning of a production/inventory study. The initial, problem identification phase is elaborated on in Section 17.3. Aggregate estimation procedures are presented in Section 17.4. Finally, the issues of control and evaluation are addressed in Section 17.5.

17.1 THE PSYCHOLOGY OF IMPLEMENTATION

The experiences of the authors and many other individuals (see, for example, Reuter, 1978), have revealed that what appear to be technically sound results developed by the management sciences and operational research (MS/OR) still have a rather low chance of ultimate successful implementation. This section is a review of possible reasons for the high failure rate, with some suggestions for ameliorating the situation.

Wolek (1975) has developed a process model for thinking about implementation in terms of three increasing levels of commitment: adoption, systematization, and institutionalization. Systematization focuses on the development of formal procedures (instructions, input and output forms, standard methods of data acquisition, software documentation, evaluation of procedures for performance control, etc.). Institutionalization involves the gradual acceptance of the decision system as evidenced by the delegation of routine operating responsibilities by the organization to the newly designed decision-making procedures. Systematization and institutionalization are gradual, sometimes painful, processes that occur over time. The decision to adopt an innovation is an event in time that precedes both these processes. The implementation of an innovation is more likely to occur if the adopter is:

1. *Predisposed to change.* It is most important that an adopter feel that there is a need for change. In particular it must be felt that the problem cannot be solved with methods currently available.

2. *Able to relate to the innovation.* New technology must be logically related to the present thinking of management. The system designer must establish that the new procedures are:

a. Definitely relevant to the manager's problem

b. Sufficiently different from existing methods

c. Meaningful in terms of the variables and conditions taken into consideration

3. *Able to assess the value of the innovation.* Benefits and costs must be made situationally specific within the adopter's own economic environment. The benefits and costs of new decision procedures are best demonstrated through actual trial use. Alternatively, simulation models and estimation procedures discussed in this chapter can be substituted.

4. *Able to justify a new invention within existing organizational norms.* The recognition by a client organization that a new technology is clearly economically beneficial does not guarantee adoption. A decision to adopt is always followed by the gradual processes of systematization and institutionalization which require, respectively, the expenditure of considerable amounts of effort on physical and social adapting of the innovation to the requirements of the particular situation. The cost of these formal and informal disruptions may be judged to be too high. Therefore, a prerequisite for the acceptance of an innovation is a determination that the impact of the resulting changes on personalities, careers, and social relationships is congruent with the client organization's desired objectives and style.

Clearly, the above discussion implies the necessity of communication between the innovator (analyst) and management. In an early study Churchman and Schainblatt (1965) postulated that successful implementation was contingent on whether a management scientist and a manager understood each other's way of thinking about the decision problem under consideration. Their conceptual model suggested that various different implementation strategies be adopted based on whether the management scientist understood the manager, and vice versa, or whether the management scientist understood the manager but the manager did not understand the scientist, and so forth. Dyckman (1967) and Duncan (1974) tested the Churchman-Schainblatt conceptual model and discovered that both managers and analysts refused to accept any specific implementation strategy as being the most desirable. In particular, mutual understanding between manager and analyst was only one of the variables that affected the success of an implementation.

Huysman (1970), as well as Doktor and Hamilton (1973), examined the different styles of reasoning used by managers and management scientists and how these reasoning modes affected the likelihood of whether a successful implementation resulted. In their work a person's cognitive style was viewed as varying along an analytic-heuristic continuum. Most management scientists are assumed to be analytic. That is, they reduce most decision problems to a key set of causal variables and then attempt to achieve an answer that optimizes some explicit mathematical objective criterion. Most managers, on the other hand, rely on heuristic reasoning, which is characterized by a global, less explicit, approach to any problem where intuition, common sense, and unsubstantiated feelings play an important role. This simply means that if a manager has a cognitive style that tends to the heuristic end of the continuum, then that individual is very likely to resist an analytic (nonsynthetic) solution, which involves mathematics, explicit assumptions, and explanations. Note that neither the manager nor the management scientist is using the "wrong" approach to problem solving. It is only a question of previous formal training and conditioning as well as psychological makeup of a person. Clearly, considerable convergence of the two models of reasoning has to occur gradually over time if management science modeling is to impact any managerial decision-making situation. At present, when this is achieved, it is usually through involving managers and management scientists in a project right from the beginning. Welsh (1979) argues strongly for having the ultimate user of any system play a primary role in its development. Participation seems to provide on-the-job training to managers in MS/OR methodology as well as an acid test for the analytical procedures being considered. Involvement also tends to lead to psychological commitment to problem resolution, on both sides, while lessening the anxiety that unavoidably must result from any change.

Primarily from the perspective of the management scientist/operational analyst Rubenstein et al. (1967) have suggested that the following factors can have an impact on effective implementation:

1. Degree and level of managerial support

2. Client's receptivity to giving the analyst freedom to select projects, gather data, and implement results
3. Organizational and technical ability of the key analyst and the MS/OR team
4. Organizational location of the MS/OR activity
5. Influence and power of the MS/OR group
6. Reputation of MS/OR activities
7. Adequacy of resources to fulfill the project
8. Relevance of the project
9. Level of opposition to MS/OR
10. General perception of the level of success of the MS/OR activity

In summary, it is clear that implementation is a long, drawn-out process whose importance and duration are both often underestimated. *Gradual* implementation, after extensive education of a wide range of associated individuals (users, those who must input data, etc.), is essential. (See Wight, 1981, for details concerning education with respect to MRP systems.) Where possible, a so-called *pilot approach* should be first utilized. Specifically, a new system should be first implemented on a trial basis on a limited class of items (for example, on only one of the several product lines manufactured by the firm). The gradual implementation should also include provision for manual overrides of the output of computerized decision rules. In this regard Bishop (1974) describes a successful implementation where the apparent key factor which led to the adoption was a design option within the new decision system that allowed manual overrides of computer decisions by the manager *whenever he disagreed with them.* "Early in the operation of the system, approximately 80 percent of the items were overriden by the use of this feature . . . a year later this proportion had declined to less than 10 percent." According to Bishop the inventory control manager, his staff, and his boss used the new decision system simply because they felt that they were in charge, rather than at the mercy, of the innovation.

Before leaving this section we recount an anecdote that points out that implementation is a never-ending process, even for systems operating on a seemingly smooth basis. It relates to the fact that the operation of *all* decision systems depends, to a considerable extent, on a number of experienced individuals to fill the gaps that are left in the formal procedures either on purpose or inadvertently.

The authors were approached by the Canadian subsidiary of a major company listed among the Fortune 500. The company was facing the possibility of a total collapse of its highly integrated computer-based inventory decision system—that automatically placed orders for s.k.u. all over the world, and that automatically released shipments to customers from its network of warehouses in Canada, the United States, and abroad. All the original system designers had left the company for other jobs. A relatively fast turnover of personnel meant that experience with the system, which had been garnered informally over the several years the system had worked marvelously, had not been properly passed on. The formal documentation and training manuals (systematization) proved inadequate, especially in that they failed to advise on the simpler tasks that, nevertheless, were crucial to the routine operation of the physical system.

One day, quite unexpectedly, some errors in the logic of the decision models came to the attention of top management. On examining the decision system it became quickly evident that it was nearly impossible for outsiders who had not spent many years tinkering with the computer-based models to untangle all the many interrelationships involved. The company faced a costly and lengthy redesign of its decision system that had evolved without a carefully thought-out plan.

The redesign involved the inclusion of many more manual overrides and statistics that would monitor the decision systems's performance more closely in the future. A *greater* dependence on inputs from more senior managers was designed into the decision rules. In the past some managers and employees had left the company because they felt that they were stuck in their jobs, unable to progress through the ranks.[1] An extensive formal training program and a planned promotion ladder were instituted (institutionalization). A permanent group was created to update and extend all documentation and training manuals on the decision system. When asked as to what he had concluded, based on his recent experiences with computer-based inventory decision systems, a top manager at the company replied, "Keep it simple!"

17.2 PLANNING A PRODUCTION/INVENTORY STUDY

As we have seen, no new decision system is completely neutral socially or politically. A systems designer must honestly and realistically face up to the following questions when planning a production/inventory study:

1. Will there be any change in the personnel who interact with the new decision system?
2. Will there be any change in criteria by which managers evaluate their skills and performance (or those of other individuals)?
3. Will there be any change in the criteria used to determine the relative status of different persons in the client organization?
4. Will there be any change in the importance of different inputs (thus the power of related persons) to the solution of problems?

[1]Needless to say, under the previous decision system the company was reluctant to promote to jobs "on the outside" persons who had garnered very specialized knowledge about the "invisible" decision system.

If the answer to any of these questions is even a conditional yes, then analysts must allow in the design of their system for the possibility that there will be significant resistance to change.

Urban (1974) has developed an approach to systems design that focuses on these questions and in which implementation is dominant throughout. We have modified somewhat the approach, originally proposed by Urban, in the diagram that appears as Figure 17.1.

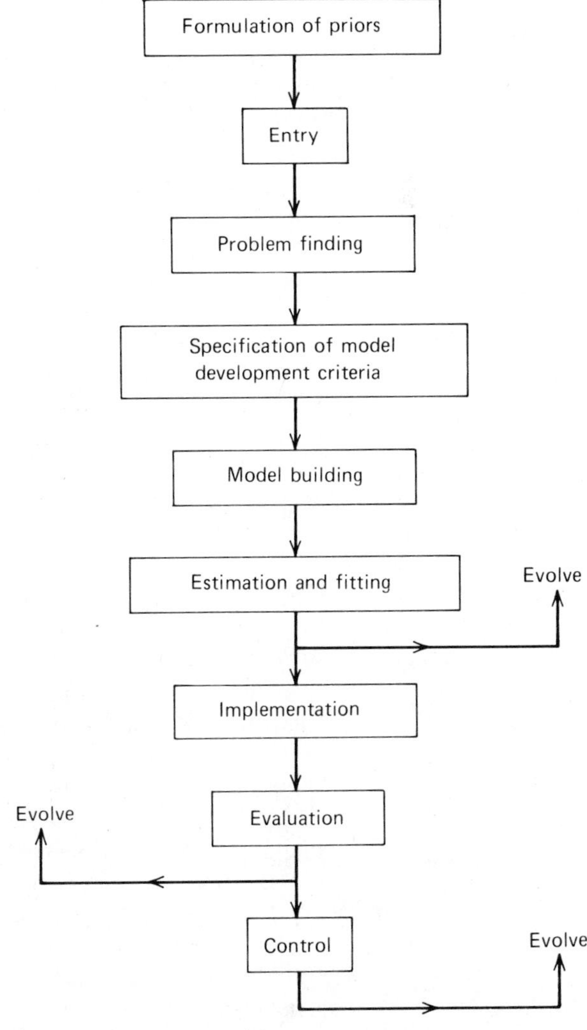

FIGURE 17.1 An Approach to Systems Design

17.2.1 Formulation of Priors

People who successfully intervene in an organization's ongoing processes must recognize and deal with their own biases and prior inclinations. Few model builders realize fully the strength of their own priors, even though they can clearly see others who are biased toward one particular technique or approach.

17.2.2 Entry

Urban recommends that entry be made at the decision point. A manager's most cherished prerogative is to make a decision, and special care must be taken to ensure that the decision models will supplement and not replace the manager in this decision making. A small team, including the decision makers, some staff people, and an agent of change who can work effectively from a relatively neutral position within the informal organization to facilitate change and gain acceptance, should be formed. Such a team must have full support from top management.

17.2.3 Problem Finding

It is important to ascertain, at the very beginning, why the systems designer has been invited to attempt intervention. More often than one may wish to admit, an "outside expert" is brought in to help tip the balance in some internal debate. Are you being asked to rubber stamp some imminent decisions or decision procedures? Does the real problem that management is ready to tackle have anything to do with inventory management and production planning? Most managers have some preconceived notions about the problem that a systems analyst is asked to solve. Unless a manager's preconceptions are proven to be in error, it is very unlikely that that individual will implement any changes that do not agree with those preconceptions.

Given managerial commitment and the resources to pursue model building, effort must be expended on defining the exact boundaries of the decision system to be designed. According to Urban, in his experience, 14 to 21 days is sometimes needed at this stage even for relatively simple situations. Studies must be carried out to identify existing decision models and rules of thumb as well as to determine answers to the four questions about the effects of the proposed changes on the social and political structure of the organization stated at the beginning of this section. Too many systems designers skip over this step or treat it lightly and thereby fail subsequently at implementation.

If a systems designer is new to an organization, it may be wise to identify at the initial stages a trial problem that has a quick and demonstrable payoff and that is currently on management's mind. This is by far the best way to establish credibility. It is possible that at times the trial problem chosen may be one that has nothing or little to do with inventory or production planning decision systems. If top management has had little previous experience with such decision systems, credibility may have to be established in some other arena, where top management can evaluate a system designer's output in a context that is familiar to them.

17.2.4 Specification of Model Development Criteria

Given a good problem definition and a clear understanding of what has to be done, a number of design options must be decided on. Which parts of the decision system should be descriptive, predictive, or normative? The physical, organizational, and external constraints must be ranked in order of priority. In the case of normative decision models, criteria used to define "optimal" and "heuristic" must be agreed on. Explicit implementation criteria must be identified along with the expected evolutionary steps that will lead to the desired final decision system.

17.2.5 Model Building

Considerable discussions on modeling strategy and on the details of modeling were presented in Section 2.6 of Chapter 2 and in Section 3.7 of Chapter 3, respectively. The reader is encouraged to review that material.

17.2.6 Estimating and Fitting

Data for model building and fitting, as we have seen, may come from subjective managerial judgment, the analysis of past numerical data, or experimentation. Generally speaking, it is wise to let the decision models (developed through the sequence of steps specified above) specify the data that needs to be henceforth collected routinely in a data base, rather than to try and collect all the data that could be in some way relevant to production/inventory decisions.

17.2.7 Implementation

See the detailed discussion of this topic presented in Section 17.1.

17.2.8 Evaluation

Monitoring of new decision systems, both during a break-in period and in subsequent use, is crucial to successful implementation. Differences from expectations and errors will undoubtedly occur. An implementation must be designed so that discrepancies resulting from (1) errors in forecasting model inputs, (2) inappropriate cost estimates, (3) incorrect model structuring, (4) changes in the real environment being modeled, or (5) random (nonrecurrent) events can be identified quickly and as a matter of routine.

17.2.9 Control

As a decision system is used over time, tracking of how an implementation is progressing (relative to agreed on model development criteria) is an important process that increases managerial confidence in decision models generally and usually leads to useful elaboration and evolution. The three components of a decision system—data base, decision models/monitoring statistics, and input/output capability—should be built up and refined gradually. Urban suggests that a five-year evolutionary period should not be considered unusual. The controls that continually monitor a decision system should be designed to last the lifetime of the system.

17.3 PRELIMINARY PROBINGS

Most analysts start the design of decision systems by a series of probing questions designed to reveal the major strengths and weaknesses of the existing procedures quickly. By this approach the analysts attempt to locate the tips of the iceberg, so to speak, leaving the more precise identification of the larger body for later on. Surprisingly simple questions usually suffice for this purpose. Such questions also have the advantage of helping to establish an immediate working rapport with top management. Woolsey (1975) describes this stage in a rather picturesque fashion:

When I do work with production and inventory management, I have the funny feeling that I am wandering through machine shops and manufacturing plants like Columbo, the rumpled cop, asking dumb questions . . . questions so stupid that nobody that works there would dare to ask. . . . (In the tool room) I go to the bins, select one at random, pull a tool from it and ask the supervisor to produce the card that matches the tool. . . . As a rule he cannot find it. . . . We have learned that the beautiful, computerized ordering system is not kept up to date . . . the second stop on the required tour is the production line . . . pick up a gear and ask. . . . How much is this worth? . . . How many of these are there in the bin? . . . How long has this bin been here? . . . What's your cost of money for this company?

One usually discovers that management is unable to answer some of the above, apparently simple, questions, thereby revealing possible shortcomings that need to be examined further. For example, if management is unclear about its cost of money, it is also very likely that it is unaware how much its inventory investment is costing the company. If management cannot tell how much a s.k.u. costs, for example, because of overhead accounting and transfer costs, then it is unlikely that the total funds tied up in inventories have been effectively rationed among the many purposes for which inventories are held.

In our experience, in response to simple probes, we have encountered situations where management did not believe that it costs money to place an order (see MIDAS Case B). As a result the company placed many small orders to keep "the delivery pipeline full and the total inventory investment low." The decision system eventually proved too expensive to run, especially because of the need for constant expediting of the small orders that inevitably failed to arrive on schedule.

A medium-sized company, run by an entrepreneur-engineer with a Ph.D., replied to one of our simple questions that he placed an order for more transistors whenever the box on the shelf was empty. Furthermore, because of a shortage of funds, he said he was keeping inventory low by ordering only in minimum quantities from his suppliers. The man's problem was immediately obvious; he was not allowing for delivery lead times. Furthermore, by ordering as few as six transistors at a time from his suppliers, he received poor delivery and service. The suppliers, because it cost them much more to process such small orders than they were worth, routinely held up the small orders for several weeks by grouping five or six orders together before shipment.

A revealing probe, at this stage, can be in the form of an attempt to calculate economic order quantities and reorder points (with the help of management) for a selected few representative A, B, and C items. A comparison with existing decision rules can be dramatic. Similarly, it is usually revealing to trace the decision to place an order through all the subsequent procedural and record-keeping steps that must be followed until stock keeping units (s.k.u.) are on the shelf ready for use.

Every decision system is capable of some improvement at a point in time. Some savings can always be achieved without a loss in effectiveness and often at little cost. The challenge that the analyst faces during these early stages involves the determination of whether the potential savings and the costs (including the attendant social costs) are of a sufficient magnitude to warrant immediate intervention. In our experience we have found that the largest potential savings that can be identified relatively easily occur at the preliminary probing stage. Almost always the allocation of safety stock and record-keeping procedures need improvement.

Because inventory decision systems evolve over time, an analyst should try through early probings to establish the level of sophistication in existing decision procedures. We have found Table 17.1 useful in fixing in our minds the

TABLE 17.1 Stages of Development in Inventory Decision Systems

Stage	Inventory Investment Is:
1	Residual
2	Recorded
3	Monitored
4	Controlled
5	Managed
6	"Optimized"

expectations we should have about improving an existing inventory decision system.

Residual inventory decision systems are the most primitive. Inventory investment is viewed as that which is left over at the end of the year when stock is counted because of the requirements of tax law. Daily, implict decision rules emphasize hand-to-mouth replenishments with no clearly defined responsibility for the replenishment function.

A more sophisticated decision system involves the periodic *recording* of inventory transactions rather than only once at the end of the year. Such systems are often motivated by accounting/cash management requirements. Replenishment decisions often tend to be more centralized in such circumstances.

Monitored inventory decision systems require the periodic reporting of inventory levels to responsible managers. While this feedback is very valuable, usually only a few formal replenishment rules exist at this stage. However, it is not uncommon for individual clerks to develop myopic rules of thumb that they follow themselves in order to cope with the workload, especially the paperwork involved.

Controlled inventory decision systems include well-defined weekly, monthly, and so on, inventory investment targets. For example, it is common in some department stores to allow buyers to procure up to a monthly limit. If the buyer has spent all of her allotment by the end of the third week, then she must wait until the beginning of the next month to place any further orders. How she spends her monthly allotment is not always controlled. Personalized and sometimes formal rules, such as required turnover ratios, are prevalent. A control system, such as an (s, Q) system, can be used at this stage, but the values of the control parameters are specified by management or clerks (without any explicit economic considerations).

Managed production/inventory decision systems involve formal rules that usually attempt limited (heuristic) tradeoffs between competing costs. Most of the decision systems in this book fall into this category. Usually the management of inventories is functionalized by the creation of a formal department at this stage.

Optimized production/inventory decision systems are comprehensive and automatic (usually computerized) replenishment procedures that attempt to control production and inventories in several locations.

Surprisingly, many decision systems in use today are at stage 1, even in fairly large companies. Only a few organizations have reached stage 6—most notable among these decision systems in the United States and Canada are those in the military establishments and in some of the larger multinational oil companies. The decision systems discussed in this book are primarily aimed at organizations in stages 3, 4, and 5, and to some extent, stage 6. In stages 1 to 3 one should recognize that the first order of business is to ensure the recording of basic demand and supply transactions to provide files of reliable information for decision-making purposes. Moreover, *an analyst should expect considerable resistance to change if an attempt is made to upgrade an existing decision system several stages at a time!*

17.4 ESTIMATION OF AGGREGATE MEASURES OF EFFECTIVENESS

If on the basis of the preliminary probings it is decided to proceed further, then the next thing that an analyst must establish is an agreed on point of reference. That is, what are the overall performance characteristics of the existing decision system; for example, what is the total average cycle stock, number of replenishments per year, and level of customer service provided? Such information is needed to estimate the potential savings and improvements possible (there may be several alternative strategies) and subsequently to ascertain any actual gains garnered when the new decision system has been implemented.

At this preliminary estimation stage one typically has a limited budget and limited time available. Thus, in a population of thousands of items it simply does not make sense to perform calculations for every single s.k.u. for each strategy under consideration. Consequently, some form of sampling or other *aggregate* estimation procedure is necessary.

17.4.1 Estimating the Aggregate Characteristics of an Existing System

To establish the overall performance characteristics of an existing system, a Distribution by Value (DBV) table or curve for *all* s.k.u. in inventory must be derived first. This requires the ranking of all s.k.u. according to their Dv values (see Section 1.5.2 of Chapter 1 for details).

Even if data were in machine-readable form, we could face two problems. First, there will undoubtedly be some missing data on annual demand D or variable cost v. Second, for large data sets, the cost of data entry and computer time may be deemed prohibitive by management.

When there are some data missing, there is not much else one can do but ask a knowledgeable clerk or manager who is familiar with the s.k.u. to make a "guesstimate." We believe that the development of a complete DBV is warranted at this stage. There is a good chance that a full-scale intervention into existing decision procedures is going to take place (otherwise we should not have proceeded beyond the stage of preliminary probings). A DBV will become mandatory eventually if new order quantities and order points must be derived for *all* s.k.u. Moreover, the expenditure of money on a DBV is unavoidable if top management wishes to specify the aggregate operating characteristics that they wish to achieve with a new decision system. Without such a specification an analyst cannot select appropriate values for A, r, or the customer service level in the subsequent calculation of order quantities and reorder points.

In Chapters 5 and 7 we developed a methodology for deriving exchange curves. We also discussed the estimation of current operating points. Figures 17.2 and 17.3 were developed for all s.k.u. in the Professional Products Division at MIDAS.[2] The exchange curves permit the determination of potential savings available if MIDAS reverted to an EOQ-type decision system, which was described in detail in Part Two of the book. (For details on this example and on the computation of exchange curves, see Section 5.9 of Chapter 5 and Section 7.9 of Chapter 7.)

If management is unwilling to spend the money needed to estimate the aggregate characteristics of the existing inventory decision system as discussed above, then we have no other option but to proceed on the basis of sample data. That is, we must develop a DBV using only a sample of s.k.u. and then *proceed as if the sample DBV was a perfect representation of that for the entire population.* (The data in Figures 17.2 and 17.3 were developed for *all* 849 s.k.u. in the Professional Products Division and took one analyst about a week to compile.)

Little guidance exists in the literature on how to select a representative sample for estimation purposes even *given that a complete DBV exists.* Obviously, stratified sampling makes sense in that certain items will contribute disproportionately to measures of effectiveness. However, well-defined stratified sampling procedures remain to be derived. Abo El-Ela (1975) has developed some preliminary results which indicate that the minimum error variance in an estimated variable (for example, total average stock, total replenishments per year, etc.) is a function of:

1. Total sample size
2. Total population size
3. Number of strata
4. The dispersion of the DBV

Abo El-Ela also derives results on how to allocate a given total sample size among the strata using as the stratification variable Dv, the annual dollar usage of each s.k.u. An important, intuitive finding is that the more important (that is, larger Dv) items dominate the sample.

Two crucial problems in this area remain unsolved. How large a sample should one select? Obviously, this should involve the balancing of the cost of sampling (recognizing a budget constraint) versus the cost of errors in the estimates, the latter being very difficult to measure. Second, if a complete DBV is not available, how should one physically carry out the stratified sampling?

Experience, judgment, and negotiations with the client determine in practice the size of the sample and its stratification. Table 17.2 shows the composition of an illustrative actual judgment sample that was used successfully in a consulting study for a large manufacturer of industrial machinery (see Hausman,

[2]Figures 17.2 and 17.3 are identical to Figures 5.11 and 7.10a, respectively.

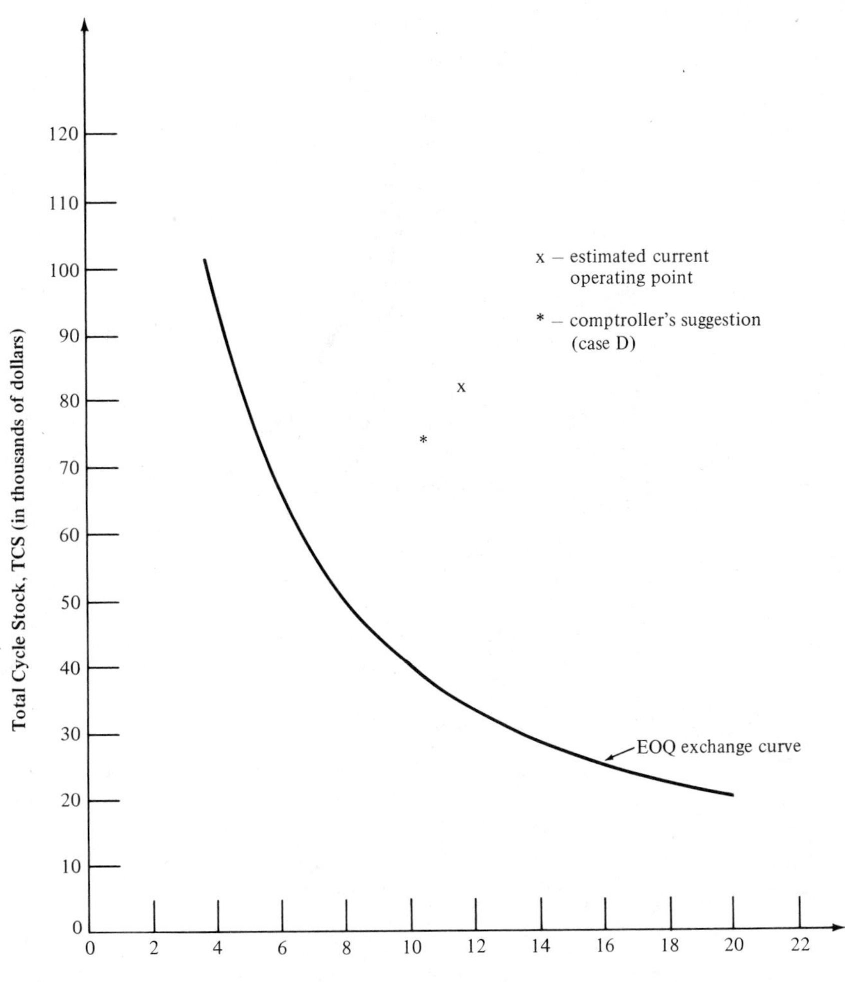

FIGURE 17.2 Order Quantity Exchange Curve for the Professional Products Division of MIDAS

1969). Within each strata the parts were chosen randomly using a complete DBV. Note that the sample of 500 s.k.u. were selected from a total current inventory of 27,600 items. Normally, sufficient accuracy is achieved with no more than 1000 s.k.u. in a sample (regardless of the size of the population).

For each s.k.u. in the sample, the information specified in Table 17.3 was collected. By summing, for example, column 7 for each of the six categories (see

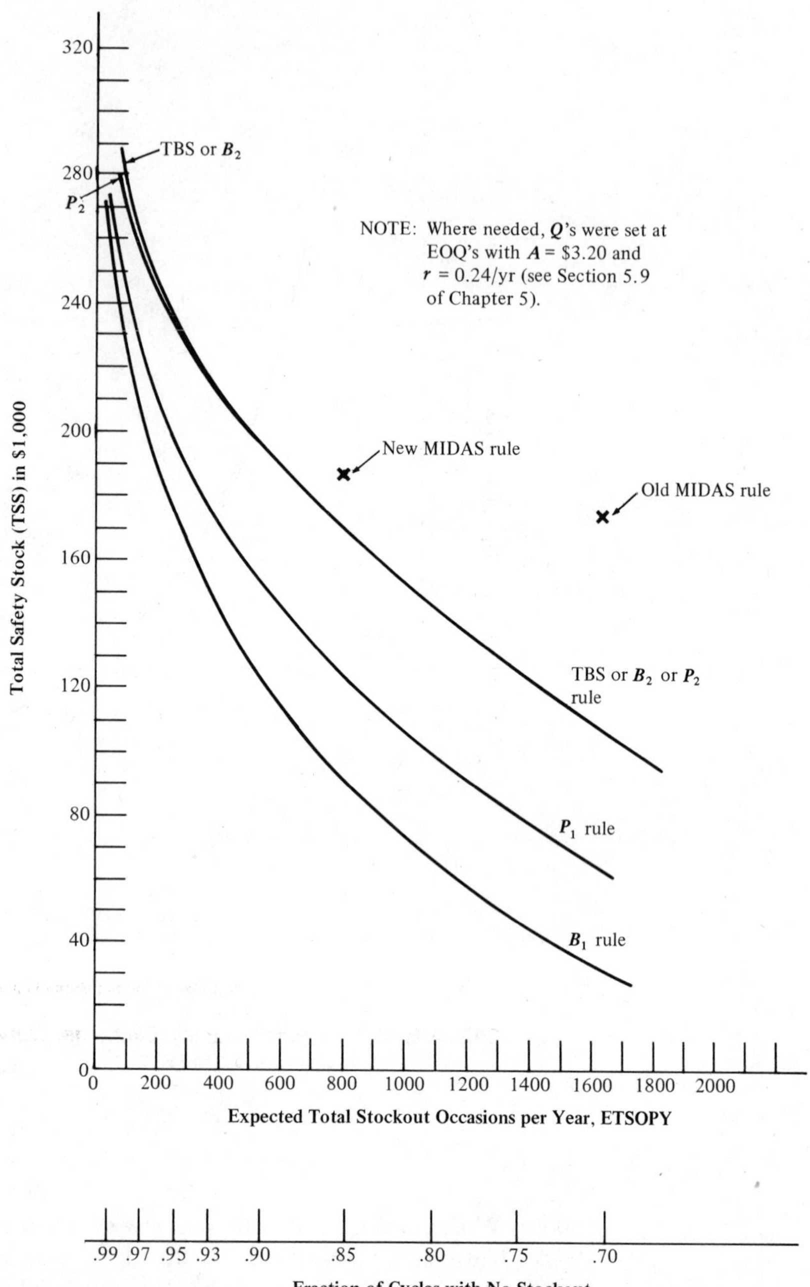

FIGURE 17.3 Exchange Curves of Safety Stock versus Expected Stockout Occasions for the Professional Products Division of MIDAS

TABLE 17.2 Composition of an Illustrative Judgment Sample

Category	Strata
1	First 100 s.k.u. from DBV
2	50 of the next 300
3	50 of the next 1600
4	100 of the next 4935
5	100 of the next 8065
6	100 of the next 12,600

Table 17.2), we estimated the total inventory investment in the population as follows:[3]

Estimated total inventory investment
= (100/100) × Total column 7 for Category 1 items +
+ (300/50) × Total column 7 for Category 2 items + · · · +
+(12,600/100) × Total column 7 for Category 6 items

A similar calculation was carried out to estimate the total number of stockouts in the population, and so on. Note that these estimated values should be compared to existing accounting data whenever possible. For example, how close is the estimated inventory investment derived above to that currently reported by the accountants? If the two are within say 5 percent, we probably can conclude that we have selected a reasonably representative sample. If not, then it is usually not obvious what one should do. In particular, one should be careful in concluding that the sample is not representative. Accounting data are probably somewhat out of date, they may not include exactly the same population of s.k.u. for which we are trying to derive estimates, and so on. In such circumstances the analyst should consult with a knowledgeable manager in trying to define what is wrong.

The classes (or categories) in a stratified sample need not be selected solely on the basis of the Dv value. Bitran et al. (1981) suggest possibly also categorizing by seasonal versus nonseasonal, dependent versus independent items, perisha-

[3]Rather than scaling each category's results up by the ratio

$$\frac{\text{Total number of s.k.u. in the category}}{\text{Number of s.k.u. in the category included in the sample}}$$

Brown (1982) suggests the, perhaps more appropriate, scale factor

$$\frac{\text{Total annual usage value } (\Sigma Dv) \text{ of s.k.u. in the category}}{\text{Total annual usage value of s.k.u. in the category included in the sample}}$$

TABLE 17.3 Data To Be Collected on Existing Inventory System for Sample of s.k.u.

S.k.u. Identification (1)	Annnual Usage D (2)	Unit Cost v (3)	Order Cost A (4)	Reorder Point (5)	Recent Average Order Size Q (6)	Current Inventory Level (7)	Estimate of M.A.D. (8)	Assumed Lead Time L (9)	Number of Stockouts in Last 12 Months (10)

Notes:

Column 2 If demand is seasonal, then the demand for each of the last 12 months should be recorded. Most of the estimation procedures described in this chapter do not allow for seasonal fluctuation. But we do eventually need an estimate of seasonal demand to derive ordering decision rules.

Column 4 It is likely that for many items A will be unavailable and will have to be assumed.

Column 5 It is likely that an average of the positions at the times of the last few orders will have to be used.

Column 6 It is likely that an average of the last few orders will have to be used.

Column 8 Only if a forecasting system such as discussed in Chapter 4 exists, will the value of M.A.D. be available. Otherwise one will have to estimate this value from one of the formulas given in Chapter 4 that related annual demand and forecast error variance. Sometimes the monthly variation in demand is calculated and used here for each s.k.u.

Column 9 Actual lead times will usually be different for each order placed in the past. There are basically two ways to develop a value for L. One could use the more precise methodology described at the end of Chapter 7. Alternatively, we suggest that a number of recent lead times be ranked and that the lead time that occurs at about the 80th percentile be assumed to be L. (This is an approximate method that the authors have resorted to when no other data were available. The 80th percentile is used to crop the outliers.)

Column 10 It is likely that this data may not be recorded. One may have to ask knowledgeable persons to make an estimate.

ble versus nonperishable, and so forth. Furthermore, they suggest an iterative classification scheme. If the sample indicates too high a variability within a category, then that category is further subdivided.

17.4.2 Estimating the Aggregate Consequences of a Proposed Decision System—The Grouping Method

In earlier chapters we derived the aggregate characteristics of the EOQ decision system proposed for the MIDAS Professional Products Division. These exchange curves were derived using all 849 s.k.u. in the Division. There is no reason why the calculations could not be done for only a sample of items, whereupon some method of extrapolation to population values would have to be used. For example, one could extrapolate in the manner we did for the sample in Table 17.2 in the previous section. Two other methodologies, which usually give somewhat less accurate results, but require less computational effort, are also available. The first, known as a *grouping method*, will be described here. The second will be treated in Section 17.4.3.

Brown (1967, Chapter 2) has recommended the grouping of s.k.u. according to annual dollar usage (Dv) from the DBV so that the upper limit for each interval is approximately three times the lower limit (see also Problem 17.9). For each category the data in Table 17.4 must be collected.

TABLE 17.4 Example Data for Brown's Typical Item Grouping Method

Category (1)	Lower Limit of Annual Usage (in \$) (2)	Number of Items n (3)	Value of Annual Usage $\Sigma_i D_i v_i$ in Category (4)	Total Ordering Cost $\Sigma_i A_i$ in Category (5)	Total Value of Safety Stock $\Sigma_i SS_i v_i$ in Category (6)	Total Value of Std. Deviation $\Sigma_i \sigma_{Li} v_i$ in Category (7)	Total Value of Orders $\Sigma_i Q_i v_i$ in Category (8)
.	.	.	.	.	.	.	.
.	.	.	.	.	.	.	.
D	30,000	.	.	.	.	.	.
E	10,000	31	\$383,287	\$2,523	\$19,622.20	\$15,337.80	\$552,323.90
F	3,000	.	.	.	.	.	.
G	1,000	.	.	.	.	.	.
H	300	.	.	.	.	.	.
I	100	.	.	.	.	.	.
.	.	.	.	.	.	.	.
.	.	.	.	.	.	.	.

Brown defines for each class a hypothetical item that has the average characteristics of that class. For that one typical item in each class, all calculations, such as the EOQ, are then carried out. Subsequently, to get the aggregate estimates for the class, all calculations for a typical item are multiplied by the number of items in a category. Then these aggregate estimates for each class are summed to yield overall estimates for the entire system. Note, for example, that category E includes all items whose Dv lies between \$30,000 and \$10,000. From Table 17.4 we get for *a typical average item in category E* that:

$$\bar{A} = \frac{\$2{,}523}{31} = \$81.39$$

$$\overline{Dv} = \frac{\$383{,}287}{31} = \$12{,}364.10$$

Therefore using Eqs. 5.27 and 5.28 from Chapter 5, we can calculate that for category E the total cycle stock (in dollars) and the total number of replenishments per year, as functions of r, are given by:

$$\begin{aligned}
\text{TCS}(E) &\simeq \sqrt{\frac{\bar{A}}{2r}}\,(31)\,\sqrt{\overline{Dv}} \\
&= \sqrt{\frac{81.39}{2r}}\,(31)\,\sqrt{12{,}364.10} \\
&= \frac{31097.71}{\sqrt{2r}}
\end{aligned}$$

$$\begin{aligned}
N(E) &\simeq \sqrt{\frac{r}{2\bar{A}}}\,(31)\,\sqrt{\overline{Dv}} \\
&= \sqrt{\frac{r}{2(81.39)}}\,(31)\,\sqrt{12{,}364.10} \\
&= 382.08\sqrt{\frac{r}{2}}
\end{aligned}$$

The total cycle stock for all categories would simply be the sum of the individual category estimates:

$$\text{TCS} = \text{TCS}(A) + \text{TCS}(B) + \cdots + \frac{1}{\sqrt{2r}}(31{,}097.71) + \text{TCS}(F) + \cdots$$

The total number of replenishments per year N would be obtained in a similar fashion. Finally, using Eq. 5.29 of Chapter 5, we can also estimate the exchange curve given in Figure 17.2:

$$(\mathrm{TCS})(N) = \tfrac{1}{2}\left(\sum_{i=1}^{n} \sqrt{D_i v_i}\right)^2$$

In addition, we can develop estimates of aggregate service under current and proposed systems. To illustrate consider category E in Table 17.4. From columns 6 and 7 the typical or average item has characteristics.

$$\begin{aligned} \bar{k} &= \$19{,}622.20/15{,}337.80 = 1.28 \\ \overline{Qv} &= \$552{,}323.90/31 = 17{,}816.90 \end{aligned}$$

Then, using Eq. 7.4.3 of Chapter 7, expected total stockout occasions per year for category E

$$\begin{aligned} &= \sum_{i \text{ in } E} \frac{D_i}{Q_i} p_{u\geq}(k_i) \\ &\simeq (31)\, p_{u\geq}(\bar{k}) \left(\frac{\overline{Dv}}{\overline{Qv}}\right) = 31\,(0.10)\left(\frac{12{,}364.10}{17{,}816.90}\right) \\ &= 2.15 \end{aligned}$$

17.4.3 Estimating the Aggregate Consequences of a Proposed Decision System—The Lognormal Method

In Section 1.5.2 of Chapter 1 we showed a procedure for developing a DBV table and curve. Empirically, it has been found that quite often the distribution of usage values across a population of items can be adequately represented by a lognormal distribution. In the Appendix of this chapter, we show (1) the mathematical form of the distribution, (2) its moments (expected values of various powers of the variable), (3) a graphic procedure for testing the adequacy of the fit to a given DBV, and (4) a graphic method of estimating the two parameters of the distribution (m, the average value of Dv, and b which is a measure of the dispersion or spread of the Dv values[4]).

---

[4]The parameter b is *not* the standard deviation of Dv. It is the standard deviation of the underlying normally distributed variable, namely $\ln(Dv)$.

From the Appendix, if for a population of n items (numbered $i = 1, 2, \ldots n$) a variable x has a lognormal distribution with parameters m and b, then

$$\sum_{i=1}^{n} x_i^j = nm^j \exp[b^2 j(j-1)/2] \tag{17.1}$$

Suppose a quantity of interest (for example, the cycle stock in dollars) for item i, call it y_i, can be expressed in the form

$$y_i = \sum_{h=1}^{H} c_h (D_i v_i)^{j_h} \tag{17.2}$$

where the c_h's and j_h's are coefficients and H is a constant, that is, a linear combination of the annual dollar usage raised to various powers. Let

$$Y = \sum_{i=1}^{n} y_i \tag{17.3}$$

be the aggregate across the population of the quantity of interest (for example, the total cycle stock in dollars). Then, because the annual dollar usage is approximately lognormally distributed (with parameters m and b), we have from Eqs. 17.1, 17.2, and 17.3

$$Y = n \sum_{h=1}^{H} c_h m^{j_h} \exp[b^2 j_h (j_h - 1)/2] \tag{17.4}$$

We now present two illustrative uses.

Illustration 1: EOQ Exchange Curve

The cycle stock of item i in dollars is

$$\frac{Q_i v_i}{2} = \sqrt{\frac{A_i D_i v_i}{2r}}$$

$$= \sqrt{\frac{A}{2r}} (D_i v_i)^{1/2}$$

assuming the same A for all items.

This is a special case of Eq. 17.2 with $H = 1$, $c_1 = \sqrt{A/2r}$, and $j_1 = \frac{1}{2}$. Thus, from Eq. 17.4 we have that the total cycle stock in dollars is given by

$$\text{TCS} = n\sqrt{A/2r}\, m^{1/2} \exp(-b^2/8)$$

For the MIDAS Professional Products Division we have from the Appendix that $n = 849$, $m = 2048$, and $b = 1.56$. Thus

$$\begin{aligned} \text{TCS} &= (849)\sqrt{A/2r}\,(2048)^{1/2} \exp[-(1.56)^2/8] \\ &= 20042\sqrt{A/r} \end{aligned} \tag{17.5}$$

The number of replenishments per year of item i is

$$\begin{aligned} D_i/Q_i &= D_iv_i/Q_iv_i \\ &= D_iv_i/\sqrt{2AD_iv_i/r} \\ &= \sqrt{\frac{r}{2A}}\,(D_iv_i)^{1/2} \end{aligned}$$

As above, we have that the total number of replenishments per year N is given by

$$N = n\sqrt{r/2A}\; m^{1/2} \exp(-\,b^2/8)$$

and for the MIDAS division

$$N = 20042\sqrt{r/A} \tag{17.6}$$

Multiplication of Eqs. 17.5 and 17.6 gives

$$(\text{TCS})N \simeq 401{,}700{,}000 \tag{17.7}$$

which is the lognormal approximation of the exchange curve of TCS versus N.

The exact exchange curve is

$$(\text{TCS})N = 406{,}500{,}000$$

The latter was developed by a complete item-by-item computation (extremely time-consuming without the aid of a computer routine). It is shown in Figure 17.2. The lognormal approximation of Eq. 17.7 falls a negligible amount above the exact curve in Figure 17.2, such a small amount that one would have difficulty in discerning any difference between the curves.

Illustration 2: Safety Stock Considerations

Herron (1974), with some reasonable approximations, has extended the lognormal approach to allow aggregate estimates of safety stocks and service measures. We indicate the nature of his methods with a particular case, namely, the B_2 shortage costing method (a charge of B_2v_i is made for each unit short of item i). The appropriate decision rule for selecting the safety factor k_i under these circumstances is, from Eq. 7.21 of Chapter 7, to select k_i such that

$$p_{u\geq}(k_i) = \frac{Q_i r}{D_i B_2}$$

where $p_{u\geq}(k_i)$ is the probability that a unit normal variable takes on a value of at least k_i. Using an EOQ for Q_i, we obtain

$$p_{u\geq}(k_i) = \frac{\sqrt{2Ar}}{B_2}(D_i v_i)^{-1/2} \tag{17.8}$$

Suppose we are interested in the total safety stock in dollars (TSS). The safety stock of item i in dollars is given by

$$\mathrm{SS}_i v_i = k_i \sigma_{L_i} v_i \tag{17.9}$$

Herron uses an approximation similar to one that we discussed earlier in the book, namely, that $\sigma_{L_i} v_i$ is given *approximately* by (see Equation 4.73 of Chapter 4)

$$\sigma_{L_i} v_i \simeq c_1 (D_i v_i)^{c_2} \tag{17.10}$$

Thus Eq. 17.9 can be expressed as

$$\mathrm{SS}_i v_i \simeq k_i c_1 (D_i v_i)^{c_2} \tag{17.11}$$

Now, we know that k_i depends on $D_i v_i$ through Eq. 17.8. However, we want Eq. 17.11 to end up as a linear combination of powers of $D_i v_i$ (in order to be able to use Eqs. 17.2 and 17.4). Herron accomplishes this by using the following fitted approximation for k_i in terms of $p_{u\geq}(k)$:[5]

$$k \simeq 1.391p^{-0.123} - 2.325p^{0.618} \tag{17.12}$$

Substitution of Eqs. 17.8 and 17.12 into Eq. 17.11 gives

$$\begin{aligned}\mathrm{SS}_i v_i &\simeq c_1 (D_i v_i)^{c_2}[1.391(\sqrt{2Ar}/B_2)^{-0.123}(D_i v_i)^{0.0615} \\ &\quad -2.325(\sqrt{2Ar}/B_2)^{0.618}(D_i v_i)^{-0.309}] \\ &= 1.319c_1(\sqrt{2Ar}/B_2)^{-0.123}(D_i v_i)^{c_2+0.0615} \\ &\quad -2.325c_1(\sqrt{2Ar}/B_2)^{0.618}(D_i v_i)^{c_2-0.309}\end{aligned}$$

[5]For simplicity in notation in Eq. 17.12 we drop the subscript on k_i and let p represent $p_{u\geq}(k_i)$.

But this is in the form of Eq. 17.2. Hence, the lognormal distribution of Dv can be used to find the total safety stock by means of Eq. 17.4.

To permit the derivation of aggregate measures of service (such as the expected total value short per year) and to deal with other safety stock decision rules, Herron makes use of other approximations (similar to Eq. 17.12), for example,

1. The $G_u(\cdot)$ function expressed as a linear combination of powers of the $p_{u\geq}(\cdot)$ function
2. k expressed as a linear combination of powers of the $G_u(\cdot)$ function

All of the above discussion concerning safety stocks hinges on having estimates of the parameters c_1 and c_2 in Eq. 17.10. As Bitran et al. (1981) point out, this may be rather difficult to accomplish at the early stages of a study where we are seeking the aggregate estimates of system performance.

17.5 EVALUATION AND CONTROL

We have described implementation as a process, consisting of a decision to adopt, followed by systematization, and by gradual institutionalization. The last of these three phases tends to get the least attention from analysts, yet many implementation failures occur at this stage. After all, it is here that the integrity of a new system is finally (if ever) proven. The claims of estimation procedures, such as discussed in Section 17.4, no matter how well conceived, seldom are a match to proven success in daily use. Actual performance should be compared to that under the old (previous) system. In this regard, it is important, during the system development stage, to collect information as quickly as possible on the operating performance of the old system. The actual performance of the new system should also be compared against that predicted by the underlying model. Even under ideal conditions, some deviation is expected for two reasons. First, the model is only an approximation of reality. Second, random processes are involved and one is only seeing a sample outcome of performance.

A number of monitoring procedures need to be designed. These procedures should ensure that undesirable and unexpected situations are quickly detected, evaluated, and remedial action initiated. Backorder levels, erroneous forecasts, manufacturing variances, deviations between physical and book inventories, and so on, all need to be continually monitored, because they may reveal some design flaws in the new decision system. Saipe (1979) provides a framework for analyzing variances from predicted (or planned) performance. Some of the most important control functions include:

1. Daily comparison of actual production with that being scheduled
2. Periodic checking of actual sales activity versus forecast

3. Periodic review of the backorder situation and the expediting of requirements
4. Periodic taking of physical inventory
5. Periodic monitoring of the design assumptions of the decision models implemented

If these activities are not carried out routinely, then the institutionalization of an innovative decision system is likely not to follow.

17.5.1 Physical Stock Counts

Physical stock counts, taken annually in many organizations, are intended to satisfy the auditors that account records reasonably represent the value of inventory investment. But the accuracy of stock records is also an important aspect of production planning and inventory management. Most of the decision systems described in this book would be seriously crippled by inaccurate records.

As a check on records some physical counting of s.k.u actually in stock has always been deemed necessary. But physical counts have proven to be expensive and time-consuming.[6] The authors recall the words of a general manager during a tour of a steel manufacturing operation: "I am deliberatly letting the inside inventory drop down to facilitate the annual stock counting." Taking a physical stock count has in the past in many companies involved the shutting down of all operations, and thereby the losing of valuable productive time. Because of this large opportunity cost, many companies have adopted different procedures that achieve the same purpose. Given a limited budget allocation to be spent on corroborating inventory records with physical inventory, a system that more effectively rations the available clerical resources is known as *cycle counting*.

In cycle counting, as the name might suggest, a physical inventory of each particular item is taken once during each of its replenishment cycles. There are several versions of cycle counting (see Jordan, 1975); probably the most effective one involves counting the remaining physical stock of an s.k.u. just as a replenishment arrives. This has two key advantages. First, the stock is counted at its lowest level. Second, a clerk is already at the stocking position delivering the replenishment; hence a special trip is not needed for counting purposes. Clearly, one drawback is that, if the records are faulty on the high side, we may already have gone into an unexpected stockout position. Note that cycle counting automatically ensures that low-usage s.k.u. are counted less often than high-usage items because the frequency of reordering increases with Dv (at least under a decision system based on economic order quantities). Most auditors agree with physically counting low-value items less often than the more expensive ones.

[6]Counting need not be done in a literal sense. An effective, accurate way of estimating the number of units of certain types of products is the use of weigh scales.

Paperwork, relating to a s.k.u. being counted, can be outstanding at any point in time. When outstanding paperwork exists, a disagreement between counted and recorded inventory may not necessarily mean that the written records are in error. Cycle counts are for this reason in some companies confined to first thing in the morning, or the last thing in the day, or on the off shift, when outstanding paperwork should be at a minimum. In any case, some form of cutoff rule such as the following is required:

1. If a discrepancy is less than some low percent of the reorder point level, adjust your records to the lower of the two figures and report any loss to accounting.
2. If the discrepancy is greater than some low percent, one must wait a few days and request a recount. One hopes by this time outstanding paperwork will have been processed. If the discrepancy is the same on both counts, we have probably found an error and should adjust the records accordingly. If the second count results in a different discrepancy, the problem requires investigation.

There are some practical disadvantages and problems with cycle counting. (Plossl and Wight, 1967). Cutoff rules are not easy to follow while normal everyday activity is going on. Checking up on the paperwork in the system, so that stock levels may be properly corroborated, requires considerable perseverance and diplomacy. Responsibility for cycle counting is often assigned to stockroom employees. As a result, too often cycle counting gets relegated a lower priority and, more often than it should, is discontinued, when business activity picks up and stockroom personnel find it difficult to carry out their regular activities as well as stock counting. One solution in such cases is to assign a permanent team to carry out cycle counting all year round.

Cycle counting rations effort in proportion to annual dollar usage Dv. It is important to recognize that not all causes of stock discrepancies are a function of Dv. Recently, the authors encountered a situation illustrating this point. Items that could be resold on the black market tended to be out of stock more often. Although it could not be proven, the distinct possibility existed that some of the stolen parts were being resold back to the company through supposedly legitimate wholesalers. Therefore, the accessibility, physical size, and resalability of items, as well as their Dv, had to be considered in establishing procedures for stock counts.

Stratified sampling procedures can also be useful for reducing required sample sizes, particularly for audit purposes. Buck and Sadowski (1983) suggest this approach.

17.5.2 Monitoring the Design Assumptions

In Chapter 3 we explored the difficulties encountered in estimating the various parameters for the decision rules developed in the rest of the book. Resistance to new decisions systems results in part from the fact that management science decision models require a greater amount of explicitness and preciseness than most managers can comfortable deliver. For example, the cost of carrying inventories, through a company's cost of capital, is affected almost daily by world events. Therefore, the total dollar investment in inventories and the quality of customer service that is "right" in keeping with these events should ideally also be subject to constant revision by top management. In a dynamic environment, models must keep pace with changes in the environment to maintain management's confidence in the production/inventory decision system. Decision systems whose design assumptions become outdated are the most frequent cause of failure over the long implementation period.

Most managers are by necessity results-oriented. When a decision system fails to be supportive of managerial actions, more often than not, a manager under such circumstances is unwilling to distinguish between problems of data measurement and a failure to appropriately model the decision environment. Therefore, a systems designer must accept responsibility for monitoring whether the model is appropriate, as well as whether the model parameters (data) are being properly estimated.

In Chapter 4 we discussed various methods for monitoring the accuracy of forecasts and the continuing appropriateness of different forecasting procedures. Such monitoring and control systems are relatively common in practice. Often ignored in practice, though, is the routine monitoring of the appropriateness of the individual-item cost parameters such as A, v, r, the shortage costs or service levels, and the more aggregate parameters such as the cost of hiring and firing, and regular and overtime production. From our experience we have found that the cost (and other) parameters for the individual-item order quantity and reorder point (order-up-to-level) decision rules should be updated once or twice a year. For the important A items these parameters should be reviewed monthly or bimonthly. The maintenance of the cost parameters for the more aggregate planning models should be integrated with regular cost accounting procedures using revised costs reported at least once a year.

17.5.3 Transient Effects

Each time the parameters of a decision model are adjusted, a series of transient effects result that must be carefully monitored and controlled. Consider the recommendation of an analyst that affects the reallocation of inventory tied up in safety stocks in such a manner that *total inventory investment is not changed in the long run*. The reorder points for some s.k.u. are raised, for others the reorder points are lowered, and for the balance there is no change. If management implemented all of the new reorder points at the *same* time, some of the newly calculated reorder points, raised from previous levels, would immediately trigger orders. If there were many changes, then a sudden wave of orders could overload a company's manufacturing plant or order department and also result, after a lead time, in an increase in on-hand dollar inventory investment, as shown in Figure 17.4.

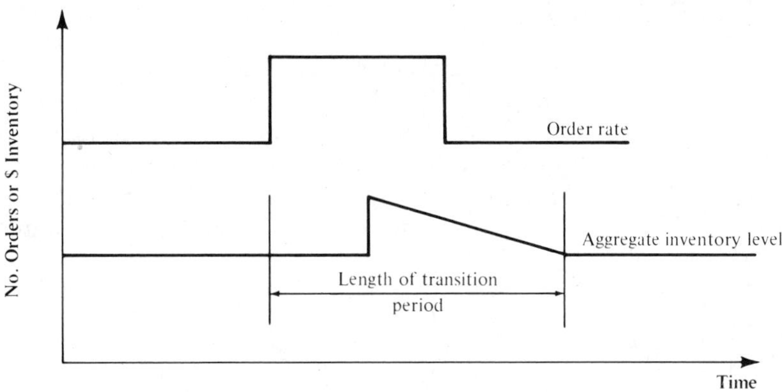

FIGURE 17.4 Schematic Diagram of a Transient Effect

The obvious solution is, of course, not to make all the changes at the same time. Some form of phased implementation strategy that lengthens the period of transition and thereby dampens the disruptions in the system must be chosen. To determine an acceptable transition strategy, the following need to be balanced:

1. The cost of carrying extra inventories during the transition period
2. The expense of a higher than normal ordering rate
3. The opportunity cost of delaying benefits from a new production/inventory decision system that is not implemented all at once
4. Any benefits resulting from the better than normal service level resulting from extra inventory on hand during the transition period

In practice, the changeover to new decision rules is often carried out at the time when an s.k.u. is reordered, the assumption being made that a dispersion of transitory effects will result through "random" times when a particular item reaches its reorder point. There is of course no guarantee that large blips such as illustrated in Figure 17.4 would not occur. Alternatively, revised decision rules are implemented in phases, starting with the most important, A items first.

In either case, it is best to try and plan a large transition carefully; in particular, one should carefully monitor the resulting stockout rate, the net increase in orders placed, and the rise in total dollar inventory. It is unlikely that the costs of transition can ever be determined and balanced analytically. Therefore, a simulation of transient effects that result from alternative implementation strategies should be undertaken whenever the scope of the problem warrants such an expense.

17.6 SUMMARY

In this chapter we have returned to a number of issues raised in the introductory chapters of the book. Of necessity, much of the discussion of planning, estimation, evaluation, and control had been rather qualitative in contrast with the modeling efforts of the main portion of the book. However, these softer issues are of vital importance in realizing the increased effectiveness of management science efforts in production and inventory management.

APPENDIX TO CHAPTER 17
THE LOGNORMAL DISTRIBUTION

1. PROBABILITY DENSITY FUNCTION AND CUMULATIVE DISTRIBUTION FUNCTION

The density function of a lognormal variable x is given by[7]

$$f_x(x_0) = \frac{1}{bx_0\sqrt{2\pi}} \exp\left[-(\ln x_0 - a)^2/2b^2\right] \qquad 0 < x_0 < \infty \tag{17.13}$$

where a and b are the two parameters of the distribution.

It is seen that the range of the lognormal is from 0 to ∞. It has a single peak in this range. A sketch of a typical lognormal distribution is shown in Figure 17.5.

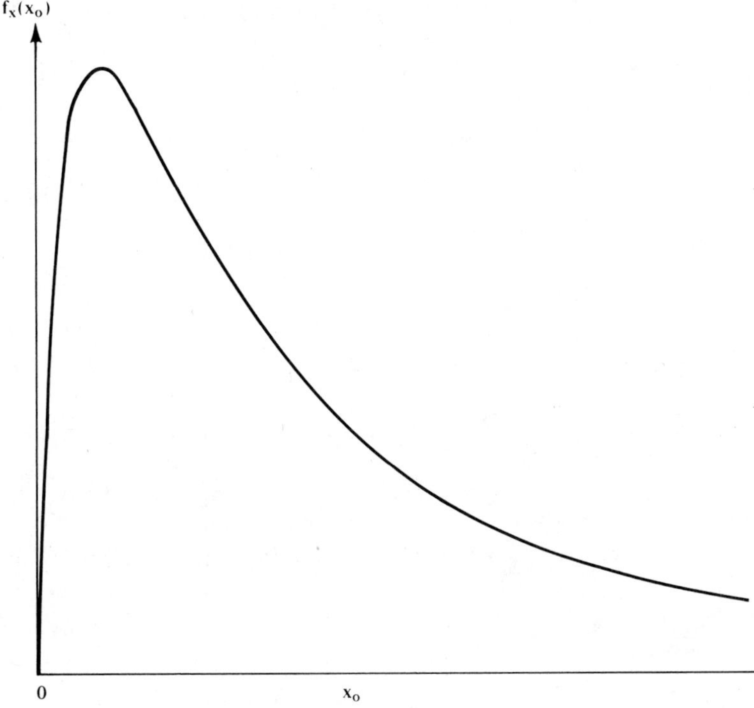

FIGURE 17.5 The Lognormal Probability Density Function

[7] $f_x(x_0)dx_0$ represents the probability that x takes on a value between x_0 and $x_0 + dx_0$.

The name is derived from the fact that the logarithm of x has a normal distribution (with mean a and standard deviation b).

The cumulative distribution function

$$p_{x\leqslant}(x_0) = \int_{-\infty}^{x_0} f_x(z)dz$$

can be shown to be given by

$$p_{x\leqslant}(x_0) = 1 - p_{u\geqslant}\left(\frac{\ln x_0 - a}{b}\right) \tag{17.14}$$

where $p_{u\geqslant}(u_0)$ is the probability that a unit normal variable takes on a value of u_0 or larger, a function tabulated in Appendix B.

2. MOMENTS

One can show (see, for example, Aitchison and Brown, 1957) that the expected value of the jth power (for any real j) of x is given by[8]

$$E(x^j) = m^j \exp[b^2 j(j-1)/2] \tag{17.15}$$

where

$$m = \exp[a + b^2/2] \tag{17.16}$$

is the mean or expected value of x itself.

The variance of x, defined by

$$\sigma_x^2 = E(x^2) - [E(x)]^2$$

can be shown, through straightforward use of Eqs. 17.15 and 17.16, to be

$$\sigma_x^2 = [E(x)]^2[\exp(b^2) - 1]$$

Hence, the standard deviation σ_x is given by

$$\sigma_x = E(x)\sqrt{\exp(b^2) - 1}$$

---

[8] In general,

$$E(x^j) = \int_{-\infty}^{\infty} x_0^j f_x(x_0)dx_0 \tag{17.17}$$

and the coefficient of variation by

$$\sigma_x/E(x) = \sqrt{\exp(b^2) - 1}$$

the latter depending only on the value of b.

If, as in a DBV of a population of n items, x is actually a discrete variable that takes on the values x_i $(i = 1, 2, \ldots, n)$ and the x_i's can be represented by a lognormal distribution with parameters m and b, then

$$E(x^j) = \frac{\sum_{i=1}^{n} x_i^j}{n} \tag{17.18}$$

and from Eq. 17.15 it follows that

$$\sum_{i=1}^{n} x_i^j = nm^j \exp[b^2 j(j - 1)/2] \tag{17.19}$$

Note that the parameter m can be estimated using the sample mean, that is,

$$m = \frac{\sum_{i=1}^{n} x_i}{n} \tag{17.20}$$

3. A GRAPHIC PROCEDURE FOR ESTIMATING b AND TESTING THE FIT OF A LOGNORMAL

Herron (1976) describes a graphic method for testing the fit of the lognormal distribution to a DBV and for estimating the value of the parameter b. The DBV table (see Table 1.4 of Chapter 1) gives us, item by item (by decreasing value of Dv), the cumulative percent of the items and the cumulative percent of total annual dollar usage. If these two quantities are plotted on a graph, where both axes are marked off according to normal probability scales, then for a lognormal distribution the resulting points would lie on a straight line with a slope of 1, as in Figure 17.6. This straight line will intersect an ordinate erected at the 50 percent mark of the horizontal scale of Figure 17.6, and allow the reading off of the value of parameter b. (Problem 17.11 deals with proving these last two statements.) The other parameter m is found from Eq. 17.20 as

$$m = \frac{\sum_{i=1}^{n} D_i v_i}{n} \tag{17.21}$$

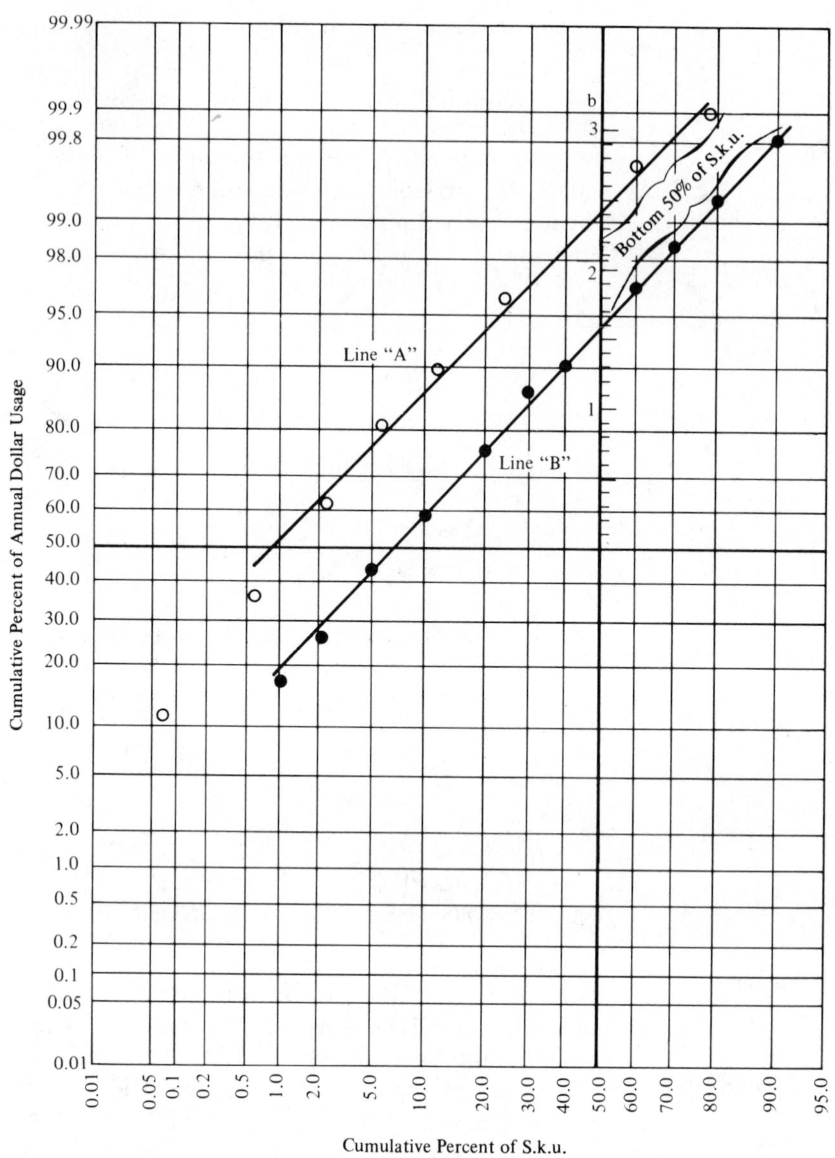

FIGURE 17.6 DBV Curves for Two Different Multi-item Inventories

The straight line labeled *A* in Figure 17.6 is for the 4,886 s.k.u. in the Warmdot Company inventory, a manufacturer of heating and air conditioning equipment described and analyzed in detail in Brown (1967). For line *A* the value of *m* is $2,923 (not on graph), and that of *b* can be read from the graph as 2.40. Line *B* describes the 849 s.k.u. in the inventory of the Professional Products Division of MIDAS (Canada) Corporation for which *m* equals $2,048 and *b* is equal to 1.56. Note that the bottom 50 percent of s.k.u. account for less than 1 percent of total annual dollar usage for Warmdot and about 6 percent of total annual dollar usage for MIDAS. According to Herron, typically the inventories of merchants (wholesalers, retailers, etc.) have b's in the range of 0.8 to 2.0; industrial producers are in the range 2 to 3; and highly sophisticated hardware suppliers (who are subject to rapid technological innovations) have b's in the 3 to 4 range.

PROBLEMS

17.1 A large wholesaler carried out a preliminary study in which they estimated the effects of introducing an order-point, order-quantity inventory control system in place of their current system. Because significant potential savings were estimated to be available, the new decision system was installed. Actual savings in carrying costs, replenishment costs, and shortage costs during the first year of operation turned out to be much lower than the estimated values. Give some possible reasons for why this might have happened. What action would you take? Elaborate.

17.2 "It is important that the operating characteristics of an existing inventory management or production planning decision be established before any revisions are started." Do you agree? Give at least 5 reasons for your opinion. Discuss.

17.3 Visit a business of your choice and try to establish on the basis of, at most, a one-hour interview how sophisticated its existing decision systems are. Write a two-page memorandum describing the decision rules and summarize your impressions in terms of the concepts presented in Table 17.1. What is the highest priority problem? Where would you start to revise the decision systems? How large are the potential savings and improvements likely to be? Does top management appear to be receptive to some changes in the existing procedures?

17.4 During the preliminary probing of an existing inventory decision system you collect the following data:

Item A	Item B
$A = \$10$	$A = \$10$
$v = \$4.58$	$v = \$1.82$
$D = 4000$ (last year)	$D = 6100$ (last year)
Current order quantity $= 1000$	Current order quantity $= 500$
Current reorder point $\simeq 350$	Current reorder point $\simeq 500$
$L = 1$ to 3 weeks	$L \simeq 1$ month

Here is your chance to play rumpled cop. Based on these data, what would you conclude? What questions would you pose to management? What other data would you seek? Would you request a full-scale investigation? Assume that A was estimated by the bookkeeper and v was the value assigned by accountants for purposes of evaluating inventories. The rest of the data were compiled by you from available records.

17.5

a. What would you conclude about the inventory decision system described, in part, in Problem 17.4 above if in addition you were able to compile (using the methodology in Section 5.9 of Chapter 5 and in Section 7.9.2 of Chapter 7) for a total of 50 items the exchange curves given in Figure 17.7?

b. Discuss some of the general approaches you would consider in attempting to improve the existing decision-making procedures.

17.6 Suppose for category H of Table 17.4 the following values were obtained:

$$n = 1203$$

$$\sum Dv = \$638{,}720/\text{yr}$$

$$\sum A = \$11{,}764.34$$

$$\sum SSv = \$100{,}539$$

$$\sum \sigma v = \$70{,}307$$

$$\sum Qv = \$83{,}808$$

Use the grouping method (Section 17.4.2) to estimate for category H the EOQ exchange

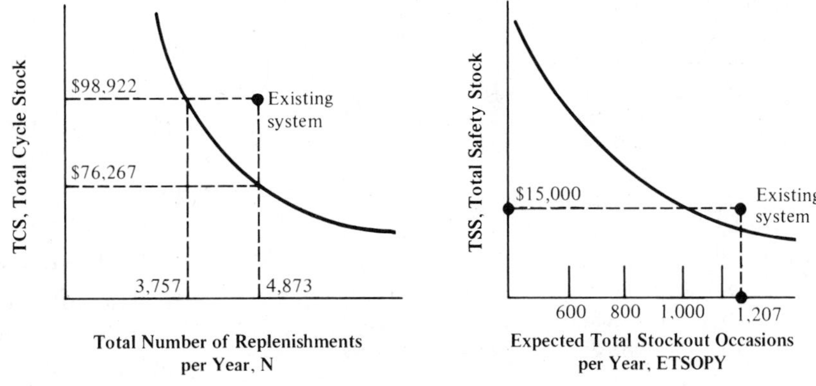

FIGURE 17.7 Exchange Curves for Problem 17.5

curve and the expected number of stockout occasions per year with the current safety stock (assuming a P_1 service measure).

17.7 For the data in Problem 17.6, estimate the total safety stock, expected number of shortages per year, and the expected value short per year (see Eq. 7.41 in Chapter 7) for each of the following strategies:

a. A five-week safety stock for each item.

b. A value of $k = 1.2$.

c. A 96.3 percent service level (fraction of demand satisfied without backorders).

d. How do the values obtained in this question compare to those you derived in Problem 17.6? Discuss.

17.8 Using the methodology described in Section 17.4.3, estimate the value of total cycle stock (TCS) and the total number of orders per year (N) for a lognormal DBV consisting of 12,387 s.k.u. with the following parameters:

$$m = \$1856/\text{yr}$$

$$b = 2.03$$

$$\bar{A} \simeq \$10.00$$

$$r = 0.20/\text{yr}$$

17.9 Consider the situation where all the items in a population have the same values of A and r. Suppose aggregation into ranges of Dv is to be done as described in Table 17.4 and the *mid-value* $\overline{Dv}$ of each range is to be used for the EOQ calculations for all items in the range. The ranges are to be selected so as to not make a percent cost error greater than p. Let $(Dv)_B$, $(Dv)_T$, and $\overline{Dv}$ be the bottom, top, and middle points of a particular range.

a. Verify that

$$\frac{(Dv)_B}{\overline{Dv}} = \frac{\overline{Dv}}{(Dv)_T} = \text{Constant}$$

where the constant is a function of p, but is independent of the particular range.

b. Show that, because of the result in part a, ranges should not be chosen to be of equal width, but should have a constant difference between the logarithms of the upper and lower limits.

17.10 A random sample of 20 items was selected from a population of 500 items. The Dv values found are as follows:

i	D_iv_i (\$/yr)	i	D_iv_i (\$/yr)
1	706.27	11	1522.33
2	304.90	12	20.01
3	339.68	13	1036.91
4	416.55	14	28.33
5	835.47	15	327.67
6	23.10	16	339.68
7	2980.96	17	42.10
8	5177.10	18	202.76
9	529.54	19	1822.56
10	988.31	20	49.80

a. Develop a DBV for these 20 items using a graph similar to Figure 17.6 to check if a lognormal distribution is a reasonable fit. If so, what is the estimated value of b?

b. What percent of the total usage is represented by the top 20 percent (fastest movers) of the items?

c. What is your estimate of the total dollar usage of all 500 items?

d. Assuming a lognormal distribution, what is your estimate of $\Sigma_i \sqrt{D_iv_i}$?

17.11 Prove the two statements made in Section 3 of the Appendix concerning Figure 17.6; namely, that if the underlying distribution is lognormal, then

a. The resulting plot will be a straight line.

b. The value of b can be determined from the intersection with a straight line, having an appropriate scale, erected at the 50 percent mark of the horizontal axis.

17.12 Discuss the economic considerations, physical constraints, and other possible factors that could influence the choice of the method, the frequency, and the timing of physical inventory counts. Illustrate your discussion with actual examples from your experience whenever possible.

REFERENCES

Abo El-Ela, M. A. (1975). "Statistical Sampling for Inventory Parameters." Unpublished M.A.Sc. thesis, Department of Management Sciences, University of Waterloo, Waterloo, Ontario.

Aitchison, J., and J. A. C. Brown (1957). *The Lognormal Distribution.* Cambridge University Press, Cambridge, England.

Bishop, J. L. (1974). "Experience with a Successful System for Forecasting and Inventory Control." *Operations Research*, Vol. 22, No. 6, pp. 1224–1231.

Bitran, G. R., A. C. Hax, and J. Valor-Sabatier (1981). "Diagnostic Analysis of Inventory Systems: A Statistical Approach." *Working Paper No. 1272–81*, Alfred P. Sloan School of Management, Massachusetts Institute of Technology, Cambridge, Massachusetts.

Brown, R. G. (1967). *Decision Rules for Inventory Management.* Holt, Rinehart and Winston, New York.

Brown, R. G. (1982). *Advanced Service Parts Inventory Control.* Materials Management Systems, Inc., Norwich, Vermont, pp. 366–369.

Buck, J. R., and R. P. Sadowski (1983). "Optimum Stratified Cycle Counting." *IEE Transactions*, Vol. 15, No. 2, pp. 119–126.

Churchman, C. W., and A. H. Schainblatt (1965). "The Researcher and the Manager: A Dialectic of Implementation." *Management Science*, Vol. 11, No. 4, pp. B69–B87.

Doktor, R. H., and W. F. Hamilton (1973). "Cognitive Style and Acceptance of Management Science Recommendations." *Management Science*, Vol. 19, No. 8, pp. 884–894.

Duncan, W. J. (1974). "The Researcher and the Manager: A Comparative View of the Need for Mutual Understanding." *Management Science*, Vol. 20, No. 8, pp. 1157–1163.

Dyckman, J. R. (1967). "Management Implementation of Scientific Research: An Attitudinal Study." *Management Science*, Vol. 13, No. 10, pp. B612–B620.

Hausman, W. H. (1969). "Minimizing Customer Line Items Backordered in Inventory Control." *Management Science*, Vol. 15, No. 12, pp. B628–B634.

Herron, D. P. (1974). "Profit Oriented Techniques for Managing Independent Demand Inventories." *Production and Inventory Management*, Vol. 15, No. 3, pp. 57–74.

Herron, D. P. (1976). "Industrial Engineering Applications of ABC Curves." *AIIE Transactions*, Vol. 8, No. 2, pp. 210–218.

Huysman, J. H. B. M. (1970). *The Implementation of Operations Research.* Wiley-Interscience, New York.

Iglehart, D., and R. Morey (1972). "Inventory Systems with Imperfect Asset Information." *Management Science*, Vol. 18, No. 8, pp. B388–B394.

Jordan, H. (1975). "How to Start a Cycle Counting Program." *Proceedings of the 18th Annual International Conference of the American Production and Inventory Control Society*, pp. 190–198.

MacCormick, A. (1978). "Predicting the Cost Performance of Inventory Control Systems by Retrospective Simulation." *Naval Research Logistics Quarterly*, Vol. 25, pp. 605–619.

Miller, W. (1978). "Giving Yourself an Inventory Checkup." *Production and Inventory Management*, Vol. 19, No. 2, pp. 68–80.

Plossl, G. W., and O. W. Wight (1967). *Production and Inventory Control.* Prentice-Hall, Englewood Cliffs, New Jersey.

Reuter, V. G. (1978). "Are We Using the Inventory Management Tools?" *Industrial Management*, Vol. 20, No. 3, pp. 26–30.

Rubenstein, A., M. Radnor, N. R. Baker, D. R. Heiman, and J. B. McColly (1967). "Some Organizational Factors Related to the Effectiveness of Management Science Groups in Industry." *Management Science*, Vol. 13, No. 8, pp. B508–B518.

Saipe, A. L. (1979). "Diagnosing Production-Inventory Systems Using Variance Analysis." *INFOR*, Vol. 17, No. 1, pp. 42–51.

Urban, G. (1974). "Building Models for Decision Makers." *INTERFACES*, Vol. 4, No. 3, pp. 1–11.

Welsh, W. E. (1979). "Management's Role in Inventory Control." *Production and Inventory Management*, Vol. 20, No. 3, pp. 85–95.

Wharton, F. (1975). "On Estimating Aggregate Inventory Characteristics." *Operational Research Quarterly*, Vol. 26, No. 3i, pp. 543–551.

Wight, O. W. (1981). *MRP II: Unlocking America's Productivity Potential.* Oliver Wight Publications, Inc., Williston, Vermont, Chapter 18.

Wolek, F. F. (1975). "Implementation and the Process of Adopting Managerial Technology." *INTERFACES*, Vol. 5, No. 3, pp. 38–46.

Woolsey, R. E. D. (1975). "On Doing Good Things and Dumb Things in Production and Inventory Control." *INTERFACES*, Vol. 5, No. 3, pp. 65–67.

CHAPTER 18

Computerized Systems

Throughout the book we have advocated a decision systems approach to inventory management and production planning, where decision systems consist of three basic elements: a data-collection and processing subsystem, a set of decision rules and a built-in capability for intervention, at will, by human decision makers. Section 18.1 addresses the need for any specific firm to have computerized versus noncomputerized decision systems. If computerization is selected, then the organization must choose between developing a software package in-house versus purchasing it from a supplier. This decision is the topic of Section 18.2. In Section 18.3 a number of guidelines are offered for the development of a computerized system. Finally, Section 18.4 provides some concluding remarks concerning the entire book.

18.1 IS A COMPUTERIZED DECISION SYSTEM NEEDED?

The reader might think that, with the widespread availability of digital computers, almost all firms involved in the production or distribution of goods would utilize computerized decision systems. The tendency will continue to be in this direction, particularly with the increased availability of powerful, relatively inexpensive mini- and micro-computers. However, many organizations have plunged headlong into computerized systems with painful results, including a not infrequent return to prior manual procedures. As reported by Burch and Gooding (1976), this is primarily the result of not having first carried out an appropriate feasibility study. Such a study should encompass the following:

1. An analysis of the current manual system with identification of needed changes.[1]
2. An estimation of the costs and benefits of using one or more computerized systems.

---

[1]Without such an analysis one runs the risk of simply computerizing ineffective manual procedures. Burch and Gooding report on a related case study. Furthermore, with respect to the design of decision systems, Heller (1972) has stated that "eight-tenths of the savings will come from better recordkeeping."

3. An estimation of calendar time needed for development and implementation of any new system.
4. An organizational impact analysis.

In essence, this is what we have argued, particularly in Chapter 17, with respect to the possible adoption of *any* new decision system, whether computerized or not.

There are obvious tangible costs of buying or leasing the required computer hardware. If a software package is purchased or leased, again the associated costs are quite clear. The costs of the development of software are more difficult to predict. In addition, there are intangible costs such as those associated with possible errors in decision making, at least in the early stages of use of a new system, and possible alienation of valuable employees.

Again, the benefits of a computerized system may be difficult to pinpoint quantitatively. In a qualitative sense, a computer permits more rapid (faster response time) and dependable collection and processing of data, including carrying out the calculations of complex (and, one hopes, more appropriate) decision rules that would be impractical to use on a manual basis. However, the usefulness of the results of such calculations is highly dependent on the validity of the input data. (Garbage-in, garbage-out!) Another important benefit of a computerized system is the ability to deal with "what-if" questions in an essentially simulation mode. In addition, a computerized system affords the opportunity to provide specially designed reports to different designated users (for example, information on an aggregated basis for senior management, on an exception basis for middle management, and on a detailed basis for clerical personnel).

In larger organizations it would appear that fairly extensive use of computerized systems is inevitable. However, the outcome is not so clear-cut for smaller firms. Unless a computerized system permits the continued use of judgmental input (personalized attention), its costs and increased rigidity (relative to a manual system) may very well make its use unattractive to smaller organizations. Nevertheless, properly designed software systems on a personal (micro) computer offer great potential for aiding decision makers in production planning and inventory management in *all* sizes of organizations. As an illustration Hohenstein (1984) describes the use of microcomputer spreadsheets in connection with physical inventory counts (see Section 17.5.1 of Chapter 17). Spreadsheet programs could also be used in developing a Distribution by Value (see Section 1.5.2 of Chapter 1) or a Coverage Analysis (see Section 9.4.1. of Chapter 9). In fact, the increased availability of *effective* decision systems on relatively inexpensive microcomputers may well be the single, most important catalyst in reducing the gap between theory and practice in production planning, scheduling, and inventory management.

18.2 TO MAKE OR BUY

In considering the problem of how to improve existing inventory management and production planning decision-making procedures, top management in effect faces the familiar *make or buy decision*. Management has the choice of either building a decision system from scratch or, more likely, gradually improving their existing procedures, using some of the ideas we have presented. Alternatively, management could adopt one of the many computerized software (canned) packages or one of the manual systems (as in the MIDAS cases) available on the market. These prepackaged systems contain decision rules and concepts that try to deal with problems similar to the ones we have discussed in this book. But the quality and sophistication of the decision-making technology used in *some* of these systems can be open to question. This appears to be a reflection of the fact that prepackaged systems are being sold by a variety of organizations: computer software/hardware companies, consulting firms, data-processing companies, computer service bureaus, and private manufacturing concerns attempting to recoup some of the investment that went into developing a custom-built decision system for themselves. Some of these organizations do not possess the know-how required to properly develop such systems or to provide appropriate assistance in their implementation.

Some of the considerations involved in deciding on whether to make or buy a software system have been spelled out by Hoyt (1975) who spent 4 months as a member of a team of managers from the Sundstrand Corporation looking at alternative prepackaged decision systems. Table 18.1 contains a partial listing of the factors considered by this management team.

Perhaps the most striking factor that stands out from the listing in Table 18.1 is the fact that it is highly probable that *all* prepackaged decision systems would have to be customized (to some degree) to be useful in a specific application. Presumably, larger companies, because of their financial and technical capabilities, are more able to develop their own customized compilers, languages, and other specialized features that are needed to increase the operational efficiency of generalized prepackaged decision systems. Smaller companies, on the other hand, if they adopt a prepackaged decision system, usually must resort to the expedient of simply suppressing (rather than eliminating) many of the options and routines available in a software package that was designed for a wider range of market needs. Suppression, rather than elimination, leads to inefficiencies from a computational standpoint. Thus, the repeated use of such a package is relatively quite expensive.

It would appear that medium-sized firms are the ones who tend to find computerized software packages to their advantage. Larger companies, because of the complexities of their management information systems, either undertake considerable customization of the prepackaged software that they purchase or they simply design their own systems.

TABLE 18.1 The Software Make-or-Buy Decision[a]

A. Why Buy a Package?

Packages, in theory, are supposed to:

1. Take less time to install since the thinking, coding, and documentation have been done already.
2. Provide quicker benefits so that payback can start sooner.
3. Involve less development cost.
4. Yield better computer utilization since vendors can afford to fine-tune their coding to use the most efficient programming techniques.
5. Come with superior documentation since vendors can amortize their efforts across all future buyers.
6. Utilize vendors' "Project Management Know-how" since they act as consultants and presumably have installed many packages before.
7. Provide an avenue for technology exchanges more easily than in-house developed programs. Packages make it easier to talk the same language as other users of the same package.

Other reasons to buy a package:

1. Why re-invent the wheel? Supposedly packages have undergone several generations of logic iterations. They are said to include a more advanced state-of-the-art than your own company people could hope to produce.
2. Projects are often too big for in-house development. The size of many projects often means getting outside help in order to get results in a reasonable period of time. Packages are one form of help.
3. Packages may free up your data-processing resource. In-house projects typically consume a larger percentage of your data-processing (D.P.) staff. A package may leave some analysts and programmers for other worthwhile projects.
4. D.P. personnel who developed and who programmed existing systems are often gone. D.P. has a high turnover rate. The technical understanding of your current systems may be just as foreign to your staff as a package.
5. Packages are tangible and in-house development proposals are not. This means a lot to top management.
6. Packages get more visibility than in-house projects, mainly since a substantial amount of cash had to be justified and paid out. In-house projects are "sunk costs" and don't get the same exposure.
7. Package cost may be capitalized, which can mean a considerable tax advantage.

B. Why Not Buy a Package?

If packages are so great, why aren't there more success stories? It's estimated that U.S. companies spend 50 times as much on in-house development as they do on packages. In other words, packages are hardly making a dent in their potential market. Some of the reasons include:

1. It's an infant industry—technology is just now developing to make packages a viable alternative. As is the case with all infant industries, there is a high mortality rate. What may be the best buy today may be obsolete overnight. The vendor may go out of business.
2. All packages must be customized to some degree.

3. Package evaluation is hard—each package has hundreds, even thousands, of features. No two packages are alike, or even close. Each has its strengths and weaknesses. It becomes mind-boggling to compare packages in a rational way.
4. Pride of authorship phenomenon—packages are an affront to D.P. As a result, they have a hard time being objective in the evaluation process. They would normally rather do it themselves. It's hard to motivate them to change somebody else's code.
5. Packages use different conventions—naturally, whoever wrote the package was familiar with different terminology. Different codes, data names, and formats will be a certainty.
6. People resist change—packages mean more change to the users than in-house projects since additional and different codes, input forms, and output reports will naturally result.
7. Packages are frequently overly sophisticated—part of the customization process includes de-tuning the package or suppressing features not immediately desired.
8. Maintenance is harder—since your D.P. staff didn't originate the programs it will definitely be harder for them to incorporate changes resulting from bugs or enhancements. Your turnaround time will deteriorate.

[a]Adopted from G. S. Hoyt (1975).

18.3 GUIDELINES FOR THE DEVELOPMENT AND IMPLEMENTATION OF A COMPUTERIZED DECISION SYSTEM

Throughout the book we have made frequent suggestions concerning procedures for the development and implementation of new systems for production planning and inventory management. Here we restrict attention to guidelines specifically oriented to *computerized* systems. (For further details see, for example, Ahituv and Neumann, 1982; Keen and Scott Morton, 1978; or Kochhar 1979.)

1. An appropriate feasibility study should be carried out, as discussed in Section 18.1.

2. Three types of documentation should be provided.

   a. General overview basis for senior management to provide an appreciation of the concepts, objectives, and control options.

   b. More detailed documentation for direct users of the system. This includes training and reference material.

   c. Extremely detailed information for the system analysts who are expected to maintain and upgrade the systems.

3. Appropriate training, different in nature for each of the three audiences mentioned in point 2, is essential.

4. In system development it should be recognized that different users require different forms of information for decision making; specifically aggregated, infrequent information for senior managers down to very detailed, frequent data for clerical personnel (see also Section 13.2.1 of Chapter 13 and Gorry and Scott Morton, 1971).

5. Related to the previous point it is desirable, where possible, to make use of graphic displays of information (for example, the presentation of exchange curves). Moreover, ideally, provision should be made for an interactive mode of operation so that the systems can respond to "what-if" scenarios posed by users.
6. As discussed in Chapter 17, gradual implementation, such as on a pilot study basis, should be used.
7. For ease in testing and modification, any system should be developed on a modular basis. At least three distinct segments should be maintained: data files, computational routines, and report generators. Perhaps surprisingly, the majority of the development effort and time typically has to be devoted to the first and third of these segments.
8. In setting up files, adequate space should be provided for expansion of the product line.
9. The tendency is for more and more systems to operate on an on-line, as opposed to a batch, basis. However, the choice should depend on the frequency of key events such as demand and production/supply status changes.

18.4 IN SUMMARY

Throughout the text we have proposed production/inventory decision systems appropriate for different environments. These have been based, where possible, on a solid theoretical foundation, but have frequently been modified in a heuristic sense to cope with factors not explicitly included in the underlying theory. Continuing in this vein, this chapter has provided some guidance concerning the possible computerization of an existing or proposed new decision system.

Most organizations face an increasingly competitive environment, both nationally and internationally, in the production and distribution of their goods. It is hoped that this book has prepared the reader to better cope with this complex decision environment, thus helping to return production and materials management to its deserved strategic role in most organizations.

REFERENCES

Ahituv, N., and S. Neumann (1982). *Principles of Information Systems for Management.* Wm. C. Brown, Dubuque, Iowa.

Burch, E. E., and C. Gooding (1976). "To Computerize or Not to Computerize." *Proceedings of the 19th Annual International Conference of the American Production and Inventory Control Society*, pp. 49–53.

Fogarty, D. W. (1977). "Utilization and Effectiveness of EDP in PIC: An Industrial Survey." *Production and Inventory Management*, Vol. 18, No. 2, pp. 8–28.

Gorry, G. A., and M. S. Scott Morton (1971). "A Framework for Management Information Systems." *Sloan Management Review*, Vol. 11, No. 3, pp. 55–70.

Hohenstein, C. L. (1984). "Microcomputer Spreadsheets for Inventory—A Schematic." *Production and Inventory Management Review*, Vol. 4, No. 1, pp. 26–50.

Heller, R. (1972). *The Great Executive Dream.* Delacorte Press, New York.

Hoyt, G. S. (1975). "The Art of Buying Software: Honest Salesmen, Successful Software Packages . . . and Other Fairy Tales." *Proceedings of the 18th Annual International Conference of the American Production and Inventory Control Society*, pp. 316–324.

Keen, P. G. W., and M. S. Scott Morton (1978). *Decision Support Systems: An Organizational Perspective.* Addison-Wesley, Reading, Massachusetts.

Kochhar, A. K. (1979). *Development of Computer-Based Production Systems.* Edward Arnold, London.

APPENDIX A

Elements of Lagrangian Optimization

We consider the case where we wish to maximize (or minimize) a function $f(x, y)$ of two variables x and y, but subject to a constraint or side condition that x and y must satisfy, denoted by

$$g(x, y) = 0 \tag{A.1}$$

x and y are not independent; selection of a value of one of them implies a value (or values) of the other through Eq. A.1. Therefore, we cannot find the maximum (or minimum) of $f(x, y)$ by simply equating the partial derivatives of f (with respect to x and y) equal to zero. Instead, we could solve Eq. A.1 for y in terms of x, then substitute this expression into $f(x, y)$ to obtain a new function, call it $h(x)$, which depends only on the single variable x. Then a maximum (or minimum) of $h(x)$ could be found by setting $dh(x)/dx = 0$, and so on. The associated value of y would be found from Eq. A.1.

Illustration

Suppose we wish to minimize

$$f(x, y) = \frac{x}{2} + 2y$$

subject to both variables being positive and

$$xy = 4$$

This constraint can be rewritten as

$$xy - 4 = 0$$

which, from Eq. A.1, shows us that

$$g(x, y) = xy - 4$$

The constraint can also be written as

$$y = 4/x \tag{A.2}$$

By substituting into $f(x, y)$, we obtain

$$\frac{x}{2} + 2(4/x) = \frac{x}{2} + 8/x$$

which we call $h(x)$. Then,

$$\frac{dh(x)}{dx} = \frac{1}{2} - \frac{8}{x^2}$$

Also

$$\frac{d^2h(x)}{dx^2} = \frac{16}{x^3}$$

At a minimum we require

$$\frac{dh(x)}{dx} = 0$$

In other words,

$$\frac{1}{2} - \frac{8}{x^2} = 0$$

or

$$x^2 = 16$$

Because x must be positive, the only valid solution is

$$x = 4$$

At $x = 4$

$$\frac{d^2h(x)}{dx^2} = \frac{16}{(4)^3} = \frac{1}{4} > 0$$

Therefore, we have a minimum at $x = 4$. The y value corresponding to $x = 4$ is found from Eq. A.2 to be $y = 1$. Finally, the minimum value of $f(x, y)$ is

$$f(4, 1) = \tfrac{4}{2} + 2(1) = 4$$

We now state, without proof, an alternative method for finding the maximum (or minimum) value of $f(x, y)$ subject to the constraint

$$g(x, y) = 0 \tag{A.3}$$

We set up the new function

$$L(x, y, M) = f(x, y) - Mg(x, y)$$

where M is called a *Lagrange multiplier*. This new function is now treated as a function of the three *independent* variables x, y, and M. Therefore, we set

$$\frac{\partial L}{\partial x} = 0 \qquad \text{that is,} \qquad \frac{\partial f}{\partial x} - M\frac{\partial g}{\partial x} = 0 \tag{A.4}$$

$$\frac{\partial L}{\partial y} = 0 \qquad \text{that is,} \qquad \frac{\partial f}{\partial y} - M\frac{\partial g}{\partial y} = 0 \tag{A.5}$$

$$\frac{\partial L}{\partial M} = 0 \qquad \text{that is,} \qquad g(x, y) = 0 \tag{A.6}$$

The last equation simply regenerates the constraint of Eq. A.3. For any given value of M, Eqs. A.4 and A.5 can be solved for the two unknowns x and y. Of course, this (x, y) pair will likely not satisfy the condition of Eq. A.3. Therefore, we keep trying different M values until this method leads to an (x, y) pair satisfying Eq. A.3. In some cases the appropriate value of M can be found analytically by substituting expressions for x and y, found from Eqs. A.4 and A.5, into Eq. A.3.

Illustration

Consider the same problem treated earlier, namely, for positive variables x and y

$$\text{Minimize} \qquad f(x, y) = \frac{x}{2} + 2y$$

$$\text{Subject to} \qquad g(x, y) = xy - 4 = 0 \tag{A.7}$$

Our new function is

$$L(x, y, M) = \frac{x}{2} + 2y - M(xy - 4)$$

Equations A.4 and A.5 give

$$\tfrac{1}{2} - My = 0 \quad \text{or} \quad y = \frac{1}{2M} \tag{A.8}$$

and

$$2 - Mx = 0 \quad \text{or} \quad x = \frac{2}{M} \tag{A.9}$$

The following table illustrates values of x, y, and $g(x, y)$ for various values of M.

M	$x = \dfrac{2}{M}$	$y = \dfrac{1}{2M}$	$g(x, y) = xy - 4$
2	1	1/4	−15/4
1	2	1/2	−3
1/2	4	1	0←
1/4	8	3	12
1/5	10	5/2	21

The behavior of $g(x, y)$ as a function of M is also sketched in Figure A.1. It is clear that there is but a single value of M, namely $\frac{1}{2}$, where $g(x, y) = 0$; that is, the constraint of Eq. A.7 is satisfied. (In this example the value of M could be found more directly, without trial-and-error, by substituting Eqs. A.8 and A.9 into Eq. A.7.) From the above table we see that the corresponding (x, y) pair is

$$x = 4 \qquad y = 1$$

precisely the same result we obtained by the earlier more direct method involving substitution, and so on.

At this stage, the reader may be asking "Who needs all this aggravation when the direct substitution method seems so much simpler?" For the example analyzed we certainly do not need the Lagrange multiplier approach. However, the method is directly extendable to the case where there are several, instead of just two, variables involved. Also, in the substitution method we can quickly run into problems if the constraint is of such a form that one variable cannot be

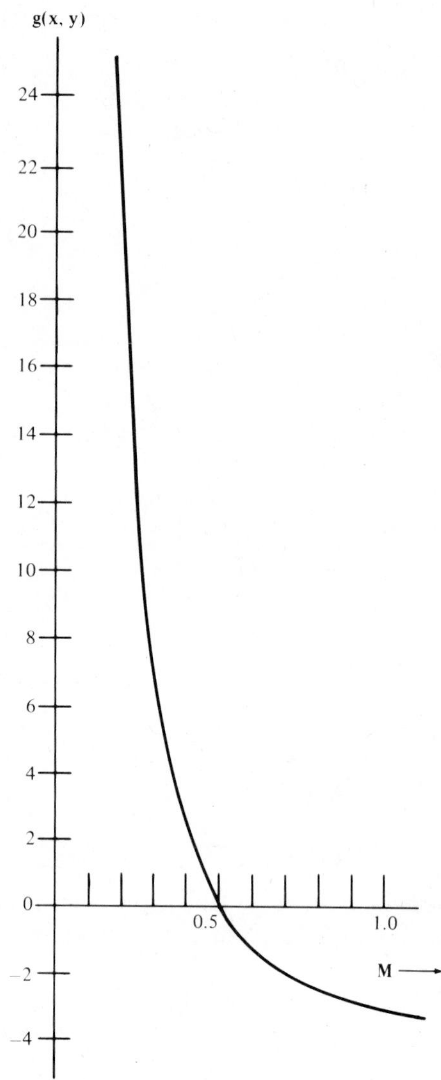

FIGURE A.1 Illustration of $g(x, y)$ as a Function of the Lagrange Multiplier M

easily expressed in terms of the other variables. This would have been the case in the above illustration if the constraint had been instead, for example,

$$x^3y^2 - 3xy^4 = 6$$

This type of complexity does not hamper the Lagrange approach.

We now present, without proof,[1] the general Lagrange approach for maximizing (or minimizing) a function $f(x_1, x_2, \ldots, x_n)$ of n variables $x_1, x_2, \ldots, x_n$ subject to a single equality constraint

$$g(x_1, x_2, \ldots, x_n) = 0 \tag{A.10}$$

Step 1 Form the function

$$L(x_1, x_2, \ldots, x_n, M) = f(x_1, x_2, \ldots, x_n) - Mg(x_1, x_2, \ldots, x_n)$$

Step 2 Evaluate the n partial derivatives and set each equal to zero.

$$\frac{\partial L}{\partial x_1} = 0$$

$$\frac{\partial L}{\partial x_2} = 0$$

$$\vdots$$

$$\frac{\partial L}{\partial x_n} = 0$$

This gives n equations in the $n + 1$ variables $x_1, x_2, \ldots, x_n$, and M.

Step 3 For a particular value of M, solve the set of equations (obtained in Step 2) for the x's. Then evaluate $g(x_1, x_2, \ldots, x_n)$.

Step 4 If $g(x_1, x_2, \ldots, x_n) = 0$, we have found a set of x's which are candidates for maximizing (or minimizing) the function f subject to satisfying the condition of Eq. A.10. Otherwise, we return to step 2 with a different value of M. There are different methods available for searching for the M values where the constraint is satisfied. At the very least we can develop graphs, similar to Figure A.1, as we proceed. This certainly would indicate in what direction to explore M values. In some cases one can obtain analytic solutions for the required M values.

[1]A proof is provided in Sokolnikoff, I. S., and R. M. Redheffer (1958). *Mathematics of Physics and Modern Engineering*. McGraw-Hill, New York, pp. 249–251.

APPENDIX B

The Normal Probability Distribution

The normal is undoubtedly the most important single probability distribution in decision rules of production planning and inventory management, as well as in general usage of probability (particularly in the area of applied statistics). This appendix is devoted to a discussion of the properties of the normal distribution, particularly those needed for the decision rules of the main text.

B.1 THE PROBABILITY DENSITY FUNCTION

The probability density function of a normal variable x, with mean $\hat{x}$ and standard deviation σ_x is denoted by

$$f_x(x_0) = \frac{1}{\sigma_x\sqrt{2\pi}} \exp[-(x_0 - \hat{x})^2/2\sigma_x^2] \qquad -\infty < x_0 < \infty \tag{B.1}$$

A typical sketch is shown in Figure B.1. This is the familiar bell-shaped curve. As the standard deviation σ_x decreases, the distribution tightens up around the mean value $\hat{x}$.

B.2 MOMENTS

The Mean, $E(x)$ or $\hat{x}$, and the Standard Deviation, σ_x

One can verify[1] that the mean and standard deviation are, indeed, the $\hat{x}$ and σ_x in Eq B.1.

[1]For details see Parzen, E. (1960). *Modern Probability Theory and Its Applications.* Wiley, New York, p. 206.

MAD

By definition, the MAD is given by

$$\text{MAD} = \int_{-} |x_0 - \hat{x}| f_x(x_0) dx_0$$

Substitution of Eq. B.1 and lengthy algebra and calculus leads to

$$\text{MAD} = \sqrt{\frac{2}{\pi}}\, \sigma_x$$

or

$$\frac{\sigma_x}{\text{MAD}} = \sqrt{\frac{\pi}{2}} \simeq 1.25$$

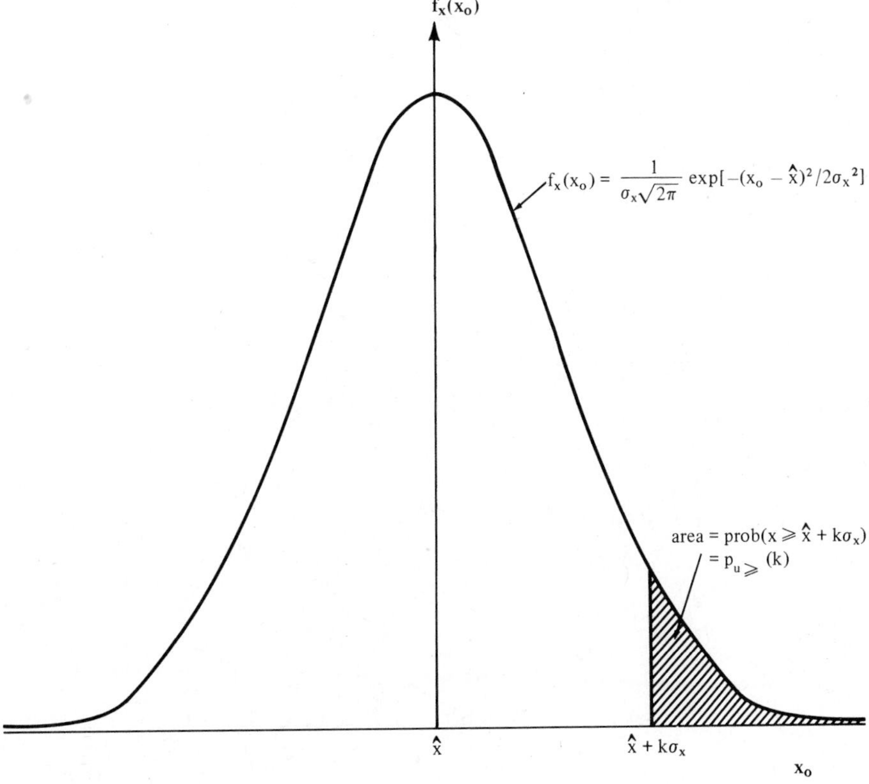

FIGURE B.1 The Normal Probability Density Function

B.3 THE UNIT (OR STANDARD) NORMAL DISTRIBUTION

A very special case of the normal distribution is the one where the mean value is 0 and the standard deviation is 1. We denote such a variable by u. Thus

$$f_u(u_0) = \frac{1}{\sqrt{2\pi}} \exp\left(-u_0^2/2\right) \qquad -\infty < u_0 < \infty \tag{B.2}$$

with $E(u)$ or $\hat{u} = 0$ and $\sigma_u = 1$. This p.d.f. is shown graphically in Figure B.2.

A quantity of frequent interest is the probability that u is at least as large as a certain value k,

$$\begin{aligned} p_{u\geqslant}(k) &= \text{prob}\,(u \geqslant k) = \int_k^\infty f_u(u_0)du_0 \\ &= \int_k^\infty \frac{1}{\sqrt{2\pi}} \exp\left(-u_0^2/2\right)du_0 \end{aligned} \tag{B.3}$$

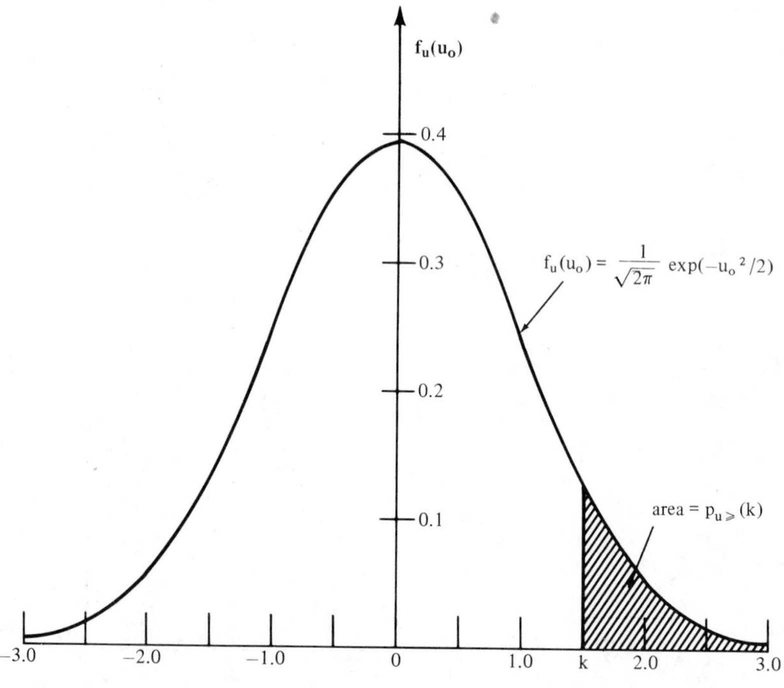

FIGURE B.2 The Unit Normal Distribution

There is no indefinite integral for

$$\exp(-x^2/2)dx$$

Therefore, Eq. B.3 has to be numerically integrated. (The result represents the hatched area in Figure B.2.) This has been done and $p_{u\geq}(k)$ has been tabulated, as in Table B.1, for a range of k values. Only positive values of k are shown in the table. If $p_{u\geq}(k)$ is needed for a negative argument, it is clear from the symmetry of Figure B.2 that

$$p_{u\geq}(-k) = 1 - p_{u\geq}(k) \tag{B.4}$$

It should be noted that, by differentiating both sides of Eq. B.3 with respect to k, and using the theorem in the Appendix of Chapter 10, we obtain

$$\frac{dp_{u\geq}(k)}{dk} = -f_u(k) \tag{B.5}$$

A second quantity of interest relative to production/inventory decision rules, denoted by $G_u(k)$, is given by

$$G_u(k) = \int_k^\infty (u_0 - k) f_u(u_0) du_0 \tag{B.6}$$

Using, a special property of the unit normal distribution, namely, that

$$\int_k^\infty u_0 f_u(u_0) du_0 = f_u(k)$$

Eq. B.6 can be expressed as

$$G_u(k) = f_u(k) - k p_{u\geq}(k) \tag{B.7}$$

Table B.1 also shows $G_u(k)$ as a function of k. Note that it can be shown that

$$G_u(-k) = G_u(k) + k \tag{B.8}$$

Differentiating both sides of Eq. B.6 with respect to k, and again using the aforementioned theorem, there results

$$\frac{dG_u(k)}{dk} = -p_{u\geq}(k) \tag{B.9}$$

B.4 RELATING ANY NORMAL DISTRIBUTION TO THE UNIT NORMAL

Consider a normally distributed variable x with mean $\hat{x}$ and standard deviation σ_x. One quantity of direct interest in measuring customer service is the probability of A where A is the event that x takes on a value greater than or equal to $\hat{x} + k\sigma_x$.

Now,

$$\begin{aligned}\text{prob}\,(A) &= \int_{\hat{x}+k\sigma_x}^{\infty} f_x(x_0)dx_0 \\ &= \int_{\hat{x}+k\sigma_x}^{\infty} \frac{1}{\sigma_x\sqrt{2\pi}} \exp\,[-\,(x_0 - \hat{x})^2/2\sigma_x^2]dx_0\end{aligned} \tag{B.10}$$

Consider

$$u_0 = (x_0 - \hat{x})/\sigma_x$$

We have that $du_0/dx_0 = 1/\sigma_x$ or $dx_0 = \sigma_x du_0$. Also, when $x_0 = \hat{x} + k\sigma_x$, we have that $u_0 = k$; and when $x_0 = \infty$, $u_0 = \infty$.

Therefore, substituting these expressions into Eq. B.10 results in

$$\text{prob}(A) = \int_k^{\infty} \frac{1}{\sqrt{2\pi}} \exp\,(-\,u_0^2/2)du_0$$

Using Eq. B.3 and the definition of event A, we thus have

$$\text{prob}\,\{x \geqslant \hat{x} + k\sigma_x\} = p_{u\geqslant}(k) \tag{B.11}$$

This is represented by the hatched area in Figure B.1.

Another quantity of interest is the expected shortage per replenishment cycle,

$$\begin{aligned}\text{ESPRC} &= \int_{\hat{x}+k\sigma_x}^{\infty} (x_0 - \hat{x} - k\sigma_x)f_x(x_0)dx_0 \\ &= \int_{\hat{x}+k\sigma_x}^{\infty} (x_0 - \hat{x} - k\sigma_x)\frac{1}{\sigma_x\sqrt{2\pi}} \exp\,[-\,(x_0 - \hat{x})^2/2\sigma_x^2]dx_0\end{aligned} \tag{B.12}$$

The key is again to substitute

$$u_0 = (x_0 - \hat{x})/\sigma_x$$

The result, after considerable simplification, is

$$\text{ESPRC} = \sigma_x \int_k^{\infty} (u_0 - k) \frac{1}{\sqrt{2\pi}} \exp{(-\, u_0^2/2)} du_0$$

From Eq. B.6 this is seen to be

$$\text{ESPRC} = \sigma_x G_u(k) \tag{B.13}$$

B.5 FURTHER PROPERTIES NEEDED FOR THE APPENDIX OF CHAPTER 10

In Chapter 10 we have a normally distributed variable x with mean $\hat{x}$ and standard deviation σ_x, and we let

$$Q = \hat{x} + k\sigma_x$$

The first quantity desired is $p_{x<}(Q)$. Clearly,

$$\begin{aligned} p_{x<}(Q) &= \text{prob}\ (x < Q) = 1 - \text{prob}\ (x \geqslant Q) \\ &= 1 - \text{prob}\ (x \geqslant \hat{x} + k\sigma_x) \end{aligned}$$

Using Eq. B.11 we have

$$p_{x<}(Q) = 1 - p_{u\geqslant}(k) = p_{u<}(k)$$

The function $p_{u<}(k)$ is sometimes denoted by $\Phi(k)$ in the literature.
The second quantity desired is

$$\int_Q^{\infty} x_0 f_x(x_0) dx_0$$

We have

$$\begin{aligned} \int_Q^{\infty} x_0 f_x(x_0) dx_0 &= \int_Q^{\infty} (x_0 - Q) f_x(x_0) dx_0 + \int_Q^{\infty} Q f_x(x_0) dx_0 \\ &= \int_{\hat{x}+k\sigma_x}^{\infty} (x_0 - \hat{x} - \mathrm{k}\sigma_x) f_x(x_0) dx_0 + Q \int_{\hat{x}+k\sigma_x}^{\infty} f_x(x_0) dx_0 \end{aligned}$$

Use of Eqs. B.11, B.12, and B.13 gives us

$$\int_Q^\infty x_0 f_x(x_0)dx_0 = \sigma_x G_u(k) + Q p_{u\geq}(k) \tag{B.14}$$

The third quantity required is

$$\int_0^Q x_0 f_x(x_0)dx_0$$

Now, if the chance of a negative value of x is very small, then

$$\begin{aligned}\int_0^Q x_0 f_x(x_0)dx_0 &\simeq \int_{-\infty}^Q x_0 f_x(x_0)dx_0 \\ &= \int_{-\infty}^{\infty} x_0 f_x(x_0)dx_0 - \int_Q^\infty x_0 f_x(x_0)dx_0 \\ &= \hat{x} - \int_Q^\infty x_0 f_x(x_0)dx_0\end{aligned}$$

Then use of Eq. B.14 leads to

$$\int_0^Q x_0 f_x(x_0)dx_0 \simeq \hat{x} - \sigma_x G_u(k) - Q p_{u\geq}(k)$$

TABLE B.1 Some Functions of the Unit Normal Distribution

k	$f_u(k)$	$p_{u\geq}(k)$	$G_u(k)$	$G_u(-k)$	k
0.00	0.3989	0.5000	0.3989	0.3989	0.00
0.01	0.3989	0.4960	0.3940	0.4040	0.01
0.02	0.3989	0.4920	0.3890	0.4090	0.02
0.03	0.3988	0.4880	0.3841	0.4141	0.03
0.04	0.3986	0.4840	0.3793	0.4193	0.04
0.05	0.3984	0.4801	0.3744	0.4244	0.05
0.06	0.3982	0.4761	0.3697	0.4297	0.06
0.07	0.3980	0.4721	0.3649	0.4349	0.07
0.08	0.3977	0.4681	0.3602	0.4402	0.08
0.09	0.3973	0.4641	0.3556	0.4456	0.09
0.10	0.3970	0.4602	0.3509	0.4509	0.10
0.11	0.3965	0.4562	0.3464	0.4564	0.11
0.12	0.3961	0.4522	0.3418	0.4618	0.12
0.13	0.3956	0.4483	0.3373	0.4673	0.13
0.14	0.3951	0.4443	0.3328	0.4728	0.14
0.15	0.3945	0.4404	0.3284	0.4784	0.15
0.16	0.3939	0.4364	0.3240	0.4840	0.16
0.17	0.3932	0.4325	0.3197	0.4897	0.17
0.18	0.3925	0.4286	0.3154	0.4954	0.18
0.19	0.3918	0.4247	0.3111	0.5011	0.19
0.20	0.3910	0.4207	0.3069	0.5069	0.20
0.21	0.3902	0.4168	0.3027	0.5127	0.21
0.22	0.3894	0.4129	0.2986	0.5186	0.22
0.23	0.3885	0.4090	0.2944	0.5244	0.23
0.24	0.3876	0.4052	0.2904	0.5304	0.24
0.25	0.3867	0.4013	0.2863	0.5363	0.25
0.26	0.3857	0.3974	0.2824	0.5424	0.26
0.27	0.3847	0.3936	0.2784	0.5484	0.27
0.28	0.3836	0.3897	0.2745	0.5545	0.28
0.29	0.3825	0.3859	0.2706	0.5606	0.29
0.30	0.3814	0.3821	0.2668	0.5668	0.30
0.31	0.3802	0.3783	0.2630	0.5730	0.31
0.32	0.3790	0.3745	0.2592	0.5792	0.32
0.33	0.3778	0.3707	0.2555	0.5855	0.33
0.34	0.3765	0.3669	0.2518	0.5918	0.34
0.35	0.3752	0.3632	0.2481	0.5981	0.35
0.36	0.3739	0.3594	0.2445	0.6045	0.36
0.37	0.3725	0.3557	0.2409	0.6109	0.37
0.38	0.3712	0.3520	0.2374	0.6174	0.38
0.39	0.3697	0.3483	0.2339	0.6239	0.39

(continued)

TABLE B.1 *(Continued)*

k	$f_u(k)$	$p_{u\geq}(k)$	$G_u(k)$	$G_u(-k)$	k
0.40	0.3683	0.3446	0.2304	0.6304	0.40
0.41	0.3668	0.3409	0.2270	0.6370	0.41
0.42	0.3653	0.3372	0.2236	0.6436	0.42
0.43	0.3637	0.3336	0.2203	0.6503	0.43
0.44	0.3621	0.3300	0.2169	0.6569	0.44
0.45	0.3605	0.3264	0.2137	0.6637	0.45
0.46	0.3589	0.3228	0.2104	0.6704	0.46
0.47	0.3572	0.3192	0.2072	0.6772	0.47
0.48	0.3555	0.3156	0.2040	0.6840	0.48
0.49	0.3538	0.3121	0.2009	0.6909	0.49
0.50	0.3521	0.3085	0.1978	0.6978	0.50
0.51	0.3503	0.3050	0.1947	0.7047	0.51
0.52	0.3485	0.3015	0.1917	0.7117	0.52
0.53	0.3467	0.2981	0.1887	0.7187	0.53
0.54	0.3448	0.2946	0.1857	0.7257	0.54
0.55	0.3429	0.2912	0.1828	0.7328	0.55
0.56	0.3410	0.2877	0.1799	0.7399	0.56
0.57	0.3391	0.2843	0.1771	0.7471	0.57
0.58	0.3372	0.2810	0.1742	0.7542	0.58
0.59	0.3352	0.2776	0.1714	0.7614	0.59
0.60	0.3332	0.2743	0.1687	0.7687	0.60
0.61	0.3312	0.2709	0.1659	0.7759	0.61
0.62	0.3292	0.2676	0.1633	0.7833	0.62
0.63	0.3271	0.2643	0.1606	0.7906	0.63
0.64	0.3251	0.2611	0.1580	0.7980	0.64
0.65	0.3230	0.2578	0.1554	0.8054	0.65
0.66	0.3209	0.2546	0.1528	0.8128	0.66
0.67	0.3187	0.2514	0.1503	0.8203	0.67
0.68	0.3166	0.2483	0.1478	0.8278	0.68
0.69	0.3144	0.2451	0.1453	0.8353	0.69
0.70	0.3123	0.2420	0.1429	0.8429	0.70
0.71	0.3101	0.2389	0.1405	0.8505	0.71
0.72	0.3079	0.2358	0.1381	0.8581	0.72
0.73	0.3056	0.2327	0.1358	0.8658	0.73
0.74	0.3034	0.2297	0.1334	0.8734	0.74
0.75	0.3011	0.2266	0.1312	0.8812	0.75
0.76	0.2989	0.2236	0.1289	0.8889	0.76
0.77	0.2966	0.2206	0.1267	0.8967	0.77
0.78	0.2943	0.2177	0.1245	0.9045	0.78
0.79	0.2920	0.2148	0.1223	0.9123	0.79
0.80	0.2897	0.2119	0.1202	0.9202	0.80
0.81	0.2874	0.2090	0.1181	0.9281	0.81

TABLE B.1 *(Continued)*

k	$f_u(k)$	$p_{u\geqslant}(k)$	$G_u(k)$	$G_u(-k)$	k
0.82	0.2850	0.2061	0.1160	0.9360	0.82
0.83	0.2827	0.2033	0.1140	0.9440	0.83
0.84	0.2803	0.2005	0.1120	0.9520	0.84
0.85	0.2780	0.1977	0.1100	0.9600	0.85
0.86	0.2756	0.1949	0.1080	0.9680	0.86
0.87	0.2732	0.1922	0.1061	0.9761	0.87
0.88	0.2709	0.1894	0.1042	0.9842	0.88
0.89	0.2685	0.1867	0.1023	0.9923	0.89
0.90	0.2661	0.1841	0.1004	1.0004	0.90
0.91	0.2637	0.1814	0.09860	1.0086	0.91
0.92	0.2613	0.1788	0.09680	1.0168	0.92
0.93	0.2589	0.1762	0.09503	1.0250	0.93
0.94	0.2565	0.1736	0.09328	1.0333	0.94
0.95	0.2541	0.1711	0.09156	1.0416	0.95
0.96	0.2516	0.1685	0.08986	1.0499	0.96
0.97	0.2492	0.1660	0.08819	1.0582	0.97
0.98	0.2468	0.1635	0.08654	1.0665	0.98
0.99	0.2444	0.1611	0.08491	1.0749	0.99
1.00	0.2420	0.1587	0.08332	1.0833	1.00
1.01	0.2396	0.1562	0.08174	1.0917	1.01
1.02	0.2371	0.1539	0.08019	1.1002	1.02
1.03	0.2347	0.1515	0.07866	1.1087	1.03
1.04	0.2323	0.1492	0.07716	1.1172	1.04
1.05	0.2299	0.1469	0.07568	1.1257	1.05
1.06	0.2275	0.1446	0.07422	1.1342	1.06
1.07	0.2251	0.1423	0.07279	1.1428	1.07
1.08	0.2227	0.1401	0.07138	1.1514	1.08
1.09	0.2203	0.1379	0.06999	1.1600	1.09
1.10	0.2179	0.1357	0.06862	1.1686	1.10
1.11	0.2155	0.1335	0.06727	1.1773	1.11
1.12	0.2131	0.1314	0.06595	1.1859	1.12
1.13	0.2107	0.1292	0.06465	1.1946	1.13
1.14	0.2083	0.1271	0.06336	1.2034	1.14
1.15	0.2059	0.1251	0.06210	1.2121	1.15
1.16	0.2036	0.1230	0.06086	1.2209	1.16
1.17	0.2012	0.1210	0.05964	1.2296	1.17
1.18	0.1989	0.1190	0.05844	1.2384	1.18
1.19	0.1965	0.1170	0.05726	1.2473	1.19
1.20	0.1942	0.1151	0.05610	1.2561	1.20
1.21	0.1919	0.1131	0.05496	1.2650	1.21

(continued)

TABLE B.1 *(Continued)*

k	$f_u(k)$	$p_{u\geq}(k)$	$G_u(k)$	$G_u(-k)$	k
1.22	0.1895	0.1112	0.05384	1.2738	1.22
1.23	0.1872	0.1093	0.05274	1.2827	1.23
1.24	0.1849	0.1075	0.05165	1.2917	1.24
1.25	0.1826	0.1056	0.05059	1.3006	1.25
1.26	0.1804	0.1038	0.04954	1.3095	1.26
1.27	0.1781	0.1020	0.04851	1.3185	1.27
1.28	0.1758	0.1003	0.04750	1.3275	1.28
1.29	0.1736	0.09853	0.04650	1.3365	1.29
1.30	0.1714	0.09680	0.04553	1.3455	1.30
1.31	0.1691	0.09510	0.04457	1.3546	1.31
1.32	0.1669	0.09342	0.04363	1.3636	1.32
1.33	0.1647	0.09176	0.04270	1.3727	1.33
1.34	0.1626	0.09012	0.04179	1.3818	1.34
1.35	0.1604	0.08851	0.04090	1.3909	1.35
1.36	0.1582	0.08692	0.04002	1.4000	1.36
1.37	0.1561	0.08534	0.03916	1.4092	1.37
1.38	0.1539	0.08379	0.03831	1.4183	1.38
1.39	0.1518	0.08226	0.03748	1.4275	1.39
1.40	0.1497	0.08076	0.03667	1.4367	1.40
1.41	0.1476	0.07927	0.03587	1.4459	1.41
1.42	0.1456	0.07780	0.03508	1.4551	1.42
1.43	0.1435	0.07636	0.03431	1.4643	1.43
1.44	0.1415	0.07493	0.03356	1.4736	1.44
1.45	0.1394	0.07353	0.03281	1.4828	1.45
1.46	0.1374	0.07215	0.03208	1.4921	1.46
1.47	0.1354	0.07078	0.03137	1.5014	1.47
1.48	0.1334	0.06944	0.03067	1.5107	1.48
1.49	0.1315	0.06811	0.02998	1.5200	1.49
1.50	0.1295	0.06681	0.02931	1.5293	1.50
1.51	0.1276	0.06552	0.02865	1.5386	1.51
1.52	0.1257	0.06426	0.02800	1.5480	1.52
1.53	0.1238	0.06301	0.02736	1.5574	1.53
1.54	0.1219	0.06178	0.02674	1.5667	1.54
1.55	0.1200	0.06057	0.02612	1.5761	1.55
1.56	0.1182	0.05938	0.02552	1.5855	1.56
1.57	0.1163	0.05821	0.02494	1.5949	1.57
1.58	0.1145	0.05705	0.02436	1.6044	1.58
1.59	0.1127	0.05592	0.02380	1.6138	1.59
1.60	0.1109	0.05480	0.02324	1.6232	1.60
1.61	0.1092	0.05370	0.02270	1.6327	1.61
1.62	0.1074	0.05262	0.02217	1.6422	1.62

TABLE B.1 *(Continued)*

k	$f_u(k)$	$p_{u\geq}(k)$	$G_u(k)$	$G_u(-k)$	k
1.63	0.1057	0.05155	0.02165	1.6516	1.63
1.64	0.1040	0.05050	0.02114	1.6611	1.64
1.65	0.1023	0.04947	0.02064	1.6706	1.65
1.66	0.1006	0.04846	0.02015	1.6801	1.66
1.67	0.0989	0.04746	0.01967	1.6897	1.67
1.68	0.0973	0.04648	0.01920	1.6992	1.68
1.69	0.0957	0.04551	0.01874	1.7087	1.69
1.70	0.0940	0.04457	0.01829	1.7183	1.70
1.71	0.0925	0.04363	0.01785	1.7278	1.71
1.72	0.0909	0.04272	0.01742	1.7374	1.72
1.73	0.0893	0.04182	0.01699	1.7470	1.73
1.74	0.0878	0.04093	0.01658	1.7566	1.74
1.75	0.0863	0.04006	0.01617	1.7662	1.75
1.76	0.0848	0.03920	0.01578	1.7758	1.76
1.77	0.0833	0.03836	0.01539	1.7854	1.77
1.78	0.0818	0.03754	0.01501	1.7950	1.78
1.79	0.0804	0.03673	0.01464	1.8046	1.79
1.80	0.0790	0.03593	0.01428	1.8143	1.80
1.81	0.0775	0.03515	0.01392	1.8239	1.81
1.82	0.0761	0.03438	0.01357	1.8336	1.82
1.83	0.0748	0.03362	0.01323	1.8432	1.83
1.84	0.0734	0.03288	0.01290	1.8529	1.84
1.85	0.0721	0.03216	0.01257	1.8626	1.85
1.86	0.0707	0.03144	0.01226	1.8723	1.86
1.87	0.0694	0.03074	0.01195	1.8819	1.87
1.88	0.0681	0.03005	0.01164	1.8916	1.88
1.89	0.0669	0.02938	0.01134	1.9013	1.89
1.90	0.0656	0.02872	0.01105	1.9111	1.90
1.91	0.0644	0.02807	0.01077	1.9208	1.91
1.92	0.0632	0.02743	0.01049	1.9305	1.92
1.93	0.0620	0.02680	0.01022	1.9402	1.93
1.94	0.0608	0.02619	0.009957	1.9500	1.94
1.95	0.0596	0.02559	0.009698	1.9597	1.95
1.96	0.0584	0.02500	0.009445	1.9694	1.96
1.97	0.0573	0.02442	0.009198	1.9792	1.97
1.98	0.0562	0.02385	0.008957	1.9890	1.98
1.99	0.0551	0.02330	0.008721	1.9987	1.99
2.00	0.0540	0.02275	0.008491	2.0085	2.00
2.01	0.0529	0.02222	0.008266	2.0183	2.01

(continued)

TABLE B.1 *(Continued)*

k	$f_u(k)$	$p_{u\geqslant}(k)$	$G_u(k)$	$G_u(-k)$	k
2.02	0.0519	0.02169	0.008046	2.0280	2.02
2.03	0.0508	0.02118	0.007832	2.0378	2.03
2.04	0.0498	0.02068	0.007623	2.0476	2.04
2.05	0.0488	0.02018	0.007418	2.0574	2.05
2.06	0.0478	0.01970	0.007219	2.0672	2.06
2.07	0.0468	0.01923	0.007024	2.0770	2.07
2.08	0.0459	0.01876	0.006835	2.0868	2.08
2.09	0.0449	0.01831	0.006649	2.0966	2.09
2.10	0.0440	0.01786	0.006468	2.1065	2.10
2.11	0.0431	0.01743	0.006292	2.1163	2.11
2.12	0.0422	0.01700	0.006120	2.1261	2.12
2.13	0.0413	0.01659	0.005952	2.1360	2.13
2.14	0.0404	0.01618	0.005788	2.1458	2.14
2.15	0.0396	0.01578	0.005628	2.1556	2.15
2.16	0.0387	0.01539	0.005472	2.1655	2.16
2.17	0.0379	0.01500	0.005320	2.1753	2.17
2.18	0.0371	0.01463	0.005172	2.1852	2.18
2.19	0.0363	0.01426	0.005028	2.1950	2.19
2.20	0.0355	0.01390	0.004887	2.2049	2.20
2.21	0.0347	0.01355	0.004750	2.2147	2.21
2.22	0.0339	0.01321	0.004616	2.2246	2.22
2.23	0.0332	0.01287	0.004486	2.2345	2.23
2.24	0.0325	0.01255	0.004358	2.2444	2.24
2.25	0.0317	0.01222	0.004235	2.2542	2.25
2.26	0.0310	0.01191	0.004114	2.2641	2.26
2.27	0.0303	0.01160	0.003996	2.2740	2.27
2.28	0.0297	0.01130	0.003882	2.2839	2.28
2.29	0.0290	0.01101	0.003770	2.2938	2.29
2.30	0.0283	0.01072	0.003662	2.3037	2.30
2.31	0.0277	0.01044	0.003556	2.3136	2.31
2.32	0.0270	0.01017	0.003453	2.3235	2.32
2.33	0.0264	0.009903	0.003352	2.3334	2.33
2.34	0.0258	0.009642	0.003255	2.3433	2.34
2.35	0.0252	0.009387	0.003159	2.3532	2.35
2.36	0.0246	0.009137	0.003067	2.3631	2.36
2.37	0.0241	0.008894	0.002977	2.3730	2.37
2.38	0.0235	0.008656	0.002889	2.3829	2.38
2.39	0.0229	0.008424	0.002804	2.3928	2.39
2.40	0.0224	0.008198	0.002720	2.4027	2.40
2.41	0.0219	0.007976	0.002640	2.4126	2.41
2.42	0.0213	0.007760	0.002561	2.4226	2.42

TABLE B.1 *(Continued)*

k	$f_u(k)$	$p_{u\geqslant}(k)$	$G_u(k)$	$G_u(-k)$	k
2.43	0.0208	0.007549	0.002484	2.4325	2.43
2.44	0.0203	0.007344	0.002410	2.4424	2.44
2.45	0.0198	0.007143	0.002337	2.4523	2.45
2.46	0.0194	0.006947	0.002267	2.4623	2.46
2.47	0.0189	0.006756	0.002199	2.4722	2.47
2.48	0.0184	0.006569	0.002132	2.4821	2.48
2.49	0.0180	0.006387	0.002067	2.4921	2.49
2.50	0.0175	0.006210	0.002004	2.5020	2.50
2.51	0.0171	0.006037	0.001943	2.5119	2.51
2.52	0.0167	0.005868	0.001883	2.5219	2.52
2.53	0.0163	0.005703	0.001826	2.5318	2.53
2.54	0.0158	0.005543	0.001769	2.5418	2.54
2.55	0.0154	0.005386	0.001715	2.5517	2.55
2.56	0.0151	0.005234	0.001662	2.5617	2.56
2.57	0.0147	0.005085	0.001610	2.5716	2.57
2.58	0.0143	0.004940	0.001560	2.5816	2.58
2.59	0.0139	0.004799	0.001511	2.5915	2.59
2.60	0.0136	0.004661	0.001464	2.6015	2.60
2.61	0.0132	0.004527	0.001418	2.6114	2.61
2.62	0.0129	0.004396	0.001373	2.6214	2.62
2.63	0.0126	0.004269	0.001330	2.6313	2.63
2.64	0.0122	0.004145	0.001288	2.6413	2.64
2.65	0.0119	0.004025	0.001247	2.6512	2.65
2.66	0.0116	0.003907	0.001207	2.6612	2.66
2.67	0.0113	0.003793	0.001169	2.6712	2.67
2.68	0.0110	0.003681	0.001132	2.6811	2.68
2.69	0.0107	0.003573	0.001095	2.6911	2.69
2.70	0.0104	0.003467	0.001060	2.7011	2.70
2.71	0.0101	0.003364	0.001026	2.7110	2.71
2.72	0.0099	0.003264	0.0009928	2.7210	2.72
2.73	0.0096	0.003167	0.0009607	2.7310	2.73
2.74	0.0093	0.003072	0.0009295	2.7409	2.74
2.75	0.0091	0.002980	0.0008992	2.7509	2.75
2.76	0.0088	0.002890	0.0008699	2.7609	2.76
2.77	0.0086	0.002803	0.0008414	2.7708	2.77
2.78	0.0084	0.002718	0.0008138	2.7808	2.78
2.79	0.0081	0.002635	0.0007870	2.7908	2.79
2.80	0.0079	0.002555	0.0007611	2.8008	2.80
2.81	0.0077	0.002477	0.0007359	2.8107	2.81

(continued)

TABLE B.1 *(Continued)*

k	$f_u(k)$	$p_{u\geq}(k)$	$G_u(k)$	$G_u(-k)$	k
2.82	0.0075	0.002401	0.0007115	2.8207	2.82
2.83	0.0073	0.002327	0.0006879	2.8307	2.83
2.84	0.0071	0.002256	0.0006650	2.8407	2.84
2.85	0.0069	0.002186	0.0006428	2.8506	2.85
2.86	0.0067	0.002118	0.0006213	2.8606	2.86
2.87	0.0065	0.002052	0.0006004	2.8706	2.87
2.88	0.0063	0.001988	0.0005802	2.8806	2.88
2.89	0.0061	0.001926	0.0005606	2.8906	2.89
2.90	0.0060	0.001866	0.0005417	2.9005	2.90
2.91	0.0058	0.001807	0.0005233	2.9105	2.91
2.92	0.0056	0.001750	0.0005055	2.9205	2.92
2.93	0.0055	0.001695	0.0004883	2.9305	2.93
2.94	0.0053	0.001641	0.0004716	2.9405	2.94
2.95	0.0051	0.001589	0.0004555	2.9505	2.95
2.96	0.0050	0.001538	0.0004398	2.9604	2.96
2.97	0.0048	0.001489	0.0004247	2.9704	2.97
2.98	0.0047	0.001441	0.0004101	2.9804	2.98
2.99	0.0046	0.001395	0.0003959	2.9904	2.99
3.00	0.0044	0.001350	0.0003822	3.0004	3.00
3.01	0.0043	0.001306	0.0003689	3.0104	3.01
3.02	0.0042	0.001264	0.0003560	3.0204	3.02
3.03	0.0040	0.001223	0.0003436	3.0303	3.03
3.04	0.0039	0.001183	0.0003316	3.0403	3.04
3.05	0.0038	0.001144	0.0003199	3.0503	3.05
3.06	0.0037	0.001107	0.0003087	3.0603	3.06
3.07	0.0036	0.001070	0.0002978	3.0703	3.07
3.08	0.0035	0.001035	0.0002873	3.0803	3.08
3.09	0.0034	0.001001	0.0002771	3.0903	3.09
3.10	0.0033	0.0009676	0.0002672	3.1003	3.10
3.11	0.0032	0.0009354	0.0002577	3.1103	3.11
3.12	0.0031	0.0009043	0.0002485	3.1202	3.12
3.13	0.0030	0.0008740	0.0002396	3.1302	3.13
3.14	0.0029	0.0008447	0.0002311	3.1402	3.14
3.15	0.0028	0.0008164	0.0002227	3.1502	3.15
3.16	0.0027	0.0007888	0.0002147	3.1602	3.16
3.17	0.0026	0.0007622	0.0002070	3.1702	3.17
3.18	0.0025	0.0007364	0.0001995	3.1802	3.18
3.19	0.0025	0.0007114	0.0001922	3.1902	3.19
3.20	0.0024	0.0006871	0.0001852	3.2002	3.20
3.21	0.0023	0.0006637	0.0001785	3.2102	3.21
3.22	0.0022	0.0006410	0.0001720	3.2202	3.22

TABLE B.1 *(Continued)*

k	$f_u(k)$	$p_{u\geq}(k)$	$G_u(k)$	$G_u(-k)$	k
3.23	0.0022	0.0006190	0.0001657	3.2302	3.23
3.24	0.0021	0.0005976	0.0001596	3.2402	3.24
3.25	0.0020	0.0005770	0.0001537	3.2502	3.25
3.26	0.0020	0.0005571	0.0001480	3.2601	3.26
3.27	0.0019	0.0005377	0.0001426	3.2701	3.27
3.28	0.0018	0.0005190	0.0001373	3.2801	3.28
3.29	0.0018	0.0005009	0.0001322	3.2901	3.29
3.30	0.0017	0.0004834	0.0001273	3.3001	3.30
3.31	0.0017	0.0004665	0.0001225	3.3101	3.31
3.32	0.0016	0.0004501	0.0001179	3.3201	3.32
3.33	0.0016	0.0004342	0.0001135	3.3301	3.33
3.34	0.0015	0.0004189	0.0001093	3.3401	3.34
3.35	0.0015	0.0004041	0.0001051	3.3501	3.35
3.36	0.0014	0.0003897	0.0001012	3.3601	3.36
3.37	0.0014	0.0003758	0.00009734	3.3701	3.37
3.38	0.0013	0.0003624	0.00009365	3.3801	3.38
3.39	0.0013	0.0003495	0.00009009	3.3901	3.39
3.40	0.0012	0.0003369	0.00008666	3.4001	3.40
3.41	0.0012	0.0003248	0.00008335	3.4101	3.41
3.42	0.0012	0.0003131	0.00008016	3.4201	3.42
3.43	0.0011	0.0003018	0.00007709	3.4301	3.43
3.44	0.0011	0.0002909	0.00007413	3.4401	3.44
3.45	0.0010	0.0002803	0.00007127	3.4501	3.45
3.46	0.0010	0.0002701	0.00006852	3.4601	3.46
3.47	0.0010	0.0002602	0.00006587	3.4701	3.47
3.48	0.0009	0.0002507	0.00006331	3.4801	3.48
3.49	0.0009	0.0002415	0.00006085	3.4901	3.49
3.50	0.0009	0.0002326	0.00005848	3.5001	3.50
3.51	0.0008	0.0002241	0.00005620	3.5101	3.51
3.52	0.0008	0.0002158	0.00005400	3.5201	3.52
3.53	0.0008	0.0002078	0.00005188	3.5301	3.53
3.54	0.0008	0.0002001	0.00004984	3.5400	3.54
3.55	0.0007	0.0001926	0.00004788	3.5500	3.55
3.56	0.0007	0.0001854	0.00004599	3.5600	3.56
3.58	0.0007	0.0001785	0.00004417	3.5700	3.57
3.58	0.0007	0.0001718	0.00004242	3.5800	3.58
3.59	0.0006	0.0001653	0.00004073	3.5900	3.59
3.60	0.0006	0.0001591	0.00003911	3.6000	3.60
3.61	0.0006	0.0001531	0.00003755	3.6100	3.61

(continued)

TABLE B.1 *(Continued)*

k	$f_u(k)$	$p_{u\geq}(k)$	$G_u(k)$	$G_u(-k)$	k
3.62	0.0006	0.0001473	0.00003605	3.6200	3.62
3.63	0.0005	0.0001417	0.00003460	3.6300	3.63
3.64	0.0005	0.0001363	0.00003321	3.6400	3.64
3.65	0.0005	0.0001311	0.00003188	3.6500	3.65
3.66	0.0005	0.0001261	0.00003059	3.6600	3.66
3.67	0.0005	0.0001213	0.00002935	3.6700	3.67
3.68	0.0005	0.0001166	0.00002816	3.6800	3.68
3.69	0.0004	0.0001121	0.00002702	3.6900	3.69
3.70	0.0004	0.0001078	0.00002592	3.7000	3.70
3.71	0.0004	0.0001036	0.00002486	3.7100	3.71
3.72	0.0004	0.00009962	0.00002385	3.7200	3.72
3.73	0.0004	0.00009574	0.00002287	3.7300	3.73
3.74	0.0004	0.00009201	0.00002193	3.7400	3.74
3.75	0.0004	0.00008842	0.00002103	3.7500	3.75
3.76	0.0003	0.00008496	0.00002016	3.7600	3.76
3.77	0.0003	0.00008162	0.00001933	3.7700	3.77
3.78	0.0003	0.00007841	0.00001853	3.7800	3.78
3.79	0.0003	0.00007532	0.00001776	3.7900	3.79
3.80	0.0003	0.00007235	0.00001702	3.8000	3.80
3.81	0.0003	0.00006948	0.00001632	3.8100	3.81
3.82	0.0003	0.00006673	0.00001563	3.8200	3.82
3.83	0.0003	0.00006407	0.00001498	3.8300	3.83
3.84	0.0003	0.00006152	0.00001435	3.8400	3.84
3.85	0.0002	0.00005906	0.00001375	3.8500	3.85
3.86	0.0002	0.00005669	0.00001317	3.8600	3.86
3.87	0.0002	0.00005542	0.00001262	3.8700	3.87
3.88	0.0002	0.00005223	0.00001208	3.8800	3.88
3.89	0.0002	0.00005012	0.00001157	3.8900	3.89
3.90	0.0002	0.00004810	0.00001108	3.9000	3.90
3.91	0.0002	0.00004615	0.00001061	3.9100	3.91
3.92	0.0002	0.00004427	0.00001016	3.9200	3.92
3.93	0.0002	0.00004247	0.000009723	3.9300	3.93
3.94	0.0002	0.00004074	0.000009307	3.9400	3.94
3.95	0.0002	0.00003908	0.000008908	3.9500	3.95
3.96	0.0002	0.00003748	0.000008525	3.9600	3.96
3.97	0.0002	0.00003594	0.000008158	3.9700	3.97
3.98	0.0001	0.00003446	0.000007806	3.9800	3.98
3.99	0.0001	0.00003304	0.000007469	3.9900	3.99
4.00	0.0001	0.00003167	0.000007145	4.0000	4.00

AUTHOR INDEX

SUBJECT INDEX